SAP PRESS e-books

Print or e-book, Kindle or iPad, workplace or airplane: Choose where and how to read your SAP PRESS books! You can now get all our titles as e-books, too:

- ► By download and online access
- ► For all popular devices
- ► And, of course, DRM-free

Convinced? Then go to **www.sap-press.com** and get your e-book today.

SAP Business One®: Business User Guide

SAP PRESS

SAP PRESS is a joint initiative of SAP and Rheinwerk Publishing. The know-how offered by SAP specialists combined with the expertise of Rheinwerk Publishing offers the reader expert books in the field. SAP PRESS features first-hand information and expert advice, and provides useful skills for professional decision-making.

SAP PRESS offers a variety of books on technical and business-related topics for the SAP user. For further information, please visit our website: *www.sap-press.com*.

Olaf Schulz
Using SAP: An Introduction for Beginners and Business Users (3rd Edition)
2017, 389 pages, paperback and e-book
www.sap-press.com/4155

Sylvia, Frye, Berg
SAP HANA: An Introduction (4th Edition)
2017, 549 pages, hardcover and e-book
www.sap-press.com/4160

Bhattacharjee, Narasimhamurti, Desai, Vazquez, Walsh
Logistics with SAP S/4HANA: An Introduction (2nd Edition)
2019, 589 pages, hardcover and e-book
www.sap-press.com/4785

Mehta, Aijaz, Duncan, Parikh
SAP S/4HANA Finance: An Introduction
2019, 397 pages, hardcover and e-book
www.sap-press.com/4784

Carl Britton Lewis

SAP Business One®: Business User Guide

Editor Emily Nicholls
Copyeditor Yvette Chin
Cover Design Graham Geary
Photo Credit Shutterstock.com: 94342093/© totophotos, 416635366/© Andrey_Popov, 146666417/© rangizzz
Layout Design Vera Brauner
Production Graham Geary
Typesetting III-satz, Husby (Germany)
Printed and bound in the United States of America, on paper from sustainable sources

ISBN 978-1-4932-1499-0

© 2019 by Rheinwerk Publishing, Inc., Boston (MA)
1st edition 2017, 1st reprint 2019

Contents at a Glance

Dear Reader,

They say that when you know, you know.

Considering the amount of proposal preparation, market research, and number crunching that our acquisitions team does ahead of each SAP PRESS Editorial Board meeting, this is a bit of a simplification—but when it came to approving the proposal for this much-requested SAP Business One user guide, we knew.

With the SAP Business One community growing at an exponential pace, we knew that practical, detailed guidance for users would find a happy home among both longstanding and brand new customers. With veteran consultant Carl Britton Lewis at the helm, we knew the project would bring together some of the most active voices in the SAP Business One network with the most insight to share. And thanks to the SAP Business One experts' invitation into this engaged ecosystem, we knew Rheinwerk Publishing would connect with a thriving, tight-knit community eager to share notes and see fellow small businesses succeed.

As always, we appreciate your feedback and want to hear what *you* know. What did you think about *SAP Business One: Business User Guide*? Your comments and suggestions are the most useful tools to help us make our books the best they can be. Please feel free to contact me and share any praise or criticism you may have.

Thank you for purchasing a book from SAP PRESS!

Emily Nicholls
Editor, SAP PRESS

Rheinwerk Publishing
Boston, MA

emilyn@rheinwerk-publishing.com
www.sap-press.com

Contents

9   Inventory 391

Foreword from Finn Backer

SAP Business One is a world-class business management software that allows small and medium-sized companies to automate their sales, purchasing, financial, customer relationship management (CRM), banking, and other business processes. Within the software, all these areas are tightly integrated and easy to use, are complemented by deep industry solution capabilities from SAP partners, and can leverage the revolutionary SAP HANA database as a platform so that users can be competitive and innovative in the digital economy.

Over the years, SAP Business One has become SAP's most successful ERP solution in terms of the number of companies using the software. More than 50,000 organizations, with a million combined users around the globe, use SAP Business One. Over the years, the solution has grown a lot in terms of its capabilities and scalability. Professionals that have used the solution for a long time will definitely have noticed a growth in functionalities and configuration options. In addition, connectivity via browsers and mobile apps, or via the cloud, for example, has not only made it possible to automate and run processes more efficiently but has also made the solution more complex, which means that, for users to master it, they have more to learn.

Further, SAP Business One has benefited from extensive R&D efforts by SAP, one of the largest software companies in the world. One of the most disruptive innovations in recent years has been SAP HANA, a revolutionary database platform. One version of SAP Business One runs on SAP HANA, which allows for unprecedented analytical power by a redesigned database, changing from row- to column-oriented structure and running in memory instead of on hard disk, which eliminates the speed limitations of the 40-year-old desktop-based architecture of most databases. Users of SAP Business One will experience new and exciting user interfaces and interactions that leverage the speed of the SAP HANA-based system. And so the SAP Business One community grows.

On behalf of these users, I am very happy and excited about this book! Not only does it contain comprehensive and extensive step-by-step guides and instructions for operating the software, but it is written by members the North America SAP

Business One Partner Advisory Council (PAC), whose recognized mastery of the software makes the book down-to-earth and practical. These SAP partners have trained tens of thousands of users over the last decade and have gained a lot of experience, which is built into the book as best practices and tips and tricks that will be extremely valuable for readers around the world. The appendix also contains a lot of links and references to other sources of information about SAP Business One, should the reader seek to deep-dive further into a specific area.

The book can of course by leveraged by new users that need to learn how to operate and master the software — but existing users will also find great value in looking up some of the specific SAP Business One functionalities they are already using and are sure to pick up some additional ideas and tips and tricks for how to work even more efficiently. Further, if an existing customer wants to expand their usage of the software, they can read the chapter associated with that topic to get a good introduction into the area before implementing the capabilities in their companies.

The application for this practical book is broad, and its audience, diverse. To all readers, I wish the great pleasure of leveraging this book to get the most out of an SAP Business One system, and to the author, Carl Lewis, and the members of the North America Partner Advisory Council, I offer my congratulations and thanks! This book is destined to be very valuable for the community of SAP Business One customers and users.

Finn Backer
Global Vice President, SAP Business One
SAP SE

Foreword from Geoff Scott

The world as we know it is undergoing tremendous change. Digital transformation, which is fueled by the Internet, mobile devices, connected sensors, and so on, is changing everything about how we do business. Once-distant markets are a mouse click away. Ordering products from a website using your mobile phone is now commonplace. The opportunities that technology is unlocking across our planet are exciting!

Running an agile business is more important now than ever. With all of this tectonic change in our business landscapes, having a technology platform that can not only keep up but stay ahead is critical. Because digital transformation doesn't recognize size, big can seem small, and small can seem big. All that matters is ease of use and speed. Technology is no longer something that can be relegated to the back office or some dark closet; it has become the fabric of our lives and something on which we are all increasingly dependent.

Readers inclined to dismiss this notion should take a look around the next time they are on a plane, or in a waiting room, or even at a sporting event. Yes, some eyes are forward, but many are tilted down, engaged in that screen firmly held between their hands. They are playing games, reading news, listening to music, taking selfies, responding to email, and buying things. And seemingly every day there are new innovations that further embed this technology into the fabric of our lives. "Screen time" is only going in one direction: up.

In stark contrast to just a few decades ago, consumers are in firm control of technology. No longer is technology the exclusive purview of business. However, you can't escape that fact that businesses, often entrepreneurial startups, are the ones providing the technical innovations that consumers are gobbling up.

This macro-level view is important to set the context of why this book on SAP Business One is so important. SAP Business One is essential to running your business. In order to compete in today's tech economy, you need simple and straightforward software that ensures your business operates to its full potential. SAP Business One answers that call, and this book provides the jumpstart you need to get the most from the software.

The pages that follow will give you great insight in how to navigate through SAP Business One: how to produce financial reports, how to manage sales, coordinate production, and govern employees—in essence, all of the things required to operate a modern, tech-savvy business.

As the CEO of the Americas' SAP Users' Group (ASUG), I am continually reminded of the richness and vastness of our collective SAP community. Whether you are a small, medium-sized, or large business, an SAP solution is available that will help you run your business in real time. SAP Business One is perfect for smaller-scale business (usually with fewer than a hundred employees). The software encompasses many of the principles found in SAP's larger ERP product, without the additional complexity that larger-scale businesses require—complexity that could slow down your business.

For years, ASUG has proudly supported the SAP Business One community, which has experienced wonderful growth. The stories that SAP Business One community members tell about their businesses and their technical journeys are impressive. This book and its team of authors underscore the vibrancy of this community and our collective commitment to ensuring that each and every customer is successful with SAP Business One.

Like all technology, understanding SAP Business One is critical to your success. There is simply no other way to unlock the real potential of the software for your business. I encourage you to read on, and I look forward to one day hearing you tell your implementation story to our amazing user community. Your journey awaits.

Geoff Scott
Chief Executive Officer
Americas' SAP Users' Group

Preface

For the past several years, many members of the SAP Business One community have inquired whether a book exists about this small and medium-sized enterprise (SME) solution from end to end. A few specialized resources can be found, but many are sorely outdated or woefully narrow in focus. With all the changes made to this enduring product in the last decade, that a new publication was needed quickly became apparent.

Joe Leimer was one of those inquisitive people. An SAP Business One user, Joe would find me every year at the Americas' SAP Users' Group (ASUG) SAP Business One Conference and ask about the possibility of a new book. I knew this information need was still unmet but also knew that finding a way to deliver such a breadth of instruction was a challenge. In early 2016, something changed: Joe reached out to SAP PRESS directly to encourage the SAP-focused publishing company to reconsider a comprehensive resource on this single SME solution—and gave them my name.

Fast-forward a few months. In conversation with the editorial team at SAP PRESS, I undertook to spearhead a collaborative effort that would curate end user-oriented instructions into a single resource. This wasn't my first rodeo; building events, training programs, and support procedures to enhance the customer experience has long been a significant slice of my professional DNA. In 2010, I helped organize our community by founding an annual SAP Business One conference that brought SAP, value-added resellers (VARs), software solution partners (SSPs), and users under the same roof. The approach to this book would borrow from this mentality: that the best material can be delivered to SAP Business One users through the strategic blend of diverse perspectives and experiences. I knew where to turn.

The SAP Business One Partner Advisory Council (PAC) has been a constant and consistent voice to SAP on behalf of SAP Business One customers everywhere. Made up of the best SAP Business One VARs and SSPs, the North America PAC collaborates with ASUG to make sure the ASUG SAP Business One Summit keeps meeting customers' needs. Many new features and functionality in SAP Business

One are the direct result of the PAC working closely with SAP product development. Though I stepped down from leading the North American PAC long ago, I remain very proud of our cooperative endeavors and the spirit of collaboration this group of professionals continues to demonstrate.

SAP Business One customers count on the software to meet all of their ERP needs—which makes for a book that is broad in scope and high in page count. Recognizing that I'd be hard-pressed to write all 600-odd pages myself, and knowing that the expertise of my colleagues and peers would similarly benefit our readers, I recruited a number of PAC member organizations and their leadership to take on chapter assignments. Some of the principals took on the writing assignments themselves, while others found quality individuals on their teams to contribute on behalf of their companies. I'm truly grateful for the content contributed by these fellow PAC member organizations and friends of SAP Business One users everywhere:

▶ Clients First Business Solutions, LLC

▶ Consensus International, LLC

▶ Forgestik, Inc.

▶ Long Business Systems, Inc.

▶ ProjectLine Solutions, Inc.

▶ Vision33, Inc.

Without their contributions, this book could not have delivered on its promise: to be the most comprehensive piece of SAP Business One user documentation ever assembled.

Target Audience

As we were writing this book, we kept a few target audiences in mind.

On average, SAP Business One customers have fifteen employees performing their daily tasks in the system. In organizations of this size and smaller, many employees wear multiple "hats" and manage processes that extend beyond a single module. (As we like to say, the typical SAP Business One customer is a small business with big ideas!) Larger organizations can have several hundred SAP Business One users; these folks, too, have a need for specialized instruction that addresses their particular workflows and processes. Users don't have time to scour websites, watch endless videos, and research how to use SAP Business One. Instead, they need a single source to guide them through the day-in and day-out usage of SAP Business One to execute the operations they conduct every day.

In any size organization, when new employees are onboarded, they need to be both taught organizational procedures and trained on the corresponding software systems. This book will help organizations bring new employees up to speed on SAP Business One—and let the would-be trainers get back to their own work sooner.

We anticipate that channel partners—the VARs, SSPs, and consulting firms that deliver new implementations or coach their clients through optimizations—will also find helpful content in this book. VARs, in particular, will be able to make use of this teaching tool to enhance the curriculum for onsite classroom training or a train-the-trainer approach.

The Objective and Structure of This Book

Our collective goal was to create a book for the everyday user of SAP Business One. Of course, we could cover the workflows and transactions that are the back-bone of any ERP system—the creation of purchase orders, the posting of G/L accounts, the printing of A/P invoices—but we also wanted to provide readers with the best practices that keep you moving forward, rather than backing up to correct mistakes. Each chapter is peppered with tips and tricks gathered from many years of working with SAP Business One that will help you avoid error messages and cross off your to-do list. We'll explain and illustrate every step of a process, making it simple for every reader to follow and learn at their own pace.

And so, bookended by guidance on navigation and design of the system on one end and guidance on reporting on the other, the table of contents of *SAP Business One: Business User Guide* is arranged in the same order as the SAP Business One main menu: Administration, Opportunities, Sales (A/R), Purchasing (A/P), Business Partners, Banking, Inventory, Resources, Production, MRP, Service, Human Resources, and Projects. The content is prioritized so that standard best practices and everyday procedures get the most coverage. We wanted to make it easy for you to read the book from front to back and, for others who wish to use the book as more of a reference guide, to gain insight into a particular business process. For example, if you're looking to learn how to create a quote, you can jump into Chapter 5; or if you're looking to process a payment, skip to Chapter 8.

Although nearly 700 pages is a lot of information, it's still not close to complete. In order to maintain our focus on the business user, we've omitted many of the strictly administrative tasks that are performed during implementation or conducted by ongoing system administration (though administrators, consultants, and developers are sure to find helpful tips here, too!). Likewise, we have chosen to focus on key reports only rather than detail every single report in every section of the application. Instead, we've referenced supplemental materials and documentation that address more specialized processes in the appendix for those wishing to go deeper or those pursuing a more technical understanding of SAP Business One.

Whether your business has been running SAP Business One for years or you've only recently encountered SAP Business One, my hope is that this book will smooth out the road along the way.

Acknowledgments

I'd like to extend special appreciation to my wife, Katherine, for her constant support and encouragement for over 20 years. The opportunity to write this book could never have been realized without her encouraging me to chase my dreams and follow my heart. Wherever I have been, and whatever success I have experienced, she has been my biggest fan, helping me reach for the stars while keeping my feet firmly on the ground.

I also want to thank the North American SAP Business One Partner Advisory Council, SAP, and ASUG. Over many years, the leaders of these three related organizations have allowed me to recruit them into my personal goals to benefit the SAP Business One community. I am indebted to each of them and their many members. I most certainly appreciate the time and effort of each individual from the PAC who contributed to the contents of the book. The contributions of Andres Castrillon, Derin Hildebrandt, Ryan Howe, Keith Taylor, and Bertrand Tougas and of our colleagues Christophe Contat, James Gibbons, Juanita Karan, Frédéric Marchand, Rob Peterson-Wakeman, Michal Raczka, and Jennifer Schmitt have made this book's quality and comprehensiveness unmatched.

Finally, I want to thank the hundreds of customer organizations and thousands of individual users of SAP Business One that I have personally met in the past 14 years. They more than anyone made this book happen. It's my most sincere hope that this volume will truly help make their business journey with SAP Business One a profitable experience.

Carl Britton Lewis
December 2016

Before exploring an ERP application as deep and wide as SAP Business One, let's get to know the basic lay of the land. This first chapter is all about the major highways and streets of SAP Business One. Learning how to navigate SAP Business One will help you on your way to success.

1   Navigation and Design

Great care has been taken by the designers and developers who created SAP Business One to ensure that the user interface (UI) is consistent throughout the application. This consistency is a great benefit, reducing the time you need to become familiar with the basic manner by which to navigate and operate the various controls and tools within SAP Business One.

In this chapter, we'll cover the basic steps for getting started with the system and provide general tips for navigation. We'll discuss login procedures, the main menu, and the general structure of the user interface, as well as printing and previewing.

1.1   Logging In

SAP Business One allows companies to deploy several databases. Typically, one will be your "production" database, which is the one you use each day to enter daily work.

1. To log in, open SAP Business One by double-clicking the SAP Business One shortcut on your desktop or by using the Windows Start menu.

2. The SAP BUSINESS ONE login screen shown in Figure 1.1 will appear. The first thing you must do is identify the database into which you wish to enter data. If your company/database is already listed, enter your user name and password and then click OK.

3. If the desired database (known as a "company" in SAP Business One) is not shown in the COMPANY NAME field, then click on the CHANGE COMPANY button at the bottom of the screen.

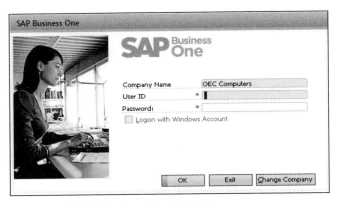

Figure 1.1 The SAP Business One Login Screen

4. The CHOOSE COMPANY screen shown in Figure 1.2 will appear. Notice the important information you are provided about each company database:

   ► Company name

   ► Database name

   ► Localization

   ► Version

5. Select your desired company from the COMPANIES ON CURRENT SERVER table. Enter your user name in the USER ID field. Enter your password in the PASS-WORD field. Once you are finished, click the OK button.

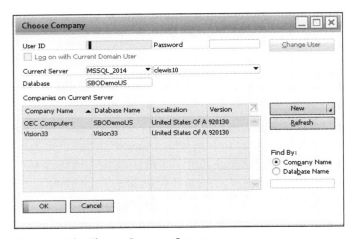

Figure 1.2 The Choose Company Screen

Tips and Tricks: Localizations

Many businesses have more than one company database for a variety of reasons—perhaps because they conduct business in a foreign country that has a different currency and tax regulations, for instance. SAP Business One refers to these differences as "localizations."

Once logged in successfully, you are now ready to explore SAP Business One. The main screen shown in Figure 1.3 is just one possible display that could appear, depending upon how SAP Business One has been configured. Much of the interface can be customized uniquely for each user's specific needs.

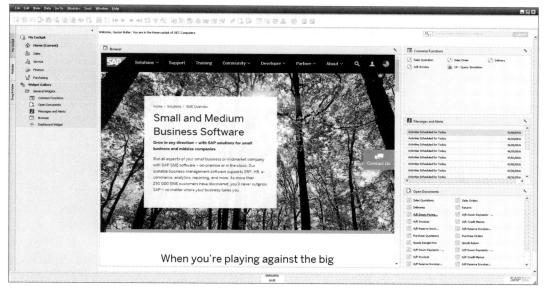

Figure 1.3 SAP Business One's Main Screen with Cockpits and Dashboards Active

1.2   Menu and General Structure

In this section, we'll examine the primary screen design and the tools available to you in the main menu, menu bar, and toolbar. We'll also explore the document screen design and built-in right-click functions. These elements are consistent throughout SAP Business One.

1.2.1 Main Menu

The main SAP Business One menu shown in Figure 1.4 is visible by default. However, this menu can be turned on or off from the WINDOW • MAIN MENU or by pressing [Ctrl]+[0]. This toggle is especially helpful for users with smaller computer screens.

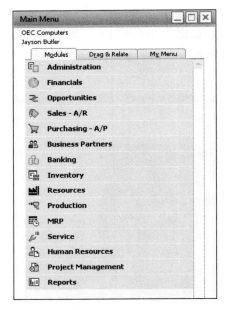

Figure 1.4 The Main Menu

The MODULES tab shown in Figure 1.4 is where the SAP Business One application and all its various parts are organized. Clicking on any of the MAIN MENU • MODULES sections will expand that section. For example, in Figure 1.5, we selected ADMINISTRATION to reveal more detail; subsequently, clicking on another section within ADMINISTRATION will show additional menu options if they exist below this level.

Two other tabs are visible in this screen. The DRAG & RELATE tab is an investigation tool—sort of an ad-hoc report writer—and the MY MENU tab enables you to arrange the program yourself and customize it to enhance convenience and productivity.

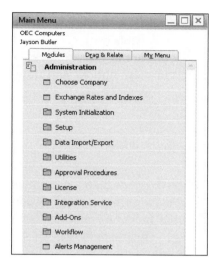

Figure 1.5 The Administration Menu

Tips and Tricks: Help with the Main Menu

For more information on the main menu and all its levels, press F1 while the main menu is open. The Context-Sensitive Help System (SAP Library) will appear, providing more detailed information regarding all the menu levels (see Figure 1.6).

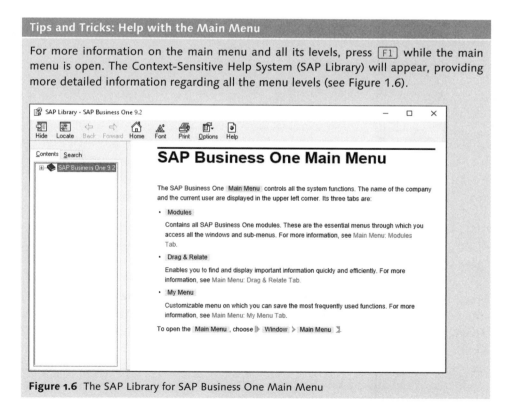

Figure 1.6 The SAP Library for SAP Business One Main Menu

1.2.2   Menu Bar

The menu bar ribbon in SAP Business One's main screen (see Figure 1.7) should look much like major command ribbons in other applications you are familiar with. Clicking the options in the menu bar will expand those options and show various functionalities.

Figure 1.7 The Menu Bar

For example, the MODULES menu option, when clicked, opens up an alternative listing of the main menu items. Hovering the cursor over a topic reveals additional potential selections. In Figure 1.8, we used the Inventory module as an example. Some users utilize this method of accessing the main menu exclusively; it helps them keep their screen clear from too much information.

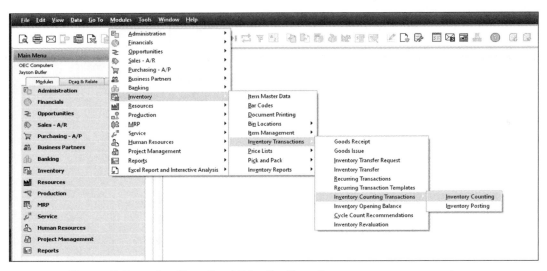

Figure 1.8 Expanding Menu Items Using the Menu Bar

Many highly valuable sections and commands are available within the overall structure of the menu bar or ribbon. Let's discuss brief examples of each menu bar (major selection) dropdown list; many of the second-level options expand for additional selections. These menus should be explored over time as you go deeper and deeper into using SAP Business One. The menus can add value and productivity to daily tasks.

Let's walk through the menu options available in the menu bar ribbon.

As shown in Figure 1.9, the FILE menu includes a number of options. Notice that the SEND and EXPORT options have small triangles immediately to their right, which signifies that these options have additional options available as well.

Figure 1.9 The File Menu

Figure 1.10 shows the menu options from the EDIT menu, which includes routine editing items such as copy and paste.

Figure 1.10 The Edit Menu

The options listed in the VIEW menu shown in Figure 1.11 focus primarily on ancillary information and display options.

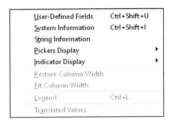

Figure 1.11 The View Menu

When you select the DATA menu, the dropdown list shown in Figure 1.12 appears. In the DATA menu, the areas where additional options are available (DUPLICATE TO and ADVANCED) is indicated by the small triangle immediately to the right.

Figure 1.12 The Data Menu

When using GO TO, different outcomes will occur depending on what else is currently in focus, meaning that this menu is *context sensitive*. The options returned will depend upon which SAP Business One object or screen is in focus at the time the GO TO selection is made. (When we talk about something being "in focus" or "active," we mean that a particular object or screen is being used at the time we selected the GO TO menu.)

Figure 1.13 displays the MODULES menu, a dropdown list reminiscent of the main menu.

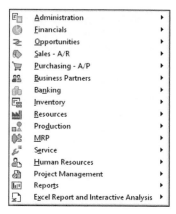

Figure 1.13 The Modules Menu

Figure 1.14 displays the TOOLS menu. Notice that certain items are grayed out, which indicates that this option is not currently available. For instance, PERVASIVE ANALYTICS is grayed out in Figure 1.14 because the Pervasive Analytics tool is only available in SAP Business One, version for SAP HANA, and the system used for these examples is not running on the SAP HANA database.

Figure 1.14 The Tools Menu

Figure 1.15 shows the WINDOW menu selection options. One option of note is the MAIN MENU checkbox. If this box is toggled off (not checked), then the main menu will not appear on the main SAP Business One screen. Toggling off the main menu might be helpful if you wanted more screen space by freeing up the area of the screen used by the main menu.

Figure 1.15 The Window Menu

The options available in the HELP menu selection shown in Figure 1.16 are important and necessary to new SAP Business One users. You should investigate each option carefully because most contain valuable additional orientation and training material available to all users.

Figure 1.16 The Help Menu

The toolbar is another design element in the layout and design of SAP Business One. Let's look specifically at how SAP Business One makes use of this common style of desktop toolkit.

1.2.3   Toolbar

The toolbar located below the menu bar is a collection of icons that provide easy access to commonly used functions. Active functions—those you are allowed to execute based on what you are doing at the moment in SAP Business One—are shown in color, while inactive ones are grayed out. Like other tools, the icons listed in Table 1.1 are context sensitive.

Icon	Description/Activity
	The PREVIEW icon enables you to view a document before printing.
	The PRINT icon prints the active document on the specified printer.
	The EMAIL icon displays the SEND MESSAGE window, in which you add the email addresses and enter the text of the message. (Note that email setup is required.)
	The TEXT icon displays the SEND MESSAGE window, in which you enter the phone number and the text for the message. (Note that this function does not work in the US localization.)
	The FAX icon displays the SEND MESSAGE window, in which you add the fax number and enter the text for the fax. (Note that fax setup is required.)
	The EXCEL icon enables you to export data to Microsoft Excel.
	The WORD icon enables you to export data to Microsoft Word.
	The PDF icon enables you to export data as a portable document format (PDF) file.
	This icon enables you to launch different applications directly from SAP Business One.
	The LOCK icon enables you to lock the active screen.
	The FIND icon switches to the Find mode.
	The ADD icon switches to the Add mode.
	The FIRST DATA RECORD, PREVIOUS RECORD, NEXT RECORD, and LAST DATA RECORD icons allow you to navigate between objects of the same type.
	The REFRESH icon updates the current screen/document.
	The FILTER icon enables you to search for and display specific data in SAP Business One.
	The SORT icon enables you to sort data in a table format.
	This icon displays a document that has been created on the basis of the selected document or as a follow-up to the selected document. For example, you can view the original sales order or the subsequent A/R invoice from a delivery.

Table 1.1 Toolbar Icons

Icon	Description/Activity
	This icon displays a document that has been created on the basis of the selected document or as a follow-up to the selected document. For example, you can view the original sales order or the subsequent A/R invoice from a delivery.
	The PROFIT icon displays the GROSS PROFIT window for a sales document.
	The PAYMENT MEANS icon enables you to specify the payment means for a document.
	The WEIGHT icon calculates the volume and weight of the items in marketing documents. The weights and volumes for inventory master data items must be set up.
	The JOURNAL icon displays the transaction journal report with the summary of all the accounting transactions.
	The JOURNAL PREVIEW icon enables you to preview the corresponding journal entry posting prior to adding a document that will generate a journal entry. If adding the document triggers more than one journal entry posting, you can preview all of them at once.
	The PRINT LAYOUT icon enables you to select a layout or printing sequence and edit the layout for printing documents and reports.
	The FORM SETTINGS icon displays a window with options specific to the active window. You can change these settings and modify the fields, rows, and tables displayed in the active window.
	This icon displays the QUERY MANAGER window.
	This icon displays WORKFLOW WORKLIST window.
	This icon displays the MESSAGES/ALERTS OVERVIEW window.
	The CALENDAR icon displays scheduled meetings, phone calls, and other task like activities.
	This icon enables you to select a default branch for the current user and document.
	The HELP icon enables you to enter the Context-Sensitive Help System (SAP Library) based on your current location in SAP Business One.

Table 1.1 Toolbar Icons (Cont.)

Icon	Description/Activity
🖳	This icon opens the COCKPIT MANAGEMENT window.
🖳	This icon opens a window that will allow you to revert cockpits to the original SAP Business One out-of-the-box designs. We recommend that you restrict this feature to only the users that require it by using authorizations as needed.

Table 1.1 Toolbar Icons (Cont.)

Note that SAP Business One, version for SAP HANA, other icons are available to connect you to Available to Promise, Delivery Schedule Management, Cash Flow Forecast, and the Pervasive Analytics Designer.

Tips and Tricks: Don't Rely Solely on Icons

Make sure you don't just rely on the icons in the toolbar. While powerful, these icons represent only a small percentage of the actions you can initiate in SAP Business One. Smart users will commit to learning more about your SAP Business One system every day by using the menus, especially by right-clicking everywhere. Context-sensitive commands are all over the place, unless you explore, you'll never know the depth of help available.

1.2.4 Document Screen Design

For SAP Business One users, SAP's commitment to consistency is valuable because consistency reduces the learning curve and elevates user competency in a much shorter period of time.

A great example is what SAP refers to as *marketing documents*. Marketing documents are any document with SAP Business One that will potentially touch or influence leads, customers, and vendors. If you learn to use one of these forms, you learn to use them all.

Table 1.2 gives a short list of A/R and A/P marketing documents. The similar design of these documents adds value to SAP Business One; let's briefly look at a few documents and pay attention to specific areas or "elements" of the screen design. The constant use of these elements throughout the application's design simplifies the user experience from one module to another.

A/R Documents	A/P Documents
	Purchase request
Sales quotation	Purchase quotation
Sales order	Purchase order
Delivery	Goods receipt PO
Return	Goods return
A/R invoice	A/P invoice
A/R credit memo	A/P credit memo

Table 1.2 Documents in the Main Menu

Take a look at the SALES QUOTATION screen in Figure 1.17 and then at the PUR-CHASE QUOTATION screen in Figure 1.18. The basic design is the same in these screens as in almost all other A/P or A/R documents. Except for the smallest of nuances, learning one screen basically means that you have learned them all.

Figure 1.17 The Sales Quotation Screen

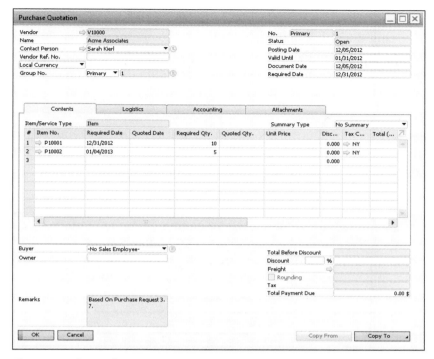

Figure 1.18 The Purchase Quotation Screen

Let's examine some of the common screen design elements found in SAP Business One.

Header

The header of the document contains what we could refer to as "introductory" information, such as the contact information, plus pertinent dates. Each header also has a document number. The information in this section links the company and contact information with the document itself.

Footer

The footer of the document contains what one might call *summary data*, which includes totals with and without taxes, plus any freight and discounts related to the entire document. The sales person and the owner of the document can use reference fields.

Tabs

The tabs are arranged in a row in the top third of the document. Clicking on each tab will open them. Much of the information in the tabs will be filled in automatically based on the choices made in the header or from other documents connected to this document. Data in tabs are generally displayed in two styles: grid and field.

In the example PURCHASE QUOTATION screen shown in Figure 1.19, notice the various screen elements. First, let's focus on the CONTENTS tab. Notice that the CONTENTS tab always uses a grid style to organize detailed data about each line item.

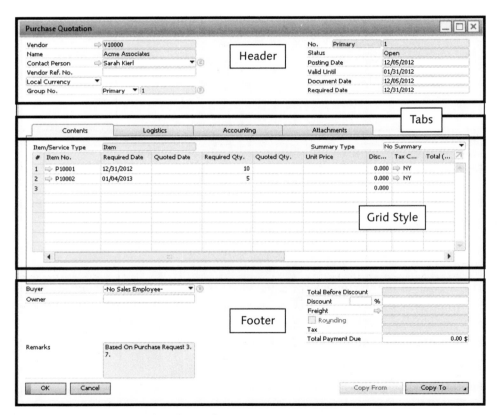

Figure 1.19 The Contents Tab in the Purchase Quotation Screen

Tips and Tricks: Grid-Style Integration with Microsoft Excel

The grid-style data entry screen of the CONTENTS tab can be exported to Excel by clicking on the EXCEL icon in the toolbar.

You can also right-click and maximize the grid to see and work with additional information.

Finally, you can also right-click and select COPY TABLE; subsequently, you can paste this table into Excel, modify the data, copy it, and paste it back into the CONTENTS tab.

Still using the PURCHASE QUOTATION screen as our example, let's turn our attention to the LOGISTICS tab shown in Figure 1.20. Notice that the LOGISTICS tab uses a field style for data entry. Some of these fields, such as SHIP TO, are filled in from the defaults on the master data record but may be edited as needed.

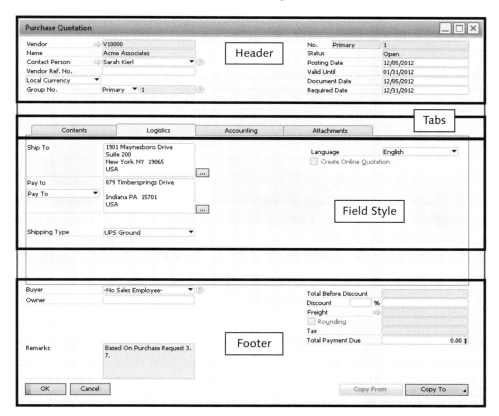

Figure 1.20 The Logistics Tab in the Purchase Quotation Screen

Let's move on to the ACCOUNTING tab shown in Figure 1.21. This tab also uses the field style, in which some fields are filled in by default and may be edited as needed.

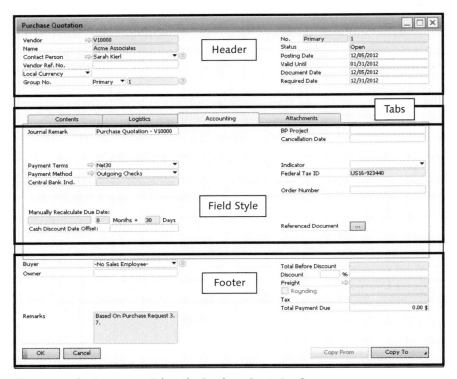

Figure 1.21 The Accounting Tab in the Purchase Quotation Screen

The last tab to examine is the ATTACHMENTS tab. Take a look at Figure 1.22 to see how this one is different. In this location, you may attach any documents type, such as a Microsoft Word or Excel document, a PDF file, or a picture or video file that is relevant to the document.

> **Tips and Tricks: Attachments Tab (Setup Required)**
>
> In order for the attachments function to work, allowing you to insert documents into the ATTACHMENTS tab, the menu path where *all* documents are stored must be specified in the ADMINISTRATION • SYSTEM INITIALIZATION • GENERAL SETTINGS • PATH TAB • ATTACHMENT folder.

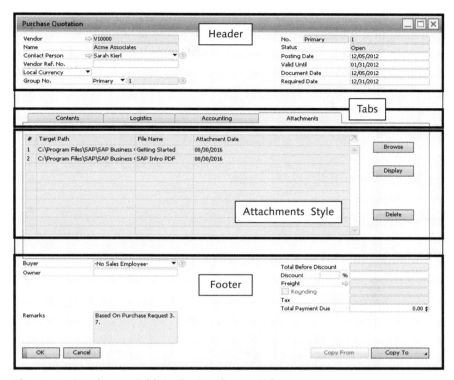

Figure 1.22 Attachments Table in the Attachments Tab

Buttons

Footers also contain buttons. The following are common buttons in standard marketing documents:

► UPDATE: Updates an existing document that has been changed.

► OK: Files the document in the designated location.

► COPY FROM: Creates a new document from an existing document.

► COPY TO: Copies the current document to another subsequent document in the business process.

► CANCEL: Cancels the document changes.

COPY TO is context sensitive and will allow you only those choices that are appropriate for the active document type. For example, in Figure 1.23, only some choices are presented when you click on the COPY TO button for a purchase quotation. All the information from the purchase quotation will be copied to the next document (e.g., a purchase order), and the documents will be linked together in the relationship map shown in Figure 1.24. A relationship map reveals the relational connections between documents in a standard SAP Business One process; we'll look at this more closely in later chapters, especially Chapter 5 and Chapter 6.

Figure 1.23 The Copy To Menu for a Purchase Order

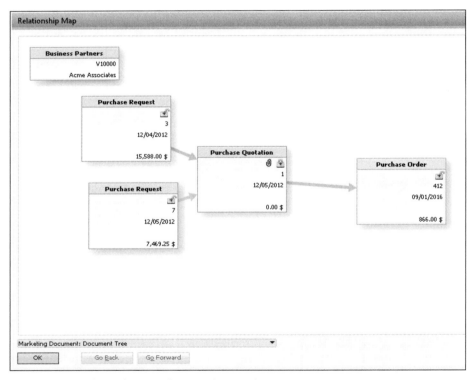

Figure 1.24 A Relationship Map for a Purchase Order

Tips and Tricks: Relationship Map

To see the relationship map for any document within SAP Business One, right-click and select RELATIONSHIP MAP while the document is open.

1.2.5   Right-Click Context-Sensitive Menu

Throughout SAP Business One, the screen design has a right-click, context-sensitive additional menu. Right-clicking in different portions of a document will result in different menus appearing.

The header and footer and all tabs, except the CONTENTS tab, will share the document-specific right-click menu shown in Figure 1.25. The CONTENTS tab has a grid-style right-click menu specific to this data region, as shown in Figure 1.26.

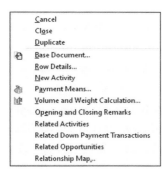

Figure 1.25 Right-Click Menu Options for the Logistics, Accounting, and Attachments Tabs

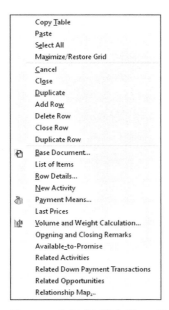

Figure 1.26 Right-Click Menu Options for the Contents Tab

1.2.6   You Can Also Menu

Throughout SAP Business One records, you are presented with the YOU CAN ALSO button, which is visible in the bottom right side of many screens. This functionality is available throughout all marketing documents in Sales (A/R), Purchasing (A/P), Inventory, and beyond. The options available in the YOU CAN ALSO menu depend on where you are, which steps have been taken, and which steps come next in the context of your SAP Business One tasks.

For an example of the YOU CAN ALSO menu in action, consult Chapter 7, Section 7.1.4, which guides you through perusing business partners' master data.

1.3   Printing

Printing documents in SAP Business One is initiated though the main menu under FILE (see Figure 1.27) or by using the PRINT icon (the printer) in the toolbar. This first option is sometimes preferable since this option allows you to pick a specific printer and other printing options. Using the PRINT icon may be a quicker approach, but the document will print only to your default printer. Notice also in Figure 1.27 that other printing options are available; SELECT LAYOUT AND PRINT, for example, allows you to choose a specific style of print layout (e.g., a style specific to a geographic region).

Figure 1.27 The Print from File Menu

1.4   Previewing

You can preview documents in SAP Business One through the main menu under
FILE (see Figure 1.28). As with printing, notice the other previewing options that
are available, such as PREVIEW LAYOUTS, which gives you the opportunity to see
what various layout styles look like prior to actual printing.

Figure 1.28 The Print from File Menu

Alternatively, you can use the PREVIEW icon (the document with a magnifying
glass) in the toolbar. This option is a fast one-click approach but is limited to previewing only the default print layout for the specific document type (for example,
a purchase quotation). Figure 1.29 shows the default preview layout when clicking on the PREVIEW icon.

You can also email an SAP Business One marketing document. When the document is open, follow the menu path FILE • SEND • OUTLOOK E-MAIL or FILE • SEND •
SAP BUSINESS ONE MAILER.

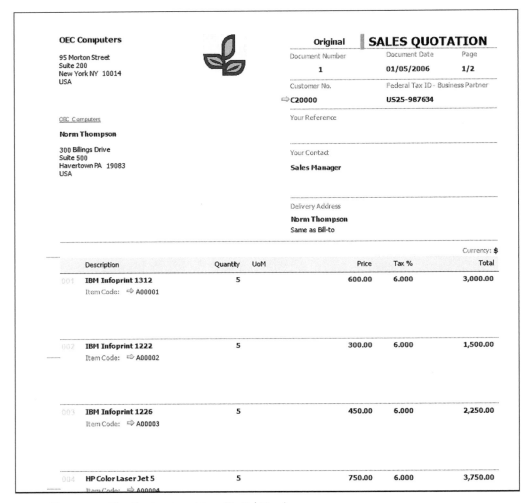

Figure 1.29 The Preview Icon View (Partial View)

1.5 Cockpits, Widgets, and Dashboards

Implementations from SAP Business One, version 8.8, onward have the option to configure and use cockpits, widgets, and dashboards. The example shown in Figure 1.30 is the plain and, some believe, sleeker offering without cockpits and dashboards.

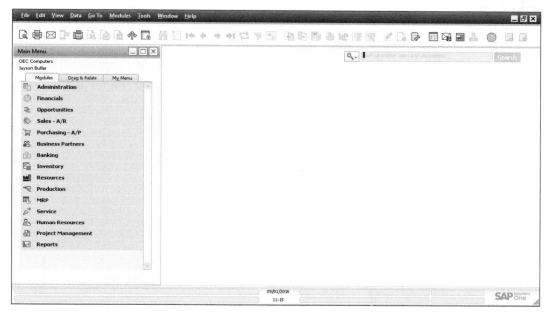

Figure 1.30 The SAP Business One Screen without Cockpits and Dashboards

Setting these screens up falls outside the scope of this book because system administrators and implementation consultants generally handle these tasks, but in the event that these have been set up, follow these steps to activate cockpits and dashboards:

1. In the main menu, go to Tools • Cockpit • Enable My Cockpit.

2. Follow the menu path Administration Menu • System Initialization • General Settings • Cockpit Tab and select Enable Cockpit. You will need to restart SAP Business One.

3. Click the More button and select Enable SAP Crystal Dashboards. Again, you will need to restart SAP Business One.

Tips and Tricks: Dashboard Activation

Dashboard activation also requires that the SAP Business One integration framework is installed, setup, configured, and activated. Again—check with your administrator or friendly consultant for this part of the implementation project.

1.6 SAP Business One, Version for SAP HANA

SAP Business One, version for SAP HANA, offers a third possible interface: the SAP Fiori interface. Unfortunately, setting up search, key performance indicators (KPIs), and analytics functionalities for SAP Fiori falls outside the scope of the book.

Now that we've mastered navigating SAP Business One, let's briefly highlight areas within the SAP Business One Administration menu that you might use in your everyday work as a business user.

2   Administration

Every ERP software involves both regular business users and system administrators. By the time the average business user gets their hands on the software, almost all the administrative decisions and processes have been made as part of the setup, design, and implementation of the product. This is the domain of system administrators and implementation consultants.

However, a small handful of administration tasks do fall within the reach of the target audience for this book: you, the business user. The goal of this chapter is not to deliver an exhaustive resource for the administration of SAP Business One but instead to cover the three important topics that every user should know: choosing a company, creating and using approval procedures, and creating and using alerts.

2.1   Choosing a Company

All SAP Business One users need to know how to change between one database (or company) and another. This skill is necessary for a few pragmatic reasons:

1. First, you must be able to switch easily between a production database and a test database. While the *production database* is used for genuine daily work and truly capturing business-related transactions, the *test database* (or *sandbox database*) is where you can go to learn, practice, investigate, and even experiment—in other words, to master SAP Business One with hands-on experience in a safe test environment.

2. Second, many companies running SAP Business One have more than one company database. One common reason is that these companies may be located in several countries and require separate databases with specific SAP Business One localizations and languages.

To change the company database, simply navigate to the main menu ADMINISTRATION • CHOOSE COMPANY. Click on CHOOSE COMPANY, and the CHOOSE COMPANY screen shown in Figure 2.1 will appear.

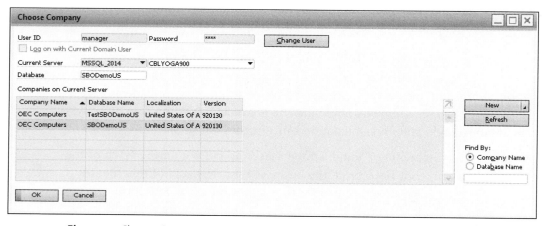

Figure 2.1 Choose Company

Notice that the company you're *currently* logged in to is highlighted in the COMPANIES ON CURRENT SERVER table. To change to any other company database, highlight the company database you wish to connect to and click the CHANGE USER button. Once you've filled in your SAP Business One user name and password, as shown in Figure 2.2, click the OK button.

Figure 2.2 User Name and Password

Now, you are logged in to the company database you selected. Take a peek at the upper left-hand corner of the SAP Business One main login screen; as shown in

Figure 2.3, this message is to remind you of your user name and to which company database you are logged in.

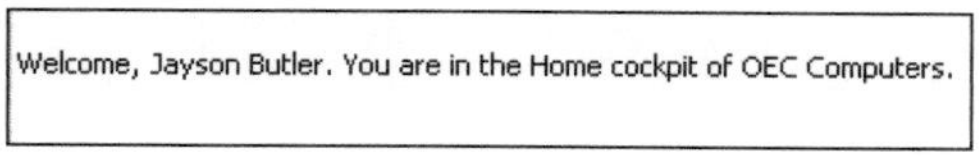

```
Welcome, Jayson Butler. You are in the Home cockpit of OEC Computers.
```

Figure 2.3 The Main Screen Login Reminder

The CHOOSE COMPANY screen also addresses a few other potential scenarios. For example, a larger company might have multiple servers with different company databases on each server. The CHOOSE COMPANY screen allows you to also change the server and then refresh the screen to list the company databases specific to that server. You can also create multiple instances of SAP Business One running at the same time and have each of them logged into the same company database or to different company databases at the same time.

However, take note you cannot use the same user name and password to simultaneously log into SAP Business One from more than one workstation.

2.2 Approval Procedures

From an administrative perspective, approval procedures may be a good fit whenever business processes require a stopping point before completion. One example might be requiring any purchase order greater than $5,000 to be approved by the purchasing manager before a commitment to a vendor is finalized. Another example might be requiring the sales manager to approve a new sales order for your customer if the total amount of the new sales order would put the customer over their credit limit.

To assist with these types of business requirements, SAP Business One has given us *approval templates*, which you can launch from the main menu by following the menu path ADMINISTRATION • APPROVAL PROCEDURES • APPROVAL TEMPLATES.

Click this menu selection to display the APPROVAL TEMPLATES SETUP screen shown in Figure 2.4. In our example, we set up an internal purchase order requisition that activates only for purchase requests that exceed $250.00.

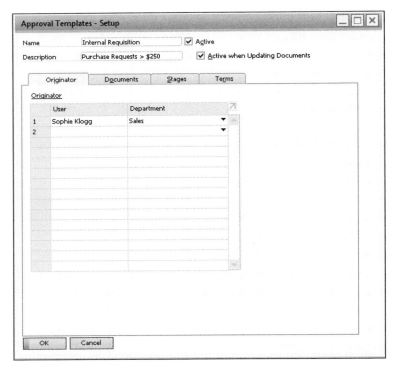

Figure 2.4 The Approval Templates Setup Screen

Notice in Figure 2.4 that you must enter a name for the approval template and a description of its general purpose. Two steps are key here: checking the ACTIVE box and checking the ACTIVE WHEN UPDATING DOCUMENTS box, which will prevent anyone from adding additional items after approval.

The APPROVAL TEMPLATES SETUP screen has four tabs:

▶ The ORIGINATOR tab contains a list of users allowed to create the situation in which this approval procedure is required. The list may contain all users, or as in the case of our example in Figure 2.4, the list may be limited to a single user, such as Sophie Klogg.

▶ The DOCUMENTS tab is a list of potential SAP Business One documents that should be included for this approval procedure. Some approval scenarios will involve multiple documents, but in our example in Figure 2.5, only one document (the purchase request) selected. Notice also that the corresponding INTERNAL REQUISITION radio button has been checked.

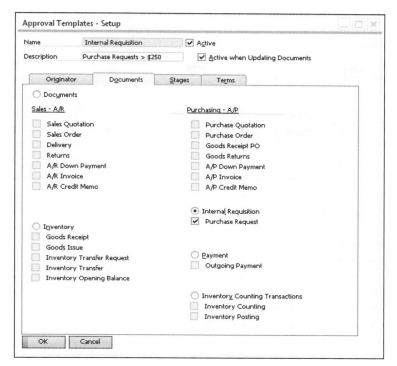

Figure 2.5 The Documents Tab of the Approval Templates Setup Screen

▶ The third tab in the APPROVAL TEMPLATES SETUP screen is the STAGES tab. Most scenarios only require a single approval stage and single approver, as is the case in our example in Figure 2.6. However, some scenarios may require multiple stages and approvers for workflows that bring a much greater level of risk for the organization and thus require higher levels of authority to authorize or approve the action being requested. You can also require multiple approvals or authorize several individuals to approve but only require one. Notice also that the approver can reject the proposed action entirely and that the approval process can even require one or more rejections.

To add a stage in the approval process, you must right-click and select ADD ROW, which brings you to the APPROVAL STAGES SETUP screen shown in Figure 2.6.

Once an approval stage has been created, you can add it to the approval template by clicking on the OK button. To edit the approval stage after it has been added, just click on the golden arrow.

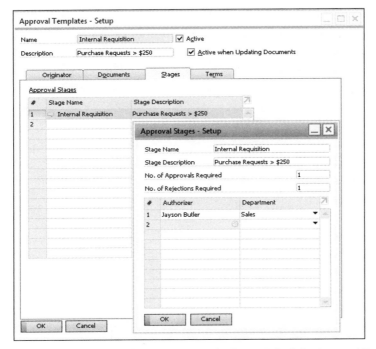

Figure 2.6 The Approval Stages Setup in the Stages Tab of the Approval Templates Setup Screen

Tips and Tricks: Editing or Deleting Approval Procedures

Once an approval procedure has been activated and a business scenario has triggered it, that procedure may not be edited or deleted until all the documents implied have been finalized. In other words, you can't edit an approval procedure when it's in the middle of an approval.

We recommend that you use approval procedures sparingly and that you be sure to create the approval correctly. The best way to ensure that the approval procedure is working properly is to test it thoroughly and completely in your test database before activating it in a production database.

▶ The final tab in the creation process is the TERMS tab shown in Figure 2.7. In this tab, we'll establish the terms or conditions under which the approval procedure will run. You have two options here: a radio button for ALWAYS and a radio button for WHEN THE FOLLOWING APPLIES, which enables you to set the various parameters that would catch the correct document. In our example, the approval procedure will run when the document's total is greater than $250.00. You may apply these conditions in a singular fashion, as in our example, or you may have multiple conditions.

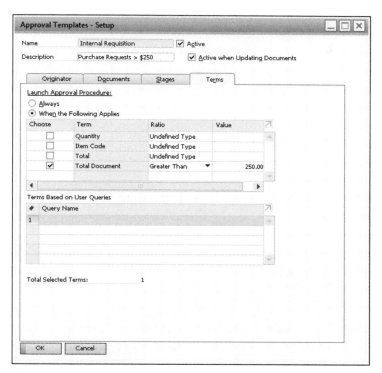

Figure 2.7 The Terms Tab of the Approval Templates Setup Screen

While our example is simple and straightforward, out-of-the-box provisions from SAP may not address all approval procedure business scenario needs. In these situations, you may create a *query*, which can be much more specific and can perform more complex evaluations.

Let's turn our attention to the bottom section of Figure 2.7, where you'll see a table labeled TERMS BASED ON USER QUERIES.

Once your query has been created, double-click on the first query row in the TERMS tab to apply your query, which will take you to the Query Manager shown in Figure 2.8; here, navigate to and select the query you created before clicking OK. The name of the query will subsequently be listed in the QUERY NAME box of the TERMS tab.

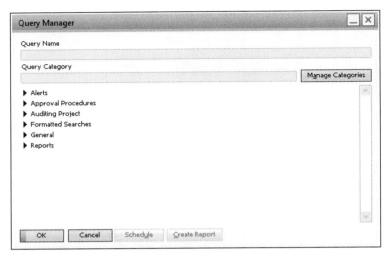

Figure 2.8 The Query Manager

> **Tips and Tricks: Query Organization**
>
> We recommend that you create special category folders for queries used for specific purposes. Notice in Figure 2.8 that category folders have been created for alerts, approval procedures, formatted searches, and reports. Having these repositories will make it far easier in the future to locate a specific query among the hundreds that you may eventually have.

Now, we've finished setting up our approval procedure and can click the OK button. Because we selected the ACTIVE checkbox, our approval procedure will now begin to take action on purchase requests created by Sophie Klogg in which the document total is greater than $250.00.

To test the procedure, you'll first need to log in as Sophie Klogg and then create a purchase request for $250.00 or more, as we've done in Figure 2.9. Notice that the REQUEST FOR DOCUMENT GENERATION screen appears when you attempt to add the document to the system. This screen displays the name of the approval procedure and a short explanation; when you click OK on the REQUEST FOR DOCUMENT GENERATION screen, the approval procedure will file the purchase request and send a notification to the approver (Jayson Butler).

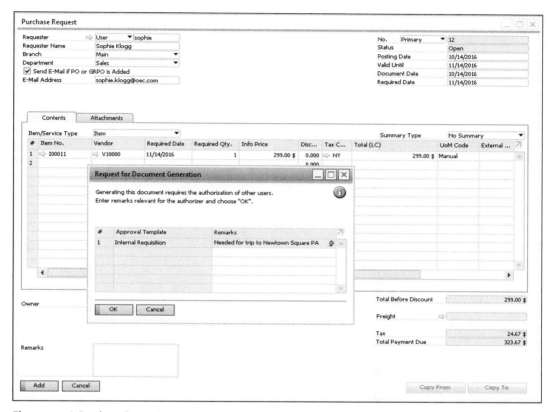

Figure 2.9 A Purchase Request

To test the next step of the approval procedure, you'll need to log out as Sophie Klogg and log in as Jayson Butler. Once you're logged into the SAP Business One as Jayson Butler, the MESSAGES AND ALERTS screen will be updated with a new alert message. As shown in Figure 2.10, the system lets you know that a new document needs to be approved or rejected.

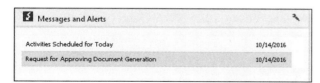

Figure 2.10 The Messages and Alerts Screen

To investigate this document approval request, double-click on the highlighted message. The MESSAGES/ALERTS OVERVIEW window shown in Figure 2.11 will open.

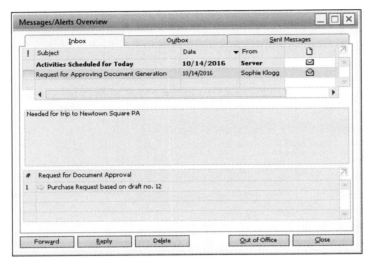

Figure 2.11 The Messages/Alerts Overview Window

Now, still logged in as Jayson, click on the golden arrow to the left of PURCHASE REQUEST BASED ON DRAFT NO. 12 to drill into this particular approval requirement. The REQUEST FOR GENERATION APPROVAL screen appears, as shown in Figure 2.12.

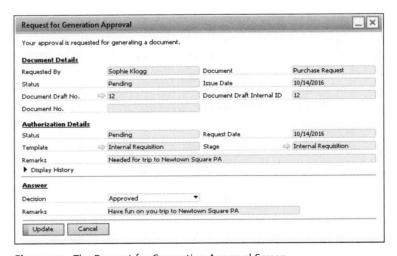

Figure 2.12 The Request for Generation Approval Screen

On this screen, you'll see summary information about this approval scenario. You can also investigate the purchase request fully by clicking on the golden arrow for the DOCUMENT DRAFT NO. or by using the golden arrow to investigate the approval procedure template and/or stage.

The most important thing you will address is the ANSWER section at the bottom of the REQUEST FOR GENERATION APPROVAL screen. Three possible responses are available in the dropdown list of the DECISION box: PENDING, APPROVED, and NOT APPROVED. All of these will send a message back to Sophie with any remarks you (as Jayson) may have added. Next, click on UPDATE • OK. As a result, Sophie will get a message saying her purchase request has been approved.

Once again, to test this next part of the process, log out as Jayson Butler and log back in as Sophie. Now, when you (as Sophie) log into SAP Business One, the MESSAGES/ALERTS OVERVIEW screen communicates that the purchase request has been approved, as shown in Figure 2.13.

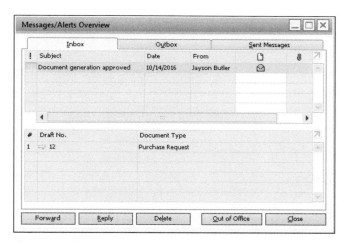

Figure 2.13 The Messages/Alerts Overview Screen

Next, click on the golden arrow to open the purchase request. Currently, the document is in draft form, but by clicking the ADD button, you actually move the document out of "draft" status and make it a true purchase request in SAP Business One.

If you retrieve the purchase request to the screen, you can also investigate the approval process this document has gone through by right-clicking in either the header or the footer of the document and selecting APPROVAL STATUS REPORT. The Approval Status Report is shown in Figure 2.14.

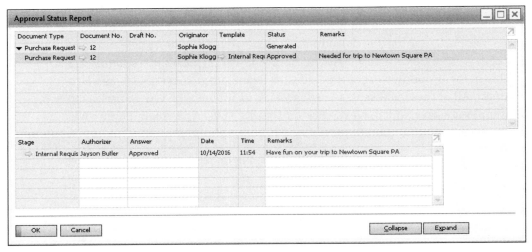

Figure 2.14 The Approval Status Report Screen

Our example was a simple illustration of the process for creating and running an approval procedure in SAP Business One. With a little practice and careful testing, you'll be able to facilitate unique approval procedures that meet the specific needs of your company.

2.3   Alerts Management

Another powerful administration feature in SAP Business One that every user should be familiar with are *alerts*. While the previous topic of approval procedures has a prevention quality built in to catch errors before they happen, alerts catch problems after they have already occurred.

You can, however, create alerts that "predict" that something will happen before it actually does—but of course, as you can imagine, that particular approach to alerts is not available out of the box. You'll need a higher degree of skill, careful calculation, and double-checking to create a query capable of prediction. Just like approval procedures, complex alerts with a powerful predictive capability will require query creation.

Out-of-the-box SAP Business One has eight alerts that you can take advantage of and adjust. Let's look at one of these—the Deviation from Percentage of Gross Profit alert—as an example. To access it, navigate to ADMINISTRATION • ALERTS MANAGEMENT and then click the green next record arrow until you arrive at the DEVIATION FROM % OF GROSS PROFIT predefined alert from SAP shown in Figure 2.15.

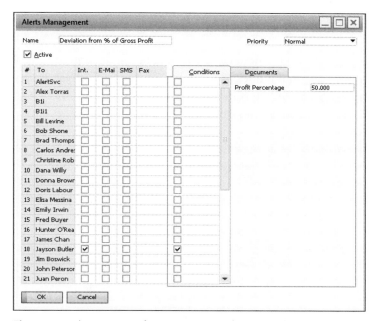

Figure 2.15 The Deviation from Percentage of Gross Profit Alert

Let's walk through the settings for this alert:

1. Set the PRIORITY field in the top-right corner to NORMAL.

2. Make sure the ACTIVE box is checked.

3. Select the approver (in our case, this is Jayson Butler) to receive an internal message.

4. On the CONDITIONS tab, the PROFIT PERCENTAGE field (in other words, the percentage below which an alert will occur) has been set to 50%.

5. In the DOCUMENTS tab shown in Figure 2.16, select SALES QUOTATION.

To file this alert and make it active, click the OK button.

Figure 2.16 The List of A/R Documents in the Document Tab

If everything works as we intended, whenever a sales quotation document is filed and the gross profit for the document does not equal 50% or better, Jayson Butler will receive an alert message. So let's test our query by creating the alert first in our test database and then creating a sales quotation as in Figure 2.17.

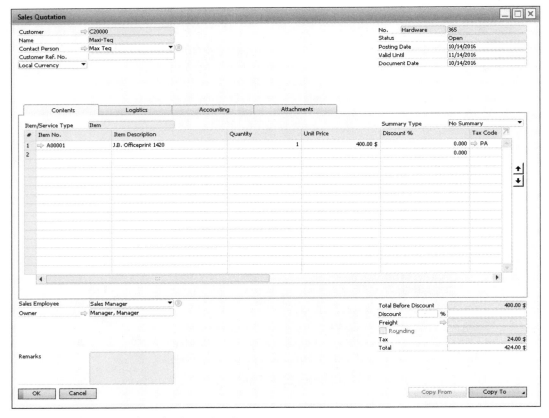

Figure 2.17 The Sales Quotation Screen

> **Tips and Tricks: Find Mode vs. Add Mode**
>
> When a screen is opened in SAP Business One, the default mode is either Find or Add. To change it from one mode to the other, use the keystrokes Ctrl+A for the Add mode or Ctrl+F for the Find mode. Alternatively, you can use the icons in the ribbon: the ADD icon (a screen with a red dot) will switch you to the Add mode, and the FIND icon (the binoculars) will switch you to the Find mode.

Because the gross profit is less than the 50% mark we set in our alert, we expect this sales quotation to send an alert to Jayson Butler. Right-click and select GROSS PROFIT just to be sure to open the gross profit analysis of this sales quotation, as shown in Figure 2.18.

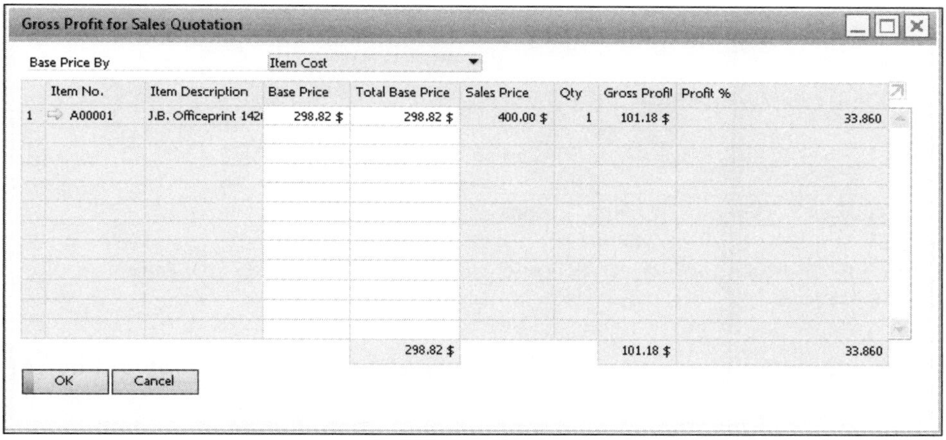
Gross Profit for Sales Quotation
Base Price By
Item Cost
Item No.
Item Description
Base Price
Total Base Price
Sales Price
Qty
Gross Profi
Profit %
1
A00001
J.B. Officeprint 142
298.82 $
298.82 $
400.00 $
1
101.18 $
33.860
298.82 $
101.18 $
33.860
OK
Cancel

Figure 2.18 The Gross Profit for Sales Quotation Screen

Look at the right column in this screen. This Gross Profit Analysis Report clearly shows that the gross profit will only be 33.86%—which would immediately launch an alert that checks sales quotations for gross profit violations called Deviation from Percentage of Gross Profit, similar to the alert shown in Figure 2.19.

With this alert, Jayson Butler and any other designated approvers can almost immediately know that a sales quotation has been processed that did not reach the established gross profit goal. Clicking on the golden arrow will open the sales quotation for further evaluation and potential corrective action.

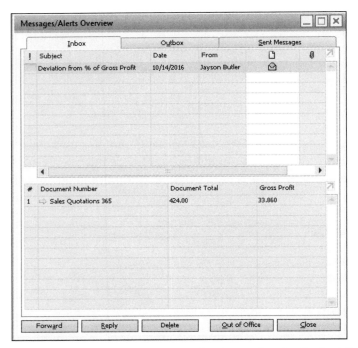

Figure 2.19 The Messages/Alerts Overview Screen Showing the Deviation from Percentage of Gross Profit Alert

But this scenario is just one example of the out-of-the-box alerts provided by SAP that are reflective of solid best practices for most businesses. In fact, another best practice is to activate these alerts one by one before creating your own customized alerts using queries. Further, we also recommend that you use alerts sparingly. Some users have created hundreds of alerts and later complained that the system is too interruptive, preventing workers from being able to pace their work due to all the interruptions.

This administration chapter has purposefully been kept short to draw a strong line between typical business user tasks and those performed by system administrators or implementation consultants, whose needs are far more complex and might require an entire book all by itself.

Financials are a crucial part of a company's day-to-day business. You'll need financial reports to get a picture of how your company is operating. In order to produce reports, each company must define and set up an approved chart of accounts. Journal entries, adjusting entries, and recurring transactions are needed to maintain and provide appropriate corrections to your financials.

3   Financials

The Financials module in SAP Business One houses the majority of what you need to maintain and provide reports. In this chapter, we'll show you how to add and maintain your chart of accounts, how to create journal entries, and how to set up recurring postings. We'll also show you how to maintain fixed assets and depreciate those assets. Finally, we'll walk you through some key financial reports to help you get a clear picture of your company's financial health.

3.1   Chart of Accounts

In SAP Business One, the chart of accounts is the foundation of your enterprise resource planning (ERP) system.

The way your chart of accounts is structured is important for how your company reports on its financials. In SAP Business One, the chart of accounts is structured like a filing cabinet that organizes each account into its appropriate drawer. For example, the ASSETS drawer on the right side of Figure 3.1 is open; in the pane to its left, the CURRENT ASSETS list of accounts, beginning with cash and cash equivalents, has been expanded. This organization gives you the ability to roll up accounts based on your defined chart of accounts.

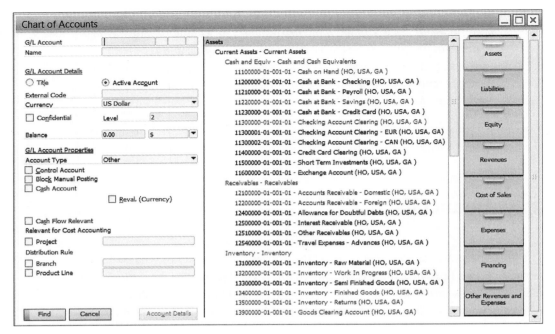

Figure 3.1 The Chart of Accounts Screen

3.1.1 Defining the Chart of Accounts

SAP Business One allows you to either select a predefined chart of accounts based on your localization or define your own chart of accounts when a new company is being created. The vast majority of customers have a very specific chart of accounts they wish to use.

The chart of accounts is structured with *title accounts* and *active accounts*. SAP Business One categorizes these accounts based on their level, moving from level 1 accounts (the highest) to level 4 accounts (the lowest, or most focused and detailed accounts). With SAP Business One, version 9.2, you can define up to ten levels in your chart of accounts.

Title accounts are used to group active accounts under a particular header, which is useful when you want to see a certain dollar figure for a group of accounts.

Active accounts are the main level of the general ledger (G/L), where all detailed transactions reside. In order to roll up an active account under a title account, the active account must be assigned to the title account. In Figure 3.1, you can see the title accounts (here, ASSETS) are at the highest level of the chart of accounts with ASSETS on level 1, CURRENT ASSETS – CURRENT ASSETS at level 2, and CASH AND EQUIV. – CASH AND CASH EQUIVALENTS at level 3.

However, you should be comfortable working with the additional fields on the left side of the CHART OF ACCOUNTS window, which we'll explain in Table 3.1.

Field	Description/Use
G/L ACCOUNT	This field displays an alphanumeric code used to create the G/L account.
NAME	Enter a descriptive name for the G/L account.
G/L ACCOUNT DETAILS	Choose either the TITLE and the ACTIVE ACCOUNT radio button to define the account.
EXTERNAL CODE	In this field, you can assign an external code to identify to the G/L account. You can use this external code later in queries to link external or internal data to the G/L account.
CURRENCY	Set a currency for each active account by choosing one of these two options: ▸ LOCAL CURRENCY: That G/L will only accept transactions in the database's local currency. ▸ ALL CURRENCIES: That G/L will accept transactions in all currencies defined in the system. This is typically recommended.
CONFIDENTIAL	Select the CONFIDENTIAL checkbox to prevent users from accessing any account in the chart of accounts.
LEVEL	Enter a value in the LEVEL field to define the structure and grouping order of the chart of accounts. Remember that level 1 is a title account. Levels 2 through 9 can be either a title account or an active account. Level 10 is an active account.
BALANCE	This field displays the current balance for each G/L account. You can click on the golden arrow to drill down into the account to learn more.

Table 3.1 Fields in the Chart of Accounts Screen

Field	Description/Use
Account Type	Select an option from the dropdown list to define the G/L account. This option places the account in either the Revenue, Expense, or Other group in the chart of accounts.
Control Account	Select this checkbox to designate the account as a control account. Control accounts are tied to a business partner. Accounts receivable and accounts payable G/Ls are considered control accounts because they are tied directly to business partner transactions.
Block Manual Posting	Select this checkbox to prevent journal entries from being created using this account.
Cash Account	Select this checkbox to define an account as a monetary account. This checkbox is only available if the account is in the Assets, Liability, or Equity balance sheet drawers.
Reval. (Currency)	Select this checkbox if your company currency is not the local currency. This option allows use the Conversion Differences tool (discussed in Section 3.9) to investigate how currency exchange impacts the business.
Cash Flow Relevant	Select this checkbox for accounts that are cash flow accounts. You'll be able to create a cash flow report out of the system.
Project	Select this checkbox if you want to assign a G/L account to a specific project. In the general settings, you can choose how to handle the postings.
Distribution Rule	If you have distribution rules defined (as we'll describe in Section 3.17), you can assign a distribution rule to a G/L account. Two subcategories are available: ▶ Branch: If you have this checkbox activated, you can assign a branch to the G/L account in the field to the right. ▶ Product Line: If you have this checkbox activated, you can assign a product line to a G/L account in the field to the right.

Table 3.1 Fields in the Chart of Accounts Screen (Cont.)

Notice the Accounts Detail button underneath these fields. Clicking on this will open an additional window for the G/L account; in this window, shown in Figure 3.2, you'll have more options for defining each G/L account.

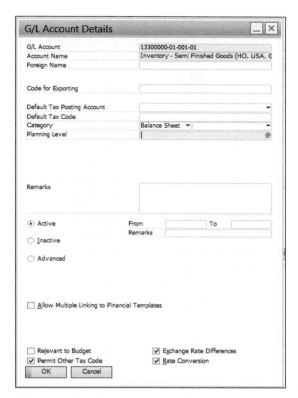

Figure 3.2 The G/L Accounts Detail Screen

We describes the fields in this window in Table 3.2; note that some fields may not be required based on your localization and company needs.

Field	Description/Use
G/L ACCOUNT and ACCOUNT NAME	These fields display information from the chart of accounts and cannot be changed.
FOREIGN NAME	In this field, you can enter an additional account name identifier; use this field to call the G/L account by a different name.
CODE FOR EXPORTING	This code is used to create a link for the chart of accounts to another software or to another chart of accounts within your organization.

Table 3.2 Fields in the G/L Accounts Detail Screen

Field	Description/Use
DEFAULT TAX POSTING ACCOUNT	Select whether the G/L account is considered a SALES TAX ACCOUNT or a PURCHASING TAX ACCOUNT from this dropdown list.
DEFAULT TAX CODE	After selecting a default tax posting account, select the DEFAULT TAX CODE from a list of tax codes defined in the system.
CATEGORY	Define the category of the account based on whether the G/L account is considered a BALANCE SHEET account or a PROFIT AND LOSS account. Once you select a category, you can further select the title account for the G/L account.
REMARKS	Use this text field to add notes regarding the G/L account.
ACTIVE or INACTIVE	These radio buttons allow you to manage any journal entry postings that impact the G/L account. Select the ACTIVE radio button if there are no restrictions. If you select INACTIVE radio button, the G/L account is locked, and no transactions can be posted to it.
FROM/TO	The FROM and TO fields allow the users to set a time frame for when a G/L account is considered ACTIVE or INACTIVE.
ADVANCED	Select this radio button if you want more flexibility than when the G/L account is considered ACTIVE or INACTIVE.
RELEVANT TO BUDGET	Select this checkbox if you want to use the G/L account when defining budgets.

Table 3.2 Fields in the G/L Accounts Detail Screen (Cont.)

3.1.2 Editing the Chart of Accounts

With SAP Business One, you can edit and rearrange the G/L accounts on your chart of accounts. You can reorganize your accounts one drawer at a time or all your drawers at once. You can always move an account from one drawer to another or even to a different title account.

Begin by navigating to MAIN MENU • FINANCIALS • EDIT CHART OF ACCOUNTS. Then place a checkmark in the box for the drawers you'd like to edit; in our example in Figure 3.3, we've selected ASSETS and LIABILITIES. You can select all or clear your selection using the corresponding buttons (SELECT ALL or CLEAR SELECTION) on the bottom right corner. When you're ready, click OK.

Figure 3.3 Edit Chart of Accounts Selection Criteria

The EDIT CHART OF ACCOUNTS window shown in Figure 3.4 opens. You'll notice that this window looks similar to the actual CHART OF ACCOUNTS window, except that after the G/L ACCOUNT DETAILS area you'll see the G/L ACCOUNT LOCATION options.

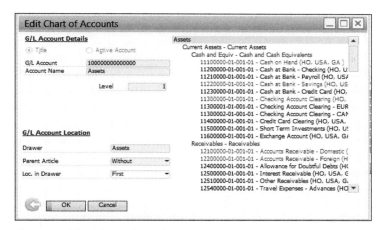

Figure 3.4 The Editing Chart of Accounts Screen

If you would like to move a G/L account to another drawer, click the DRAWER dropdown list and select the drawer where you'd like to move the G/L account to. (In Figure 3.5, our only options are ASSETS and LIABILITIES.)

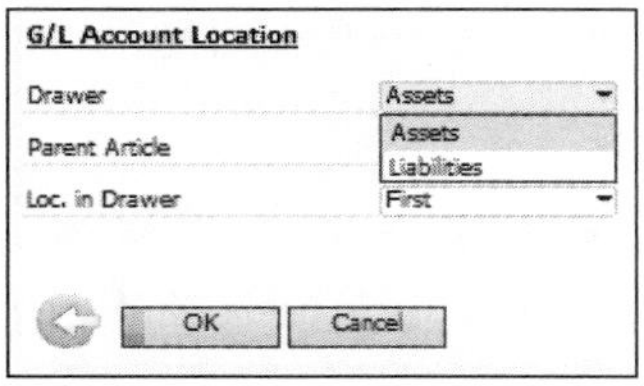

Figure 3.5 Selecting the Drawer

If you would like to move a G/L account to a different title account (called the "parent article" here), choose the corresponding placement from the PARENT ARTICLE dropdown list in Figure 3.6. The list will display the different title accounts into which you can move the G/L.

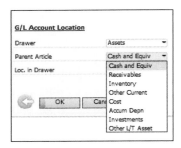

Figure 3.6 Selecting the Parent Article

Finally, let's direct the G/L account to its new home. If you would like to move the G/L account before or after another G/L account, select where you would like the G/L account to go from the LOC. IN DRAWER dropdown list shown in Figure 3.7.

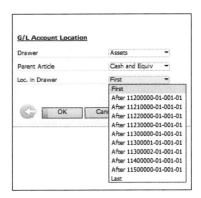

Figure 3.7 Selecting a Location in a Drawer

3.2   Account Code Generator

The Account Code Generator shown in Figure 3.8 is a helpful tool when adding new G/L accounts to the chart of accounts. This tool is especially useful if you are using a segmented chart of accounts and have multiple divisions, regions, or departments and need to create multiple G/L accounts with the same natural account.

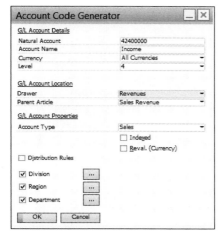

Figure 3.8 The Account Code Generator Screen

Let's use Table 3.3 to walk through the ACCOUNT CODE GENERATOR window.

Fields	Description/Use
NATURAL ACCOUNT	Enter the natural account number.
ACCOUNT NAME	Enter the account name.
CURRENCY	Select the currency type based on your organizational structure. Again, your options here are ALL CURRENCIES or LOCAL CURRENCIES.
LEVEL	Determine whether this account is a title account or an active account by choosing a level from the dropdown list.
DRAWER	Select the drawer into which you will create the new G/L account.
PARENT ARTICLE	Select the parent article (title account) into which the new G/L account will go.
ACCOUNT TYPE	Select the account type; your options here are SALES, EXPENDITURES, or OTHER.
INDEXED	N/A

Table 3.3 Fields in the Account Code Generator Screen

Fields	Description/Use
DISTRIBUTION RULES	If you have distribution rules defined (as we'll describe in Section 3.17), you can assign a distribution rule to a G/L account. There are two subcategories here: ▸ BRANCH: If you have this checkbox activated, you can assign a branch to the G/L account in the field to the right. ▸ PRODUCT LINE: If you have this checkbox activated, you can assign a product line to the G/L account in the field to the right.
DIVISION, REGION, and DEPARTMENT	To use the DIVISION, REGION, and DEPARTMENT checkboxes, click the BROWSE icons (the ellipses) to expand your selection options. As you can see in Figure 3.9, another window will open for you to select the various segments needed to create the G/L account.

Table 3.3 Fields in the Account Code Generator Screen (Cont.)

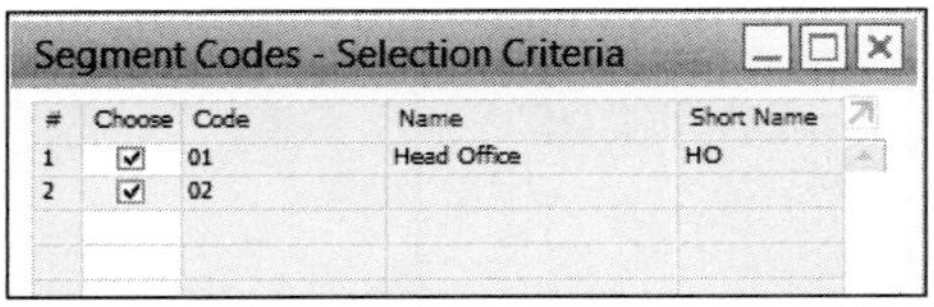

Figure 3.9 Selecting Segments

Once you have completed the selection criteria screen, click OK. The system will generate the account code list shown in Figure 3.10. Select the G/L accounts you wish to add and click ADD to create new G/L accounts.

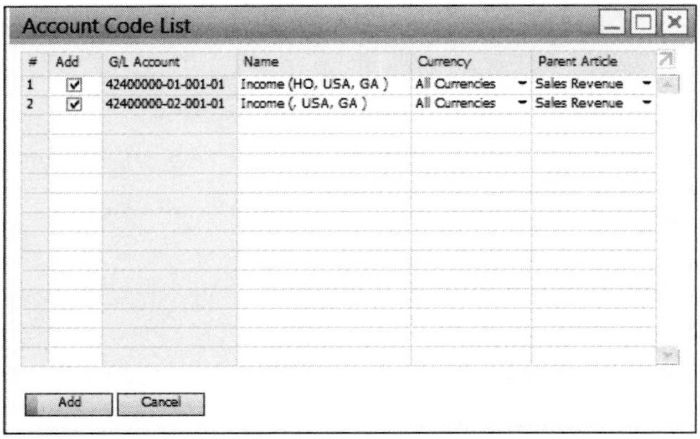

Figure 3.10 The Account Code List Screen

3.3 Journal Entries

A journal entry (JE) is used to post data directly to the database. Any marketing document that affects a G/L posting automatically creates a journal entry behind the scenes in SAP Business One. You cannot add a journal entry unless the entry is balanced (debit and credit are equal).

The JOURNAL ENTRY window is broken into two sections: the header and the corresponding table underneath. Let's look at each.

As shown in Figure 3.11, the header area of the journal entry shows you data that tells a story about the creation of the journal entry. You'll see a journal entry number, which you can use to look up existing journal entries in the system. The journal entry number can also be used externally to refer back to the journal entry. The dates on the header give you information about when the journal entry was posted (the POSTING DATE field), when the originating document was due (the DUE DATE field), and the date on the originating document (the DOC. DATE field). You can use the REMARKS field to add comments to a journal entry to help differentiate this journal entry from others in the system. All these fields, explained further in Table 3.4, can help you identify the reasoning behind the journal entry.

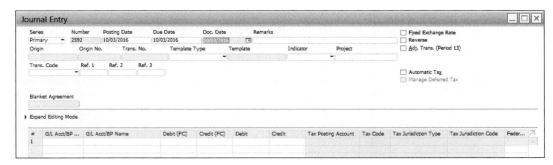

Figure 3.11 The Journal Entry Header Area

Field	Description/Use
SERIES	SAP Business One allows you to define the document number for journal entries and marketing documents. In this field, you can change the series based on company preference.

Table 3.4 Fields in the Journal Entry Header Area

Field	Description/Use
NUMBER	This field displays a sequential number, based on the chosen series, that is generated when a journal entry is added to the database.
POSTING DATE, DUE DATE, and DOC. DATE	These fields display various dates related to the journal entry. The posting date defaults to today's date and can be changed if necessary. The due date is the date the journal entry was entered. The document date is used for reporting purposes.
REMARKS	Enter additional data in this alphanumeric field. If the journal entry was created by another marketing document, the REMARKS field will have the document type and business partner associated with the transaction.
ORIGIN	This field displays an abbreviation indicating the originating document. If the journal entry was created by an A/R invoice, you will see IN in that field.
ORIGIN NO.	This field displays the number of the document that created the journal entry. Click on the golden arrow to drill down into the originating transaction.
TRANS. NO.	This field displays the number series that has been automatically assigned to journal entry.
TEMPLATE TYPE and TEMPLATE	You can create posting templates to post journal entries by percentage or for recurring postings. We'll look at how to create posting templates in Section 3.5 and how to create recurring postings in Section 3.6.
INDICATOR	Enter indicator codes to help you with report writing.
PROJECT	Enter a project code to link a journal entry to any project, which is beneficial for reporting.
TRANS. CODE	Select a user-defined transaction code for reporting. These "user-defined" codes give you yet another way to identify this transaction in any way you wish.
REF 1, REF 2, REF 3	These reference fields correspond to the document numbers of marketing documents that created the journal entry. These fields can also be left blank.
FIXED EXCHANGE RATE	Select this checkbox to create a journal entry in a different currency with a set exchange rate.

Table 3.4 Fields in the Journal Entry Header Area (Cont.)

Field	Description/Use
REVERSE	Select this checkbox to set the journal entry as a reversing transaction, which is often used at period-end closing. When you create the journal entry, you enter the date you wish to see the journal entry reversed in the POSTING DATE field. We'll discuss reverse transactions further in Section 3.7.
ADJ. TRANS. (PERIOD 13)	Select this checkbox to indicate this journal entry as a closing entry, which is beneficial for excluding journal entries from reporting.
AUTOMATIC TAX	If you select this checkbox, SAP Business One will create an additional row with any calculated tax for every row added to any G/L that has a tax group associated with it.

Table 3.4 Fields in the Journal Entry Header Area (Cont.)

Underneath the header is a table for the journal entries. Each row of a journal entry breaks the dollar amounts for each transaction into its corresponding G/L accounts. Our example in Figure 3.12 shows a journal entry to a business partner with the corresponding G/L accounts used to balance the journal entry. You cannot add a journal entry unless the journal entry amounts are balanced (debits and credits are equal).

When completing this table, you'll need to know the G/L account or business partner code and the dollar amounts to enter. To select a business partner code, press Ctrl+Tab on your keyboard. When you add a G/L account into the grid, you'll see a golden arrow next to the G/L account or business partner code. Click the golden arrow to open the chart of accounts where you can drill down into the detail behind that particular G/L account.

#	G/L Acct/BP ...	G/L Acct/BP Name	Debit	Credit	Tax Posting Account	Tax Cod
1	C40000	Earthshaker Corporation	1,090.00 $			
2	22220000-01-	Sales Tax Accrual - State (HO, U		60.00 $		
3	22240000-01-	Sales Tax Accrual - City (HO, US		10.00 $		
4	22230000-01-	Sales Tax Accrual - County (HO,		20.00 $		
5	41110000-01-	JB Printer Revenues (HO, USA,		375.00 $		
6	41100000-01-	Sales Revenues - Domestic (HO,		625.00 $		
7	13400000-01-	Inventory - Finished Goods (HO,		587.66 $		
8	51100000-01-	COGS - Domestic (HO, USA, G/	587.66 $			
			1,677.66 $	1,677.66 $		

Figure 3.12 Fields in the Journal Entry Table Area

3.4 Journal Vouchers

With SAP Business One, you can start a journal entry without finishing it (in other words, without directly posting it to the G/L) using a *journal voucher*. These journal vouchers can be useful if you have a lengthy entry to put together and need to come back to it. You can begin the data entry process and save a journal entry as a draft even if it is unbalanced.

To access the journal voucher functionality shown in Figure 3.13, from the main menu, follow the menu path FINANCIALS • JOURNAL VOUCHERS. The JOURNAL VOUCHER window contains two tables. Once started, your draft journal entry resides in this screen.

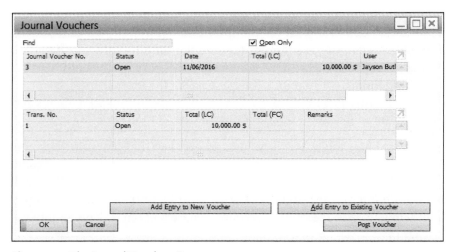

Figure 3.13 The Journal Vouchers Screen

Let's create a new voucher by following these steps:

1. Click ADD ENTRY TO NEW VOUCHER. When the JOURNAL VOUCHER ENTRY window shown in Figure 3.14 opens, notice that it looks identical to the JOURNAL ENTRY window from Figure 3.11.

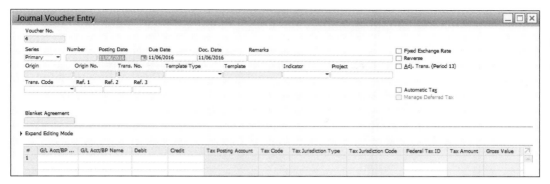

Figure 3.14 The Journal Voucher Entry Screen

2. Enter your required data into the POSTING DATES, DUE DATES, and DOC. DATES fields. You can also add any remarks you want to use to refer back to this journal entry. In the table area, add the G/L accounts you want to use to create the journal voucher, along with the necessary dollar amounts. The journal voucher does not have to be balanced to be created.

3. Click the ADD TO VOUCHER button.

4. Close the JOURNAL VOUCHER ENTRY window, which will bring you back to the JOURNAL VOUCHERS window shown previously in Figure 3.13.

5. Click UPDATE.

You can also add journal entries to existing journal vouchers. In other words, you can create one journal voucher that holds multiple journal entries. Once added, the new entry will display in the bottom frame of the JOURNAL VOUCHER window. The journal voucher entry will have the same voucher number but a different transaction number as shown in Figure 3.15.

At the top, the JOURNAL VOUCHER NO. column displays journal voucher numbers, which can be used to group several journal voucher transactions together. When you click ADD ENTRY TO EXISTING VOUCHER, the system creates a journal voucher under a different transaction number and groups it with the existing journal voucher number. At the bottom, the TRANS. NO. column will display the various journal vouchers created under the same journal voucher number.

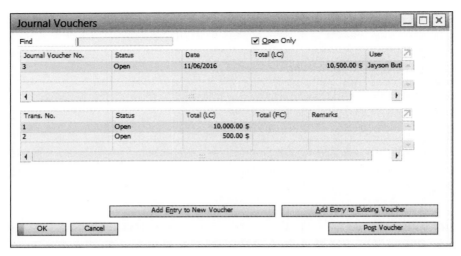

Figure 3.15 Adding an Entry to an Existing Voucher

Let's add an entry to an existing journal voucher by following these steps:

1. Open the JOURNAL VOUCHER window. In the JOURNAL VOUCHER NO. column at the top, select the journal voucher you would like to add transactions to.

2. Click ADD ENTRY TO EXISTING VOUCHER, which will open a blank JOURNAL VOUCHER ENTRY window, like the one shown in Figure 3.14.

3. Enter details about the journal voucher entry such as the posting date, due date, and document date. You can also add remarks to the journal voucher to keep track of the journal voucher or to hold further information about the journal entry. In the table area, add the G/L accounts you want to use for the journal voucher along with the necessary dollar amounts.

4. Next, click ADD VOUCHER. Your journal voucher does not have to be balanced to be added. Make sure you close the JOURNAL VOUCHER ENTRY window.

5. Back on the JOURNAL VOUCHERS window, click UPDATE.

Once you have completed your journal voucher entries, post the journal voucher by following these steps:

1. Click the Post Voucher button shown at the bottom right of Figure 3.16. Your journal vouchers must be balanced before posting (debits and credits are equal).

2. A system message will ask whether you want to save the journal voucher to a permanent file. Click Yes to finalize the posting.

If you want to delete a journal voucher, select the journal voucher in the Journal Voucher No. column at the top and select the transaction in the Trans. No. column at the bottom. Next, follow the menu path Data • Remove Entry found in the very top menu bar between View and Go To of the SAP Business One screen. Alternatively, you can right-click on the line and select Remove Entry. Finally, click the Update button on the Journal Vouchers window.

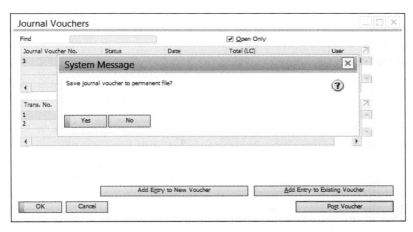

Figure 3.16 Posting a Journal Voucher

3.5 Posting Templates

Some companies have transactions that recur every month, every quarter, and so on. As shown in Figure 3.17, SAP Business One's posting template functionality simplifies data entry by enabling you to set up templates that define the G/L accounts and the percentage to distribute or allocate to. For example, you could allocate a utility bill across several departments, when the chart of accounts has a unique segment for each department. You can use posting templates when entering a journal entry manually.

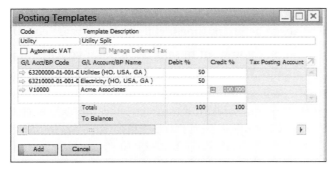

Figure 3.17 The Posting Templates Screen

To create a posting template, follow these steps:

1. Open the POSTING TEMPLATE screen by following the menu path FINANCIALS • POSTING TEMPLATES from the main menu.

2. Enter a unique code to identify the posting template in the CODE field and a description for the posting template in the TEMPLATE DESCRIPTION field.

3. Next, in the G/L ACCT/BP CODE column on the left, enter the G/L accounts or business partner codes you would like to use in the posting template.

4. In the DEBIT % and CREDIT % columns, enter the percentages for distribution. Click ADD to create the posting template.

Now, when creating a journal entry in the JOURNAL ENTRY window as discussed in Section 3.3, you'll be able to select a posting template to distribute values as specified on the posting template you created.

3.6   Recurring Postings

Every organization has transactions that recur every month, every quarter, and so on. SAP Business One allows you to streamline those transactions by setting up recurring postings that are executed automatically.

To define recurring postings, access the RECURRING POSTINGS window by following the menu path MAIN MENU • FINANCIALS • RECURRING POSTINGS and follow these steps:

1. In the header area of the RECURRING POSTINGS window shown in Figure 3.18, specify a code (up to 8 characters) that is unique to the recurring posting.

2. Add a description to the recurring posting in the DESCRIPTION field.

3. You can use any of the reference fields (REF. 1, REF. 2, REF. 3) to add any information about the recurring postings. Many users add information about the posting that is unique to the instance, like a reference number from a business partner or an invoice.

4. In the table area, enter the necessary amounts and G/L accounts or business partner codes. Make sure the DEBIT and CREDIT columns of the recurring postings are balanced.

5. In the footer area of the RECURRING POSTINGS screen, define the frequency of the transaction using the two FREQUENCY dropdown lists.

6. Define when you would like the recurring postings to begin by entering a date in the NEXT EXECUTION field.

7. You can set a limit on the recurring postings by activating the VALID UNTIL checkbox. Enter a date here to set an expiration date for the recurring postings.

8. When you're done, click OK.

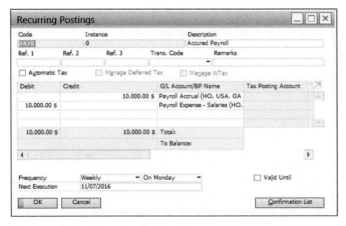

Figure 3.18 The Recurring Postings Screen

SAP Business One will remind the relevant authorized users when a recurring posting is due. This reminder appears in the form of the CONFIRMATION OF RECURRING POSTINGS window shown in Figure 3.19. To access this functionality, you must enable it in the general settings by following the menu path ADMINISTRATION • SYSTEM INITIALIZATION • GENERAL SETTINGS. In the SERVICES tab, select the DISPLAY RECURRING POSTINGS ON EXECUTION checkbox.

The CONFIRMATION OF RECURRING POSTINGS window allows you to edit the recurring postings as needed or to execute them directly either immediately (with the CURRENT SYSTEM DATE radio button) or in the future (with the RECURRING POSTINGS DATE radio button).

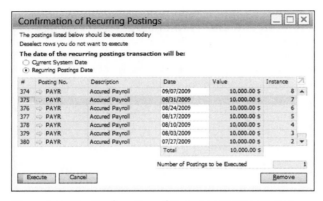

Figure 3.19 The Confirmation of Recurring Postings Screen

To edit a recurring post, follow these steps:

1. Double-click the number of the line you want to edit; in our example in Figure 3.20, we've selected 374.

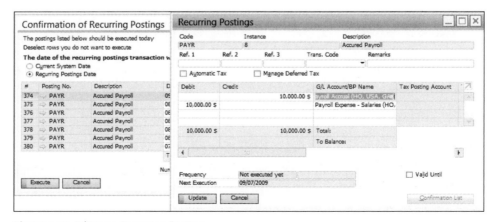

Figure 3.20 Editing a Recurring Posting

2. The RECURRING POSTING window will open. In this screen, make any necessary adjustments to the dollar amounts, remarks, or any of the reference fields.

3. Select UPDATE. Once the recurring posting has been updated, you can now go ahead and click the EXECUTE button.

Before you execute the transaction, you can select whether to post the transaction on the current system date or on the recurring posting date. If you are late executing a recurring posting, your posting period for the month may be closed. If you have finalized your financials and submitted reports, you'll want to consider using the current system date to keep your financials from the closed period the same. Also, if the posting period is closed, you cannot post a journal entry using a date in that closed period. However, if you are still in the process of closing the books and the posting period, you can use the recurring posting date to keep the transaction in the same posting period.

After you click EXECUTE, a system message will ask whether you want to save the postings to a permanent file, as shown in Figure 3.21. Select ADD to finalize the transaction.

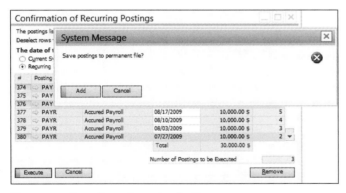

Figure 3.21 Executing a Recurring Posting

3.7 Reverse Transactions

When creating a journal entry, you have the option to set the journal entry as a reversing entry by clicking the REVERSE checkbox on the right side of the JOURNAL ENTRY window in Figure 3.22.

SAP Business One will create a reverse transaction that will post to the G/L based on the date entered in the POSTING DATE field.

Figure 3.22 Creating a Reverse Journal Entry

When the posting date of the reverse transaction occurs, SAP Business One will create the journal entry to be executed. You will either see a popup window called REVERSE TRANSACTIONS when you log into SAP Business One, or you can navigate to MAIN MENU • FINANCIALS • REVERSE TRANSACTIONS as shown in Figure 3.23.

In order to execute the reversing transaction, place a checkbox in the REVERSE column on the left and click EXECUTE to post the journal entry to the G/L.

Figure 3.23 The Reverse Transactions Screen

3.8 Exchange Rate Differences

The Exchange Rate Differences tool allows you to recalculate the local currency and foreign currency in your system based on the exchange rate on a particular day. This is a specialized tool not commonly used by SAP Business One customers; check with your organization's consultant or reseller for more information.

3.9   Conversion Differences

The Conversion Difference tool is used when a company's system currency is different from its local currency. The Conversion Difference tool is used to make adjustments for any differences between system currency and local currency. This, too, is a specialized tool; get in touch with your organization's consultant or reseller for more information.

3.10   1099 Editing

Use the 1099 EDITING window under FINANCIALS • 1099 EDITING to update and make changes to A/P invoices for 1099 vendors, which are unincorporated companies or individuals that you must report to the IRS for services performed.

Let's walk through the selection criteria screen shown in Figure 3.24. For the REPORT TYPE radio buttons, choose either OPEN INVOICES AND CREDIT MEMOS or INVOICES AND CREDIT MEMOS NOT MARKED AS SUBMITTED.

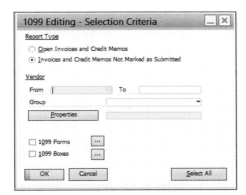

Figure 3.24 1099 Editing Selection Criteria

If you select OPEN INVOICES AND CREDIT MEMOS, SAP Business One will generate a list of A/P invoices with their 1099 form and 1099 box classification (in the middle columns in Figure 3.25). Both the 1099 FORM and 1099 BOX columns can be modified. If a vendor invoice was classified incorrectly, you can switch from, for example, a 1099-DIV to a 1099-MISC. Once you change the form, select an option in the 1099 Box column to specify how you report to the IRS.

Figure 3.25 1099 Editing Screen with Open Invoices and Credit Memos Selected

If you select INVOICES AND CREDIT MEMOS NOT MARKED AS SUBMITTED, SAP Business One will generate a list of A/P invoices with amounts reflected on the 1099 forms. In the window shown in Figure 3.26, you can make adjustments to the dollar amount that will show up in the 1099 AMOUNT column—but only down. In our example, the 1099 amount is $19,485. You can make it $19,000, but you cannot increase it to $20,000.

Figure 3.26 1099 Editing with Invoices and Credit Memos Not Marked as Submitted Selected

The next step is to specify which vendors you want to include. You can specify either ALL VENDORS by leaving the VENDOR FROM and TO fields blank, or you can select a range of vendors by clicking the LOOK UP icon (the circle) in the field and selecting a range of vendors. Additionally, you can select vendors by their vendor group from the GROUP dropdown list, which will include user-defined vendor groups used to categorize your vendors.

Click the PROPERTIES button to use properties defined on the business partner master data to select a list of A/P invoices to review. The 1099 FORMS checkbox allows you to select a certain 1099 form when viewing the list of vendors. For example, you can review either all vendors no matter the type of vendor, or you can select vendors that specifically require 1099-DIV (for dividends), 1099-MISC (for miscellaneous income), or 1099-INT (for interest) forms.

3.11 Financial Report Templates

Sometimes, the standard reports from SAP Business One may not meet your company's needs for reporting. You may need to restructure a profit and loss statement or edit the accounts that appear in it. You may want a template that calculates your company's earnings before interest, taxes, depreciation, and amortization (EBITDA).

SAP Business One's financial report templates allow you to create or modify financial reports for specific purposes. You can create financial report templates from the existing Balance Sheet, the Profit and Loss Statement, the Trial Balance, the Statement of Cash Flows, and the Asset History Sheet. When you run a financial report, you can select the financial report template you created to display the results.

To create a financial report using existing financial report templates, from the main menu, follow the menu path FINANCIALS • FINANCIAL REPORT TEMPLATES. When you open the FINANCIAL REPORT TEMPLATES window shown in Figure 3.27, you'll see a handful of options on the left side, and the right side of the window will be blank.

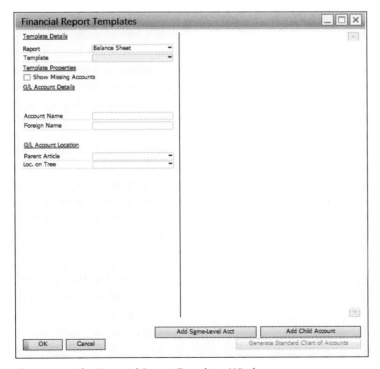

Figure 3.27 The Financial Report Templates Window

1. In the TEMPLATE DETAILS area, select the report you want to create or modify from the REPORT dropdown list and choose whether you want to define a new template or modify an existing user template from the TEMPLATE dropdown list.

2. In the TEMPLATE PROPERTIES area, if you select the SHOW MISSING ACCOUNTS checkbox, the system will still display any G/L account not selected/included in the template.

3. In the G/L ACCOUNT DETAILS area, begin adding the title accounts you would like to see in the report structure by entering them into the ACCOUNT NAME field and updating the financial report template by clicking UPDATE. Since we are creating a report template, you can create your own account naming structure. You do not need use what is seen in your chart of accounts. Once you get to the third level, you can bring in the fourth-level G/L accounts used in your chart of accounts.

4. You can also choose the GENERATE STANDARD CHART OF ACCOUNTS button shown in Figure 3.28 to bring up the complete chart of account structure for the report template. Once the standard chart of accounts is populated, double-click into the third-level title account, which will open a window called ACCOUNT CATEGORY DETAILS. In this window, you can remove or add rows. To remove a row, click on the number next to the G/L account to highlight the entire row and click DELETE ROWS. To add a G/L to a row, click on an empty box in the ACCOUNT NUMBER column and either tab through or click on the LOOK UP icon (the circle) to open a list of G/L account.

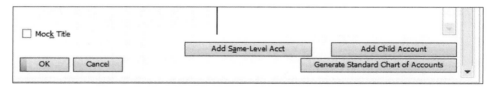

Figure 3.28 Financial Report Templates: Generate Standard Chart of Accounts

5. Once you have defined the structure of the financial report template, you can double-click into the level 4 accounts to add or remove any G/L account, as shown in Figure 3.29.

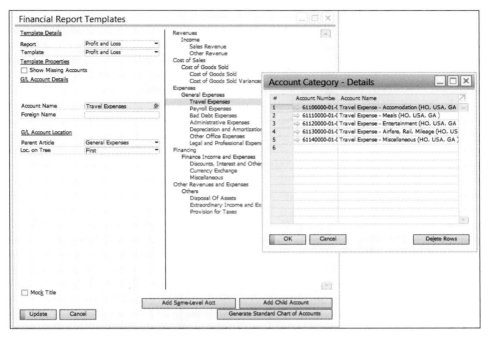

Figure 3.29 Financial Report Templates Editing the G/L Accounts

6. When you select a level 1 account, this enables the reporting template to create an automatic summary for this level 1 account, made up of the level 4 accounts you assigned.

7. Once the financial report template has been updated and saved, you can use this template to run a financial report.

3.12 Document Printing

The Document Printing tool in the Financials module gives you the option to print documents in batches.

In the DOCUMENT PRINTING window shown in Figure 3.30, you can navigate to many different document types to print. Each document type has its own set of printing criteria. Once you enter the criteria for printing and click OK, a list of documents will open. Using Ctrl you can select multiple documents to print at once.

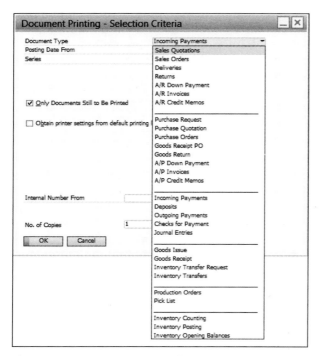

Figure 3.30 Document Printing Selection Criteria

3.13 Journal Voucher Report

If your company uses a lot of journal vouchers, the Journal Voucher Report is a good reporting tool used to get a complete list of all journal vouchers that need to be posted.

Access the Journal Voucher Report window by following the main menu path FINANCIALS • JOURNAL VOUCHER REPORT. Begin by choosing a date range, a range of journal voucher numbers, or a range of transaction numbers in the selection criteria screen shown in Figure 3.31. At the bottom of the screen, you have two options:

▶ Select the DISPLAY ONLY OPEN JOURNAL VOUCHERS checkbox to see journal vouchers that are open and either ready to post or modify.

▶ Select the DISPLAY ONLY CLOSED JOURNAL VOUCHERS checkbox to see a list of journal vouchers that have been posted to the system.

Although you must select at least one checkbox, you can use both.

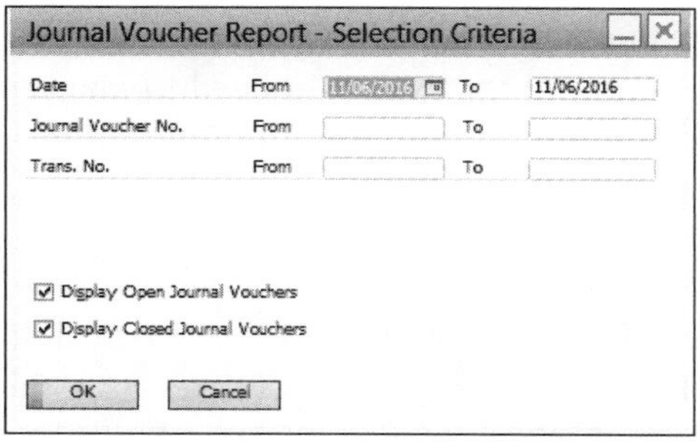

Figure 3.31 Journal Voucher Report Selection Criteria

Once you have entered your selection criteria, a Journal Voucher Report will display all journal vouchers outstanding as shown in Figure 3.32. In this report, you can review the transactions and drill down into the journal vouchers using the golden arrow for additional information. To post these journal vouchers to the G/L account, select the desired journal vouchers from the leftmost column and click POST.

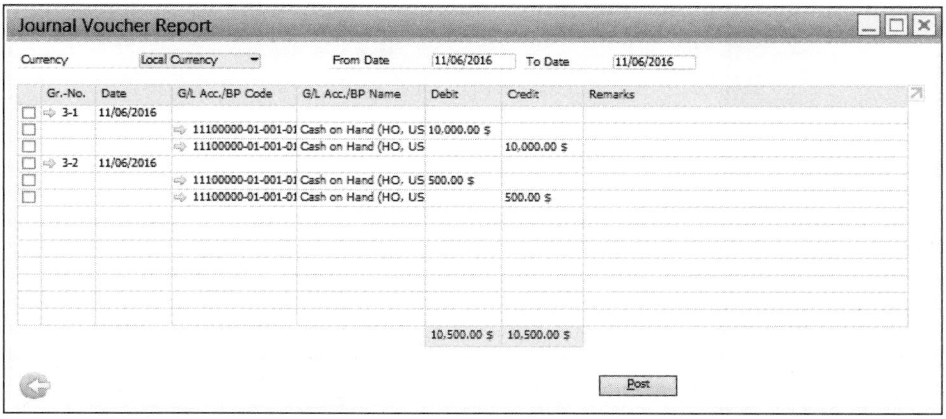

Figure 3.32 A Journal Voucher Report

3.14 Fixed Assets

Fixed assets are properties, facilities such as plants, and equipment purchased for long-term use. Fixed assets cannot be converted to cash easily and require depreciation schedules in order to represent the correct value of the asset.

SAP Business One provides the tools you need to manage your company's fixed assets within the system. You can set up asset master data to track an asset and its depreciation. You can also capitalize your assets and retire them. Follow the menu path FINANCIALS • FIXED ASSETS to access all the tools you need to manage your company's fixed assets.

3.14.1 Asset Master Data

The ASSET MASTER DATA screen in SAP Business One looks very similar to the item master data in the Inventory module, which we will discuss in Chapter 9. In the ASSET MASTER DATA screen shown in Figure 3.33, the FIXED ASSETS tab displays relevant information regarding your company's fixed assets.

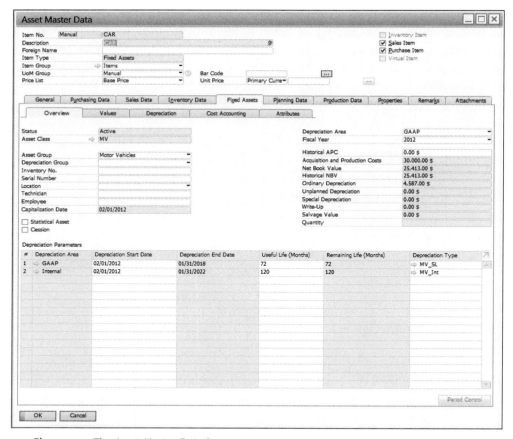

Figure 3.33 The Asset Master Data Screen

Table 3.5 lists the fields in the header of the Asset Master Data screen to define the fixed asset.

Field	Description/Use
Item No.	Enter a unique code used to identify the fixed asset.
Description	Enter a description in this alphanumeric field to describe the fixed asset.
Foreign Name	Enter an additional alphanumeric name to describe the fixed asset.
Item Type	The value in this field should be Fixed Assets.
Item Group	Use this field to assign the fixed asset to a group to use for reports.
UoM Group	The UoM group is set to Manual by default, but you can select a different UoM group if you have additional units of measure set up in the system.
Price List	The price list defaults to base price.
Bar Code	This information is not really needed here but is used more often in the item details in the Inventory module.
Unit Price	This information is not really needed here but is used more often in the item details in the Inventory module.
Sales Item	Select this checkbox to allow the fixed asset to be sold.
Purchase Item	Select this checkbox to allow the fixed asset to be purchased.

Table 3.5 Fields in the Asset Master Data Header

Overview Tab

The Overview tab of the asset master data gives a general overview of the useful life and value of the asset; as you can see in Figure 3.33, the tab contains important information for the fixed asset such as its depreciation parameters.

The first field in the Overview tab is the Status field. When a fixed asset is created manually, the status of the fixed asset is set to "New" until the asset is capitalized. Once capitalized, the status is set to "Active" until the asset is retired—at which time, the status changes to "Inactive."

Select the Asset Class based on the type of fixed asset you are defining in the fixed asset master data.

In Figure 3.33 the ASSET CLASS shown is MV, which stands for "motor vehicles." These ASSET CLASSES are created in MAIN MENU • SETUP • FINANCIALS • FIXED ASSETS • ASSET CLASSES on an as-needed basis per for your organization's requirements.

Once you select an asset class, the DEPRECIATION AREA and DEPRECIATION TYPE fields will be automatically filled based on the asset class. SAP Business One will automatically add the capitalization date when the asset has been capitalized or purchased. If the fixed asset master data was manually created, you can add the capitalization date to the fixed asset master data. We'll discuss capitalization in more detail in Section 3.14.2.

The noneditable fields on the right side of the OVERVIEW tab displays information about the fixed asset based on the year selected. Use the FISCAL YEAR dropdown list to select which year you want to review. The fiscal year will always default to the current year but can be changed to a previous year to look at historical data. The information in this area breaks down the acquisition and production cost, net book value (NBV), historical NBV, ordinary depreciation, unplanned depreciation, special depreciation, and so on for the selected fixed asset for the year selected.

Depreciation Parameters

The DEPRECIATION PARAMETER table on the bottom of the OVERVIEW tab specifies the depreciation areas of the fixed assets.

As seen at the bottom of Figure 3.33, the depreciation areas display the start date and end date for depreciation, the useful life and remaining life of the asset, and the depreciation type.

Values Tab

The VALUES tab of the fixed asset master data is another informational tab for the fixed assets. The VALUES tab details from the beginning of the selected year the value of the asset through the end of the selected year. Using the FISCAL YEAR dropdown, you can monitor the value of the asset for the selected year, as shown in Figure 3.34.

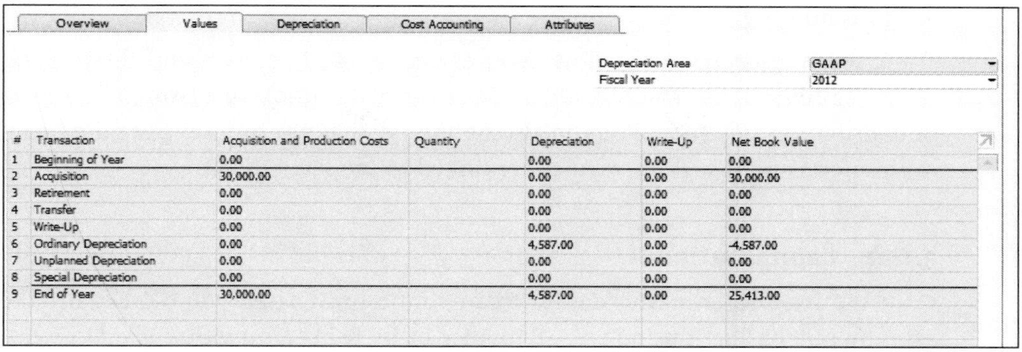

Overview | Values | Depreciation | Cost Accounting | Attributes

Depreciation Area: GAAP
Fiscal Year: 2012

#	Transaction	Acquisition and Production Costs	Quantity	Depreciation	Write-Up	Net Book Value
1	Beginning of Year	0.00		0.00	0.00	0.00
2	Acquisition	30,000.00		0.00	0.00	30,000.00
3	Retirement	0.00		0.00	0.00	0.00
4	Transfer	0.00		0.00	0.00	0.00
5	Write-Up	0.00		0.00	0.00	0.00
6	Ordinary Depreciation	0.00		4,587.00	0.00	-4,587.00
7	Unplanned Depreciation	0.00		0.00	0.00	0.00
8	Special Depreciation	0.00		0.00	0.00	0.00
9	End of Year	30,000.00		4,587.00	0.00	25,413.00

Figure 3.34 The Values Tab on the Fixed Asset Master Data Screen

Depreciation Tab

The DEPRECIATION tab lists all the planned, posted, automatic, and manual depreciation that has occurred or will occur for a specific period within the selected fiscal year. Take a look at Figure 3.35 to see the data broken into four kinds of depreciation. This window gives you an idea of what will happen to a fixed asset in the future and is a good tool for seeing the depreciation history for a particular fixed asset.

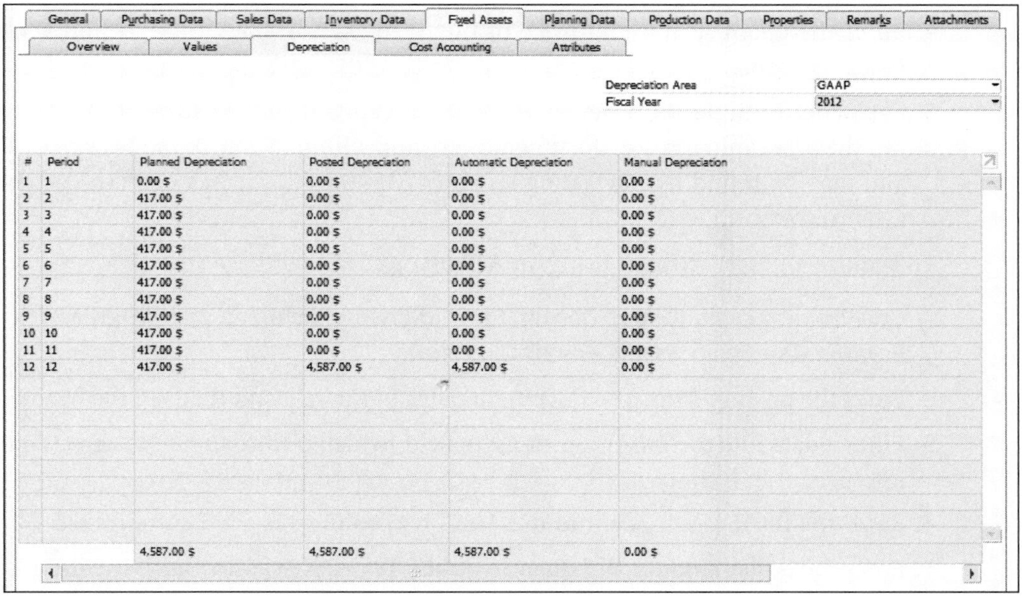

General | Purchasing Data | Sales Data | Inventory Data | Fixed Assets | Planning Data | Production Data | Properties | Remarks | Attachments

Overview | Values | Depreciation | Cost Accounting | Attributes

Depreciation Area: GAAP
Fiscal Year: 2012

#	Period	Planned Depreciation	Posted Depreciation	Automatic Depreciation	Manual Depreciation
1	1	0.00 $	0.00 $	0.00 $	0.00 $
2	2	417.00 $	0.00 $	0.00 $	0.00 $
3	3	417.00 $	0.00 $	0.00 $	0.00 $
4	4	417.00 $	0.00 $	0.00 $	0.00 $
5	5	417.00 $	0.00 $	0.00 $	0.00 $
6	6	417.00 $	0.00 $	0.00 $	0.00 $
7	7	417.00 $	0.00 $	0.00 $	0.00 $
8	8	417.00 $	0.00 $	0.00 $	0.00 $
9	9	417.00 $	0.00 $	0.00 $	0.00 $
10	10	417.00 $	0.00 $	0.00 $	0.00 $
11	11	417.00 $	0.00 $	0.00 $	0.00 $
12	12	417.00 $	4,587.00 $	4,587.00 $	0.00 $
		4,587.00 $	4,587.00 $	4,587.00 $	0.00 $

Figure 3.35 The Depreciation Tab on the Fixed Asset Master Data Screen

Cost Accounting

The Cost Accounting tab allows you to tie financial projects and distribution rules to a fixed asset. You can add a project or distribution rule using the project or distribution rule code. You can also define a date range for how long the financial projects and distribution rules are linked to the fixed assets.

3.14.2 Capitalization

Once the fixed asset master data is created for a fixed asset, you can acquire the asset by purchasing it using an A/P invoice or by using a *capitalization document*. When you use an A/P invoice to purchase the fixed asset, a capitalization document is automatically created. We'll show you how to create A/P invoices in more detail in Chapter 6.

As you can see in Figure 3.36, an A/P invoice was created by doing the following:

1. Navigate to Main Menu • Purchasing – A/P • A/P Invoice.
2. Select a vendor in the Vendor field.
3. Add the fixed asset item code to the A/P invoice in the Item No. column in the Contents tab.
4. Enter the quantity and unit price of the fixed asset in the Quantity and Unit Price columns.
5. Click OK to add the document and create the capitalization document. (Remember that the capitalization document is created automatically in the background and may be found by navigating to Main Menu • Financials • Fixed Assets • Capitalization.)

To acquire an asset without using an A/P invoice, follow these steps:

1. Create a new capitalization document by following the menu path Main Menu • Financials • Fixed Assets • Capitalization.
2. Enter the posting dates and document dates in the relevant fields in the header.
3. Enter a date into the Asset Value Date field, which is the date the asset was put into use.
4. Enter the fixed asset code into the Asset No. column in the Contents tab.
5. Enter the dollar amount and quantity in the Total (LC) and Quantity columns.
6. Click OK to add the document.

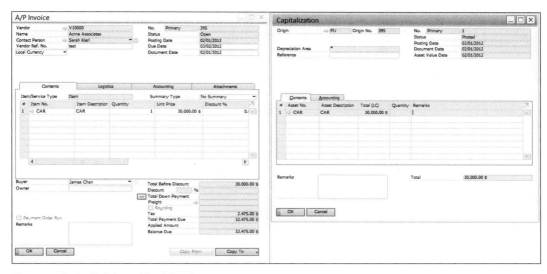

Figure 3.36 Capitalizing a Fixed Asset

3.14.3 Retirement

After a fixed asset has been fully depreciated and is no longer in use, you can retire the fixed asset by creating an A/R invoice or by creating a retirement document. If you use an A/R invoice to sell a fixed asset, SAP Business One will automatically create a retirement document in the background. We'll show you how to create A/P invoices in more detail in Chapter 5.

As shown in Figure 3.37, an A/R invoice was created by following these steps:

1. Navigate to MAIN MENU • PURCHASING – A/R • A/R INVOICE.

2. Select a customer in the CUSTOMER field.

3. Add a fixed asset item code to the ITEM NO. column in the CONTENTS tab.

4. Enter the quantity and unit price of the fixed asset in the QUANTITY and UNIT PRICE columns.

5. Click OK to add A/R invoice. Once added, the retirement document is created. (Remember that the retirement document is created in the background. You can locate it by navigating to MAIN MENU • FINANCIALS • FIXED ASSETS • RETIREMENT.)

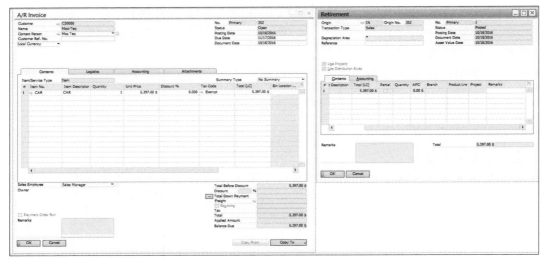

Figure 3.37 Retiring a Fixed Asset

To retire an asset without using an A/R invoice, follow these steps:

1. To create a new retirement document, navigate to FINANCIALS • FIXED ASSETS • RETIREMENT.

2. Enter the posting dates and document dates in the relevant fields in the header.

3. Enter a date in the ASSET VALUE DATE field, which is the date the asset is being retired.

4. Add the fixed asset code into the ASSET NO. column in the CONTENTS tab.

5. Enter the dollar amount and quantity in the TOTAL (LC) and QUANTITY columns.

6. Click OK to add the document.

3.14.4 Transfer

If you need to change the class of a fixed asset or combine a fixed asset with another asset, use *transfer documents* to do so. Navigate to MAIN MENU • FINAN-CIALS • FIXED ASSETS • TRANSFER and then select whether you are transferring the asset to another asset or to a different asset class; then complete the document by selecting the asset to which you want to move the current fixed asset or by selecting the asset class to which you want to change the fixed asset.

3.14.5 Manual Depreciation

Sometimes when you own a fixed asset, you need to manually depreciate the asset. If you decide to not use a depreciation schedule in SAP Business One and need to manually calculate the ordinary depreciation to post, you would utilize SAP Business One's manual depreciation functionality. You can also use a *manual depreciation document* to post any unplanned depreciation for a fixed asset.

To create a manual depreciation document, follow these steps:

1. Navigate to FINANCIALS • FIXED ASSETS • MANUAL DEPRECIATION.

2. Select the transaction type from the TRANSACTION TYPE dropdown list shown in Figure 3.38. Your options in this dropdown list are ORDINARY DEPRECIATION, UNPLANNED DEPRECIATION, SPECIAL DEPRECIATION, or APPRECIATION. (Note that appreciation of a fixed asset is usually handled with asset revaluation, so you can ignore this option for now.)

3. Enter dates into the POSTING DATE and DOCUMENT DATE fields on the right side of Figure 3.38.

4. Enter the date you want the manual depreciation to take place into the ASSET VALUE DATE field.

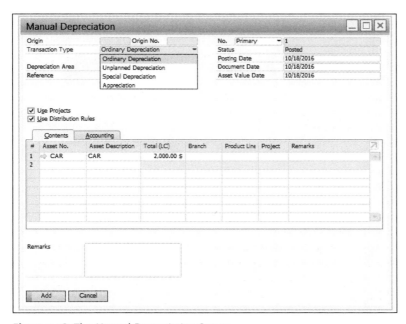

Figure 3.38 The Manual Depreciation Screen

5. In table area, in the ASSET NO. column, enter the asset number to which you want to apply the manual depreciation.

6. In the TOTAL field, enter the dollar amount to depreciate.

7. Click ADD to create the manual depreciation document.

> **Tips and Tricks: Projects and Distribution Rules**
>
> When the USE PROJECTS and USE DISTRIBUTION RULES checkboxes are checked, the system activates the columns in the table so that you can add/edit the projects or distribution rules associated with depreciating the fixed asset.

3.14.6 Depreciation Run

After you have set up your fixed asset master data and purchased or capitalized your fixed asset, you can begin the scheduled depreciation of your assets.

SAP Business One uses the Depreciation Run tool shown in Figure 3.39 to assist users in executing their scheduled depreciation runs for their fixed assets.

To execute a depreciation run, click on the LIST icon next to the DEPRECIATE TO field in Figure 3.39. Select the period for which you want to run depreciation and then click PREVIEW. By default, the depreciate to date will be the date of the next depreciation run.

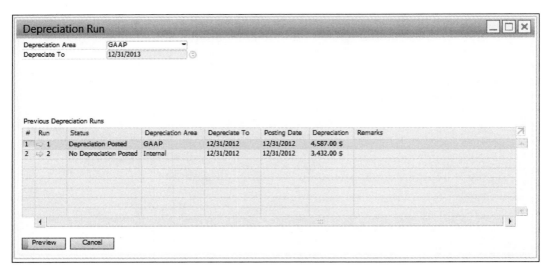

Figure 3.39 The Depreciation Run Screen

The DEPRECIATION RUN PREVIEW window shown in Figure 3.40 allows you to review the depreciation numbers for all fixed assets before you post them to the G/L.

If you select the CONSOLIDATE JOURNAL ENTRY ROWS BY PROJECT checkbox, the journal entry posted will be grouped by the project based on the G/L account, and the amount will be posted on one line instead of on multiple lines in the same G/L.

If you select the CONSOLIDATE JOURNAL ENTRY ROWS BY DISTRIBUTION RULES checkbox, the journal entry posted will be grouped based on the distribution rule, and the amount will be posted on one line instead of on multiple lines to the same G/L.

After you click EXECUTE, a system message will appear to confirm the posting as shown in Figure 3.41. Click CONTINUE to confirm and post the depreciation run for the fixed assets.

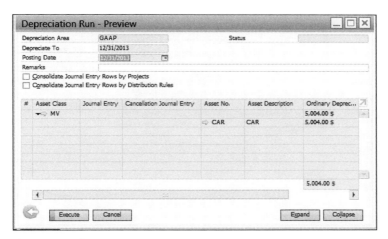

Figure 3.40 The Depreciation Run Preview Screen

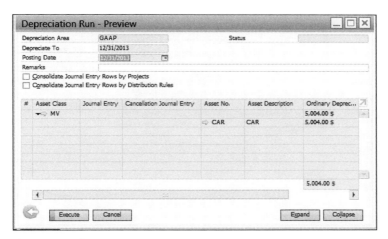

Figure 3.41 Depreciation Run Message

3.14.7 Asset Revaluation

The ASSET REVALUATION window gives you the ability to revalue any fixed asset. For example, you may notice that the net book value of an asset is not accurate or that an appraisal was done on an asset or a property that changes its value, you can use this tool to adjust the NBV of the fixed asset.

To revalue your fixed asset, go to FINANCIALS • FIXED ASSETS • ASSET REVALUATION and follow these steps:

1. Enter the posting date and document date on the right side of Figure 3.42. These dates usually default to the current date.

2. Make sure the asset value date in the ASSET VALUE DATE field is the last day of your current fiscal year.

3. Enter the fixed asset code for the asset you want to revalue in the ASSET NO. column. When you add the fixed asset code, the system will automatically populate the NBV column with the current NBV as shown in Figure 3.42.

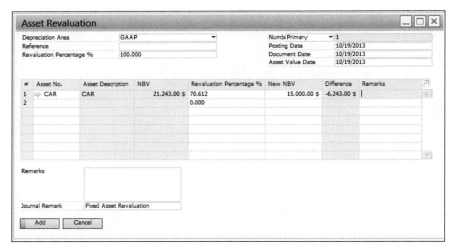

Figure 3.42 The Asset Revaluation Screen

4. Enter a new net book value in the NEW NBV column.

5. Click ADD. SAP Business One will generate a system message warning you that you cannot change the document after it is added, as shown in Figure 3.43. If you're ready to continue, click YES to post the transaction.

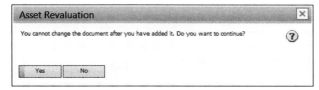

Figure 3.43 Asset Revaluation System Message

3.14.8 Fiscal Year Change

The FISCAL YEAR CHANGE window shown in Figure 3.44 calculates year-end values for the current year in order to start the new year. This window also recalculates any planned depreciation for the new fiscal year. You'll see these values on the fixed asset master data.

You can capitalize/retire assets in the middle of a fiscal year as long at the fiscal year is current. For example, if you want to retire something in 2016, the fiscal year for fixed assets needs to be set to 2016. You must change the fiscal year in order to execute depreciation runs and use any of the capitalization or retirement documents. To change the fiscal year, select the "from" year from the FROM FISCAL YEAR dropdown and the "to" year from the TO FISCAL YEAR dropdown. Next, click EXECUTE.

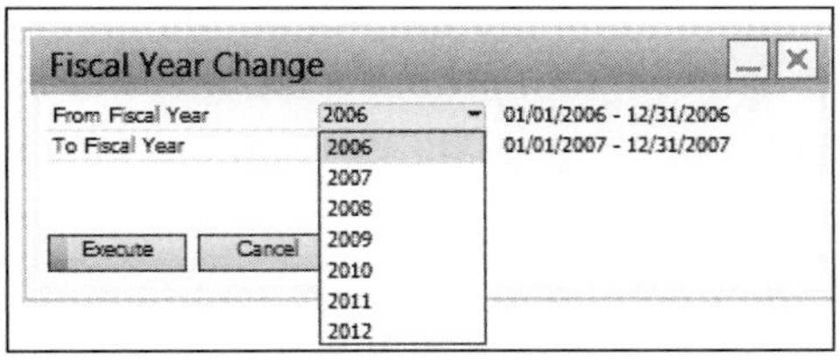

Figure 3.44 The Fiscal Year Change Window

3.14.9 Fixed Asset Reports

In the main menu under FINANCIALS • FIXED ASSETS • FIXED ASSETS REPORTS, a handful of useful reports are available for managing your fixed assets, as shown in Figure 3.45. Use these reports to obtain information on your company's fixed assets:

▸ Asset Depreciation Forecast Report: This report lets you see in detail what is scheduled for upcoming depreciation runs for your fixed assets.

▶ Asset History Sheet: This report displays any changes in the fixed asset over a selected time frame.

▶ Asset Status Report: This report gives you a breakdown of your fixed assets in one window, including details about the asset class, depreciation area, useful life, remaining life, and so on.

▶ Asset Transaction Report: This report displays any transactions that occur for the fixed assets. If a document is associated with the transactions, you can drill down into the document by clicking the golden arrow.

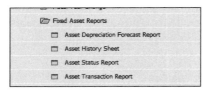

Figure 3.45 Available Fixed Asset Reports

3.15 Internal Reconciliation

As you perform your day-to-day operations and transactions for your company, you may need to reconcile accounts in your G/L. This process matches transactions in the G/L and clears them. In SAP Business One, most transactions in the system are automatically reconciled through marketing documents. However, sometimes documents are not connected to marketing documents and need to be reconciled.

The Reconciliation tool gives you the ability to perform G/L account reconciliations, offering three options for how you want to reconcile your accounts. These appear in the G/L INTERNAL RECONCILIATION window shown in Figure 3.46.

If you select MANUAL as the reconciliation type, enter a date into the RECONCILIATION DATE field and enter an account code for the account you want to reconcile into the G/L ACCOUNT field.

If you select the DATE checkbox under the TRANS. SELECTION CRITERIA heading, more options will be made available so you can enter a date range to limit the transactions you want to see. You can use either the posting date, the due date, or the document date to pull data and limit transactions.

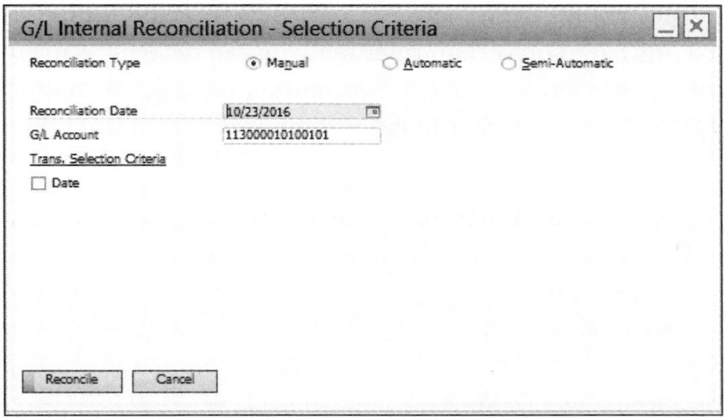

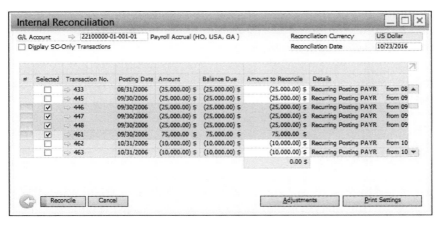

Figure 3.46 G/L Internal Reconciliation Selection Criteria

After you click RECONCILE, the INTERNAL RECONCILIATION screen shown in Figure 3.47 will open, displaying the manual reconciliation data. In order to perform the reconciliation, select the amounts to reconcile by placing a checkmark in the SELECTED column for the corresponding amounts. When you select the lines to reconcile, you must make sure values in the AMOUNT TO RECONCILE column total to zero (indicated at the bottom of the column) in order to perform the reconciliation. If you find that the balance is off, select ADJUSTMENTS to create a journal entry that will adjust the amount.

Figure 3.47 The Internal Reconciliation Screen

Let's go back to Figure 3.46, but this time, select the Automatic radio button to reconcile a range of accounts based on certain rules that you can determine using the new fields that appear: Matching Rule 1, Matching Rule 2, Matching Rule 3, Reconciliation Difference, Variation in Days, and Relate To (as shown in Figure 3.48).

Now, when you click Reconcile, the system automatically performs the reconciliation in the background.

> **Tips and Tricks: Automatic Reconciliation**
>
> Be careful when using the automatic function because the system might match transactions with the same dollar amount that do not necessarily go together.

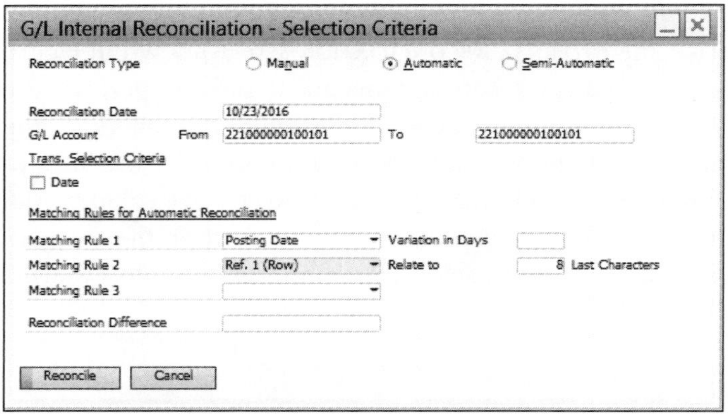

Figure 3.48 Selecting Automatic Reconciliation

The Semi-Automatic option in Figure 3.48 is reserved for external reconciliations, which we'll discuss when we cover the Banking module in Chapter 8.

3.16 Budget Setup

SAP Business One allows you to maintain a budget within the system that is based off the structure of the chart of accounts. As a result, the budget is prepared based on each G/L account, giving you the opportunity to run comparisons between your budget and actual numbers throughout the year.

To set up a budget in SAP Business One, you'll have to create a budget scenario by navigating to FINANCIALS • BUDGET SETUP • BUDGET SCENARIO, and then following these steps:

1. As shown in Figure 3.49, select a fiscal year for which you would like to set up a budget scenario from the FISCAL YEAR dropdown.

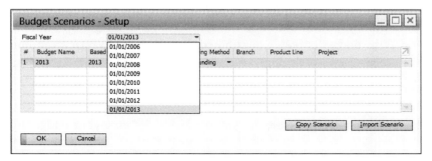

Figure 3.49 The Budget Scenario Setup Screen

2. Right-click on the first row and select ADD ROW, as shown in Figure 3.50.

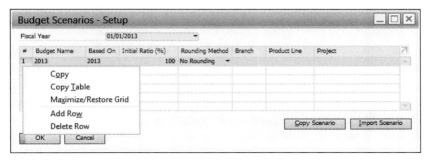

Figure 3.50 Adding a Row to a Budget Scenario

3. Give your budget scenario a name in the BUDGET NAME field.

4. Take a look at the BASED ON field next to the budget name. In this field, you can choose whether to create a budget scenario based off a previous budget scenario or based off the new scenario you just created.

5. If you decide to base your budget scenario on a previous budget scenario, use the INITIAL RATIO (%) column to determine what percentage to base the new budget scenario on. If you create a new budget, the INITIAL RATIO (%) value defaults to 100%. The ROUNDING METHOD column allows you to determine if

you want to round your budget numbers or not. If you decide to use rounding, you can choose to round to a full decimal amount, to a full amount, or to a full amount divisible by 10.

6. In the remaining columns, you can associate a budget with a branch, a product line (cost center), or a financial project. Click OK to save your scenario.

Budget distribution methods allow you to define how a budget will be distributed throughout the fiscal year. SAP Business One has three stock budget distribution methods: equal (the budget is evenly distributed throughout the year), ascending (the budget amounts increase throughout the year each month), and descending (the budget amounts decrease throughout the year each month). You can define as many budget distribution methods as necessary.

Once you have set up a budget scenario, you can begin defining your budget by following these steps:

1. Create a new budget from the main menu by following the screen path FINANCIALS • BUDGET SETUP • BUDGET.

2. In the BUDGET SCENARIO DEFINITION window shown in Figure 3.51, select the budget scenario you would like to use from the SCENARIO field on the left and select the accounts you would like to work with on the right. In our example, we have selected REVENUES. When you click OK, only the G/L accounts that are classified as revenue accounts will populate the BUDGET SCENARIO SETUP window.

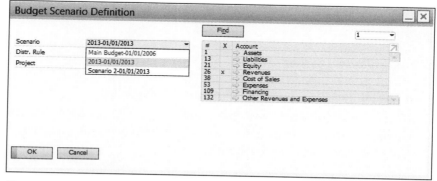

Figure 3.51 The Budget Scenario Definition Screen

3. Click OK to open the BUDGET SCENARIO SETUP window for your selected budget scenario.

4. If this is the first budget you have created, you may need to check the DISPLAY ACCOUNTS WITH NO BUDGET checkbox at the top of the window as shown in Figure 3.52.

Budget Scenarios - Setup (Scenario -2013)											
☑ Display Accounts with no Budget									Local		
#	Acct No.	Acct Name	Parent Acct	%		Method	Debit	Credit		Actual	Dis
1	41100000-01-001-01	Sales Revenues - Domestic (HO, USA, GA)			⇨	Equal ▾					
2	41200000-01-001-01	Sales Revenues - Foreign (HO, USA, GA)				Equal		500,000.00 $			
3	41300000-01-001-01	Sales Revenues - Services (HO, USA, GA)			⇨	Ascending Order		200,000.00 $			
4	41400000-01-001-01	Sales Reveues - Freight (HO, USA, GA)			⇨	Descending Series		50,000.00 $			
5	42100000-01-001-01	Sales Rebates (HO, USA, GA)			⇨	Define New		25,000.00 $			
6	42200000-01-001-01	Sales Discounts (HO, USA, GA)			⇨	Manual		30,000.00 $			
7	42300000-01-001-01	Miscellaneous Income (HO, USA, GA)			⇨	Equal		10,000.00 $			
8	44100000-01-001-01	Interest Income (HO, USA, GA)			⇨	Equal ▾		25,000.00 $			

Figure 3.52 Setting Up Budget Scenarios

5. Select the budget distribution method you would like to use for each G/L account from the METHOD column.

6. Once you have selected the distribution method, enter the year's total budget values. If you select the manual distribution method, you can double-click on that line to open the BUDGET ITEMS DETAILS window.

7. In the BUDGET ITEMS DETAILS window, enter budget values for each month as shown in Figure 3.53.

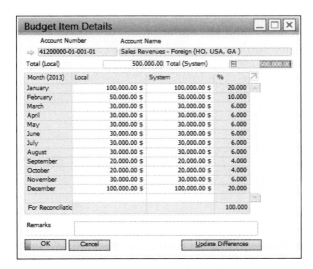

Figure 3.53 The Budget Item Details Window

8. Once all the G/L accounts have been defined with their budget numbers, select UPDATE to define your budget.

When budgets have been created they may be reported against with some out-of-the-box financials comparison reports located in MAIN MENU • FINANCIALS • FINANCIALS REPORTS.

Budgets can also be advantageously used in alerts and approval procedures to manage expense in a real time. You can use the A/P document being created to evaluate the new expense against the budget and take preventative action as designed in the alert of approval process.

3.17 Cost Accounting

In SAP Business One, the Cost Accounting functionality gives you an additional layer of reporting. Using dimensions, cost centers, and distribution rules, you can view your revenue and expenses in a more dynamic way.

Dimensions are used to define certain trackable company criteria and provide different ways to see expenses and revenues. Define dimensions by following the menu path FINANCIALS • COST ACCOUNTING • DIMENSIONS. As shown in Figure 3.54, use the DESCRIPTION column to define your dimensions. Select the ACT. checkbox to activate another dimension to use in marketing documents and reporting. When checked, you can change the name of the dimension and use it based on your business criteria.

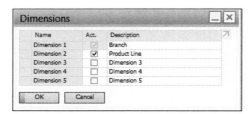

Figure 3.54 The Cost Accounting Dimensions Screen

Use *cost centers* to define a department or division within a company. Cost centers can be used to group revenues and expenses within your company into departments or divisions. To define your cost centers, input the corresponding data into the Cost Centers Setup screen as shown in Figure 3.55 and described in Table 3.6.

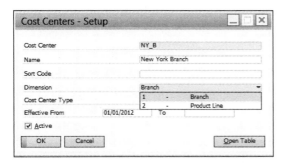

Figure 3.55 The Cost Centers Setup Screen

Field	Description/Use
Cost Center	Enter a unique code used to describe your cost center.
Name	Enter a description/title for the cost center.
Sort Code	Enter a value into this optional field to be used in reporting.
Dimension	Use this field to assign a dimension to the cost center.
Cost Center Type	Enter a cost center type, which is optional in reporting.
Effective From	Enter dates to restrict when the cost center can be used in marketing documents.
Active	Select this checkbox to make the cost center active.
Open Table	Click this button to open the table of cost centers and distribution rules.

Table 3.6 Fields in the Cost Center Screen

Distribution rule functionality, which is found at Main Menu • Financials • Cost Accounting • Distribution Rules, is used to allocate (distribute) revenue and expenses to your defined cost centers. As shown in Figure 3.56, you can fill out the fields outlined in Table 3.7 to make a distribution rule split costs or revenues between two or more cost centers using a percentage. Alternatively, you can distribute expenses or revenues directly to one cost center. The image on the left displays a direct allocation distribution rule. The image on the right displays an indirect allocation distribution rule.

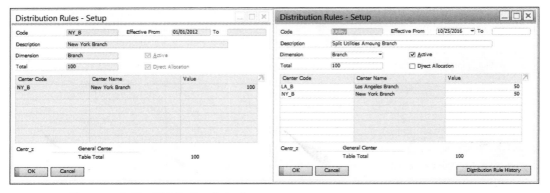

Figure 3.56 The Distribution Rules Screen

Field	Description/Use
CODE	Enter a unique descriptor for the distribution rule.
EFFECTIVE FROM	Enter dates used to restrict the use of the distribution rules.
DESCRIPTION	Enter a description that explains the distribution rule.
DIMENSION	Select an existing dimension to associate with the distribution rule.
TOTAL	Enter the amount used to determine the values to distribute.
ACTIVE	Select this checkbox to determine whether the distribution rule is active to use.
DIRECT ALLOCATION	This checkbox is used for reporting to specify when revenue or expenses are directly related to a cost center.
CENTER CODE	Enter the cost center you want to use to define the distribution rule.
VALUE	Enter the amount to be split across the cost center. This amount does not have to equal the total. If there is a difference, the remainder will go to the general cost center.
TABLE TOTAL	This field displays the sum of the amounts distributed to the cost centers in the table.
DISTRIBUTION RULE HISTORY	This button opens the DISTRIBUTION RULE HISTORY window, which details any changes that occurred with the distribution rule.

Table 3.7 Fields in the Distribution Rule Screen

SAP Business One's Table of Cost Centers and Distribution Rules functionality gives you information about all the distribution rules and cost centers defined in the system. As shown in Figure 3.57, this table lists each distribution rule and the cost centers associated with it.

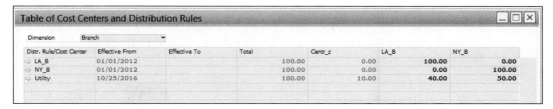

Table of Cost Centers and Distribution Rules								_ □ ×
Dimension	Branch ▾							
Distr. Rule/Cost Center	Effective From	Effective To	Total		Centr_z	LA_B	NY_B	
⇨ LA_B	01/01/2012			100.00	0.00	100.00	0.00	
⇨ NY_B	01/01/2012			100.00	0.00	0.00	100.00	
⇨ Utility	10/25/2016			100.00	10.00	40.00	50.00	

Figure 3.57 The Table of Cost Centers and Distribution Rules Screen

Under the COST ACCOUNT folder, a handful of useful reports are available for you to use:

▸ Cost Center Report: This report gives a breakdown of revenues and expenses for both indirect and direct allocations by cost center and dimension.

▸ Distribution Report: This report breaks down expenses defined by each distribution rule.

▸ Cost Accounting Summary Report: This summary reports gives more detail on each transaction associated with a cost center.

▸ Budget Versus Cost Accounting Report: This report compares the financial budget to cost centers distribution rules.

▸ Cost Accounting Reconciliation Report: Use this report to compare your company's financials to any costing accounting definitions.

3.18 Financial Reports

The FINANCIAL REPORTS folder in the Financials module groups different reports based on their category:

▸ The ACCOUNTING folder contains customer and vendor aging reports, G/L reports, 1099 reports, and so on.

▸ The FINANCIAL folder contains reports used for submitting financials, such as balance sheets, trial balances, the profit and loss statements, and so on.

▸ The COMPARISON folder contains reports that allow you to compare different reporting periods and/or different databases when running a balance sheet, trial balance, or profit and loss statement.

▶ The BUDGET folder contains reports used to compare a budget to actual numbers. You can run a balance sheet, trial balance, and profit and loss statement to compare budgets to actual numbers for specific time frames.

Since the Financial module includes so many reports, we'll only focus on printing a handful of reports. The standard reports most companies use are balance sheets, trial balances, profit and loss statements, and aging reports.

3.18.1 Balance Sheets

A balance sheet displays an account of your company's assets, liabilities, and equities on one report. From the main menu, follow the menu path FINANCIALS • FINANCIAL REPORTS • FINANCIALS • BALANCE SHEET to open the BALANCE SHEET SELECTION CRITERIA window shown in Figure 3.58. As shown in Table 3.8, many options are available to provide different ways of viewing a balance sheet.

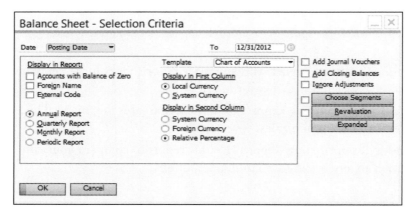

Figure 3.58 Balance Sheet Selection Criteria

Field	Description/Use
DATE	From this dropdown list, select whether you want the report to be based on either the document POSTING DATE or the DOCUMENT DATE.
TO	Enter the last date for which you would like to run the balance sheet.
TEMPLATE	Select a financial template created using the FINANCIAL REPORTS TEMPLATES menu from this dropdown list. We discussed financial report templates in Section 3.11.

Table 3.8 Balance Sheet Selection Criteria Fields

Field	Description/Use
DISPLAY IN REPORT	The checkboxes in this section determine what you would like to see when you run the report. You can display G/L accounts that have a balance of zero. You choose to include the foreign name and the external code (both found in the G/L ACCOUNTS DETAIL screen discussed in Section 3.1.1) in the report.
DISPLAY IN FIST COLUMN	Choose whether you want to see amounts in local currency or system currency in the first column of the report.
DISPLAY IN SECOND COLUMN	Choose whether you want to see amounts in local currency, system currency, or relative percentage in the second column of the report.
ANNUAL REPORT, QUARTERLY REPORT, MONTHLY REPORT, or PERIODIC REPORT	Choose one of the radio buttons to generate an ANNUAL REPORT (based on year-to-date date information), a QUARTERLY REPORT (based on fiscal year quarters), a MONTHLY REPORT (based on calendar year months), or a PERIODIC REPORT (based on the posting periods defined in the system).
ADD JOURNAL VOUCHERS	If you have an existing journal voucher in the system and you would like to see how that journal voucher will affect the balance sheet, select this checkbox to include the journal voucher in the calculation.
ADD CLOSING BALANCE	Select this checkbox to include any period-end journal entries.
IGNORE ADJUSTMENTS	Select this checkbox to exclude any journal entries that are deemed adjustment journal entries.
CHOOSE SEGMENTS	Click this button to select specific G/L segments to run on your balance sheet. For example, you might only want to see how one department (if set up as a segment) is doing.
REVALUATION	Click this button to define criteria to run a revaluated balance sheet.
EXPANDED	Click this button to narrow your selection criteria by reference fields, user-defined fields, and agreement numbers.

Table 3.8 Balance Sheet Selection Criteria Fields (Cont.)

After you have decided what information you want, click OK.

The Balance Sheet Report will show you list of your G/L accounts. Based on your selection criteria, you'll see either a total balance or a balance by month, quarter, or period. In our example shown in Figure 3.59, you'll see a total balance with foreign currency. If you select the DISPLAY SUBTOTALS checkbox, you will see subtotals for each title account in the report. If you select the HIDE TITLES checkbox, the system will hide all title accounts. You can use the LEVEL dropdown list to change what level of accounts displays on the report.

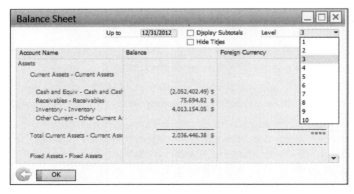

Figure 3.59 A Balance Sheet Report

3.18.2 Trial Balances

A trial balance is a report that displays both balance sheet accounts and profit and loss accounts. To print a trial balance from the main menu, go to FINANCIALS • FINANCIAL REPORTS • FINANCIALS • TRIAL BALANCE to open the BALANCE SHEET SELECTION CRITERIA window, shown in Figure 3.60. As shown in Table 3.9, this window has many options for different ways to view a trial balance sheet.

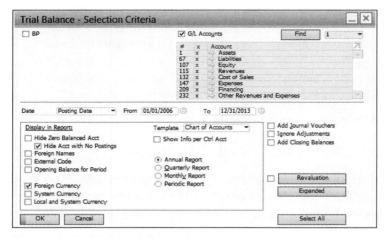

Figure 3.60 Trial Balance Selection Criteria

Field	Description/ Use
BP	Select this checkbox to select a specific business partner or a range of business partners to view in the report.
G/L ACCOUNTS	You can activate G/L accounts level selection by clicking this checkbox to reveal the G/L accounts selection criteria. Clicking on the "X" in the X column will select all or unselect all accounts. Alternatively, when all accounts have been unchecked, you may select specific accounts only by clicking in X column of the specific account you wish to include in the report.
FIND	Click FIND to open a selection box where you can narrow down which G/Ls you would like to see in your trial balance.
DATE	From this dropdown list, select whether to run the trial balance sheet based on the posting date, the due date, or the document date.
FROM/TO	Enter dates in these fields to specify a date range to run the trial balance.
HIDE ZERO BALANCED ACCT	Select this checkbox to hide G/L accounts that do not have a balance when the report is run. Additionally, you can select the HIDE ACCT WITH NO POSTINGS checkbox, which would hide G/L accounts without any transactions.
FOREIGN NAME	Select this checkbox to display the foreign name for the account, which was determined in the G/L ACCOUNTS DETAIL screen discussed in Section 3.1.1.
EXTERNAL CODE	Select this checkbox to display a user-defined external code, which was determined in that G/L ACCOUNTS DETAIL screen.
OPENING BALANCES FOR PERIOD	Select this checkbox to include the previous period's balance in the report. When selected, the system will provide two more options for you to choose from: OB FROM START OF COMPANY ACTIVITY (from the beginning of time for the company) or OB FROM START OF FISCAL YEAR (from the beginning of the new fiscal year).
FOREIGN CURRENCY	If your company uses foreign currency, select this checkbox to display amounts in the foreign currency in a separate column.
SYSTEM CURRENCY	If your system currency is different from your local currency, select this checkbox to display amounts in system currency in another column.
LOCAL AND SYSTEM CURRENCY	Select this checkbox to display amounts in both the local currency and the system currency. If checked, you cannot select either the FOREIGN CURRENCY or the SYSTEM CURRENCY checkboxes.

Table 3.9 Trial Balance Selection Criteria Fields

Field	Description/ Use
TEMPLATE	From this dropdown list, you can select a financial template created using the FINANCIAL REPORTS TEMPLATES menu.
SHOW INFO PER CRTL. ACCT	Select this checkbox to display the control account assigned to a business partner.
ANNUAL REPORT, QUARTERLY REPORT, MONTHLY REPORT, or PERIODIC REPORT	Choose one of the radio buttons to generate an ANNUAL REPORT (based on year-to-date date information), a QUARTERLY REPORT (based on fiscal year quarters), a MONTHLY REPORT (based on calendar year months), or a PERIODIC REPORT (based on the posting periods defined in the system).
ADD JOURNAL VOUCHER	If you have an existing journal voucher in the system and you would like to see how that journal voucher will affect the trial balance, select this checkbox to include the journal voucher in the calculation.
IGNORE ADJUSTMENTS	Select this checkbox to exclude any journal entries that are deemed adjustment journal entries.
ADD CLOSING BALANCES	Select this checkbox to include any period-end journal entries.
REVALUATION	Click this button to define criteria to run a revaluated trial balance.
EXPANDED	Click this button to narrow your selection criteria by reference fields, documents, transaction codes, projects, user-defined fields, branches, product line, and agreement numbers.
SELECT ALL	Click this button to select all accounts and business partners to display in the report.

Table 3.9 Trial Balance Selection Criteria Fields (Cont.)

Similar to printing a balance sheet, once you have decided what information you want to see you can click OK to display the report.

Let's explore the Trial Balance Report shown in Figure 3.61, which shows the name of the G/L accounts. At the top of the window, the DATE FROM and To fields display the date range you selected in the selection criteria screen. Select the HIDE TITLES checkbox if you want to remove any title accounts and leave all active accounts only. The LEVEL dropdown lists lets you choose at what level you want the report to display. As a result, you can view only level 1 accounts or title accounts, or you can display the deepest level of G/L accounts. In SAP Business One, the chart of active accounts can go down to ten levels.

Notice that most of the report is divided into two columns: LOCAL CURRENCY and FOREIGN CURRENCY. The LOCAL CURRENCY column contains the DEBIT, CREDIT, and BALANCE subcolumns. The FOREIGN CURRENCY column displays the dollar amount in the actual currency taken.

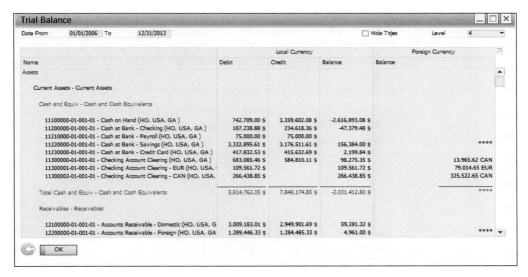

Figure 3.61 A Trial Balance Report

3.18.3 Profit and Loss Statements

A profit and loss statement summarizes total revenue, the cost of goods sold, and expenses and calculates gross profit, operating profit, and net income.

Let's explore the selection criteria fields shown in Figure 3.62 in Table 3.10.

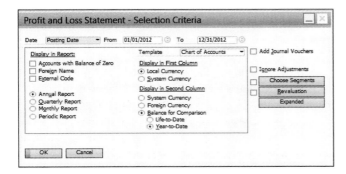

Figure 3.62 Profit and Loss Statement Selection Criteria

Field	Description/Use
DATE	From this dropdown list, choose whether the profit and loss statement will be based on the posting date, due date, or document date.
FROM/TO	Enter dates in these fields to determine the date range of the profit and loss statement.
DISPLAY IN REPORT	This area gives you options controlling what you would like to see when you run the profit and loss statement. By checking the subordinate checkboxes, you can display G/L accounts that have a balance of zero, can select to see the foreign name, and can choose to show the external code (both found in the G/L ACCOUNTS DETAIL screen discussed in Section 3.1.1).
ANNUAL REPORT, QUARTERLY REPORT, MONTHLY REPORT, or PERIODIC REPORT	Choose one of the radio buttons to generate an ANNUAL REPORT (based on year-to-date date information), a QUARTERLY REPORT (based on fiscal year quarters), a MONTHLY REPORT (based on calendar year months), or a PERIODIC REPORT (based on the posting periods defined in the system).
TEMPLATE	From this dropdown list, you can choose a financial template created using the FINANCIAL REPORTS TEMPLATES menu.
DISPLAY IN FIRST COLUMN	Choose whether you want to see amounts in local currency or in system currency in the first column of the report.
DISPLAY IN SECOND COLUMN	Choose whether you want to see amounts in local currency, system currency, or the balance in the second column of the report. When you select BALANCE FOR COMPARISON, you'll have the option to choose either LIFE TO DATE or YEAR TO DATE.
ADD JOURNAL VOUCHERS	If you have an existing journal voucher in the system and you would like to see how that journal voucher will affect the profit and loss statement, select this checkbox to include the journal voucher in the calculation.
IGNORE ADJUSTMENTS	Select this checkbox to exclude any journal entries that are deemed adjustment journal entries.
CHOOSE SEGMENTS	Click this button to select specific G/L segments to run in your profit and loss statement. For example, you might want to see how one department (if set up as a segment) is doing.
REVALUATION	Click this button to define criteria to run a revaluated profit and loss statement.

Table 3.10 Profit and Loss Statement Selection Criteria Fields

Field	Description/Use
EXPANDED	Click this button to narrow your selection criteria by project, branch, product line, reference fields, user-defined fields, and blanket agreement numbers.

Table 3.10 Profit and Loss Statement Selection Criteria Fields (Cont.)

Just like printing a Balance Sheet Report and a Trial Balance Report, once you've selected the information you want displayed in the report, click OK to display the profit and loss statement. At the top of the report, you can display subtotals for title accounts by selecting the DISPLAY SUBTOTALS checkbox and/or hide title accounts by selecting the HIDE TITLES checkbox. Similar to the Balance Sheet Report and Trial Balance Report, you can choose different G/L account levels. You can choose to display level 1 accounts or display all the way through level 10 active accounts.

In our example shown in Figure 3.63, notice the date range we selected when determining the reporting criteria: from January 1, 2012 to December 31, 2012. The columns are based on what you decided to display in the report; here, we selected the account name, balance, and year-to-date amount.

Figure 3.63 A Profit and Loss Statement

3.18.4 Aging Reports

In general, aging reports list any overdue/unpaid invoices on both the customer and vendor side. These reports provide information such as unpaid invoice dates and unpaid invoice amounts by vendor or customer.

For example, SAP Business One provides both a Customer Receivables Aging Report and a Vendor Liabilities Aging Report. Many businesses primarily use the Customer Receivables Aging Report to communicate with their customers in order to increase their cash flow.

Table 3.11 lists the selection criteria you can use in your aging reports (see Figure 3.64).

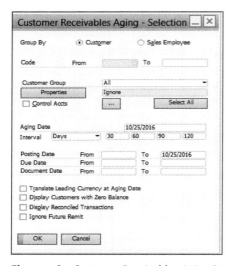

Figure 3.64 Customer Receivables Aging Report Selection Criteria

Field	Description/Use
GROUP BY	Select either the CUSTOMER or SALES EMPLOYEE radio button to determine if the aging report displays by customer/vendor or by sales employee/buyer.
CODE	Enter a range of customer or vendor codes to include in the report in the FROM and To fields. To run the aging report for all customers/vendors, leave the CODE FROM and To fields blank.

Table 3.11 Customer Receivables Aging Report Selection Criteria Fields

Field	Description/Use
CUSTOMER GROUP or VENDOR GROUP	Select a customer or vendor group from this dropdown list; in our example in Figure 3.64, we selected ALL in the CUSTOMER GROUP field.
PROPERTIES	If you have properties defined on the business partner master data, you can select one or more properties to restrict an aging report.
CONTROL ACCTS	Select this checkbox to only see transactions for the selected control accounts.
AGING DATE	This field displays the aging date, which is usually the current date. Enter a date in the future to get an idea of what will be due on that date.
INTERVAL	Set intervals by days, months, or periods. Usually this field is set to DAYS with intervals 30, 60, 90, and 120 days apart.
POSTING DATE, DUE DATE, and DOCUMENT DATE	Enter dates into these fields to determine, by date, which invoices you want to run the aging report. When you set the aging date, the POSTING DATE field automatically populates with the date you used.
DISPLAY CUSTOMERS/ VENDORS WITH ZERO BALANCE	Select this checkbox to display customers/vendors that have a zero balance.
DISPLAY RECONCILED TRANSACTIONS	Select this checkbox to show transactions that have been reconciled.
IGNORE FUTURE REMIT	Select this checkbox to hide the FUTURE REMIT column.

Table 3.11 Customer Receivables Aging Report Selection Criteria Fields (Cont.)

Once you have set your selection criteria for the aging report, click OK to display the report. The report will display the customer/vendor code and name. It will also display the document type in the TYPE column along with the document number in the DOC. NO. column. You will also see total balance due for the customer/ vendor in the BALANCE DUE column.

Look closely at the Customer Receivables Aging Report shown in Figure 3.65 to spot the aging intervals in the columns labeled 0-30, 31-60, 61-90, 91-120, and 121+. This particular aging report is a helpful snapshot of what is due from your customers and what is due from your company to pay your vendors.

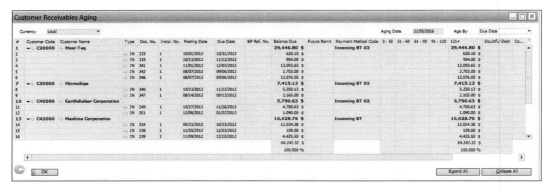

Figure 3.65 A Customer Receivables Aging Report

Organizations seeking to forecast future revenues relative to sales endeavors often run into the obstacle of organizing their opportunities — perhaps because salespeople are by nature independent or because we don't provide systems for them to centralize their collective knowledge and create reports easily. In this chapter, we'll investigate how SAP Business One helps organize opportunities.

4   Opportunities

Most ERP applications lack functionality for customer relationship management (CRM). Without internalized CRM, relationships with prospects, customers, and even vendors are often tracked in separate systems detached from the ERP system.

However, SAP Business One offers an integrated way to manage customer relationships easily, that includes basic provision for things such as activities, calendars, communication, and — of course — *opportunities*. Opportunities in this business are possible sales, so opportunity tracking is the process of monitoring these sales opportunities closely.

To begin organizing opportunities in SAP Business One, click on MAIN MENU • OPPORTUNITIES and then on OPPORTUNITY to access the opportunity management screen shown in Figure 4.1.

Tips and Tricks: Add Mode
The OPPORTUNITY screen shown here is in Add mode — but in a system that already has opportunities created, the screen will open in Find mode.

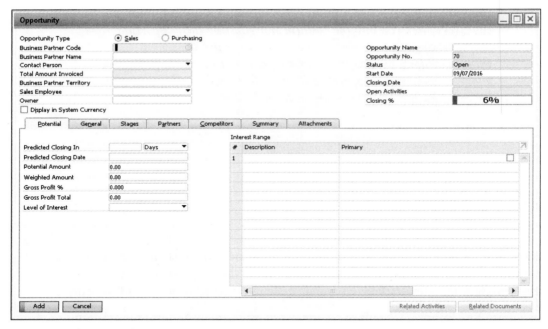

Figure 4.1 The Opportunity Screen

You can create opportunities relative to leads and customers (sales) and vendors (purchasing). Our examples will focus on sales, but rest assured, purchasing works in nearly identical fashion.

Now let's look at the basic steps to create and manage an opportunity.

4.1   Opportunity

Much of the information in the opportunity's header and seven subordinate tabs is optional. In some sales processes, the opportunity is opened and closed—or, in other words, is won or lost—almost immediately. In such cases, some details may be less important than would be necessary elsewhere; in a long and complex sales cycle, additional details and the ability to constantly evaluate the current status of an opportunity from multiple perspectives can be of great help and can provide the intelligence needed to think strategically from a sales perspective. Figure 4.2

illustrates more complex requirements and includes optional information filled in with examples to help us evaluate the potential use of each section.

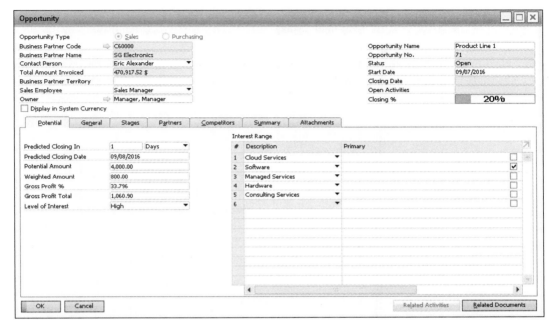

Figure 4.2 The Opportunity Screen Showing Complex Requirements

Let's take a closer look at every section starting with the header. The header area of the screen, which is the top half of Figure 4.2, provides the most basic of sales processes this information would be a requirement.

Table 4.1 lists each field in the opportunity header.

Field	Description/Use
OPPORTUNITY TYPE	Select the kind of opportunity you are creating from the SALES or PURCHASING radio buttons.
BUSINESS PARTNER CODE	This field displays the business partner code from the BUSINESS PARTNER MASTER DATA screen.
BUSINESS PARTNER NAME	This field displays the business partner name from the BUSINESS PARTNER MASTER DATA screen.

Table 4.1 Fields in the Opportunity Header

Field	Description/Use
CONTACT PERSON	Choose the contact person for the business partner master from the dropdown list of business partner contacts.
TOTAL AMOUNT INVOICED	This field displays the total invoices processed historically for this business partner.
BUSINESS PARTNER TERRITORY	This field displays the default territory from the BUSINESS PARTNER MASTER DATA screen, but you can change it as necessary.
SALES EMPLOYEE	This field displays the default salesperson from the BUSINESS PARTNER MASTER DATA screen, but you can change it as necessary.
OWNER	This field displays the default owner from the BUSINESS PARTNER MASTER DATA screen, but you can change it as necessary.
DISPLAY IN SYSTEM CURRENCY	If the box is checked, SAP Business One will use the system currency. The default value is the local currency.
OPPORTUNITY NAME	Create a unique name for this opportunity (but first check to see if your company has a pre-existing nomenclature for opportunity names for reporting purposes).
OPPORTUNITY NO.	This field is automatically generated with a unique ID number.
STATUS	In this field, the status options are OPEN, WON, or LOST.
START DATE	By default, this date is the day the opportunity was created but can be changed.
CLOSING DATE	This field is populated automatically based upon data entered in the SUMMARY tab.
OPEN ACTIVITIES	This field lists the number of all *open* activities related to this opportunity.
CLOSING PERCENTAGE	In opportunities with stages, this field is automatically populated based on data in the STAGES tab (which we'll cover in Section 4.1.3).

Table 4.1 Fields in the Opportunity Header (Cont.)

4.1.1   Potential Tab

The POTENTIAL tab shown in Figure 4.3 provides the most basic, high-level summary information regarding the opportunity record. Other tabs are used to record more detailed information. All of the fields in the POTENTIAL tab are open, meaning you'll be able to input and edit information there.

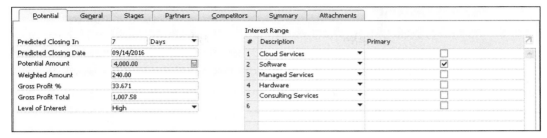

Figure 4.3 The Potential Tab

Table 4.2 describes the information that may be captured in the POTENTIAL tab. You do not need to fill in all fields.

Field	Description/Use
PREDICTED CLOSING IN	Enter an estimate in days, weeks, or months until the opportunity will close.
PREDICTED CLOSING DATE	This field will populate automatically based on your previous selection, but you can edit it manually.
POTENTIAL AMOUNT	This field is autocalculated based on documents attached to the opportunity, which is useful for complex opportunities. For more basic opportunities, you can manually edit this field.
WEIGHTED AMOUNT	In more complex opportunities with stages, each stage is weighted with a percentage; the percentage is applied to the potential amount in calculating this field automatically. You can manually edit this number as necessary.
GROSS PROFIT %	This field is calculated automatically based upon the cost and revenue analysis of the attached documents (such as a sales order). You can manually edit this number as necessary.
GROSS PROFIT TOTAL	This field is calculated automatically based upon the cost and revenue analysis of the attached documents (such as a sales order). You can manually edit this number as necessary.
LEVEL OF INTEREST	Select the level of interest from the dropdown list. You can use the DEFINE NEW option to create your custom list.
INTEREST RANGE DESCRIPTION	Select a descriptive category from the dropdown list. You can use the DEFINE NEW option to create your custom list.
INTEREST RANGE PRIMARY	Select the checkbox that corresponds to the primary area of interest.

Table 4.2 Fields in the Potential Tab

4.1.2 General Tab

The GENERAL tab shown in Figure 4.4 is used for additional information that may be important for future analysis, reporting, and target marketing. This tab provides salespeople with the ability to paste significant notes into a larger dialogue box for context.

Figure 4.4 The General Tab

In Table 4.3, let's investigate each of the fields in the GENERAL tab and their usage.

Field	Description/Use
BP CHANNEL CODE	In some opportunities, the prospective buyer is part of a larger channel. Use this field to identify the opportunity as part of a channel by selecting the "parent" of the buying channel.
BP CHANNEL NAME	This data is filled in automatically when you select the channel code; alternatively, selecting the channel name will update the channel code.
BP CHANNEL CONTACT	This data is filled in automatically from the channel name's default contact in the business partner master record. You can also select a contact from the available list of all contacts associated with that channel name's business partner master record.
BP PROJECT	If this opportunity is part of a larger project, that project's financial code may be entered.
INFORMATION SOURCE	This field helps to identify the source of the lead. The list is dynamic and may be expanded with the DEFINE NEW option.
INDUSTRY	The field helps to identify the industry specific to the opportunity. Select an industry from the dropdown list. The list is dynamic and may be expanded with the DEFINE NEW option.
REMARKS	Add general notes to this field; you can cut and paste from other sources, such as a web page, as necessary.

Table 4.3 Fields in the General Tab

Some of the data in the GENERAL tab fields may be used in the future by your marketing department, for example, or perhaps to evaluate channel impact.

4.1.3 Stages Tab

In larger and more complex opportunities, *stages* are carefully designed and managed to both organize and properly project sales forecast pipeline probabilities. Knowing the current stage of an opportunity within the overall process helps organizations focus their resources—especially sales executives—on those opportunities most likely to close. Typically, this staged approach to the sales process is appropriate for complex sales processes that take multiple encounters and time.

Of course, you'll have to create stages before you can use them. To create stages, go to ADMINISTRATION • SETUP • OPPORTUNITIES • OPPORTUNITY STAGES.

These stages are typically unique to the type of business you are in and strongly identify with the sales style of those responsible for generating new business within the organization. In the OPPORTUNITY STAGES SETUP screen shown in Figure 4.5, you can establish any number of stages or steps on the way to closing an opportunity. The stages are in numerical sequence in the STAGE NO. column; each is assigned a closing percentage that corresponds with the level of commitment this type of activity might convey.

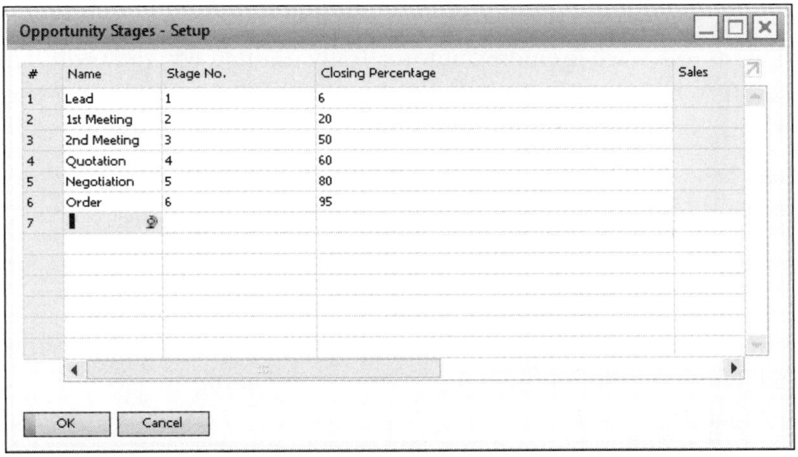

#	Name	Stage No.	Closing Percentage	Sales
1	Lead	1	6	
2	1st Meeting	2	20	
3	2nd Meeting	3	50	
4	Quotation	4	60	
5	Negotiation	5	80	
6	Order	6	95	
7				

Figure 4.5 The Opportunity Stages Setup Screen

Once you've created these stages, they're available in the STAGES tab shown in Figure 4.6, which shows two stages in process. The current stage is 1ST MEETING, and the current associated probability is 20%.

#	Start Date	Closing Date	Sales E...	Stage	%	Potential Amount	Weighted A...	Sho...	Document Type	Doc....	Acti...	Owner	
													↗
1	09/07/2016	09/07/2016	Sales Mana Lead		6.00	4,000.00	240.00	✔	Sales Quotations ⇨	363	⇨	Manager, Manager	
2	09/08/2016	09/08/2016	Sales Ma ▼	1st Meeti ▼	20.0	4,000.00	800.00	✔	Sales Quotatio ▼ ⇨	363	⇨	Manager, Manager	⊙

Figure 4.6 The Stages Tab

To add another stage to the sales process and manage the corresponding details, walk through the following steps:

1. Right-click on the pound sign in the left column of the STAGES tab. From the menu shown in Figure 4.7, select ADD ROW to create and edit a new row.

Copy
Copy Table
Maximize/Restore Grid
Add Row
Delete Row
Duplicate Row
Form Settings...

Figure 4.7 Adding a Stage Using the Right-Click Menu

2. The start date for this stage is entered automatically (though you may edit this date as necessary), but you'll need to enter the estimated closing date for this stage (and perhaps revisit it later for precision).

3. Edit the SALES EMPLOYEE field if it has changed.

4. Edit the STAGE by selecting the desired stage from the dropdown list.

5. Notice the % (probability) column is populated automatically but may be edited.

6. If you're using documents to update the opportunity, both the POTENTIAL AMOUNT and the WEIGHTED AMOUNT fields are updated automatically but may be edited manually.

7. Make sure the SHOW BP DOCS checkbox is checked to filter the next step for documents associated with this business partner only.

8. In the DOCUMENT TYPE field, select the SAP Business One document type you would like to use. For example, perhaps the opportunity is getting more serious, and a sales order would be more appropriate than a quotation.

9. In the DOC. NO. field, either enter the number of the document you want to use or click on the BROWSE icon (the ellipsis). Locate the document you desire, highlight the line, and select CHOOSE; to begin a new document altogether, click NEW.

10. As you're selecting your document, the system will warn that the document selected is already attached to an opportunity (even this same opportunity). If you are certain this is the document you want, select CONTINUE, as shown in Figure 4.8. If not, click SUSPEND to return to the stage line for another try.

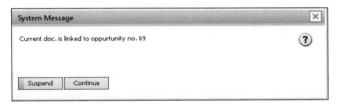

Figure 4.8 An Opportunity Link System Message

11. You won't get far before another warning like the one in Figure 4.9 will appear. This SAP Business One control allows you to either attach the document to the stage and automatically update all the sales revenue estimates or to attach the document but continue manually editing your sales figures. If you are managing the sales amount fields manually, select NO. If you want the system to automatically calculate and evaluate probabilities for you, select YES.

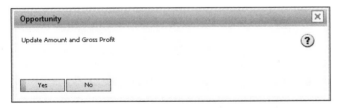

Figure 4.9 An Update Amount and Gross Profit Warning

12. Notice that the POTENTIAL AMOUNT field and the WEIGHTED AMOUNT field have been updated for the stage.

13. In the ACTIVITY field, click the golden arrow to open a screen to create a new activity related to this opportunity. This new activity will be easily visible by clicking on the RELATED ACTIVITIES button.

    This SAP Business One control allows you to either attach the document to the stage and automatically update all the sales revenue estimates or to attach the document but continue manually editing your sales figures.

14. Edit the OWNER field if necessary.

15. Be sure to click the UPDATE button and then select OK.

The STAGES tab is by far the most complex of the tabs within the opportunity management screen—but it has many benefits. A sales professional that masters this tab will find that the resulting detail has made them a more accurate predictor of what will really happen, rather than simply guessing about the proficiency of their sales forecast pipeline evaluations.

4.1.4   Partners Tab

The PARTNERS tab allows you to make references to anyone who is part of the sales team, as shown in Figure 4.10. If you create a record in SAP Business One for your own company, you can even refer to internal team members as well as external sales partners. These capabilities work well when you have an extended and more collaborative sales referral network and want to track the identities of anyone who can influence the outcome of the opportunity.

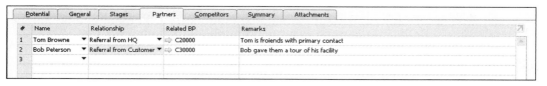

Figure 4.10 The Partners Tab

Table 4.4 describes the four available fields in more detail.

Field	Description/Use
NAME	This field is intended to hold a unique name. Select a sales partner from the dropdown list.

Table 4.4 Fields in the Partners Tab

Field	Description/Use
RELATIONSHIP	Select from the dropdown list to identify the relationship between this partner in the sales process and the prospect you are selling to.
RELATED BP	Link the sales partner to a business partner record in SAP Business One, if possible.
REMARKS	Add any pertinent notes in this field, but note that space is limited to 50 characters.

Table 4.4 Fields in the Partners Tab (Cont.)

4.1.5 Competitors Tab

The COMPETITORS tab shown in Figure 4.11 helps the sales professionals track the performance of the competition to get insight into its strengths and weaknesses. Trends become easier to see when you consistently win or lose against the same competitor, thus enabling you to analyze why that might be the case.

One field in the COMPETITORS tab also allows you to note when you lose a deal to one of your competitors. The checkbox in the WON column signifies that *they* won; in other words, you have lost the opportunity.

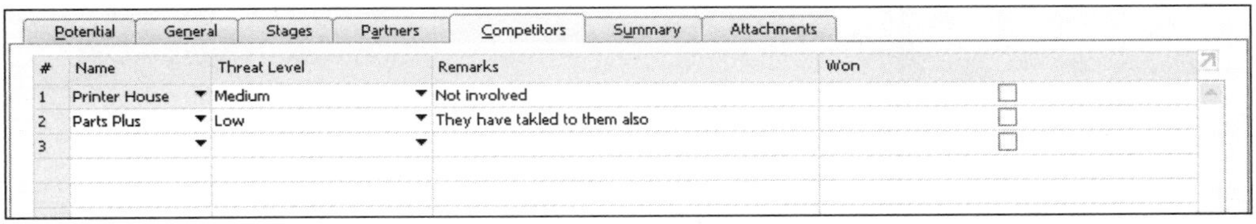

Figure 4.11 The Competitors Tab

Let's discuss the four fields in the COMPETITORS tab in Table 4.5.

Field	Description/Use
NAME	Specify the competitor by name. When using the DEFINE NEW option, this field makes these entries available for all other opportunities.
THREAT LEVEL	Classify competitors with categories that you create, which can be as simple as "low," "medium," and "high" or a more complex weighted numerical system.

Table 4.5 Fields in the Competitors Tab

Field	Description/Use
REMARKS	Add brief and pertinent notes in this field (up to 50 characters).
WON	If you lose the deal to one of these competitors, check this box to signify that the competitor has "won."

Table 4.5 Fields in the Competitors Tab (Cont.)

Because we don't really use the SUMMARY tab until we finalize an opportunity, let's momentarily skip over this tab and proceed instead to the ATTACHMENTS tab.

4.1.6 Attachments Tab

The ATTACHMENTS tab (see Figure 4.12) provides a place for the salesperson to file all the discovery material that was generated in the sales process. If other employees will follow up on the long-term relationship with the customer, having easy access to notes, pictures, brochures, websites, videos, statements of work, and contracts (to name just a few examples) could be of tremendous assistance to another salesperson or other employees after the sale has been accomplished.

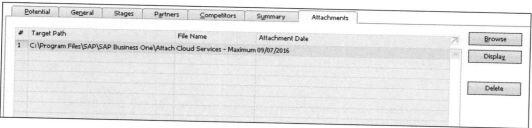

Figure 4.12 The Attachments Tab

All the fields in the ATTACHMENTS tab area are filled in automatically when you click on the BROWSE button and select the attachment you wish to connect to the opportunity. After these attachments have been placed into the ATTACHMENTS tab, use the DISPLAY button to view them at any time. The system automatically opens the appropriate type of viewer. If you need to delete a document, select the line for that document and click the DELETE button.

Let's now return to look at the SUMMARY tab, which is where we truly keep score on our opportunities.

4.1.7 Summary Tab

The SUMMARY tab shown in Figure 4.13 is where an opportunity is filed for historical purposes. Generally speaking, an opportunity is either "won" or "lost" and is "open" only while being actively worked on.

An opportunity may go dormant; sometimes, other business opportunities or challenges get in the way of the sale and cause the prospect to delay a decision. In those cases, we recommend marking the opportunity as LOST with a reason that articulates the delay. A lost opportunity can always be reopened for additional work at a future date.

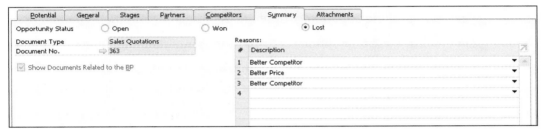

Figure 4.13 The Summary Tab

In Table 4.6, you can see a brief explanation of the fields within the SUMMARY tab. The SUMMARY tab is the final score card for the opportunity. Opportunities have no gray area; in the end, an opportunity is either won or lost.

Field	Description/Use
OPPORTUNITY STATUS	Select OPEN, WON, or LOST. (If lost to a competitor, use the COMPETITORS tab to identify the winner.)
DOCUMENT TYPE	This field displays the last document referenced on the last stage of the STAGES tab; the data in this field is populated automatically.
DOCUMENT NUMBER	This field displays the document number of the last document. Click on the golden arrow to open this document in SAP Business One.
SHOW DOCUMENTS RELATED TO BP	Check this box to display the available documents for the business partner referenced on the opportunity only.

Table 4.6 Fields in the Summary Tab

Field	Description/Use
REASONS	Specify the reasons the opportunity was either won or lost. The dropdown list is only available when the status is either WON or LOST. You can create additional reasons with the DEFINE NEW option in the dropdown list.

Table 4.6 Fields in the Summary Tab (Cont.)

4.1.8 Footer Buttons

Four buttons appear in the footer of the OPPORTUNITY screen. These buttons help us manage the data associated with the opportunity throughout SAP Business One and to file the opportunity record in the database forever.

Let's look at these four buttons in just a little more detail:

▸ UPDATE: This button replaces the standard OK button whenever changes have been made to remind you to save your work. Clicking this button will save your edits, and then the button will change back to OK. Clicking OK will close the OPPORTUNITY window entirely.

▸ CANCEL: This button simply closes the windows. If you have made edits and do not wish to save them, clicking CANCEL will close the windows without saving any of the changes you may have made.

▸ RELATED ACTIVITIES: This button will open the ACTIVITY OVERVIEW window, which lists all activities associated with this opportunity (as shown in Figure 4.14). The ACTIVITY OVERVIEW window features three special characteristics. Select the DISPLAY ONLY OPEN ACTIVITIES checkbox in the top left corner to limit the activity list to only open activities. An ATTACHMENT icon (a paperclip) signifies that the activity has an attachment, and a DOCUMENT icon (a folded page) signifies that an SAP Business One document is attached. Of course, you can also immediately drill down into these items using the golden arrow to open the activity.

▸ RELATED DOCUMENTS: This button will open the LINKED DOCUMENTS window shown in Figure 4.15, which lists all of the SAP Business One documents that are related in any way to this opportunity. Recall that these documents were specifically noted in the STAGES tab. Each line on the STAGES tab has the option of referencing a specific SAP Business One document. The list may show several different documents if a new document was used for each stage or may have the same document listed multiple times if the choice was to simply update the document along the way. Notice in Figure 4.15 that one quotation document was referenced twice and a sales order was referenced three times.

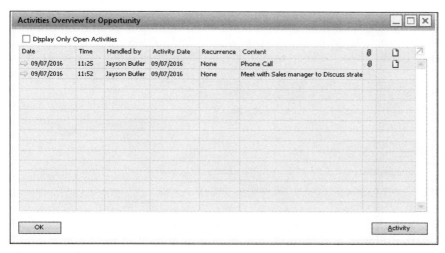

Figure 4.14 The Activities Overview for Opportunity Screen

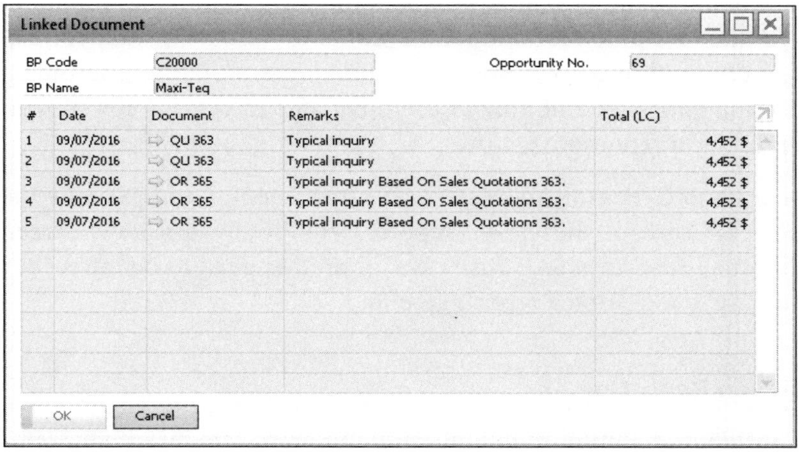

Figure 4.15 The Linked Document Window

Before we can file away this opportunity, we'll need to designate it as either "won" or "lost" by following these steps:

1. Navigate to the SUMMARY tab.

2. Change the status to WON or LOST and select a reason or reasons why.

3. Click the UPDATE button.

At this point, the system will generate a message like the one shown in Figure 4.16 to inquire whether you want to automatically close any related activities that have not already been closed. To keep things tidy, we recommend that you select YES.

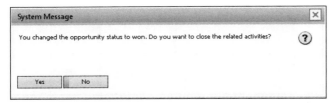

Figure 4.16 A System Message for Closing Related Items

4.2 Opportunity Reports

Eleven out-of-the-box report templates are available for opportunities in SAP Business One to help you understand the statuses and investigate the efficiency of opportunities as they are processed and recorded. Using these templates, you can filter, sort, and slice and dice the report's output in numerous ways. Becoming familiar with these templates and how to use them amplifies these eleven templates into hundreds of report possibilities.

Before we navigate to OPPORTUNITIES • OPPORTUNITIES REPORTS and examine the report template for each of the eleven reports, let's briefly discuss onscreen reporting. Almost all reports in SAP Business One are designed to be interactive onscreen reports first and printed reports second.

4.2.1 Onscreen Reporting

The screen version of the output is intended as a live and interactive tool. Take a look at the Opportunity Forecast Report shown in Figure 4.17; the onscreen version of this report data is embedded with golden arrows to drill down deeper into the information they deliver. We recommend that you investigate each of these reports in detail, running test scenarios to understand the use of each template and some of their possibilities.

Tips and Tricks: Optional Fields

Recall from Section 4.1 that only a few fields in the header, footer, and the various tabs are actually required. However, many of the out-of-the-box reports make use of these optional fields. Sometimes the onscreen reports have blank columns because that data has not been entered into the opportunity.

Opportunities Forecast Report

#	Oppr. No.	BP Name	Contact Person	Last Sales Emp.	Territory	Last Stage	Closing %	Potential Amount (LC)	Weighted Amount (LC)	Predicted Closing Date
1	1	Maxi-Teq	Max Teq	Brad Thompson		Quotation	60	29,005	17,403	03/02/2006
2	3	Parameter Technology	Daniel Brown	Jim Boswick		1st Meeting	20	50,000	10,000	02/16/2006
3	4	Earthshaker Corporation	Bob McKensly	Brad Thompson		Quotation	60	15,005	9,003	01/15/2006
4	10	Werner Richter	Vince Wilfork	Bill Levine		Quotation	60	60,000	36,000	02/25/2006
5	11	Mashina Corporation	Anthony Smith	Sophie Klogg		1st Meeting	20	25,000	5,000	02/20/2006
6	12	Mashina Corporation	Anthony Smith	Brad Thompson		Quotation	60	30,000	18,000	02/04/2006
7	13	Mashina Corporation	Anthony Smith	Brad Thompson		2nd Meeting	50	50,000	25,000	02/15/2006
8	14	Mashina Corporation	Anthony Smith	Sophie Klogg		Lead	6	10,000	600	02/24/2006
9	15	Earthshaker Corporation	Bob McKensly	Brad Thompson		Negotiation	80	40,000	32,000	03/19/2006
10	16	Maxi-Teq	Max Teq	Brad Thompson		Lead	6	10,000	600	01/19/2006
11	17	Parameter Technology	Daniel Brown	Bill Levine		Lead	3	25,000	750	01/19/2006
12	18	Microchips	Judy Brown	Sophie Klogg		1st Meeting	20	7,000	1,400	01/19/2006
13	19	Werner Richter	Vince Wilfork	Sophie Klogg		Lead	6	7,000	420	01/17/2006
14	21	Mashina Corporation	Anthony Smith	-No Sales Employ		2nd Meeting	50	50,000	25,000	05/06/2006
15	25	Maxi-Teq	Max Teq	Brad Thompson		Quotation	60	29,005	17,403	03/02/2007
16	27	Microchips	Judy Brown	Jim Boswick		1st Meeting	20	50,000	10,000	02/16/2007
17	28	Earthshaker Corporation	Bob McKensly	Brad Thompson		Quotation	60	15,005	9,003	01/15/2007
18	34	Werner Richter	Vince Wilfork	Bill Levine		Quotation	60	60,000	36,000	02/25/2007
19	35	Andreas Ackermann	James Sanders	Sophie Klogg		1st Meeting	20	25,000	5,000	02/20/2007
20	36	Werner Richter	Vince Wilfork	Brad Thompson		Quotation	60	30,000	18,000	02/04/2007
21	37	Maxi-Teq	Max Teq	Brad Thompson		Quotation	60	30,000	18,000	04/16/2007
22	39	Parameter Technology	Daniel Brown	Brad Thompson		Quotation	60	50,000	30,000	06/18/2007
23	40	Earthshaker Corporation	Bob McKensly	Bill Levine		Quotation	60	15,000	9,000	08/19/2007
24	46	Aquent Systems	Troy Brown	Brad Thompson		1st Meeting	20	60,000	12,000	02/21/2008
25	47	Mashina Corporation	Anthony Smith	Brad Thompson		1st Meeting	20	25,000	5,000	03/21/2008
26	48	Mashina Corporation	Anthony Smith	Brad Thompson		1st Meeting	20	30,000	6,000	04/21/2008
27	49	Mashina Corporation	Anthony Smith	Jim Boswick		1st Meeting	20	50,000	10,000	05/21/2008
28	50	Mashina Corporation	Anthony Smith	Jim Boswick		1st Meeting	20	10,000	2,000	06/21/2008
29	52	Maxi-Teq	Max Teq	Sophie Klogg		Quotation	60	10,000	6,000	08/21/2008
30	53	Parameter Technology	Daniel Brown	Sophie Klogg		Quotation	60	25,000	15,000	09/21/2008
31	54	Microchips	Judy Brown	Sophie Klogg		Quotation	60	70,000	42,000	10/21/2008
32	55	ADA Technologies	Mary Brown	Sophie Klogg		Quotation	60	70,000	42,000	11/21/2008
33	57	Mashina Corporation	Anthony Smith	Sophie Klogg		Quotation	60	50,000	30,000	01/21/2009
34	64	Maxi-Teq	Max Teq	Bill Levine		1st Meeting	20	25,000	5,000	08/21/2009
35	65	Parameter Technology	Daniel Brown	Bill Levine		1st Meeting	20	70,000	14,000	09/21/2009
36	66	ADA Technologies	Mary Brown	Bill Levine		1st Meeting	20	50,000	10,000	10/21/2009
37	67	SG Electronics	Eric Alexander	Bill Levine		1st Meeting	20	50,000	10,000	11/21/2009
38	68	Aquent Systems	Troy Brown	Bill Levine		1st Meeting	20	88,888	17,777.6	12/21/2009
39	70	Earthshaker Corporation	Bob McKensly	Sales Manager		Negotiation	80	4,200	3,360	09/09/2016
40	71	SG Electronics	Eric Alexander	Sales Manager		1st Meeting	20	4,000	800	09/08/2016

OK

Figure 4.17 An Opportunities Forecast Report

Let's look more closely at this example for the OPPORTUNITIES FORECAST REPORT menu item. Notice that the TERRITORY column in Figure 4.17 is blank because our example company OEC Computers doesn't use the TERRITORY field in the opportunity. So if the TERRITORY field isn't necessary in our report, how do we remove this field from the report? With this onscreen report open, click the FORM SETTINGS icon (a blank sheet with a green gear) in the toolbar to gain access to the TABLE FORMAT tab for this report, which is shown in Figure 4.18. The TABLE FORMAT tab allows you to select the fields you wish to have visible in the onscreen report. (Notice that, in this example, many more fields are available to choose from!)

For now, unselect the TERRITORY field checkbox, which will hide it from our report. Click OK to save this choice.

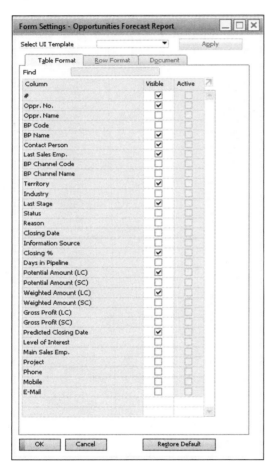

Figure 4.18 The Table Format Screen

The onscreen report will automatically refresh with your changes in place. Notice that now the Territory column has been removed from the report shown in Figure 4.19.

#	Oppr. No.	BP Name	Contact Person	Last Sales Emp.	Last Stage	Closing %	Potential Amount (LC)	Weighted Amount (LC)	Predicted Closing Date
1	1	Maxi-Teq	Max Teq	Brad Thompson	Quotation	60	29,005	17,403	03/02/2006
2	3	Parameter Technology	Daniel Brown	Jim Boswick	1st Meeting	20	50,000	10,000	02/16/2006
3	4	Earthshaker Corporation	Bob McKensly	Brad Thompson	Quotation	60	15,005	9,003	01/15/2006
4	10	Werner Richter	Vince Wilfork	Bill Levine	Quotation	60	60,000	36,000	02/25/2006
5	11	Mashina Corporation	Anthony Smith	Sophie Klogg	1st Meeting	20	25,000	5,000	02/20/2006
6	12	Mashina Corporation	Anthony Smith	Brad Thompson	Quotation	60	30,000	18,000	02/04/2006
7	13	Mashina Corporation	Anthony Smith	Brad Thompson	2nd Meeting	50	50,000	25,000	02/15/2006
8	14	Mashina Corporation	Anthony Smith	Sophie Klogg	Lead	6	10,000	600	02/24/2006
9	15	Earthshaker Corporation	Bob McKensly	Brad Thompson	Negotiation	80	40,000	32,000	03/19/2006
10	16	Maxi-Teq	Max Teq	Brad Thompson	Lead	6	10,000	600	01/19/2006
11	17	Parameter Technology	Daniel Brown	Bill Levine	Lead	3	25,000	750	02/07/2006
12	18	Microchips	Judy Brown	Sophie Klogg	1st Meeting	20	7,000	1,400	01/19/2006
13	19	Werner Richter	Vince Wilfork	Sophie Klogg	Lead	6	7,000	420	01/17/2006
14	21	Mashina Corporation	Anthony Smith	-No Sales Employ	2nd Meeting	50	50,000	25,000	05/06/2006
15	25	Maxi-Teq	Max Teq	Brad Thompson	Quotation	60	29,005	17,403	03/02/2007
16	27	Microchips	Judy Brown	Jim Boswick	1st Meeting	20	50,000	10,000	02/16/2007
17	28	Earthshaker Corporation	Bob McKensly	Brad Thompson	Quotation	60	15,005	9,003	01/15/2007
18	34	Werner Richter	Vince Wilfork	Bill Levine	Quotation	60	60,000	36,000	02/25/2007
19	35	Andreas Ackermann	James Sanders	Sophie Klogg	1st Meeting	20	25,000	5,000	02/20/2007
20	36	Werner Richter	Vince Wilfork	Brad Thompson	Quotation	60	30,000	18,000	02/04/2007
21	37	Maxi-Teq	Max Teq	Brad Thompson	Quotation	60	30,000	18,000	04/16/2007
22	39	Parameter Technology	Daniel Brown	Brad Thompson	Quotation	60	50,000	30,000	06/18/2007
23	40	Earthshaker Corporation	Bob McKensly	Bill Levine	Quotation	60	15,000	9,000	08/19/2007
24	46	Aquent Systems	Troy Brown	Brad Thompson	1st Meeting	20	60,000	12,000	02/21/2008
25	47	Mashina Corporation	Anthony Smith	Brad Thompson	1st Meeting	20	25,000	5,000	03/21/2008
26	48	Mashina Corporation	Anthony Smith	Brad Thompson	1st Meeting	20	30,000	6,000	04/21/2008
27	49	Mashina Corporation	Anthony Smith	Jim Boswick	1st Meeting	20	50,000	10,000	05/21/2008
28	50	Mashina Corporation	Anthony Smith	Jim Boswick	1st Meeting	20	10,000	2,000	06/21/2008
29	52	Maxi-Teq	Max Teq	Sophie Klogg	Quotation	60	10,000	6,000	08/21/2008
30	53	Parameter Technology	Daniel Brown	Sophie Klogg	Quotation	60	25,000	15,000	09/21/2008
31	54	Microchips	Judy Brown	Sophie Klogg	Quotation	60	70,000	42,000	10/21/2008
32	55	ADA Technologies	Mary Brown	Sophie Klogg	Quotation	60	70,000	42,000	11/21/2008
33	57	Mashina Corporation	Anthony Smith	Sophie Klogg	Quotation	60	50,000	30,000	01/21/2009
34	64	Maxi-Teq	Max Teq	Bill Levine	1st Meeting	20	25,000	5,000	08/21/2009
35	65	Parameter Technology	Daniel Brown	Bill Levine	1st Meeting	20	70,000	14,000	09/21/2009
36	66	ADA Technologies	Mary Brown	Bill Levine	1st Meeting	20	50,000	10,000	10/21/2009
37	67	SG Electronics	Eric Alexander	Bill Levine	1st Meeting	20	50,000	10,000	11/21/2009
38	68	Aquent Systems	Troy Brown	Bill Levine	1st Meeting	20	88,888	17,777.6	12/21/2009
39	70	Earthshaker Corporation	Bob McKensly	Sales Manager	Negotiation	80	4,200	3,360	09/09/2016
40	71	SG Electronics	Eric Alexander	Sales Manager	1st Meeting	20	4,000	800	09/08/2016

OK

Figure 4.19 An Opportunities Forecast Report without Territories

> **Tips and Tricks: Manipulating Onscreen Reports**
>
> To sort by any single column, just double-click on the column header. To filter the onscreen report, use the FILTER icon (the funnel) in the toolbar. To sort in a more complicated, multilevel fashion, use the SORT icon (the grid with A and Z) in the toolbar.

Now let's take a brief tour of the eleven out-of-the-box opportunity reports, their templates, and their printouts.

4.2.2 Opportunity Forecast Report

The Opportunities Forecast Report shown in the system in Figure 4.20 and as a printout in Figure 4.21 gives a simple listing of open opportunities. Use this template or form to select the data you wish to include in the report, such as stages or industries.

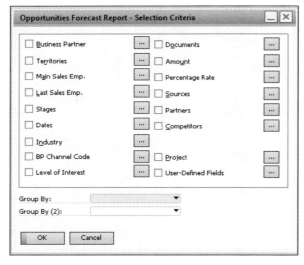

Figure 4.20 Selection Criteria for an Opportunities Forecast Report

Opp. ID	Opp. Name	BP Code	Territory	Sales Employee	Industry	Projected Amt	Probability	Pred. Date	Stage

OEC Computers

Opportunities - Forecast

Date 3/08/2016

Time 11:28

Opp. ID	Opp. Name	BP Code	Territory	Sales Employee	Industry	Projected Amt	Probability	Pred. Date	Stage
1		C20000		Brad Thompson		29,005.00	60.000	03/02/2006	Quotation
3		C23900		Jim Boswick		50,000.00	20.000	02/16/2006	1st Meeting
4		C40000		Brad Thompson		15,005.00	60.000	01/15/2006	Quotation
10		L10002		Bill Levine		60,000.00	60.000	02/25/2006	Quotation
11		C42000		Sophie Klogg		25,000.00	20.000	02/20/2006	1st Meeting
12		C42000		Brad Thompson		30,000.00	60.000	02/04/2006	Quotation
13		C42000		Brad Thompson		50,000.00	50.000	02/15/2006	2nd Meeting
14		C42000		Sophie Klogg		10,000.00	6.000	02/24/2006	Lead
15		C40000		Brad Thompson		40,000.00	80.000	03/19/2006	Negotiation
16		C20000		Brad Thompson		10,000.00	6.000	01/19/2006	Lead
17		C23900		Bill Levine		25,000.00	3.000	02/07/2006	Lead
18		C30000		Sophie Klogg		7,000.00	20.000	01/19/2006	1st Meeting
19		L10002		Sophie Klogg		7,000.00	6.000	01/17/2006	Lead
21		C42000		Jim Boswick		50,000.00	50.000	05/06/2006	2nd Meeting
25		C20000		Brad Thompson		29,005.00	60.000	03/02/2007	Quotation
27		C30000		Jim Boswick		50,000.00	20.000	02/16/2007	1st Meeting
28		C40000		Brad Thompson		15,005.00	60.000	01/15/2007	Quotation
34		L10002		Bill Levine		60,000.00	60.000	02/25/2007	Quotation
35		L10001		Sophie Klogg		25,000.00	20.000	02/20/2007	1st Meeting
36		L10002		Brad Thompson		30,000.00	60.000	02/04/2007	Quotation
37		C20000		Brad Thompson		30,000.00	60.000	04/16/2007	Quotation
39		C23900		Jim Boswick		50,000.00	60.000	06/18/2007	Quotation
40		C40000		Brad Thompson		15,000.00	60.000	08/19/2007	Quotation
46		C70000		Bill Levine		60,000.00	20.000	02/21/2008	1st Meeting
47		C42000		Sophie Klogg		25,000.00	20.000	03/21/2008	1st Meeting

Figure 4.21 An Opportunities Forecast Report Printout

4.2.3 Opportunity Forecast Over Time Report

The Opportunity Forecast Over Time Report shown in Figure 4.22 and as a printout in Figure 4.23 gives a summary analysis of opportunity performance over time. You can use this template or form to select the data you wish to include in the report, for example, using the GROUP BY dropdown list, as we have done for MONTH in this example.

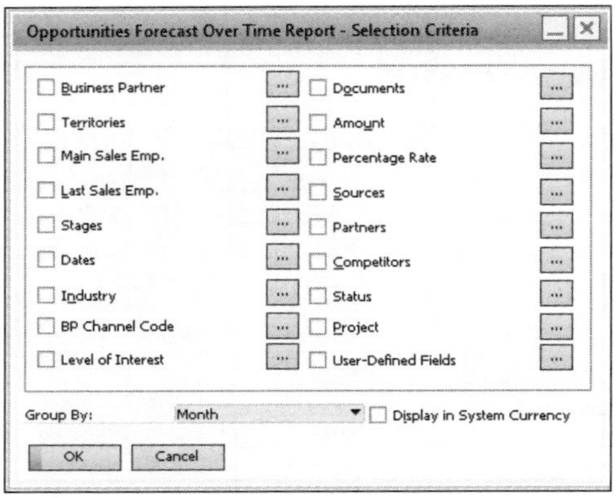

Figure 4.22 Selection Criteria for an Opportunities Forecast Over Time Report

OEC Computers

Date 09/08/2016
Time 11:33

Opportunities - Forecast Over Time

Month	Open Amount	Total Open	Total Won	Total Lost	Total Close
1 - 2006	39,005.00	4	4		4
2 - 2006	250,000.00	7	1	2	3
3 - 2006	69,005.00	2		1	1
4 - 2006	0.00		2		2
5 - 2006	50,000.00	1			
1 - 2007	15,005.00	1	2		2
2 - 2007	165,000.00	4		2	2
3 - 2007	29,005.00	1		1	1
4 - 2007	30,000.00	1	1		1
5 - 2007	0.00		1		1
6 - 2007	50,000.00	1			
8 - 2007	15,000.00	1			
9 - 2007	0.00			1	1
10 - 2007	0.00			1	1
11 - 2007	0.00		1		1
12 - 2007	0.00			1	1
1 - 2008	0.00		1		1
2 - 2008	60,000.00	1			
3 - 2008	25,000.00	1			
4 - 2008	30,000.00	1			
5 - 2008	50,000.00	1			
6 - 2008	10,000.00	1			
7 - 2008	0.00		1		1
8 - 2008	10,000.00	1			
9 - 2008	25,000.00	1			
10 - 2008	70,000.00	1			
11 - 2008	70,000.00	1			
12 - 2008	0.00		1		1
1 - 2009	50,000.00	1			
2 - 2009	0.00		1		1

Figure 4.23 An Opportunities Forecast Over Time Report Printout

4.2.4 Opportunity Statistics Report

The Opportunity Statistics Report shown in the system in Figure 4.24 and as a printout in Figure 4.25 gives a statistical analysis of opportunity performance by business partner. Use this template or form to select the data you wish to include in the report; in our example, we have grouped our data by business partner code, as shown in the left column of Figure 4.25.

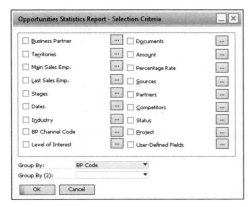

Figure 4.24 Selection Criteria for an Opportunity Statistics Report

OEC Computers

Opportunities List

Date 09/08/2016

Time 11:34

BP Code	Total	Total Open	Total Won	Total Lost	Total Close	Success %	Projected Open Amt	Won Amount	Lost Amount
C20000	8.00	6.00	1.00	1.00	2.00	50.00	133,010.00	4,200.00	10,000.00
C23900	11.00	5.00	5.00	1.00	6.00	83.00	220,000.00	180,010.00	60,000.00
C30000	4.00	3.00	1.00	0.00	1.00	100.00	127,000.00	100,000.00	0.00
C40000	7.00	5.00	1.00	1.00	2.00	50.00	89,210.00	40,000.00	10,000.00
C42000	14.00	10.00	3.00	1.00	4.00	75.00	330,000.00	115,005.00	10,000.00
C50000	5.00	2.00	1.00	2.00	3.00	33.00	120,000.00	61,000.00	160,000.00
C60000	5.00	2.00	2.00	1.00	3.00	66.00	54,000.00	50,005.00	45,000.00
C70000	4.00	2.00	1.00	1.00	2.00	50.00	148,888.00	10,000.00	100,000.00
L10001	6.00	1.00	4.00	1.00	5.00	80.00	25,000.00	82,470.00	10,000.00
L10002	7.00	4.00	1.00	2.00	3.00	33.00	157,000.00	16,005.00	160,000.00

Figure 4.25 An Opportunity Statistics Report Printout

4.2.5 Opportunities Report

The Opportunities Report shown in the system in Figure 4.26 and as a printout in Figure 4.27 gives a rather simple listing of all opportunities, either open, won, or lost. Use this template or form to select the data you wish to include in the report. In our example in Figure 4.27, the STATUS column is visible to the right of the page.

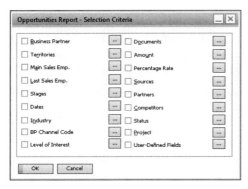

Figure 4.26 Selection Criteria for an Opportunities Report

Opp. ID	Opp. Name	BP Code	Sales Employee	Industry	Projected Amt	Probability	Status	Stage
1		C20000	Brad Thompson		29,005.00	60.000	Open	Quotation
2		C23900	Bill Levine		20,005.00	95.000	Won	Order
3		C23900	Jim Boswick		50,000.00	20.000	Open	1st Meeting
4		C40000	Brad Thompson		15,005.00	60.000	Open	Quotation
5		L10001	Jim Boswick		10,000.00	20.000	Lost	1st Meeting
6		L10002	Sophie Klogg		60,000.00	60.000	Lost	Quotation
7		L10001	Sophie Klogg		10,005.00	95.000	Won	Order
8		L10002	Sophie Klogg		100,000.00	80.000	Lost	Negotiation
9		L10001	Bill Levine		36,005.00	95.000	Won	Order
10		L10002	Bill Levine		60,000.00	60.000	Open	Quotation
11		C42000	Sophie Klogg		25,000.00	20.000	Open	1st Meeting
12		C42000	Brad Thompson		30,000.00	60.000	Open	Quotation
13		C42000	Brad Thompson		50,000.00	50.000	Open	2nd Meeting
14		C42000	Sophie Klogg		10,000.00	6.000	Open	Lead
15		C40000	Brad Thompson		40,000.00	80.000	Open	Negotiation
16		C20000	Brad Thompson		10,000.00	6.000	Open	Lead
17		C23900	Bill Levine		25,000.00	3.000	Open	Lead
18		C30000	Sophie Klogg		7,000.00	20.000	Open	1st Meeting
19		L10002	Sophie Klogg		7,000.00	6.000	Open	Lead
20		C42000	Jim Boswick		25,005.00	95.000	Won	Order
21		C42000	Jim Boswick		50,000.00	50.000	Open	2nd Meeting
22		C23900	Bill Levine		10,000.00	60.000	Won	Quotation
23		L10002	Sales Manager		16,005.00	95.000	Won	Order

OEC Computers

Date 09/08/2016 Time 11:37

Opportunities List

Page 1   Continued on next page

Figure 4.27 An Opportunities Report Printout

4.2.6 Stage Analysis Report

The Stage Analysis Report shown in the system in Figure 4.28 and as a printout in Figure 4.29 gives a summary of stage performance by salespersons for open opportunities. Use this template or form to select the data you wish to include in the report; you can use the START DATE and PREDICTED CLOSING DATE fields to restrict the data, for example.

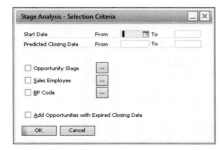

Figure 4.28 Selection Criteria for a Stage Analysis Report

OEC Computers

		Date	09/08/2016
		Time	11:39

Stage Analysis Report

Stage	Defined %	Sales Employee	Actual %	Leads in Stage
Lead	6.00	General	62.00	29
		Sales Manager	100.00	1
		Bill Levine	62.00	8
		Sophie Klogg	58.00	12
		Brad Thompson	100.00	3
		Jim Boswick	40.00	5
1st Meeting	20.00	General	60.00	23
		Sales Manager	100.00	1
		Bill Levine	50.00	6
		Sophie Klogg	70.00	10
		Brad Thompson	100.00	2
		Jim Boswick	25.00	4
2nd Meeting	50.00	General	50.00	10
		Bill Levine	100.00	1
		Sophie Klogg	33.00	6
		Brad Thompson	100.00	1
		Jim Boswick	50.00	2
Quotation	60.00	General	76.00	13
		Bill Levine	100.00	4
		Sophie Klogg	66.00	6
		Brad Thompson	100.00	1
		Jim Boswick	50.00	2
Negotiation	80.00	General	33.00	3
		Sales Manager	100.00	1
		Sophie Klogg	0.00	2
Order	95.00	General	100.00	9
		Sales Manager	100.00	1
		Bill Levine	100.00	4
		Sophie Klogg	100.00	3
		Jim Boswick	100.00	1
Closed	100.00	General	100.00	1
		Sales Manager	100.00	1

Page   1

Figure 4.29 A Stage Analysis Report Printout

4.2.7 Information Source Distribution Over Time Report

The Information Source Distribution Over Time Report shown in the system in Figure 4.30 and as a printout in Figure 4.31 summarizes the performance or information sources (also known as leads) over time—in our case, measured in weeks. This report helps to answer the question, "Where am I getting my leads?" Use this template or form to select the data you wish to include in the report.

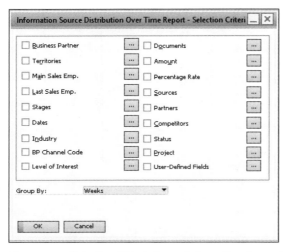

Figure 4.30 Selection Criteria for an Information Source Distribution Over Time Report

OEC Computers

| | | | Date | 09/08/2016 |
| | | | Time | 11:45 |

Opportunities - Source Distribution

Weeks	Global Lead List	Customer Referral	Internal Referral	Purchased List 20	Total
1 - 2006	3	3	3	3	22
2 - 2006					1
4 - 2006					1
	3	3	3	3	

Figure 4.31 An Information Source Distribution Over Time Report Printout

4.2.8 Won Opportunities Report

The Won Opportunities Report shown in the system in Figure 4.32 and as a print-out in Figure 4.33 gives you a high-level summary of open opportunities grouped by days until close. You use this template or form to select the data you wish to include in the report. In our example, we chose to view this data in 10-day ranges.

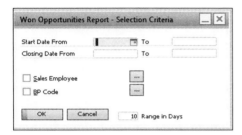

Figure 4.32 Selection Criteria for a Won Opportunities Report

OEC Computers

Date 09/08/2016
Time 11:46

Successful Opportunities Report

Days Until Closing	No. of Opportunities	Total Amount
0 - 10	3	14,655.00
11 - 20	9	471,000.00
21 - 30	5	108,025.00
31 - 40	0	0.00
41 - 50	0	0.00
51 - 60	0	0.00
61 - 70	0	0.00
71 - 80	0	0.00
81 - 90	1	25,005.00
91 - 100	2	40,010.00

Page 1

Figure 4.33 A Won Opportunities Report Printout

4.2.9 Lost Opportunities Report

The Lost Opportunities Report shown in the system in Figure 4.34 and as a print-out in Figure 4.35 gives a detailed listing of all lost opportunities. Take a look at the LAST STAGE column on the far right of Figure 4.35 to see where each opportunity was lost.

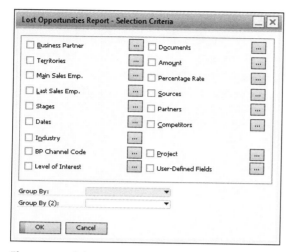

Figure 4.34 Selection Criteria for a Lost Opportunities Report

	**OEC Computers** Date 9/08/2016 — **Opportunities - Lost** Time 11:48
Opp. ID	Opp. Name	BP Code	Territory	Salesperson	Industry	Projected Amt	Days in Pipeline	Reason for Loss	Last Stage
5		L10001		Jim Boswick		10,000.00	462		1st Meeting
6		L10002		Sophie Klogg		60,000.00	463		Quotation
8		L10002		Sophie Klogg		100,000.00	459		Negotiation
29		C42000		Jim Boswick		10,000.00	98		1st Meeting
30		C50000		Sophie Klogg		60,000.00	99		Quotation
32		C70000		Sophie Klogg		100,000.00	95		Negotiation
41		C20000		Jim Boswick		10,000.00	848		1st Meeting
42		C23900		Sophie Klogg		60,000.00	817		1st Meeting
44		C50000		Sophie Klogg		100,000.00	754		Quotation
60		C60000		Brad Thompson		45,000.00	269		1st Meeting
63		C40000		Jim Boswick		10,000.00	178		1st Meeting

Figure 4.35 A Lost Opportunities Report Printout

4.2.10 My Open Opportunities Report

The My Open Opportunities Report shown in Figure 4.36 does not require you to fill out a template or form. Instead, this report is generated by a simple query that is filtered automatically for the currently signed-on user, thus delivering a quick listing of that user's open opportunities.

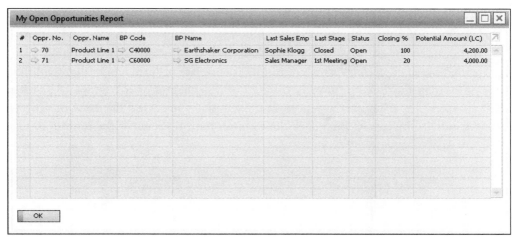

Figure 4.36 My Open Opportunities Report

4.2.11 My Closed Opportunities Report

Similarly, the My Closed Opportunities Report shown in Figure 4.37 lacks a template or form. This report is a simple query that is filtered automatically for the currently signed-on user, thus delivering a quick listing of that user's closed opportunities.

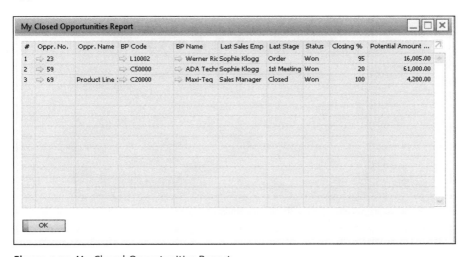

Figure 4.37 My Closed Opportunities Report

4.2.12 Opportunities Pipeline

The Opportunities Pipeline Report shown in the system in Figure 4.38 and as a printout in Figure 4.39 summarizes and evaluates what has traditionally been called the *sales pipeline* or *sales funnel*. This template or form works slightly differently than those we've already covered in this chapter as the template or form also serves as the onscreen report. In the template, you select the data you wish to include in the report, then click the REFRESH button shown at the bottom of Figure 4.38 to update the report.

Tips and Tricks: Drill to the Details

When viewing the onscreen version of the Opportunities Pipeline Report, you can do one of two things to drill down into the details of a stage:

▸ Double-click any STAGE section of the chart.

▸ Double-click the ID number of the stage in the list below the chart.

Either method will return a detailed list of the open opportunities in that stage.

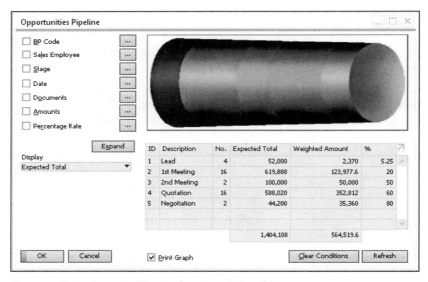

Figure 4.38 An Opportunities Pipeline Report Template

Page 1 of 1

OEC Computers

| | | Date | 10/30/2016 |
| | | Time | 09:48 |

Opportunity Analysis

#	Description	Number	Expected Total	Weighted Amount	%
1	Lead	4	52,000	2,370	5.25
2	1st Meeting	16	619,888	123,977.6	20
3	2nd Meeting	2	100,000	50,000	50
4	Quotation	16	588,020	352,812	60
5	Negotiation	2	44,200	35,360	80
			1,404,108	564,519.6	

Figure 4.39 An Opportunities Pipeline Report Printout

Tips and Tricks: Dynamic Opportunity Analysis

While the Opportunity Pipeline Report is visible onscreen, click the Go-To menu and select DYNAMIC OPPORTUNITY ANALYSIS. The SAP Business One system will load a unique approach to analyzing the same data.

Many simplistic accounting packages only include an A/R invoice. However, more sophisticated businesses need more functionality than that. SAP Business One's Sales (A/R) module was created with this in mind. What's more, it's all integrated with your customer's master record, ensuring that accurate and relevant CRM information is at your fingertips.

5   Sales (A/R)

Once an opportunity starts turning into a sale, a different SAP Business One module is applicable: Sales (A/R). The Sales (A/R) module is the place to go in SAP Business One when you want to quote your customer, take an order, send an invoice, and much more. This module captures both simple and complex variations on the traditional sales process. Because the Sales (A/R) module is almost the mirror image of its sister module, Purchasing (A/P), which we'll cover in Chapter 6, paying careful attention to what each document does in the sales process will set you up for success once you move into the purchasing process. The Sales (A/R) module is also linked with many of the other modules in SAP Business One. In particular, sales documents will automatically incorporate data from business partner master data (Chapter 7) and item master data (Chapter 9).

This chapter will walk through the sales process in SAP Business One and help you tailor its transactions and tools to your business. We'll take a deeper dive on each sales document's intended purpose, from sales blanket agreements through A/R reserve invoices. We'll also see how wizards and tools such as the Document Generation Wizard and the Dunning Wizard can automate time-consuming and repetitive sales processes such as an invoicing run or regularly recurring transactions. We'll conclude this chapter by looking at the reports and report generators that are available in SAP Business One's standard toolkit.

5.1   Sales Process

Let's get right down to revenue generation! Every business has a sales process that progresses a little bit differently. *Sales documents*—the first menu items in the module—capture unique aspects of the sales process from start to finish. We'll go into detail about what each document does and how they can lend themselves to variations in the sales processes of different companies. We'll also study the similarities between all documents in the module and see how they interact together. By the end of this section, you should have a better understanding of which sales documents you'd like to use and which ones you may not need.

As you work your way through the sales documents, you'll eventually see an A/R invoice—the only sales document that is absolutely required in the sales process. A few different versions of the A/R invoice are available to capture a diversity of needs in invoicing and payment scenarios.

With the exception of the sales blanket agreement, the sales documents described from sales quotation through A/R reserve invoice are all considered marketing documents; consequently, each displays a header and four tabs: CONTENTS, LOGISTICS, ACCOUNTING, and ATTACHMENTS. In this chapter, we'll focus on the specific purpose of each sales document and any unique aspects of its function. First, however, note that the sales blanket agreement is actually not considered a marketing document but, rather, a *master data style document*, similar to the item master or business partner master data record. That sales blanket agreement is where we begin the sales process.

5.1.1   Sales Blanket Agreement

The *sales blanket agreement* is a virtual handshake between you (as the vendor) and your customer that captures the details of what has been agreed to for a certain period of time. Just like its sister document (the purchase blanket agreement), the sales blanket agreement can record the details of what you'll sell to your customer as well as the volume, price, and period. The sales blanket agreement then works in concert with other sales documents to track the fulfillment of the contract while it remains open. This information can then be used to negotiate future contracts with a customer based on the performance of previous agreements.

Figure 5.1 shows the SALES BLANKET AGREEMENT window in Add mode. The header of the document includes fields where you can enter customer information into the record. Certain fields on the sales blanket agreement will not allow any inputs until a customer is selected. Table 5.1 provides a detailed description of each data field in the header.

Figure 5.1 The Draft Sales Blanket Agreement Header

Field	Description/Use
BP CODE	This field displays the customer's business partner record code.
BP NAME	This field displays the customer's name.
CONTACT PERSON	This field will default to the default contact on the customer's business partner record. If more than one contact exists in the business partner record, you can choose an alternative from the dropdown list.
TELEPHONE NO.	This field displays the telephone number of the business partner contact selected.
E-MAIL	This field displays the email address of the business partner contact selected.
NO.	This field displays the number (in series) of the blanket sales agreement. You may have more than one numbering series for sales blanket agreements.
AGREEMENT METHOD	You must choose from two kinds of agreement methods: ▶ ITEMS METHOD: Use the items method if you are selling something specific (inventory items) that has an item master data record associated with it. You will be able to select the quantity and special price for this item over the period specified in the header of the agreement. ▶ MONETARY METHOD: In the monetary method, you will specify not items, but rather the overall sales amounts that you and the customer agreed to. These overall sales volumes can also come with special global discounts.

Table 5.1 Fields in the Sales Blanket Agreement Header

Field	Description/Use
START DATE	This field displays the start date of the agreement. Special pricing, discounts, and the tracking of fulfillment against the agreement will not be possible prior to the start date.
END DATE	This field displays the end date of the agreement. Special pricing, discounts, and the tracking of fulfillment against the agreement will not be possible past the end date.
TERMINATION DATE	This field displays the date that the agreement status is changed to TERMINATED.
SIGNING DATE	This field displays the signing date of the agreement. Note that the field will default to the start date of the agreement but can be overridden to reflect a different signing date.
DESCRIPTION	Input a helpful description of the agreement here.

Table 5.1 Fields in the Sales Blanket Agreement Header (Cont.)

General Tab

The GENERAL tab shown in Figure 5.2 allows you to specify certain high-level terms on the agreement, as well as the agreement's current status. Table 5.2 describes how the fields in the GENERAL tab can be used.

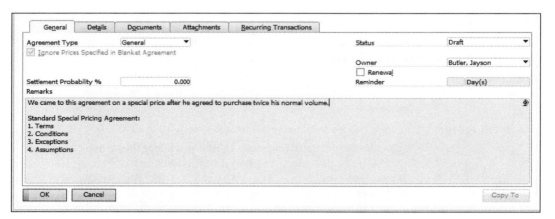

Figure 5.2 The Sales Blanket Agreement General Tab

Field	Description/Use
AGREEMENT TYPE	Specify an agreement type if different from the agreement method with one of these options: ▶ GENERAL: This agreement type will ignore any special prices specified in the details of the agreement. ▶ SPECIFIC: This agreement type will respect any special prices specified in the details of the agreement.
IGNORE PRICES IN SPECIFIED BLANKET AGREEMENT or IGNORE DISCOUNT SPECIFIED IN BLANKET AGREEMENT	This checkbox cannot be edited manually and will be autofilled based on whether you chose the GENERAL or SPECIFIC agreement types: ▶ If you specified using the items method for the agreement, then this checkbox will be called IGNORE PRICES IN SPECIFIED BLANKET AGREEMENT. ▶ If you specified using the monetary method for the agreement, then this checkbox will be called IGNORE DISCOUNT SPECIFIED IN BLANKET AGREEMENT.
SETTLEMENT PROBABILITY %	Assign a percentage of certainty that the agreement will be fulfilled.
STATUS	Blanket sales agreements have four possible statuses: ▶ DRAFT: This status is initially selected. You can change most of the agreement variables when still in "draft" status. The agreement will enforce special pricing or be tracked against sales documents if still in "draft" status. ▶ ON HOLD: This status places an agreement on hold and can be used either prior to, or following, the agreement being approved. As with "draft" status, the terms of the agreement are suspended, and the agreement does not impact the sales process. ▶ APPROVED: The agreement is active in this status and will dictate special pricing, as well as track against relevant sales documents. Certain details of the agreement cannot be changed when active. ▶ TERMINATED: This status is selected when the agreement is finished. You can select this status after the end date or at any time during the course of the agreement. Terminating a sales blanket agreement is irreversible.

Table 5.2 Fields in the Sales Blanket Agreement General Tab

Field	Description/Use
PRICE LIST	This field will only appear below the STATUS field if the monetary method is specified (not depicted in Figure 5.2). In this field, specify a special price list other than the customer's default for the period of the agreement (in a monetary method scheme). This option is not relevant for the items method.
OWNER	This (optional) field refers to the SAP Business One user who has ownership of the document.
RENEWAL	Check this box if the agreement can be renewed.
REMINDER	If you check the RENEWAL checkbox, you must now specify an alert to remind you to follow up on agreement renewal prior to the end date.
REMARKS	This field allows you to record additional comments about the agreement.

Table 5.2 Fields in the Sales Blanket Agreement General Tab (Cont.)

Details Tab

Use the DETAILS tab of the sales blanket agreement to define the specifics of the agreement, such as whether the agreement is based on the items method or the monetary method. In the items method variant shown in Figure 5.3, you would specify the items included in the agreement. You would then specify the planned quantities of the item and special prices for the period of the agreement. Alternatively, if you are creating an agreement based on the monetary method, the planned amount and special discount can be specified as in Figure 5.4. (Note that, in Figure 5.4, the "LC" in the columns indicates that the system is using local currency.)

Figure 5.3 The Sales Blanket Agreement Details Tab (Item Method)

Figure 5.4 The Sales Blanket Agreement Details Tab (Monetary Method)

For a more detailed description of the data fields on the DETAILS tab, refer to Table 5.3.

Field	Description/Use
ITEM NO. and ITEM DESCRIPTION	If using the item method, choose an item and add a description.
PLANNED QUANTITY or PLANNED AMOUNT	Depending on your agreement method, select the planned quantity (for the item method) or planned amount (for the monetary method).
UNIT PRICE or LINE DISCOUNT	Specify a special price for an item when using the item method. If UNIT PRICE is left blank, then the price will be blank when a sales document is created. Specify a special discount for a customer when using the monetary method. If LINE DISCOUNT is left blank, then the discount will be zero when a sales document is created.
CUMULATIVE QUANTITY or CUMULATIVE AMOUNT	The CUMULATIVE QUANTITY and CUMULATIVE AMOUNT fields will track the sum of all sales that match the criteria of the agreement to date.
OPEN QUANTITY or OPEN AMOUNT	The OPEN QUANTITY and OPEN AMOUNT fields will track the remaining sales required to fulfill the agreement according to the original planned quantity/amounts.
FREE TEXT	Enter line-specific notes to the details of the agreement.

Table 5.3 Fields in the Sales Blanket Agreement Details Tab

You can also drill down on any detail row and specify a more advanced schedule for the release of inventory over subperiods of the agreement. Figure 5.5 shows the Row Details window that will appear when you double-click the item line. You may also right-click on the row and choose Details from the menu to create as many sublines as necessary to specify the release of inventory over as many subperiods as desired. Of course, the sum of the item quantities for release must not exceed the overall planned quantity on the agreement. Activities can be placed against each row in order to schedule tasks associated with a subperiod of a sales blanket agreement.

Figure 5.5 Row Details of Items When Using the Item Method

Documents Tab

Once a sales blanket agreement becomes active (in other words, has an approved status and is between its start and end dates), SAP Business One will begin to track the sales documents that are created and are relevant to the agreement. These documents will update the running totals seen in the Cumulative Quantity and Cumulative Amount fields explained in Table 5.3. Figure 5.6 shows a sample of sales documents being tracked against this agreement.

Take a look at the bottom right corner of Figure 5.6. Use the Copy To button to create a sales document—a quotation, order, delivery, A/R invoice, or A/R down payment invoice—that is linked to the sales blanket agreement.

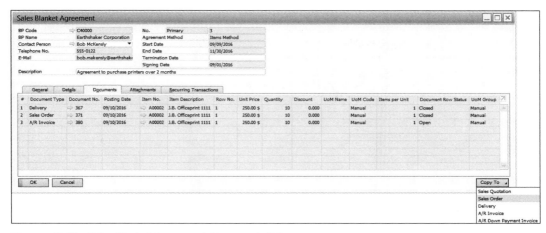

Figure 5.6 The Sales Blanket Agreement Documents Tab

Tips and Tricks: Autolinking of In-Scope Sales Documents

SAP Business One will automatically link sales documents to a blanket agreement number if the parameters of the sales document fall within the scope of an existing sales blanket agreement.

Attachments Tab

The ATTACHMENTS tab of the sales blanket agreement is consistent with ATTACHMENTS tabs in all documents. Chapter 1, Section 1.2.4, describes how to attach files to documents.

Recurring Transactions Tab

SAP Business One can schedule and create templates for recurring transactions. You can use this helpful functionality if, for example, you're confident about a customer's agreement to buy from you, and you simply want to automatically create sales documents throughout the period of the blanket agreement. Figure 5.7 shows that recurring transaction templates can be linked against the sales blanket agreement. In addition, once a recurring transaction has been executed, the transaction is recorded in the table on the right part of this tab. We'll go into much more detail about recurring transactions in Section 5.3.

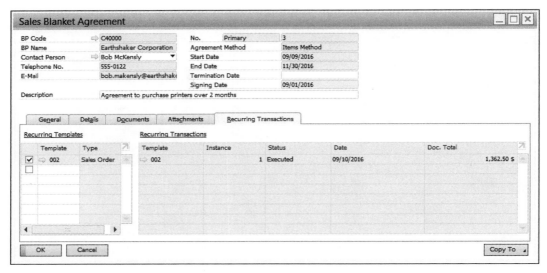

Figure 5.7 The Sales Blanket Agreement Recurring Transactions Tab

5.1.2 Sales Quotation

A *sales quotation* is a customer-facing document that you can use to quote the price and availability of an item or service. Although sales quotations share many characteristics with other sales documents, two major differences distinguish them: With a sales quotation, inventory is not committed; nor are balance transactions posted against the general ledger (G/L) account. Sales quotations can be modified once added to the system (although the business partner cannot be changed after the sales quotation is initially created).

Tips and Tricks: Change the Business Partner on a Document

Although the business partner cannot be changed on a sales or purchasing document, you can create a new document with the same information fairly easily: right-click on the document where you'd like to change the business partner and select DUPLICATE. A new document will be created with all the same information except for the business partner.

You'll find this method particularly handy for large documents where re-creating them is too time consuming.

Let's take a look at some of the fields in the SALES QUOTATION screen shown in Figure 5.8, which are slightly unique from other sales documents, as outlined in Table 5.4.

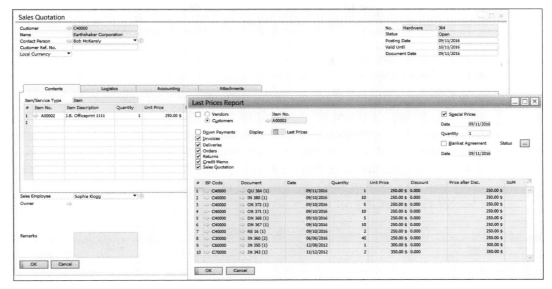

Figure 5.8 The Sales Quotation Screen: Last Prices Report

Field	Description/Use
VALID UNTIL	This date field is found between the POSTING DATE and DOCUMENT DATE fields in the header and specifies the start date of the sales quotation.
PROCUREMENT DOCUMENT (LOGISTICS tab)	This checkbox is found on the sales quotation and the sales order. If checked, it will launch the Procurement Confirmation Wizard.
JOURNAL REMARK (ACCOUNTING tab)	This field is found on all marketing documents; however, no journal remark is created when a sales quotation is added to the system.

Table 5.4 Fields in the Sales Quotation Screen

> **Tips and Tricks: Last Prices Report**
>
> With your cursor in the UNIT PRICE field of a line inside a sales order, pressing
> ⌈Ctrl⌉+⌈Tab⌉ will bring up the Last Prices Report, which is a comprehensive log of all
> pricing related to the item in focus. This report includes many filters that allow more
> detail about the history of the pricing of an item.

5.1.3 Sales Order

A *sales order* is used to capture the commitment of your customer to purchase
something with a defined price, quantity, and delivery date as shown in Figure
5.9. Prior to this commitment, a potential sale was represented by a sales blanket
agreement or a sales quote, but an order becomes real with a sales order. If you
already had a blanket agreement or a sales quotation, you can easily create a sales
order based on one of these by simply using the COPY TO button described in
Chapter 1, Section 1.2.4.

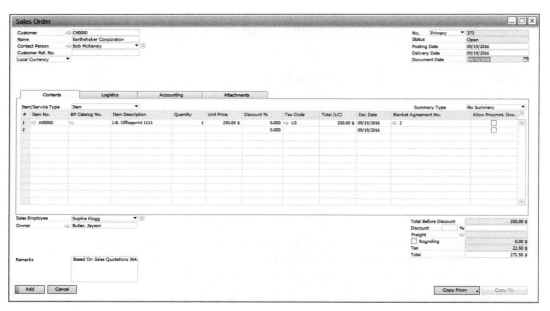

Figure 5.9 The Sales Order Screen

Table 5.5 lists the fields in the SALES ORDER screen.

Field	Description/Use
DELIVERY DATE	This field exists in the header of the document, as well as on each date of each line in the contents. As a result, you can set the requested delivery date on the entire order or specify different delivery dates for individual items on a sales order.
	When setting the delivery date in the header, the system will ask you if you want to set the same delivery date for each line in the contents field as well. If each line has a unique delivery date, choose NO; if not, choose YES.
	Note that, if you don't enter a delivery date, you will not be able to add the sales order to the system.
PRINT PICKING SHEET (LOGISTICS tab)	Selecting this box will automatically print a pick list based on the sales order to the default printer.
PROCUREMENT DOCUMENT (LOGISTICS tab)	This checkbox is found on the sales quotation and sales order. If checked, it will launch the Procurement Confirmation Wizard.
APPROVED (LOGISTICS tab)	This checkbox can be set to default to checked (approved) or unchecked (unapproved) in the global system settings.
	If you set this checkbox to default to unchecked (unapproved), then a new sales order will be prevented from being promoted to a delivery document or to a pick list. The status in the document header will change to "unapproved"—which can be useful if a secondary check is required to ensure the sales order is correct.
ALLOW PARTIAL DELIVERY (LOGISTICS tab)	This checkbox is checked by default and will enable you to only partially deliver on a sales order. Uncheck this box if it is important that the whole order be shipped in one delivery.
CANCELLATION DATE (ACCOUNTING tab)	This date specifies the last day on which the customer will accept the goods in the sales order. This date will default to 30 days after the delivery date on the document. Note that this date is for reference only and will not automatically close the document on this date.
REQUIRED DATE (ACCOUNTING tab)	This field allows the user to specify the date on which the customer expects to take delivery of goods. By default, this date is equal to the delivery date on the document.

Table 5.5 Fields in the Sales Order Screen

Because your customer is now committed to buy from you, a sales order will place a commitment on the quantity for that item in inventory. This commitment doesn't mean you have the item quantity in stock, but rather, a committed quantity will appear in the item master INVENTORY tab of any item and will represent the total amount of that item committed across all sales orders. Further, if you place an item on order that does not have sufficient stock available to promise by the delivery date chosen on the sales order, an availability check will appear as shown in Figure 5.10.

Figure 5.10 The Item Availability Check Screen

Tips and Tricks: Taking a Down Payment on a Sales Order

You can take a payment on a sales order as down payment or deposit against placing the order. With the sales order open, click on the PAYMENT MEANS icon (the moneybag and coins) in the top ribbon bar in Figure 5.11. Alternatively, you can right-click on the sales order and select PAYMENT MEANS from the menu. A special type of invoice called the *A/R down payment invoice* will be created to allow you to take a payment. We'll discuss A/R down payment invoices in more detail in Section 5.1.6.

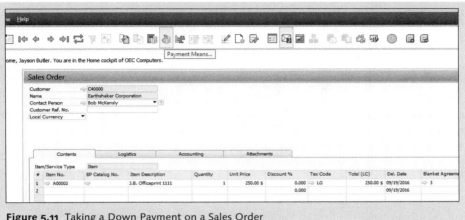

Figure 5.11 Taking a Down Payment on a Sales Order

5.1.4 Delivery

Once you are ready to deliver goods or services against a sales order, the *delivery document* is specially designed for this purpose. When a delivery document is added, the system will reduce the delivered quantity specified for any inventory items in the CONTENTS tab of the document. The cost of goods is typically recorded at this point, but the revenue associated with the transaction is left up to the A/R invoice.

For any company that ships physical goods, the delivery document performs a very similar function as a bill of lading. You can generate a bill of lading, freight waybill, or packing slips from the information contained within the delivery document. You can make partial deliveries against a sales order by using multiple delivery documents and then invoicing either individually or all together.

> **Tips and Tricks: Partial Delivery against a Sales Order**
>
> Sales order lines that are only partially delivered against will stay open until full delivery, though you can also manually close them (as with all other marketing documents). Use the Backorder Report covered in Section 5.7.4 to quickly assess partial deliveries and open quantities on customer orders.

The delivery document can also be used to indicate the delivery of services that are not physical inventory. In Table 5.6, we'll take a look at some of the fields in the DELIVERY screen shown in Figure 5.12.

Field	Description/Use
DELIVERY DATE	The date in this field is similar to the date of a sales order, except that, on a delivery document, this date is the date that the order is actually shipped (not requested).
SHIPPING TYPE (LOGISTICS tab)	Specify a shipping type on all sales documents, which is especially important for a delivery document. From the SHIPPING TYPE dropdown list, select the shipping type that matches the actual shipping method of the delivery.
TRACKING NUMBER (LOGISTICS tab)	Fill in the tracking (waybill) number provided by your freight carrier. If your company handles its own freight, you may use an internal tracking number system.
STAMP NUMBER (LOGISTICS tab)	Fill out the international standard stamp number for postage-type shipments.
USE SHIPPED GOODS ACCOUNT (ACCOUNTING tab)	This checkbox will enable you to post inventory values into a shipped goods account instead of the usual cost of goods account. This alternative is particularly useful if deliveries are routinely happening in different accounting periods than the invoices that follow.

Table 5.6 Fields in the Delivery Screen

The delivery document can be used to create packing slips, either for the shipment or to indicate the contents of individual packages. Access the packing slip menu by right-clicking on the DELIVERY document window. As shown in Figure 5.12, the contents of a delivery are being packaged into multiple boxes for shipment. This packing slip lays out the contents of two boxes that contain the entire shipment. You can define package types to match any description. Note that, once the packing contents is completed, you can print an overall manifest for the order and also individual package content slips to attach to each box.

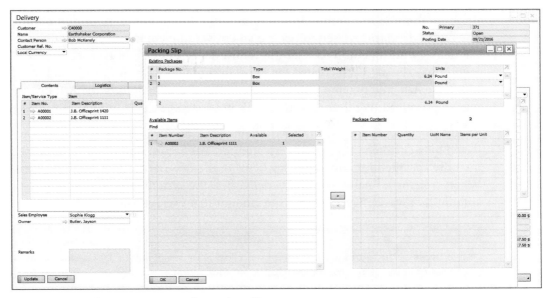

Figure 5.12 A Delivery Document with a Packing Slip

Tips and Tricks: Volume and Weight Calculation

SAP Business One can calculate and summarize the overall volume and weight of the contents of any marketing document. For instance, Figure 5.13 shows a delivery document with two items for shipment.

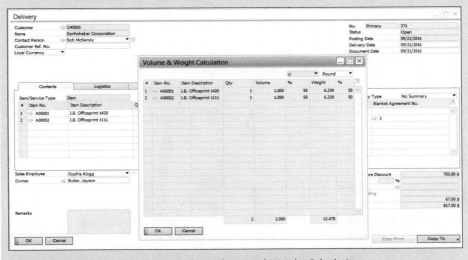

Figure 5.13 A Delivery Document with a Volume and Weight Calculation

5.1.5 Return

The *return document* is used to reverse an outward inventory movement done by the delivery document. Note that the return document cannot be used if an A/R invoice has already been created for the delivered goods. In this case, you'll need to use the A/R credit memo instead, as the revenue transactions of the A/R invoice must be reversed. We'll discuss A/R credit memos more detail in Section 5.1.9.

Return documents are usually used when items or services are returned or rejected by a customer after a delivery attempt. The return document will add the quantity specified for any inventory items in the CONTENTS tab of the document. When creating a final invoice from deliveries, the system takes into account the amount that was delivered minus the amount that was returned.

Tips and Tricks: Relationship Maps

An example of the return in a document workflow is shown in Figure 5.14, which shows the *relationship map* run from its related return document.

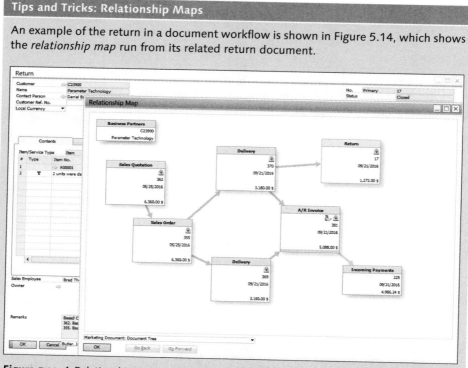

Figure 5.14 A Relationship Map Featuring a Return

To use this SAP Business One functionality, right-click on any marketing document and choose RELATIONSHIP MAP from the menu. This map paints a picture of the complex set of transactions that all start from the same sales order, then branch into two deliveries, and eventually end up in one A/R invoice. Along the way, one of the deliveries has a return placed against it due to a portion of damaged goods that were rejected by the customer. The user can keep track of all ins and outs if everything remains linked in the document chain.

5.1.6   A/R Down Payment Invoice

Use an *A/R down payment invoice* when you'd like to take a full or partial payment on an order before those goods or services are actually delivered. What's unique is that the transaction will typically be recorded as deferred revenue, meaning that, regardless of whether the payment on an A/R down payment invoice is partial or full, a final A/R invoice will have to be generated to recognize the revenue associated with the transaction (and settle any outstanding balance).

The relationship map in Figure 5.15 shows a scenario where a customer placed a special order—let's say on a new fireplace for their home—and a 50% deposit was taken. The A/R down payment invoice was paid, and the down payment was later applied to the final A/R invoice after the fireplace was delivered and installed, and the remaining amount paid.

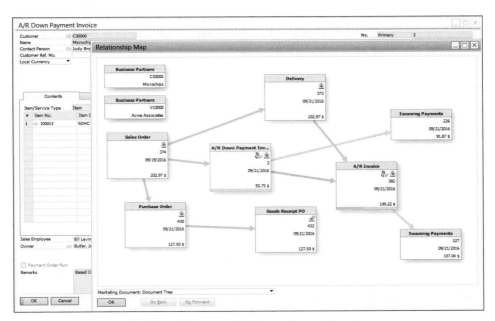

Figure 5.15 A Relationship Map Featuring an A/R Down Payment Invoice

The map shows the entire flow of this transaction chain, including the purchasing documents that were created to special order the fireplace for the customer.

> **Tips and Tricks: DPM versus Discount Amount**
>
> On most marketing documents, a DOCUMENT LEVEL DISCOUNT field will appear just below the TOTAL BEFORE DISCOUNT field on the document footer. In the case of an A/R down payment invoice, this field is labeled DPM (down payment). Instead of setting a discount percentage, use this field to specify a down payment as a percentage of the sales order total.

5.1.7   A/R Invoice

An *A/R invoice* is the only sales document that is absolutely required. Even if your sales process doesn't include sales quotes, sales orders, or deliveries, the sale will always require some form of A/R invoice. For instance, if you do not use a delivery document in your process, then the A/R invoice will not only recognize revenue but also reduce the inventory and record the cost of goods transaction.

Let's examine the key fields found on the A/R INVOICE screen in Table 5.7.

Field	Description/Use
DUE DATE	This field in the header displays the payment due date of the invoice. This date will be autofilled according the payment terms specified on the business partner record associated with the invoice.
BLOCK DUNNING LETTERS (LOGISTICS tab)	This checkbox will block the current document from being included in dunning letters.
PAYMENT BLOCK (ACCOUNTING tab)	This checkbox will allow you to block the A/R invoice from payment and specify a reason.
MAX. CASH DISCOUNT (ACCOUNTING tab)	This checkbox will force the document to calculate the maximum cash discount (if applicable) that applies to the document for favorable payment terms even if the cash discount due date has already occurred.
PAYMENT TERMS (ACCOUNTING tab)	This field displays the default payment terms for the business partner associated with the document. The value in the PAYMENT TERMS field can be overridden on a per-document basis.

Table 5.7 Fields in the A/R Invoice Screen

Field	Description/Use
PAYMENT METHOD (ACCOUNTING tab)	This field displays the default payment method for the business partner associated with the document. The value in the PAYMENT METHODS field can be overridden on a per-document basis.
INSTALLMENTS (ACCOUNTING tab)	Clicking on the golden arrow adjacent to the INSTALLMENTS field will allow you to define payment installments for the A/R invoice.
MANUAL RECALCULATE DUE DATE (ACCOUNTING tab)	These fields allow you to manually calculate a new due date for the A/R invoice at the time it is being generated. (These fields are not active after the A/R invoice is added.) You may specify a number of months or days to recalculate the due date as of the posting date of the document. You may also from choose one of the predefined, commonly used recalculation periods as follows: ▸ MONTH END ▸ HALF MONTH ▸ MONTH START
CASH DISCOUNT DATE OFFSET (ACCOUNTING tab)	You may specify an offset of the usual payment terms using this field. For example, if the customer normally gets a 2% discount for paying within 15 days, entering a value of "5" in this field will extend these terms for 5 more days (to 20 days total for the 2% discount). You can also enter a zero or a negative number in this field, thereby maintaining or shortening the normal payment terms.
BP PROJECT (ACCOUNTING tab)	By default, this field displays the business partner project, which appears on the business partner master data GENERAL tab for the associated business partner. Alternatively, a different code might be inherited from a base document, or you can specify a different project code at the level of the A/R invoice.
INDICATOR (ACCOUNTING tab)	By default, this field displays the factoring indicator, which appears on the business partner master data GENERAL tab for the associated business partner.
FEDERAL TAX ID (ACCOUNTING tab)	This field displays the tax ID indicated on the business partner record associated with the A/R invoice.
TOTAL DOWN PAYMENT	This field in the footer will show a value if an A/R down payment invoice is associated with the document chain. This amount will be applied against the overall balance of the A/R invoice.

Table 5.7 Fields in the A/R Invoice Screen (Cont.)

Tips and Tricks: Invoice Installments

You can set up payment installments on A/R invoices (and other similar documents) as shown in Figure 5.16. To do this, select the golden arrow next to the INSTALLMENTS field in the ACCOUNTING tab of the A/R invoice to specify an installment plan for collection on the A/R invoice.

Note that this only works when you are creating an A/R invoice; you cannot add payment installments once an A/R invoice is added to the system.

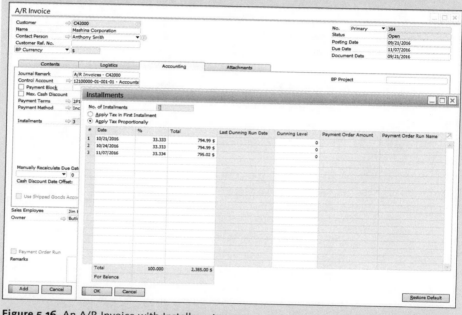

Figure 5.16 An A/R Invoice with Installments

5.1.8 A/R Invoice + Payment

The A/R invoice + payment is a specialized form of the A/R invoice that helps to automate creating documents for quick transactions where the invoice and the payment are generated at the same time.

You should note two interesting things about an A/R invoice + payment:

▶ First, when you click the A/R INVOICE + PAYMENT button, a generic business partner is populated in the header to save time. You can enter a specific business partner into this field.

▶ Second, when the invoice is added, an incoming payment is automatically launched against the invoice. The payment must be for the exact amount of the A/R invoice (the payment cannot be partial).

Once the payment information is filled in and updated, the A/R invoice can then be finalized. The result is an A/R invoice and corresponding incoming payment as shown in Figure 5.17.

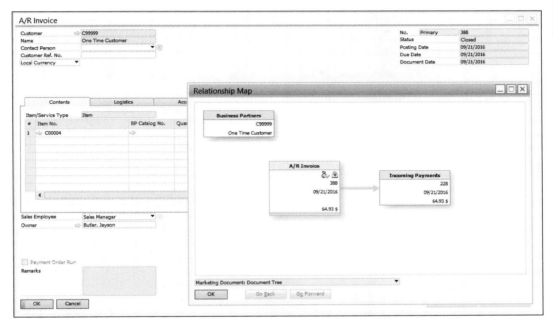

Figure 5.17 An A/R Invoice + Payment for a One-Time Customer

Tips and Tricks: A/R Invoice + Payment

You can use an A/R invoice + payment at a sales counter, for example, where the customer is purchasing goods and paying for them at the same time.

5.1.9 A/R Credit Memo

An A/R credit memo (rather than a return) is typically used whenever there is a return of goods or services *after* the creation of an A/R invoice. Think of the A/R credit memo as the opposite of the A/R invoice. However, an A/R credit memo does not require an A/R invoice as its base. For example, you can credit a customer for items or amounts at a date far removed for the original transaction. In general, an A/R credit memo includes most of the same fields as an A/R invoice. In Figure 5.18, we see an A/R credit memo applied to an A/R invoice and the resulting settlement of the outstanding balance.

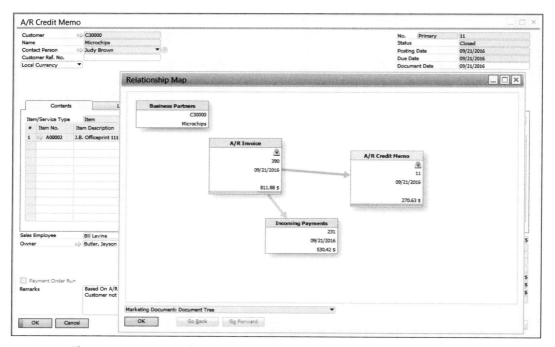

Figure 5.18 An A/R Credit Memo Applied against an A/R Invoice

Tips and Tricks: Specifying Return Costs

With SAP Business One, you can specify a cost for items that are being returned into inventory when the return document does not have a base document (an original delivery or A/R invoice) associated with it; you can specify this cost on each item line as shown in Figure 5.19. If the return or credit document does have a base document, the cost from the base document will be used for the items inventory value.

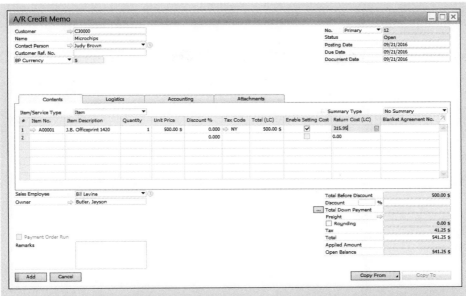

Figure 5.19 Specifying the Return Cost of an Inventory Item on an A/R Credit Memo with No Base Document

5.1.10   A/R Reserve Invoice

An *A/R reserve invoice* is a special form of the A/R invoice that allows for revenue recognition (and payment) ahead of the delivery of goods or services.

You'll likely use the A/R reserve invoice in cases where a pro forma invoice may be necessary for special declarations (such as customs) or your customer simply requires one—but you can also use an A/R reserve invoice in any situation where you'd essentially like to be prepaid for the order. Because this invoice type will recognize revenue, A/R reserve invoices are not appropriate for a sales process where deferred revenue is preferred. Since an A/R reserve invoice is a special form of an A/R invoice, the A/R RESERVE INVOICE screen includes most of the same fields listed in Table 5.7.

Figure 5.20 shows how the progression of sales documents differs when using an A/R reserve invoice. The A/R reserve invoice will precede the delivery document.

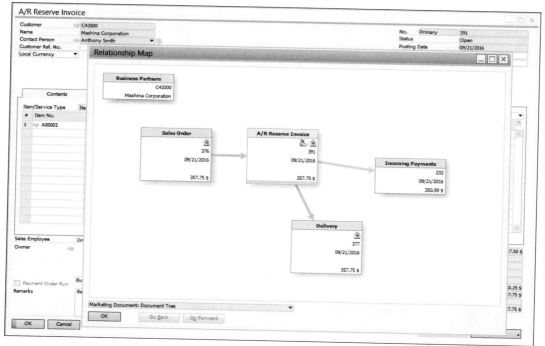

Figure 5.20 An A/R Reserve Invoice with Corresponding Incoming Payment and Subsequent Delivery

5.2 Document Generation Wizard

The Document Generation Wizard allows you to create a number of documents in batches, instead of one by one—kind of like doing a mass copy/paste from one type of marketing document to another.

This tool can be very useful when you need to generate a high volume of documents. You'll also have various options when running the wizard as to the selection criteria of the base and target documents, as well as options on how to consolidate multiple base documents into one target document.

Bear in mind that the Document Generation Wizard converts one type of sales document to another. The wizard cannot create documents without a base document; for this, you'd use recurring transactions, which we'll cover in Section 5.3.

The most typical example using this tool would be the automated generation of A/R invoices based on open deliveries in the system. In our example, an A/R invoicing clerk wants to automatically create A/R invoices from the previous day's delivery. Customers should only receive one invoice for the previous day's deliveries, even if they received multiple deliveries in the same day.

You'll find the Document Generation Wizard in the SALES (A/R) menu just under the sales documents, as shown in Figure 5.21. Click DOCUMENT GENERATION WIZARD to run the wizard, and after reading the initial message, click NEXT to get to Step 1. Note that Figure 5.21 shows the three open deliveries from the previous day that we'll use to create target documents in our example.

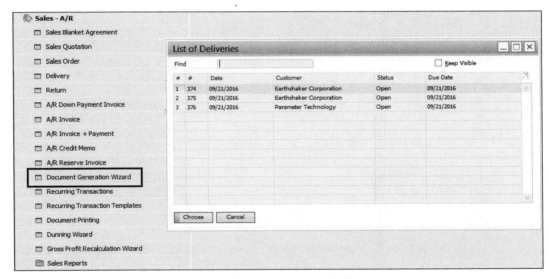

Figure 5.21 Running Document Generation Wizard against Open Deliveries

Once the wizard is up and running, follow these steps:

1. In the DOCUMENT GENERATION OPTIONS window shown in Figure 5.22, you can define a new parameter set for an automated document creation run. In other words, you can save their settings for the automated run and use them again in the future. Saving these parameters is useful in our scenario where our A/R invoicing clerk wants to generate A/R invoices every day based on the previous day's deliveries. In this window, give your parameter set a short name and a

long description. (The option to save the parameter set comes later in the process.) The next time the wizard is launched, you'll get the option to load an existing parameter set.

Click NEXT to move to the next step.

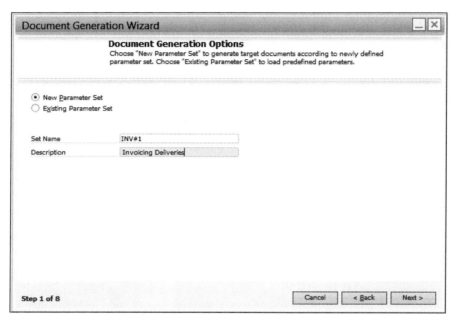

Figure 5.22 Document Generation Options (Step 1 of the Wizard)

2. In the TARGET DOCUMENT window shown in Figure 5.23, specify what type of target documents you'd like to create as part of the automated document creation run. In our example, we would like to create invoices, but you may also create sales orders, deliveries, or returns. You may also specify other attributes of the document such as the posting date, document date, number series, type (item based or service based), and exchange rate options. Notice also that you have the option to create the target documents as drafts, which can be useful if the resulting target documents need to be reviewed.

Click NEXT to move to the next step.

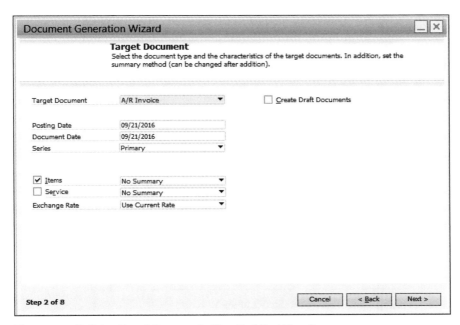

Figure 5.23 Defining Target Documents (Step 2 of the Wizard)

3. In Step 3 of the Document Generation Wizard, you'll define the selection criteria for which base documents will be included in the automated document creation run. Take a look at the DOC. TYPES area on the left side of Figure 5.24 and choose one of three documents types: SALES QUOTATIONS, SALES ORDERS, or DELIVERIES. Next, select a range of posting dates, delivery dates, or a numbering series. Beyond these criteria, you may also select a set of expanded selection criteria (five additional criteria in total). The expanded selection criteria include many standard SAP Business One fields but can also accommodate custom data fields.

The SORT BY area will allow you to specify what in what order the base documents are turned into target documents based on a filter set of three different criteria.

The DO NOT CREATE DOCS. CONT. ZERO QTY. LINES OR NO LINES checkbox will suppress the creation of new documents that would contain zero quantity lines or no lines at all.

Click NEXT to move to the next step.

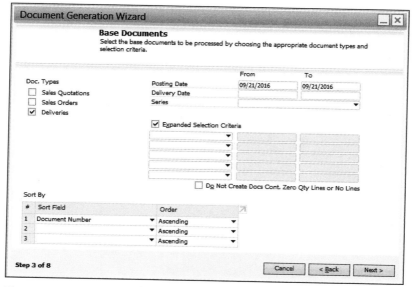

Figure 5.24 Choosing a Base Document (Step 3 of the Wizard)

4. Choose specific options for which base documents should be consolidated into one target document from the CONSOLIDATION window shown in Figure 5.25. In this window, you have two consolidation options, shown as radio buttons:

   ▸ NO CONSOLIDATION: Choose this option if the customer wants to see one invoice for each delivery.

   ▸ CONSOLIDATION: In the consolidation model, the system always defaults to consolidating base documents of the same business partner. (Consolidating across different business partners would not make sense.) Beyond this basic system default, you can choose to consolidate on the basis of SHIP-TO ADDRESS, PAYMENT TERMS, or PAYMENT MEANS by checking those boxes and other expanded criteria. As before, you can configure user-defined fields to serve as the basis of consolidation.

   Click NEXT to move to the next step.

5. In Step 5 of the Document Generation Wizard, you'll select a certain range or grouping of customers on which to automatically generate documents. In our example, we simply clicked on the ADD CUSTOMERS button near the bottom right-hand part of the window shown in Figure 5.26; by not specifying any customer selection criteria, all customers were added.

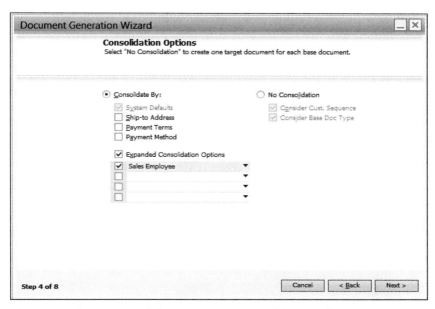

Figure 5.25 Choosing Consolidation Options (Step 4 of the Wizard)

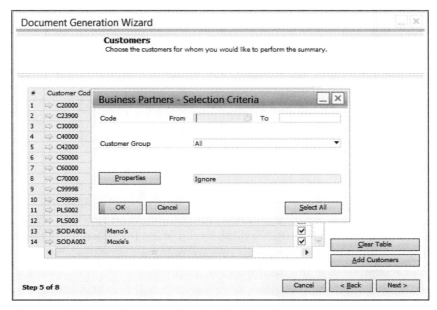

Figure 5.26 Selecting Customers (Step 5 of the Wizard)

6. In the MESSAGES AND ALERTS screen shown in Figure 5.27, you'll define what the system should do if data is missing or if document-based alerts come up when generating target documents from base documents.

A typical example of an alert would be if the system does not have a current exchange rate on which to base documents for customers that have different currencies. However, alerts can also be triggered by deviations from credit limits or insufficient inventory.

Using the dropdown lists in the MISSING DATA, BOOKKEEPING, and INVENTORY fields, specify what action should be taken if these exceptions occur: SKIP TO NEXT CUSTOMER, SKIP TO NEXT DOCUMENT, or ASK FOR USER CONFIRMATION.

Figure 5.27 Setting Up Messages and Alerts (Step 6 of the Wizard)

7. Before you can run the automated creation process, you have the option to save and/or execute the document generation run that has been specified. Figure 5.28 shows the SAVE AND EXECUTE OPTIONS screen of the Document Generation Wizard, where you'll elect whether to execute only, save your parameter set and then execute, or save the parameter set and exit rather than executing. If you choose to execute the parameter set, a message will pop up warning you that moving ahead will likely result in creating documents on the system. Click YES to execute the parameter set.

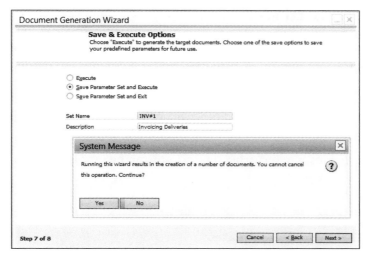

Figure 5.28 Save and Execute Options (Step 7 of the Wizard)

8. The last step of the wizard is to review the Summary Report to learn whether the automated document run was successful and what documents were created as a result. This Summary Report, shown in Figure 5.29, will also log any errors that were encountered during the run. In our example scenario, two target documents were created from three base documents, and no errors occurred. The new A/R invoices are now added to the system and can be found through the new document numbers provided in the SUMMARY REPORT screen.

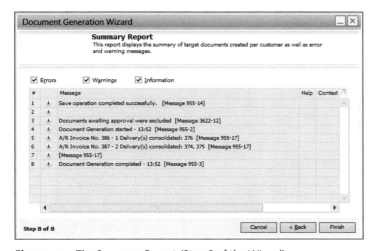

Figure 5.29 The Summary Report (Step 8 of the Wizard)

5.3 Recurring Transactions

Recurring transactions in SAP Business One allow you to set up a repeating sales type transaction with a customer—much like how you'd set up a repeating appointment in your calendar. Recurring transactions are ideal if you have a recurring charge such as a service contract or subscription-based regular fee, but they can also be used to automate a standard order of goods for your customer on whatever periodic basis you'd like.

Apart from sales transactions, the recurring transactions can be used to generate purchasing and inventory transaction documents; we'll revisit this functionality in Chapter 6 and Chapter 9.

5.3.1 Recurring Transactions Templates

Though the RECURRING TRANSACTIONS TEMPLATES menu item in the Sales (A/R) module comes *after* the RECURRING TRANSACTIONS menu item, you'll probably want to set up the templates first.

Open the RECURRING TRANSACTIONS TEMPLATES screen shown in Figure 5.30. In this screen, you'll specify a unique code and description for the recurring transaction you'd like to create, followed by the transaction type, frequency, and date range of your recurring transaction. Consult Table 5.8 for more details on using the fields of the RECURRING TRANSACTIONS TEMPLATES screen. After selecting a document type for your template, choose from an existing document number of that type or create a new sales document. Remember, you aren't actually creating a document of this type but, rather, a template of the desired document that can be stored and triggered according to the periods you specify.

#	Template	Description	Type	Doc No.	Recurrence Period	Recurrence Date	Start Date	Next Execution	Valid Until	Total No. of Instances	BP	BP Name	BP Priority	Warehouse	Doc Total (LC)	Remarks
1	SODA-01	Monthly Regular Order	Sales Order	367	Weekly	On Tuesday	08/02/2016	08/02/2016	12/27/2016	22	SODA001	Mano's		01	500.67 $	
2	002		Sales Order	372	Weekly	On Saturday	09/10/2016	09/24/2016	11/30/2016	12	C40000	Earthshaker Corporation	Second	01	1,362.50 $	
3	001	Regular Service Charge	A/R Invoice	359	Monthly	On 25	05/25/2016	09/25/2016			C23900	Parameter Technology	First	01	39.75 $	
4					Monthly	On 1	10/13/2016	11/01/2016								

Figure 5.30 Recurring Transactions Templates

Field	Description/Use
TEMPLATE	Give the template a unique alphanumeric code (required).
DESCRIPTION	Describe the recurring transaction template.
TYPE	Choose the type of recurring sales document: ▶ SALES QUOTATION ▶ SALES ORDER ▶ DELIVERY ▶ RETURN ▶ A/R DOWN PAYMENT ▶ A/R INVOICE ▶ A/R CREDIT MEMO ▶ A/R RESERVE INVOICE
DOC. NO.	Enter the document number of the existing sales document or a newly created document that is used as the template for the recurring transaction.
RECURRENCE PERIOD	Choose the type of calendar recurrence the transaction template follows: ▶ DAILY ▶ WEEKLY ▶ MONTHLY ▶ QUARTERLY ▶ SEMIANNUALLY ▶ ANNUALLY ▶ ONE TIME
RECURRENCE DATE	Enter the date of recurrence that is relevant to the recurrence period.
START DATE	Enter the beginning date for the range of recurring transactions.
NEXT EXECUTION	Enter the date of the next recurring transaction execution for the template.
VALID UNTIL	Enter the end date for the range of recurring transactions.
TOTAL NO. OF OCCURRENCES	Enter the number of occurrences of the recurring transaction according to the specified date range and recurrence frequency.
BP	Enter the business partner code for which the template applies.
BP NAME	Enter the business partner name for which the template applies.

Table 5.8 Fields in Recurring Transactions Templates

Field	Description/Use
BP PRIORITY	This field displays the priority as defined in the business partner master data record.
WAREHOUSE	This field displays the warehouse for the recurring transaction.
DOC TOTAL	This field displays the document total of the recurring transaction. By clicking on the FORM SETTINGS icon (a blank sheet with a green gear), you can choose whether the DOC TOTAL field uses local currency (LC), foreign currency (FC), or system currency (SC).
REMARKS	Add extended remarks for this recurring transaction template.

Table 5.8 Fields in Recurring Transactions Templates (Cont.)

Recurring transaction templates can also be linked to a sales blanket agreement (or a purchase blanket agreement) as well as a service contract record.

5.3.2 Executing Recurring Transactions

Now that you've set up the recurring transactions template, let's check in on the recurring transactions you've scheduled.

Select the RECURRING TRANSACTIONS menu item in the Sales (A/R) module to process any recurring transactions that are now due. Figure 5.31 shows how each recurring transaction that is currently due will have row in the table.

These fields are similar to those in the recurring transactions templates, so you should refer to Table 5.8 for reference. You can also filter the recurring transactions in this window with the FILTER RECURRING TRANSACTIONS button or access the recurring transactions templates with the TEMPLATES button in the bottom-right corner of the window.

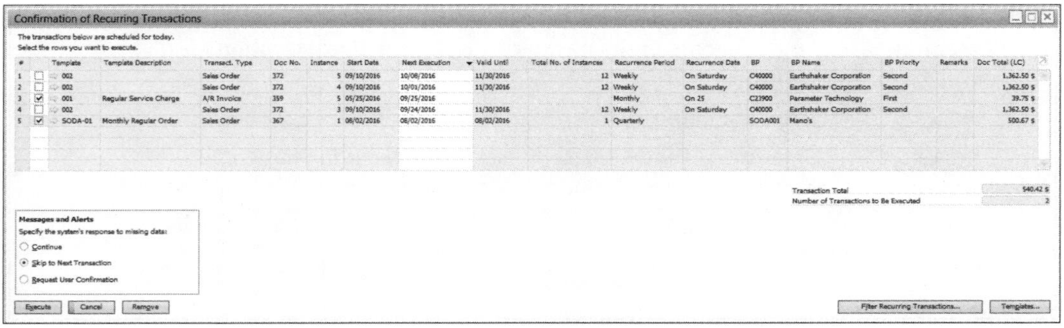

Figure 5.31 The Confirmation of Recurring Transactions Screen

To execute the transactions, select the checkboxes that correspond to the rows lines for the transactions you wish to execute. (In our example in Figure 5.31, we selected REGULAR SERVICE CHARGE and MONTHLY REGULAR ORDER.)

Take a peek at the MESSAGES AND ALERTS box shown at the bottom left of the window; you can also choose what happens if important data is missing when the recurring transactions are created. We chose to skip to the next transaction

Once you click EXECUTE, a RECURRING TRANSACTIONS MESSAGE dialogue window, such as the one shown in Figure 5.32, will appear. This window will log whether the documents were created successfully or not according the recurring transactions in the queue. You may also drill down on the documents that have been created from this dialogue box by clicking on the golden arrows.

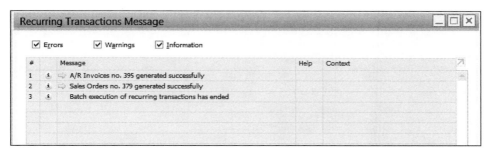

Figure 5.32 The Recurring Transactions Message Screen

5.4 Document Printing

You can use the Document Printing tool to print a run of documents based on multiple selection criteria. The tool can print documents on paper or in an electronic format such as PDF across many modules of SAP Business One. While numerous documents can be printed, as shown in the DOCUMENT TYPE dropdown list in Figure 5.33, for the purposes of this section, we'll focus on using the Document Printing tool with sales documents.

You can use this tool to automatically print a batch run for seven sales documents: sales quotation, sales order, deliveries, returns, A/R down payment, A/R invoices, and A/R credit memos.

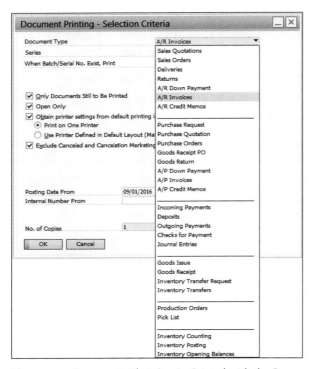

Figure 5.33 Documents That Can Be Printed with the Document Printing Tool

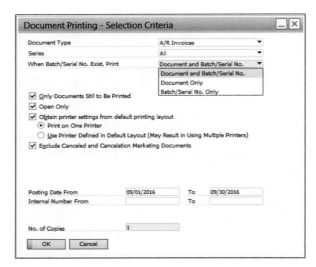

Figure 5.34 Document Printing Options Depending on Document Type

Let's walk through the options for sales documents in this DOCUMENT PRINTING window (see Figure 5.34) in Table 5.9.

Field	Description/Use
DOCUMENT TYPE	From this dropdown list, specify the type of SAP Business One document for which you would like to print a batch run. Your sales-related options here are the following: SALES QUOTATION, SALES ORDER, DELIVERIES, RETURNS, A/R DOWN PAYMENT, A/R INVOICES, A/R CREDIT MEMOS.
SERIES	This dropdown list specifies the numbering series of the document(s) being printed or specifies documents from all series.
WHEN BATCH/ SERIAL NO. EXIST, PRINT	From this dropdown list, specify what to print if the document includes batch or serial numbers. This option is only available for sales documents that are related to the release or receipt of batch or serial numbers (in other words, for deliveries, returns, A/R invoices, and A/R credit memos).
ONLY DOCUMENTS STILL TO BE PRINTED	Select this checkbox to exclude printing documents that have a status indicating they have already been printed.
OPEN ONLY	Select this checkbox to restrict printing to "open" documents only.
OBTAIN PRINTER SETTINGS FROM DEFAULT PRINTING LAYOUT	Choose one of these two options to select printer settings as laid out by the document printing template in SAP Business One for the document being printed: ▶ PRINT ON ONE PRINTER ▶ USE PRINTER DEFINED IN DEFAULT LAYOUT (MAY RESULT IN USING MULTIPLE PRINTERS)
EXCLUDE CANCELED AND CANCELATION MARKETING DOCUMENTS	Select this checkbox to exclude printing documents (of the type you have selected) that have a "canceled" status or that are cancelation type marketing documents.
POSTING DATE FROM and TO	Specify a range of posting dates for document printing in these two fields.
INTERNAL NUMBER FROM and TO	Specify a range of internal numbers (document series number range) for document printing in these two fields.
NO. OF COPIES	Specify the number of copies of each document to be made in this field (unless OBTAIN PRINTER SETTINGS FROM DEFAULT PRINTING LAYOUT is selected).

Table 5.9 Fields in the Document Printing Screen

5.5   Dunning Wizard

The Dunning Wizard enables you to create and send letters to customers that have not paid their open invoices within a given time range and remind them of their overdue payments.

Open the Dunning Wizard by following the menu path Sales – A/R • Dunning Wizard. The Dunning Wizard has six steps:

1. Begin in the Wizard Options window. As with other wizards in SAP Business One, you can create and save the parameters of a wizard run. In our example in Figure 5.35, we don't have any previously saved parameter sets for this wizard, so let's choose Start a Dunning Run rather than Load a Saved Dunning Run. You may also search for keywords in an existing saved dunning run, which can be useful if there are several saved runs.

   Click Next to move to the next step.

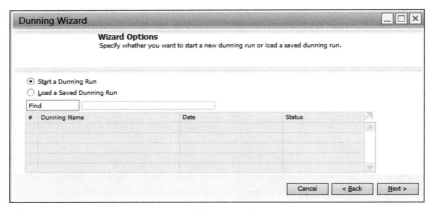

Figure 5.35 Wizard Options (Step 1 of the Wizard)

2. Now, in the General Parameters screen of the wizard, shown in Figure 5.36, SAP Business One will automatically create a dunning name and input that into the Dunning Name field, but you can override that name based on your company's nomenclature or personal preference. The Date of Dunning Run field is fixed to the current date, but you can specify your own dunning level and dunning term sets being used for the run using the Dunning Level and Dunning Term fields. (Note that the dunning level and terms for each of your customers are specified in the business partner master record!) You can set the wizard to

generate letters only for customers who match these criteria, *or* you can simply leave both DUNNING LEVEL and DUNNING TERM values as ALL, which will create letters for all dunning terms and levels.

Click NEXT to move to the next step.

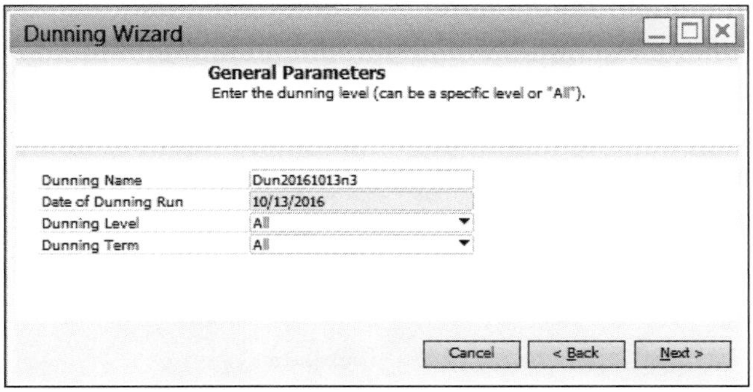

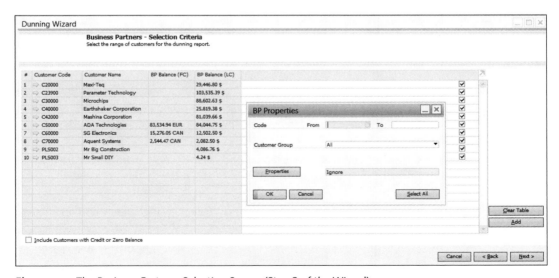

Figure 5.36 Setting Up General Parameters (Step 2 of the Wizard)

3. Next, you must specify a specific customer, range of customers, customer group, or property into your dunning letter run using the BUSINESS PARTNERS SELECTION CRITERIA window shown in Figure 5.37.

Figure 5.37 The Business Partners Selection Screen (Step 3 of the Wizard)

In the selection criteria window, bring up the customer selection criteria by clicking on the ADD button on the bottom-right side of Figure 5.37.

Click NEXT to move to the next step.

4. From the DOCUMENT PARAMETERS screen in Figure 5.38, choose which transactional documents to consider for the dunning run. Apart from selecting the POSTING DATE and DUE DATE range, there are seven additional parameters for the run; let's walk through them in Table 5.10.

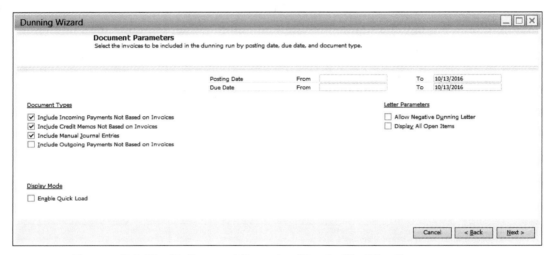

Figure 5.38 Setting Up Document Parameters (Step 4 of the Wizard)

Field	Description/Use
INCLUDE INCOMING PAYMENTS NOT BASED ON INVOICES	Select this checkbox to include incoming payments that are not linked to open overdue invoices in the dunning calculation.
INCLUDE CREDIT MEMOS NOT BASED ON INVOICES	Select this checkbox to include A/R credit memos that are not linked to open overdue invoices in the dunning calculation.
INCLUDE MANUAL JOURNAL ENTRIES	Select this checkbox to include manual journal entries that are not linked to open overdue invoices in the dunning calculation.
INCLUDE OUTGOING PAYMENTS NOT BASED ON INVOICES	Select this checkbox to include outgoing payments that are not linked to open overdue invoices in the dunning calculation.

Table 5.10 Document Parameters Options for the Dunning Wizard

Field	Description/Use
ALLOW NEGATIVE DUNNING LETTER	Select this checkbox to create a negative (credit) dunning letter to your customer. The dunning calculation must determine that your customer account has a negative balance.
DISPLAY ALL OPEN ITEMS	Select this checkbox to display all open documents of the customer, overdue or not. This option has two suboptions: ▶ FOR SELECTED BPS ▶ FOR BPS WITH OVERDUE ITEMS ONLY
ENABLE QUICK LOAD	Select this checkbox to abbreviate the data on the next screen to only show dunning letter summary information, which could be useful if your dunning Recommendation Report is taking too long to load.

Table 5.10 Document Parameters Options for the Dunning Wizard (Cont.)

5. The RECOMMENDATION REPORT screen of the Dunning Wizard shown in Figure 5.39 is where you'll set the date by which you expect payment from the customer, modify the relevant columns, and change the selection of invoices to be dunned. You can edit columns that are white on this report to adjust the terms of dunning letters created; we describe these columns in Table 5.11. Changing the values in any of these columns will update the data in the adjacent columns to the right. You can change the amounts of interest charged to your customer on overdue transactions or, alternatively, apply a flat fee for overdue payment. Only the rows that are selected with a checkbox on the left side will be included when dunning letters are generated.

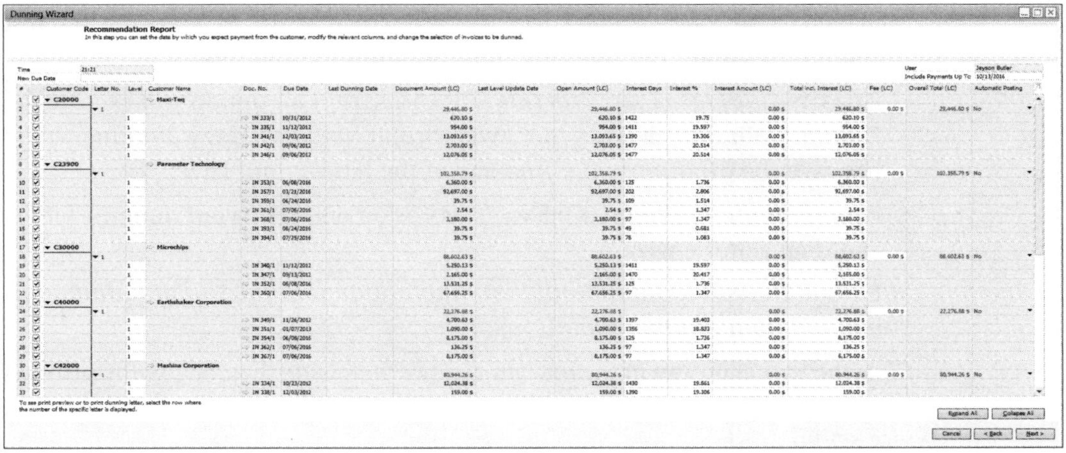

Figure 5.39 The Recommendation Report (Step 5 of the Wizard)

Using this wizard is different from simply printing a customer statement because the Dunning Wizard allows for a high level of control over what goes into your payment demand to a customer.

Field	Description/Use
INTEREST DAYS	This column shows the number of days of interest that should be applied to the line in the dunning Recommendation Report.
INTEREST %	This column shows the interest percentage that should be applied to the line in the dunning report.
INTEREST AMOUNT (LC)	This column shows the total amount of interest applicable to the line in the dunning report.
TOTAL INCL. INTEREST	This column shows the total of the dunning line or letter and includes the principal plus any interest specified.

Table 5.11 Fields in the Recommendation Report of the Dunning Wizard

6. The final step of the Dunning Wizard is to formalize the action of creating dunning letters or to save the dunning run parameters according to your preference. In the PROCESSING screen shown in Figure 5.40, select the processing option that is most appropriate from the following options:

   ▶ SAVE SELECTION PARAMETER AND EXIT: This option will save the Dunning Wizard parameters you have specified and close the Dunning Wizard without execution. You may run your saved parameter set in the future.

   ▶ SAVE RECOMMENDATION REPORT AS DRAFT AND EXIT: Beyond saving the parameters of the dunning run, this option will also save any specific changes you make to the RECOMMENDATION REPORT screen (such as updating interest charge amounts).

   ▶ EXECUTE ONLY AND EXIT. PRINT OR E-MAIL LATER: This option will execute the Dunning Wizard run and generate electronic versions of the dunning letters but save the printing or the emailing of the letters until later.

   ▶ PRINT DUNNING LETTERS AND EXIT: This option will print your dunning letters and then exit the wizard.

   ▶ E-MAIL DUNNING LETTERS AND EXIT: This option will email your dunning letters and then exit the wizard.

Click the FINISH button in the bottom-right corner. Note that, before the printing or emailing dunning letters, you'll need to have your default printer or email service set up.

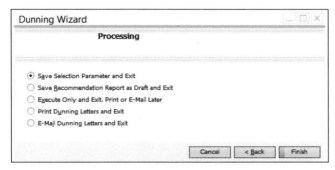

Figure 5.40 The Processing Screen (Step 6 of the Wizard)

7. Once you have executed the dunning letter run, SAP Business One will generate a Recommendation Report, as shown in Figure 5.41.

Tips and Tricks: Dunning Wizard Print Preview

You may preview any dunning letter in the Recommendation Report. Simply select the line of the recommended dunning letter that you'd like to view, and click the PRINT PREVIEW button in the ribbon bar to display the dunning letter preview for that line, as shown in Figure 5.41.

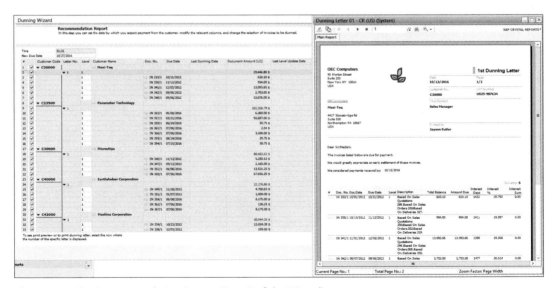

Figure 5.41 The Recommendation Report (Step 7 of the Wizard)

5.6 Gross Profit Recalculation Wizard

The Gross Profit Recalculation Wizard is used to manage items by the batch/serial valuation method. The wizard enables you to recalculate the gross profit of batches/serials in sales documents using the current cost of the batch/serials. If any of those batches/serials were received from production, the system first reconstructs the cost of the product using the current cost of batch/serial components and then recalculates gross profit.

5.7 Sales Reports

Sales reports available in SAP Business One include both revenue analysis tools and reports that fulfill a specific purpose. By the end of this section, you should be able to create reports that slice and dice your revenue in several different ways. You'll also learn about reports that can provide insights into sales processes to help you know where to intervene.

5.7.1 Open Items List Report

The Open Items List Report applies to documents across many modules in SAP Business One. With respect to sales documents, you can access this report to get a quick listing of how many documents are open on the system. The Open Items List Report can include the following kinds of sales documents:

- Sales quotations
- Sales orders
- Deliveries
- Returns
- A/R down payments (unpaid)
- A/R down payments (not yet fully applied)
- A/R invoices
- A/R credit memos
- A/R reserve invoices (unpaid)
- A/R reserve invoices (not yet delivered)

Access the Open Items List Report by following the menu path SALES – A/R • SALES REPORTS • OPEN ITEMS LIST.

Figure 5.42 shows an example Open Items List Report that lists sales documents. The columns in the Open Items List Report are a summary list of the open documents in focus. Use the golden arrows to drill down into the document or the business partner associated with the document. Additionally, you can also access summary data on document dates and amounts, giving you a quick window on the magnitude of the open documents in view.

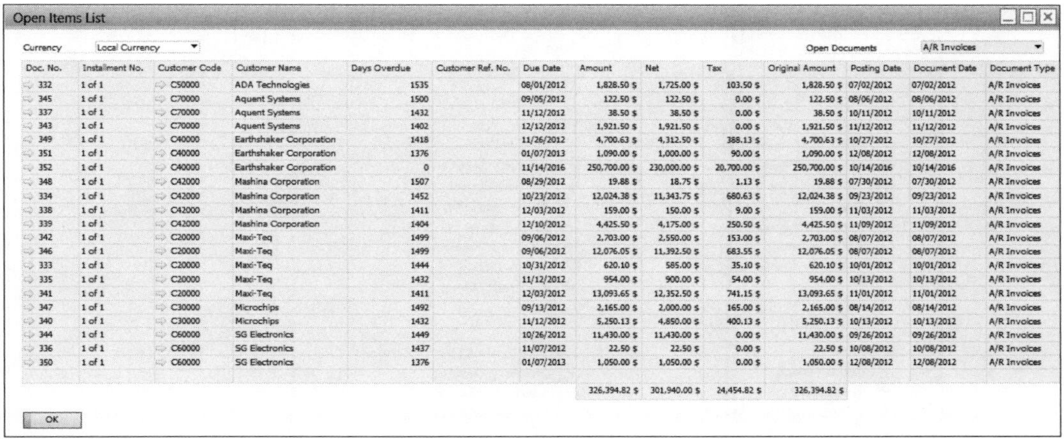

Doc. No.	Installment No.	Customer Code	Customer Name	Days Overdue	Customer Ref. No.	Due Date	Amount	Net	Tax	Original Amount	Posting Date	Document Date	Document Type
332	1 of 1	C50000	ADA Technologies	1535		08/01/2012	1,828.50 $	1,725.00 $	103.50 $	1,828.50 $	07/02/2012	07/02/2012	A/R Invoices
345	1 of 1	C70000	Aquent Systems	1500		09/05/2012	122.50 $	122.50 $	0.00 $	122.50 $	08/06/2012	08/06/2012	A/R Invoices
337	1 of 1	C70000	Aquent Systems	1432		11/12/2012	38.50 $	38.50 $	0.00 $	38.50 $	10/11/2012	10/11/2012	A/R Invoices
343	1 of 1	C70000	Aquent Systems	1402		12/12/2012	1,921.50 $	1,921.50 $	0.00 $	1,921.50 $	11/12/2012	11/12/2012	A/R Invoices
349	1 of 1	C40000	Earthshaker Corporation	1418		11/26/2012	4,700.63 $	4,312.50 $	388.13 $	4,700.63 $	10/27/2012	10/27/2012	A/R Invoices
351	1 of 1	C40000	Earthshaker Corporation	1376		01/07/2013	1,090.00 $	1,000.00 $	90.00 $	1,090.00 $	12/08/2012	12/08/2012	A/R Invoices
352	1 of 1	C40000	Earthshaker Corporation	0		11/14/2016	250,700.00 $	230,000.00 $	20,700.00 $	250,700.00 $	10/14/2016	10/14/2016	A/R Invoices
348	1 of 1	C42000	Mashina Corporation	1507		08/29/2012	19.88 $	18.75 $	1.13 $	19.88 $	07/30/2012	07/30/2012	A/R Invoices
334	1 of 1	C42000	Mashina Corporation	1452		10/23/2012	12,024.38 $	11,343.75 $	680.63 $	12,024.38 $	09/23/2012	09/23/2012	A/R Invoices
338	1 of 1	C42000	Mashina Corporation	1411		12/03/2012	159.00 $	150.00 $	9.00 $	159.00 $	11/03/2012	11/03/2012	A/R Invoices
339	1 of 1	C42000	Mashina Corporation	1404		12/10/2012	4,425.50 $	4,175.00 $	250.50 $	4,425.50 $	11/09/2012	11/09/2012	A/R Invoices
342	1 of 1	C20000	Maxi-Teq	1499		09/06/2012	2,703.00 $	2,550.00 $	153.00 $	2,703.00 $	08/07/2012	08/07/2012	A/R Invoices
346	1 of 1	C20000	Maxi-Teq	1499		09/06/2012	12,076.05 $	11,392.50 $	683.55 $	12,076.05 $	08/07/2012	08/07/2012	A/R Invoices
333	1 of 1	C20000	Maxi-Teq	1444		10/31/2012	620.10 $	585.00 $	35.10 $	620.10 $	10/01/2012	10/01/2012	A/R Invoices
335	1 of 1	C20000	Maxi-Teq	1432		11/12/2012	954.00 $	900.00 $	54.00 $	954.00 $	10/13/2012	10/13/2012	A/R Invoices
341	1 of 1	C20000	Maxi-Teq	1411		12/03/2012	13,093.65 $	12,352.50 $	741.15 $	13,093.65 $	11/01/2012	11/01/2012	A/R Invoices
347	1 of 1	C30000	Microchips	1492		09/13/2012	2,165.00 $	2,000.00 $	165.00 $	2,165.00 $	08/14/2012	08/14/2012	A/R Invoices
340	1 of 1	C30000	Microchips	1432		11/12/2012	5,250.13 $	4,850.00 $	400.13 $	5,250.13 $	10/13/2012	10/13/2012	A/R Invoices
344	1 of 1	C60000	SG Electronics	1449		10/26/2012	11,430.00 $	11,430.00 $	0.00 $	11,430.00 $	09/26/2012	09/26/2012	A/R Invoices
336	1 of 1	C60000	SG Electronics	1437		11/07/2012	22.50 $	22.50 $	0.00 $	22.50 $	10/08/2012	10/08/2012	A/R Invoices
350	1 of 1	C60000	SG Electronics	1376		01/07/2013	1,050.00 $	1,050.00 $	0.00 $	1,050.00 $	12/08/2012	12/08/2012	A/R Invoices
							326,394.82 $	301,940.00 $	24,454.82 $	326,394.82 $			

Figure 5.42 The Open Items List Screen

Notice that sales blanket agreements are not listed in this report; they are considered a form of master data (not transactional documents). The Open Items Report provides an excellent quick summary of important information on open documents and, in many cases, can act as a trigger for users to deal with the next task in the sales document chain.

5.7.2 Document Drafts Report

The Document Drafts Report will generate a list of all sales documents that have been saved in "draft" status—a helpful functionality because these draft documents do not show up in the main records with all the other marketing documents.

Access the Document Drafts Report by following the menu path SALES – A/R •
SALES REPORTS • DOCUMENT DRAFTS REPORT, which opens the selection criteria
screen shown in Figure 5.43. As with other tools, select a number of parameters
to filter the results, including filtering the owner of document drafts (USER), specifying open drafts only (OPEN ONLY), or defining various date ranges of drafts
(DATE checkbox and selector). Various draft document types are available when
selecting the checkboxes next to SALES – A/R, PURCHASING – A/P, INVENTORY, and
INVENTORY COUNTING TRANSACTIONS.

Figure 5.43 Selection Criteria for a Document Drafts Report

After completing the selection criteria, running the Document Drafts Report will
give you a summary report of your document drafts, similar to the result shown
in Figure 5.44. In our example, we can see a draft that was previously added to
the system because the customer was not 100% sure they wanted to commit to
the order. Once your customer is ready to commit, you can quickly run the Document Drafts Report, open the document, and add it to the open sales orders. In
situations where an approval process exists, a user seeking approval will add a
new sales document, fill out the approval request, and the document will automatically be saved in "draft" status. The Document Drafts Report summarizes
information for each draft document including the approval status.

Many additional options for summary data are possible by clicking the FORM SETTINGS icon (a blank sheet with a green gear) while in the Document Drafts Report.

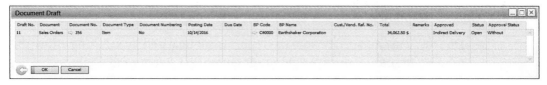

Figure 5.44 Document Drafts Report Results

5.7.3 Sales Analysis Tool

The Sales Analysis is not simply a sales report but a tool that allows you to select a broad set of criteria to create a customized sales report.

Once you open the Sales Analysis tool by following the menu path SALES – A/R • SALES REPORTS • SALES ANALYSIS, you are presented with three major groupings for viewing sales data: by customer, by item, or by sales employee; each of these options has its own tab. (Figure 5.45 shows the selection criteria available when the ITEMS tab is selected.)

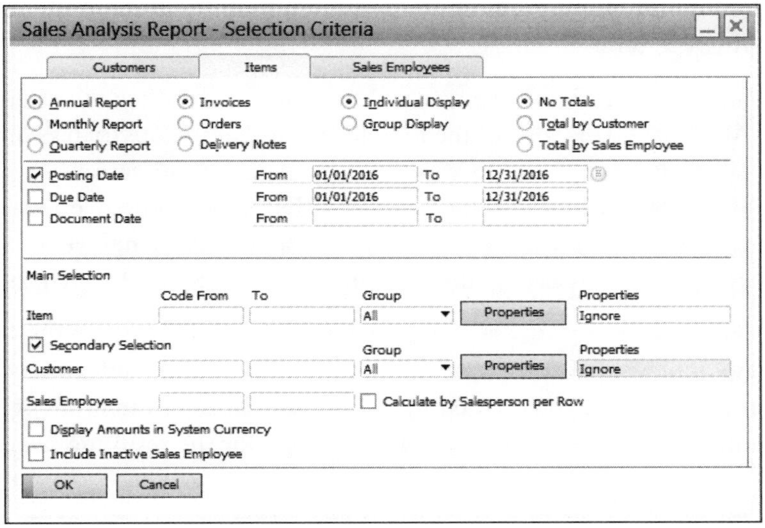

Figure 5.45 Selection Criteria for the Sales Analysis Report

Once this major dimension is selected, the Sales Analysis tool provides much more detailed selection criteria on which to generate the resulting sales report. As shown in Figure 5.45, the top area of the Sales Analysis tool allows you to further choose how the report is displayed and filtered. The top of the tool offers four choices, as follows:

▶ Time dimension: Specify how the report is summarized by selecting either the ANNUAL REPORT, MONTHLY REPORT, or QUARTERLY REPORT radio button.

▶ Document type: Specify whether to run the report for INVOICES, SALES ORDERS, or DELIVERIES by selecting the respective radio button.

▶ Individual/group display: Choose to show the report either by INDIVIDUAL DIS-PLAY (for individual customers/items) or by GROUP DISPLAY (by customer/item group). This option is not available when the SALES EMPLOYEE tab is selected because there are no sales employee groups.

▶ Totals by: Specify whether to show NO TOTALS, TOTALS BY CUSTOMER, or TOTALS BY SALES EMPLOYEE. This option is only available when you have selected the ITEMS tab.

The second set of selection criteria allows you to specify date ranges associated with documents. Specify a range of posting dates, due dates, and/or document dates from the document type selected. The date range selector is available on all tabs of the Sales Analysis tool.

Next, choose a range of customers, items, or sales employees to filter the sales report under the MAIN SELECTION area of the tool. In the case of the CUSTOMERS or SALES EMPLOYEE tab, you may choose to view the results in system currency by selecting the DISPLAY AMOUNTS IN SYSTEM CURRENCY checkbox. Further, on the SALES EMPLOYEE tab, you may also choose to include inactive sales employees in the resulting sales report by selecting the INCLUDE INACTIVE SALES EMPLOYEES checkbox.

The ITEMS tab has a much expanded set of selection criteria possible under SEC-ONDARY SELECTION. In this area, you can go further and also specify a range of customers or sales employees (in addition to a range of items) for the resulting sales report.

The resulting sales report should return results based on the selection criteria. Figure 5.46 shows an example of the type of report that is typically generated when using the CUSTOMER or SALES EMPLOYEE tab of the Sales Analysis tool. Sales reports grouped by customers or sales employee will include total sales amount data, gross profit, gross profit percent, and the total of any open invoices for the relevant customer or sales employee.

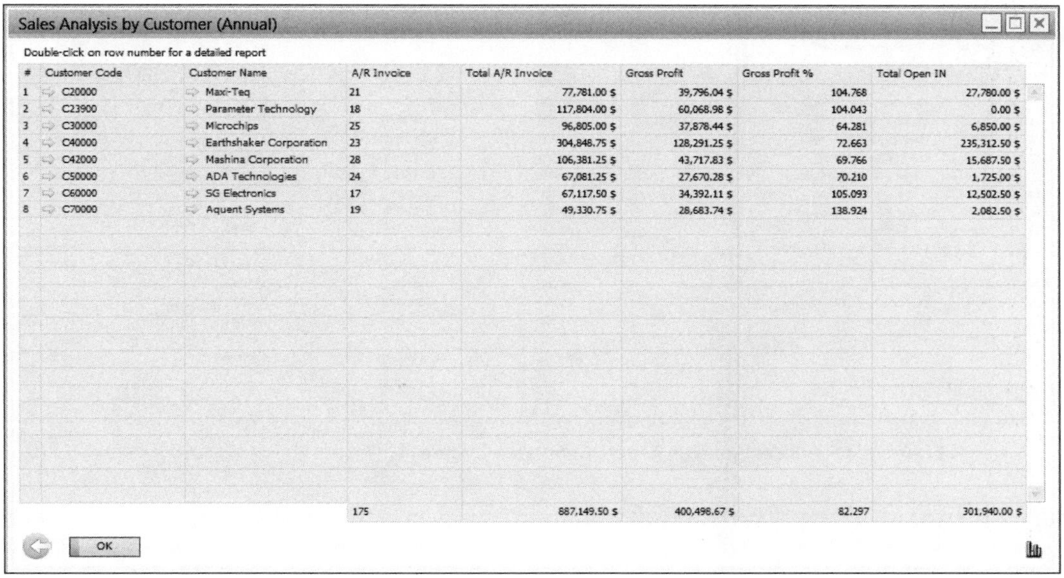

Sales Analysis by Customer (Annual)

Double-click on row number for a detailed report

#	Customer Code	Customer Name	A/R Invoice	Total A/R Invoice	Gross Profit	Gross Profit %	Total Open IN
1	C20000	Maxi-Teq	21	77,781.00 $	39,796.04 $	104.768	27,780.00 $
2	C23900	Parameter Technology	18	117,804.00 $	60,068.98 $	104.043	0.00 $
3	C30000	Microchips	25	96,805.00 $	37,878.44 $	64.281	6,850.00 $
4	C40000	Earthshaker Corporation	23	304,848.75 $	128,291.25 $	72.663	235,312.50 $
5	C42000	Mashina Corporation	28	106,381.25 $	43,717.83 $	69.766	15,687.50 $
6	C50000	ADA Technologies	24	67,081.25 $	27,670.28 $	70.210	1,725.00 $
7	C60000	SG Electronics	17	67,117.50 $	34,392.11 $	105.093	12,502.50 $
8	C70000	Aquent Systems	19	49,330.75 $	28,683.74 $	138.924	2,082.50 $
			175	887,149.50 $	400,498.67 $	82.297	301,940.00 $

OK

Figure 5.46 A Sales Analysis Report Generated by Customer

In contrast, Figure 5.47 shows the typical result when running the sales report from the ITEMS tab of the Sales Analysis tool. This report will show sales quantities for each item, total sales amounts, gross profit, and gross profit percentage.

You may also choose to open a visualization of the Sales Analysis Report by clicking on the VISUALIZATION icon (the bar graph) in the bottom-right corner of the screen in these reports. Figure 5.48 shows a visualization of an item-based Sales Analysis Report.

Sales Analysis by Items (Annual)

Double-click on row number for a detailed display of all sales

#	Item No.	Item Description	Quantity	Sales Amt	Gross Profit	Gross Profit %
1	A00001	J.B. Officeprint 1420	114.000	60,700.00 $	26,344.97 $	76.684
2	A00002	J.B. Officeprint 1111	126.000	35,050.00 $	16,326.64 $	87.199
3	A00003	J.B. Officeprint 1186	70.000	29,550.00 $	14,063.98 $	90.817
4	A00004	Rainbow Color Printer 5.0	88.000	60,000.00 $	27,454.55 $	84.358
5	A00005	Rainbow Color Printer 7.5	60.000	32,500.00 $	15,622.25 $	92.561
6	C00001	Motherboard BTX	48.000	25,800.00 $	12,058.66 $	87.755
7	C00002	Motherboard MicroATX	81.000	33,525.00 $	16,246.88 $	94.032
8	C00003	Quadcore CPU 3.4 GHz	65.000	11,635.00 $	5,707.55 $	96.290
9	C00004	Tower Case with Power supply	68.000	3,097.50 $	1,435.98 $	86.426
10	C00005	WLAN Card	62.000	4,725.00 $	2,004.75 $	73.697
11	C00006	Gigabit Network Card	85.000	1,668.75 $	792.04 $	90.342
12	C00007	Hard Disk 3TB	62.000	44,625.00 $	22,425.63 $	101.019
13	C00008	Computer Monitor 24" HDMI	50.000	14,550.00 $	7,402.79 $	103.576
14	C00009	Keyboard Comfort USB	78.000	2,410.00 $	1,304.94 $	118.088
15	C00010	Mouse USB	106.000	3,085.00 $	1,588.18 $	106.104
16	C00011	Memory DDR RAM 8GB	96.000	5,560.00 $	2,687.29 $	93.545
17	I00001	Blu-Ray Disc 10-Pack	78.000	313.50 $	146.48 $	87.702
18	I00002	Blu-Ray DL Disc 10-Pack	104.000	1,707.00 $	812.83 $	90.903
19	I00003	USB Flashdrive 128GB	105.000	2,825.00 $	1,275.25 $	82.287
20	I00004	USB Flashdrive 256GB	117.000	4,725.00 $	2,170.34 $	84.956
21	I00005	J.B. Laptop Batteries X1 series	88.000	10,980.00 $	5,548.50 $	102.154
22	I00006	J.B. Laptop Batteries X2 series	77.000	8,340.00 $	3,869.37 $	86.551
23	I00007	Rainbow Printer 9.5 Inkjet Cartridge	77.000	2,926.00 $	1,417.03 $	93.907
24	I00008	Rainbow Nuance Ink 6-Pack and Photo Paper Kit	80.000	4,182.75 $	2,006.63 $	92.211
25	I00009	SLR PreciseShot PX1500	81.000	16,200.00 $	7,433.77 $	84.800
26	I00010	SLR M-CAM 40C	71.000	59,550.00 $	28,453.62 $	91.501
27	I00011	KG USB Travel Hub	72.000	1,239.00 $	634.56 $	104.983
			2,590.000	887,149.50 $	399,962.36 $	82.096

OK

Figure 5.47 A Sales Analysis Report Generated by Item

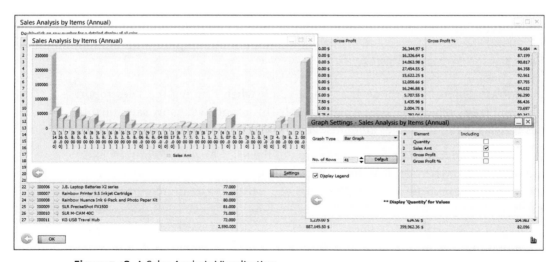

Figure 5.48 A Sales Analysis Visualization

Tips and Tricks: Sales Report Details

In many of the sales reports generated by the Sales Analysis tool, you can drill down to further details of the sales report using the golden arrows. As shown in Figure 5.49, we have drilled down from the item on row 1 of the sales report by double-clicking on the line. The resulting detail shows us the individual invoices where this item is present for the specified criteria of the report. Try drilling down into other sales reports generated by the Sales Analysis tool.

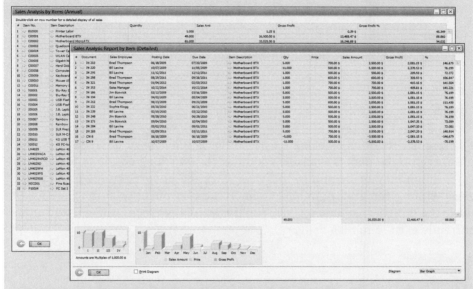

Figure 5.49 Further Details Available in Sales Analysis Reports

5.7.4 Backorder Report

The Backorder Report allows you to compile a summary of all items that are on backorder, that is, all open lines on sales orders.

To generate a Backorder Report, follow the menu path SALES – A/R • SALES REPORTS • BACKORDER REPORT. Figure 5.50 shows the selection criteria that you can use when running the Backorder Report. Select a range of DELIVERY DATES, CUSTOMER NUMBERS, or DOCUMENT NUMBERS to filter the output of the Backorder Report. In the ITEMS section of the screen, you may also specify a range of items, item group, or item properties in order to filter the output of the report. The last section of the screen allows you to specify certain warehouses for your Backorder Report; in this case, all warehouses are selected.

Figure 5.50 Selection Criteria for a Backorder Report

The number reported as being on backorder is the sum of all open sales order lines, even if the item is available and in stock. Switching on the IN STOCK quantity column may be helpful in this case. Click the FORM SETTINGS icon (a blank sheet with a green gear) right next to the BACKORDER quantity, as in Figure 5.51 to make the IN STOCK column visible. You'll immediately see if sufficient quantities currently exist to fulfill a delivery.

#	Item No.	Description	Doc No.	Customer Code	Delivery Date	Whse	Unit of Measure	Items per Unit	Ordered	Delivered	Backorder	In Stock
1	A00001	J.B. Officeprint 1420	343	C40000	11/10/2012	01		1.000	3		3	994
2	A00001	J.B. Officeprint 1420	361	C40000	10/30/2014	01		1.000	3		3	994
3	A00002	J.B. Officeprint 1111	350	C20000	09/12/2012	01		1.000	5		5	959
4	A00002	J.B. Officeprint 1111	361	C40000	10/30/2014	01		1.000	3		3	959
5	A00002	J.B. Officeprint 1111	366	C23900	02/17/2016	01		1.000	1		1	959
6	A00003	J.B. Officeprint 1186	342	C30000	08/26/2012	01		1.000	2		2	1,037
7	A00003	J.B. Officeprint 1186	361	C40000	10/30/2014	01		1.000	3		3	1,037
8	A00003	J.B. Officeprint 1186	366	C23900	02/17/2016	01		1.000	1		1	1,037
9	A00004	Rainbow Color Printer 5.0	351	C23900	08/04/2012	01		1.000	3		3	1,047
10	A00004	Rainbow Color Printer 5.0	339	C50000	09/23/2012	01		1.000	3		3	1,047
11	A00004	Rainbow Color Printer 5.0	341	C42000	12/07/2012	01		1.000	4		4	1,047
12	A00004	Rainbow Color Printer 5.0	349	C20000	12/07/2012	01		1.000	1		1	1,047
13	A00004	Rainbow Color Printer 5.0	338	C30000	12/12/2012	01		1.000	4		4	1,047
14	A00004	Rainbow Color Printer 5.0	366	C23900	02/17/2016	01		1.000	1		1	1,047
15	A00005	Rainbow Color Printer 7.5	337	C23900	10/07/2012	01		1.000	2		2	1,115
16	C00001	Motherboard BTX	346	C40000	08/05/2012	01		1.000	4		4	1,280
17	C00001	Motherboard BTX	344	C20000	09/08/2012	01		1.000	5		5	1,280
18	C00002	Motherboard MicroATX	342	C30000	08/26/2012	01		1.000	3		3	1,182
19	C00002	Motherboard MicroATX	355	C23900	10/30/2014	01		1.000	5		5	1,182
20	C00002	Motherboard MicroATX	363	C30000	02/16/2016	01		1.000	1		1	1,182
21	C00002	Motherboard MicroATX	364	C23900	02/16/2016	01		1.000	1		1	1,182
22	C00002	Motherboard MicroATX	365	C40000	02/16/2016	01		1.000	400		400	1,182
23	C00003	Quadcore CPU 3.4 GHz	338	C30000	12/12/2012	01		1.000	5		5	1,077
24	C00004	Tower Case with Power supply	340	C50000	08/29/2012	01		1.000	4		4	1,135
25	C00004	Tower Case with Power supply	343	C40000	11/30/2012	01		1.000	1		1	1,135
26	C00005	WLAN Card	355	C23900	10/30/2014	01		1.000	3		3	1,086
27	C00006	Gigabit Network Card	318	C20000	02/02/2012	01		1.000	3		3	1,029
28	C00006	Gigabit Network Card	351	C23900	08/04/2012	01		1.000	5		5	1,029
29	C00006	Gigabit Network Card	343	C40000	11/10/2012	01		1.000	1		1	1,029
30	C00008	Computer Monitor 24" HDMI	351	C23900	08/04/2012	01		1.000	5		5	1,116
31	C00008	Computer Monitor 24" HDMI	345	C30000	09/11/2012	01		1.000	1		1	1,116

Date From To — Items All
Customers From To — Warehouses 05, 02, 01, 04

OK

Figure 5.51 A Backorder Report

Tips and Tricks: Cancel a Backordered Row

You can cancel a customer backorder directly from the backorder report. If you know which row you'd like to cancel, right-click on it, and select CLOSE ROW, as shown in Figure 5.52. The corresponding row on the sales order related to this line in the Backorder Report will be canceled.

In certain situations, cancelling backorders in this way can save time because you won't have to open sales orders one by one.

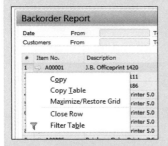

Figure 5.52 Canceling a Backorder Row

5.7.5   Blanket Agreement Fulfillment Report

The Blanket Agreement Fulfillment Report allows you to analyze whether customers have made good on their purchase commitments and to identify what is remaining.

The selection criteria shown in Figure 5.53 are based on properties of blanket agreements; refer to Section 5.1.1 for a more complete list of these fields. The last selection criteria, FULFILLED, allows you to filter the report to only include fulfilled agreements, unfulfilled agreements, or both.

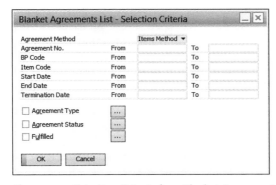

Figure 5.53 Selection Criteria for a Blanket Agreement Fulfillment Report

An example Blanket Agreement Fulfillment Report is shown in Figure 5.54. The report shows all contract lines from the sales blanket agreement and shows the fulfillment status. You can quickly assess which agreements are fulfilled and which agreements still have open amounts remaining to fulfill. In this case, we can see two customers in the report: One has fulfilled their volume commitment to buy a certain type of printer, but the other still has a remaining quantity to order per the agreement. This information can be useful when renegotiating agreements with customers for special prices or terms.

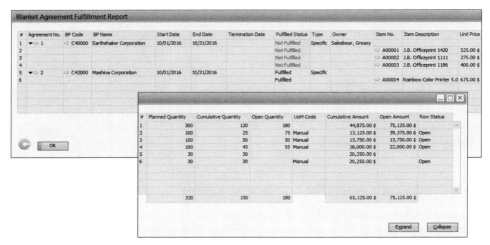

Figure 5.54 A Blanket Agreement Fulfillment Report

5.7.6 Specialized Reports

The reports covered in this section differ slightly from their previous counterparts as they have fewer selection criteria to slice and dice your data and have more specific purposes in mind. Less about analysis, these tools are more focused on providing finished reports that answer specific questions about your sales data.

Let's consider these reports in the order in which they appear under the SALES REPORTS menu.

Locate Exceptional Discount in Invoice Report

The Locate Exceptional Discount in Invoice Report will list all invoices that include a discount you specify. Figure 5.55 shows the selection criteria box where you'll indicate a discount amount prior to running the report. The resulting report lists the A/R invoices that include this discount level. Note that this report will find document-level discounts but not line-level discounts.

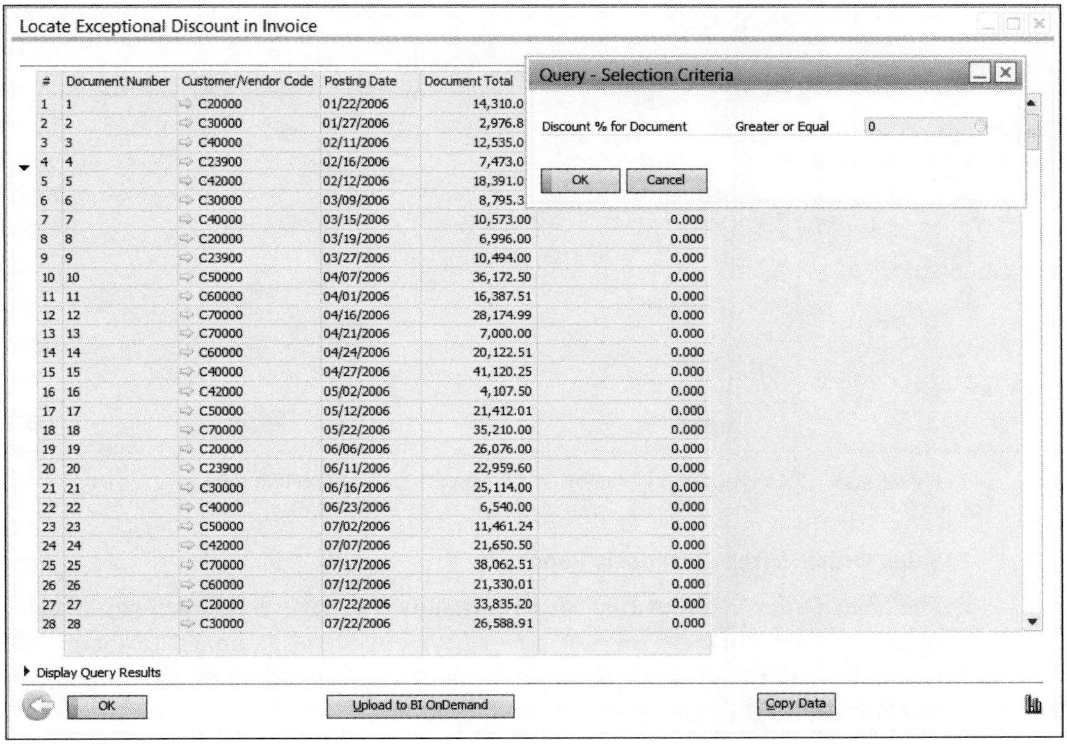

#	Document Number	Customer/Vendor Code	Posting Date	Document Total	
1	1	C20000	01/22/2006	14,310.0	
2	2	C30000	01/27/2006	2,976.8	
3	3	C40000	02/11/2006	12,535.0	
4	4	C23900	02/16/2006	7,473.0	
5	5	C42000	02/12/2006	18,391.0	
6	6	C30000	03/09/2006	8,795.3	
7	7	C40000	03/15/2006	10,573.00	0.000
8	8	C20000	03/19/2006	6,996.00	0.000
9	9	C23900	03/27/2006	10,494.00	0.000
10	10	C50000	04/07/2006	36,172.50	0.000
11	11	C60000	04/01/2006	16,387.51	0.000
12	12	C70000	04/16/2006	28,174.99	0.000
13	13	C70000	04/21/2006	7,000.00	0.000
14	14	C60000	04/24/2006	20,122.51	0.000
15	15	C40000	04/27/2006	41,120.25	0.000
16	16	C42000	05/02/2006	4,107.50	0.000
17	17	C50000	05/12/2006	21,412.01	0.000
18	18	C70000	05/22/2006	35,210.00	0.000
19	19	C20000	06/06/2006	26,076.00	0.000
20	20	C23900	06/11/2006	22,959.60	0.000
21	21	C30000	06/16/2006	25,114.00	0.000
22	22	C40000	06/23/2006	6,540.00	0.000
23	23	C50000	07/02/2006	11,461.24	0.000
24	24	C42000	07/07/2006	21,650.50	0.000
25	25	C70000	07/17/2006	38,062.51	0.000
26	26	C60000	07/12/2006	21,330.01	0.000
27	27	C20000	07/22/2006	33,835.20	0.000
28	28	C30000	07/22/2006	26,588.91	0.000

Figure 5.55 A Locate Exceptional Discount in Invoice Report

SP Commission by Invoices in Posting Date Cross-Section Report

This report allows you to calculate sales commissions based on a date range of invoices. (Here, SP stands for salesperson.) In order for this report to work, you must set up commission amounts in the Administration module. This report will calculate commissions based on the total of sales invoices, not including tax (see Figure 5.56).

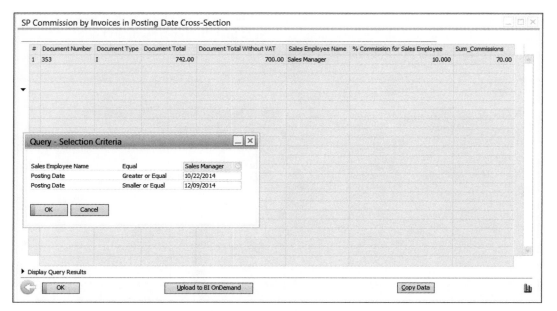

Figure 5.56 SP Commission by Invoices in a Posting Date Cross-Section Report

Sales Order Without Deposit Report

The Sales Order Without Deposit Report shown in Figure 5.57 returns all sales orders that do not have an A/R down payment (deposit) linked to them. The report does not have selection criteria but can be filtered using the FILTER icon (the funnel) on the ribbon bar.

Sales Order Linked to Deposit

The Sales Order Linked to Deposit Report shown in Figure 5.58 returns all sales orders that have an A/R down payment (deposit) linked to them. The report does not have selection criteria but can be filtered using the FILTER icon (the funnel) on the ribbon bar.

Sales Order Without Deposit

#	Customer Code	Customer Name	Sales Order No.	Document Date	Due Date	Total Amount of Order
1	C20000	Norm Thompson	1	01/10/2006	01/20/2006	14,310.00
2	C30000	Microchips	2	01/15/2006	01/25/2006	2,976.88
3	C40000	Earthshaker Corporation	3	01/20/2006	01/30/2006	12,535.00
4	C23900	Parameter Technology	4	01/25/2006	02/04/2006	7,473.00
5	C42000	Mashina Corporation	5	01/30/2006	02/10/2006	18,391.00
6	C30000	Microchips	6	02/15/2006	02/25/2006	8,795.31
7	C40000	Earthshaker Corporation	7	02/21/2006	03/03/2006	10,573.00
8	C20000	Norm Thompson	8	02/25/2006	03/07/2006	6,996.00
9	C23900	Parameter Technology	9	03/05/2006	03/15/2006	10,494.00
10	C50000	ADA Technologies	10	03/16/2006	03/26/2006	29,835.45
11	C60000	SG Electronics	11	03/20/2006	03/30/2006	19,202.61
12	C70000	Aquent Systems	12	03/25/2006	04/04/2006	33,014.99
13	C70000	Aquent Systems	13	03/30/2006	04/09/2006	8,202.48
14	C60000	SG Electronics	14	04/02/2006	04/12/2006	23,579.23
15	C40000	Earthshaker Corporation	15	04/05/2006	04/15/2006	41,120.25
16	C42000	Mashina Corporation	16	04/10/2006	04/20/2006	4,107.50
17	C50000	ADA Technologies	17	04/20/2006	04/30/2006	17,660.84
18	C70000	Aquent Systems	18	04/30/2006	05/10/2006	41,258.50
19	C20000	Norm Thompson	19	05/15/2006	05/25/2006	26,076.00
20	C23900	Parameter Technology	20	05/20/2006	05/30/2006	22,959.60
21	C30000	Microchips	21	05/25/2006	06/04/2006	25,114.00
22	C40000	Earthshaker Corporation	22	06/01/2006	06/11/2006	6,540.00
23	C50000	ADA Technologies	23	06/10/2006	06/20/2006	8,937.35
24	C42000	Mashina Corporation	24	06/15/2006	06/25/2006	21,650.50
25	C70000	Aquent Systems	25	06/25/2006	07/05/2006	41,882.14
26	C60000	SG Electronics	26	06/30/2006	07/10/2006	23,470.51
27	C20000	Norm Thompson	27	07/07/2006	07/20/2006	33,835.20
28	C30000	Microchips	28	07/11/2006	07/20/2006	20,743.41
29	C42000	Mashina Corporation	29	07/18/2006	07/28/2006	8,851.00
30	C60000	SG Electronics	30	07/23/2006	07/31/2006	31,236.80
31	C23900	Parameter Technology	31	08/01/2006	08/10/2006	8,649.60
32	C40000	Earthshaker Corporation	32	08/08/2006	08/17/2006	19,783.50
33	C50000	ADA Technologies	33	08/14/2006	08/23/2006	17,265.03
34	C70000	Aquent Systems	34	08/20/2006	08/30/2006	14,728.51
35	C20000	Norm Thompson	35	08/25/2006	09/05/2006	45,760.20

▶ Display Query Results

[OK]   [Upload to BI OnDemand]   [Copy Data]

Figure 5.57 A Sales Order Without Deposit Report

Sales Order Linked to Deposit

#	Customer Code	Customer Name	Sales Order No.	Document Date	Due Date	Total Amount of Order	Document Currency	Down Payment Invoice No.	Amount Paid	Percentage Paid
1	C40000	Earthshaker Corporation	358	10/22/2014	10/22/2014	817.50	$	1	400.00	53.33
2	C40000	Earthshaker Corporation	360	10/22/2014	10/22/2014	14,933.00	$	3	7,500.00	54.74

▶ Display Query Results

[OK]   [Upload to BI OnDemand]   [Copy Data]

Figure 5.58 A Sales Order Linked to Deposit Report

Monthly Customer Status Report

The Monthly Customer Status Report provides a summary view of customer sales performance broken down by month over a certain time period.

Figure 5.59 shows an overlay of the selection criteria for the report. You can specify a date range for the report, as well as a range of customers, if desired. The first page of this report (Figure 5.59) provides a bar graph that shows the top five customers by invoice (and collected amounts) and a pie graph that shows the top five customers by current outstanding business partner balance. Each page thereafter (Figure 5.60) is a detailed monthly breakdown of sales transactions and payments grouped by customer.

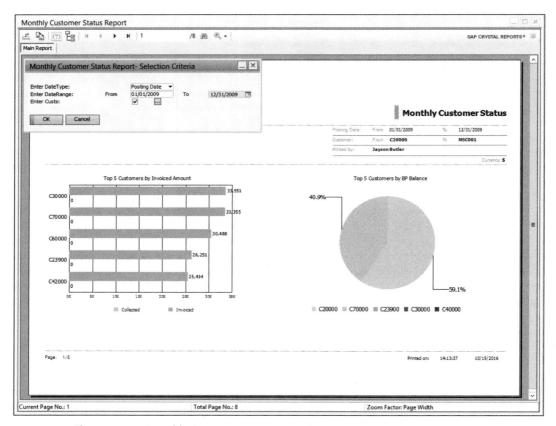

Figure 5.59 A Monthly Customer Status Report (Page 1)

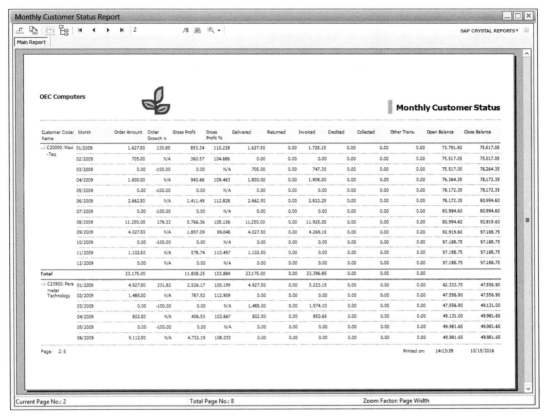

Figure 5.60 A Monthly Customer Status Report (Page 2 Onward)

Annual Sales Analysis (by Quarter) Report

The Annual Sales Analysis (by Quarter) Report provides a quarterly revenue analysis between the current year and the last year, as well as a revenue breakdown by customer group as shown in Figure 5.61. The bar graph on the left side shows quarterly revenue for the current year compared to last year. On the right side, a stacked column graph shows total revenue by customer group separated into cost of sales and gross margin. The table below the graph gives a quarterly breakdown of revenue and margin by customer group.

Figure 5.61 An Annual Sales Analysis (by Quarter) Report

Small to medium-sized businesses purchase raw materials, products, services, and other items in order to produce goods and services or for resale to their customers. The Purchasing (A/P) module in SAP Business One manages the flow of purchasing documents and their corresponding data throughout the chain of custody.

6   Purchasing (A/P)

The Purchasing (A/P) module in SAP Business One covers the entire procurement process including purchase requisitions, purchase quotations, blanket agreements, purchase orders (POs), PO goods receipts, PO goods returns, A/P invoices, A/P credits, and other purchasing documents.

In this chapter, you'll gain a broad understanding of the entire purchasing process in SAP Business One. Using step-by-step instructions and screenshots, the chapter will teach you how to create and maintain all of the purchasing screens and functions in SAP Business One; we'll also look at recurring transactions and landed costs, as well as a few helpful wizards that will aid you in your purchasing document management. Of course, since SAP continues to introduce additional functionality with every new release of SAP Business One, we could not possibly include all of the menu options and details in this chapter, but what we'll cover will be enough for most purchasing processes.

6.1   Purchasing Process

Every company, no matter how big or small, purchases some type of materials, goods, or services in order to run their business. This function is often defined as the *purchase-to-pay* or *purchasing process*.

In SAP Business One, the purchasing process includes everything from purchase blanket agreements to the A/P invoice. If desired, the purchasing process allows you to perform a document flow from a purchase request to a purchase quotation and onto a purchase blanket agreement, a purchase order, a goods receipt PO, and finally an A/P invoice with further capability to create PO returns and A/P credit memos; all of these can be linked together so that you have complete visibility and traceability using the relationship map in SAP Business One.

In Chapter 5 you learned about the relationship map functionality of SAP Business One, which is used to visualize the flow of information. Figure 6.1 gives an example of a relationship map for some of the documents that we'll cover during our examination of the purchasing process in SAP Business One.

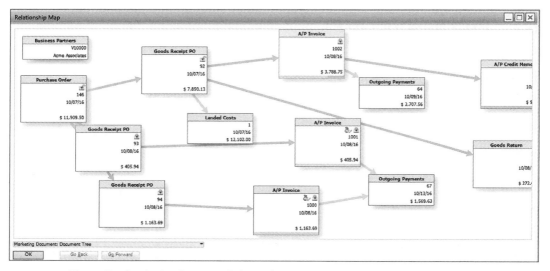

Figure 6.1 Purchasing Processes Relationship Map

Most of the Purchasing (A/P) module screens throughout the process offer you the capability of working with items or services by choosing the corresponding type from the dropdown list on the CONTENTS tab of the screen:

▶ An *item* type document can be created only for items identified in your item master. These items may be inventory items, or they can be noninventoried items for things you may commonly purchase such as shipping supplies, maintenance supplies, etc. An advantage of item type documents is that the accounting transactions are typically predefined in general ledger (G/L) account determination, item groups, or warehouses with the added benefit of visibility into all the purchases and their related documents.

▸ Meanwhile, *service* type documents are used when purchasing goods or services that do not have item numbers. These transactions require you to enter G/L account numbers whenever recording transactions that affect accounting. Additionally, you cannot enter quantities and unit prices. Because of these limitations, you may consider creating item numbers for your common "non-inventoried" items. When doing so, make sure that you create these items as noninventory items and set the G/L accounts appropriately.

By now, you should have a good understanding of how the marketing document screens look and feel from the explanations in Chapter 1 and in Chapter 5, which covered the Sales (A/R) module in SAP Business One, so we won't bore you with detailed explanations of all the fields and tabs on all the Purchasing (A/P) module screens that all share in this similarity, which include the purchase request, the purchase quotation, the purchase order, the goods receipt PO, the PO goods return, the A/P invoice, the A/P credit, the A/P down payment invoice, and the A/P reserve invoice; instead, we'll focus on the differences and important features of each subsection.

6.1.1 Purchase Request

Purchase requests (commonly referred to as *purchase requisitions*) can be used to request items, services, or supplies. Although purchase requests can be used to request *all* purchases for a company, they are typically used for goods that exceed a certain dollar amount; are special items, like supplies and equipment; or require approvals from management.

Once submitted, purchase requests are reviewed by the purchasing department, which would obtain price and delivery information from vendors for the items or services requested. The information can then be routed back to the requestor and then ultimately turned into a *purchase order* by copying the purchase request to a purchase order as shown in Figure 6.2.

To access the purchase request functionality in SAP Business One, follow the menu path PURCHASING – A/P • PURCHASE REQUEST. Notice that the PURCHASE REQUEST screen shown in Figure 6.2 contains a header and two tabs: CONTENTS and ATTACHMENTS.

The header displays the following information: the purchase requestor, purchase requestor name, and the branch and department. (The branch and department are determined from a dropdown list, although the BRANCH option is only visible if your organization uses multibranch functionality.) Check the SEND EMAIL IF PO OR GRPO IS ADDED checkbox if you want the system to send an email to the requestor if a PO or goods receipt PO is added. The header also displays the email address of the person designated to receive that email.

Additional data is shown on the right side of the header, including the purchase request number, the status, the posting and valid-until dates, the document date, and the date by which the items are required.

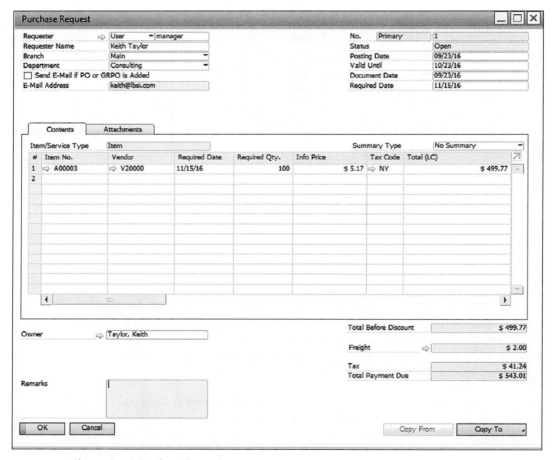

Figure 6.2 A Purchase Request

Table 6.1 lists some key fields visible in the CONTENTS tab of the purchase request shown in Figure 6.2.

Field	Description/Use
REQUIRED DATE	Input the date the items is required by (in our example in Figure 6.2, this date is November 15, 2016).
REQUIRED QTY	Input the quantity of items required (e.g., 100).
INFO PRICE	Identify the price of the items (e.g., $5.17).

Table 6.1 Fields of the Purchase Request Contents Tab

6.1.2 Purchase Blanket Agreements

Blanket agreements are long-term arrangements between a purchasing organization and a vendor. Purchase blanket agreements allow you to provide an agreement or contract to your vendors for goods or services without defining exact delivery dates. These purchase blanket agreements are a great way to define all the terms and conditions of the agreement to your supplier; later, you can tie in purchase orders that contain delivery dates.

Two types of blanket agreements are available:

▸ *General blanket agreements* are used to track purchases in order to obtain a rebate or bonus at the end of the year for either purchasing a certain quantity or dollar amount.

▸ *Specific blanket agreements* are used to track purchases and terms to obtain a special discount or price for items or services.

In addition, purchase blanket agreements can be based on specific items (where you state specific items) or on a monetary method (where no items are specified and instead you specify a total dollar amount). The monetary method works well for suppliers who provide you a discount based on total dollars purchased.

Once purchase blanket agreements are created and the status is changed to approved, documents are automatically linked to the purchase blanket agreement.

Let's look closer at how SAP Business One handles purchasing blanket agreements. Access this functionality by following the menu path PURCHASING – A/P • PURCHASE BLANKET AGREEMENTS. The PURCHASE BLANKET AGREEMENTS screen consists of a header and five different tabs (GENERAL, DETAILS, DOCUMENTS, ATTACHMENTS, and RECURRING TRANSACTIONS), each of which is explained in the following subsections.

In the header of the PURCHASE BLANKET AGREEMENTS screen, you'll input the business partner code, the business partner name, the corresponding contract person (chosen from a dropdown list), and their corresponding telephone number and email address. The right side of the screen displays information about the document number; the agreement method (your options here are ITEMS METHOD or MONETARY METHOD); and the start, end, termination, and signing dates.

General Tab

Let's walk through the fields shown in the GENERAL tab shown in Figure 6.3 using Table 6.2.

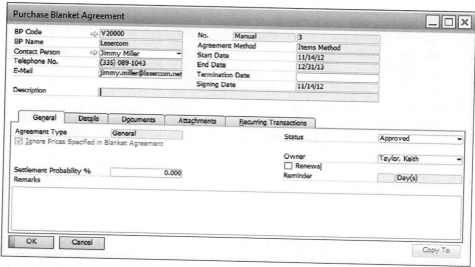

Figure 6.3 The Purchase Blanket Agreement General Tab

Field	Description/Use
AGREEMENT TYPE	Choose an agreement type from this dropdown list: ▸ GENERAL: Use this type to track purchases in order to obtain a rebate or bonus at the end of the year for either purchasing a certain quantity or dollar amount. ▸ SPECIFIC: Use this type to track purchases and terms to obtain a special discount or price for items or services.

Table 6.2 Fields of the Purchase Blanket Agreement General Tab

Field	Description/Use
IGNORE PRICES SPECIFIED IN THE BLANKET AGREEMENT	Select this checkbox if you want to ignore the process specified in the blanket agreement.
STATUS	Choose from the following status options: ▶ DRAFT ▶ APPROVED ▶ ON HOLD ▶ TERMINATED
OWNER	This field displays the user that created the document.
RENEWAL	Select this checkbox if you want a reminder to renew the blanket agreement before it expires.
REMINDER	Enter a number of days to send a reminder before the blanket agreement expires.
SETTLEMENT PROBABILITY %	Enter the percentage of probability that you will purchase all items and quantities. Normally, this probability is set to 100%.
REMARKS	Add other remarks here.

Table 6.2 Fields of the Purchase Blanket Agreement General Tab (Cont.)

Details Tab

The DETAILS tab of the purchase blanket agreement shown in Figure 6.4 contains the detailed item information about quantities, pricing, cumulative quantity and cumulative dollar amounts, and open quantity and open dollar amounts.

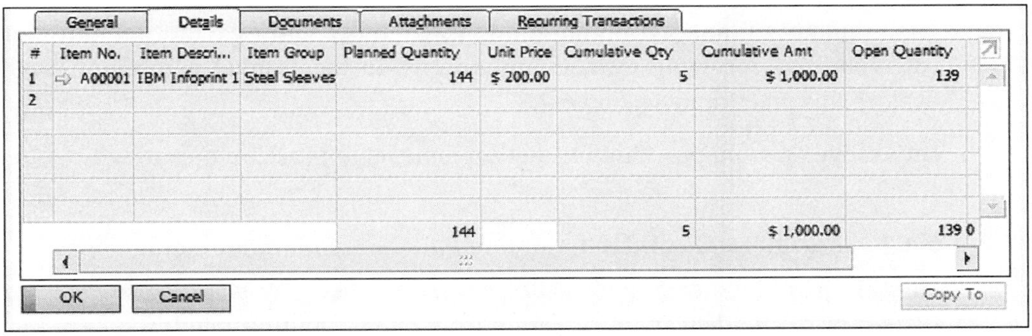

Figure 6.4 The Purchase Blanket Agreement Details Tab

231

Documents Tab

The DOCUMENTS tab contains all of the transactional documents that are tied to this purchase blanket agreement. Documents such as the purchase order, PO goods receipts, PO goods returns, A/P invoices, and A/P credit memos will be displayed, as well as the transactional details for each.

Our example in Figure 6.5 contains a goods receipt PO, an A/P invoice, and a purchase order.

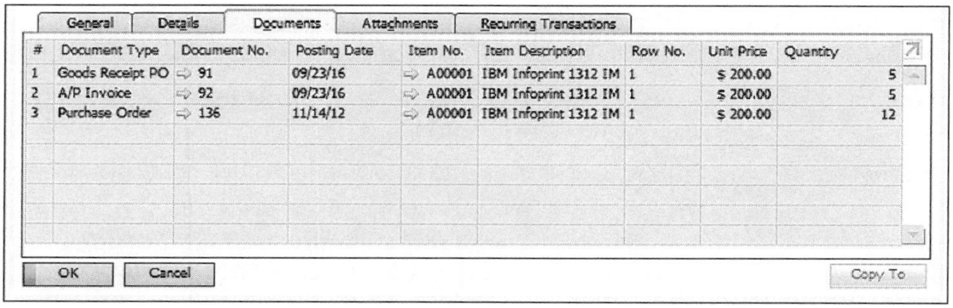

	General	Details	Documents	Attachments		Recurring Transactions				
#	Document Type	Document No.	Posting Date	Item No.	Item Description	Row No.	Unit Price	Quantity	
1	Goods Receipt PO	91	09/23/16	A00001	IBM Infoprint 1312 IM	1	$ 200.00	5	
2	A/P Invoice	92	09/23/16	A00001	IBM Infoprint 1312 IM	1	$ 200.00	5	
3	Purchase Order	136	11/14/12	A00001	IBM Infoprint 1312 IM	1	$ 200.00	12	

OK   Cancel   Copy To

Figure 6.5 The Purchase Blanket Agreement Documents Tab

Attachments Tab

The ATTACHMENTS tab is provided so that you can attach various files that apply directly to the purchase blanket agreement.

Recurring Transactions Tab

The RECURRING TRANSACTIONS tab allows you to link recurring templates and their corresponding recurring transactions directly to the blanket agreement; we'll explore this practice in Section 6.2.

Let's move on from purchase blanket agreements to purchase quotations.

6.1.3   Purchase Quotation

Purchase quotations (commonly called *purchase requests for quotation*) are used to request price and delivery information from one or multiple vendors.

You can create purchase quotations directly from the PURCHASE QUOTATION screen shown in Figure 6.6 or, if you had received a purchase request from one of your departments, you could copy the purchase request form to the purchase quotation. The screen allows you to complete limited information including the vendor, item details, quantities requested, dates required, etc. and forward to your vendor(s) so that they can use the information to provide a quotation to you.

Once you've received pricing and delivery information, you would update the purchase quotation with the quoted costs, the quantities quoted, and other information supplied from the vendor. You are then able to review and compare the quotations received and determine from whom to purchase the goods or services. You can then copy the information from the purchase quotation to the purchase order and close other purchase quotations that were sent to other vendors that you did not extend the purchase order to.

You can access this functionality by following the menu path: PURCHASING – A/P • PURCHASE QUOTATION. Let's take a closer look at this PURCHASE QUOTATION screen, which has a header and four tabs: CONTENT, LOGISTICS, ACCOUNTING, and ATTACHMENTS.

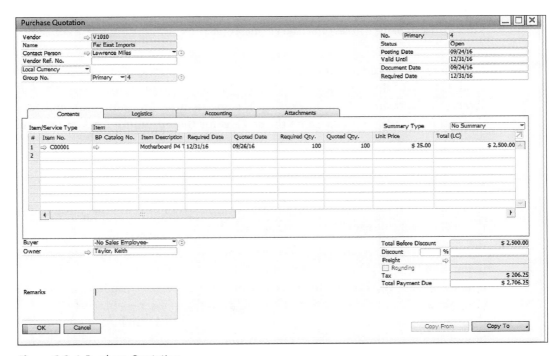

Figure 6.6 A Purchase Quotation

The left side of the header displays much of the same information as the purchase request just covered, with the addition of a vendor reference number (the vendor's quotation number), the local currency, and the group type and number. The right side of the header similarly has VALID UNTIL and REQUIRED DATE fields to designate the date the vendor's quotation expires and the date that you require the item at your receiving location, respectively.

Table 6.3 lists key fields that appear in the CONTENTS tab.

Field	Description/Use
BP CATALOG NO.	Enter your vendor's part number.
REQUIRED DATE	Enter the date you require the item at your receiving location. (This field is automatically populated from the field in the header.)
QUOTED DATE	Enter the date the vendor responded to your quotation request.
PURCHASE QUANTITY	Enter the purchase quantity the quote is valid for.
QUOTED QTY.	Enter the quoted quantity. In many cases, the quoted quantity will be identical to the requested quantity.

Table 6.3 Fields of the Purchase Quotation Contents Tab

From here on, we can pick up the pace on our journey through the Purchasing (A/P) module because SAP Business One applies the same design concept to most of its screens. As a result, all the marketing documents have the same look and feel. Consequently, we won't examine the screens for the upcoming marketing documents so closely.

6.1.4 Purchase Order

A purchase order (PO) is a document sent from a buyer to a seller that outlines the items and quantities sought and the agreed-upon prices.

In SAP Business One, you can create or access a purchase order by following the menu path PURCHASING – A/P • PURCHASE ORDER. From the PURCHASE ORDER maintenance screen, you can create a purchase order directly, or if you have a purchase quotation, you could copy the quotation to a purchase order—a process similar to the one you just saw for copying a purchase request to a purchase quotation. By now, you should be comfortable creating one screen from another one using the COPY TO and COPY FROM buttons on the various marketing document screens, but you can refer back to Chapter 1, Section 1.2.4, if you need a refresher.

If you are copying from a PURCHASE QUOTATION screen, you'll receive a message inquiring whether you want to close other purchase quotations with the same group number—in other words, to close any other purchase quotations sent to suppliers other than the one who'll get the purchase order. You would typically respond YES to this message.

Fields that are unique to the PURCHASE ORDER document are listed in Table 6.4.

Field	Description/Use
DELIVERY DATE	This field exists in the header of the document, as well as on each date of each line in the contents. As a result, you can set the requested delivery date on the entire order or specify different delivery dates for individual items on a purchase order.
	When setting the delivery date in the header, the system will ask you if you want to set the same delivery date for each line in the contents field as well. If each line has a unique delivery date, choose No; if not, choose YES.
	Note that, if you don't enter a delivery date, you will not be able to add the purchase order to the system.
SPLIT PURCHASE ORDER (LOGISTICS tab)	This field enables you to divide purchase orders that involve more than one warehouse.
APPROVED (LOGISTICS tab)	This checkbox can be set to default to checked (approved) or unchecked (unapproved) in the global system settings.
	If you set this checkbox to default to unchecked (unapproved), then a new purchase order will be prevented from being promoted to a goods receipt document. The status in the document header will change to "unapproved"—which can be useful if a secondary check is required to ensure the purchase order is correct.
CANCELLATION DATE (ACCOUNTING tab)	This date specifies the last day on which the customer will accept the goods in the sales order. This date will default to 30 days after the delivery date on the document. Note that this date is for reference only and will not automatically close the document on this date.
REQUIRED DATE (ACCOUNTING tab)	This field allows the user to specify the date on which the goods should leave the vendor's site, in order to arrive at the company's site by the delivery date.

Table 6.4 Fields of the Purchase Order

6.1.5 Goods Receipt PO

The Goods Receipt PO screen (reached by following the menu path Purchasing – A/P • Goods Receipt PO) is used to receive the products or services that you purchased via a purchase order.

This process is normally performed by your receiving department or warehouse personnel. Using this screen, you can easily compare your vendor's packing slip to your purchase order in real time. You won't need a hard copy of the printed purchase order in front of you while you are performing the receiving function since all of the details are on the Goods Receipt PO screen. (Remember that you can "hide" various fields such as the vendor's cost on the Goods Receipt PO screen from the person performing the receiving function if you feel that this information is confidential.)

The goods receipt PO transaction will automatically receive the goods or services into your inventory when the items being received are inventory items.

Tips and Tricks: Goods Receipt PO

It's important for the information on the purchase order to be accurate when you are performing the goods receipt PO. If the items are classified as "inventory items," items will be received into inventory at the costs on the purchase orders. Goods receipt PO transactions for noninventory items and services do not affect inventory, but that goods receipt PO transaction will be used to review and create the A/P invoice when you receive the invoice from your vendor.

6.1.6 Goods Return

The Goods Return screen is used to return purchased products or services to a vendor. The goods return transaction will automatically remove the products you are returning from your inventory if they are classified as *inventory items*.

Access the Goods Return screen by following the menu path Purchasing – A/P • Goods Return.

6.1.7 A/P Down Payment Invoice

You'll use *A/P down payment invoices* when you need to provide a vendor a payment in advance for purchases or services prior to receiving them. The down payment invoice posting affects accounting but does not affect inventory until the PO goods receipt is created when the product or service is received.

In this scenario, the process flow goes from purchase order to the A/P down payment invoice, the incoming payment, the PO goods receipt, the final A/P invoice, and finally to vendor payment. Using the built-in process that SAP Business One provides for A/P down payment invoices, proper accounting transactions are performed throughout this process flow. Access this functionality by following the menu path PURCHASING – A/P • A/P DOWN PAYMENT INVOICE.

Tips and Tricks: A/P Down-Payment Invoices

Refer to the DOWN PAYMENT INVOICE PROCESS section in SAP Business One's Context-Sensitive Help System (SAP Library) for more information on A/P down payment invoices.

6.1.8   A/P Invoice

A/P invoices (commonly referred to *vouchers* in other business systems) are used to set up the payment for goods and services received from a vendor, such as rent, utilities, and consulting services. You would create these A/P invoices when you receive the invoices from your vendors.

Access the A/P invoice management functionality in SAP Business One by following the menu path PURCHASING – A/P • A/P INVOICE. If the invoice you received is for products or services that were originally received using a goods receipt PO, then you would base your A/P invoice off of a goods receipt PO by choosing either the COPY TO feature from the goods receipt PO to an A/P invoice or by starting with an A/P invoice and using the COPY FROM feature and selecting the goods receipt PO.

Table 6.5 lists important fields in the A/P invoice.

Field	Description/Use
DUE DATE	This field in the header displays the payment due date of the invoice. This date will be autofilled according the payment terms specified on the business partner record associated with the invoice.

Table 6.5 Fields of the A/P Invoice

Field	Description/Use
STAMP NUMBER (LOGISTICS tab)	Use this field to fill out the international standard stamp number for postage type shipments.
PAYMENT BLOCK (ACCOUNTING tab)	This checkbox will allow you to block the A/P invoice from payment and specify a reason.
MAX. CASH DISCOUNT (ACCOUNTING tab)	This checkbox will force the document to calculate the maximum cash discount (if applicable) that applies to the document for favorable payment terms even if the cash discount due date has already occurred.
PAYMENT TERMS (ACCOUNTING tab)	This field displays the default payment terms for the business partner associated with the document. The value in the PAYMENT TERMS field can be overridden on a per-document basis.
PAYMENT METHOD (ACCOUNTING tab)	This field displays the default payment method for the business partner associated with the document. The value in the PAYMENT METHODS can be overridden on a per-document basis.
CENTRAL BANK IND.	Specify a central bank indicator for documents created for foreign business partners.
INSTALLMENTS (ACCOUNTING tab)	Clicking on the golden arrow adjacent to the INSTALLMENTS field will allow you to define payment installments for the A/P invoice.
MANUAL RECALCULATE DUE DATE (ACCOUNTING tab)	These fields allow you to manually calculate a new due date for the A/P invoice at the time it is being generated. (These fields are not active after the A/P invoice is added.) You may specify a number of months or days to recalculate the due date as of the POSTING DATE of the document. You may also from choose one of the predefined, commonly used recalculation periods as follows: ▸ MONTH END ▸ HALF MONTH ▸ MONTH START
CASH DISCOUNT DATE OFFSET (ACCOUNTING tab)	You may specify an offset of the usual payment terms using this field. For example, if the customer normally gets a 2% discount for paying within 15 days, entering a value of "5" in this field will extend these terms for 5 more days (to 20 days total for the 2% discount). You can also enter a zero or a negative number in this field, thereby maintaining or shortening the normal payment terms.

Table 6.5 Fields of the A/P Invoice (Cont.)

Field	Description/Use
BP PROJECT (ACCOUNTING tab)	By default, this field displays the business partner project, which appears on the business partner master data GENERAL tab for the associated business partner. Alternatively, a different code might be inherited from a base document, or you can specify a different project code at the level of the A/P invoice.
INDICATOR (ACCOUNTING tab)	By default, this field displays the factoring indicator, which appears on the business partner master data GENERAL tab for the associated business partner.
FEDERAL TAX ID (ACCOUNTING tab)	This field displays the tax ID indicated on the business partner record associated with the A/P invoice.
TOTAL DOWN PAYMENT	This field in the footer will show a value if an A/P down payment invoice is associated with the document chain. This amount will be applied against the overall balance of the A/P invoice.

Table 6.5 Fields of the A/P Invoice (Cont.)

6.1.9 A/P Credit Memo

The *A/P credit memo* is the clearing document for the A/P invoice. You would create an A/P credit memo if you received products or services from a vendor that need to be returned or if you need to reverse the transaction of an A/P invoice either partially or completely.

Access the A/P credit memo functionality in SAP Business One by following the menu path PURCHASING – A/P • CREDIT MEMO.

6.1.10 A/P Reserve Invoice

A/P reserve invoices are yet another method to use when you want to pay for purchases prior to receiving them. When using A/P reserve invoices, you will create a G/L transaction in accounting, but no inventory transaction will be performed. You can create an A/P reserve invoice with a zero dollar amount before you receive no-charge items. The A/P reserve invoice is not available for service documents.

Access the A/P reserve invoices functionality in SAP Business One by following the menu path PURCHASING – A/P • RESERVE INVOICE.

Now that we've walked through the purchasing process, let's dig into additional SAP Business One functionality that can speed things up and make transactions easier—such as the recurring transactions and templates.

6.2   Recurring Transactions and Templates

Recurring transactions are a great time-saver for business transactions that repeat periodically. You can define templates for recurring transactions using sales or purchasing document drafts. The templates would contain information such as the business partner, items, accounting, and shipping information.

The following recurring transaction types can be created in the purchasing section of SAP Business One:

▶ Purchase requests

▶ Purchase quotations

▶ Purchase orders

▶ Goods receipt POs

▶ Goods returns

▶ A/P down payments

▶ A/P invoices

▶ A/P credit memos

▶ A/P reserve invoices

As an example, let's create a recurring transaction for an A/P invoice that will be used for monthly rent payments. You can apply the principles learned in this example to any other type of recurring transaction that you may want to set up.

Access the recurring transactions functionality by following the menu path PUR-CHASING – A/P • RECURRING TRANSACTIONS.

Figure 6.7 shows the CONFIRMATION OF RECURRING TRANSACTION screen. To begin, click on the TEMPLATES button in the bottom-right corner to create or select an existing template.

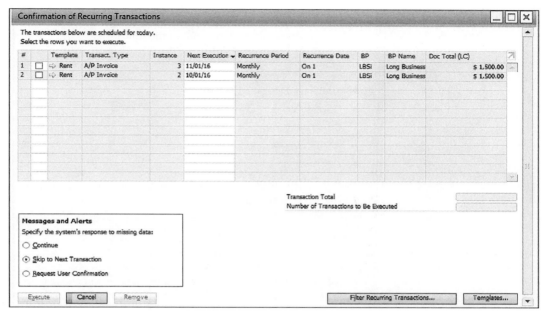

Figure 6.7 Confirmation of Recurring Transactions

The next screen is the RECURRING TRANSACTIONS TEMPLATES screen, as shown in Figure 6.8. You'll populate this screen with the data listed in Table 6.6.

#	Template	Type	Doc No.	Recurrence Period	Recurrence Date	Start Date	Next Exe...	Valid Until	
1	Rent	A/P Invoice	⇨ 93	Monthly	On 1	09/01/16	10/01/16	12/31/20	
2				Monthly	On 1	11/03/16	12/01/16		

Figure 6.8 Recurring Transaction Template

Field	Description/Use
TEMPLATE	Choose an existing template or create a new template by clicking in the TEMPLATE column and entering a template name up to 8 characters long.

Table 6.6 Fields in Recurring Transaction Templates

Field	Description/Use
Type	Select a document type from one of the following: ▶ Purchase Request ▶ Purchase Quotation ▶ Purchase Order ▶ Goods Receipt PO ▶ Goods Return ▶ A/P Down Payment ▶ A/P Invoice ▶ A/P Credit Memo ▶ A/P Reserve Invoice Note that, although you can select sales and inventory type transactions, we are only listing purchasing type templates here.
Doc. No.	Enter or look up a document number to use with this recurring transaction. Click on the Search icon (yellow arrow) to pull up a list of documents that equal the document type you chose in the Type field. You can also create a new document from this window by clicking on the New button. In our example, we created an A/P invoice for monthly rent as shown in Figure 6.9.
Recurrence Period	Select from the following recurrence period options: ▶ Daily ▶ Weekly ▶ Monthly ▶ Quarterly ▶ Semiannually ▶ Annually ▶ One Time
Recurrence Date	Choose the day of the recurrence period for this transaction from the Recurrence Date dropdown list.
Start Date	Enter the start date the recurring transaction.
Next Execution	Enter the date the transaction will next be executed.

Table 6.6 Fields in Recurring Transaction Templates (Cont.)

Let's continue with our task of creating a monthly recurring A/P invoice. Notice that, since we created the template from within the Recurring Transaction window, the words Template – Rent were automatically added to the A/P Invoices document header shown in Figure 6.9. Two other key things happened in the header: The STATUS field changed to DRAFT, and the value in the POSTING DATE field is the date that we entered when creating the A/P invoice.

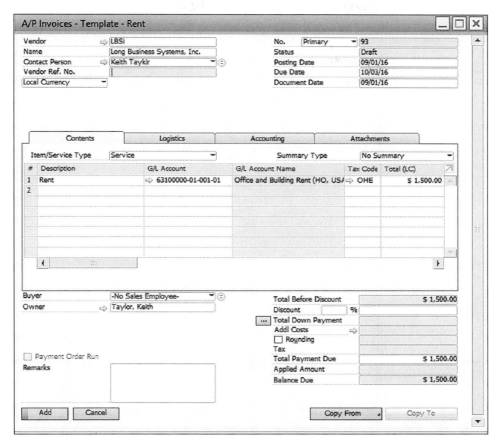

Figure 6.9 A/P Invoice Template for Rent

The RECURRING TRANSACTIONS screen is where you'll review and post recurring transactions that are due to be executed. If there are transactions due, the name of the screen will change from RECURRING TRANSACTIONS to CONFIRMATION OF

RECURRING TRANSACTIONS when you open the screen; the latter is shown in Figure 6.10. Remember that you can access this screen through the menu path PURCHASING – A/P • RECURRING POSTINGS.

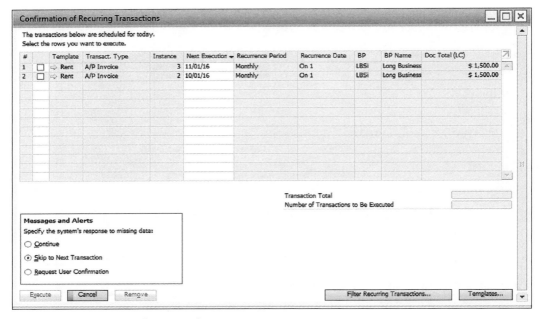

Figure 6.10 Confirmation of Recurring Transactions

Let's walk through the process of executing recurring postings.

1. Select the rows for the transactions that you want to execute. In our example in Figure 6.10, we will execute only one transaction: the A/P invoice template for rent. Note that, for each row, the following data is filled out:

   ▶ TEMPLATE NAME

   ▶ TRANSACTION TYPE (document type)

   ▶ INSTANCE

- NEXT EXECUTION (date)
- RECURRENCE PERIOD
- RECURRENCE DATE
- BP (business partner code)
- BP NAME
- DOC TOTAL (total value of the document for this execution date only)

2. Enter a date in the NEXT EXECUTION field.

3. In the MESSAGES AND ALERTS box, choose how the system should respond to missing data from the available radio buttons:

- CONTINUE
- SKIP TO NEXT TRANSACTION
- REQUEST USER CONFIRMATION

4. Take a look at the TRANSACTION TOTAL field shown on the right side of the screen. This field displays the total of all transactions that you have selected, which in our case is still $1,500.00.

The buttons at the bottom of Figure 6.10 give you a few options for how to proceed:

- EXECUTE: Click this button to post the transaction.
- CANCEL: Click this button to cancel the transaction (does not post).
- REMOVE: To remove a posting, select the row you want to remove and click REMOVE.
- FILTER RECURRING TRANSACTIONS: Select which documents you want to display on this screen.
- TEMPLATES: Access a list of all templates and create others if needed.

Once you've executed the postings, you'll receive a confirmation message displaying the transactions that posted, any errors, and related information. You can further review the postings by clicking on the golden arrow for any of the transactions.

6.3   Landed Costs

When importing goods from other countries, you'll likely incur additional costs, such as customs, transportation costs, insurance fees, and taxes. These additional costs, called *landed costs*, can be allocated to the imported items and reflected in the accounting system using the landed costs feature in SAP Business One. Before you can use landed costs, though, you have to first define measurements for imported goods and assign the goods to a customs group. Customs groups can be created on the CUSTOMS GROUPS SETUP screen shown in Figure 6.11 and accessed by following the menu path ADMINISTRATION • SETUP • INVENTORY • CUSTOMS GROUPS.

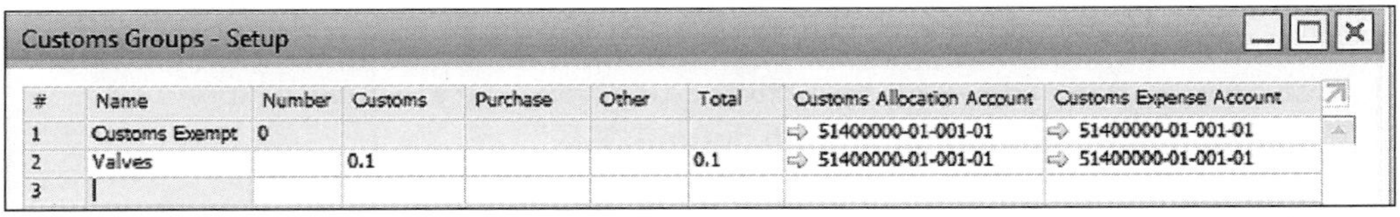

#	Name	Number	Customs	Purchase	Other	Total	Customs Allocation Account	Customs Expense Account
1	Customs Exempt	0					⇨ 51400000-01-001-01	⇨ 51400000-01-001-01
2	Valves		0.1			0.1	⇨ 51400000-01-001-01	⇨ 51400000-01-001-01
3								

Figure 6.11 Customs Group Setup

After assigning customs groups, you'll need to assign the items being imported to their respective customs group on the ITEM MASTER screen shown in Figure 6.12. The menu path for this screen is INVENTORY • ITEM MASTER • PURCHASING DATA tab. At the bottom of our example, you can see that VALVES is an option for the CUSTOMS GROUP dropdown list.

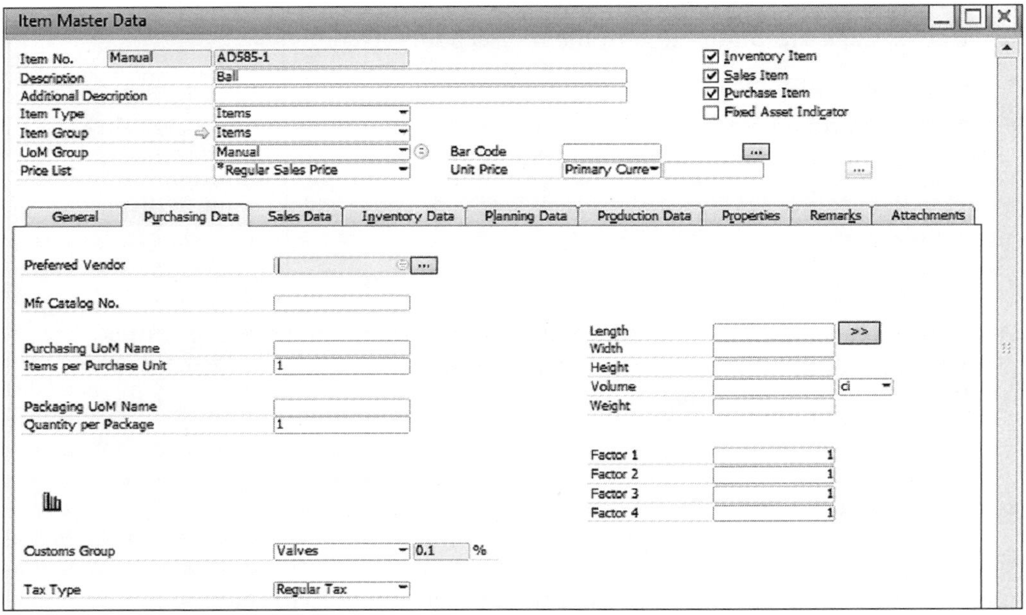

Figure 6.12 Item Master Data Customs Group

In order to use landed costs, you must have already defined landed cost types and G/L accounts for landed costs (by following the menu path ADMINISTRATION • SETUP • PURCHASING • LANDED COSTS). Access the LANDED COSTS SETUP maintenance screen shown in Figure 6.13 by following the menu path PURCHASING – A/P • LANDED COSTS.

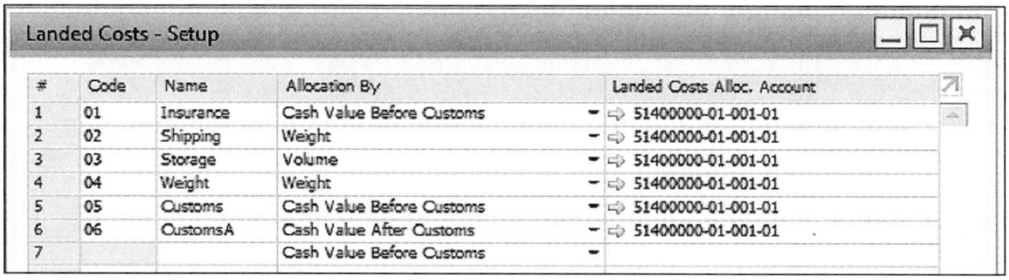

#	Code	Name	Allocation By	Landed Costs Alloc. Account
1	01	Insurance	Cash Value Before Customs	51400000-01-001-01
2	02	Shipping	Weight	51400000-01-001-01
3	03	Storage	Volume	51400000-01-001-01
4	04	Weight	Weight	51400000-01-001-01
5	05	Customs	Cash Value Before Customs	51400000-01-001-01
6	06	CustomsA	Cash Value After Customs	51400000-01-001-01
7			Cash Value Before Customs	

Figure 6.13 Landed Costs Setup

Now that landed costs have been set up, we can begin to use them. Let's walk through the LANDED COST screen tab by tab.

6.3.1 Items Tab

The first step of creating a landed cost transaction includes filling out some header information and fields in the ITEMS tab. Note that most of the information on this tab can be populated by using the COPY FROM button and copying from a PO goods receipt, an A/P invoice, or another LANDED COST screen (as seen in Figure 6.14).

Tips and Tricks: The Add Button

Do not click the ADD button until the required information is entered on all of the tabs. The ADD button will create a G/L transaction and adjust the inventory cost for the items to reflect the total cost on the PO goods receipt plus each item's share of the additional charges on the landed cost transaction.

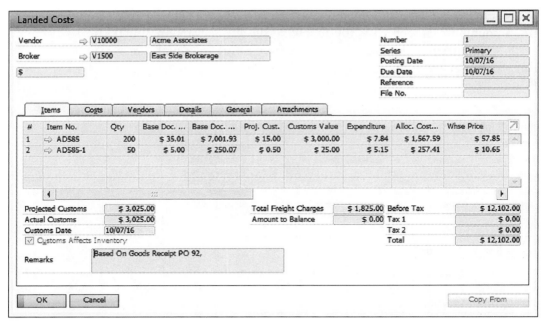

Figure 6.14 Landed Costs Items Tab

The ITEMS tab of the LANDED COST screen has many fields to fill out, so let's explore key fields for creating a landed costs transaction in Table 6.7.

Field	Description/Use
VENDOR	Select the vendor you purchased the product from.
BROKER	Select a broker.
NUMBER	This field refers to the landed cost document number, which is autopopulated by the system.
SERIES	Enter the series number.
POSTING DATA	This field contains the posting data, which is autopopulated by the system.
DUE DATE	Enter the due date.
REFERENCE NUMBER	Enter a reference number if desired.
FILE NO.	Enter a file number if desired.
ITEM NO.	Enter the item number.
QTY.	Enter the quantity.

Table 6.7 Fields of the Landed Costs Items Tab

Field	Description/Use
BASE DOC.	This field refers to the unit price cost, which is autopopulated by the system.
BASE DOC.	This field refers to extended price cost, which is autopopulated by the system.
PROJECTED CUSTOMS FEE	This field defaults to percentage from the customs group assigned to each item.
CUSTOMS VALUE	This field displays the extended customs value based on the quantity received multiplied by the projected customs fee.
EXPENDITURE	This field displays the expenses for each item as calculated in this document.
ALLOCATED COST	This field displays the value of landed costs allocated to this item row.
PROJECTED CUSTOMS TOTAL	This field displays a number based on the total of all items on this landed cost transaction.
ACTUAL CUSTOMS FEE	This field displays a number based on the total of all items on this landed cost transaction.
CUSTOMS DATE	Enter the date the line cleared customs.
TOTAL FREIGHT CHARGES	This field displays a number based on the sum of the (expenditure multiplied by quantity) for all lines.
AMOUNT TO BALANCE	This field shows the difference between the sum of amounts on the COSTS tab and the total freight charges value on the ITEMS tab.
TOTAL BEFORE TAX	This field displays the total before tax.
TAX 1	This field displays one level of tax if used.
TAX 2	This field displays a second level of tax if used.
TOTAL INCLUDING TAX	This field displays the grand total including taxes.
CUSTOMS AFFECTS INVENTORY	Select this checkbox if customs fees affect the inventory value. This field is only available for companies managing perpetual inventory.
COPY FROM	Use this button to copy a PO goods receipt, an A/P invoice, or the information in another LANDED COST screen.

Table 6.7 Fields of the Landed Costs Items Tab (Cont.)

6.3.2   Costs Tab

The COSTS tab shown in Figure 6.15 is used to enter the various fixed or variable costs for the landed cost transaction.

Note the two subtabs on this screen: the FIXED COSTS tab is enabled if you're using perpetual inventory. The VARIABLE COSTS tab is enabled when you're not using perpetual inventory.

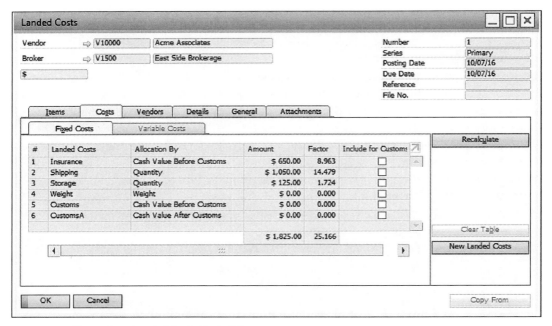

Figure 6.15 Landed Costs Costs Tab

Let's walk through the remaining fields that are shown in the FIXED COSTS subtab in Table 6.8.

Field	Description/Use
LANDED COSTS	This field displays the type of landed cost expense.
ALLOCATION BY	Choose from one of the following allocation options: ▶ CASH VALUE BEFORE CUSTOMS ▶ CASH VALUE AFTER CUSTOMS ▶ QUANTITY ▶ WEIGHT ▶ VOLUME ▶ EQUAL

Table 6.8 Fields of the Landed Costs Fixed Costs Tab

Field	Description/Use
AMOUNT	This field displays the total cost for this expenditure, which is autopopulated by the system.
FACTOR	This field displays the percentage of the total FOB costs of the shipment.
INCLUDE FOR CUSTOMS	Select this checkbox to INCLUDE FOR CUSTOMS.
AMOUNT	The bottom of the AMOUNT column displays the total expenditure amount.
FACTOR	The bottom of the FACTOR column displays the total percentage all lines of the FOB costs of the shipment.

Table 6.8 Fields of the Landed Costs Fixed Costs Tab (Cont.)

When you're done, choose from these three buttons:

▶ RECALCULATE: This button recalculates the landed costs amounts if you updated any values in the table.

▶ CLEAR TABLE: This button resets all table amounts and changes the allocation amounts back to their original default values.

▶ NEW LANDED COSTS: This button is used to add additional landed cost expenditure types to the LANDED COST SETUP screen.

6.3.3 Vendors Tab

The VENDORS tab includes vendor information for all vendors attached to a landed cost. The vendor information will be populated automatically when adding a PO goods receipt or other document.

6.3.4 Details Tab

This tab contains detailed information about each item associated with a landed cost, including items, the warehouse price, the price list, and expenditures, as shown in Figure 6.16.

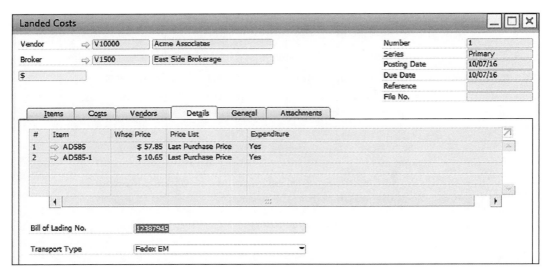

Figure 6.16 Landed Costs Details Tab

Let's walk through some key fields in the DETAILS tab in Table 6.9.

Field	Description/Use
ITEM	This field is populated automatically based on the master item record
WHSE PRICE	In this field, the warehouse price is calculated for a single imported item after all landed costs are allocated.
PRICE LIST	Specify the price list that you want to update with the item price and landed costs.
EXPENDITURE	Choose either YES or NO. If no costs should be allocated to this row, choose NO.
BILL OF LADING NO.	Enter a bill of lading number as a reference.
TRANSPORT TYPE	Specify a shipping method in this field.

Table 6.9 Fields of the Landed Costs Details Tab

6.3.5 General Tab

This tab is only available if your company is using perpetual inventory. This tab contains the golden arrow drilldown functionality into the journal entry that was created when this landed cost transaction was added.

6.3.6 Attachments Tab

The ATTACHMENTS tab can be used to attach documents to this screen.

6.4 Procurement Confirmation Wizard

The Procurement Confirmation Wizard is a tool that SAP Business One provides that allows you to create purchasing documents (purchase orders, purchase quotations, or purchase requests) and production orders based on sales quotations or sales orders. The wizard contains several steps that will allow you to select certain business partners, certain documents and document types, specify delivery dates, consolidate similar items to one vendor, and print the documents at the same time if desired. Access the Procurement Confirmation Wizard by following the menu path PURCHASING – A/P • PURCHASE CONFIRMATION WIZARD.

Let's walk through the steps for creating purchasing documents using this wizard:

1. In the BASE DOCUMENT TYPE AND CUSTOMERS screen of the wizard shown in Figure 6.17, select the customers to review and the type of document (a sales quotation or a sales order) you want to process.

   ▶ Select the base document from the BASE DOC. dropdown list. Our example in Figure 6.17 uses a sales order.

   ▶ Click the CLEAR TABLE button to the left of the table to remove the selected business partners on the screen and then select a checkbox in the column for the corresponding business partners you want to consider during the procurement confirmation process. Click ADD.

   ▶ Select the INCLUDE ALL OPEN BASE DOCUMENTS checkbox for the selected business partners.

   After you have made your selections, click NEXT.

2. The next screen of the Procurement Confirmation Wizard is the BASE DOCUMENTS screen shown in Figure 6.18. In this screen, you identify which base documents you want to select and process in the wizard. The table displays the base documents of the customers that were selected in the previous step.

   You have two main options here: You can either select the GO TO THE FINAL STEP checkbox to jump ahead (perhaps you had someone first create the wizard, and then another user wanted to review and just go to the final step to finalize the wizard) or click NEXT to move on to the next step in the wizard.

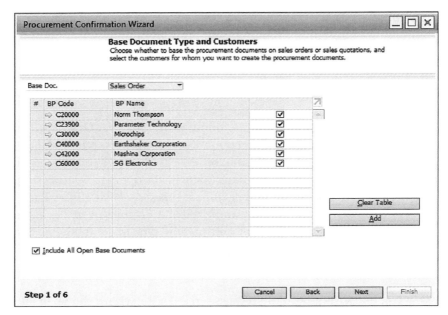

Figure 6.17 Choosing Base Document Type and Customers (Step 1 of the Wizard)

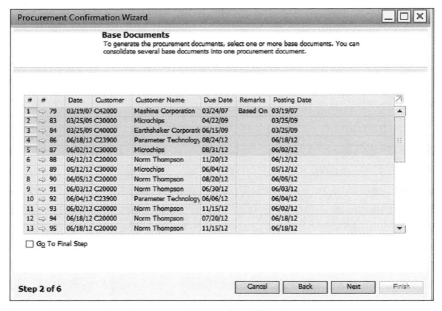

Figure 6.18 Select Base Documents (Step 2 of the Wizard)

3. In Step 3 of the wizard shown in the Base Document Line Items screen in Figure 6.19, we'll get into the details.

- ▸ In the Target Document dropdown list, choose from among the following types of target documents: Purchase Request, Purchase Quotation, Purchase Order, and Production Order.

- ▸ Select the vendor in the Vendor field; the Name field will display that vendor's name.

- ▸ Select either the Print Target Documents checkbox to print your target documents as each one is created or select the Create Draft Documents checkbox. *Draft documents* allow you to review and assure everything is correct on each document before you click Add.

- ▸ From the Target Doc. Series dropdown list, select the target document series to be used when creating documents. In our example, we've chosen Primary for this value.

- ▸ For the Delivery Date field, select a date to be used when creating the documents from the calendar on the right.

- ▸ Select the items by highlighting the rows that will be used when creating the documents and then click Next to move to the next step of the wizard.

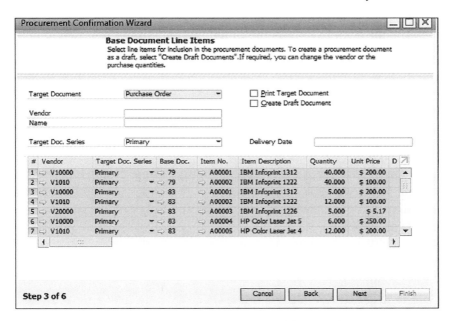

Figure 6.19 Select Base Document Line Items (Step 3 of the Wizard)

4. The fourth step of the Procurement Confirmation Wizard consolidates base documents into a single procurement document.

You have a few important options in this window, as shown in Figure 6.20. If you select NO CONSOLIDATION, the documents are grouped by vendor, and one document is created for each vendor and sales documents. If you select CONSOLIDATE BY, you can make further specifications:

▸ If you put a checkmark in the VENDOR (SYSTEM DEFAULT) box, then the documents are grouped by vendor, and one purchase order is created per vendor.

▸ If you put a checkmark in the TARGET DOC. SERIES (SYSTEM DEFAULT) box, then the documents are grouped by the target document series.

▸ If you put a checkmark in the WAREHOUSE (SPLIT BY) box, then the documents are grouped by the warehouse that ships the items. If multiple warehouses are on the same sales document, one procurement document will be created for each warehouse.

Notice the blank fields below WAREHOUSE (SPLIT BY). You can also consolidate by the following items: DELIVERY DATES, SHIPPING TYPE, SHIP-TO-ADDRESS, LANGUAGE, SERIES, POSTING DATE, BP REFERENCE NO., DOCUMENT CURRENCY, and PROJECT CODE.

Take a look at the IF AN ERROR OCCURS dropdown list. Make a selection to help the system know how to proceed; in our example in Figure 6.20, we've chosen SKIP TO THE NEXT VENDOR.

After you have made your selections, click NEXT.

5. Step 5 of the wizard involves the PREVIEW RESULTS window shown in Figure 6.21; in this window, you'll preview the results that the system has generated based on your parameters.

▸ The header will summarize the details about the target document, vendor, document series, and delivery date, but you can drill down into or out of the results shown in the table using the EXPAND and COLLAPSE buttons, respectively.

▸ Click NEXT to create the documents. You'll receive a message asking you to confirm that you want to create the documents.

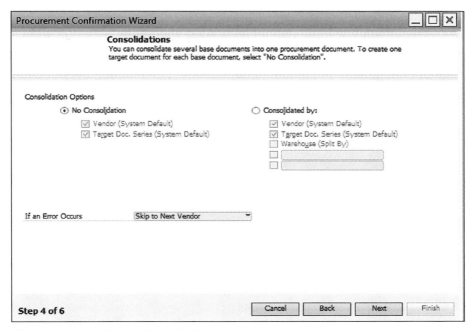

Figure 6.20 Consolidations (Step 4 of the Wizard)

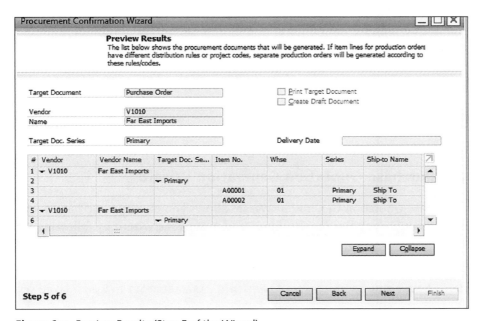

Figure 6.21 Preview Results (Step 5 of the Wizard)

6. The final step of the Procurement Confirmation Wizard is shown in the SUMMARY REPORT window displayed in Figure 6.22. The results of the documents you created and any errors will be displayed on this screen in the SUMMARY REPORT window.

▸ You can drill down into the individual documents to review them using the golden arrows on the left side of the screen in the MESSAGE column.

▸ Click on the CLOSE button to exit the wizard.

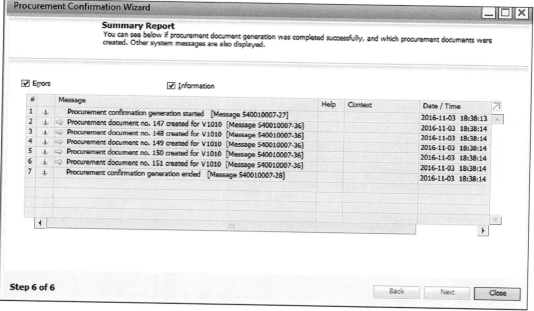

Figure 6.22 Summary Report (Step 6 of the Wizard)

6.5   Purchase Quotation Generation Wizard

The Purchase Quotation Generation Wizard allows you to create purchase quotations for multiple vendors for the same item(s). Start the wizard by following the menu path PURCHASING – A/P • PURCHASE QUOTATION GENERATION WIZARD.

1. To create this purchase quotation, begin by selecting NEW PARAMETER SET to start a brand new parameter set or EXISTING PARAMETER SET to load a saved set.

Once you fill out the SET NAME and DESCRIPTION fields shown in Figure 6.23, click NEXT.

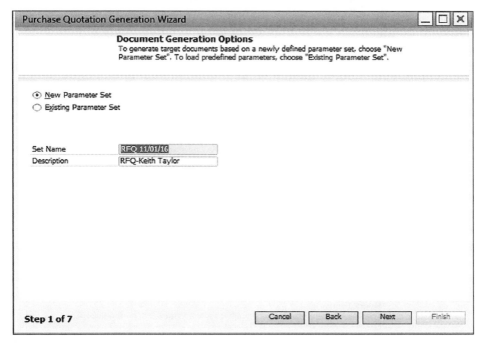

Figure 6.23 Document Generation Options (Step 1 of the Wizard)

2. Choose either the BASE ON ITEMS or the BASE ON PURCHASE REQUESTS radio button, as shown in Figure 6.24. Depending on your selection, the system will provide different prompts. If you selected ITEMS, you'll be prompted for details of the items; if you chose to base your quote on PURCHASE REQUESTS, the system will require information on the PURCHASE REQUESTS you'll be copying from.

   Enter the required information and click NEXT.

3. Now let's choose the items. You also have the option to select open purchase requests that other users may have created. In our example shown in Figure 6.25, let's choose ITEMS. Enter or choose the items and quantities and enter the required date and how long you would like the quotation to be valid for.

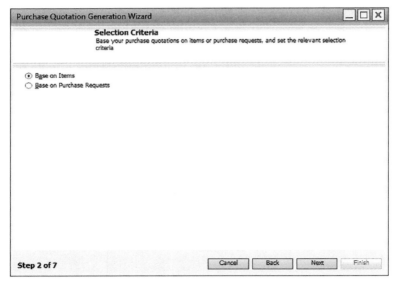

Figure 6.24 Selection Criteria (Step 2 of the Wizard)

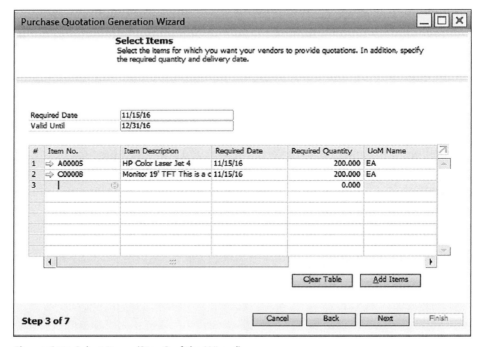

Figure 6.25 Select Items (Step 3 of the Wizard)

4. The next step is to choose the vendors. The system will display preferred vendors for the items you have selected, but you can add additional vendors as necessary. Select whether you want to group by business partner or by item and update the values in corresponding fields if desired. When you're done, click NEXT (see Figure 6.26).

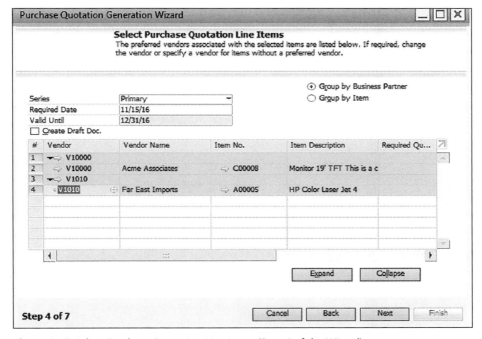

Figure 6.26 Select Purchase Quotation Line Items (Step 4 of the Wizard)

5. The next screen shown in Figure 6.27 will display the vendors and the items that will be included on the purchase requests. Review these and click NEXT to continue.

6. Select EXECUTE, SAVE PARAMETER SET AND EXECUTE, or SAVE PARAMETER SET AND EXIT and then choose whether to create an online quotation or a print quotation from the CREATE ONLINE QUOTATION or PRINT QUOTATIONS options. The screen shown in Figure 6.28 will display the set's name and description. Choose how you want to handle errors and then click NEXT. To continue, click YES; to stop the process, click NO.

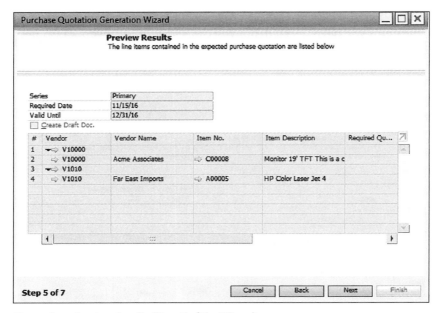

Figure 6.27 Preview Results (Step 5 of the Wizard)

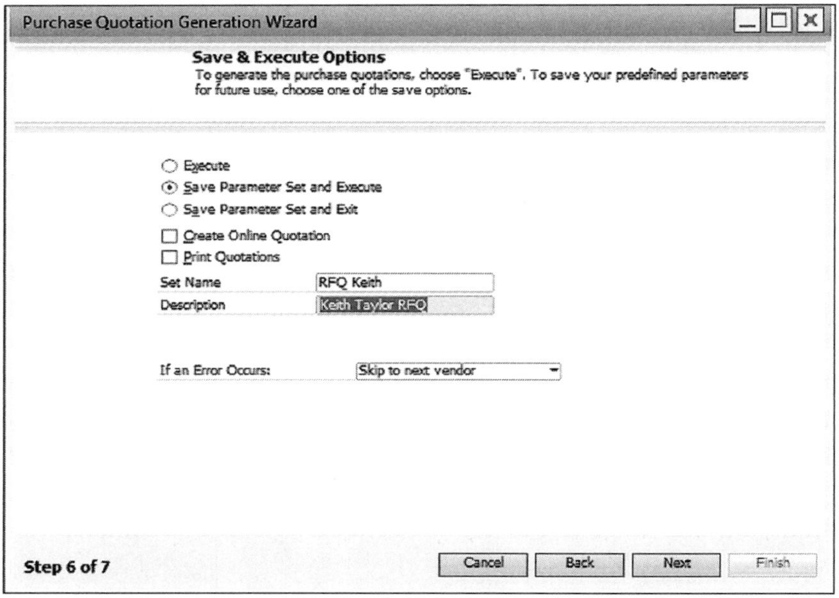

Figure 6.28 Save and Execute Options (Step 6 of the Wizard)

7. Finally, the SUMMARY REPORT screen shown in Figure 6.29 will show the purchase quotations and information that were generated. The system will display any errors encountered. You can drill down into the purchase quotation using the golden arrow to take a closer look. Click CLOSE to exit the wizard.

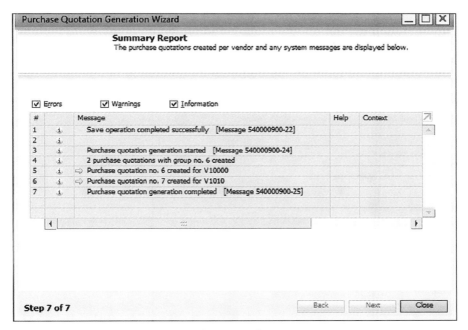

Figure 6.29 Summary Report (Step 7 of the Wizard)

6.6   Document Printing

The DOCUMENT PRINTING screen shown in Figure 6.30 is used to print documents en masse rather than printing them one at a time or having SAP Business One auto-print the document when you click the ADD button during document creation.

The DOCUMENT PRINTING screen allows you to print documents of all types, and its selection capabilities enable you to refine the printing down to certain date ranges, statuses, number of copies, and other information. (Of course, the selection fields change depending on which document you select to print!)

Although you can use this screen to print most documents, we'll focus on A/P invoice documents where the fields are representative of most of the purchasing document screens. You should be able to print other documents from this same screen by following the principles you learned when performing document printing for the A/P invoices.

To begin, follow the menu path PURCHASING – A/P • DOCUMENT PRINTING. As we've done throughout this chapter, let's walk through the fields displayed in Figure 6.30 in Table 6.10.

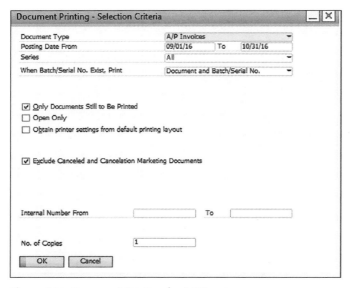

Figure 6.30 Document Printing for A/P Invoices

Field	Description/Use
DOCUMENT TYPE	Select the document type that you want to print.
POSTING DATE FROM	This field allows you to select a date range of documents; for example, on the current screen, we are going to select all documents for the months of September and October.
SERIES	Select the particular series you want to print or accept ALL as the default to print documents for all series.
WHEN BATCH/ SERIAL NO. EXIST, PRINT	Choose one of the following to tell the system what to do when both a batch number and a serial number exist: ▸ DOCUMENT AND BATCH/SERIAL NO. ▸ DOCUMENT ONLY ▸ BATCH/SERIAL NO. ONLY

Table 6.10 Fields for A/P Invoice Document Printing

Field	Description/Use
ONLY DOCUMENTS STILL TO BE PRINTED	Select this checkbox to print only documents that haven't yet been printed.
OPEN ONLY	Select this checkbox to print only documents that are open.
OBTAIN PRINTER SETTINGS FROM DEFAULT PRINTING LAYOUT	Select this checkbox to apply the default print layout's printer settings.
EXCLUDE CANCELED AND CANCELATION MARKETING DOCUMENTS	Select this checkbox to exclude canceled or cancelation marketing documents; any canceled document matching the document type you selected in from the DOCUMENT TYPE dropdown list at the top of the screen will be ignored.
INTERNAL NUMBER FROM	This field allows you to select certain internal documents
NO. OF COPIES	Enter the number of copies to print for each document. In our example, we're only printing one.

Table 6.10 Fields for A/P Invoice Document Printing (Cont.)

When you're done, click on the OK button to print the documents selected.

6.7 Purchasing Reports

Several purchasing reports are included in SAP Business One. Most of the reports have a selection screen with options, allowing you to take one report and turn it into many different reports using the selection criteria fields. Access the PURCHASING REPORTS menu by following the menu path PURCHASING – A/P • PURCHASING REPORTS.

6.7.1 Open Items List Report

Like many report screens in SAP Business One, the Open Items List Report allows you to run many different reports from one screen. The OPEN ITEMS LIST screen allows you to view or print a report of almost all open documents by selecting the appropriate documents from the dropdown list.

You can view and print the open items list for the following different purchasing documents, among others:

- ▶ Purchase requests
- ▶ Purchase quotations (shown in Figure 6.31)

- Purchase orders (shown in Figure 6.32)
- Goods receipt POs
- Goods returns
- A/P down payments (unpaid)
- A/P down payments (not yet fully applied)
- A/P invoices (shown in Figure 6.33)
- A/P credit memos
- A/P reserve invoices (unpaid)
- A/P reserve invoices (not yet delivered)

To access the Open Items List Report, follow the menu path PURCHASING – A/P • PURCHASING REPORTS • OPEN ITEMS LIST.

Tips and Tricks: Open Items List

Open items lists are used for more than just reporting. Since the golden arrows are available on the documents, you can use the screens like a to-do list. For instance:

- A list of open goods receipt POs shows all your purchase order receipts that you have not yet received the vendor's invoice for.
- A list of open goods returns shows all open returns that you should consider creating A/P credit memos for.
- A list of open purchase quotations shows all outstanding purchase quotes where vendors have not yet gotten back to you with the cost and delivery information. Click on the golden arrow and use this screen to expedite responses from your vendor(s) right from this screen.
- A list of open A/P down payments shows all payments that you have paid vendors in advance of receiving products or services that you have not yet received.

Figure 6.31, Figure 6.32, and Figure 6.33 display a few open items report samples to give you some examples. Some features these samples all have in common include the following:

- These open items lists generally include information at the header level and do not show item details.
- These open items lists will include totals of things such as total purchase quotations gross, net, and total taxes.

▶ These open items lists can be viewed easily in different currencies using the CURRENCY field in the top-left corner.

▶ You do not have any selection options; these reports simply list all of the open documents of a particular type.

▶ You can down drill into more detail using the golden arrows on the left side of the screen.

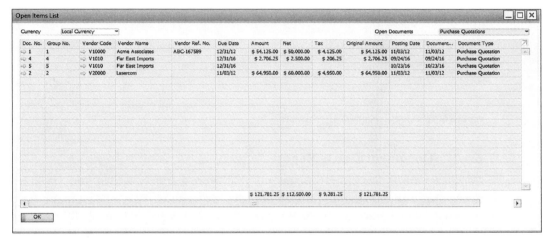

Figure 6.31 Open Items List: Purchase Quotations

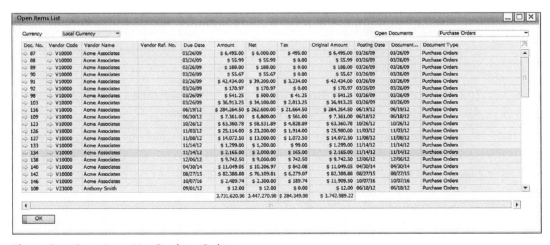

Figure 6.32 Open Items List: Purchase Orders

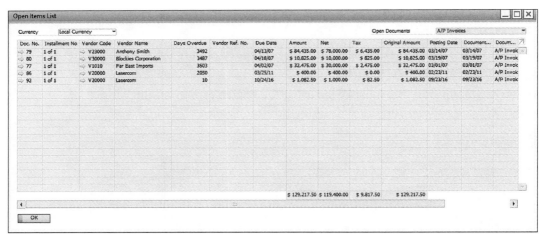

Figure 6.33 Open Items List: A/P Invoices

6.7.2 Document Drafts Report

Document drafts are either documents that were partially added and saved as drafts or documents that require an approval procedure. A saved document draft is stored in a separate area of SAP Business One and is only accessible by running the Document Drafts Report.

The first step is to choose the drafts that you want to review and then review the documents and add each one you want added as a permanent document. The Document Drafts Report can be used to view purchasing, sales, inventory, and inventory counting drafts. In our examples, we'll focus on the purchasing drafts, although you can follow the same procedures to view any document draft.

To begin creating a Document Drafts Report, follow the menu path PURCHASING – A/P • PURCHASING REPORTS • DOCUMENT DRAFTS REPORT.

To print the Document Drafts Report in order to review the drafts and add the documents as permanent documents, we'll walk through the key fields shown in Figure 6.34 in Table 6.11.

Figure 6.34 Document Drafts Report

Field	Description/Use
USER	Select one particular user or all users.
OPEN ONLY	Select this checkbox to view/display only drafts that are open.
DATE	Select this checkbox to choose documents for a specific date range. For the dropdown list beside the DATE checkbox, select one of the following: ▶ CREATION DATE ▶ DATE OF UPDATE ▶ POSTING DATE ▶ VALUE DATE ▶ DOCUMENT DATE
FROM	When the DATE checkbox is selected, the FROM (starting) date field is visible. Enter the first date to be considered in the report.
TO	When the DATE checkbox is selected, the To (ending) date field is visible. Enter the last date to be considered in the report.
SALES A/R	Select which sales documents to view.

Table 6.11 Fields for Document Drafts Report

Field	Description/Use
PURCHASING A/P	Select which purchasing documents to view.
INVENTORY	Select which inventory documents to view.
INVENTORY COUNTING TRANSACTIONS	Select which inventory counting documents to view.

Table 6.11 Fields for Document Drafts Report (Cont.)

Each draft that was selected in Table 6.11 is shown on the DOCUMENT DRAFTS PRE-VIEW SCREEN shown in Figure 6.35. When you click on the corresponding golden arrow, the draft document is displayed.

Two key things to note here: the reference to the draft status and the document number. Note that, if and when this document is added, SAP Business One will assign a permanent document number that most likely will not correlate to the one shown in our example on the screen.

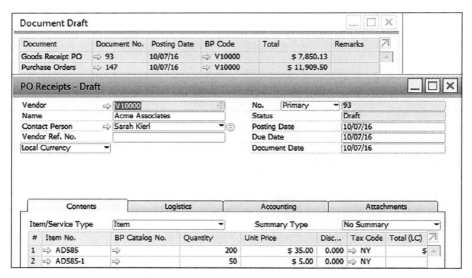

Figure 6.35 Document Drafts Report and Preview Screen

6.7.3 Purchase Analysis Report

The PURCHASE ANALYSIS REPORT selection screen allows you to specify selection criteria for the Purchasing Analysis Report. The screen consists of three tabs: the

VENDORS tab in Figure 6.36, the ITEMS tab in Figure 6.37, and the SALES EMPLOYEES tab in Figure 6.38.

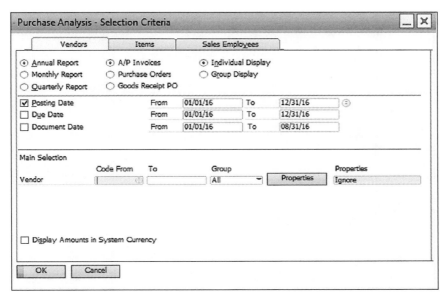

Figure 6.36 Purchase Analysis Vendors Tab

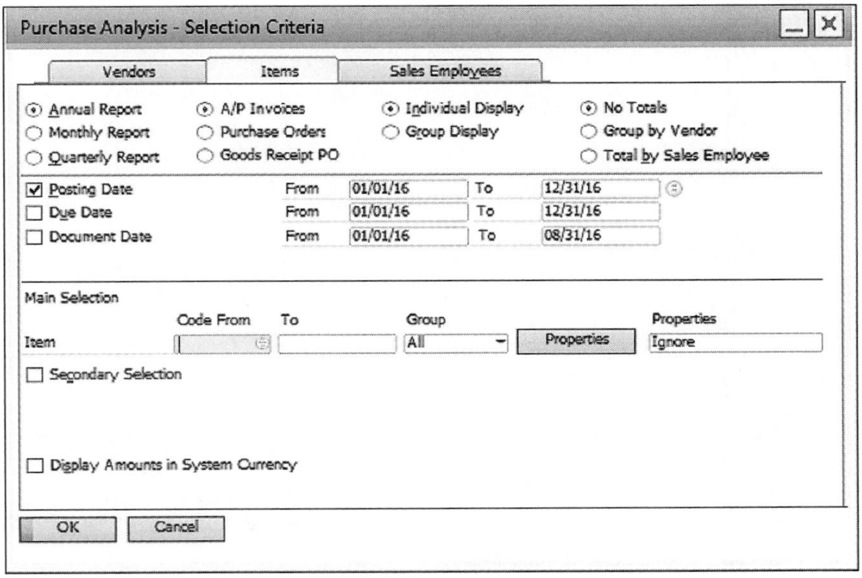

Figure 6.37 Purchase Analysis Items Tab

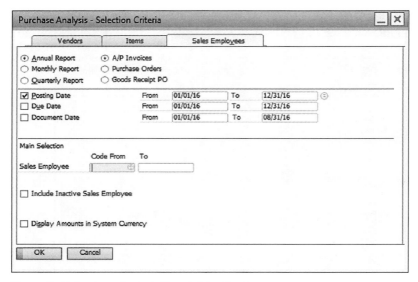

Figure 6.38 Purchase Analysis Report Sales Employees

Each tab contains selection fields that allow you to customize the report for your specific requirements, such as the following:

▸ Type of report (annual, monthly, quarterly)

▸ Type of document (purchase orders, PO goods receipts, or A/P Invoices)

▸ Date type and ranges

▸ One vendor, a range of vendors, or all vendors

▸ One vendor group, all vendor groups, or certain vendor GROUPS

▸ One or more vendor properties

▸ One item, a range of items, or all items

▸ One item group, a range of item groups, or all item groups

▸ One or more item properties

▸ One sales employee (buyer) or a range of sales employees (buyers)

To begin creating a Purchase Analysis Report, follow the menu path PURCHASING – A/P • PURCHASING REPORTS • PURCHASE ANALYSIS REPORT.

Let's look briefly at some sample reports that can be generated from the PUR-CHASE ANALYSIS REPORT selection screen.

Figure 6.39 shows the Purchase Analysis by Vendors Report with a monthly view. The report summarizes purchases by vendor, sorted by vendor, with the total purchased for each month. Double-click on any line item to show its detail and a graph of purchases for each vendor on the report. This report is helpful for determining what your total purchases are for each of your vendors.

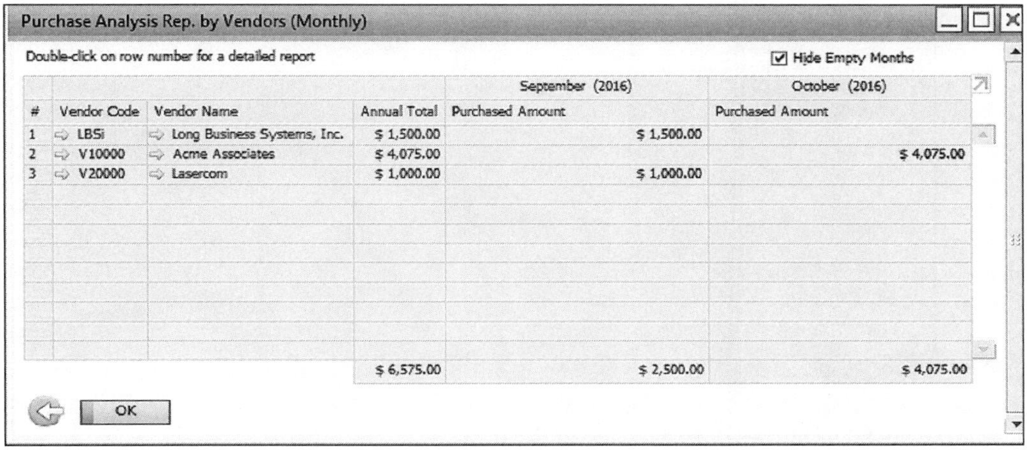

Figure 6.39 Purchase Analysis Report by Vendors (Monthly)

Figure 6.40 shows the Purchase Analysis by Item Report with a monthly view. The report summarizes purchases by item and is sorted by item. Double-click on each line item to see its detailed transactions and a graph. This report is useful to quickly see what your total purchases are for an item for a particular month.

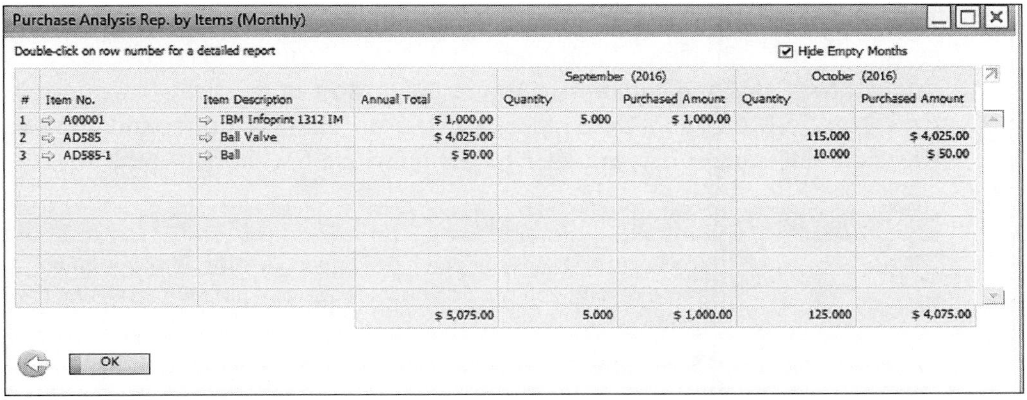

Figure 6.40 Purchase Analysis Report by Items (Monthly)

Figure 6.41 shows Purchase Analysis by Item Report with a yearly view, sorted by item. Double-click on each line item to view the item's details and a graph. This report is great for showing items purchased, but in our example, this report is based on total purchases for a year.

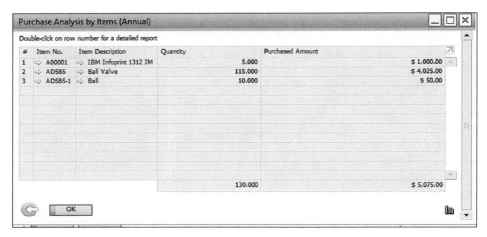

Figure 6.41 Purchase Analysis Report by Items (Annual)

6.7.4 Purchase Request Report

The Purchase Request Report is really much more than a report; the selection screen generates an interactive onscreen report that can be used to review purchase requests and then ultimately turn the purchase requests into purchase quotations or purchase orders.

To begin, access the Purchase Request Report by following the menu path PURCHASING – A/P • PURCHASING REPORTS • PURCHASE REQUEST REPORT. Let's walk through the fields and columns in Figure 6.42. Most of the fields here such as ITEM CODE, BP CATALOG NO., ITEM DESCRIPTION, VENDOR CODE, and VENDOR NAME are self-explanatory, but we'll follow up with a few more in Table 6.12.

Field	Description/Use
PR NO.	This field contains the purchase request number. If you require more details, you can drill down to the purchase request using the golden arrow.
ONLINE QUOTATION	Select this checkbox to create an online quotation.

Table 6.12 Fields for Purchase Request Report

Field	Description/Use
TARGET PRICE	This field displays the target price for this item.
DISCOUNT %	This field displays the discount for this item.
GROUP BY VENDOR or GROUP BY ITEM	Select either the GROUP BY VENDOR or the GROUP BY ITEM radio button to organize your purchase requests.
PRINT TARGET DOCUMENTS	Select this checkbox to print the target documents after they are created.

Table 6.12 Fields for Purchase Request Report (Cont.)

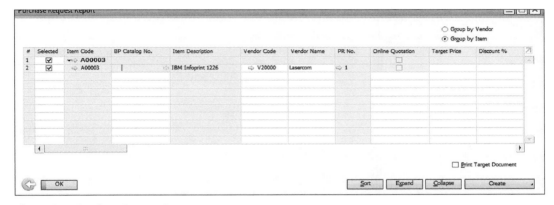

Figure 6.42 Purchase Request Report

When you're done, choose from one of the buttons shown at the bottom of Figure 6.42:

▸ SORT: Opens the PURCHASE REQUEST SORT table, which gives you several options for sorting the purchase requests.

▸ EXPAND: Expands the list.

▸ COLLAPSE: Collapses the list.

▸ CREATE: Creates purchase quotations or purchase orders for the line items selected.

6.7.5 Blanket Agreement Fulfillment Report

The Blanket Agreement Fulfillment Report compares blanket agreements to the purchase orders to help you determine whether the agreements need to be extended and to generally analyze purchases and rebate statuses.

Access the report by following the menu path PURCHASING – A/P • PURCHASING REPORTS • BLANKET AGREEMENT FULFILLMENT REPORT. A sample of the report is shown in Figure 6.43.

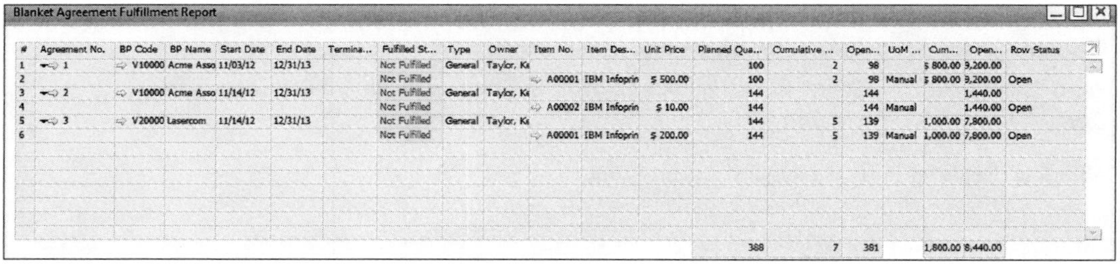

#	Agreement No.	BP Code	BP Name	Start Date	End Date	Termina...	Fulfilled St...	Type	Owner	Item No.	Item Des...	Unit Price	Planned Qua...	Cumulative ...	Open...	UoM ...	Cum...	Open...	Row Status
1	1	V10000	Acme Asso	11/03/12	12/31/13		Not Fulfilled	General	Taylor, Ki				100	2	98		$800.00	9,200.00	
2							Not Fulfilled			A00001	IBM Infoprin	$500.00	100	2	98	Manual	$800.00	9,200.00	Open
3	2	V10000	Acme Asso	11/14/12	12/31/13		Not Fulfilled	General	Taylor, Ki				144		144			1,440.00	
4							Not Fulfilled			A00002	IBM Infoprin	$10.00	144		144	Manual		1,440.00	Open
5	3	V20000	Lasercom	11/14/12	12/31/13		Not Fulfilled	General	Taylor, Ki				144	5	139		1,000.00	7,800.00	
6							Not Fulfilled			A00001	IBM Infoprin	$200.00	144	5	139	Manual	1,000.00	7,800.00	Open
													388	7	381		1,800.00	8,440.00	

Figure 6.43 Blanket Agreement Fulfillment Report

Managing relationships with business partners is critical to customer and vendor acquisition, retention, and satisfaction while fostering opportunities to drive revenue, control cost, maximize cash flow, and, in the for-profit sector, profitability.

7　Business Partners

Let's turn our attention to the processes that administer your business partner relationships. The Business Partners module manages all the information relevant for your relationship with customers, vendors, and leads. This module provides a foundation for customer relationship management (CRM) by giving you many ways to categorize, segment, and identify customers during the setup stage. Similarly, supply chain management (SCM) is facilitated with the many fields associated with the vendor. The strategic tools in your arsenal include master data, activities, campaigns, reports, and internal reconciliations for business partners.

In this chapter, we'll discuss the SAP Business One tasks and transactions that enable relationship management. In this chapter, you'll explore the strategic relationship toolkit available to you in SAP Business One to set up master records and execute business processes via these menu options: BUSINESS PARTNER MASTER DATA, ACTIVITY, CAMPAIGN GENERATION WIZARD, CAMPAIGN, INTERNAL RECONCILIATION, and BUSINESS PARTNER REPORTS.

> **Tips and Tricks: Business Partner Master Data Display**
>
> The BUSINESS PARTNER MASTER DATA display contains several icons that can guide you through the data and tables.
>
> First, the black down arrow indicates a dropdown list. The LIST icon (three horizontal lines) reveals a table with relevant values. Many of the lists have a DEFINE NEW option or an ADD option, which you can use to add data to the table on the fly. The golden arrow enables you to drill further into the detail supporting the summary data. The BROWSE icon (an ellipsis or three dots) will allow you to browse records in a table where you'll be presented multiple items to select via checkboxes. The VISUALIZATION icon (the bar graph) opens a graphical and table view of the financial data.
>
> We'll refer to these buttons and icons throughout this chapter.

7.1 Business Partner Master Data

SAP Business One offers three categories for business partner data: lead, customer, or vendor. From the main screen, select MODULES • BUSINESS PARTNER • BUSINESS PARTNER MASTER DATA. Figure 7.1 illustrates the style of master records in SAP Business One: the records contain a header above the tabs, which hold the details required for marketing documents.

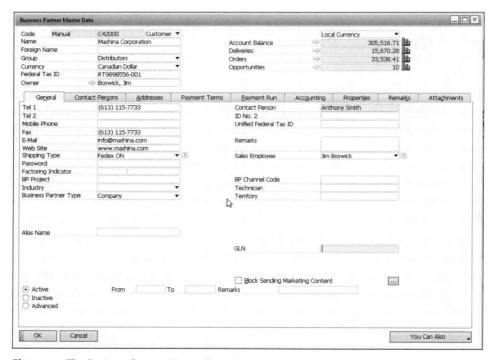

Figure 7.1 The Business Partner Master Data Screen

A lead is an opportunity to conduct business in the future; in the system, a lead data record provides data to support the company's sales and marketing programs. When you close a sale with the lead, you change the category of the record from lead to customer.

A customer data record contains people and organizations to whom you sell goods and services or clients to whom you deliver not-for-profit services. The information in the customer/client master record provides the foundation for the completion of sales marketing documents and the Dunning Wizard.

A vendor data record contains the people and organizations from whom you purchase goods and services and to whom you provide government tax and fee payments or donate funds. Vendor master data records are used to create purchasing documents, receive goods and services, and process payments to vendor business partners.

7.1.1 Adding Business Partner Master Data

Adding the business partner is the first step in your relationship management strategy. This CRM functionality is woven throughout SAP Business One. Ensuring that your setup is detailed and specific to your partners will enable many of the fields in the business partner master data record to be populated by default values that give useful and accurate information. Your suppliers play an important role in the success of your organization, so they require similar relationship management activities. Supply chain management is crucial to meeting the needs of your customers while controlling costs over the long run.

The header of the record shows basic business partner data and includes the preset fields defined in ADMINISTRATION • SYSTEM INITIALIZATION • GENERAL • BP tab and in ADMINISTRATION • SETUP • BUSINESS PARTNERS.

The header also provides financial business partner information and the ability to drill down to details by clicking on the golden arrow. The VISUALIZATION icon (the bar graph) will present financial information in a variety of graphic formats. Clicking on ACCOUNT BALANCES drills down into the A/R data; the DELIVERIES button presents a table with delivery detail (as does the ORDERS option), and the OPPORTUNITIES option drills down to the CRM functions.

Before you add business partners, though, consider the logical grouping of your business partners. Grouping provides an opportunity to define customer market segments that have similar dimensions and may be used to filter reports and target marketing campaigns. We suggest that you group vendors that supply identical products so that a request for purchase quotation can be sent to the group to determine which supplier best meets your company's needs. To add a new customer, vendor, or lead, follow these steps:

1. From the SAP Business One main screen, follow the menu path Modules • Business Partner • Business Partner Master Data.

2. Switch from Find mode to the Add mode by choosing the Add icon (a sheet with a red dot).

> **Tips and Tricks: Business Partner Master Data Record**
>
> The business partner data entry screen opens in the Find mode, which displays fields with yellow fill. Switching to the Add mode presents fields with white fill. To switch to the Add mode, use the shortcut Ctrl+A; alternatively, you can use the Add icon (a sheet with a red dot) on the toolbar or follow the Data • Add from the menu options. To switch back to the Find mode, use the shortcut Ctrl+F or select the Find icon (the binoculars) or the menu options Data • Find.

3. In the field to right of the Code field, select the business partner type from the dropdown list shown in Figure 7.2.

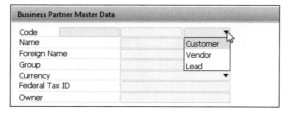

Figure 7.2 Choosing a Business Partner Type

> **Tips and Tricks: Vendors, Customer, and Leads**
>
> If a vendor is also one of your customers, you must create two different master data records (one customer record and one vendor record) containing the same data but with different codes.
>
> When a business partner is defined as a lead and a sales order is generated, the lead becomes a customer; you'll need to change the business partner type to Customer.

4. Enter the other information into the relevant fields of the Business Partner Master Data window.

5. Choose the Add button or click Cancel to abandon your changes.

7.1.2 Removing Business Partners

If a business partner is set up in error or no longer exists, you can remove the business partner master data record—but only if the following conditions are met:

▸ The business partner balance is zero.

▸ The business partner is not defined as a consolidation business partner.

▸ The business partner is not connected to any document.

Find and display the relevant business partner by following the menu path Mod-ules • Business Partners • Business Partner Master Data and then clicking on the Find icon (binoculars). Do one of the following:

▸ From the menu bar, choose Data • Remove Business Partner.

▸ Right-click the Business Partner Master Data window and choose Remove Business Partner, as illustrated in Figure 7.3.

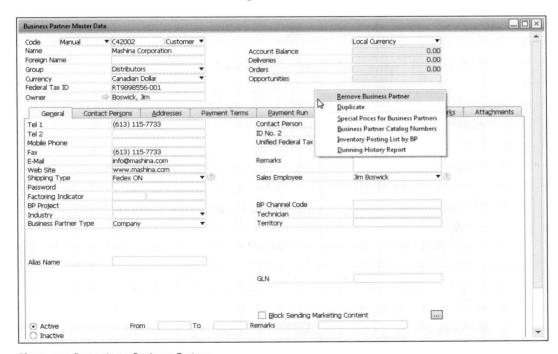

Figure 7.3 Removing a Business Partner

In the BUSINESS PARTNER MASTER DATA system message shown in Figure 7.4, either choose OK to permanently delete the business partner or click the CANCEL button to keep the business partner and return to the BUSINESS PARTNER MASTER DATA window.

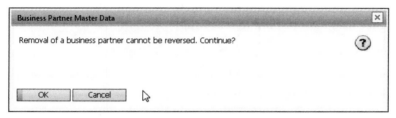

Figure 7.4 A Permanent Record Removal Warning

7.1.3 Displaying and Updating Business Partners

Once you have established your list of business partners, you will frequently access the records to manage your relationship and update the various fields found on the master records. To display and update these partners, follow these steps:

1. From the SAP Business One main menu or the MODULES tab, follow the menu path MODULES • BUSINESS PARTNER • BUSINESS PARTNER MASTER DATA. The BUSINESS PARTNER MASTER DATA window appears in Find mode.

2. Enter the search criteria in one or several fields. The searchable fields are highlighted in yellow. Limit your search to a specific business partner type by selecting LEAD, CUSTOMER, or VENDOR in the CODE field. You can also specify search criteria on the multiple tabs of the window as shown in Figure 7.5. Once you've finished inputting your search criteria, click the FIND icon (the binoculars).

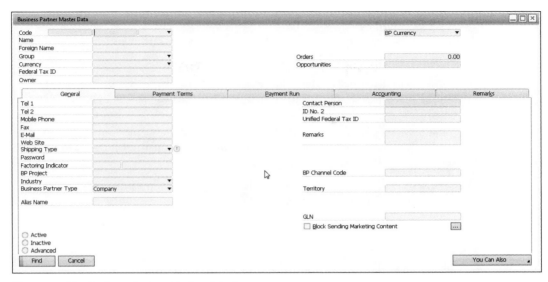

Figure 7.5 The Business Partner Master Data Screen

3. Select the business partner you want to display and click the CHOOSE button. Alternatively, you can browse through existing business partners, using the master data browsing icons:

- ▶ FIND icon (binoculars): Switches to the Find mode
- ▶ ADD icon (a sheet with a red dot): Switches to the Add mode
- ▶ FIRST RECORD icon (far-left arrow): Goes to the first record
- ▶ PREVIOUS RECORD icon (left arrow): Goes to the previous record
- ▶ NEXT RECORD icon (right arrow): Goes to the next record
- ▶ LAST RECORD icon (far-right arrow): Goes to the last record
- ▶ REFRESH icon (circular arrows): Refreshes the screen

4. To edit the data, modify the required fields.

5. To save your changes, click UPDATE.

Tips and Tricks: Changing Code, Type, or Currency

You can change the code, type, or currency of a business partner only if the following conditions are met:

- ▶ The business partner account balance is zero.

▸ The business partner is not defined as a consolidation business partner.

▸ The business partner is not connected to any marketing document.

The following are the exceptions to these rules:

▸ If the business partner is connected to a sales opportunity, sales order, sales quotation, or activity, you can change the business partner code and the business partner type.

▸ If the business partner is connected to a sales opportunity, sales order, sales quotation, activity, item, or draft, you can change the business partner currency to another currency.

You can set the business partner currency to ALL CURRENCIES, regardless of the object to which the business partner is connected.

7.1.4 Basic Data

The basic data on the left side of the header record shown in Figure 7.6 is the starting point for setting up business partner. The code you create for the customer may be up to 15 characters long.

A common practice is to begin with business partner code with a "C" for a customer, a "V" for a vendor, or an "L" for a lead. While this practice may seem redundant, since you will identify the business partner in the field to the right of the code by selecting the business partner type, including the business partner type in the code simplifies creating queries and reports by providing an additional filter method. The other fields in the basic data header are described in Table 7.1.

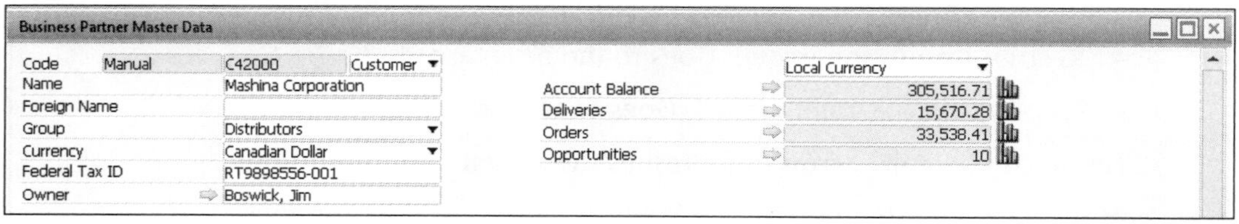

Figure 7.6 The Business Partner Master Data Header

Field	Description/Use
CODE	The code is a unique alphanumeric string of up to 15 characters used to identify the business partner.

Table 7.1 Basic Data Fields in the Business Partner Master Data Header

Field	Description/Use
TYPE	From the dropdown list to the right of the code, select the partner type. The types of transactions that can be completed are determined by the partner type: ▶ CUSTOMER: Enables sales transactions, activities, sales opportunities, and service calls ▶ VENDOR: Enables purchasing transactions and activities ▶ LEAD: Enables sales opportunities, sales quotations, sales orders, and activities
FOREIGN NAME	The partner's foreign name can be up to 100 characters. When using a foreign language marketing document template, the name in this field is displayed on the document.
GROUP	Select the group from the preset list to classify the business partner.
CURRENCY	Choose the currency designated for transactions with the business partner.
FEDERAL TAX ID	The federal tax ID of the business partner is transferred to marketing documents. In Canada, for example, this number would be the GST number.
OWNER	Assign the employee who is the "owner" (designated manager) of the business partner. You can manage data ownership by BUSINESS PARTNER ONLY or BUSINESS PARTNER and DOCUMENTS. The OWNER field becomes a filter to access the business partner; by default, this field contains the document owner.
CURRENCY	Select the currency type to display in the ACCOUNT BALANCE, DELIVERIES, ORDERS, and OPPORTUNITIES fields. The last three fields are not relevant for vendors.

Table 7.1 Basic Data Fields in the Business Partner Master Data Header (Cont.)

Financial Information: Customers

The header record gives you a snapshot of your financial relationship with a business partner.

The financial values shown represent future incoming cash, so the data presented enables you to access vital information to manage customer relations and cash flow. This screen can help answer several key questions: How much does the customer on this account owe us? What deliveries are outstanding for this customer?

What is the value of the orders on the books? Finally, what is the value of opportunities with this client?

You can make strategic decisions that impact cash flow using the summary data shown in Figure 7.6. If the company appears to be owed receivables past a certain benchmark, you can drill further into the data to gain a better understanding of the situation by clicking on the golden arrow. Further investigation into the Accounts Receivable Aging Report may indicate long-outstanding invoices, thus putting a dunning strategy into action to speed up cash collection.

Or, for example, you may also be compelled to create and distribute an activity throughout the organization to facilitate working with the customer to resolve issues. Because collection issues often arise from poor service or problems with invoices, communicating with the business partner is important for understanding the reason for delayed payment and mitigating credit risk. To trigger that report, go to MODULES • BUSINESS PARTNER • BUSINESS PARTNER MASTER DATA • ACCOUNT BALANCE and click on the golden arrow. The selection criteria for the Customer Receivable Aging Report are illustrated in Figure 7.7.

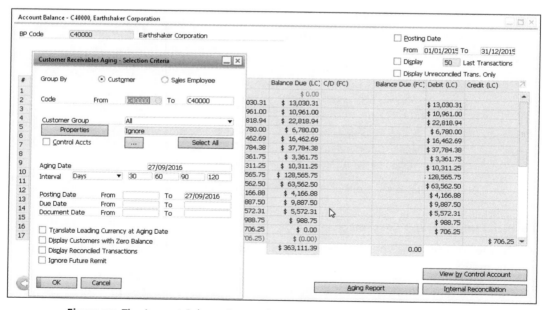

Figure 7.7 The Account Balance Screen: Customer Receivables Aging Report

Monitoring deliveries will mitigate potential late shipment issues. The value of deliveries shown in Figure 7.8 may represent the value of the inventory on the floor awaiting shipment or the amounts of deliveries to be copied into an invoice marketing document. Perhaps your observations regarding your deliveries will compel you to drive additional activity into the process. Generate the Delivery Balance Report by following the menu path MODULES • BUSINESS PARTNER • BUSINESS PARTNER MASTER DATA • DELIVERIES and clicking on the golden arrow.

Delivery Balance					
BP Code	C42000		Display Currency	Canadian Dollar	
BP Name	Mashina Corporation				
Date	Document ...	Remarks	Amount	Balance	
27/09/2016	254	Based On Sales Quotations 241. Based On Sales Orders 239.	7,768.75	7,768.75	
27/09/2016	255	Based On Sales Quotations 249. Based On Sales Orders 245.	2,223.28	9,992.03	
27/09/2016	256	Based On Sales Quotations 250. Based On Sales Orders 255.	64,240.50	74,232.53	
27/09/2016	257	Based on Sales Quotation 560	2,223.28	76,455.81	
27/09/2016	258	Direct Telephone order RUSH	9,294.25	85,750.06	
13/09/2016	259	Base on Discussion with Anthony	2,223.28	87,973.34	

Figure 7.8 A Delivery Balance Report

The value of orders is cash sitting on the system waiting for delivery and invoicing. Drilling into the orders brings up the Sales Order Balance Report shown in Figure 7.9.

Sales Order Balance					
BP Code	C42000		Display Currency	Canadian Dollar	
BP Name	Mashina Corporation				
Date	Order No.	Remarks	Amount	Balance	
27/09/2016	255	Based On Sales Quotations 250.	64,240.50	64,240.50	
27/09/2016	256	Based On Sales Quotations 251.	1,589.06	65,829.56	
27/09/2016	257	Based On Sales Quotations 252.	1,398.38	67,227.94	
27/09/2016	258	Based On Sales Quotations 253.	3,608.94	70,836.88	
27/09/2016	259	Based On Sales Quotations 254.	7,090.75	77,927.63	
27/09/2016	260	Based On Sales Quotations 255.	64,240.50	142,168.13	

Figure 7.9 A Sales Order Balance Report

Sales orders are future cash flow, so it's imperative to turn these orders into cash as soon as possible. Drilling further down into the sales order data may indicate the need to expedite inventory purchase orders or schedule production. To bring up the Sales Order Balance Report, follow the menu path MODULES • BUSINESS PARTNER • BUSINESS PARTNER MASTER DATA • ORDERS and click on the golden arrow.

If you follow the menu path MODULES • BUSINESS PARTNER • BUSINESS PARTNER MASTER DATA • ORDERS and click on the VISUALIZATION icon (the bar graph), you'll get a graphical view of the same report, as shown in Figure 7.10.

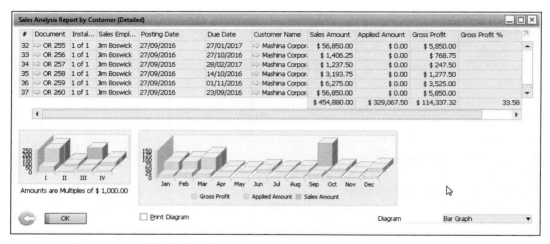

Sales Analysis Report by Customer (Detailed)

#	Document	Instal...	Sales Empl...	Posting Date	Due Date	Customer Name	Sales Amount	Applied Amount	Gross Profit	Gross Profit %
32	OR 255	1 of 1	Jim Boswick	27/09/2016	27/01/2017	Mashina Corpor.	$ 56,850.00	$ 0.00	$ 5,850.00	
33	OR 256	1 of 1	Jim Boswick	27/09/2016	27/10/2016	Mashina Corpor.	$ 1,406.25	$ 0.00	$ 768.75	
34	OR 257	1 of 1	Jim Boswick	27/09/2016	28/02/2017	Mashina Corpor.	$ 1,237.50	$ 0.00	$ 247.50	
35	OR 258	1 of 1	Jim Boswick	27/09/2016	14/10/2016	Mashina Corpor.	$ 3,193.75	$ 0.00	$ 1,277.50	
36	OR 259	1 of 1	Jim Boswick	27/09/2016	01/11/2016	Mashina Corpor.	$ 6,275.00	$ 0.00	$ 3,525.00	
37	OR 260	1 of 1	Jim Boswick	27/09/2016	23/09/2016	Mashina Corpor.	$ 56,850.00	$ 0.00	$ 5,850.00	
							$ 454,880.00	$ 329,067.50	$ 114,337.32	33.58

Amounts are Multiples of $ 1,000.00

Gross Profit   Applied Amount   Sales Amount

OK   Print Diagram   Diagram   Bar Graph

Figure 7.10 A Sales Order Balance Report in Graphical Form

Financial Information: Vendors

The header record gives you a snapshot of your financial relationship with the business partner as shown in Figure 7.11. Whereas the financial values shown in Section 7.5.2 represent future incoming cash from customers, the financial values shown in the vendor header record represent future outgoing cash. The data presented in the header enables you to work from the business partner master data record to access vital information to manage vendor relations and cash flow. Related questions might include the following: How much do we owe the vendor on this account? What is the value of goods receipt POs from the vendor? Finally, what is the value of the outstanding POs with this business partner? To access the vendor record, follow the menu path MODULES • BUSINESS PARTNERS • BUSINESS PARTNER MASTER DATA and drill down into the ACCOUNT BALANCE, GOODS RECEIPT POs, or PURCHASE ORDERS using the corresponding golden arrows shown in Figure 7.11.

Figure 7.11 Business Partner Master Data Header for a Vendor Record

Drilling down into the financial balances produces reports that provide detail to support summary data. The Account Balance Report presents further reporting options as seen in Figure 7.12. The Accounts Payable Aging Report provides a view of future cash outflow. You can look at the balance of the control accounts via the VIEW BY CONTROL ACCOUNTS button on the ACCOUNTS BALANCE screen and can access the Internal Reconciliation function from this screen.

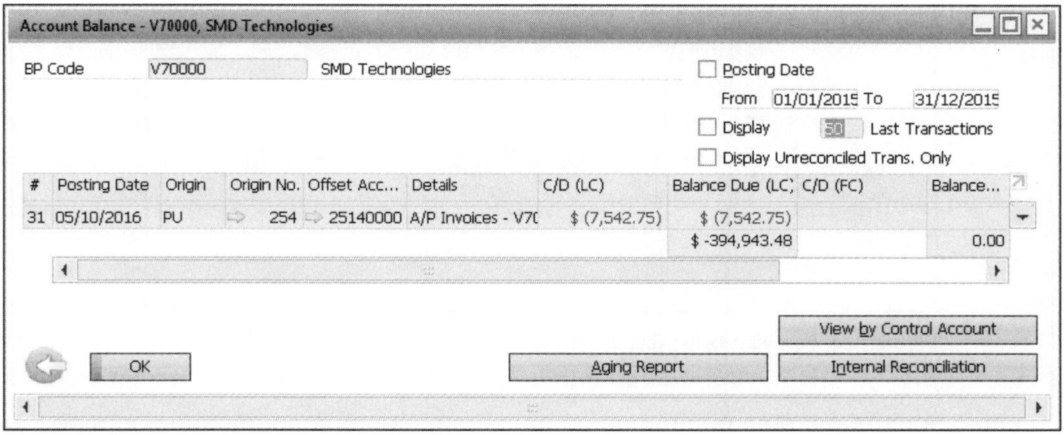

Figure 7.12 A Vendor Accounts Report

The Goods Receipt PO Report shown in Figure 7.13 provides the value of inventory received but not yet invoiced. The goods receipt PO is copied into the A/P invoice; then, the amount will appear in the account's summary total. Access the report by following the menu path MODULES • BUSINESS PARTNERS • BUSINESS PARTNER MASTER DATA and clicking on the golden arrow for GOODS RECEIPT PO.

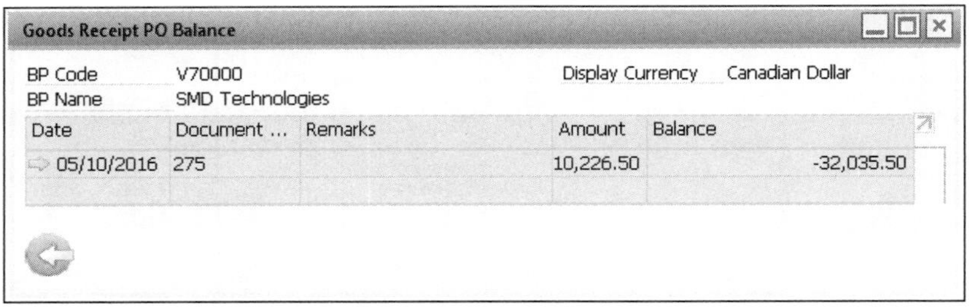

Figure 7.13 A Goods Receipt PO Report for a Vendor

The Purchase Order Balance Report in Figure 7.14 lists all outstanding purchase orders in the system. Monitoring outstanding purchase orders is important to maintain required inventory levels. Aging POs should drive activities to expedite the shipment of goods. Access the report by going to MODULES • BUSINESS PARTNERS • BUSINESS PARTNER MASTER DATA and clicking on the golden arrow for PURCHASE ORDERS.

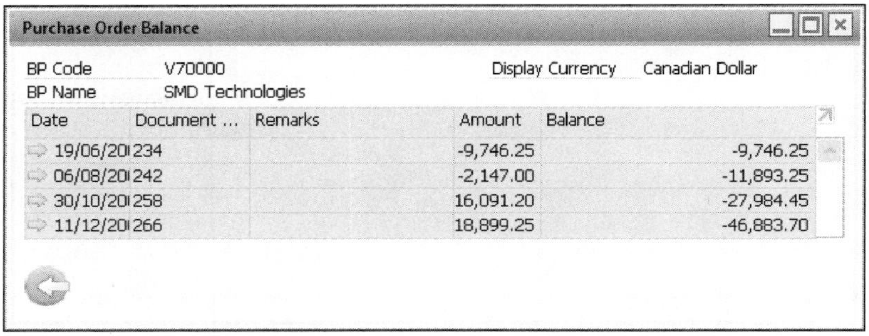

Figure 7.14 Purchase Order Balance Report

Right-Click Menu

The menu illustrated in Figure 7.15 displays several options related to the business partner. An explanation of each of the options is presented in Table 7.2.

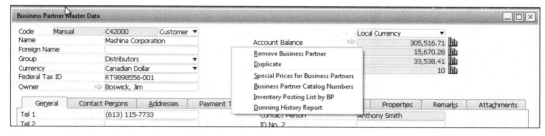

Figure 7.15 Business Partner Master Data Record: Right-Click Menu

Fields	Description/Use
REMOVE BUSINESS PARTNER	This option will remove (or delete) a business partner.
DUPLICATE	This option allows you to create duplicate master data, which is useful if you have a vendor that you want to set up as customer.
SPECIAL PRICES FOR BUSINESS PARTNERS	In addition to the standard price lists, you can define special prices for specific business partners or by discount groups according to item groups, properties, manufacturers, or items. Special prices can only be in one currency, based on one of the item's prices; items can have up to three unit prices with different currencies. In addition, you can set different special prices for each unit of measurement (UoM) of the item.
BUSINESS PARTNER CATALOG NUMBERS	Right-click the BUSINESS PARTNER MASTER DATA record and choose BUSINESS PARTNER CATALOG NUMBERS. Selecting this option brings up a table where you can maintain a business partner catalog that lines up your item numbers with those of the business partner.
INVENTORY POSTING LIST BY BP	You can view a list of inventory-related postings for each item or business partner or other criteria, depending on your selection. Alternatively, you can obtain the report from the MAIN MENU • INVENTORY • INVENTORY • INVENTORY POSTING LIST.
DUNNING HISTORY REPORT	Dunning is the practice of sending letters to customers requesting payment for outstanding account balances. The Dunning History Report provides the history of payment patterns of customers and dunning letters sent.

Table 7.2 Right-Click Options in Business Partner Master Data Record

You Can Also Menu Options

Throughout SAP Business One records, you are presented with the YOU CAN ALSO menu button. Attached to a business partner master data record, this button enables you to create and view service calls, activities, opportunities, recurring transactions, blanket agreements, and service contracts related to the business partner. As shown in Figure 7.16, the command can be reached via MODULES • BUSINESS PARTNER • BUSINESS PARTNER MASTER DATA • YOU CAN ALSO.

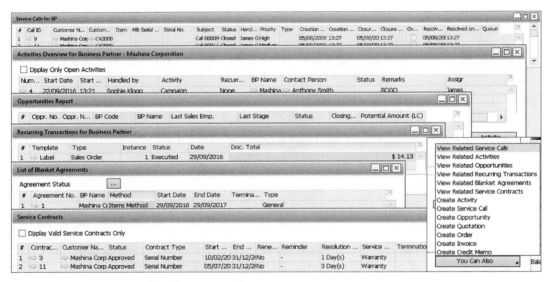

Figure 7.16 Finding the You Can Also Button

7.1.5 General Tab

The GENERAL tab shown in Figure 7.17 contains basic information about the business partner. Access the GENERAL tab by selecting MODULES • BUSINESS PARTNER • BUSINESS PARTNER MASTER DATA • GENERAL.

Notice that slight differences exist between the business partner master data GENERAL tab for the customer, vendor, and lead records: The customer card in Figure 7.17 contains SALES EMPLOYEE, BP CHANNEL CODE, TECHNICIAN, and TERRITORY business partner fields on the right side. The vendor card refers to a buyer, and the lead record does not have an associated technician.

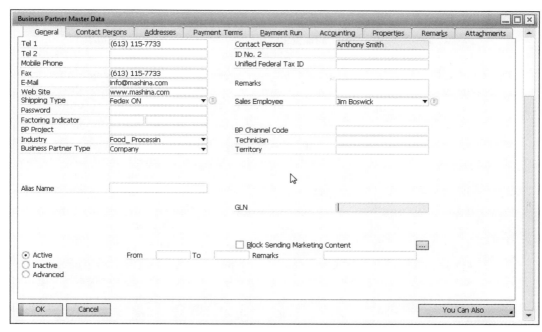

Figure 7.17 General Information about the Customer

CRM and SCM strategies are enhanced by providing several fields found in Table 7.3 to provide communication, classify business partners, provide a basis for market segmentation, and assign employees that interact with the business partner. You can design marketing campaigns that target specific market segments via email and fax, or you can prevent sending marketing materials to certain segments.

Field	Description/Use
Tele1, Tele2, Mobile Phone, Fax, and Email	These fields set up the communication capability with the business partner. The telephone fields can be used to autodial partners when Microsoft Auto Dialer is installed. Email and fax can be utilized in daily contact with the business partners and in marketing campaigns.
Website	Input the business partner's website address or uniform resource locator (URL).
Shipping Type	Define the shipping types used by your company, such as FedEx, UPS, ground transport, and air freight, to create the dropdown list. You can define an unlimited number of options to select from.

Table 7.3 Fields in the Business Partners General Tab

Field	Description/Use
Password	Enter a password for the business partner to conduct e-commerce transactions when utilized.
Factoring Indicator	Factoring is the practice of selling your accounts receivables to a creditor. Any payments to a business partner will be directed to the creditor when the Factoring Indicator field contains data.
BP Project	Identify a project associated with the business partner.
Industry	Define the industry types served or targeted by your company, such as automotive, aerospace, government, and retail, to create the dropdown list. You can define an unlimited number of options to select from.
Business Partner Type	Select a business partner type. Business partner types determine if a business partner is a company or a private contact.
Alias Name	Enter an additional name for the business partner.
Active, Inactive, or Advanced	Select the status of the business partner. Enter the date range during which the status is valid. Add remarks to explain the status.
Contact Person	This field displays the contact person, which is the main person that is available by default from the Contact Persons tab.
ID no. 2	Enter an additional identifying number for the business partner.
Unified Federal Tax ID	Enter a Unified Federal Tax ID associated with a group of companies or a subsidiary associated with a parent company.
Remarks	Enter remarks to facilitate further understanding of the business partner's circumstances.
Sales Employee or Buyer	For customers, this field displays Sales Employees; for vendors, this field displays a Buyer.
BP Channel Code	Insert the business partner code of an associated channel partner of the customer.
Technician	Enter the service technician that works with this business partner.
Territory	Use this field to enter the territory associated with the business partner.
GLN	This field displays the global location number (GLN), which identifies an address for the business partner. The GLN is fed from the company detail record.
Block Sending Marketing Content	This checkbox controls which business partners will receive email or fax campaign material.

Table 7.3 Fields in the Business Partners General Tab (Cont.)

7.1.6 Contact Persons Tab

The CONTACT PERSONS tab shown in Figure 7.18 contains names of contacts and communication information to enable you to manage your relationships and conduct your communication strategy with the business partners. Access the CONTACT PERSONS tab by selecting MODULES • BUSINESS PARTNER • BUSINESS PARTNER MASTER DATA • CONTACT PERSONS.

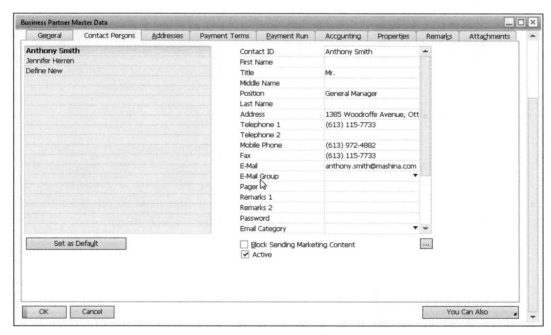

Figure 7.18 Contact Persons Detail Record

To add a contact, follow the menu path MODULES • BUSINESS PARTNER • BUSINESS PARTNER MASTER DATA • CONTACT PERSONS • DEFINE NEW. Input the data to the fields in the CONTACT PERSONS tab; when you've completed the record, click on the UPDATE button.

Many of the fields in the CONTACT PERSONS detail record are self-explanatory, but we've given some tips for the others in Table 7.4.

Field	Description
EMAIL GROUP	Identifying your contact with an email group indicates that an email sent to the group will be delivered to the contact person. To add an email group, choose the DEFINE NEW option from the dropdown list.
REMARKS 1 and REMARKS 2	The REMARKS field gives you the opportunity to collect additional information about the partner. In this field, you can enrich your CRM with data to manage your relationship with the partner.
PASSWORD	The password enables the business partner to conduct e-commerce transactions when utilized.
BLOCK SENDING MARKETING MATERIAL	To block marketing material from being sent to the business partner, click on the BROWSE icon (the ellipsis) to open the COMMUNICATION MEDIA dialog box. Next, select the BLOCK SENDING MARKETING MATERIAL checkbox.

Table 7.4 Fields in the Business Partners Contact Persons Tab

We want to call your attention to two more buttons in Figure 7.18. The SET AS DEFAULT button identifies the contact that you want to be the default contact. The default contact is displayed on the GENERAL tab. The YOU CAN ALSO option shown in Figure 7.19 enables you to create activities or view related activities, opportunities, recurring transactions, and blanket agreements.

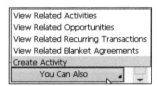

Figure 7.19 The You Can Also Menu

You can permanently remove a contact record by right-clicking on the CONTACT PERSONS tab and choosing REMOVE CONTACT PERSON or by selecting DATA • REMOVE CONTACT PERSONS from the menu bar.

Tips and Tricks: User-Defined Fields

One of the powerful features of SAP Business One is the ability to create *user-defined fields* (UDFs) that can be attached to the master data records. Some organizations collect additional information to add personal data to manage relations and run marketing campaigns.

For example, a local retailer might collect birthday information to run a campaign offering the customer a 20% discount during the month of their birthday. To accommodate the marketing strategy, the BIRTHMONTH UDF was added. You can access these menu options by following the path TOOLS • CUSTOMIZATION TOOLS • USER DEFINED FIELDS – MANAGEMENT.

7.1.7   Addresses Tab

Input the customer and vendor ship-to addresses into the ADDRESSES tab. The bill-to customer and the pay-to vendor addresses are also stored in the ADDRESSES tab.

Tips and Tricks: Business Partner Master Data Addresses

The business partner master data ADDRESSES tab displays BP SHIP TO, BILL TO, and PAY TO addresses and provides an opportunity to create an ADDRESS ID field filter.

A useful trick is to add a prefix to your ADDRESS ID in order to differentiate the SHIP TO addresses from the BILL TO and PAY TO addresses, perhaps by using "S_" or "B_" or "P_" or any other combination of prefixes.

7.1.8   Payment Terms Tab

The PAYMENT TERMS tab shown in Figure 7.20 contains information to implement credit policies; to establish links with the business partner's bank; to store credit card information; and to select options that affect the shipping, discount, and check handling policies.

Access the PAYMENT TERMS tab by selecting MODULES • BUSINESS PARTNER • BUSINESS PARTNER MASTER DATA • PAYMENT TERMS. Table 7.5 discusses some of the more complicated fields that require additional information.

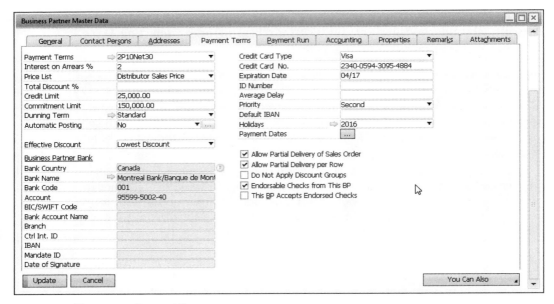

Figure 7.20 Payment Terms

Field	Description/Use
PAYMENT TERMS	Payment terms determine the due date of the marketing document associated with the business partner. Select the established payment terms from the dropdown list or DEFINE NEW to create a new term. To change the payment terms, select YES when prompted to overwrite the business partner's existing payment terms or select No to leave the data that exists.
INTEREST ON ARREARS %	Input the interest rate to be applied to overdue accounts.
PRICE LIST	Input the price list to apply to sales and purchasing documents. Item prices in this list are automatically displayed in marketing documents.
TOTAL DISCOUNT %	The discount is specific to the payment term. This discount is linked to the sales and purchasing marketing documents where the payment term is used for this business partner.
CREDIT LIMIT	Input the credit limit linked to the payment terms or an amount consistent with your company's credit policy.

Table 7.5 Fields in the Business Partners Payment Terms Tab

Field	Description/Use
COMMITMENT LIMIT	If a sales or purchasing commitment has been negotiated with the business partner, input an amount linked to the payment term or an amount agreed to with your business partner.
DUNNING TERM	The term determines which dunning letter the customer will receive. You can send out a default letter as a standard practice as necessary. Select the dunning term for the customer business partner from the dropdown list. Determine the dunning level based on your customer, customer group, or your credit policy.
AUTOMATIC POSTING	This field only applies if a dunning term has been selected. If selected, interest and late fees are automatically posted to general ledger (G/L) accounts, and a service invoice is created for other charges during the dunning run.
EFFECTIVE DISCOUNT	You can define multiple discounts in any discount group. When more than one discount could be applied to the business partner in the DISCOUNTS GROUP window, select one of the following: LOWEST DISCOUNT (default), HIGHEST DISCOUNT, AVERAGE, TOTAL, or DISCOUNT MULTIPLES. For example, say the group is entitled to a 15% discount and another available discount is 10%; if LOWEST is selected in the business partner master, the 10% discount would apply to this business partner.
BUSINESS PARTNER BANK	Payments created by the Payment Wizard and incoming payments are associated with this bank. Choose from the list by clicking on LIST icon (three horizontal lines).
CREDIT CARD TYPE	Select the type of credit card from the dropdown list or use DEFINE NEW to create a new type.
ID NUMBER	Input the identification of the credit card holder. You can use this field to input the card holder's name or apply a CONTACT ID code from the CONTACT PERSON tab.
AVERAGE DELAY	Input the average delay in receipt of cash flow from customers and payment to vendors. The value provides data used in cash flow analysis.
PRIORITY	Specify the business partner priority in the pick and pack process.
DEFAULT IBAN	Input the International Bank Account Number (IBAN). The default IBAN number will be used during bank file generation; otherwise, the IBAN number is taken from this record.

Table 7.5 Fields in the Business Partners Payment Terms Tab (Cont.)

Field	Description/Use
Holidays	Since business does not occur during holidays, input the holiday schedule to adjust due dates of marketing documents.
Allow Partial Delivery per Sales Orders	Relevant to sales only, check this box to allow shipping partial deliveries even when a sales order is not complete.
Allow Partial Delivery per Row	Select this checkbox to allow shipments to the customer if one row in the order is incomplete.
Do Not Apply Discount Groups	Select the checkbox if the business partner should be submitted to discount definitions. The discount in the header is not affected; when not selected, discounts can be applied manually. When copying a document to a target document, discounts are copied.
Endorsable Check from This BP	This checkbox determines whether a business partner's check can be endorsed. Selecting the option allows endorsement through a manual journal entry or outgoing payments.
This BP Accepts Endorsed Checks	This checkbox signifies that the business partner accepts endorsed checks.

Table 7.5 Fields in the Business Partners Payment Terms Tab (Cont.)

Once you've input the requisite payment terms, click the UPDATE button to apply the data or CANCEL to leave the record in its current state.

Following the menu path MODULES • BUSINESS PARTNER • BUSINESS PARTNER MASTER DATA • PAYMENT TERMS • YOU CAN ALSO will bring up different options depending on whether the record type is customer or vendor, as shown in Figure 7.21 and Figure 7.22, respectively. The YOU CAN ALSO menu provides a quick way to create new transactions and follow up on business partner activities.

Figure 7.21 The You Can Also Menu for a Customer Record

Figure 7.22 The You Can Also Menu for a Vendor Record

7.1.9 Payment Run Tab

A payment run is the process of preparing to pay business partners.

The PAYMENT RUN tab shown in Figure 7.23 provides options for using the Payment Wizard for a business partner. You can access the PAYMENT RUN tab by selecting MODULES • BUSINESS PARTNER • BUSINESS PARTNER MASTER DATA • PAYMENT RUN. The data on this tab, explained in Table 7.6, combined with values pulled from various setup tables, provides the necessary information to complete the payment process.

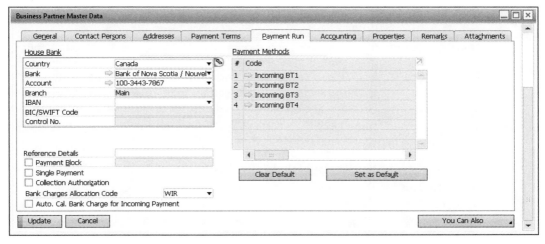

Figure 7.23 Payment Run Settings

The house bank information in the COUNTRY, BANK, ACCOUNT, BRANCH, IBAN, BIC/SWIFT CODE, and CONTROL NO. fields are populated by selecting the corresponding bank from the dropdown list. Alternatively, you can access this data via the CHOOSE FROM TREE icon (the stacked boxes). The house bank account links the offset G/L account in journal entries created by the payment wizard. Click the golden arrow for the BANK and ACCOUNT fields to open the BANKS SETUP or the HOUSE BANK ACCOUNTS SETUP windows.

Fields	Description/Use
REFERENCE DETAILS	This field is relevant to the creation of OPEX export bank transfer files and applicable to European localizations only.
PAYMENT BLOCK	Checking this box blocks business partners from receiving payments.
SINGLE PAYMENT	Check this box to tell the Payment Wizard to create a separate payment for each invoice. Unchecking this box summarizes all open invoices into one payment per payment method.
COLLECTION AUTHORIZATION	Check this box when the customer authorizes you to automatically collect from the company bank account.
BANK CHARGES ALLOCATION CODE	From the dropdown list, select the required bank charges allocation code to be assigned to the business partner.
AUTO. CAL. BANK CHARGE FOR INCOMING PAYMENT	Select the checkbox to automatically calculate the difference between the payment amount and the total amount due. When the business partner bank transfers funds, the amount that arrives may have had bank charges levied.
PAYMENT METHODS	Customer records display all incoming payment methods. Vendor records display all outgoing methods. When the ENABLE NEGATIVE PAYMENT FOR PAYMENT WIZARD checkbox is checked via MODULES • ADMINISTRATION • DOCUMENT SETTINGS • GENERAL tab, the options differ. The customer record displays all incoming payment methods and all outgoing payment methods where the payment means is bank transfer. The vendor record displays all outgoing payment methods and all incoming payment methods where the payment means is bank transfer.
CLEAR DEFAULT	Select the CLEAR DEFAULT button to deactivate this payment method's default status.
SET AS DEFAULT	Select the payment method as the default method in all marketing documents for the business partner.

Table 7.6 Fields in the Business Partners Payment Run Tab

7.1.10 Accounting Tab

Access the ACCOUNTING tab by selecting MODULES • BUSINESS PARTNER • BUSINESS PARTNER MASTER DATA • ACCOUNTING. The options in Table 7.7 in the GENERAL subtab are used to set the accounting properties for business partners as shown in

Figure 7.24; the Tax subtab is used to set the business partner as Tax Liable or Tax Exempt as shown in Figure 7.25.

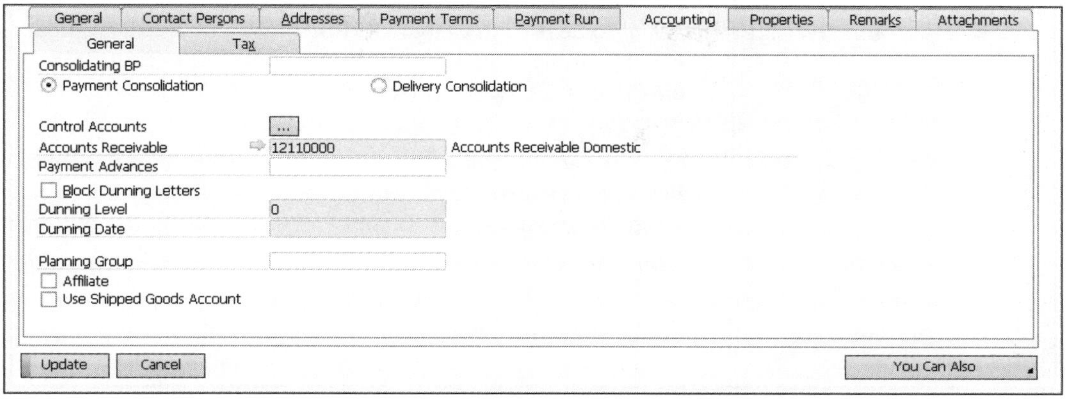

Figure 7.24 Control Accounts Options in the General Subtab of the Accounting Tab

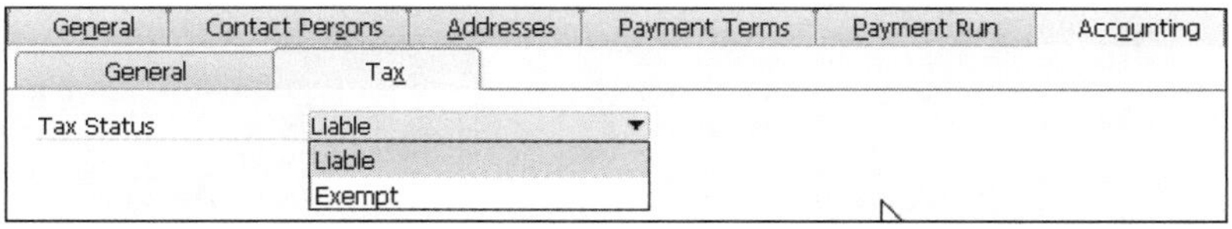

Figure 7.25 Business Partner's Tax Liability in the Tax Subtab of the Accounting Tab

Fields	Description/Use
CONSOLIDATING BP	This function consolidates the business transactions of many partners under one partner. Select the consolidating business partner by using the List icon (three horizontal lines). This partner becomes the parent record, and the partners being consolidated become child records.
	▶ PAYMENT CONSOLIDATION: Click this button to display invoices of the same consolidating business partner in the incoming or outgoing payments.
	▶ DELIVERY CONSOLIDATION: Click this button to display deliveries linked to the consolidating parent business partner in the INVOICE window.
CONTROL ACCOUNT	Open the CONTROL ACCOUNTS window by selecting the BROWSE icon (the ellipsis) and display the open debts for both A/R and A/P.

Table 7.7 Fields in the Business Partners Accounting Tab

Fields	Description/Use
Accounts Receivable/ Accounts Payable	Click the golden arrow to choose the A/R control account to be used in all journal entries for a customer or the A/P control account to be used in all journal entries associated with a vendor. Default control accounts are defined in Modules • Administration • Setup • G/L Account Determination • G/L Account Determination.
Payment Advances	Choose the account for posting payment advances from customers by using the List icon (three horizontal lines) to display the account list. Highlight the account and select the Choose button.
Block Dunning Letters	This checkbox blocks the customers from receiving dunning letters.
Dunning Level	This field represents the highest dunning level for the customer. Each dunning level is used to address the severity of the overdue account. Dunning 0 may be a friendly reminder whereas Dunning 3 may be demand for payment and a threat of collection.
Dunning Date	This field displays the dunning date, which is the last date that a dunning letter was issued.
Planning Group	This field displays the planning group used for liquidity forecasting and is used to process the Liquidity Forecasting Report.
Use Shipped Goods Account (Customer)	Setup is required by selecting the Use Shipped Goods Account for Customer checkbox via Modules • Administration • System Initialization • General Settings • BP. Once setup is complete, checking this box on the business partner record enables you to post the delivery of inventory to the shipped goods account instead of the cost of goods sold account when the delivery and issue of invoice occur in different posting periods.
Affiliate	An affiliate is a related company; thus, the control account for this business partner should be an intercompany account versus your A/R or A/P control accounts.

Table 7.7 Fields in the Business Partners Accounting Tab (Cont.)

7.1.11 Properties Tab

The Properties tab offers sixty-four items that can be coded to provide further information about the business partner according to your business requirements. Access the Properties tab by selecting Modules • Business Partner • Business Partner Master Data • Properties. Properties provide a way to make your business partner data more granular to facilitate filtering, reporting, and data processing—but they're optional; you can have none or all sixty-four items, based on how you want to format reports, sort data, and select master records.

Properties are set up under MODULES • ADMINISTRATION • BUSINESS PARTNER PROP-ERTIES as shown in Figure 7.26. All of the properties are presented with the PROP-ERTY NAME As business partner's property and the record number in the table. Click on the partner name and change it to a value that enables your business partner strategy; in Figure 7.27, these properties can be used to provide classification that are useful when filtering partners.

Figure 7.26 Business Partners Properties Setup

You'll need to collect information on the business partner to drive growth and meet the firm's long-term goals and objectives. With properties, you can classify the business partner in a way tailored to your strategy, policy, and process. If desired, you can segment these business partners further based on market, financial potential, risk management, and other dimensions, so give consideration to your strategy when you build your sixty-four business partner properties to manage your business partner relations.

Once you have set up the properties, put a check in the middle column for those properties relevant to your strategic purpose. In our example in Figure 7.27, the business partner has been identified as a LEVEL 1 customer with 51 TO 100 EMPLOYEES in the DISTRIBUTION business.

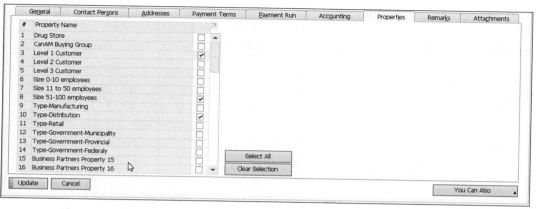

Figure 7.27 Business Partner Properties

Whenever the PROPERTIES window is open, the YOU CAN ALSO button provides options related to the business partner as shown in Figure 7.28.

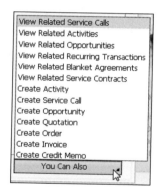

Figure 7.28 The You Can Also Menu

7.1.12 Remarks Tab

The REMARKS tab provides you with another tool in your business partner management strategy by permitting you to add descriptions, comments, notes, and images related to the business partner.

Access the REMARKS tab by selecting MODULES • BUSINESS PARTNER • BUSINESS PARTNER MASTER DATA • REMARKS. The REMARKS field shown in Figure 7.29 can contain 256,000 characters, giving you ample room to store information about the business partner. The IMAGE icon (the camera) enables you to attach images to your remarks. Once you have completed your input, select UPDATE to save your data or CANCEL to abort the update.

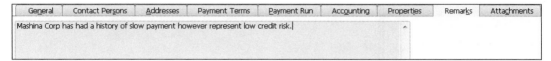

General	Contact Persons	Addresses	Payment Terms	Payment Run	Accounting	Properties	Remarks	Attachments

Mashina Corp has had a history of slow payment however represent low credit risk.|

Figure 7.29 Remarks on the Business Partner Master Record

7.1.13 Attachments Tab

You can attach documents, spreadsheets, images, and other files to the business partner. First, make sure you have set up the path to the ATTACHMENTS tab by following the menu path MODULES • ADMINISTRATION • SYSTEM INITIALIZATION • GENERAL SETTINGS • PATH, as shown in Figure 7.30. Once you have completed the setup, you can access the ATTACHMENTS tab by selecting MODULES • BUSINESS PARTNER • BUSINESS PARTNER MASTER DATA • ATTACHMENTS as illustrated in Figure 7.31.

General Settings

BP	Budget	Services	Display	Font & Bkgd	Path	Inventory	Resources	Cash Flow	Cockpit

Microsoft Word Templates Folder	D:\B1_SHR\Word\
Microsoft Excel Folder	D:\B1_SHR\Excel\
Pictures Folder	D:\B1_SHR\Images\
Attachments Folder	D:\B1_SHR\Attachments\
Extensions Folder	
Current Scanner	Integrated Camera TWAIN
XML File Folder	D:\B1_SHR\XML\

Refresh Paths in Documents

Figure 7.30 The Path Subtab in the General Settings Screen

To attach a file to the business partner, use the BROWSE icon (the ellipsis) to navigate to your document. Double-click on the desired document to pull the file into the attachments folder. To open the file, select the DISPLAY button to display the attachment. To remove an attached file, select the DELETE button. You can complete the process of attaching a file by selecting the UPDATE button; to abandon any changes, select the CANCEL button shown in Figure 7.31.

Figure 7.31 Adding Attachments

7.2 Activity

The key to a successful relationship management system is managing activities that promote business partner acquisition, retention, and satisfaction. Activity functionality in SAP Business One allows you design and tailor your system to drive a focus on business partner relations. You can create or update activity data by selecting MODULES • BUSINESS PARTNERS • ACTIVITY as shown in Figure 7.32 or by selecting the YOU CAN ALSO button from the business partner master data record.

Figure 7.32 The Activity Menu Path from the Business Partners Menu

7.2.1 Creating and Updating an Activity

To create an activity, follow the menu path MODULES • BUSINESS PARTNERS • ACTIVITY.

1. From the ACTIVITY field in the window, select the type of activity.

2. Link the activity to a BP CODE or check it as PERSONAL if the activity is only related to you.

3. Enter any other required information and select ADD to save the activity.

You can update existing activities by following these steps:

1. Bring up the ACTIVITY window by selecting MODULES • BUSINESS PARTNERS • ACTIVITY.

2. Select a search field to the display the required activity.

3. Modify the activity record with the information required and then choose UPDATE to save the modifications.

7.2.2 Creating an Activity from the Calendar

The calendar enables you to view, add, or update meetings, phone calls, tasks, and other activities. To open the CALENDAR window, choose the CALENDAR icon. When the calendar is displayed, as shown in Figure 7.33, a new set of icons will appear in the top right corner that, when selected, will then display the associated activity:

▶ Phone calls

▶ Meetings

▶ Campaigns

▶ Tasks

▶ Service calls

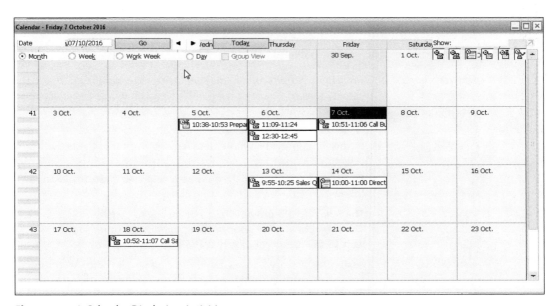

Figure 7.33 A Calendar Displaying Activities

Select the icon to display the activity on the calendar. The activity will be displayed on the date block with an icon identifying the type of activity scheduled. To add an activity to the calendar, double-click on the date block, and the ACTIVITY window will appear. Input the appropriate information to the window and select ADD to save your activity.

7.2.3 Activity Record Header

Activities come predefined in the first dropdown list shown in Figure 7.34 under the ACTIVITY field. Table 7.8 lists the predefined options.

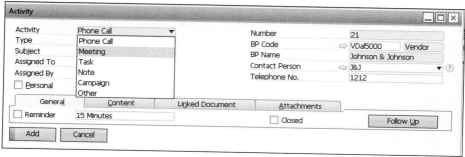

Figure 7.34 The Activity Dropdown List

Field	Description/Use
ACTIVITY	An activity is a phone call, meeting, task, note, campaign, or other activity that can be scheduled and placed on the calendar. Your options here are PHONE CALL, MEETING, TASK, NOTE, CAMPAIGN, or OTHER.
TYPE	In this field, provide a more detailed description of the activity by selecting DEFINE NEW. For example, a phone call could be a cold call, a return call, or a follow-up call.
SUBJECT	The SUBJECT field provides another means to classify your activity. The subject could be your product, service, or other topics relevant to the activity directed at the business partner.
ASSIGNED TO	Assign the activity to a system user or an employee by selecting the corresponding dropdown lists to reveal the list of users or employees.

Table 7.8 Fields in the Header Record of an Activity

Field	Description/Use
ASSIGNED BY	The field displays the person assigning the activity to the assigned user or employee.
NUMBER	This field displays a system-generated activity reference number.
BP CODE	Click the LIST icon (three horizontal lines) to bring up a list of business partners and select one. Your options are the CHOOSE, CANCEL, and NEW buttons.
BP NAME	This field displays data from the business partner record.
CONTACT PERSON	Choose from the list of contact persons or click CANCEL.
TELEPHONE NO.	This field displays data based on the contact person you selected.

Table 7.8 Fields in the Header Record of an Activity (Cont.)

Tips and Tricks: Add New Business Partner from an Activity

When selecting the business partner with the LIST icon (three horizontal lines), you are presented with the List of Business Partners Report. From the report screen, you are able to select the NEW icon to add a new business partner.

7.2.4 General Tab

The options in the GENERAL tab provide a basis to schedule, prioritize, locate, and record the frequency of an activity. Select an activity by following the menu path MODULES • BUSINESS PARTNER • ACTIVITY and then clicking on the GENERAL tab; the corresponding fields displayed will vary based on the activity selected or the recurrence frequency.

You are required to input data into the REMARKS, START DATE, END DATE, and DURATION fields as shown in Figure 7.35 to provide data for your activity calendar. Activities can have a single occurrence or can be designated to reoccur in the frequency options found in the dropdown list: NONE, DAILY, WEEKLY, MONTHLY, and ANNUALLY, as shown in Figure 7.36. The PRIORITY field designates the importance of the activity, while MEETING LOCATION provides the location for the activity. Return to Table 7.8 for further discussion of the GENERAL tab options.

RECURRENCE fields allow you to manage your CRM and SCM relationship management activities through scheduling. These schedules create alerts that are delivered into the MESSAGES AND ALERTS window. The display on the GENERAL tab changes based on the selection on the RECURRENCE dropdown lists shown in Figure 7.37.

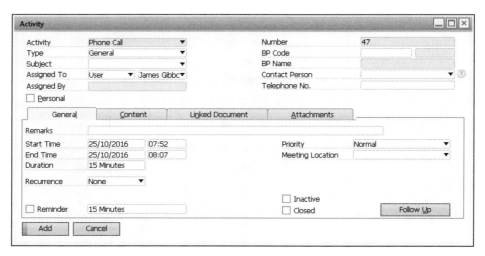

Figure 7.35 The General Tab of the Activity Screen

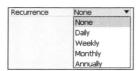

Figure 7.36 Setting the Frequency of Recurrence for an Activity

Recurrence	None ▼	
Recurrence	Daily ▼	
Repeat Every	⦿ 1	Day(s)
	○ Every Weekday	
Recurrence	Weekly ▼	
Repeat Every	1	Week(s)
Repeat on	☐ Mon ☐ Tue ☐ Wed ☑ Thu ☐ Fri ☐ Sat ☐ Sun	
Recurrence	Monthly ▼	
Repeat Every	1	Month(s)
Repeat on	⦿ Day 6	
	○ first Thursday	
Recurrence	Annually ▼	
Repeat Every	1	Year(s)
Repeat on	⦿ October ▼ 6	
	○ first Thursday of October	
Range		
Start	06/10/2016	
End	⦿ No End Date	
	○ After 1 Occurrence(s)	
	○ By	

Figure 7.37 Setting Activity Recurrence

7.2.5 Content Tab

The CONTENT tab allows you to input remarks, with 256,000 characters at your disposal for recording information relevant to the ACTIVITY.

You can select an activity via MODULES • BUSINESS PARTNER • ACTIVITY • CONTENT tab. Once you have recorded your comments, click on the ADD button or, alternatively, the CANCEL button to abandon your changes; these are shown in Figure 7.38.

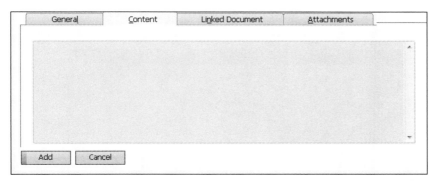

Figure 7.38 The Activity Content Tab

7.2.6 Linked Document

The LINKED DOCUMENT tab allows you to link a marketing document, such as a sales quotation or an A/R invoice, to an activity; the list of documents that can be attached is shown in Figure 7.39. Select an activity via MODULES • BUSINESS PARTNER • ACTIVITY • LINKED DOCUMENT tab. For example, you can view the linked service call used to create an activity on the SERVICE CALL record for the business partner. You can also view the original activity if the current view is a FOLLOW-UP. You can also link document drafts by checking the LINK DRAFT checkbox.

Choose a document type and then input the requisite data for the fields listed in Table 7.9.

Field	Description/Use
DOCUMENT NUMBER	Input the document number related to the document type selected.
SHOW DOCUMENTS RELATED TO THE BP	Check this checkbox to create a filter that ensures only documents related to the business partner are listed to select from.

Table 7.9 Fields in the Business Partners Linked Document Tab

Field	Description/Use
SOURCE OBJECT TYPE	This field displays the system number associated with an activity that was created from a service or sales opportunity.
SOURCE OBJECT NUMBER	This field displays the system number associated with the service or sales opportunity from which the activity was created.
PREVIOUS ACTIVITY	This field displays the number of the activity from which the follow-up activity was created.

Table 7.9 Fields in the Business Partners Linked Document Tab (Cont.)

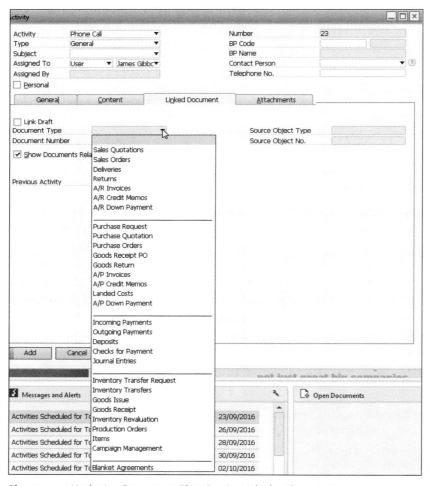

Figure 7.39 Marketing Documents That Can Be Linked with an Activity

7.2.7   Attachments Tab

Use this tab to attach files to your ACTIVITY via MODULES • BUSINESS PARTNER • ACTIVITY • ATTACHMENTS. You can attach as many files as is required. A complete discussion of attachments can be found in Section 7.1.13.

7.3   Campaigns

You can create campaigns in two ways: using the Campaign Generation Wizard or manually. In this section, we'll look at each method.

7.3.1   Campaign Generation Wizard

The Campaign Generation Wizard shown in Figure 7.40 guides you through the steps to create your customer and vendor campaigns.

To start the wizard, follow the menu path MODULES • BUSINESS PARTNERS • CAMPAIGN GENERATION WIZARD. When the wizard window appears, select NEXT to bring up the CAMPAIGN GENERATION OPTIONS window shown in Figure 7.41. Each step can be reached by completing the information and selecting NEXT, selecting BACK to return to the previous step, or choosing CANCEL.

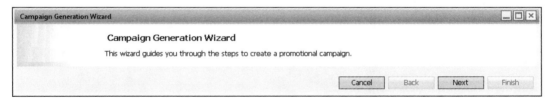

Figure 7.40 The Campaign Generation Wizard

The wizard will take you through a five-step process to manage the campaign:

1. In the first step, the CAMPAIGN GENERATION OPTIONS screen provides three radio buttons: CREATE NEW CAMPAIGN, CREATE CAMPAIGN BASED ON EXISTING CAMPAIGN, and RUN AN EXISTING CAMPAIGN AGAIN. In our example shown in Figure 7.41, we've selected the CREATE NEW CAMPAIGN option. Input a name for your new campaign in the CAMPAIGN NAME field and add any necessary remarks to clarify the purpose of the campaign. When you're ready, click the NEXT button.

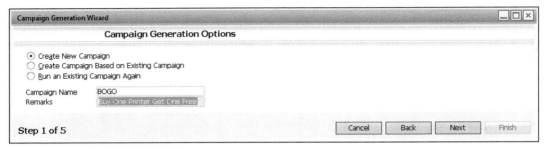

Figure 7.41 Create New Campaign (Step 1 of the Wizard)

2. Next, select the campaign details from the CAMPAIGN DETAILS screen shown in Figure 7.42. As listed in Table 7.10, these details extend beyond just the campaign.

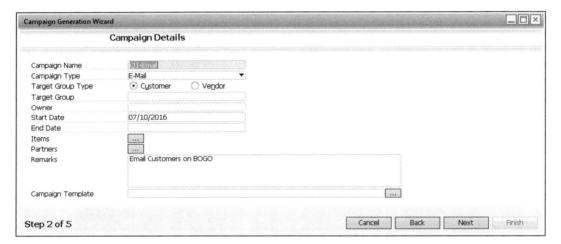

Figure 7.42 New Campaign (Step 2 of the Wizard)

Field	Description/Use
CAMPAIGN NAME	Input a name for your campaign (Step 1).
CAMPAIGN TYPE	Select the type of campaign you are running from this dropdown list.
TARGET GROUP TYPE	Using the radio buttons, select whether your group consists of customers or vendors.

Table 7.10 Fields in the Campaign Details Screen

Field	Description/Use
TARGET GROUP	The LIST icon (three horizontal lines) will bring up the LIST OF TARGET GROUP table. You'll then have the option to create a new target group, choose from an existing group, or cancel the transaction.
OWNER	The LIST icon (three horizontal lines) will bring up the LIST OF EMPLOYEES table. Select the employee, choose the list, or cancel the transaction.
START AND END DATE	Identify the period of time the campaign will run.
ITEMS	The BROWSE icon (the ellipsis) will bring up the item list. Select the list icon and choose the items for the promotion. You may also add a new item to the item master file or cancel.
PARTNERS	The BROWSE icon (the ellipsis) will bring up the PARTNERS table. Use the dropdown list to select the partner name and then again use the dropdown list for relationship to further classify the partner. To maintain partner data, follow the menu path MODULES • ADMINISTRATION • SALES OPPORTUNITIES • PARTNERS.
REMARKS	Input remarks to clarify information concerning the campaign.
CAMPAIGN TEMPLATE	The field opens the file manager. Choose a template to import into the campaign. The following file types are supported: TXT, HTML, JPG, GIF, BMP, PNG, and Word templates.

Table 7.10 Fields in the Campaign Details Screen (Cont.)

Once you've entered the requisite campaign details, select NEXT.

3. The next step is to designate the business partners targeted by the campaign. Take a look at the buttons to the right of Figure 7.43; you can remove all partners with the CLEAR button, add new partners with the ADD button, and import partner data with the IMPORT button. You can update business partner information, if necessary. When put your cursor over the BP CODE column, the LIST icon (three horizontal lines) appears; click this icon to bring up the list of business partners to choose from or add a new partner.

As always, when you're finished selecting your target business partners, select NEXT to move ahead. Alternatively, you can click CANCEL or click BACK to return to the previous step.

4. Once you've targeted your business partners, you can save your campaign using the radio buttons shown in Figure 7.44 and listed in Table 7.11.

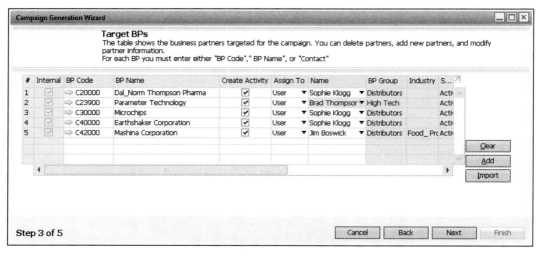

Figure 7.43 Target BPs (Step 3 of the Wizard)

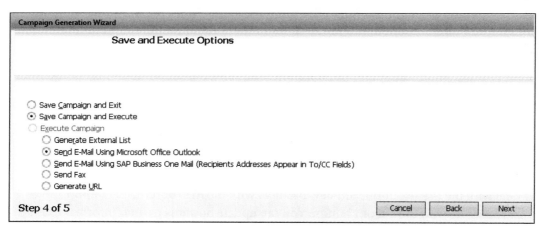

Figure 7.44 Save and Execute Options (Step 4 of the Wizard)

Field	Description/Use
SAVE CAMPAIGN AND EXIT	This radio button appears if you selected CREATE NEW CAMPAIGN or CREATE CAMPAIGN BASED ON EXISTING CAMPAIGN in Step 1 of the wizard. Save your campaign data by choosing the NEXT button. You can view the campaign data select MODULES • BUSINESS PARTNERS • CAMPAIGN.

Table 7.11 Save and Execute Options

Field	Description/Use
Save Campaign and Execute	This radio button appears if you selected Create New Campaign or Create Campaign Based on Existing Campaign in Step 1 of the wizard. You have further options for executing the campaign, shown in subordinate radio buttons: ▶ Generate External List ▶ Send E-Mail Using Microsoft Office ▶ Send E-Mail Using SAP Business One Mail (Recipients Addresses Appear in To/CC Fields) ▶ Send Fax ▶ Generate URL To execute, select the Next button.
Execute Campaign	This option is available if you selected Run an Existing Campaign in Step 1. You have further options for executing the campaign, shown in subordinate radio buttons: ▶ Generate External List ▶ Send E-Mail Using Microsoft Office ▶ Send E-Mail Using SAP Business One Mail (Recipients Addresses Appear in To/CC Fields) ▶ Send Fax ▶ Generate URL

Table 7.11 Save and Execute Options (Cont.)

5. The final step in the Campaign Generation Wizard process is the Summary Report shown in Figure 7.45. Select Close to complete the Campaign Generation Wizard process.

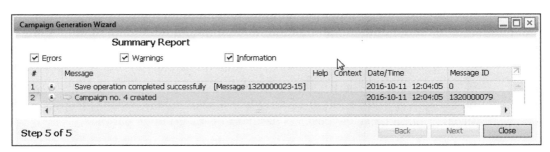

Figure 7.45 Summary Report (Step of the Wizard)

7.3.2 Manual Campaign Creation

An alternative to the Campaign Generation Wizard is to manually generate your campaign by selecting MODULES • BUSINESS PARTNER • CAMPAIGN to open the CAMPAIGN window shown in Figure 7.46. Many of the options presented are the same as discussed in the Table 7.10, so we won't revisit them here.

Select the TARGET GROUP TYPE as CUSTOMER or VENDOR and complete the rest of the header. Then, move through the TARGET BPS, ITEMS, PARTNERS, and ATTACHMENTS tabs, adding details as necessary. Finally, select ADD to save the campaign information.

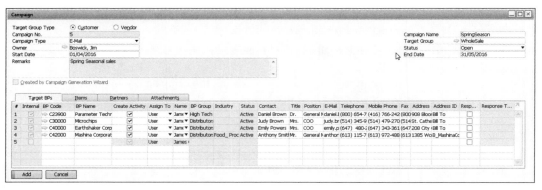

Figure 7.46 Manual Campaign Management

7.4 Internal Reconciliation

SAP Business One's Internal Reconciliation function allows you to match transactions posted to business partner accounts.

Two types of reconciliation are available in the SAP Business One: *Manual reconciliation* (shown in Figure 7.47) is required when you have a payment on account or create a document such as a credit memo that is unrelated to a specific invoice or transaction, whereas *automatic reconciliation* is handled by SAP when you have incoming and outgoing payments that are applied to invoices and when credit memos are copied from an invoice (shown in Figure 7.48). Reconciliation can be partial or full for a single business partner or for a group of partners.

To access the Internal Reconciliation function, navigate to the menu path MOD-ULE • BUSINESS PARTNER • INTERNAL RECONCILIATIONS • RECONCILIATION to bring up the BP INTERNAL RECONCILIATION SELECTION CRITERIA window. Another route is to go through MODULE • BUSINESS PARTNERS • BUSINESS PARTNER MASTER DATA • ACCOUNT and then use the golden arrow to drill down into BP INTERNAL RECONCILIATION on the ACCOUNT BALANCE window.

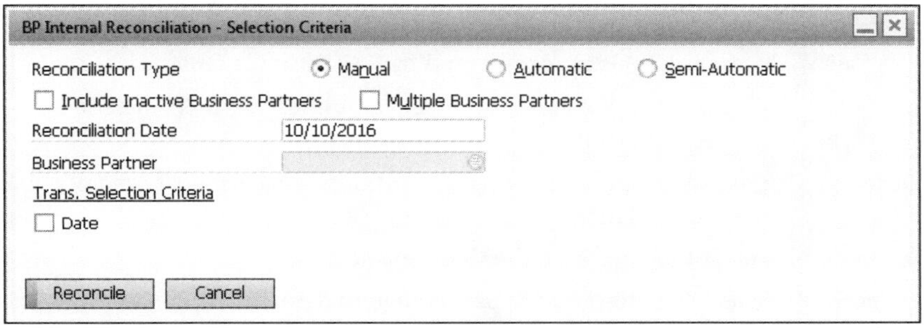

Figure 7.47 Selection Criteria for Manual Internal Reconciliation

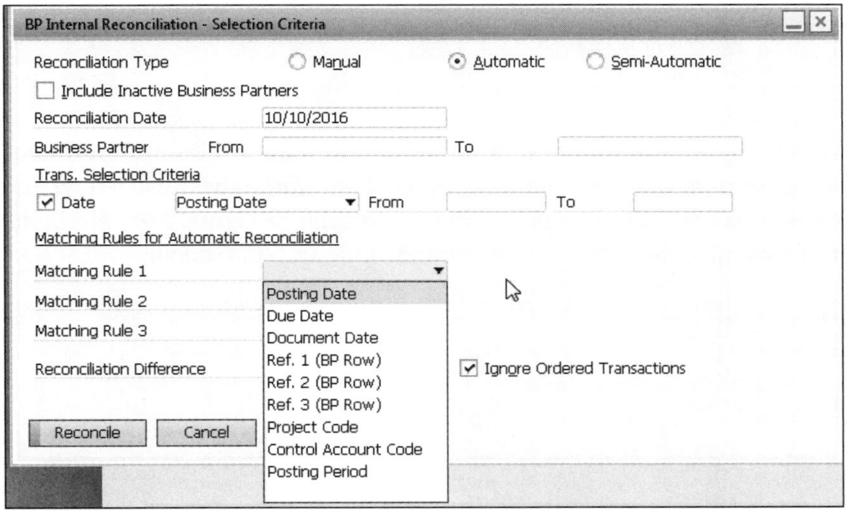

Figure 7.48 Selection Criteria for Automatic Internal Reconciliation

Table 7.12 lists the cumulative fields in the BP INTERNAL RECONCILIATION SELEC-TION CRITERIA screens for both manual and automatic reconciliation.

Field	Description/Use
RECONCILIATION TYPE	Choose from three options for the RECONCILIATION TYPE field: ▶ MANUAL: Choose this option when you only have a small number of transactions to reconcile or when partial reconciliation is required. ▶ AUTOMATIC: Choose this option when you have many transactions and business partners to reconcile. ▶ SEMI-AUTOMATIC: Choose this option to manually reconcile transactions as recommend by SAP Business One.
INCLUDE INACTIVE BUSINESS PARTNERS	Check this box if you want inactive business partners included in the reconciliation.
MULTIPLE BUSINESS PARTNERS	Check this box to bring up a list of business partners to include in the reconciliation.
RECONCILIATION DATE	Select the date from the CALENDAR icon.
TRANS. SELECTION CRITERIA	Select this checkbox to use a range of dates and alternatives for posting date, due date, or document date.
MATCHING RULE 1, MATCHING RULE 2, and MATCHING RULE 3	You can specify up to three matching rules to govern the reconciliation, as shown in Figure 7.48.

Table 7.12 Internal Reconciliation Selection Criteria

Once you have input your selection criteria, the INTERNAL RECONCILIATION window is available. For the reconciliation process to work, the total below the AMOUNT TO RECONCILE column needs to be $0, as seen in Figure 7.49. No items have been selected, so the RECONCILE button is hidden in this screen.

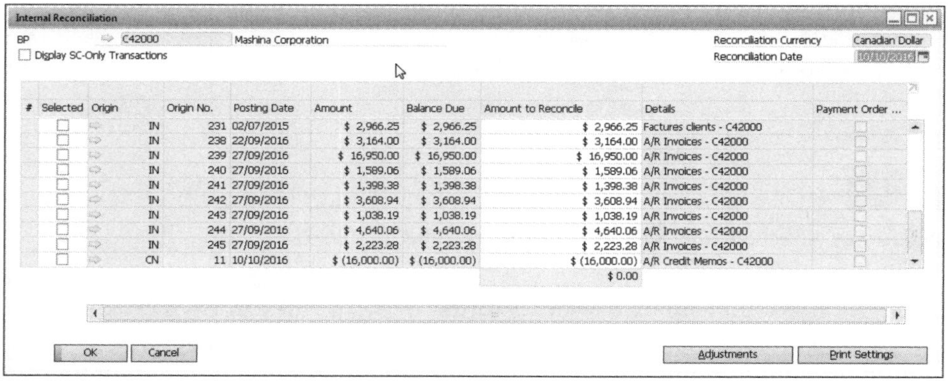

Figure 7.49 The Internal Reconciliation Window

But let's go ahead and select some items for Internal Reconciliation by putting a checkmark into the SELECTED column shown in Figure 7.50. The AMOUNT TO RECONCILE total is still $0.00; thus, the RECONCILE button is now available. Select RECONCILE to continue the reconciliation process. When the system generates a message inquiring whether you want to reconcile the selected transactions, select YES to complete the reconciliation or NO to abandon the process.

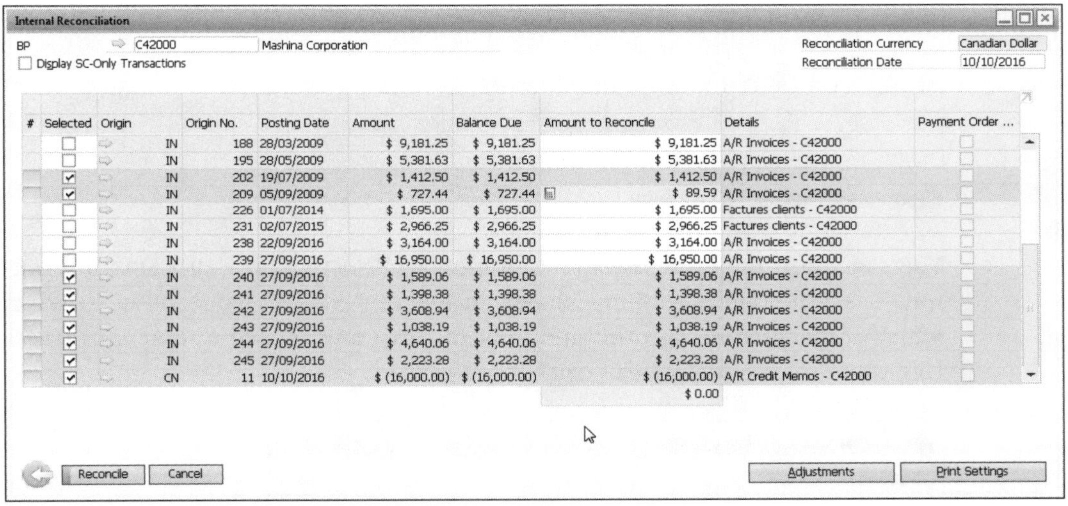

Figure 7.50 Items Reconciled

The client was issued a $16,000 credit memo and has requested it be applied to outstanding invoices. In Figure 7.50, the $16,000 credit amount was applied to eight invoices with one invoice still short due to a remaining balance of $89.59. The short invoice will display a balance due of $637.85 when you drill down into the invoice detail using the golden arrow.

Sometimes, the transactions may result in small balances. When small balances occur, you can create an adjusting journal entry by selecting the CREATE JOURNAL ENTRY and then the ADJUSTMENTS button. Additional adjustments are available to add an incoming payment or an outgoing payment using the corresponding radio buttons shown in Figure 7.51.

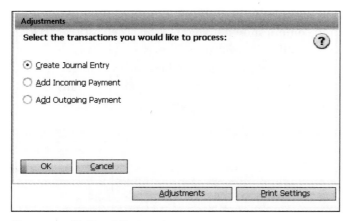

Figure 7.51 Making Adjustments

You can adjust the print setting preferences by selecting the PRINT SETTINGS button. The print setting options shown in Figure 7.52 give you option to select which reconciliations to print and how to sort unreconciled transactions. Press UPDATE to set the preferences or choose CANCEL.

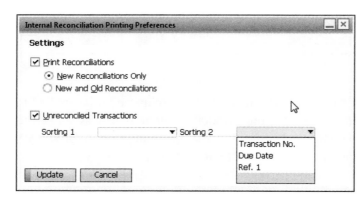

Figure 7.52 Internal Reconciliation Printing Preferences

7.5   Business Partner Reports

The strategic tools in your arsenal include reports on activity, cash management, internal reconciliations, and campaigns for business partners. Many of the business partner reports have already been displayed throughout the chapter in the various figures under the menu options associated with the report. The selection criteria typically display fields that are either self-explanatory or that have been discussed in many areas of the chapter, so we won't go into detail here.

Access business partner reports by following the menu path MODULES • BUSINESS PARTNER • BUSINESS PARTNER REPORTS.

7.5.1 Activity Reports

Activity reports provide you with numerous ways to look at your activities. You can select criteria from a comprehensive list of master record fields and drop-down lists as well as date criteria, as shown in Figure 7.53. You can execute the report by following the menu path MODULES • BUSINESS PARTNERS • BUSINESS PARTNERS REPORTS • ACTIVITY OVERVIEW.

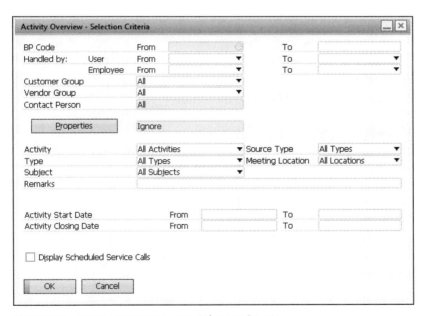

Figure 7.53 Activity Overview Report Selection Criteria

The output from leaving the default data in all fields as shown in Figure 7.53 is the ACTIVITIES OVERVIEW report in Figure 7.54. A similar report tailored to the current user can be generated by selecting the MODULES • BUSINESS PARTNERS • BUSINESS PARTNERS REPORTS • MY ACTIVITIES from the menu.

Number	Start Date	Start Time	Handled by	Activity	Recurrence	BP Name	Contact Person	Status	Remarks	Assigned By
32	01/04/2016	13:53	James Gibbons	Campaign	None	Dal_Norm Thompson Pharma	Norm Thompson		SpringSeason	James Gibbons
33	01/04/2016	13:53	James Gibbons	Campaign	None	Parameter Technology	Daniel Brown		SpringSeason	James Gibbons
34	01/04/2016	13:53	James Gibbons	Campaign	None	Microchips	Judy Brown		SpringSeason	James Gibbons
35	01/04/2016	13:53	James Gibbons	Campaign	None	Earthshaker Corporation	Emily Powers		SpringSeason	James Gibbons
36	01/04/2016	13:53	James Gibbons	Campaign	None	Mashina Corporation	Anthony Smith		SpringSeason	James Gibbons
1	21/09/2016	16:20	James Gibbons	Meeting	None	Forgestik Inc				James Gibbons
3	22/09/2016	13:21	Sophie Klogg	Campaign	None	Forgestik Inc			BOGO	James Gibbons
4	22/09/2016	13:21	Sophie Klogg	Campaign	None	Mashina Corporation	Anthony Smith		BOGO	James Gibbons
5	22/09/2016	13:14	James Gibbons	Phone Call	None	Mashina Corporation	Anthony Smith		BOGO	James Gibbons
18	05/10/2016		James Gibbons	Task	None			Not Started	Prepare HANA Demo	James Gibbons
21	06/10/2017	11:09	James Gibbons	Phone Call	Annually	Johnson & Johnson	J&J			James Gibbons
22	06/10/2016	12:30	James Gibbons	Phone Call	None	Mashina Corporation	Anthony Smith			James Gibbons
14	06/11/2016	08:47	Fred Buyer	Meeting	Monthly	Earthshaker Corporation	Emily Powers			James Gibbons
16	07/10/2016	10:51	James Gibbons	Phone Call	None				Call Buyer	James Gibbons
15	13/10/2016	09:55	James Gibbons	Meeting	None	Earthshaker Corporation	Emily Powers		Sales Quote to be followed up	James Gibbons
19	14/10/2016	10:00	James Gibbons	Campaign	None	Acme Associates	Sarah Kierl		Direct Mail 001	James Gibbons
17	18/10/2016	10:52	James Gibbons	Phone Call	None	Acme Associates	Sarah Kierl		Call Sarah	James Gibbons
13	19/11/2016	18:00	Dana Willy	Meeting	Monthly				Customer is unhappy with invoice 235	James Gibbons
20	21/10/2016	03:00	John	Campaign	None	Acme Associates	Sarah Kierl			James Gibbons

Figure 7.54 An Activities Overview Report

You can also generate a list of business partners for whom no activity exists using the Inactive Customers Report. Select MODULES • BUSINESS PARTNERS • BUSINESS PARTNERS REPORTS • INACTIVE CUSTOMERS report from the menu. The selection criteria dialog box shown in Figure 7.55 will appear; input your selection criteria and then choose CANCEL, OK, or SELECT ALL.

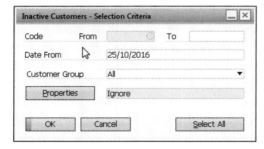

Figure 7.55 Inactive Customers Report Selection Criteria

The resulting list of customers in the report shown in Figure 7.56 are those business partners where the INACTIVE radio button has been selected.

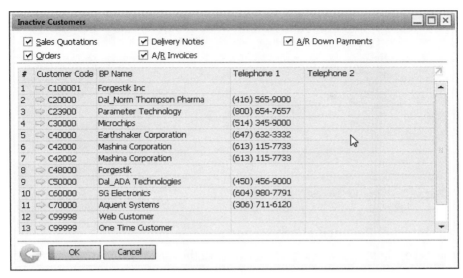

Figure 7.56 An Inactive Customers Report

7.5.2 Cash Management Reports

Four report options are available to facilitate cash flow management: the Dunning History Report, the Customer Receivables by Customer Report, the Customer Credit Limit Deviation Report, and the Aging Report, which includes customer receivables aging and vendor liabilities aging.

The Dunning History Report displays the history of collection activities directed at the business partner through the Dunning Wizard found under the Sales (A/R) module menu options. The wizard creates letters based on the severity of the credit limit deviation.

The Customer Receivables by Customer Report allows you to manage your collection activity down the customer level, whereas the Customer Receivables Aging Report in Figure 7.57 provides you with the age of the A/R invoices by customer to highlight those customers who deviated from the credit limit established on the business partner master record.

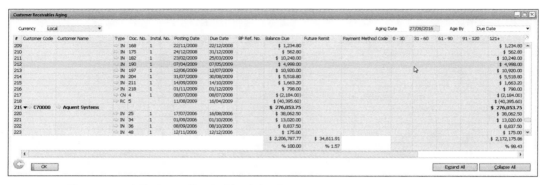

Figure 7.57 A Customer Receivables Aging Report

7.5.3 Internal Reconciliations Reports

Internal reconciliation reports provide you with the information you need to reconcile your system accounts. These reports provide three query options to pull the data: by total reconciliation amount, by transaction key, and by total reconciliation amount. Figure 7.58 shows the Internal Reconciliation by Due Date Report and the three selection criteria windows.

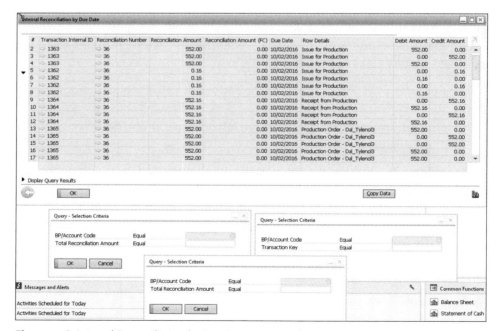

Figure 7.58 Internal Reconciliation by Due Date Report Selection Criteria

7.5.4   Campaign Reports

The final business partner report type we'll discuss are campaign reports. During your campaigns, you'll collect the results of your marketing efforts; to parse this data, you can use the Campaign List Report shown in Figure 7.59. Access this report via the menu path MODULES • BUSINESS PARTNERS • BUSINESS PARTNERS REPORTS • CAMPAIGN LIST.

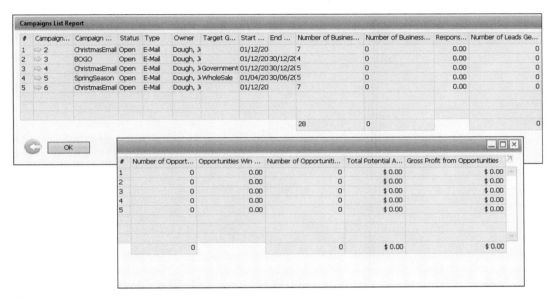

Figure 7.59 A Campaign List Report

Banking tasks generally cover transactions such as paying bills, collecting money from customers, balancing your bank accounts, and performing other reconciliations. Like all ERP systems, SAP Business One provides customers control over these common banking transactions to help companies manage their day-to-day business.

8   Banking

In SAP Business One, banking processes are generally divided into *incoming payments*, *deposits*, *outgoing payments*, and *reconciliations*. This chapter focuses on SAP Business One tasks that are stored and executed in the Banking module. Using step-by-step instructions and screenshots, you'll learn how to perform transactions related to incoming payments, deposits, outgoing payments, bank statements, reconciliations, and so on. We'll walk through each of these tasks and any corresponding wizards; after reading this chapter, you'll be able to navigate easily through these screens and functions, which generally finalize the processes in SAP Business One that were started in sales or purchasing.

8.1   Incoming Payments

The Incoming Payments menu option contains the following processes for incoming payments: Incoming Payments, Check Register, and Credit Card Management.

8.1.1   Incoming Payments

The Incoming Payments window—accessed by following the menu path Banking • Incoming Payments • Incoming Payments—is used to create a transaction each time your company receives a payment from a customer, a vendor, or a general ledger (G/L) account.

Incoming payments can be created for four different payment means or methods: by cash, check, credit card, or bank transfer. When you add an incoming payment, a journal entry is automatically created. When you create an incoming payment to clear a partial or fully paid transaction, a process called an *internal reconciliation* takes place automatically. Incoming payments can be created manually or via the Payment Wizard, which you'll learn about later in Section 8.4.

Creating an incoming payment involves two basic steps. The first step is to create the information on the main screen, and the second is to select and enter the appropriate information to set up a payment means.

Main Screen

This window contains information about the business partner or G/L account from which you are receiving the incoming payment as well as the dates of the transaction and all open invoices for the customer or vendor selected. Note that, in our example, we are recording an incoming payment for a customer. If the incoming payment applies to a G/L account, the screen will change slightly; instead of showing customer transactions on the rows, the screen shows fields for the G/L account number and related information.

If you are creating a new incoming payment (as opposed to viewing an existing incoming payment), you would first complete the main INCOMING PAYMENTS screen and then click on the PAYMENT MEANS icon (the moneybag and coins) near the bottom right of Figure 8.1, before you click ADD on the bottom left.

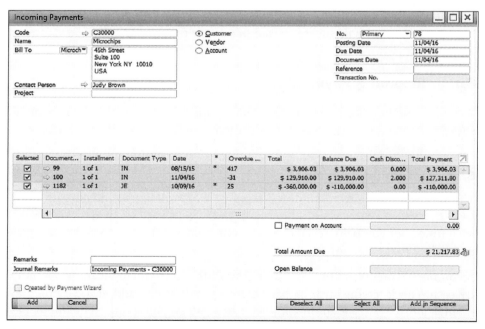

Figure 8.1 The Incoming Payments Screen

Let's walk through the important fields in the main INCOMING PAYMENTS screen in Table 8.1.

Field	Description/Use
CUSTOMER, VENDOR, or ACCOUNT	Select from one of the following: ▸ CUSTOMER (selected by default) ▸ VENDOR ▸ G/L ACCOUNT
CODE	Enter either the business partner code or the G/L account number, depending on your previous selection. The business partner name or the G/L account description will also be shown in the NAME field.
BILL TO	This field displays the business partner's address information.
CONTACT PERSON	This field displays the contact person.
PROJECT	Enter a project number (if desired) for this transaction.
NO.	This field displays the document number for the incoming payment.
POSTING DATE	Enter the posting date for this transaction.
DUE DATE	Enter the due date for this transaction.
DOCUMENT DATE	Enter the document date for this transaction.
REFERENCE	Enter a reference number if desired.
TRANSACTION NO.	This field displays a transaction number. When this incoming payment is added, a golden arrow icon will be made available so you can drill down to the journal entry transaction.
SELECTED	Use this field to select the documents that you want to mark as "paid" with this incoming payment. Note that, as you select transactions, the value in the TOTAL AMOUNT DUE field will be adjusted.
DOCUMENT NO.	This field displays the document number for the transaction. You can drill down to the specific document for further information using the golden arrow icon.
INSTALLMENT	This field displays whether the transaction is one of several planned; in our example, only one transaction is planned.
DOCUMENT TYPE	This field displays the document type.
DOCUMENT DATE	This field displays the document date.
*	An asterisk (*) designates that the invoice is past due.

Table 8.1 Fields in the Incoming Payments Screen

Field	Description/Use
OVERDUE	This field displays the number of days overdue. A negative amount signifies that the document is not yet due.
TOTAL	This field displays the total of the document.
BALANCE DUE	This field displays the balance due for the document.
CASH DISCOUNT	This field displays the cash discount. Note that you can override a cash discount when creating the incoming payment.
TOTAL PAYMENT	This field displays the total payment. Note that you can override the total payment amount, for example, when a customer is short-paying an invoice.
PAYMENT ON ACCOUNT	Select this checkbox if you are receiving a payment on account; you will be prompted to enter a value in the corresponding field.
TOTAL AMOUNT DUE	This field displays the total of all documents selected.
PAYMENT MEANS icon (the moneybag and coins)	Click on this icon to enter the payment means (method) and information that applies to the payment means you are receiving for this incoming payment.
OPEN BALANCE	This field displays an open balance that is not yet applied to open documents.
REMARKS	Enter any remarks desired.
JOURNAL REMARKS	This field displays the journal remarks that will be created after the incoming payment has been added.
CREATED BY PAYMENT WIZARD	This checkbox will be selected if the incoming payment was generated from the Payment Wizard.

Table 8.1 Fields in the Incoming Payments Screen (Cont.)

Payment Means

The PAYMENT MEANS window is used to record the payment means for an incoming payment. Each of the four possible payment methods (check, bank transfer, credit card, or cash) has its own tab.

Check Tab

The CHECK tab shown in Figure 8.2 is used to record the payment means for an incoming payment when the incoming payment method is by check.

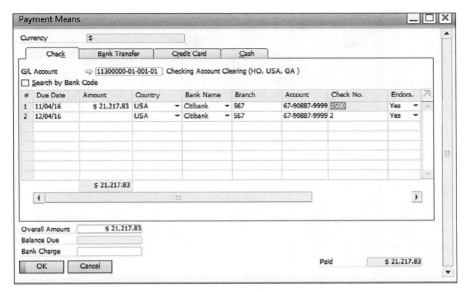

Figure 8.2 The Incoming Payment Means Check Tab

As we did for the main screen, in Table 8.2, let's walk through the fields that you'll need to focus on when creating an incoming payment.

Field	Description/Use
G/L ACCOUNT	Select the G/L account to post the transaction to.
SEARCH BY BANK CODE	Select this checkbox to search G/L accounts by bank code. This checkbox is helpful if you have numerous accounts to choose from.
DUE DATE	This field contains the due date of the transaction; the value in this column defaults to today's date.
AMOUNT	This field displays the amount of the transaction. You can bring the total over from the main INCOMING PAYMENTS window using the keyboard command $\boxed{\text{Ctrl}}+\boxed{\text{B}}$. Note that the total from this column will appear at the bottom.
COUNTRY	This field displays the country of the bank.
BANK NAME	This field displays the bank name.
BRANCH	This field displays the branch.
ACCOUNT	This field displays the bank account number.

Table 8.2 Fields in the Incoming Payment Means Check Tab

Field	Description/Use
CHECK NO.	Enter the check number of the check supplied by the payer.
ENDORS.	Select whether the check should be endorsed or not.
OVERALL AMOUNT	This field displays the overall amount.
BALANCE DUE	This field displays the balance due.
BANK CHARGE	Enter any bank charges.
PAID	This field displays the total paid amount.

Table 8.2 Fields in the Incoming Payment Means Check Tab (Cont.)

Bank Transfer Tab

Use the BANK TRANSFER tab shown in Figure 8.3 when you want to record the payment means for an incoming payment when the incoming payment method is a bank transfer. Table 8.3 lists the corresponding fields.

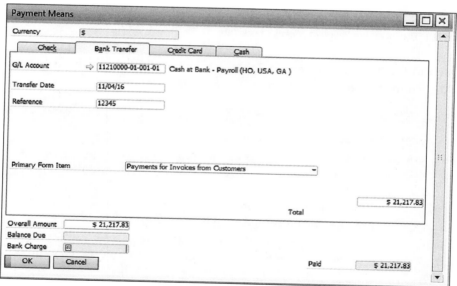

Figure 8.3 The Incoming Payment Means Bank Transfer Tab

Field	Description/Use
G/L ACCOUNT	Enter the G/L account to post the transaction to.
TRANSFER DATE	This field displays the transfer date, which defaults to today's date.

Table 8.3 Fields in the Incoming Payment Means Bank Transfer Tab

Field	Description/Use
REFERENCE	Enter the transfer reference.
PRIMARY FORM ITEM	This field is visible only if the G/L account selected is a cash flow-relevant account. After you have defined the cash flow line items in the CASH FLOW LINE ITEMS SETUP window, you can then specify the primary form line items that should be assigned to the cash flow-relevant transaction from the COMBINED CASH FLOW ASSIGNMENT window from this dropdown list.
TOTAL	This field displays the total.
OVERALL AMOUNT	This field displays the overall amount of the transaction.
BALANCE DUE	This field displays the balance due.
BANK CHARGE	In this field, enter any bank charges that apply to this transaction.

Table 8.3 Fields in the Incoming Payment Means Bank Transfer Tab (Cont.)

Credit Card Tab

The CREDIT CARD tab shown in Figure 8.4 is used to record the payment means for the incoming payment when the incoming payment method is a credit card. Table 8.4 provides details on how to complete this tab.

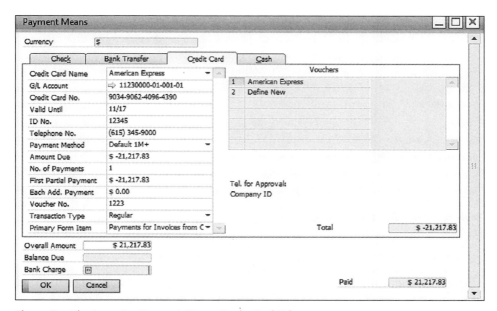

Figure 8.4 The Incoming Payment Means Credit Card Tab

Field	Description/Use
CREDIT CARD NAME	Select a credit card name from the dropdown list.
G/L ACCOUNT	Select the G/L account.
CREDIT CARD NO.	Enter the credit card number (last 4 digits only recommended).
VALID UNTIL	Enter the credit card expiration date.
ID NO.	Enter the ID or reference number.
TELEPHONE NO.	Enter the telephone number.
PAYMENT METHOD	Choose a payment method for the credit card from the dropdown menu.
AMOUNT DUE	Enter the amount due.
NO. OF PAYMENTS	Enter the number of payments.
FIRST PARTIAL PAYMENT	Enter the amount of the payment or the first partial payment.
EACH ADD. PAYMENT	Enter additional installment payments as needed.
VOUCHER NO.	Enter the voucher number.
TRANSACTION TYPE	Select one of the following: ▸ TELEPHONE TRANSACTION ▸ REGULAR ▸ INTERNET TRANSACTION
PRIMARY FORM ITEM	This field is visible only if the G/L account selected is a cash flow-relevant account. After you have defined the cash flow line items in the CASH FLOW LINE ITEMS SETUP window, you can then specify the primary form line items that should be assigned to the cash flow-relevant transaction from the COMBINED CASH FLOW ASSIGNMENT window from this dropdown list.
VOUCHERS	Add additional credit card vouchers if needed.
TOTAL	This field displays the total.
OVERALL AMOUNT	This field displays the overall amount of the transaction.
BALANCE DUE	This field displays the balance due.
BANK CHARGE	Enter any bank charges that apply to this transaction.
PAID	This field displays the paid amount.

Table 8.4 Fields in the Incoming Payment Means Credit Card Tab

Cash Tab

The last payment method for an incoming payment is cash. The CASH tab shown in Figure 8.5 is used to record the payment means this method. Fill the tab using the instructions listed in Table 8.5.

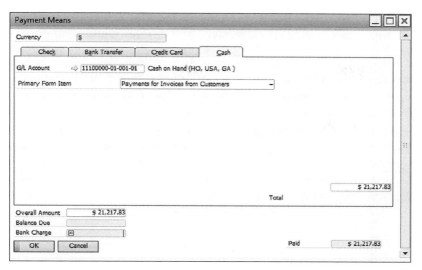

Figure 8.5 The Incoming Payment Means Cash Tab

Field	Description/Use
G/L ACCOUNT	Select the G/L account.
PRIMARY FORM ITEM	This field is visible only if the G/L account selected is a cash flow-relevant account. After you have defined the cash flow line items in the CASH FLOW LINE ITEMS SETUP window, you can then specify the primary form line items that should be assigned to the cash flow-relevant transaction from the COMBINED CASH FLOW ASSIGNMENT window from this dropdown list.
TOTAL	Enter the total.
PAID	This field displays the total paid.
OVERALL AMOUNT	This field displays the overall amount of the transaction.
BALANCE DUE	This field displays the balance due.
BANK CHARGE	Enter any bank charges that apply to this transaction.

Table 8.5 Fields in the Incoming Payment Means Cash Tab

8.1.2 Check Register

SAP Business One uses the check register to store details of all the checks that have been received by the company. The check details are recorded in the PAYMENT MEANS window while creating an incoming payment. In addition, the check information is updated when the check is deposited. The CHECK REGISTER screen shows the status of every check received and enables you to find out the status of when a check was received and deposited and whether it was endorsed.

To access the check register functionality, follow the menu path BANKING • INCOMING PAYMENTS • CHECK REGISTER. As shown in Figure 8.6, a selection screen will be displayed where you can enter specific data to narrow down the report. After you click OK, a report will be displayed containing the details of the checks and deposits that met the requirements of the data that you entered on the selection screen, as shown in Figure 8.7.

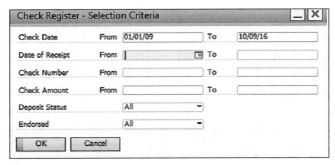

Figure 8.6 Check Register Selection Criteria

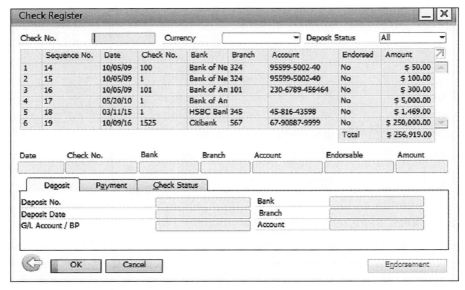

Figure 8.7 The Check Register Screen

8.1.3 Credit Card Management

The CREDIT CARD MANAGEMENT screen is used to store information about all the credit card vouchers that are recorded in the PAYMENT MEANS window when incoming payments are created. When a credit card voucher is deposited, the information is updated so that you can see the status of all credit card transactions. The CREDIT CARD MANAGEMENT screen shows the status of every credit card transaction received and enables you to find out the status of when a transaction was received or deposited. To access the CREDIT CARD MANAGEMENT screen, follow the menu path BANKING • INCOMING PAYMENTS • CREDIT CARD MANAGEMENT. As shown in Figure 8.8, a selection screen will be displayed where you can enter specific data to narrow down the report. After you click OK, a report will be displayed containing the details of the credit card transactions that met the requirements of the data that you entered in the selection screen, as shown in Figure 8.9.

Figure 8.8 Credit Card Management Selection Criteria

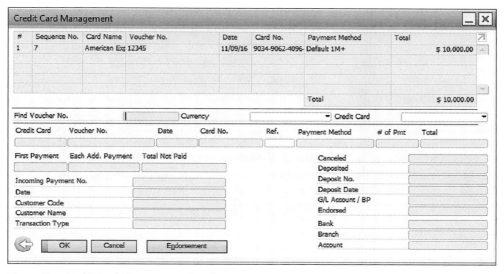

Figure 8.9 Credit Card Management Details

8.2   Deposits

The DEPOSIT screen is used to deposit checks, credit cards, and cash that you have received. The screen contains header information that applies to the deposit plus three tabs (the CHECKS, CREDIT CARD, and CASH tabs). Access the DEPOSIT screen by following the menu path BANKING • DEPOSITS • DEPOSIT.

The header shown in Figure 8.10 contains the main information about the deposit.

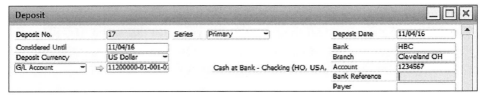

Figure 8.10 The Deposit Screen Header Details

Table 8.6 contains the details and instructions for creating the header details on the DEPOSIT screen.

Field	Description/Use
DEPOSIT NO.	This field displays a number that is automatically assigned for each deposit.
CONSIDERED UNTIL	Enter the date to be considered until for this deposit. This field will default to today's date.
DEPOSIT CURRENCY	Enter the currency to be used for this deposit.
G/L ACCOUNT	Enter the G/L account you'll deposit into.
DEPOSIT DATE	Enter the deposit date.
BANK	Enter the bank where the deposit was made.
BRANCH	Enter the bank branch where the deposit was made.
ACCOUNT	Enter the bank account number.
BANK REFERENCE	Enter the bank reference assigned to the deposit by the bank.
PAYER	Enter the payer (person that made the deposit).

Table 8.6 Fields in the Deposit Screen

A deposit may take one of three forms: check, credit card, or cash. Let's examine the requisite information for each.

8.2.1 Check Tab

The CHECK tab of the DEPOSIT screen is used to select incoming checks to be deposited, as shown in Figure 8.11.

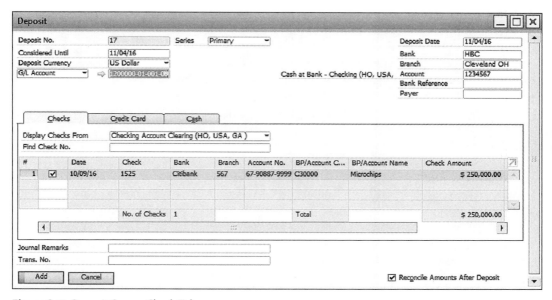

Figure 8.11 Deposit Screen Check Tab

Table 8.7 contains the details and instructions for creating the CHECK tab on the DEPOSIT screen.

Field	Description/Use
DISPLAY CHECKS FROM	Select the G/L account to display checks from.
FIND CHECK NO.	Enter a check number if searching for a specific check.
#	Select this checkbox to choose this check to deposit.
DATE	This field displays the date of the check.

Table 8.7 Fields in the Deposits Screen Check Tab

Field	Description/Use
CHECK	This field displays the check number of the check.
BANK	This field displays the bank.
BRANCH	This field displays the bank branch information.
ACCOUNT No.	This field displays the bank account number.
BP/ACCOUNT CODE	This field displays the business partner code or G/L account code of the transaction.
BP/ACCOUNT DESC.	This field displays the business partner name or G/L account description.
No. OF CHECKS	This field displays the total number of checks selected for this deposit.
TOTAL	This field displays the total for this deposit.
JOURNAL REMARKS	After a deposit is added, a journal remark will be added automatically.
TRANS. No.	After a deposit is added, a journal entry transaction number will be added automatically, and a golden arrow will appear so that you can drill down to the journal entry transaction.
RECONCILE AMOUNTS AFTER DEPOSIT	Select this checkbox to automatically reconcile amounts after the deposit has been created.

Table 8.7 Fields in the Deposits Screen Check Tab (Cont.)

Once you've entered this information, either click ADD to add the deposit or click CANCEL to cancel the deposit. Take these steps for each tab.

8.2.2 Credit Card Tab

Figure 8.12 shows the CREDIT CARD tab of the DEPOSIT screen, which is used to select incoming credit card payments to be deposited.

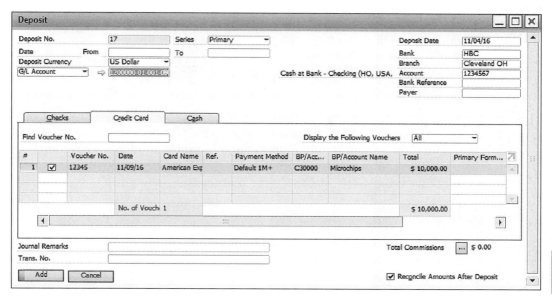

Figure 8.12 Deposit Screen Credit Card Tab

Table 8.8 contains the details and instructions for creating the CREDIT CARD tab on the DEPOSIT screen.

Field	Description/Use
FIND VOUCHER NO.	Enter a voucher number if searching for a specific voucher.
DISPLAY THE FOLLOWING VOUCHERS	Choose whether to display the vouchers for all G/L accounts or a select G/L account.
#	Select this checkbox to choose this credit card to deposit.
VOUCHER NO.	This field displays the credit card voucher number.
DATE	This field displays the date.
REF.	This field displays the reference.
PAYMENT METHOD	This field displays the payment method.
BP/ACCOUNT CODE	This field displays the business partner code or G/L account code of the transaction.

Table 8.8 Fields in the Deposit Screen Credit Card Tab

Field	Description/Use
BP/ACCOUNT DESCR.	This field displays the business partner name or G/L account description.
TOTAL	This field displays the total.
JOURNAL REMARKS	After a deposit is added, a journal remark will be added automatically.
TRANS. NO.	After the deposit is added, a journal entry transaction number will be added automatically and a golden arrow will appear so that you can drill down to the journal entry transaction.
TOTAL COMMISSIONS	This field displays total commissions.
RECONCILE AMOUNTS AFTER DEPOSIT	Select this checkbox to automatically reconcile amounts after the deposit has been created.

Table 8.8 Fields in the Deposit Screen Credit Card Tab (Cont.)

8.2.3 Cash Tab

The CASH tab of the DEPOSIT screen shown in Figure 8.13 is used to select incoming cash payments to be deposited, the last of the three deposit payment options. We'll discuss the important fields in this tab in Table 8.9.

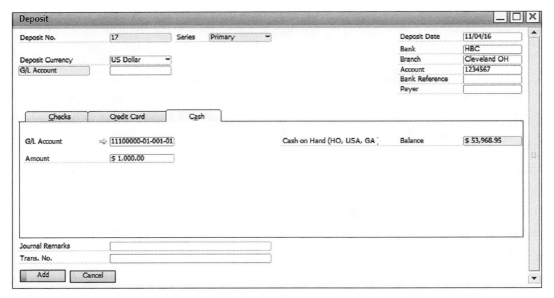

Figure 8.13 The Deposit Screen Cash Tab

Field	Description/Use
G/L ACCOUNT	Select the G/L account to deposit to.
AMOUNT	This field displays the amount to be deposited.
CASH ON HAND	This field displays the G/L account name for the deposit.
BALANCE	This field displays the balance.
JOURNAL REMARKS	After the deposit is added, a journal remark will be added automatically.
TRANS NO.	After the deposit is added, a journal entry transaction number will be added automatically, and a golden arrow will appear so that you can drill down to the journal entry transaction.

Table 8.9 Fields in the Deposits Cash Tab

8.3 Outgoing Payments

If you're already familiar with the incoming payment process, you'll find that the outgoing payment process is similar. The OUTGOING PAYMENTS menu option contains the following processes: OUTGOING PAYMENTS, CHECK FOR PAYMENT, VOID CHECKS FOR PAYMENT, and CHECKS FOR PAYMENT DRAFTS REPORT.

8.3.1 Outgoing Payments

This window is used to create a transaction each time your company makes a payment to a vendor, customer, or G/L account. Just like incoming payments, outgoing payments can be created for the following different payment means (methods): cash, check, credit card, or bank transfers. When you add the outgoing payment, a journal entry is automatically created. When you create an outgoing payment to clear a partial or fully paid transaction a process called an *internal reconciliation* takes place automatically. You can either create outgoing payments manually or by using the Payment Wizard, which we'll cover in Section 8.4; after you have learned and mastered the Payment Wizard process, you will most likely utilize the Payment Wizard to make most of your payments.

Creating an outgoing payment involves two basic steps. The first step is to create the information on the main screen, and the second is to select and enter the appropriate information for a payment means. Start by following the menu path BANKING • OUTGOING PAYMENTS • OUTGOING PAYMENTS.

Main Screen

This window contains the information about the business partner or the G/L account to which you are paying the outgoing payment as well as the dates of the transaction and all open items for the vendor or customer selected. Note that, in our example, we are recording an outgoing payment for a vendor. If the outgoing payment applies to a G/L account or a customer, the screen will change slightly; instead of showing open items transactions on the rows, the screen would instead show fields for the G/L account number and related information.

If you are creating a new outgoing payment (as opposed to viewing an existing outgoing payment), you would first complete the main OUTGOING PAYMENTS screen and then click on the PAYMENT MEANS icon (the moneybag and coins), shown in Figure 8.14, before you click ADD on the document.

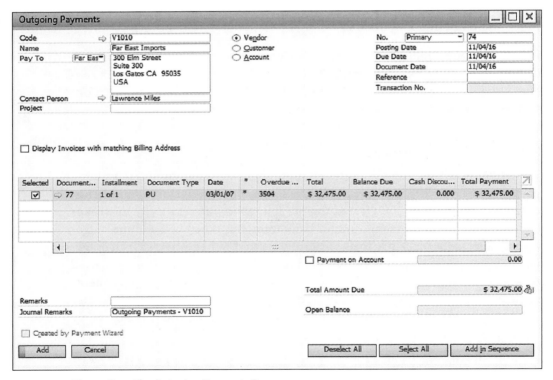

Figure 8.14 The Outgoing Payments Screen

Table 8.10 contains details and instructions for the main OUTGOING PAYMENTS screen.

Field	Description/Use
VENDOR, CUSTOMER, and ACCOUNT	Select from one of the following: ▶ VENDOR (selected as the default) ▶ CUSTOMER ▶ G/L ACCOUNT
CODE	Enter either the business partner code or the G/L account number depending on your selection for the first field. The business partner name or the G/L account description will also be shown.
PAY TO	This field displays the business partner's address information.
CONTRACT PERSON	This field displays the contact person.
PROJECT	Enter a project number (if desired) for this transaction.
NO.	This field displays the automatically assigned document number for this outgoing payment.
POSTING DATE	Enter the posting date for this transaction.
DUE DATE	Enter the due date.
DOCUMENT DATE	Enter the document date.
REFERENCE	Enter a reference number if desired.
TRANSACTION NO.	This field will display a transaction number when this outgoing payment is added. To drill down into the journal entry transaction, use the golden arrow.
SELECTED	Use this field to select the documents that you want to mark as "paid" with this outgoing payment. Note that, as you select invoices and other open items, the TOTAL AMOUNT DUE field will be adjusted.
DOCUMENT NO.	This field displays the document number for the transaction. In this field, you can use the golden arrow to drill down to the specific document for further information.
INSTALLMENT	This field displays the installment number.
DOCUMENT TYPE	This field displays the document type.
DATE	This field displays the document date.
*	An asterisk (*) designates that the invoice or open item is past due.

Table 8.10 Fields in the Outgoing Payments Screen

Field	Description/Use
OVERDUE	This field shows the number of days either overdue or a negative amount will signify that the document is not yet due.
TOTAL	This field displays the total of the document.
BALANCE DUE	This field displays the balance due for the document.
CASH DISCOUNT	This field displays the cash discount. Note that you can override this value when creating the outgoing payment.
TOTAL PAYMENT	This field displays the total payment. Note that you can override this amount when you want to short-pay an invoice.
PAYMENT ON ACCOUNT	Select this checkbox if you are making a payment on account and then enter a value in the corresponding field.
TOTAL AMOUNT DUE	This field displays the total of all documents selected.
PAYMENT MEANS icon (the moneybag and coins)	Click on this icon to enter the payment means and the information that applies to the payment means for this outgoing payment.
OPEN BALANCE	This field displays an open balance that is not yet applied to open documents.
REMARKS	Enter any remarks desired.
JOURNAL REMARKS	This field displays the journal remarks after the outgoing payment has been added.
DISPLAY INVOICES WITH MATCHING BILLING ADDRESS	This checkbox will be selected if the outgoing payment was generated from the Payment Wizard.

Table 8.10 Fields in the Outgoing Payments Screen (Cont.)

Payment Means

This window is used to record the payment means for an outgoing payment. The four possible payment methods (check, bank transfer, credit card, or cash) each have their own tabs within the PAYMENT MEANS window.

Check Tab

The CHECK tab shown in Figure 8.15 is used to record the payment means for the outgoing payment when the outgoing payment method is a check.

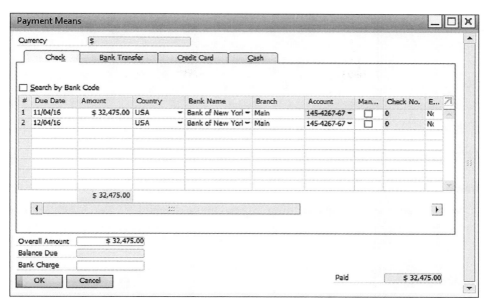

Figure 8.15 The Outgoing Payment Means Check Tab

Table 8.11 outlines the fields for you to focus on and contains details and instructions for creating an outgoing payment with this method.

Field	Description/Use
SEARCH BY BANK CODE	Select this field to search by bank code.
DUE DATE	This field displays the posting date of the transaction; the field will default to today's date, but you can change it as necessary.
AMOUNT	This field displays the amount of the transaction. The keyboard stroke $\boxed{Ctrl}+\boxed{B}$ will bring the total over from the main INCOMING PAYMENT screen.
COUNTRY	This field displays the country of the bank.
BANK NAME	This field displays the bank name.
BRANCH	This field displays the branch.
ACCOUNT	This field displays the bank account number.
MANUAL and CHECK NO.	Select the MANUAL checkbox if you are entering the check number after a check was manually created and put the check number in the adjacent CHECK NO. field.

Table 8.11 Fields in the Outgoing Payment Means Check Tab

Field	Description/Use
ENDORS.	Select whether the check should be endorsed or not.
OVERALL AMOUNT	This field displays the overall amount.
BALANCE DUE	This field displays the balance due.
BANK CHARGE	Enter any bank charges.
PAID	This field displays the total paid amount.

Table 8.11 Fields in the Outgoing Payment Means Check Tab (Cont.)

Bank Transfer Tab

If the payment method for your outgoing payment is a bank transfer, then use the BANK TRANSFER tab shown in Figure 8.16 to record the payment means. Table 8.12 provides details on how to complete this tab.

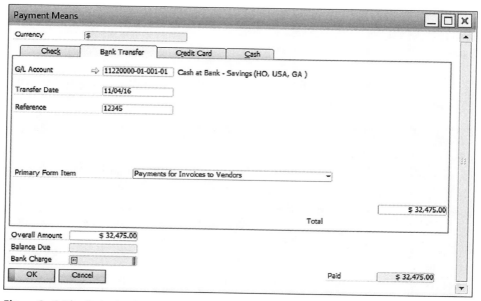

Figure 8.16 The Outgoing Payment Means Bank Transfer Tab

Field	Description/Use
G/L AMOUNT	Enter the G/L account to post the transaction to.
TRANSFER DATE	Input the transfer date; this field will default to today's date.

Table 8.12 Fields in the Outgoing Payment Means Bank Transfer Tab

Field	Description/Use
REFERENCE	Enter the transfer reference.
PRIMARY FORM ITEM	This field is visible only if the G/L account selected is a cash flow-relevant account. After you have defined the cash flow line items in the CASH FLOW LINE ITEMS SETUP window, you can then specify the primary line items that should be assigned to the cash-relevant transaction from the COMBINED CASH FLOW ASSIGNMENT window from this dropdown list.
TOTAL	This field displays the total.
OVERALL AMOUNT	This field displays the overall amount of the transaction.
BALANCE DUE	This field displays the balance due.
BANK CHARGE	Enter any bank charges that apply to this transaction.
PAID	This field displays the total paid.

Table 8.12 Fields in the Outgoing Payment Means Bank Transfer Tab (Cont.)

Credit Card Tab

Use the CREDIT CARD tab shown in Figure 8.17 to record the payment means for an outgoing payment when the outgoing payment method is a credit card. We've outlined the important fields with corresponding instructions in Table 8.13.

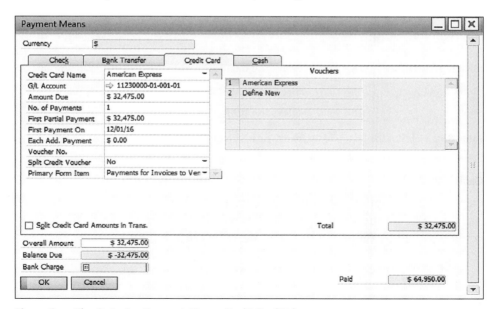

Figure 8.17 The Outgoing Payment Means Credit Card Tab

Field	Description/Use
CREDIT CARD NAME	Select a credit card name.
G/L ACCOUNT	Select the G/L account.
AMOUNT DUE	Enter the amount due.
NO. OF PAYMENTS	Enter the number of payments.
FIRST PARTIAL PAYMENT	Enter the amount of the payment or the first partial payment.
FIRST PAYMENT ON	Enter the date of the first payment.
EACH ADD. PAYMENT	Enter additional installment payments.
VOUCHER NO.	Enter the voucher number.
SPLIT CREDIT VOUCHER	Designate whether to split the credit voucher by selecting YES or NO.
VOUCHERS	This field is used to define new credit vouchers types.
SPLIT CREDIT CARD AMOUNT IN TRANS.	Select this checkbox to split credit card amounts in transaction.
TOTAL	This field displays the total, or you can enter an amount.
OVERALL AMOUNT	Select one of the following: ▶ TELEPHONE TRANSACTION ▶ REGULAR ▶ INTERNET TRANSACTION
BALANCE DUE	This field displays the balance due, or you can enter an amount.
BANK CHARGE	Enter any bank charges that apply to this transaction.
PAID	This field displays the total paid.

Table 8.13 Fields in the Outgoing Payment Means Credit Card

Cash Tab

Cash is the last option for outgoing payment methods with SAP Business One. Use the CASH tab shown in Figure 8.18 to record the payment means for the outgoing payment by filling out the fields described in Table 8.14.

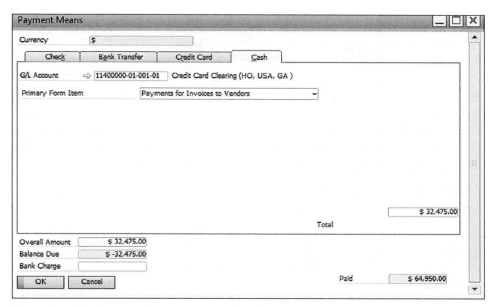

Figure 8.18 The Outgoing Payment Means Cash Tab

Field	Description/Use
G/L AMOUNT	Select the G/L account.
PRIMARY FORM ITEM	This field is visible only if the G/L account selected is a cash flow-relevant account. After you have defined the cash flow line items in the CASH FLOW LINE ITEMS SETUP window, you can then specify the primary form line items that should be assigned to the cash flow-relevant transaction from the COMBINED CASH FLOW ASSIGNMENT window from this dropdown list.
TOTAL	Enter the total.
OVERALL AMOUNT	This field displays the overall amount of the transaction.
BALANCE DUE	This field will display the balance due.
BANK CHARGE	Enter any bank charges that apply to this transaction.
PAID	This field displays the total paid.

Table 8.14 Fields in the Outgoing Payment Means Cash Tab

8.3.2 Checks for Payment

The CHECKS FOR PAYMENT screen is used to define or review the checks that you need to pay. Although SAP Business One allows you to create a check directly from this screen, we don't recommend using this method because it does not meet standard accounting practices. Instead, you should either create the outgoing payments manually or use the Payment Wizard. Both methods will automatically create the transactions on the CHECKS FOR PAYMENT screen when the checks are processed. We'll limit our discussion on this screen to reviewing the screen shown in Figure 8.19 and explaining the fields in Table 8.15.

To access the CHECKS FOR PAYMENT screen, follow the menu path BANKING • OUTGOING PAYMENTS • CHECKS FOR PAYMENT.

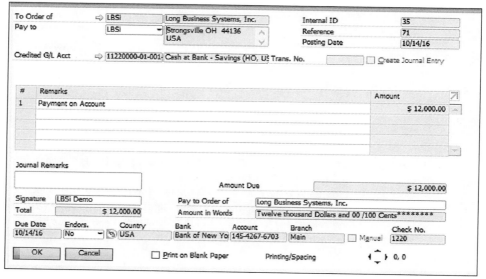

Figure 8.19 The Checks for Payment Screen

Field	Description/Use
TO ORDER OF	This field will display the payee on the check.
PAY TO	This field will display the address of the payee
INTERNAL ID	This field displays internal ID of the check (not the check number!).

Table 8.15 Fields in the Checks for Payment Screen

Field	Description/Use
REFERENCE	This field is for a reference if one was noted when creating the payment.
POSTING DATE	This field displays the date of the check.
CREDITED G/L ACCOUNT	This field displays the G/L account for the cash side of the transaction
REMARKS	Input any required or helpful remarks line by line, including remarks made by the Payment Wizard if the checks were produced from that tool.
AMOUNT	This field displays the amount of the check.
TOTAL	This field displays the total.
PAY TO ORDER OF	This field displays the entity to whom the check is made.
CHECK NO.	This field displays the check number.
DUE DATE	This field displays the due date.
COUNTRY	This field displays the country of the bank that issues the check.
BANK, ACCOUNT, and BRANCH	This field displays the bank name, account and branch information.

Table 8.15 Fields in the Checks for Payment Screen (Cont.)

Tips and Tricks: Checks for Payment
Are you looking for information about a check, but all you have is the check number? You can find the check by navigating to BANKING • OUTGOING PAYMENTS • CHECKS FOR PAYMENTS and entering the check number to perform a search on the CHECK NUMBER field.

8.3.3 Void Checks for Payments

The VOID CHECKS FOR PAYMENTS screen is used to void any checks that were previously created and not yet cashed.

To void checks, follow the menu path BANKING • OUTGOING PAYMENTS • VOID CHECKS FOR PAYMENTS. As shown in Figure 8.20, the system will first prompt you to enter selection criteria to bring up a filtered list of checks; enter a range of dates, check numbers, or internal document numbers. If you click on the BANK CODE button, you will further be able to select checks based on particular banks that you identify. Select which checks you wish to cancel and click OK.

After you've complete the selection criteria, the VOID CHECKS FOR PAYMENT screen shown in Figure 8.21 will be displayed. Table 8.16 outlines the fields shown in this screen.

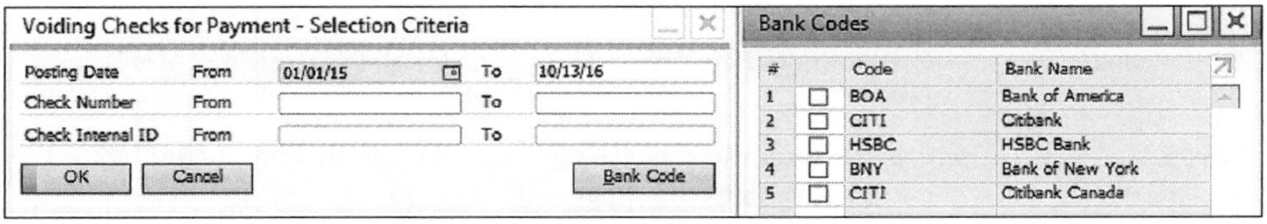

Figure 8.20 Void Checks for Payment Selection Criteria

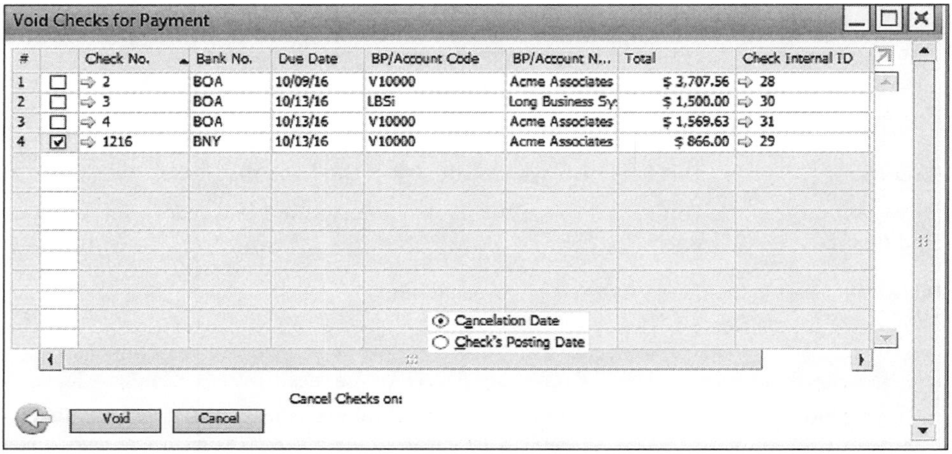

Figure 8.21 Void Checks for Payment Results

Field	Description/Use
(blank column)	Select this checkbox if you want to void this check.
CHECK NO.	This field displays the check number.
BANK NO.	This field displays the bank information.
DUE DATE	This field displays the due date.
BP/ACCOUNT CODE	This field displays the business partner or account code.
TOTAL	This field displays the check total.
CHECK INTERNAL ID	This field displays the internal ID of the check.

Table 8.16 Fields in the Void Checks for Payment Results Screen

Field	Description/Use
CANCEL CHECKS ON	Choose the date to use when the check is voided: ▸ CANCELATION DATE: Cancels the check on the current date of the void transaction). ▸ CHECK POSTING DATE: Cancels the check on the original check posting date.

Table 8.16 Fields in the Void Checks for Payment Results Screen (Cont.)

At the end of this process, you'll have two options:

▸ Click the VOID button to cancel or void the checks you selected.

▸ Click the CANCEL button to cancel the transaction and not void any checks.

8.3.4 Checks for Payments Draft Report

Use the CHECKS FOR PAYMENT DRAFTS screen to process drafts created for checks for payment. To access the function, choose BANKING • OUTGOING PAYMENTS • CHECKS FOR PAYMENT DRAFTS.

8.4 Payment Wizard

The Payment Wizard is the process that most users will utilize to create incoming and outgoing payments by entering criteria on all the screens of the Payment Wizard. If you are also creating checks while using the Payment Wizard, you will be prompted to print the checks and confirm that the checks are printed correctly.

Let's walk through the process of using the Payment Wizard. Start by navigating to the wizard following the menu path BANKING • PAYMENT WIZARD. Note that, between each step, you'll have three options:

▸ Click the NEXT button to the next step of the Payment Wizard.

▸ Click the BACK button to return to the last step of the Payment Wizard.

▸ Click the CANCEL button to cancel the Payment Wizard.

Let's begin. Start the Payment Wizard by clicking the NEXT button.

1. The first step is to decide whether you want to start a new payment run or choose an existing saved payment run using the corresponding radio buttons shown in Figure 8.22. Once you've made your selection, click NEXT.

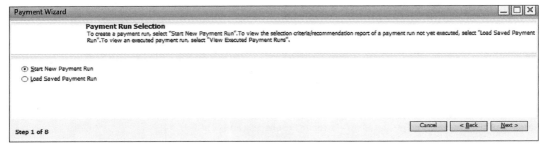

Figure 8.22 Payment Run Selections (Step 1 of the Wizard)

2. The GENERAL PARAMETERS window of the Payment Wizard shown in Figure 8.23 walks you through selecting the general parameters for the payment run. A dozen important fields appear in this window; we'll explain them in Table 8.17.

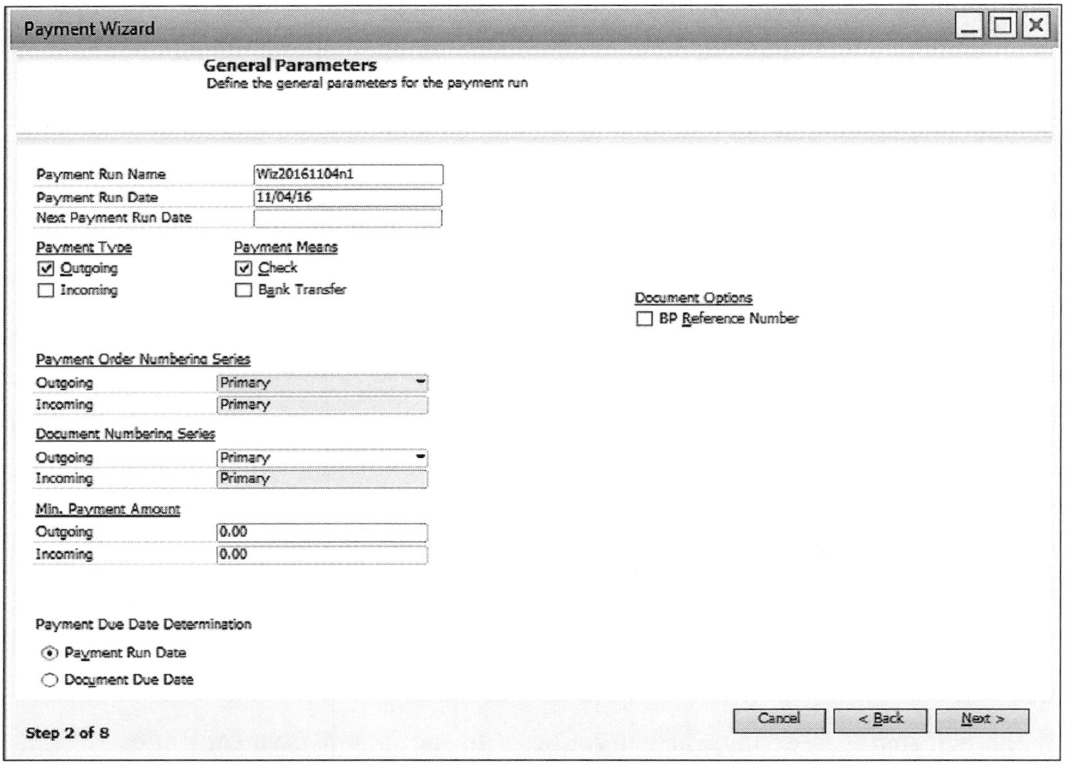

Figure 8.23 The General Parameters (Step 2 of the Wizard)

Field	Description/Use
PAYMENT RUN NAME	This field displays an automatically assigned name that can be overwritten manually, as necessary.
PAYMENT RUN DATE	This field displays the run date, which defaults to today's date.
NEXT PAYMENT RUN DATE	Enter the date of your planned next payment run. You can use this date to take advantage of cash discounts. For example, if any due payments with cash discounts are to be made prior to the date of the next payment run date, the wizard will include those payments as suggestions in the Payment Wizard results. Of course, you may choose to accept these suggestions or ignore them and not process those payments.
PAYMENT TYPE	Select either the OUTGOING PAYMENTS or INCOMING PAYMENTS checkbox. If you select OUTGOING PAYMENTS, then all open A/P transactions matching your selection criteria will be displayed. If you select INCOMING PAYMENTS, then all open A/R transactions matching your selection criteria will be displayed.
PAYMENT MEANS	By putting a checkmark in the respective boxes, select whether to process payments for checks, bank transfers, or both. (Note that you can combine these payment means in one Payment Wizard, and SAP Business One will only print checks for the outgoing payments created for checks.)
DOCUMENT OPTIONS	Select this checkbox to display the BP REFERENCE NUMBER column instead of the DOCUMENT column in the GENERATED PAYMENTS review screen.
PAYMENT ORDER NUMBERING SERIES	Specify the payment order numbering series to be considered for this wizard. (If you are not using a custom numbering series, then the PRIMARY default is correct; otherwise, select a series from the OUTGOING and INCOMING dropdown lists.)
DOCUMENT NUMBERING SERIES	Specify the document numbering series to be considered for this wizard. (If you are not using a custom numbering series, then the PRIMARY default is correct; otherwise, select a series from the OUTGOING and INCOMING dropdown lists.)
MINIMUM PAYMENT AMOUNT	Specify the minimum amount for a single payment generated by the current payment run for both outgoing and incoming payments. If you leave the OUTGOING or INCOMING field blank, then no payment amount limitation will be considered for that respective payment.

Table 8.17 Fields in the General Parameters Screen

Field	Description/Use
PAYMENT DUE DATE DETERMINATION	Select one of the values to determine the payment due date. You have two options: ▸ PAYMENT RUN DATE (most common selection) ▸ DOCUMENT DUE DATE

Table 8.17 Fields in the General Parameters Screen (Cont.)

Once you've made your selections, click NEXT.

3. The next step is to choose selection criteria to determine the business partners (customers and vendors) for the payment run. The BUSINESS PARTNER SELECTION CRITERIA screen is shown in Figure 8.24; its key fields are described in Table 8.18.

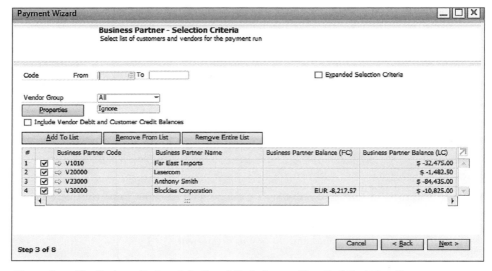

Figure 8.24 The Business Partner Selection Criteria Screen (Step 3 of the Wizard)

Field	Description/Use
CODE	Select the first and last business partner code to be considered. To add all business partners, click the ADD TO LIST button.
EXPANDED SELECTION CRITERIA	Select this checkbox to utilize additional selection fields from the BUSINESS PARTNER screen.
VENDOR GROUP	Select specific vendor or customer groups or select ALL to include all vendor or customer groups.

Table 8.18 Fields in the Business Partner Selection Criteria Screen

Field	Description/Use
PROPERTIES	Use the PROPERTIES button to select transactions based on specific business partner property codes.
INCLUDE VENDOR DEBIT AND CUSTOMER CREDIT BALANCES	Select this checkbox to include vendor debit and customer credit balances. Note that you cannot create payments for vendor debit or customer credit balances. By default, this checkbox is *not* selected.
ADD TO LIST	Click this button to add the business partners selected to the display list.
REMOVE FROM LIST	Click this button to remove business partners from the display list.
REMOVE ENTIRE LIST	Click this button to clear the entire list of business partners.
BUSINESS PARTNERS	This table displays all the business partners you selected. You can choose to deselect business partners from this list.

Table 8.18 Fields in the Business Partner Selection Criteria Screen (Cont.)

Once you've made your selections, click NEXT.

4. Now that you've identified the desired business partners, the Payment Wizard walks you through selecting document parameters for the payment run. This DOCUMENT PARAMETERS screen is shown in Figure 8.25, and its fields are listed in Table 8.19.

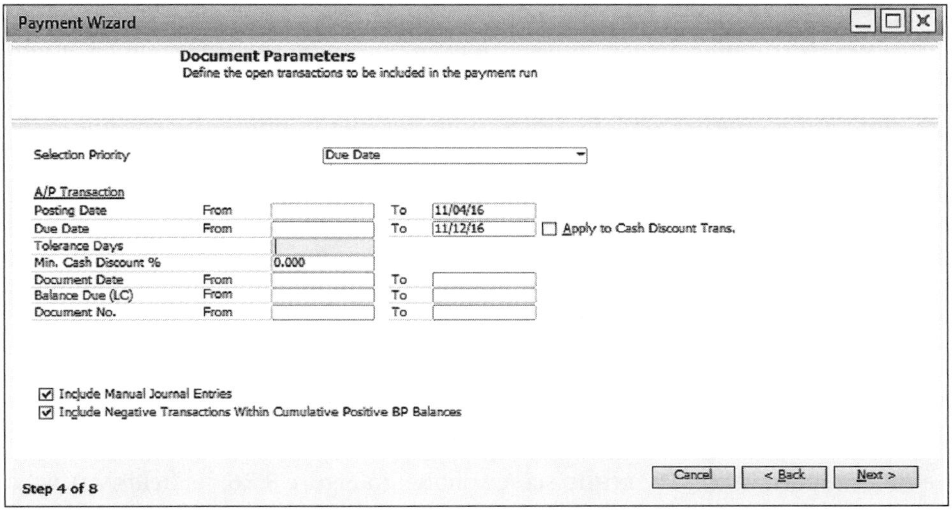

Figure 8.25 The Document Parameters Screen (Step 4 of the Wizard)

Field	Description/Use
SELECTION PRIORITY	Select from one of the following: ▸ POSTING DATE ▸ DUE DATE ▸ CASH DISCOUNT ▸ PAY TO DETAILS
POSTING DATE	Enter a range of dates. Normally, these fields are left blank, since usually you want to base payments on their due dates rather than their posting dates.
DUE DATE	Enter an ending due date to be considered. For example, if you want to process payments for all transactions through 10/15/16, then enter that date in this field. Select the APPLY TO CASH DISCOUNT TRANSACTIONS checkbox if you want this date used for cash discounts also. This checkbox is normally not selected.
TOLERANCE DAYS	Specify the number of days to adjust the due date range of A/P transactions. If tolerance days are entered, then the date for the payment run will be calculated as the original due date minus tolerance days.
MINIMUM CASH DISCOUNT %	Enter the amount to be considered.
DISCOUNT DATE	Enter the document date range. This field is typically left blank.
BALANCE DUE (LC)	Enter the balance due range. This field is typically left blank.
DOCUMENT NO.	Enter the document number range. This field is typically left blank.
INCLUDE MANUAL JOURNAL ENTRIES	Select this checkbox to include manual journal entries. This field is typically left blank.
INCLUDE NEGATIVE TRANSACTIONS WITHIN CUMULATIVE POSITIVE BP BALANCES	Select this checkbox to include negative transactions within cumulative positive business partner balances. This checkbox is normally selected.

Table 8.19 Fields in the Document Parameters Screen

Once you've made your selections, click NEXT.

5. The next step is to choose one or more payment methods for the payment run. Refer to the PAYMENT METHOD screen shown in Figure 8.26; its fields are listed in Table 8.20.

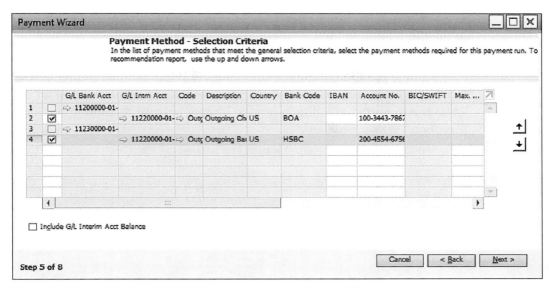

Figure 8.26 The Payment Method Selection Criteria Screen (Step 5 of the Wizard)

Field	Description/Use
(blank column)	The checkboxes in the second column are used to select which payment methods you want to include in the Payment Wizard.
MAX. OUTGOING AMOUNT	This field displays the maximum outgoing amount that is considered for this payment method based on the cash balance of the G/L account. Note that, if your cash in the bank account is not up to date, you may need to override this amount because SAP Business One will not create payments for more than the values shown in this field for each payment method.
INCLUDE G/L INTERIM ACCT. BALANCE	Select this checkbox to include the G/L interim account balance.

Table 8.20 Fields in the Payment Method Selection Criteria Screen

Once you've made your selections, click NEXT.

6. The Recommendation Report from the Payment Wizard provides you with suggestions for the payment run. The screen shown in Figure 8.27 allows you to

select the checkboxes of the business partners for whom you intend to generate payments.

Table 8.21 offers a few suggestions on how to use this screen. To select specific transactions, you can choose the EXPAND ALL button. You can further choose to include or exclude specific transactions within the detail window of the EXPAND ALL button. To display errors, always be sure to choose the NON-INCLUDED TRANSACTION button.

To recalculate the totals, click the REFRESH button.

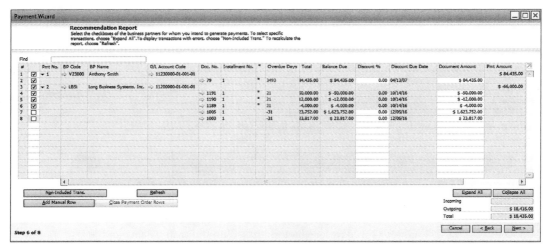

Figure 8.27 The Recommendation Report Screen (Step 6 of the Wizard)

Field	Description/Use
FIND	Enter search terms in this field to find certain transactions.
(blank column)	Select or deselect business partners and/or details.
DISCOUNT AMOUNT	This field displays the discount amount. You can overwrite it as necessary.
DOCUMENT TOTAL	This field displays the document total. You can overwrite it as necessary.
NON-INCLUDED TRANS.	Click this button to display the nonincluded transaction errors. (This should be done on every payment run!)

Table 8.21 Fields in the Recommendation Report Screen

Field	Description/Use
ADD MANUAL ROW	Click this button to add a manual row to the wizard and include a payment not already included. Any additions here are not tied to any specific transactions.
REFRESH	Click this button to refresh the screen to recalculate the Recommendation Report and to display all transactions not included in the Recommendation Report with errors.
CLOSE PAYMENT ORDER ROWS	Click this button to close payment order rows.
EXPAND ALL	Click this button to expand all transactions and include all details.
COLLAPSE ALL	Click this button to collapse all detailed transactions and only show summary information for each business partner.
INCOMING	This field displays the total of all incoming payments.
OUTGOING	This field displays the total of outgoing payments.
TOTAL	This field displays the total of all payments.

Table 8.21 Fields in the Recommendation Report Screen (Cont.)

Once you've made your selections, click NEXT.

7. The SAVE OPTIONS screen shown of the Payment Wizard in Figure 8.28 comes next. You can select from the following radio buttons:

   ▸ Select SAVE SELECTION CRITERIA ONLY to save the selection criteria without saving the Recommendation Report.

   ▸ Select SAVE RECOMMENDATIONS to save both the selection criteria and the Recommendation Report. This option is typically used if you need another manager to review and approve your payment run.

   ▸ Select EXECUTE PAYMENT ORDER RUN to generate payment orders. This option allows you generate outbound bank files without creating payment documents. Note that this option only affects the transactions for this payment order run. You cannot include transactions from another payment run or payment order run. Consult Context-Sensitive Help Menu (SAP Library) for more information on payment orders.

   ▸ Select EXECUTE PAYMENT RUN to execute the payment run.

   Once you've made your selections, click NEXT.

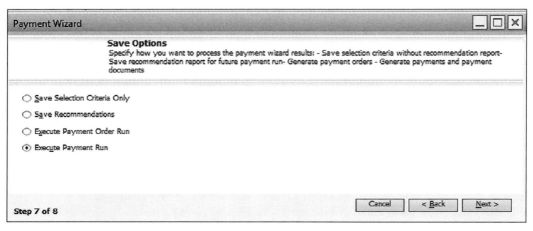

Figure 8.28 Save Options (Step 7 of the Wizard)

8. The final step of the Payment Wizard contains the PAYMENT RUN SUMMARY AND PRINTING window, shown in Figure 8.29; Table 8.22 describes the fields in this window.

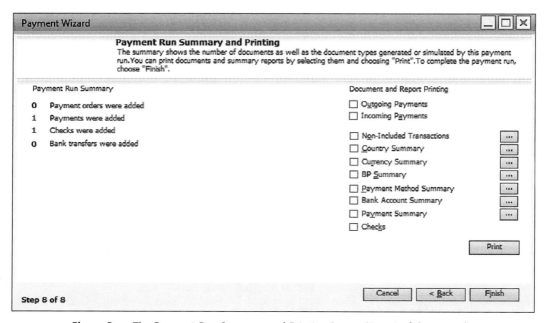

Figure 8.29 The Payment Run Summary and Printing Screen (Step 8 of the Wizard)

Field	Description/Use
PAYMENT RUN SUMMARY	This field displays summary information about this payment run.
OUTGOING PAYMENTS	Select this checkbox to print outgoing payments, which are not normally printed.
INCOMING PAYMENTS	Select this checkbox to print incoming payments, which are not normally printed.
NON-INCLUDED TRANSACTIONS	Select this checkbox to print nonincluded transactions, which are not normally printed.
COUNTRY SUMMARY	Select this checkbox to print a country summary, which is not normally printed.
CURRENCY SUMMARY	Select this checkbox to print a currency summary, which is not normally printed.
BP SUMMARY	Select this checkbox to print a business partner summary, which is not normally printed.
PAYMENT METHOD SUMMARY	Select this checkbox to print a payment method summary, which is not normally printed.
BANK ACCOUNT SUMMARY	Select this checkbox to print a bank account summary, which is not normally printed.
PAYMENT SUMMARY	Select this checkbox to print a payment summary, which is not normally printed.
CHECKS	Select this checkbox to print the checks. When printing, additional dialog boxes will prompt you for the printer and the starting check number to ensure that you have inserted any required check forms into the printer.
BROWSE icon (the ellipsis)	This field is used to choose refine the printing based on further selection criteria that you can enter.
PRINT	After choosing each item to print, select the PRINT button to execute all printing.

Table 8.22 Fields in the Payment Run Summary and Printing Screen

The Payment Wizard gives you three buttons on the final wizard screen:

▶ Click the FINISH button if you have completed with the Payment Wizard process.

▶ Click the BACK button to return to the last step of the Payment Wizard.

▶ Click the CANCEL button to cancel the Payment Wizard.

8.5 Bank Statements and External Reconciliations

Reconciliations can include internal reconciliations for various G/L accounts or bank reconciliations for your bank accounts.

This menu option offers various types of reconciliations and gives you the ability to manage previous external reconciliations and to check and restore previous external reconciliations that were performed with SAP Business One.

8.5.1 Manual (External Bank) Reconciliation

This screen is used to reconcile your *bank accounts* in SAP Business One to your bank's statements. The first part of this process is to complete the selection criteria outlined in the EXTERNAL BANK RECONCILIATION screen shown in Figure 8.30; the second part of the process is to review and reconcile the transaction details.

Follow the menu path BANKING • BANK STATEMENTS AND EXTERNAL RECONCILIATIONS • MANUAL RECONCILIATIONS and consult Table 8.23 for details about the fields in the EXTERNAL BANK RECONCILIATION screen.

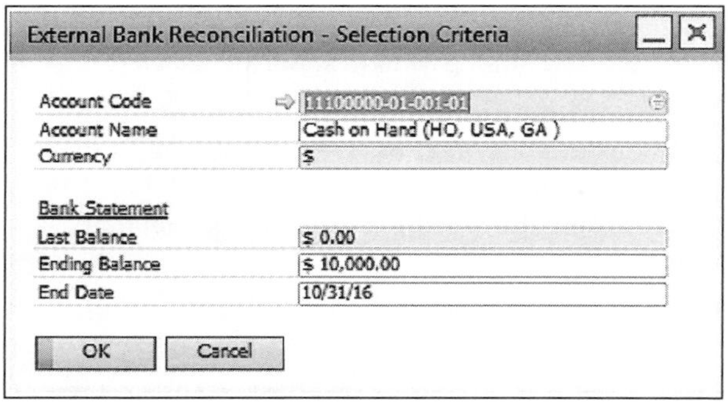

Figure 8.30 External Bank Reconciliation Selection Criteria

Field	Description/Use
ACCOUNT CODE	Choose a bank account to reconcile.
ACCOUNT NAME	This field displays the G/L account name.
CURRENCY	This field displays the currency of the selected G/L account.

Table 8.23 Fields in the External Bank Reconciliation Selection Criteria Screen

Field	Description/Use
Last Balance	Enter the last balance of the bank statement.
Ending Balance	Enter the ending balance of the current statement you are reconciling.
End Date	Enter the ending date of the statement you are reconciling.

Table 8.23 Fields in the External Bank Reconciliation Selection Criteria Screen (Cont.)

Once you've input these fields, you can either click OK to begin the reconciliation process and display the Bank Statement Reconciliation screen shown in Figure 8.31, or you can click Cancel to cancel the current reconciliation.

Use the Reconciliation Bank Statement to review and check line items (outgoing checks, payments received, adjustments, and bank fees). This screen contains several options to help you reconcile your statements expediently; we'll walk through them in Table 8.24.

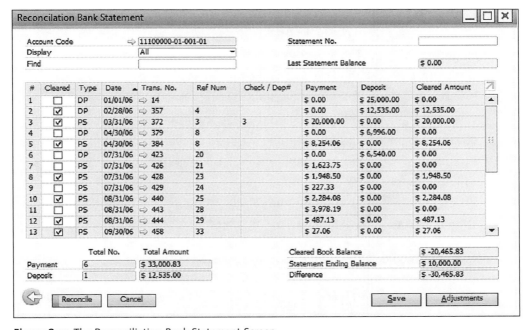

Figure 8.31 The Reconciliation Bank Statement Screen

Field	Description/Use
ACCOUNT CODE	This field displays the account code selected.
DISPLAY	Choose one of the options below to restrict display of transactions or to display all transactions: ▸ ALL ▸ CLEARED ▸ UN-CLEARED
FIND	Use this field to find certain transactions.
STATEMENT NO.	Enter a statement number that matches your bank's statement.
LAST STATEMENT BALANCE	This field displays the last statement balance.
CLEARED	Select to reconcile or clear lines.
TYPE	This field displays the transaction type.
DATE	This field displays the transaction date.
TRANS. NO.	This field displays the transaction number and allows for drill down to the detail.
REF. NUM.	This field displays the reference number.
CHECK/DEP. #	This field displays the check/deposit number.
PAYMENT	This field displays the payment amount.
DEPOSIT	This field displays the deposit amount.
CLEARED AMOUNT	This field displays the cleared amount.
PAYMENT	This field displays the number of cleared payments and the total amount.
DEPOSIT	This field displays the number of cleared deposits and the total.
CLEARED BOOK BALANCE	This field displays the cleared book balance.
STATEMENT ENDING BALANCE	This field displays the statement ending balance.
DIFFERENCE	This field displays the difference between the statement ending balance and the cleared book balance.

Table 8.24 Fields in the Reconciliation Bank Statement Screen

Notice the four buttons of interest at the bottom of Figure 8.31:

▶ Click RECONCILE to clear all line items and reconcile the statement.

▶ Click CANCEL to cancel the reconciliation and return to the selection criteria screen.

▶ Click SAVE to save the selection and settings but not reconcile at this time. When choosing this option, you will be able to pull up the existing saved recommendations at a later time.

▶ Click ADJUSTMENT to enter adjustment entries such as bank fees and minor adjustments that may be necessary in order to reconcile the bank statement.

8.5.2 Manage Previous External Reconciliations

SAP Business One's MANAGE PREVIOUS EXTERNAL RECONCILIATIONS screen is used to view the history of all external reconciliations performed for business partners or G/L accounts. You can then cancel and re-create previously created external reconciliations for business partners or G/L accounts and can cancel incorrect external reconciliations.

To manage a previous external reconciliation, follow the menu path BANKING • BANK STATEMENTS AND EXTERNAL RECONCILIATIONS • MANAGE PREVIOUS EXTERNAL RECONCILIATIONS.

The first step to managing previous external reconciliations is to choose whether to manage previous reconciliations for G/L accounts or business partners. Consult the selection criteria screen shown in Figure 8.32 with its corresponding fields listed in Table 8.25.

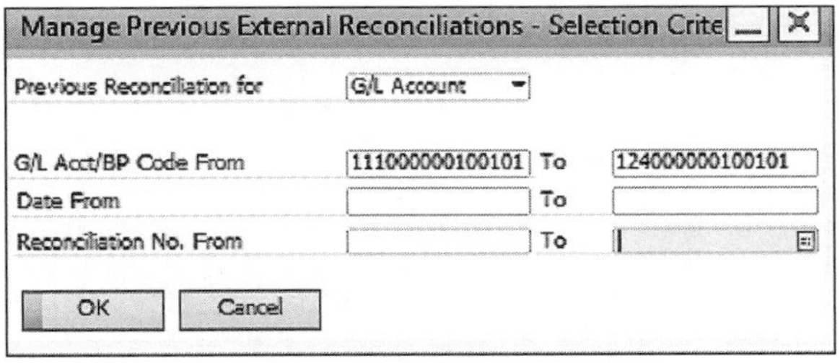

Figure 8.32 Manage Previous External Reconciliations Selection Criteria

Field	Description/Use
PREVIOUS RECONCILIATION FOR	Select from one of the following: ▶ G/L ACCOUNT ▶ BP CODE
G/L ACCT/BP CODE FROM	Choose a range of G/L accounts or business partners; the value here is dependent upon your selection for the previous field.
DATE FROM	Choose a range of dates.
RECONCILIATION NO. FROM	Choose a range of reconciliation numbers.

Table 8.25 Fields in the Manage Previous External Reconciliations Selection Criteria

Click the OK button to proceed to the next step or click the CANCEL button to cancel and close the screen.

The second step to managing previous external reconciliations is to review the screen shown in Figure 8.33; determine if you want to cancel the reconciliations and perhaps redo the reconciliation.

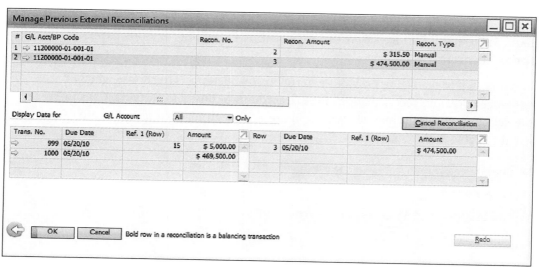

Figure 8.33 The Manage Previous External Reconciliations Screen

The top section of the screen lists the reconciliations that meet your requirements. To view the detail of each reconciliation, highlight the line of the reconciliation you want to review, cancel, or redo. The bottom section displays the transaction detail of the reconciliation you highlighted. Use the DISPLAY DATA FOR...G/L ACCOUNT dropdown list to view all accounts or to display certain accounts.

In this screen, you have a few options:

- Click on the CANCEL RECONCILIATION button to cancel the highlighted reconciliation.
- Click the OK button to save the reconciliation.
- Click the CANCEL button to cancel and close the screen.
- Click the REDO button to redo a transaction that has been cancelled.

8.5.3 Check and Restore Previous External Reconciliations

Incorrect external reconciliations can contain instances where the amounts in the debit and the credit side do not match. You can display and cancel only incorrect external reconciliations that were initiated by users for a specific G/L account or business partner. Follow the menu path BANKING • BANK STATEMENTS AND EXTERNAL RECONCILIATIONS • CHECK AND RESTORE PREVIOUS EXTERNAL RECONCILIATIONS.

8.6 Document Printing

The DOCUMENT PRINTING screen allows you to print several different documents, including sales, purchasing, inventory, production, financial, and banking documents. In the Banking module, you can use document printing for the following documents:

- Incoming payments
- Deposits
- Outgoing payments
- Checks for payments

We'll focus on using this feature to print checks for payments—but you can apply the same technique to other documents. Document printing can be accessed by following the menu path BANKING • DOCUMENT PRINTING.

The first step of the process is to enter selection criteria for the documents or checks for payment to print, as shown in Figure 8.34 and listed in Table 8.26.

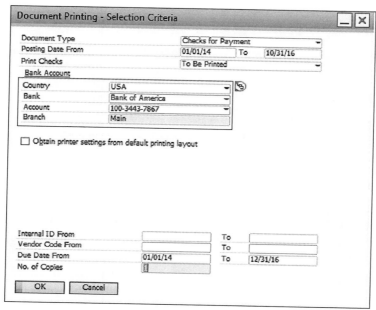

Figure 8.34 The Document Printing Screen

Field	Description/Use
DOCUMENT TYPE	Select the document type to be printed (in our example, CHECKS FOR PAYMENT).
POSTING DATE FROM	Enter a posting date range.
PRINT CHECKS	Select from one of the following: ▸ TO BE PRINTED: Prints the check(s) for the first time ▸ FOR REISSUING: Voids the original check and print a new check ▸ CHECK DETAILS ONLY: Prints remittance information only
BANK ACCOUNT	Select the bank account to print checks for. Clicking on the BROWSE icon (the ellipsis) will bring up a list of all banks to choose from. From this list, double-click on the bank account number, and all the fields for the bank will be filled in.

Table 8.26 Fields in the Document Printing Screen

Field	Description/Use
OBTAIN PRINTER SETTINGS FROM DEFAULT PRINTING LAYOUT	Select this checkbox to obtain printer settings from the default printing layout.
INTERNAL ID FROM	Enter a starting and ending internal ID or leave blank for all.
VENDOR CODE FROM	Enter a starting and ending vendor code or leave blank for all.
DUE DATE FROM	Enter a starting and ending due date. Entering a date range is required.
NO. OF COPIES	Enter the number of copies to print of each check.

Table 8.26 Fields in the Document Printing Screen (Cont.)

When you're done, click on the OK button to print the checks or click on the CANCEL button to cancel printing and close the screen.

The second step of the process is to review and confirm which checks for payment you want to print from the PRINT CHECKS FOR PAYMENT – TO BE PRINTED screen shown in Figure 8.35; the corresponding fields are described in Table 8.27.

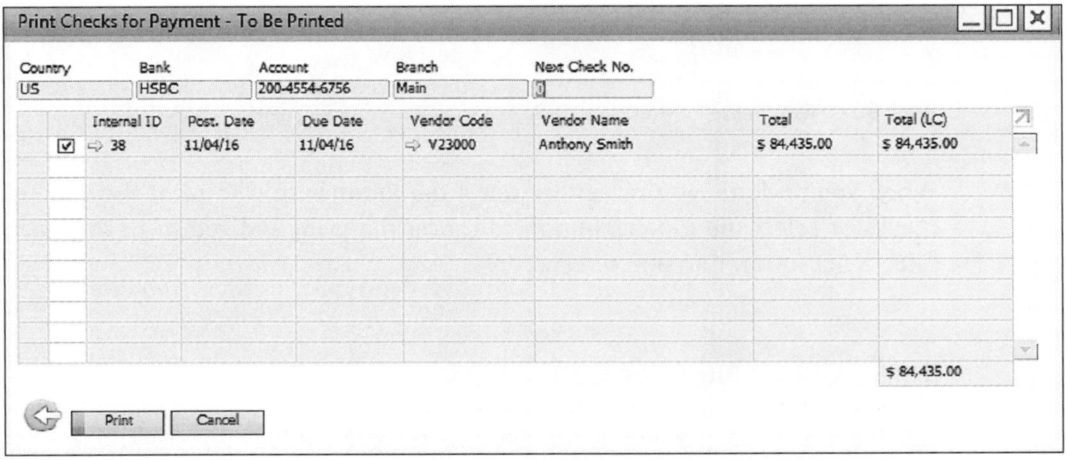

	Internal ID	Post. Date	Due Date	Vendor Code	Vendor Name	Total	Total (LC)	
☑ ⇨ 38		11/04/16	11/04/16	⇨ V23000	Anthony Smith	$ 84,435.00	$ 84,435.00	
							$ 84,435.00	

Country: US Bank: HSBC Account: 200-4554-6756 Branch: Main Next Check No.: 0

Figure 8.35 The Print Checks for Payment To Be Printed Screen

Field	Description/Use
COUNTRY	This field displays the country of the selected bank.
BANK	This field displays the selected bank name.
AMOUNT	This field displays the selected bank account.
BRANCH	This field displays the selected branch.
NEXT CHECK NO.	This field displays the next check number—but you can overwrite it as necessary.
	Select each checkbox of the checks you want to print.
INTERNAL ID	This field displays the internal ID of the checks for payment.
POST. DATE	This field displays the posting date.
DUE DATE	This field displays the due date.
VENDOR CODE	This field displays the vendor code.
VENDOR NAME	This field displays the vendor name.
TOTAL	This field displays the check total.
TOTAL LC	This field displays the total in local currency.
Total from TOTAL LC column	This field displays the total of all checks.
PRINT	Select the PRINT button to print the selected checks.
CANCEL	Select the CANCEL button to cancel the print and return to the PRINT CHECKS SELECTION CRITERIA screen.

Table 8.27 Fields in the Print Checks for Payment To Be Printed Screen

When you're done, you can either select the PRINT button to print the selected checks or select the CANCEL button to cancel the print and return to the PRINT CHECKS SELECTION CRITERIA screen.

8.7 Check Number Confirmation

This function enables you to verify that checks were printed correctly and that the numbers assigned to the checks match the numbers on the printed checks. To access this function, follow the menu path BANKING • CHECK NUMBER CONFIRMATION.

Note that, when you are using document printing, the CHECK NUMBER CONFIRMATION screen should appear at the end of your check run requesting that you review and confirm the checks.

The first step of the process is to enter selection criteria for the checks to confirm using CHECK NUMBER CONFIRMATION. The selection criteria are shown in Figure 8.36 and listed in Table 8.28.

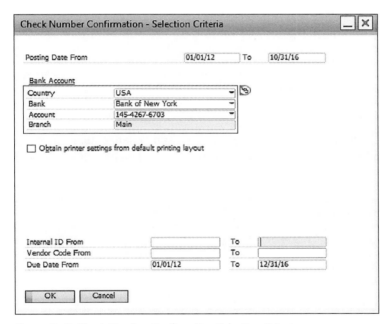

Figure 8.36 Check Number Confirmation Selection Criteria

Field	Description/Use
POSTING DATE FROM	Enter a posting date range.
BANK ACCOUNT	Select the bank account to print checks for. Clicking on the BROWSE icon (the ellipsis) will bring up a list of all banks to choose from. From this list, double-click on the bank account number, and all the fields for the bank will be filled in.

Table 8.28 Check Number Confirmation Selection Criteria Fields

Field	Description/Use
OBTAIN PRINTER SETTINGS FROM DEFAULT PRINTING LAYOUT	Select this checkbox to obtain printer settings from the default printing layout.
INTERNAL ID FROM	Enter a starting and ending internal ID or leave blank for all.
VENDOR CODE FROM	Enter a starting and ending vendor code or leave blank for all.
DUE DATE FROM	Enter a starting and ending due date.

Table 8.28 Check Number Confirmation Selection Criteria Fields (Cont.)

When you're done, choose from the buttons at the bottom of Figure 8.36:

▸ Click on the OK button to process and bring up the CHECK NUMBER CONFIRMATION screen shown in Figure 8.37.

▸ Click on the CANCEL button to cancel return to the previous screen.

Review the list of checks that have *not* been confirmed and change the print status for each check. Table 8.29 describes the information in each column on this screen.

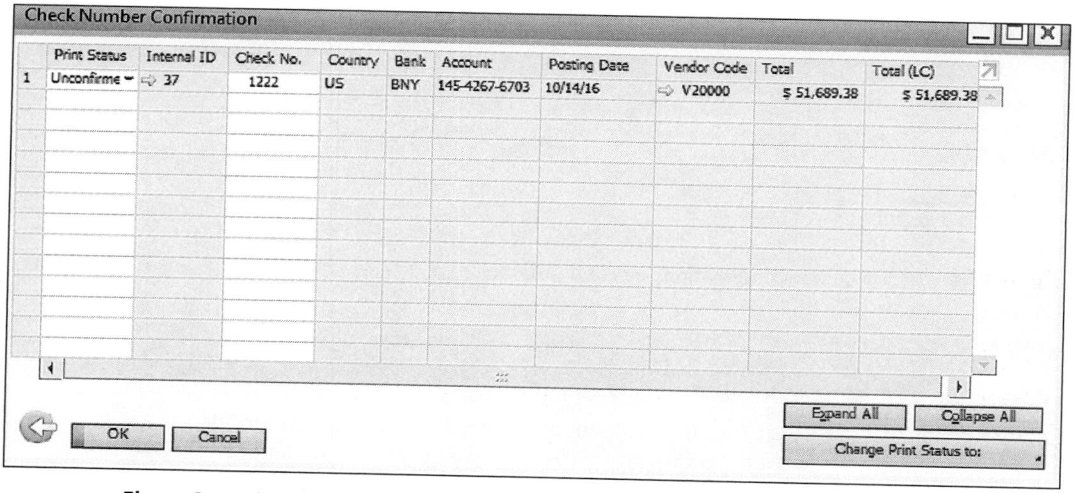

Figure 8.37 The Check Number Confirmation Screen

Field	Description/Use
PRINT STATUS	Select from the following: ▶ UNCONFIRMED: The document was printed, but its status has not been changed. ▶ CONFIRMED: The document was printed, and it was confirmed to have been printed correctly. ▶ DAMAGED: This document was printed but was damaged. The damaged check's number will be voided, and a new check will need to be printed. ▶ NOT PRINTED: This document was not printed. The same check can be printed again without voiding the check. Select this option if, for example, you forgot to insert the check forms into the printer.
INTERNAL ID	This field displays the internal ID (checks for payment internal ID).
CHECK NO.	This field displays the check number.
COUNTRY	This field displays the country of the selected bank.
BANK	This field displays the selected bank name.
ACCOUNT	This field displays the selected bank account.
POSTING DATE	This field displays the posting date.
VENDOR CODE	This field displays the vendor code.
TOTAL	This field displays the check total.
TOTAL LC	This field displays the total in local currency.

Table 8.29 Fields in the Check Number Confirmation Screen

When you're done, you can use two buttons to change how much data you see on the screen and one button to manage several checks at once:

▶ Click on the EXPAND ALL button to expand the transactions.

▶ Click on the COLLAPSE ALL button to collapse the transactions.

▶ Use the CHANGE PRINT STATUS TO button to change the status of several checks at one time.

Finally, you only have one more decision to make:

▸ Click on the CANCEL button to cancel and close the screen.

▸ Click on the OK button to close the screen.

8.8 Banking Reports

This menu option contains the various banking reports and queries that you can use to analyze the banking features in SAP Business One.

Like most reports within SAP Business One, you'll use a selection criteria screen to select which records you want to appear on each report.

8.8.1 Check Register Report

The Check Register Report prints out a report of all outgoing checks. To access this report, follow the menu path BANKING • BANKING REPORTS • CHECK REGISTER REPORT. You can use selection criteria to include or exclude voided checks and to choose information to be printed based on ranges of due dates, check numbers, vendor codes, payment numbers, and checking accounts. In addition, the DISPLAY RESULTS AS A LIST option reformats the data for easy export to Excel.

Refer to Figure 8.38 for the selection criteria. Figure 8.39 shows the standard report output, while Figure 8.40 shows the report output in list view.

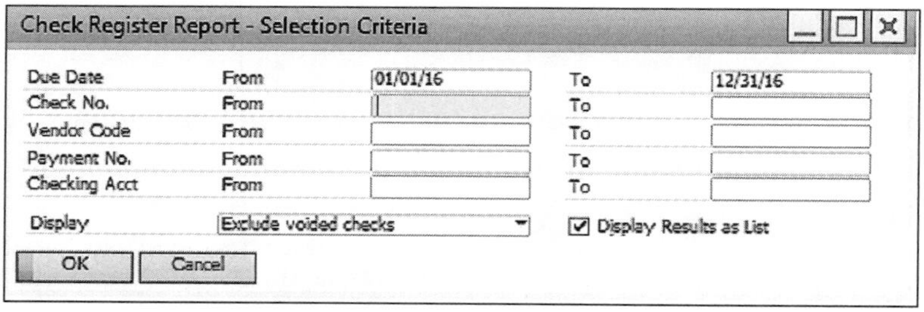

Figure 8.38 Check Register Report Selection Criteria

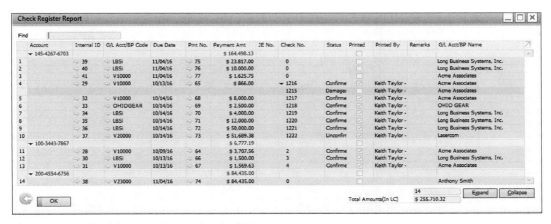

Figure 8.39 A Check Register Report: Standard View

	Account	Internal ID	G/L Acct/BP Code	Due Date	Pmt No.	Payment Amt	JE No.	Check No.	Status	Printed	Printed By	Remarks	G/L Acct/BP Name	
1	145-4267-6703	39	LBSi	11/04/16	75	$ 23,817.00		0		☐			Long Business Systems, Inc.	
2	145-4267-6703	40	LBSi	11/04/16	76	$ 10,000.00		0		☐			Long Business Systems, Inc.	
3	145-4267-6703	41	V10000	11/04/16	77	$ 1,625.75		0					Acme Associates	
4	145-4267-6703	29	V10000	10/13/16	65	$ 866.00		1216	Confirme	☑	Keith Taylor -		Acme Associates	
4	145-4267-6703	29	V10000	10/13/16	65	$ 866.00		1215	Damagec	☑	Keith Taylor -		Acme Associates	
5	145-4267-6703	32	V10000	10/14/16	68	$ 8,000.00		1217	Confirme	☑	Keith Taylor -		Acme Associates	
6	145-4267-6703	33	OHIOGEAR	10/14/16	69	$ 2,500.00		1218	Confirme	☑	Keith Taylor -		OHIO GEAR	
7	145-4267-6703	34	LBSi	10/14/16	70	$ 4,000.00		1219	Confirme	☑	Keith Taylor -		Long Business Systems, Inc.	
8	145-4267-6703	35	LBSi	10/14/16	71	$ 12,000.00		1220	Confirme	☑	Keith Taylor -		Long Business Systems, Inc.	
9	145-4267-6703	36	LBSi	10/14/16	72	$ 50,000.00		1221	Confirme	☑	Keith Taylor -		Long Business Systems, Inc.	
10	145-4267-6703	37	V20000	10/14/16	73	$ 51,689.38		1222	Unconfir	☑	Keith Taylor -		Lasercom	
11	100-3443-7867	28	V10000	10/09/16	64	$ 3,707.56		2	Confirme	☑	Keith Taylor -		Acme Associates	
12	100-3443-7867	30	LBSi	10/13/16	66	$ 1,500.00		3	Confirme	☑	Keith Taylor -		Long Business Systems, Inc.	
13	100-3443-7867	31	V10000	10/13/16	67	$ 1,569.63		4	Confirme	☑	Keith Taylor -		Acme Associates	
14	200-4554-6756	38	V23000	11/04/16	74	$ 84,435.00		0		☐			Anthony Smith	

Figure 8.40 A Check Register Report: List View

8.8.2 Payment Drafts Report

The Payment Drafts Report allows you to report on incoming and/or outgoing payment drafts. The selection criteria screen allows you to choose incoming or outgoing payments, to display open drafts only, and to select drafts created for specific users.

For this report, follow the menu path BANKING • BANKING REPORTS • PAYMENT DRAFTS REPORT.

8.8.3 Checks for Payment in Date Cross Section Report

This query prompts you for a starting and ending check date and will display a list of checks with the information shown in Figure 8.41.

For this report, follow the menu path BANKING • BANKING REPORTS • CHECKS FOR PAYMENT IN DATE CROSS SECTION REPORT.

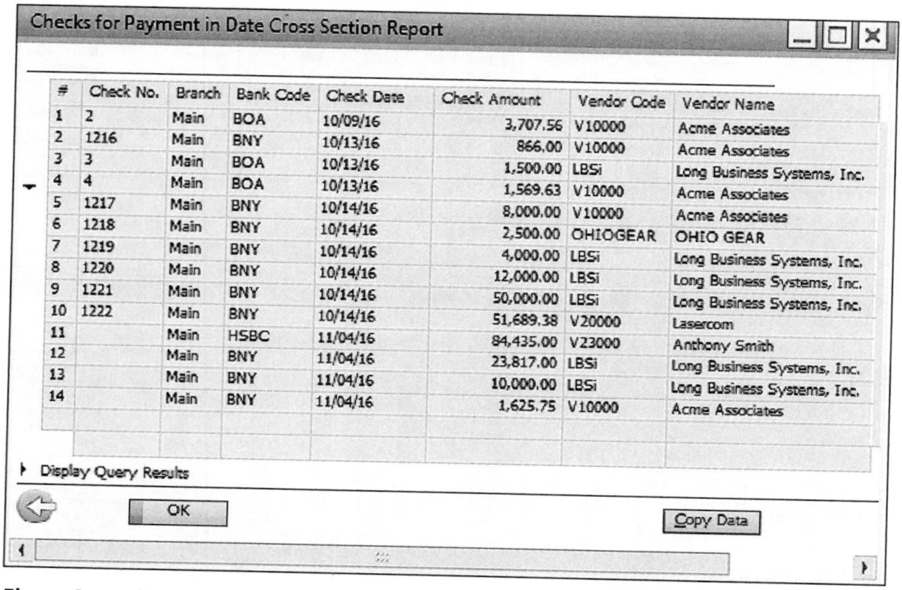

#	Check No.	Branch	Bank Code	Check Date	Check Amount	Vendor Code	Vendor Name
1	2	Main	BOA	10/09/16	3,707.56	V10000	Acme Associates
2	1216	Main	BNY	10/13/16	866.00	V10000	Acme Associates
3	3	Main	BOA	10/13/16	1,500.00	LBSi	Long Business Systems, Inc.
4	4	Main	BOA	10/13/16	1,569.63	V10000	Acme Associates
5	1217	Main	BNY	10/14/16	8,000.00	V10000	Acme Associates
6	1218	Main	BNY	10/14/16	2,500.00	OHIOGEAR	OHIO GEAR
7	1219	Main	BNY	10/14/16	4,000.00	LBSi	Long Business Systems, Inc.
8	1220	Main	BNY	10/14/16	12,000.00	LBSi	Long Business Systems, Inc.
9	1221	Main	BNY	10/14/16	50,000.00	LBSi	Long Business Systems, Inc.
10	1222	Main	BNY	10/14/16	51,689.38	V20000	Lasercom
11		Main	HSBC	11/04/16	84,435.00	V23000	Anthony Smith
12		Main	BNY	11/04/16	23,817.00	LBSi	Long Business Systems, Inc.
13		Main	BNY	11/04/16	10,000.00	LBSi	Long Business Systems, Inc.
14		Main	BNY	11/04/16	1,625.75	V10000	Acme Associates

Display Query Results

OK   Copy Data

Figure 8.41 Checks for Payment in Date Cross Section Report (Query)

8.8.4 BP Bank Accounts Query

This query displays a list of all business partners for which you have entered banking information on the PAYMENT TERMS tab of the Business Partner module as shown in Figure 8.42. Follow the menu path BANKING • BANKING REPORTS • BP BANK ACCOUNTS QUERY.

8.8.5 House Bank Accounts Query

This query displays a list of all house bank accounts that you have created for your company, as shown in Figure 8.43. For this report, follow the menu path BANKING • BANKING REPORTS • HOUSE BANK ACCOUNTS QUERY.

BP Bank Accounts Query

#	BP Name	BP Code	Bank Country	Bank Code	Bank Name	Branch	Bank Account Number	IBAN	BIC/SWIFT Code
1	Norm Thompson	C20000	US	BOA	Bank of America	101	230-6789-456464		
2	Parameter Technology	C23900	US	HSBC	HSBC Bank	345	45-816-43598		
3	Microchips	C30000	US	CITI	Citibank	567	67-90887-9999		
4	Earthshaker Corporation	C40000	US	BOA	Bank of America	345	230-1123-403958		
5	Mashina Corporation	C42000	US	BNY	Bank of New York	324	95599-5002-40		
6	ADA Technologies	C50000	US	HSBC	HSBC Bank	6	45-276-98888		
7	SG Electronics	C60000	CA	CITI	Citibank Canada	45	67-91567-9022		
8	Aquent Systems	C70000	CA	CITI	Citibank Canada	43	67-44387-9748		
9	Acme Associates	V10000	US	CITI	Citibank	234	67-55887-2349		
10	Far East Imports	V1010	US	BOA	Bank of America	234	230-6001-905646		

Display Query Results

OK   Copy Data

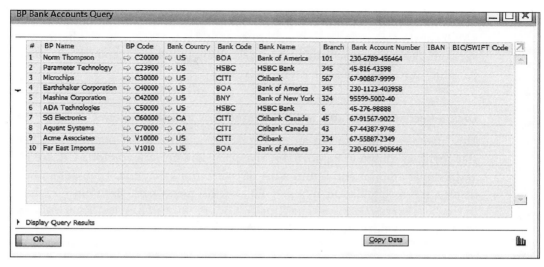

Figure 8.42 A BP Bank Accounts Query

House Bank Accounts Query

#	Bank Country	Bank Code	Bank Name	Branch	Bank Account Number	IBAN	BIC/SWIFT Code
1	US	BNY	Bank of New York	Main	145-4267-6703		
2	US	BOA	Bank of America	Main	100-3443-7867		
3	US	CITI	Citibank	Main	300-4562-7690		
4	US	HSBC	HSBC Bank	Main	200-4554-6756		

Display Query Results

OK   Copy Data

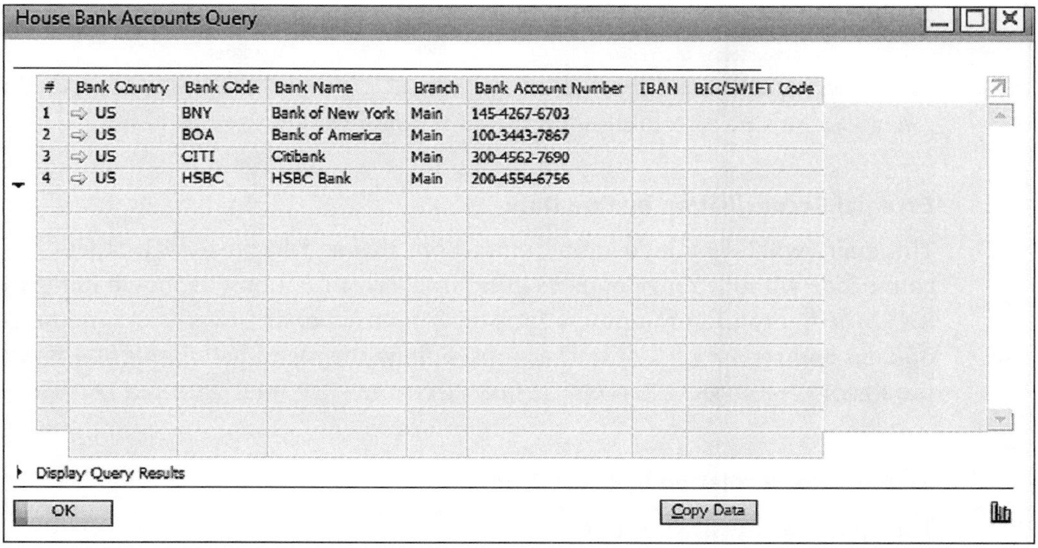

Figure 8.43 A House Bank Accounts Query

8.8.6 External Reconciliation

SAP Business One offers you several queries and reports to help you better manage your external reconciliations. To access them, follow the menu path BANKING • BANKING REPORTS • EXTERNAL RECONCILIATION.

Locate Reconciliation/Row in Bank Statements by Exact Amount

This query will help you to locate a specific value for a G/L account in a bank statement, as shown in Figure 8.44. The query will prompt you for a G/L account and a dollar amount and return a list of transactions that equal that amount and display the reconciliation number. Follow the menu path BANKING • BANKING REPORTS • EXTERNAL RECONCILIATION • LOCATE RECONCILIATION/ROW IN BANK STATEMENTS BY ROW NUMBER & EXACT AMOUNT.

Locate Reconciliation/Row in Bank Statements by Exact Amount

#	Sequence No.	Account Number	Due Date	Details	Debit Amount (FC)	Credit Amount (FC)	Reconciliation No.
1	1	_SYS00000000002	03/31/06		0.00	25,184.50	1
2	2	_SYS00000000002	05/18/10		0.00	315.50	2
3	3	_SYS00000000002	05/20/10		0.00	474,500.00	3
4	4	_SYS00000000002	03/31/06		0.00	-25,184.50	1

Figure 8.44 A Locate Reconciliation/Row in Bank Statements by Exact Amount Report

External Reconciliation by Due Date

This query will help you to locate transactions that equal a business partner or account code within a range of dates in external reconciliations, as shown in Figure 8.45. The query will prompt you for a business partner or G/L account and range of dates and return a list of transactions. Follow the menu path BANKING • BANKING REPORTS • EXTERNAL RECONCILIATION • EXTERNAL RECONCILIATION BY DUE DATE.

External Reconciliation by Exact Sum

This query will help you to locate transactions that equal a business partner or account code within a range of dates in external reconciliations, as shown in Figure 8.46. This query will prompt you for a business partner or G/L account and exact debit amount and return a list of transactions. Follow the menu path BANKING • BANKING REPORTS • EXTERNAL RECONCILIATION • EXTERNAL RECONCILIATION BY EXACT SUM.

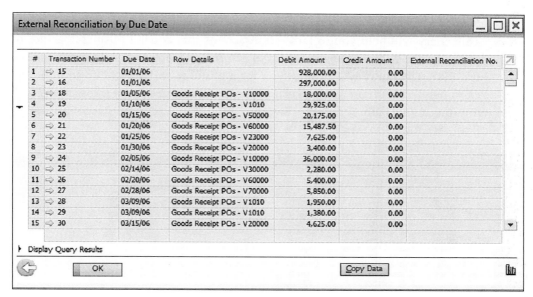

Figure 8.45 An External Reconciliation by Due Date Report

#	Transaction Number	Due Date	Row Details	Debit Amount	Credit Amount	External Reconciliation No.
1	⇨ 15	01/01/06		928,000.00	0.00	
2	⇨ 16	01/01/06		297,000.00	0.00	
3	⇨ 18	01/05/06	Goods Receipt POs - V10000	18,000.00	0.00	
4	⇨ 19	01/10/06	Goods Receipt POs - V1010	29,925.00	0.00	
5	⇨ 20	01/15/06	Goods Receipt POs - V50000	20,175.00	0.00	
6	⇨ 21	01/20/06	Goods Receipt POs - V60000	15,487.50	0.00	
7	⇨ 22	01/25/06	Goods Receipt POs - V23000	7,625.00	0.00	
8	⇨ 23	01/30/06	Goods Receipt POs - V20000	3,400.00	0.00	
9	⇨ 24	02/05/06	Goods Receipt POs - V10000	36,000.00	0.00	
10	⇨ 25	02/14/06	Goods Receipt POs - V30000	2,280.00	0.00	
11	⇨ 26	02/20/06	Goods Receipt POs - V60000	5,400.00	0.00	
12	⇨ 27	02/28/06	Goods Receipt POs - V70000	5,850.00	0.00	
13	⇨ 28	03/09/06	Goods Receipt POs - V1010	1,950.00	0.00	
14	⇨ 29	03/09/06	Goods Receipt POs - V1010	1,380.00	0.00	
15	⇨ 30	03/15/06	Goods Receipt POs - V20000	4,625.00	0.00	

#	Transaction Number	Due Date	Row Details	Debit Amount	Credit Amount	External R...
1	⇨ 3	01/01/06	G/L Accounts Opening Balance	450,000.00	0.00	
2	⇨ 346	01/31/06	Recurring Posting ELEC from 01/30/2006	0.00	250.00	
3	⇨ 349	01/31/06	Incoming - C30000	2,917.34	0.00	
4	⇨ 350	01/31/06	Outgoing - V10000	0.00	19,485.00	
5	⇨ 355	02/28/06	Recurring Posting ELEC from 02/28/2006	0.00	250.00	
6	⇨ 358	02/28/06	Outgoing - V1010	0.00	32,393.81	
7	⇨ 359	02/28/06	Outgoing - V60000	0.00	16,765.22	
8	⇨ 364	03/31/06	Recurring Posting ELEC from 03/30/2006	0.00	250.00	
9	⇨ 367	03/31/06	Incoming - C42000	18,391.00	0.00	
10	⇨ 368	03/31/06	Incoming - C40000	10,573.00	0.00	
11	⇨ 370	03/31/06	Deposit - 11220000-01-001-01	22,819.11	0.00	
12	⇨ 371	03/28/06	Deposit - 11220000-01-001-01	7,473.00	0.00	
13	⇨ 377	04/30/06	Recurring Posting ELEC from 04/30/2006	0.00	250.00	
14	⇨ 382	04/30/06	Incoming - C50000	36,172.50	0.00	

Figure 8.46 An External Reconciliation by Exact Sum Report

External Reconciliation by Sum (FC)

This query will help you to locate transactions that equal a business partner or account code within a range of dates in external reconciliations, as shown in Figure 8.47. The query will prompt you for a business partner or G/L account and exact debit amount (in foreign currency, FC) and return a list of transactions. Follow the menu path Banking • Banking Reports • External Reconciliation • External Reconciliation by Sum (FC).

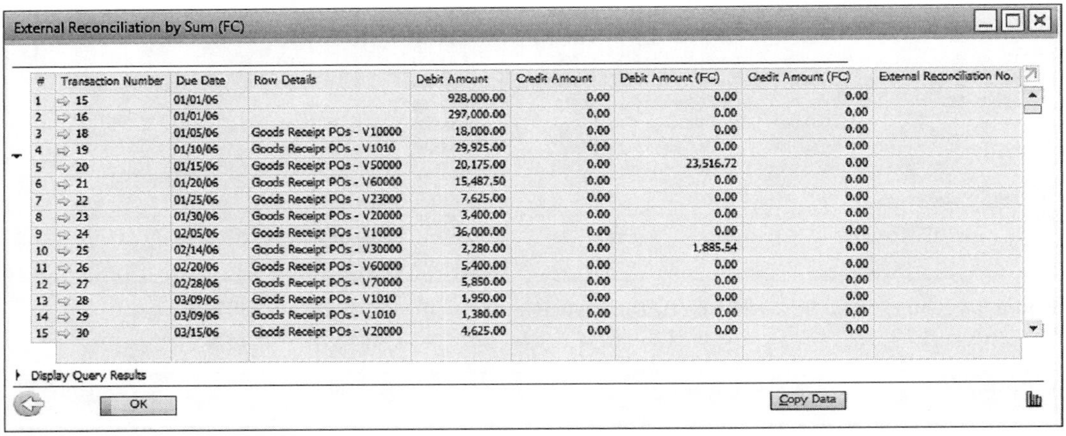

Figure 8.47 An External Reconciliation by Sum (FC) Report

External Reconciliation by Transaction Number

This query will help you to locate transactions that equal a business partner or account code within a range of dates in external reconciliations. The query will prompt you for a business partner or G/L account and transaction number and return a list of transactions. Follow the menu path Banking • Banking Reports • External reconciliation • External Reconciliation by Transaction Number.

Bank Reconciliation Report

SAP Business One includes the Bank Reconciliation Report to help you report on your external bank reconciliations, as shown in Figure 8.48. This report will prompt you for a G/L account code and a reconciliation number and display a Bank Reconciliation Report that contains all of the pertinent details of the reconciliation.

Follow the menu path BANKING • BANKING REPORTS • EXTERNAL RECONCILIATION • BANK RECONCILIATION REPORT.

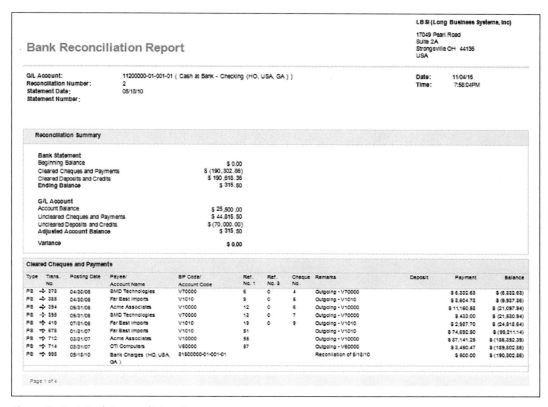

Figure 8.48 A Bank Reconciliation Report

Alongside the charts of accounts and the business partners, items are the foundation of all ERP systems. The same is true in SAP Business One—which makes a close examination of its inventory functionality crucial.

9   Inventory

The Inventory module in SAP allows you to create and manage item master data, define pricing structures, perform inventory-related transactions, define bin locations, and generate inventory-related reports.

In this chapter, we'll walk through key inventory management transactions, beginning with item master data in Section 9.1; from there, we'll follow the menu from top to bottom, going through bar codes, document printing, bin locations, item management, inventory transactions, price lists, pick and pack, and inventory reports.

9.1   Item Master Data

In the ITEM MASTER DATA window shown in Figure 9.1, you can add, update, search, and delete any item that can be sold, purchased, manufactured, or kept in inventory. To access this screen, follow the menu path INVENTORY • ITEM MASTER DATA.

The ITEM MASTER DATA window is composed of a header section at the top and nine tabs for defining additional information. Note that the ITEM MASTER DATA window will open by default in Find mode. At this point, you can search for an item by typing in any field on the screen and clicking on the FIND button at the bottom. If multiple items match the search criteria you entered, the system will display a list of those items. You can select the required item and click on the CHOOSE button at the bottom of the list. The selected item will then be displayed in the main ITEM MASTER DATA window.

In order to *create* an item, you'll have to switch to Add mode by clicking on the ADD icon (document with red dot) in the toolbar. A screen will appear with fields for you to enter information related to the item. Note that the only *required* field to add the item is the ITEM NO. field. Once you are ready to save the item, click on the ADD button at the bottom of the window.

> **Tips and Tricks: The Right-Click Menu**
>
> In addition to all the available tabs and fields described in this section, you can right-click anywhere on the window to display a list of transactions, such as creating a new activity or reports (items list, inventory status, etc.), that are related to the displayed item.

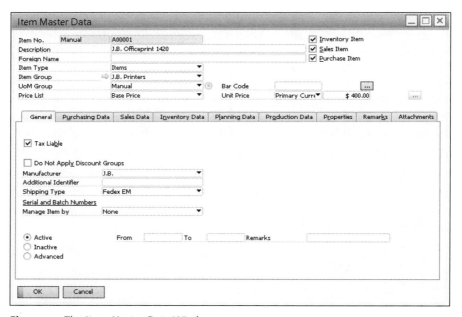

Figure 9.1 The Item Master Data Window

The header of the ITEM MASTER DATA window displays basic item information such as the item number, description, item group, and unit of measure group (UOM GROUP); you can also define whether the item can be sold or purchased or even whether the item is managed in inventory or not.

Assign bar codes to an item by clicking on the BROWSE icon (the ellipsis) beside the BAR CODES field. Note that, if the item is assigned to a unit of measure group, you can also assign a bar code or a price by unit of measure (UoM).

9.1.1 General Tab

In this tab (see Figure 9.2), you can define whether an item is tax liable and whether discounts groups are applicable (for more information about discount groups, refer to Section 9.7.3). In the MANAGE ITEM BY field, you can also define the release method for the item. Select from one of the following choices:

▶ NONE

▶ SERIAL NUMBERS

▶ BATCHES

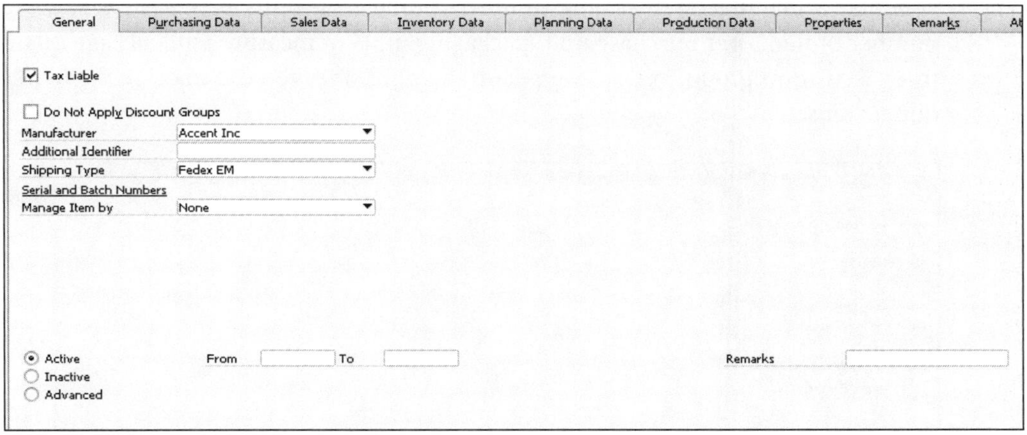

Figure 9.2 The General Tab

If the item is managed either by serial numbers or by batches, two additional fields will appear on screen: MANAGEMENT METHOD and ISSUE PRIMARILY BY. The management method allows you to define if the serial numbers or batches need to be entered and tracked on every single inventory transaction (ON EVERY TRANSACTION) for a complete traceability or only upon delivery or AR/invoicing (ON RELEASE ONLY).

Tips and Tricks: Management Method

You won't be able to change the inventory management method if there is inventory for the item.

For existing items that do have inventory in stock, you will need to perform a goods issue, change the management method to NONE, SERIAL NUMBERS, or BATCHES, and then perform a goods receipt in order to adjust the inventory back with the right method.

At the bottom of the GENERAL tab, you can set items to be ACTIVE or INACTIVE. SAP offers great flexibility for this classification; not only can an item be set as ACTIVE or INACTIVE by date range, but you can also add exceptions. To add exceptions, select the ADVANCED radio button and the simultaneously use the ACTIVE RANGE and INACTIVE RANGE options.

9.1.2 Purchasing Data Tab

The PURCHASING DATA tab is where all purchasing-related information is defined for an item. On the left side of Figure 9.3, you can assign one or many preferred vendors, a manufacturer catalog number, purchasing units of measure and the number of items per purchase unit, packaging units of measure and package quantities, a customs group, and a tax type; on the right side, you can manage the item's dimensions.

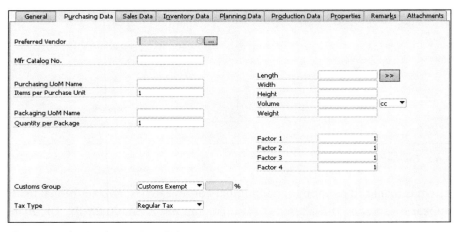

Figure 9.3 The Purchasing Data Tab

Let's look more closely about how to input data into these fields.

Both the PURCHASING UoM NAME field and the PACKAGING UoM NAME field will behave differently, depending on whether the item has been assigned a unit of measure group. If the item has *not* been assigned a unit of measure group (in other words, if the MANUAL option is selected), you can edit these two fields freely. You can also enter the number of items per purchase unit and the quantity per package in the ITEMS PER PURCHASE UNIT and QUANTITY PER PACKAGE fields, respectively. When purchasing the item, the system will purchase in the purchasing UoM and receive in stock the quantity purchased multiplied by the number of items per purchase unit.

If a unit of measure group *is* assigned to the item, you'll need to select from the predefined PURCHASING UOM NAME and PACKAGING UOM NAME fields as follows:

1. Click on the BROWSE icon (the ellipsis) located next to the PURCHASING UOM CODE field or the PACKAGING TYPE field. Both will open the PURCHASING UOM AND PACKAGE TYPES window shown in Figure 9.4.

2. Select the appropriate purchasing unit of measure from the PURCHASING UOM list in the left portion of the window and click on the SET AS DEFAULT button below.

3. Select the appropriate package type from the PACKAGE TYPES list in the right portion of the window and click on the SET AS DEFAULT button below.

4. Enter the number of default purchasing units of measures contained in the default package type in the QTY PER PACKAGE field.

5. You can also define the DIMENSIONS (LENGTH, WIDTH, HEIGHT, VOLUME, and WEIGHT) for both the purchasing UoM and packaging UoM.

6. Click on the UPDATE button to apply changes to the item.

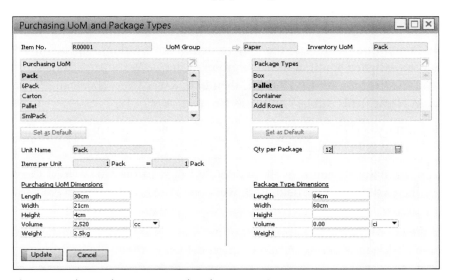

Figure 9.4 The Purchasing UoM and Package Types Screen

Tips and Tricks: Set As Default

Another way to set the values for PURCHASING UoM CODE or PACKAGING TYPE values as default is to simply click on the LIST icon (three horizontal lines) in those fields and select the required value in the list that appears.

9.1.3 Sales Data Tab

The SALES DATA tab shown in Figure 9.5 is where you'll manage the default sales units of measure, packaging type, and dimensions of an item.

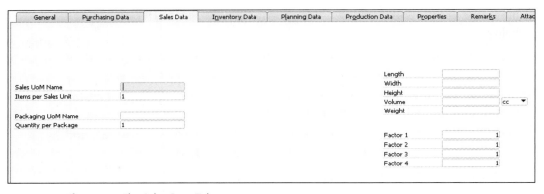

Figure 9.5 The Sales Data Tab

As in the PURCHASING DATA tab, the way to define those values depends if the item has been assigned a unit of measure group. If the UoM GROUP field is set to MANUAL in the item master data header, then both SALES UoM NAME and PACKAGING UoM NAME fields can be entered as free text.

If, on the contrary, a UoM group has been assigned to the item, you need to select values for the SALES UoM NAME and PACKAGING UoM fields as follows:

1. Click on the BROWSE icon (the ellipsis) located next to the SALES UoM CODE field or the PACKAGING TYPE field. Both will open the SALES UoM AND PACKAGE TYPES window.

2. Select the appropriate purchasing unit of measure on the left side of the window and click on the SET AS DEFAULT button below.

3. Select the appropriate package type on the right side of the window and click on the SET AS DEFAULT button below.

4. Enter the number of default purchasing units of measures contained in the default package type in the QTY PER PACKAGE field.

5. Note that on the right side of the SALES DATA tab, you can also define dimensions (length, width, height, volume, and weight) for both the purchasing UoM and packaging UoM items.

6. Click on the UPDATE button to apply changes to the item.

9.1.4 Inventory Data Tab

The INVENTORY DATA tab shown in Figure 9.6 is used to view and maintain the warehouse, inventory, and costing information of the items.

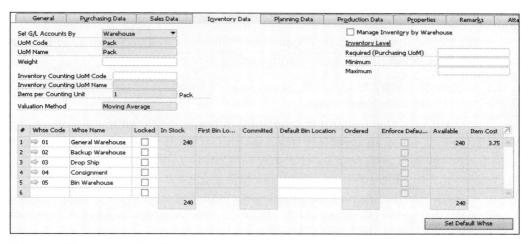

Figure 9.6 The Inventory Data Tab

The SET G/L ACCOUNTS BY field determines the default G/L method for an item. Choose one of the following options from the dropdown list:

▸ WAREHOUSE: G/L accounts for the item are defined at the warehouse level.

▸ ITEM GROUP: G/L accounts for the item are defined at the item group level.

▸ ITEM LEVEL: G/L accounts for the item are defined directly in the item. If you select this method, all account fields in the table of the INVENTORY DATA tab will become editable; otherwise they are grayed out.

The UOM CODE field appears only if a UoM group is assigned to the item; in this case, you can select the code by clicking on the LIST icon (three horizontal lines) and selecting the required code from the list. If there is no UoM group assigned to the item, you can directly enter a value in the UoM NAME field.

Tips and Tricks: The Default UoM Code
By default, the system will set the UoM CODE as the default UoM of the item's UoM GROUP. Changing the UoM code of an item (which is possible only if the item does not have any posted inventory transactions) will remove all UoM prices defined for the item.

Three other fields are available only for items with assigned UoM groups: INVENTORY COUNTING UoM CODE, INVENTORY COUNTING UoM NAME, and ITEMS PER COUNTING UNITS. Use these fields to define the default unit of measure for the inventory counting process. (We'll go into more detail on this process in Section 9.6.6 and Section 9.6.7.)

The VALUATION METHOD field applies only for items with perpetual inventory. In this field, select one of the following costing methods:

- ▸ MOVING AVERAGE: This method is calculated based on averages from each sales and purchasing transaction.
- ▸ STANDARD: The item cost is defined by you and used for all transactions. If the item is set as an inventory item, the cost needs to be defined via inventory revaluation (which we'll cover in Section 9.6.10). Otherwise, you can enter the cost value directly in the ITEM COST field.
- ▸ FIFO (first in, first out): This valuation method is based on the assumption that the first goods purchased are the first to be sold. When defined as FIFO, an item will potentially have multiple costing layers.

An item's inventory may be managed by warehouse or for the whole company. When the MANAGE INVENTORY BY WAREHOUSE field is checked, the REQUIRED (PURCHASING UoM), MINIMUM, and MAXIMUM fields can only be defined in the table for each warehouse. If the item's inventory is *not* managed by warehouse but managed instead by company, those three fields must be maintained in the main area of the INVENTORY DATA tab.

Table 9.1 defines the main fields that appear in the table of the INVENTORY DATA tab.

Field	Description/Use
LOCKED	When this checkbox is check, the item becomes locked for the warehouse and cannot be added to any A/R or A/P document.

Table 9.1 Fields in the Inventory Data Tab

Field	Description/Use
IN STOCK	This column displays the total on-hand quantity.
COMMITTED	This column displays the sum of units committed on sales orders, A/R reserve invoices, or production orders for child items.
ORDERED	This column displays the sum of ordered units for the item from purchase orders, A/P reserve invoices, and production orders for parent items.
AVAILABLE	This column displays the number of "available" items; in other words, the number of items in stock minus the number committed plus the number ordered.
FIRST BIN LOCATION	This column displays the first bin location, which is the bin from which the item will be allocated automatically by the system.
DEFAULT BIN LOCATION	This column displays the default bin location that used to store incoming goods by default.
ENFORCE DEFAULT BIN LOC.	Check this field to enforce the use of the default bin location when receiving incoming goods.
REQUIRED (PURCHASING UoM)	Enter the required inventory level of the item for the company or the warehouse.
MINIMUM	Enter the minimum inventory level of the item for the company or the warehouse.
MAXIMUM	Enter the maximum inventory level of the item for the company or the warehouse.

Table 9.1 Fields in the Inventory Data Tab (Cont.)

From the following available options, choose the default G/L method for this item:

▶ WHSE: Uses all G/L accounts that you have defined at the warehouses level.

▶ ITEMGROUP: Uses all G/L accounts that you have defined at the item group level.

▶ ITEMLEVEL: Uses any G/L accounts that you have defined at the item level.

9.1.5 Planning Data Tab

Maintain production and materials requirements planning (MRP)-related information in the PLANNING DATA tab shown in Figure 9.7.

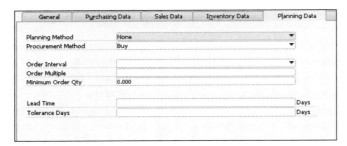

Figure 9.7 The Planning Data Tab

The PLANNING METHOD dropdown list defines whether the item is to be planned by the MRP system (MRP) or not (NONE). For more information about MRP, check out Chapter 12.

Take a look at the second field in Figure 9.7: PROCUREMENT METHOD. In a manufacturing environment, parent items (finished or semi-finished goods) will be set as MAKE (the MRP system will suggest quantities to make via production orders), while component items will be set as BUY (the MRP system will suggest quantities to purchase via purchase orders).

Tips and Tricks: Procurement Methods

If the PROCUREMENT METHOD value is set to MRP, another field (COMPONENT WAREHOUSE) will appear to determine the warehouse source for the component item that needs to be purchased or produced. Two warehouse source options are available:

▸ FROM BILL OF MATERIAL LINE: Uses the warehouse from the bill of materials (BOM).

▸ FROM PARENT ITEM DOCUMENT LINE: Uses the warehouse from the lines of the document generating the demand for the parent item.

The MRP run will also consider the order interval (i.e., weekly, monthly, and so on); the order multiple (make or purchase by multiple of); the minimum quantity to make or buy; the lead time (time interval in days between order and receipt); and the tolerance days (additional days to fulfill the requirements based on the MRP's recommendations). You'll make these selections in the five bottom fields shown in Figure 9.7.

9.1.6 Production Data Tab

The PRODUCTION DATA tab shown in Figure 9.8 mostly contains informative data related to a bill of materials such as the BOM type, the number of item components, and the number of resource components. For more information about BOMs, please refer to Chapter 11 on bills of materials.

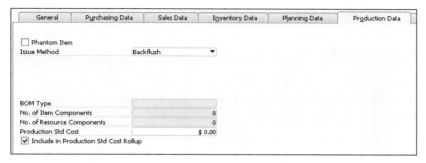

Figure 9.8 The Production Data Tab

We want to draw your attention to two key fields on the PRODUCTION DATA tab:

▶ The PHANTOM ITEM checkbox: A *phantom item* is a noninventory item used to regroup multiple components under one single line in a multilevel BOM. The purpose of creating a phantom item is to facilitate data entry in a case where multiple BOMs would share the same components. Note that, when used in a production order, all individual components of the phantom item will appear.

▶ The ISSUE METHODS dropdown list: You can choose from two options here:

  ▶ BACKFLUSH: After reporting completion of the finished goods (parent items), this method automatically consumes the components according to the BOM definition (i.e. the issue for components for those components is automatically created).

  ▶ MANUAL: In this method, you'll need to create each issue for components manually and specify exactly the amounts to issue for production.

Tips and Tricks: Backflush Method

For a batch-managed or serialized item, you cannot select a backflush method because you will need to indicate which batch or serial number to issue for production.

You can also define the item's standard production cost and define whether the system should include it in the standard production cost rollup by checking the INCLUDE IN PRODUCT STD. COST ROLLUP field. When this field is checked, you'll be able to recalculate the item's standard cost based on the standard cost of its components defined in its BOM (see Chapter 11 for more details).

9.1.7 Properties Tab

You can use the PROPERTIES tab to assign up to sixty-four different properties to an item. Those properties are user defined and are maintained with binary values (Y or N).

Tips and Tricks: Properties versus UDF
Using properties instead of user-defined fields brings certain advantages. Since the properties are built into the item master table, they are also integrated as selection criteria in many standard sales reports; hence, properties enhance built-in reporting capabilities.

You can also click on the SELECT ALL button to check all properties at once or click on the CLEAR SELECTION button to uncheck them.

9.1.8 Remarks Tab

You can use the REMARKS tab to enter additional notes for an item or even insert an image by clicking on the IMAGE icon (the camera).

Tips and Tricks: The Picture Folder
In order to insert an image, you must ensure the picture folder is defined under ADMINISTRATION • SYSTEM INITIALIZATION • GENERAL SETTINGS.

9.1.9 Attachments Tab

In this tab, you can attach documents to the current items. You can:

- Attach a new document by clicking on the BROWSE button.
- Display an attached document by clicking on the DISPLAY button.
- Delete an attached document by clicking on the DELETE button.

For any attached document, the system will display the target path of the file, the file name, and the attachment date.

Tips and Tricks: The Attachment Folder
In order to attach a document, you must ensure the attachment folder is defined under ADMINISTRATION • SYSTEM INITIALIZATION • GENERAL SETTINGS.

9.2   Bar Codes

Before SAP Business One, version 9.0, you could enter only one bar code per item. From version 9.0 onward, you can associate an unlimited number of bar codes per item and an unlimited number of bar codes per unit of measure.

Access the bar code functionality by following the screen path INVENTORY • BAR CODES. The BAR CODES window opens in Find mode (see Figure 9.9). You can search for an item by typing in its item number and clicking on the FIND button. You can also click on the BAR CODE LIST button to get the whole list of existing bar codes to select from.

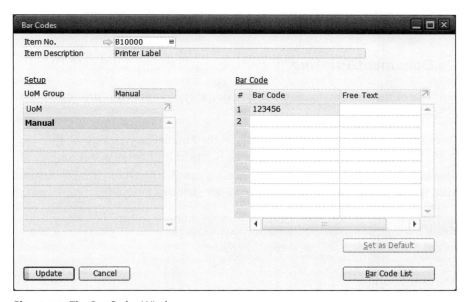

Figure 9.9 The Bar Codes Window

To add a new bar code or modify an existing bar code, you must do the following:

1. Select an item.
2. Select the unit of measure on the left pane and modify an existing bar code or create a new one on the right pane.
3. Click on the UPDATE button.

Tip and Tricks: Bar Code Defaults

In the BAR CODES window, only the FIND icon (the binoculars) is available, and you cannot create a new item from the BAR CODES window. If you have multiple bar codes for the same items or units of measure, you can set one of them as the default bar code via the SET AS DEFAULT button.

Tips and Tricks: Duplicate Bar Codes

By default, the system displays a warning message when you associate the same bar code to different items. Instead of a warning, SAP Business One can send an error message that would not allow those duplicates. Discuss this setting with your SAP Business One consultant.

9.3   Document Printing

The purpose of the Document Printing functionality is to preview print, email, or fax documents in batches.

The DOCUMENT PRINTING menu is available in the Financials, Sales (A/R), Purchasing (A/P), Banking, and Inventory modules, but in this chapter, we'll only cover printing inventory-related transactions (see Figure 9.10). Open the DOCUMENT PRINTING menu by following the menu path INVENTORY • DOCUMENT PRINTING.

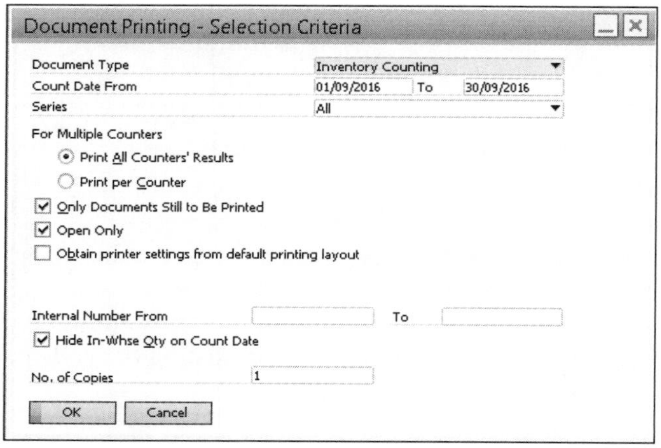

Figure 9.10 Document Printing Selection Criteria

As we've done throughout this chapter, let's walk through the fields displayed in Figure 9.10 in Table 9.2.

Field	Description/Use
DOCUMENT TYPE	Select the document type that you want to print. Every document that exist in SAP is listed: sales documents (from the sales quotation to the A/R credit memo), purchasing documents (from the purchase request to the A/P credit memo), accounting documents (from an incoming payment to the journal entries), inventory documents (from the goods issue to the transfers), production documents (from the production orders to the pick lists) and inventory counting transactions (from inventory counting to opening balances).
COUNT DATE FROM	Select a date range of documents to print. In our example shown in Figure 9.10, we are selecting all documents for the month of September.
SERIES	Select the particular series you want to print or accept ALL as the default to print documents for all series.
FOR MULTIPLE COUNTERS	Choose one of the following radio buttons to tell the system how to print when there are multiple counters: ▶ PRINT ALL COUNTERS' RESULTS ▶ PRINT PER COUNTER
ONLY DOCUMENTS STILL TO BE PRINTED	Select this checkbox to print only documents that haven't yet been printed.
OPEN ONLY	Select this checkbox to print only documents that are open.
OBTAIN PRINTER SETTINGS FROM DEFAULT PRINTING LAYOUT	Select this checkbox to apply the default printing layout's printer settings.
INTERNAL NUMBER FROM	This field allows you to select certain internal documents by entering a number range.
HIDE IN-WHSE QTY. ON COUNT DATE	Select this checkbox to hide the quantity of items in the warehouse on the date they were counted.
NO. OF COPIES	Enter the number of copies to print for each document. In our example, we're only printing one copy.

Table 9.2 Fields in the Document Printing Selection Criteria Screen

9.4   Bin Locations

Bin locations are the smallest storage space units in a warehouse. When bin locations are enabled for a warehouse, every inventory transaction will require a bin location in order to designate from where to issue the stock or where to receive the stock.

9.4.1   Bin Location Master Data

The BIN LOCATION MASTER DATA window shown in Figure 9.11 is where you can add, update, search, and delete a bin location. You can access this window by following the menu path INVENTORY • BIN LOCATIONS • BIN LOCATION MASTER DATA.

The structure of a bin location is composed of a warehouse and at least one sublevel (i.e., aisle, shelf, level, etc.).

To create a bin location, follow these steps:

1. Select a warehouse from the dropdown list of the WAREHOUSE field.

2. Select at least one warehouse sublevel.

3. Fill in the fields under BIN LOCATION PROPERTIES, which are all optional. We describe these fields in Table 9.3.

4. Click on the ADD button to save the bin location.

Tips and Tricks: Enable Bin Locations

Only warehouses that have the option ENABLE BIN LOCATIONS checked will be available in the WAREHOUSE field dropdown list (from the WAREHOUSE SETUP window in the menu ADMINISTRATION • SETUP • INVENTORY • WAREHOUSE), and only the defined warehouse sublevels will be available in the sublevel fields.

As you fill the bin location information, you'll see that the BIN LOCATION CODE field will automatically populate with the selected warehouse and warehouse sublevels. The warehouse and warehouse sublevels will be separated by the code separator defined in the BIN LOCATIONS tab of the WAREHOUSES SETUP window.

You can also click on the MANAGE BIN LOCATIONS button to access the BIN LOCATION MANAGEMENT window. To access the BIN LOCATION CODE MODIFICATION window, click on the MODIFY BIN LOCATION CODES button shown at the bottom of Figure 9.11.

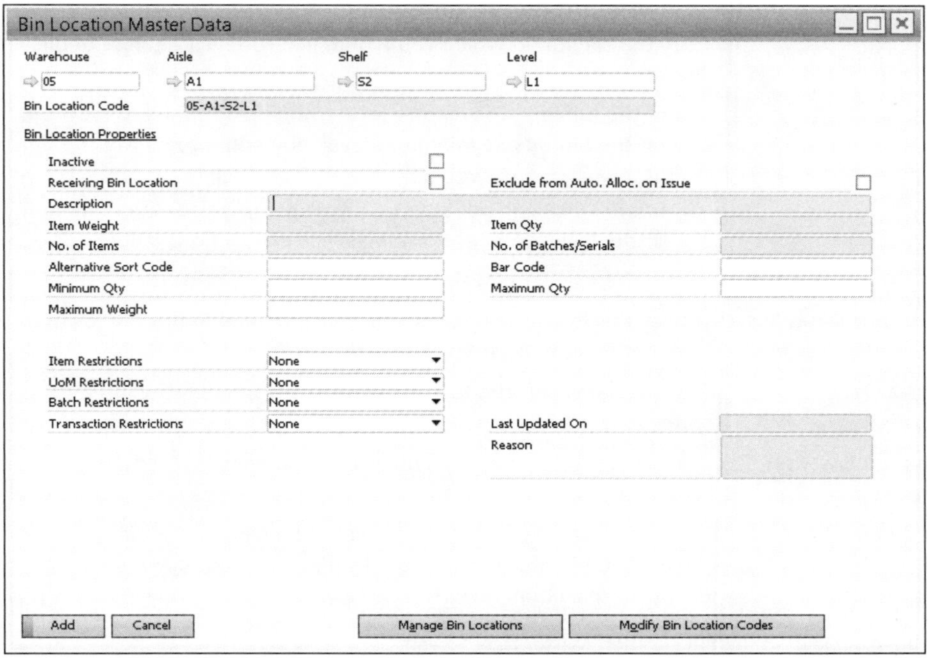

Figure 9.11 The Bin Location Master Data Screen

Fields	Description/Use
INACTIVE	Check this box to deactivate a bin location—but only if the bin does not contain any inventory. Once inactive, the bin will not be usable in any transaction.
RECEIVING BIN LOCATION	This field displays the receiving bin location, which is automatically assigned when receiving inventory. Typically, items will reside temporarily in the receiving bin in order to be counted and inspected prior to the put away process, which would place them into storage locations.
ITEM WEIGHT	This field displays the sum of items' weights located in this particular bin location. This field is for information only. To define an item weight, use the INVENTORY DATA tab of the ITEM MASTER window, which we discussed in Section 9.1.4.
NO. OF ITEMS	This field displays the number of different items contained in the bin location.
ALTERNATIVE SORT CODE	Enter an alternative sort code for the bin location, if necessary. Alternative sort codes might be useful when performing an inventory transaction in which you would like to select a range of bin locations.
MINIMUM QTY	Enter the minimum inventory level to be held in the bin location. When the bin hits its minimum level, you could replenish the bin to hit its maximum level. Be careful: SAP will not stop you from going below the minimum inventory level when performing an inventory transaction.
MAXIMUM WEIGHT	Enter the maximum weight allowed for this bin location.
EXCLUDE FROM AUTO. ALLOC. ON ISSUE	Check this box so that the inventory contained in this bin location will not be automatically allocated.
ITEM QTY	This field displays the total inventory contained in the bin location.
NO. OF BATCHES/ SERIALS	This field displays the total quantity of batches and serial numbers contained in the bin location.
MAXIMUM QTY	Enter the maximum inventory level to be held in the bin location. When the bin hits its minimum level, you could replenish the bin to hit its maximum level.

Table 9.3 Fields in the Bin Location Master Data Screen

You can add restrictions to bin locations by selecting from the four dropdown lists in the bottom left of Figure 9.11.

You can assign one of the following item restrictions in the ITEM RESTRICTIONS dropdown list:

▶ NONE: No item-related restrictions are applied, which means that the bin can store any item.

▶ SPECIFIC ITEM: You can select a specific item code in the ITEM field that appears on the right so the bin can store only that particular item.

▶ SPECIFIC ITEM GROUP: You can select a specific item group in the ITEM GROUP field that appeared on the right so the bin can only store that particular group.

▶ SINGLE ITEM GROUP: When this option is selected, the bin can only hold one item group at a time. Any other item group than the one already contained in the bin location will be refused by the system.

You can also assign one of the following restrictions in the UoM RESTRICTIONS dropdown list:

▶ NONE: No UoM-related restrictions are applied. The bin can store any UoM.

▶ SPECIFIC UoM: You can select a specific UoM code in the UoM field that appears on the right so the bin can store only that particular unit of measure.

▶ SPECIFIC UoM GROUP: You can select a specific UoM group in the UoM GROUP field that appeared on the right so the bin can only store that particular unit of measure group.

▶ SINGLE UoM GROUP: When this option is selected, the bin can only hold one UoM group at a time. Any other UoM group than the one already contained in the bin location will be refused by the system.

You can also assign one of the following restrictions in the BATCH RESTRICTIONS dropdown list:

▶ NONE: No batch-related restrictions are applied. The bin can store any batch.

▶ SINGLE BATCH: When this option is selected, the bin can only hold one batch at a time. Any other batch than the one already contained in the bin location will be refused by the system. You can view the CURRENT BATCH in the field located next to the BATCH RESTRICTION.

You can also assign one of the following restrictions in the TRANSACTION RESTRICTIONS dropdown list:

▶ NONE: No transaction-related restrictions are applied. The bin can be used for any transaction.

- ALL TRANSACTIONS: The bin cannot be used for any transaction.

- INBOUND TRANSACTIONS: The bin cannot be used for inbound transactions (goods receipts, goods receipts PO, A/P invoices, etc.).

- OUTBOUND TRANSACTIONS: The bin cannot be used for outbound transactions (goods issues, deliveries, A/R invoices, etc.).

- ALL EXCEPT INVENTORY TRANSFER AND COUNTING TRANSACTIONS: The bin location *can only* be used for transfers, inventory counting, and inventory posting.

Tips and Tricks: Transaction Restrictions

When setting transaction restrictions, you must fill the REASON field with a brief explanation. This is a mandatory field. Once the transaction restriction changes to the bin location are saved, the LAST UPDATED ON field will display the date of the last update.

9.4.2   Bin Location Management

The BIN LOCATION MANAGEMENT window shown in Figure 9.12 is where you add, update, and delete bin locations in batches.

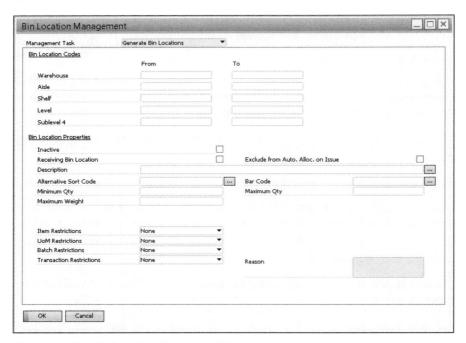

Figure 9.12 The Bin Location Management Screen

Access the BIN LOCATION MANAGEMENT window by following the menu path INVENTORY • BIN LOCATIONS • BIN LOCATION MANAGEMENT.

The first field in Figure 9.12 is the MANAGEMENT TASK field. Choose one of the following tasks from the dropdown list:

- GENERATE BIN LOCATION: This action generates bin locations in batches for selected warehouses and warehouse sublevels.

- UPDATE BIN LOCATIONS PROPERTIES: This action updates the bin location properties for selected warehouses and warehouse sublevels.

- DELETE BIN LOCATIONS: This action deletes bin locations for selected warehouses and warehouse sublevels.

Let's look at the steps for generating bin locations; note, however, that the process is similar to updating or deleting bin locations. Select the appropriate task (that is, to generate, update, or delete bin locations) and fill the fields to be updated or deleted for locations matching the selected warehouse and warehouse sublevels.

To generate bin locations, follow these steps:

1. Select GENERATE BIN LOCATION in the MANAGEMENT TASK field.

2. Fill the BIN LOCATION CODES, including the relevant warehouse sublevel fields, with values in the FROM and TO fields.

3. Fill in the BIN LOCATION PROPERTIES. Refer to Table 9.3 for more information about each specific field.

Tips and Tricks: Automatic String Creation

For each bin you create, you can automatically generate a description, an alternative sort code, or a bar code using the Automatic String Create function shown in Figure 9.13.

The AUTOMATIC STRING CREATION window allows you to generate string details for batches. You can enter the string to be generated in the STRING field and its type in the TYPE field (either STRING or NUMBER). For numbers, you can also specify an INCREASE or DECREASE operation in the OPERATION field.

In the example shown in Figure 9.14, the system will generate an ascending string for every created bin location (i.e., A5-001, A5-002, and so on).

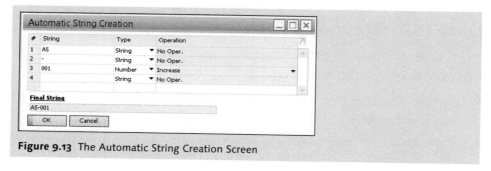

Figure 9.13 The Automatic String Creation Screen

4. Once all required fields are filled out in the BIN LOCATION MANAGEMENT window, click OK. The BIN LOCATION MANAGEMENT GENERATION PREVIEW window shown in Figure 9.14 will be displayed; review the list of bin locations to be created, and when you're done, click the GENERATE button.

#	Bin Location Code	Inactive	Receiving Bin Location	Exclude from ...	Alternative Sort Code	Description	Item Weight	Item Qty
1	05-A5-S1-L1	No	No	No	A5-001			
2	05-A5-S1-L2	No	No	No	A5-002			
3	05-A5-S1-L3	No	No	No	A5-003			
4	05-A5-S1-L4	No	No	No	A5-004			
5	05-A5-S2-L1	No	No	No	A5-005			
6	05-A5-S2-L2	No	No	No	A5-006			
7	05-A5-S2-L3	No	No	No	A5-007			
8	05-A5-S2-L4	No	No	No	A5-008			
9	05-A5-S3-L1	No	No	No	A5-009			
10	05-A5-S3-L2	No	No	No	A5-010			
11	05-A5-S3-L3	No	No	No	A5-011			
12	05-A5-S3-L4	No	No	No	A5-012			
13	05-A5-S4-L1	No	No	No	A5-013			

Figure 9.14 The Bin Location Management Generation Preview Screen

9.4.3   Bin Location Code Modification

Access the BIN LOCATION CODE MODIFICATION screen shown in Figure 9.15 by following the menu path INVENTORY • BIN LOCATION • BIN LOCATION CODE MODIFICATION.

Use this window to rename bin location codes in batches based on certain selection criteria. For example, our second sublevel in our warehouse is the aisle; using this functionality, we could easily rename the aisle structure from "A1" to "A01" for thousands of bin locations.

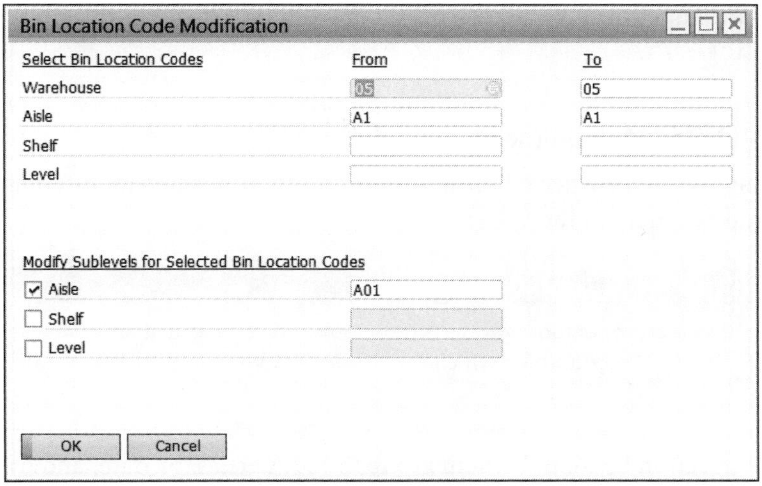

Figure 9.15 Bin Location Code Modification Screen

When you click on OK, the system will prompt the BIN LOCATION CODE MODIFI-CATION PREVIEW window shown in Figure 9.16. Select each record to be updated and click MODIFY.

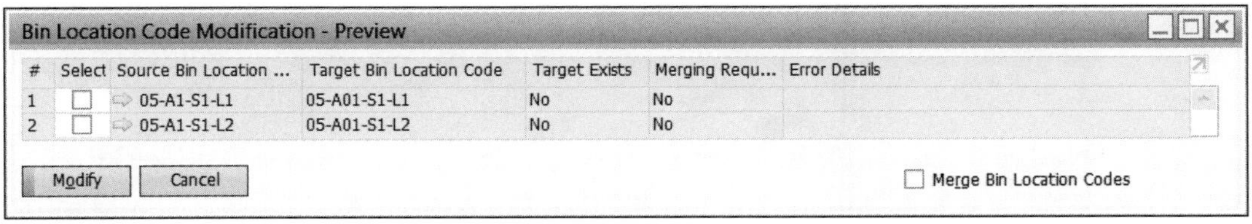

Figure 9.16 Bin Location Code Modification Preview Screen

In this example, the target bin location 05-A01-S1-L1 was created and the source bin location 05-A1-S1-L1 was not deleted, but set to INACTIVE.

9.5 Item Management

You can use the Item Management functionality to manage item serial numbers, item batches, alternatives items, and business partner catalog numbers; globally update business partner catalog numbers; and modify the inventory valuation method. Item Management can be accessed by following the menu path INVEN-TORY • ITEM MANAGEMENT.

9.5.1 Serial Number Management

The SERIAL NUMBER MANAGEMENT window allows you to either update or complete (create) serial numbers in the system.

> **Tips and Tricks: The Complete Operation**
>
> You can use the COMPLETE operation for serialized items that have a management method set to ON RELEASE ONLY and for which serial numbers were not created upon receipt.

You can filter the selection by item, by item group, by properties, by date, and by transaction types. Once you've entered your selection criteria, the SERIAL NUMBER MANAGEMENT window shown in Figure 9.17 will be displayed; this is where you can perform the required updates.

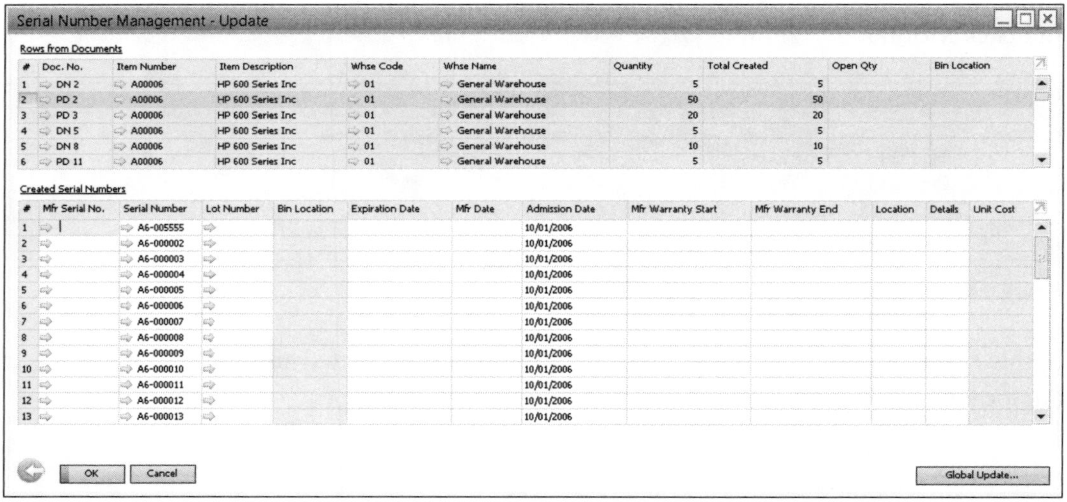

Figure 9.17 The Serial Number Management Screen

The SERIAL NUMBERS DETAILS window shown in Figure 9.18 allows you to view and update serial numbers. Note that, in this window, only the Find mode is available—meaning that you cannot create serial numbers from this screen.

Figure 9.18 The Serial Number Details Screen

9.5.2 Batch Management

The BATCH MANAGEMENT window has the same functionality and displays the same fields as the SERIAL NUMBER MANAGEMENT window but applies to batches instead of serial numbers. Similarly, the BATCH MANAGEMENT DETAILS window allows you to view and update batch numbers. Pay close attention to the STATUS field, which controls whether the batch is ready for shipping.

9.5.3 Alternative Item

The ALTERNATIVE ITEMS window allows you to link two items together. An alternative item is used to replace another item in case the original item is not available for sale. When a sales order is created, if the AUTOMATIC AVAILABILITY CHECK option is enabled, the system would offer an option to display and replace the missing item by one of its alternative items.

9.5.4 Business Partner Catalog Numbers

The BUSINESS PARTNER CATALOG NUMBERS window shown in Figure 9.19 allows you to maintain business partner catalog numbers either by item or by business partner. You can assign multiple business partner catalog numbers for the same item number. In our example, both business partner catalog numbers 1234 and 3345 were assigned to item number A0001.

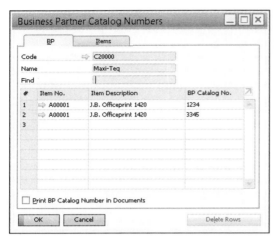

Figure 9.19 The Business Partner Catalog Numbers Screen

Tips and Tricks: Adding Business Partner Catalogs

When creating or adding items to a marketing document, you can enter items either by item number or by the business partner catalog number.

9.5.5 Global Updates to BP Catalog Numbers

Maintaining business partner catalog numbers can become tedious, so SAP Business One offers the global update to simplify this process. You can select a source business partner and copy its catalog numbers to a new business partner using the following options:

▶ REPLACE ALL ITEMS: This option will copy all the business partner catalog numbers from one business partner to another.

▶ REPLACE ONLY EXISTING ITEMS: This option will only update items that exist for both business partners.

▶ DO NOT REPLACE ITEMS: This option will copy new items but will not affect existing items in the destination business partner.

Tips and Tricks: Using the Test Database

For this kind of batch maintenance, we always recommend backing up the database first or testing the update in a test environment. No undo feature is available.

9.5.6   Inventory Valuation Method

This feature allows you to perform updates on item valuation methods. You can select a range of items by item number, by group, or by item properties and can update their valuation methods in batches.

> **Tips and Tricks: Valuation Method Changes**
>
> Changing a valuation method is only possible if the item has zero stock in inventory for each warehouse.

9.6   Inventory Transactions

The Inventory Transaction submodule of the Inventory module allows you to do every inventory movement in your warehouses such as goods receipts, goods issues, inventory transfers, inventory counting, and postings; it allows you to enter inventory opening balances and even perform an inventory revaluation.

9.6.1   Goods Receipt

Use the *goods receipt* function shown in Figure 9.20 to perform a positive inventory adjustment.

This function is available by following the menu path INVENTORY • INVENTORY TRANSACTIONS • GOODS RECEIPT. By default, the window will open in Add mode.

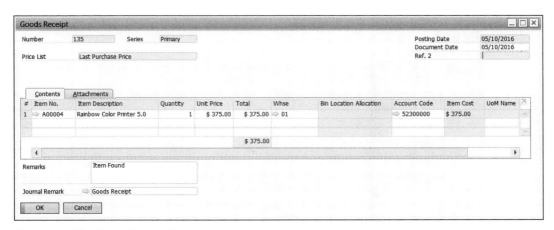

Figure 9.20 The Goods Receipt Screen

To create a goods receipt, select the price list that contains the right price (if available) and add the item via the ITEM NO. field, the ITEM DESCRIPTION field, or the LIST OF ITEM window, which is accessible from the LIST icon (three horizontal lines).

Make sure the data in the POSTING DATE, QUANTITY, WAREHOUSE, and UoM fields are correct. You can also enter remarks in the text box above the OK button.

The unit price (and thus the total) is important in a goods receipt, whether derived from a price list or manually inputted. The value in the TOTAL column will drive the corresponding journal entries: a debit on the inventory account and a credit on the cost of goods sold (COGS) account.

> **Tips and Tricks: Goods Receipt**
>
> Pay particular attention to the ACCOUNT CODE field. The number here should reference an expense account in the COGS account. If this G/L account determination is incorrectly linked to the inventory account, then the inventory audit report will not match the corresponding G/L account.

9.6.2 Goods Issue

The *goods issue* function performs a negative inventory adjustment. Access this transaction by following the menu path INVENTORY • INVENTORY TRANSACTIONS • GOODS ISSUE.

Creating a goods issue is exactly the same process as for a goods receipt, so you can follow the same steps as before. Note, however, that there is no need to input a price in a goods issue document. SAP Business One will input the item cost of the item.

> **Tips and Tricks: Goods Issue**
>
> Particular attention should be paid to the ACCOUNT CODE field. The number here should be an expense account in the COGS drawer. If this G/L account determination is incorrectly linked to the inventory account, then the inventory audit report will not match the corresponding G/L account.

> **Tips and Tricks: Goods Issue**
>
> Think about which users you should authorize to create goods issues. We recommend you consider setting up an approval procedure or an alert so that a manager is aware of these transactions when they happen.

9.6.3 Inventory Transfer Request

Sometimes, you may notice a shortage of certain goods. Inventory transfer requests can be done from one warehouse to another or within the same warehouse from one bin location to another.

The INVENTORY TRANSFER REQUEST screen shown in Figure 9.21 can be used as a source of demand in the Pick and Pack Manager, described in Section 9.8, and in the MRP Wizard, described in Chapter 12. Access this screen by following the menu path INVENTORY • INVENTORY TRANSACTIONS • INVENTORY TRANSFER REQUEST.

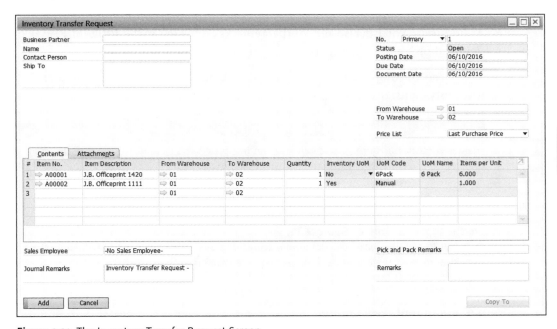

Figure 9.21 The Inventory Transfer Request Screen

To create an inventory transfer request, enter the following fields shown in Figure 9.21:

▸ ITEM NO.: Use the tab key to access the CHOOSE FROM LIST window or simply enter the item code manually.

▸ FROM WAREHOUSE: You can enter this code at the header level, which would then copy it to each line. The FROM WAREHOUSE field comes from the field specified in the GENERAL SETTINGS • INVENTORY tab.

▸ To WAREHOUSE: Similarly, you can enter this code at the header level on the right side, which would then copy it to each line.

▸ QUANTITY: Enter the quantity to be transferred. Keep in mind that this field goes with the UoM Code field.

▸ INVENTORY UOM and UOM CODE: When INVENTORY UOM is set to YES, we'll transfer the quantities in STOCK UOM (e.g., units, chosen from the UOM CODE dropdown list); when INVENTORY UOM is set to NO, then we transfer in the SALES UOM (e.g., six-pack or twelve-pack, chosen from the UOM CODE dropdown list).

As necessary, you can also add journal remarks on the left in the JOURNAL REMARKS field and pick and pack remarks in the REMARKS field on the right.

When you've completed your selections, click on the ADD button to complete the inventory transfer request.

Tips and Tricks: Inventory Transfer Request

The inventory transfer request will have an impact on the quantities ordered and committed in the ITEM MASTER DATA WINDOW • INVENTORY tab.

Tips and Tricks: Transfer Requests for Business Partners

In the top left corner of Figure 9.21, you can associate a transfer request to a business partner in the header of the document to reserve a certain quantity of inventory into a physical or logical warehouse for a particular customer.

9.6.4 Inventory Transfer

You can move inventory from one warehouse to another or from one bin location to another within the same warehouse using inventory transfer. Access this function by following the menu path INVENTORY • INVENTORY TRANSACTIONS • INVENTORY TRANSFER.

Creating a new inventory transfer can be done in one of two ways:

▸ To create an inventory transfer from scratch, follow the same steps as for the inventory transfer request in the previous section. When creating a transfer, the system will default to the item's inventory unit of measure as the default unit of measure to transfer. If the item is sold or purchased in different units of measure, those units of measure can be used in the transfer process. To change the unit of measure on a transfer, you can set the field INVENTORY UoM to NO and then change the UoM CODE for the appropriate unit of measure.

If one of the items is managed by serial numbers or batches on every transaction, the SERIAL NUMBER SELECTION window or the BATCH NUMBER SELECTION window will open so that serial number or batches can be selected.

▸ You can also create a transfer from an existing transfer request by clicking on the COPY FROM button and selecting INVENTORY TRANSFER REQUEST. This function will copy all information previously entered on the transfer request, and the remarks field will specify that this inventory transfer is based on the original inventory transfer request. Confirm the quantities and click on the ADD button.

Tips and Tricks: Inventory Transfer

Fill in the FROM BIN LOCATION and TO BIN LOCATION fields only if the Bin Location feature is enabled in at least one warehouse.

Tips and Tricks: Transferring a Business Partner

You can associate a transfer to a business partner in the header of the document, perhaps to reserve a certain quantity of inventory into a physical or logical warehouse for a particular customer.

9.6.5   Recurring Transactions

You can define recurring transactions in SAP Business One. For example, maybe you want to create a purchase order every week until the end of year or perform an inventory transfer every Monday from one warehouse to another warehouse.

Recurring transactions are available by following the menu path INVENTORY • INVENTORY TRANSACTION • RECURRING TRANSACTIONS. Figure 9.22 shows the screen to define recurring transactions.

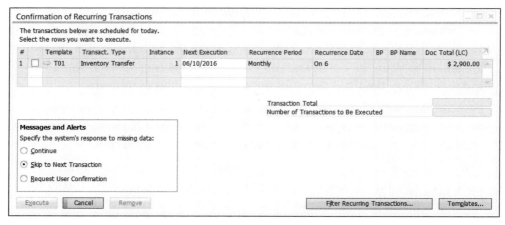

Figure 9.22 The Confirmation of Recurring Transactions Screen

From the CONFIRMATION OF RECURRING TRANSACTIONS window, you can drill down to a recurring transaction template by clicking on the golden arrow next to it. Make sure you *do not* click on the ADD button at this point. When you are ready to post a transaction, select the transaction to be executed in the CONFIRMATION OF RECURRING TRANSACTIONS window and click on the EXECUTE button.

The system will display a confirmation message that the transaction was created.

> **Tips and Tricks: Recurring Transactions**
>
> The DISPLAY RECURRING TRANSACTIONS ON EXECUTION option has to be activated in the general settings so that you get the recurring transactions confirmation popup.

Of course, before you can use recurring transactions, you must have previously created a recurring transaction template by following the menu path INVENTORY • INVENTORY TRANSACTION • RECURRING TRANSACTIONS TEMPLATES.

To create a new recurring transaction template, simply go to the next line available (in our example in Figure 9.22, line 2) and fill out the following fields:

► TEMPLATE: Enter a template number for the new template to create.

► TYPE: Most A/R documents, A/P documents, and inventory transaction documents are available to be chosen.

► RECURRENCE PERIOD: Your options here are the following: DAILY, WEEKLY, MONTHLY, QUARTERLY, SEMIANNUALLY, ANNUALLY, and ONE TIME.

- RECURRENCE DATE: This date will be dependent on the information provided in the RECURRENCE PERIOD field. For instance, if we chose DAILY for the recurrence period, the recurrence date will be EVERY1 (day), EVERY2 (day), etc. If we chose weekly, the RECURRENCE DATE options will be ON MONDAY, ON TUESDAY, and so on.

- VALID UNTIL: Specify an end date.

Click on the UPDATE button. On the date entered in the NEXT EXECUTION field, the recurring transaction will pop up in SAP Business One.

9.6.6 Inventory Counting

The *inventory counting* process in SAP Business One offers a structured process for the inventory counting: counting by individual counters or by team counters. Access Inventory Counting by following the menu path INVENTORY • INVENTORY TRANSACTIONS • INVENTORY COUNTING TRANSACTIONS • INVENTORY COUNTING (see Figure 9.23).

The first step is to select the items that will be counted using one of three ways:

- By selecting ADD ITEM • SELECT ITEMS
- By selecting ADD ITEM • IMPORT ITEMS
- By copying and pasting from an Excel file

> **Tips and Tricks: Inventory Counting and Serial Number/Batches**
>
> If some items are managed by serial number or batches, we recommend that you use the ADD ITEM • IMPORT ITEMS option, which will allow each item to insert the serial number/batch number directly from the *.txt* file.
>
> If you use the ADD ITEM • SELECT ITEMS or copy and paste from Excel instead, then you have to right-click each counted line and select the SERIAL AND BATCH SELECTION menu.

The second step is to freeze the inventory by activating the checkbox in the FREEZE column shown in Figure 9.23. This optional step is useful because it will prevent any inventory movement (delivery, return, transfer, etc.). You can freeze every line quickly by double-clicking on the title of the FREEZE column. Click on the UPDATE button to save the inventory counting list.

At this stage, you can print the list of items to give to the counting team. You can also show or hide the quantities in inventory.

Some SAP Business One customers do their inventory count by hand and write the quantities on a sheet of paper. These counted quantities will have to be entered manually by clicking on the COUNTED columns and by filling in the quantities in the UoM COUNTED QTY or COUNTED QUANTITY column shown in Figure 9.23.

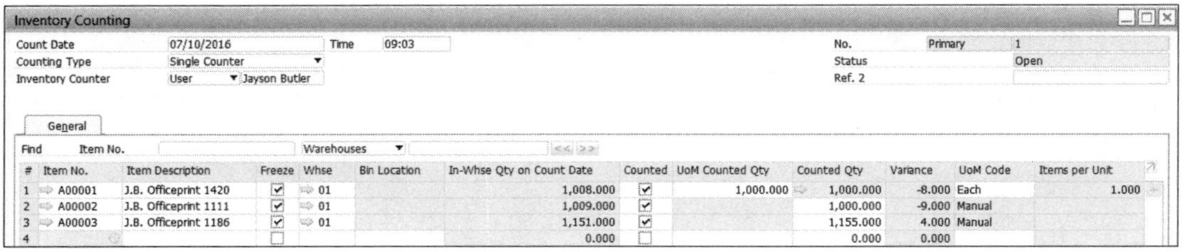

Figure 9.23 Counted Quantities in the Inventory Counting Screen

If the items are bar coded, the inventory can be scanned with a handheld device and directly saved on file (a *.txt* file for instance) making the update of the UoM COUNTED QTY or COUNTED QUANTITY more efficient. All the columns can then be updated using the ADD ITEM • IMPORT ITEMS option.

If bin locations have been activated for the warehouse, the BIN LOCATION field becomes active and must be filled in. You might want to use this filter in the selection criteria when adding the items to a list by using the ADD ITEM • IMPORT ITEM option; in the event that the warehouse is counted by more than one counter, you may want to split the item list by bin location in the INVENTORY COUNTING • ITEMS SELECTION CRITERIA and in INVENTORY COUNTING • BIN LOCATION SELECTION CRITERIA.

This method will result in selecting only the combination of item and bin location for the inventory counter assigned to count these bin locations, as shown in Figure 9.24.

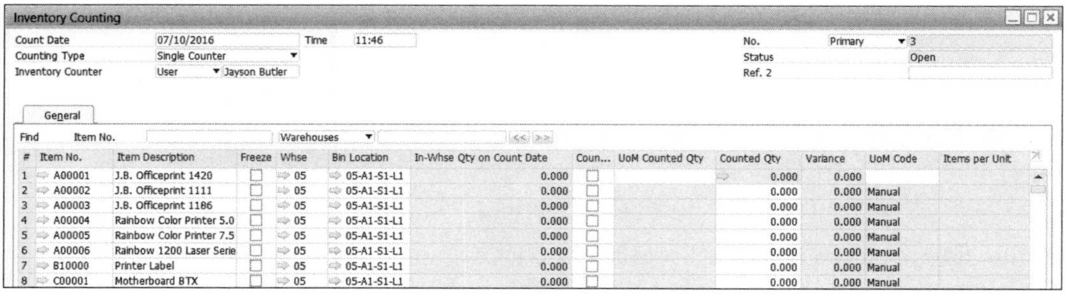

Figure 9.24 Bin Location in the Inventory Counting Screen

The inventory count can be entered under one individual counter or multiple counters in the COUNTING TYPE field. If the counting type is set to a SINGLE COUNTER, then the user or the employee needs to be selected below. If the counting type is set to MULTIPLE COUNTERS, then two additional fields will be displayed to specify the number of individual counters (the NO. OF INDIVIDUAL COUNTERS field) for multiple counters to count individually or the number of team counters (the NO. OF TEAM COUNTERS field) for multiple counters to count in teams.

The purpose of having multiple counters working *individually* is to compare the result of the counting; this duplication will help identify any discrepancies and result in verification before the inventory posting. The counted information is displayed for each of the counters.

The purpose of having multiple counters working *as a team* for an item or bin location is to spread out the work. When stock is high, adding up each counter's quantity is easier than having one person count all the stock.

Two fields located in the GENERAL tab of the INVENTORY COUNTING screen require particular attention:

▸ MAXIMUM VARIANCE: This field displays the maximum difference between the counted quantities by the counters and the value in the IN-WAREHOUSE QUANTITY ON COUNT DATE column.

▸ COUNTER'S DIFFERENCE: This field displays the maximum difference between the counted quantities by the counters.

Click UPDATE to save the count.

Tips and Tricks: Inventory Counting

Creating an inventory counting document does not change any quantity or value in SAP Business One. The new quantities and values will be posted to the system when the inventory posting document is created. That inventory posting document will be copied from one or many inventory counting documents.

9.6.7 Inventory Posting

Once you have created one or many inventory counting documents, you can post them to SAP Business One by following the menu path INVENTORY • INVENTORY TRANSACTIONS • INVENTORY COUNTING TRANSACTIONS • INVENTORY POSTING.

You could enter the quantities directly in the INVENTORY POSTING window, but we recommend that you use the INVENTORY COUNTING window first and then copy the information from there into the inventory posting.

To do so, you need to perform the following steps:

1. Click on the COPY FROM INVENTORY COUNTING button at the bottom.

2. Select the required inventory counting documents from the LIST OF INVENTORY COUNTING window.

3. Click on the CHOOSE button.

4. Select the option DRAW ALL DATA in the DRAW DOCUMENT WIZARD window.

5. Click on the FINISH button.

   If discrepancies between multiple individual counters exist, correct them before the inventory posting. If you don't correct those discrepancies, you will have to choose which quantities to post. You can select counted quantities from a specific counter (in our example in Figure 9.25, Bill Levine or Jayson Butler) or only those quantities without discrepancies (the ITEMS WITH NO COUNTERS' DIFF. option).

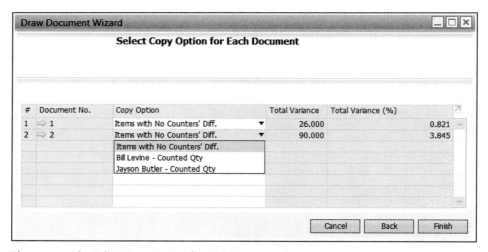

Figure 9.25 The Select Copy Option for Each Document Screen

6. Once all the data has been imported and validated, click on the ADD button at the bottom to post the inventory.

9.6.8   Inventory Opening Balance

Use the INVENTORY OPENING BALANCE window only for the first inventory count. For inventory counts that occur after the first one, you should use INVENTORY COUNTING and INVENTORY POSTING.

You can access the INVENTORY OPENING BALANCE window shown in Figure 9.26 by following the menu path INVENTORY • INVENTORY TRANSACTIONS • INVENTORY OPENING BALANCE.

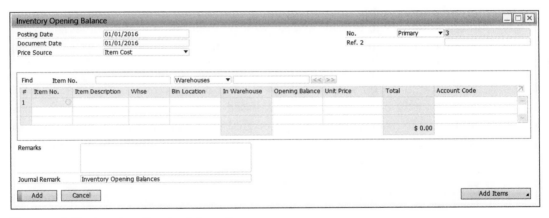

Figure 9.26 The Inventory Opening Balance Screen

To create an inventory opening balance transaction, enter the following information:

▸ POSTING DATE: Enter date of the first inventory count.

▸ PRICE SOURCE and UNIT PRICE: We can create a price list (let's call it "Opening Balance Item Cost") and use this price list for the cost. Alternatively, we may decide not to worry about the price list and simply fill in the UNIT PRICE column with the actual cost.

▸ ITEM NO.: Enter the item number in this field.

- WHSE: Enter the warehouse code in this field.

- OPENING BALANCE: This field displays the opening value. Set the opening balance quantity in that field.

- ACCOUNT CODE: The field displays the offsetting account of the inventory account. The offsetting account must an account in the equity drawer. Importing a trial balance will reverse an offsetting account.

- REMARKS: Add any important notes here.

> **Tips and Tricks: Inventory Opening Balance**
>
> If bin locations are enabled for the specified warehouse, you have to enter the bin location in the BIN LOCATION field next to the warehouse code. If the items are managed by serial number or batch number, the BATCH SETUP or the SERIAL NUMBER SETUP window will prompt and you will have to enter the required batch number or serial number information, respectively.

You have three options for importing the line items of your inventory opening balance:

1. You could use the ADD ITEM • SELECT ITEMS option shown in Figure 9.27. Items will simply be added to the grid, based on certain selection criteria, such as item code from, item code to, preferred vendor, item group, item properties, and warehouse code. Once you enter the quantities, verify the unit price and enter the account code. Click the ADD button.

Figure 9.27 Adding an Item

> **Tips and Tricks: Inventory Opening Balance**
>
> The total should exactly match the amount that will be entered in the trial balance for that offsetting account and should match exactly the amount in the legacy system.

2. You could use the ADD ITEM • IMPORT ITEMS option also shown in Figure 9.27. This option can be more user friendly than the SELECT ITEM option because you can use a *.txt* file that contains all the information that needs to be filled in. As shown in Figure 9.28, select the fields to be imported, making sure you add these fields in the same order as they appear in the *.txt* file (which should

contain tab-delimited data) and link the file to this window using the BROWSE icon (the ellipsis) next to the FILE TO IMPORT field. Click IMPORT.

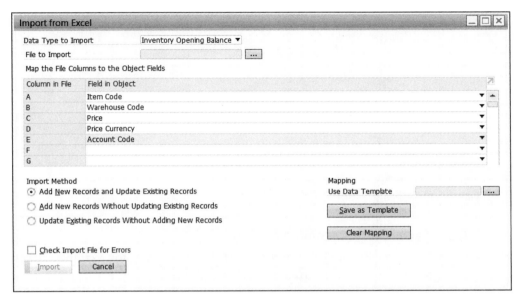

Figure 9.28 Importing Items from Excel

Tips and Tricks: Importing a .txt File

If the *.txt* file has a header, the system will generate an error for the first line, but the information of the rest of the file will be imported.

3. You could copy and paste from an Excel file, which is an easy way of copying a large amount of data into the inventory opening balance. Begin with an Excel file like the one shown in Figure 9.29 and then simply copy and paste! Use the keyboard shortcut Ctrl+C in Excel and Ctrl+V in SAP Business One as shown in Figure 9.30. If any columns are inactive, or if you don't want to import all columns (for instance, you want to exclude the ITEM DESCRIPTION column), make sure that you have an empty column in Excel.

	A	B	C	D	E	F	G	H	I
1	Item No.	Item Description	WhsCode	Empty column	Empty column	Opening Balance	Price	Empty column	Offsetting Account
2	I00001	Blu-Ray Disc 10-Pack	01			10	80		33999999
3	I00002	Blu-Ray DL Disc 10-Pack	01			10	85		33999999
4	C00008	Computer Monitor 24" HDMI	01			10	90		33999999

Figure 9.29 Copying Items from Excel

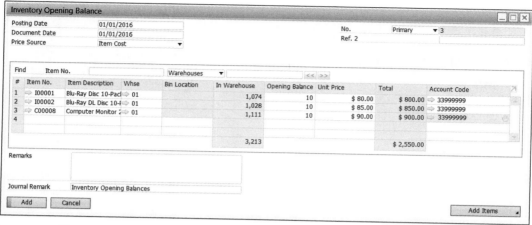

Figure 9.30 Pasting Items from Excel

9.6.9 Cycle Count Recommendations

You could proceed to a cycle count in SAP Business One, for example, if you wanted better control over certain critical or high-value items. Perhaps you want to simply count a certain percentage of the total inventory regularly so that, at period end, the whole inventory can be counted without stopping the whole warehouse or stopping production for days.

To create a cycle count inventory, you must fulfill two prerequisites: setting up the inventory cycle and setting up the cycle count determination:

▶ Inventory cycle setup is available by following the menu path ADMINISTRATION • SETUP • INVENTORY • INVENTORY CYCLES. This window is used to define the recurrence of the cycle count and offers great flexibility in setting up the date and time for cycle count. We could, for instance, define a monthly cycle count that will take place every first Sunday of the month. The recurrence could be daily, weekly, monthly, or annually or have no recurrence. You can also set up a time and an end date.

▶ The cycle count determination setup is available by following the menu path ADMINISTRATION • SETUP • INVENTORY • CYCLE COUNT DETERMINATION SETUP. Use this window to define, for each warehouse and for each item group, the recurrence of the cycle count, whether an alert should be sent, and to which user. On the planned date for the inventory count, that user will receive an alert in SAP Business One.

For more on the inventory counting process, please refer to the Section 9.6.6.

9.6.10 Inventory Revaluation

Under certain circumstances, the value of the inventory can increase or decrease over the time. If you need to revaluate your inventory, use the INVENTORY REVAL-UATION window shown in Figure 9.31. To access this function, follow the menu path INVENTORY • INVENTORY TRANSACTIONS • INVENTORY REVALUATION. By default, this window will open in Add mode rather than in Find mode.

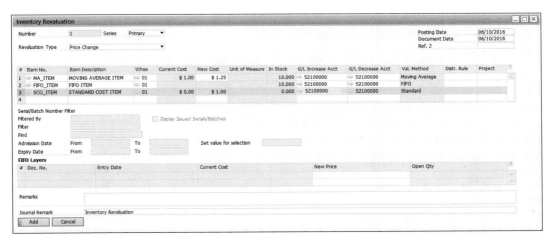

Figure 9.31 Moving Average and Standard Inventory Revaluation

Let's perform a revaluation for three items: one that uses the moving average valuation method, one that uses FIFO, and one that uses standard cost:

1. Enter the items that you want to revaluate.

2. For items using the moving average or standard valuation methods, simply enter a new cost in the NEW COST column. For items using the FIFO valuation method, you must enter a new price in each layer (at the bottom of the window).

3. Click the ADD button.

> **Tips and Tricks: Inventory Revaluation**
>
> G/L INCREASE ACCT and G/L DECREASE ACCT are two important columns. These two offsetting accounts increase or decrease values in the inventory account and should be linked to an expense account.

9.7 Price Lists

SAP Business One offers a comprehensive price management module that considers units of measure, currencies, quantities, dates, and other characteristic from the ITEM MASTER DATA window.

You can create different price management logics that are hierarchized in the following way:

- Are there special prices for business partners?
- Are there period and volume discounts?
- Are there discount groups?
- Is there a price in the price list linked to the business partner?

For a marketing document (for instance, a sales quotation), SAP Business One will verify among these four different hierarchized options if they are configured and, if so, will use the corresponding price.

9.7.1 Price Lists

The price list functionality shown in Figure 9.32 is available by following the menu path INVENTORY • PRICE LIST • PRICE LIST.

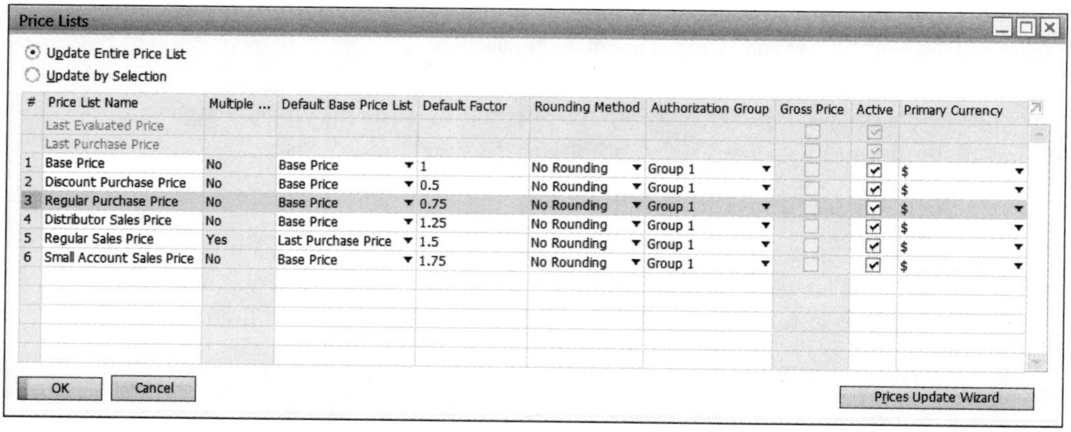

#	Price List Name	Multiple ...	Default Base Price List	Default Factor	Rounding Method	Authorization Group	Gross Price	Active	Primary Currency
	Last Evaluated Price								
	Last Purchase Price								
1	Base Price	No	Base Price	1	No Rounding	Group 1		✓	$
2	Discount Purchase Price	No	Base Price	0.5	No Rounding	Group 1		✓	$
3	Regular Purchase Price	No	Base Price	0.75	No Rounding	Group 1		✓	$
4	Distributor Sales Price	No	Base Price	1.25	No Rounding	Group 1		✓	$
5	Regular Sales Price	Yes	Last Purchase Price	1.5	No Rounding	Group 1		✓	$
6	Small Account Sales Price	No	Base Price	1.75	No Rounding	Group 1		✓	$

Figure 9.32 The Price Lists Screen

To link a price to a price list in a marketing document, you must fulfill two prerequisites:

- A price list must be linked to the business partner in the PAYMENT TERMS tab.
- A price must exist in the price list for the item.

By default, ten price lists are available, but you can easily delete unused price lists or create any additional price lists as required by right-clicking a price list and navigating to the SUMMARY menu.

A price list can be based on itself (for instance, a purchase price list) or on a base price list with a factor. For instance, a sales price list can be based on the purchase price list with a factor of 1.5, meaning that the sales price would be 1.5 times the purchase price for a nice profit. The sales price will automatically be calculated for every item that has a price in the purchase price list.

At the top of the PRICE LIST window, you'll have two options for updating a given price list:

- UPDATE ENTIRE PRICE LIST: Select this radio button to retrieve every item from the base price list, which is a fast and easy way to maintain prices based on a base price list and a factor. To update the prices, enter a new factor and click OK. Read the confirmation window carefully (see Figure 9.33) because every price will be overridden!
- UPDATE BY SELECTION: Select this radio button to change the base price list or factor only for certain items chosen based on certain selection criteria. This option gives you more flexibility to set sales price with different factors depending on the item's preferred vendor, item group, or item properties.

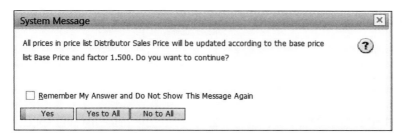

Figure 9.33 The Confirmation Window

Tips and Tricks: Deleting and Modifying Price Lists
Two price lists cannot be deleted or modified: the last purchase list and the last evaluated list.

In fact, the last purchase price list should be updated only in special circumstances—during A/P invoice and freight transactions. The last evaluated price list is updated when an Inventory Audit Report or an Inventory Valuation Report is created.

Tips and Tricks: Price List and Authorization Groups

You can link a price list to an authorization group (Group 1 to Group 4) to prevent certain users from accessing a confidential price list.

Once that the structure of the price list is defined, we can also maintain the prices from the ITEM MASTER DATA window shown in Figure 9.34.

To define a price, simply enter the price in the right price list. The price that you see is the price linked to the price list displayed. You can view only one price list at a time. Use the PRICE LIST dropdown list to display the prices on other price lists.

In addition to defining the primary currency for the unit price, you can also define two additional currencies for a price, as shown in Figure 9.34. Make sure to type in the corresponding currency before the price.

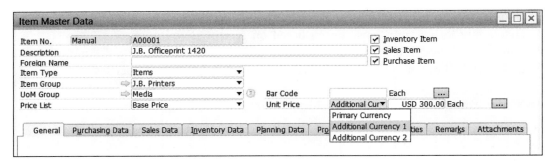

Figure 9.34 Additional Currency in the Item Master Data Screen

If the item is linked to a UoM group, the price linked to the price list will specify the unit of measure (each, pack of 6, etc.).

To define a price by UoM, you must click on the BROWSE icon (the ellipsis) for the DEFINE UOM PRICES button and assign a price in the UNIT PRICE column.

Alternatively, you can have the system calculate the price for packages by entering a discount percent for packs in the Reduce By % column shown in Figure 9.35.

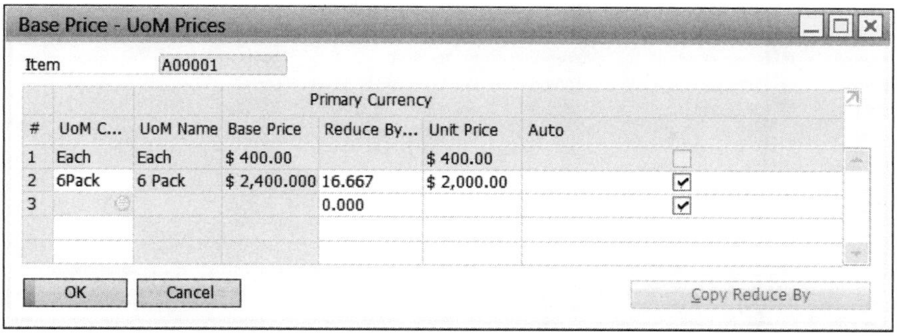

Base Price - UoM Prices						
Item		A00001				
			Primary Currency			
#	UoM C...	UoM Name	Base Price	Reduce By...	Unit Price	Auto
1	Each	Each	$ 400.00		$ 400.00	☐
2	6Pack	6 Pack	$ 2,400.000	16.667	$ 2,000.00	☑
3				0.000		☑

OK   Cancel   Copy Reduce By

Figure 9.35 Prices Assigned by UoM Code with a Discount Percent

Tips and Tricks: The Auto Column

The checkboxes in the Auto column will be selected automatically. As a result, if the price changes for the Base UoM (for instance, Each), then the price for the Alt. UoM will also change (for instance, 6Pack).

If the Auto checkbox is unselected, then the Alt. UoM will remain the same price when the Base UoM changes.

By following the menu path Administration • System Initialization • General Setting and Pricing tab, you'll have the option to display inactive price lists in reports, documents, or settings and to display no prices if the price source is based on an inactive price list.

Use the Remove Unpriced Items from Price List in Database option if many items in price lists for which the price is zero. You can increase the performance of your documents and reports by deleting these unused records.

9.7.2 Period and Volume Discounts

A period and volume discount will take precedence over the price list and can be set up by following the menu path Inventory • Price List • Period and Volume Discounts (as shown Figure 9.36).

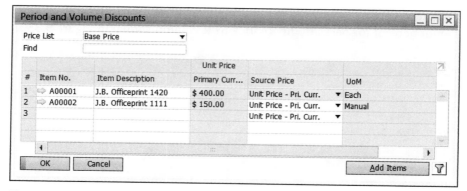

Figure 9.36 The Period and Volume Discounts Screen

To create period and volume discounts, select the price list for which you would like to have a period and volume discount. Add the items using the LIST OF ITEMS option (the funnel in the bottom right corner) or the ADD ITEMS button.

To add a period discount (in other words, a discount that runs from one date to another), double-click on the line of the item (in the # column shown in Figure 9.36). This will bring up the PERIOD DISCOUNTS screen shown in Figure 9.37.

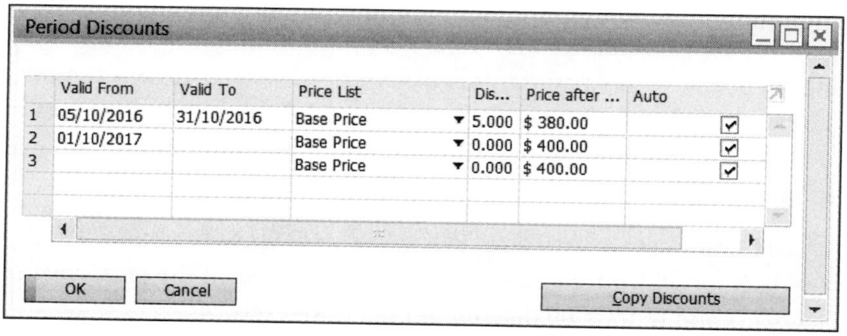

Figure 9.37 The Period Discounts Screen

To add a discount based on a volume rebate, double-click on the line of the PERIOD DISCOUNT window (for example, 1 or 2) and enter a quantity and a percentage discount or the discounted price. In our example in Figure 9.38, we've entered a quantity of 5 and a special price of $380.00.

Figure 9.38 The Volume Discount for Price List Screen

9.7.3 Discount Groups

Discount groups take precedence over period and volume discounts and the price list. You can access discount groups by following the menu path INVENTORY • PRICE LIST • DISCOUNT GROUPS. By default, the DISCOUNT GROUP is in Add mode.

You can create a discount group for every business partner, for one customer group, for one vendor group, or for one specific business partner. You can then copy that discount group to another business partner or business partner group using the COPY TO option.

Base your discount groups on the following four options: ITEM GROUPS, PROPERTIES, MANUFACTURERS, and ITEMS, as shown in Figure 9.39. For each of these options, you can specify a percentage discount that will be granted for the type of business partner specified.

For the item groups, manufacturers, and items, the discount will be mutually exclusive. But for the properties, one item could be linked to two or more properties. In this situation, the discount relations selected in the DISC. RELATIONS dropdown list will manage the discount applied. Your options are as follows:

- ► LOWEST DISCOUNT
- ► HIGHEST DISCOUNT
- ► AVERAGE
- ► TOTAL (the discounts are summed up)
- ► MULTIPLE DISCOUNT (the discounts are multiplied)

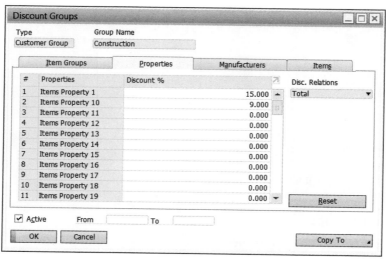

Figure 9.39 The Discount Groups Screen

For a given marketing document, one item could be linked to different discounts (for example, one discount for the item group, one for the properties, and one for manufacturer). This conflict will be resolved with the value specified in the EFFECTIVE DISCOUNT field in the PAYMENT TERMS tab of the BUSINESS PARTNER MASTER DATA window. These options are the same as those we have seen in PROPERTIES tab of the discount groups: LOWEST DISCOUNT, HIGHEST DISCOUNT, AVERAGE, TOTAL, and MULTIPLE DISCOUNT.

Note that you can exclude a particular business partner from the discount groups by selecting the DO NOT APPLY DISCOUNT GROUPS field in the PAYMENT TERMS tab of the BUSINESS PARTNER MASTER DATA window.

Tips and Tricks: Discount Groups

A discount group can be set as inactive, or you can make the discount group valid only for a limited period of time.

9.7.4 Special Prices for Business Partners

Special Prices for Business Partners is a pricing management option that takes precedence over all the others in SAP Business One. Access this functionality by following the menu path INVENTORY • PRICE LIST • SPECIAL PRICES • SPECIAL PRICES FOR BUSINESS PARTNERS. By default, this window will open in Add mode.

Enter the business partner code and the price list in the BP CODE and PRICE LIST fields in Figure 9.40. You can also enter a discount using the DISCOUNT PERCENTAGE field, which will apply the discount on each line. You can also enter the discount line by line, or you can leave the discount at zero.

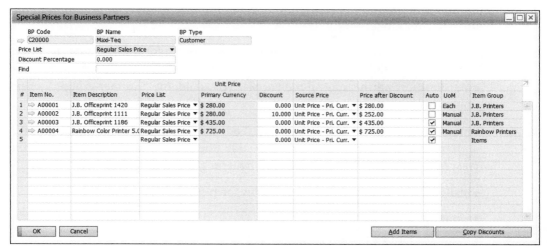

Figure 9.40 The Special Prices for Business Partners Screen

Tips and Tricks: Special Prices for Business Partners

The price list that appears in this window is just a base for calculating the price after discount of the Special Price for Business Partner. If a business partner is linked to another price list, the price after discount will still apply to this special price.

If the special price for a business partner is available only for a limited time, double-click on the number of the line (in the # column) and enter a validity period in the PERIOD DISCOUNT window. If there is a special price based on a volume rebate, double-click on the line of the PERIOD DISCOUNT window (in the # column) and enter a quantity and either the percentage discount or the discounted price. The special price for business partners (PERIOD DISCOUNT window and VOLUME DISCOUNT window) looks similar to the period and volume discount.

Tips and Tricks: Price Source

When in doubt about the price source in a marketing document, you can rely on the PRICE SOURCE field available in every marketing document in the FORMS SETTINGS.

9.7.5 Copy Special Prices to Selection Criteria

Copy Special Prices to Selection Criteria is a fast and easy tool that you can use to copy part or all of a special price to one or more other business partners. Access this functionality by following the menu path INVENTORY • PRICE LIST • SPECIAL PRICES • COPY SPECIAL PRICES TO SELECTION CRITERIA. By default, the window will open in Add mode.

First, enter the business partner that will be the source for the other special prices and then enter the business partners that will inherit the special prices. You can enter business partners using the FROM _ TO _ field, by customer group, by vendor groups, or by properties.

Enter the items that should be copied. You can filter items by using the FROM _ and TO _ option, by using the vendor code (the PREFERRED VENDOR field on the ITEM MASTER DATA • PURCHASING tab), by item groups, or by properties.

Finally, chose between the three options for replacement:

▶ REPLACE ALL ITEMS

▶ REPLACE ONLY EXISTING ITEMS

▶ DO NOT REPLACE ITEMS

When choosing the DO NOT REPLACE ITEMS option, only the records that do not exist in the destination will be created. The records that already exist will not be replaced.

> **Tips and Tricks: Copy Special Prices to Selection Criteria**
>
> Be careful here! We recommend you back up your database before using this function.

9.7.6 Update Special Prices Globally

Update Special Prices Globally is an efficient tool to rapidly update a significant amount of special prices for business partners. Access this functionality by following the menu path INVENTORY • PRICE LIST • SPECIAL PRICES • UPDATE SPECIAL PRICES GLOBALLY.

Four options are available for updating prices:

▶ CHANGE DISCOUNT %

▶ CHANGE PRICE %

- REFRESH BY PRICE LIST (used to refresh special prices when the price in the price list has changed and the AUTO field is not ticked)
- DELETE

> **Tips and Tricks: Update Special Prices Globally**
>
> As with the Copy Special Prices to Selection Criteria functionality, you should consider backing up your database before proceeding.

9.7.7 Update Parent Item Prices Globally

Use the UPDATE PARENTS ITEM PRICES GLOBALLY window to change the price of parent items or component items in a bill of materials (BOM). Access this functionality by following the menu path INVENTORY • PRICE LIST • UPDATE PARENTS ITEM PRICES.

9.7.8 Prices Update Wizard

The Prices Update Wizard is available from the PRICE LIST window (at the bottom right corner of Figure 9.32) to provide great flexibility for a mass change in the prices. Access this wizard by following the menu path INVENTORY • PRICE LIST • PRICES UPDATE WIZARD.

The Prices Update Wizard offers four methods for updating prices:

- ITEM PRICES: Choose this option to multiply, divide, add, subtract, or set a price based on a factor or a monetary amount.
- BASE PRICE LIST: Choose this option to change the factor for a price list.
- CONVERT TO: Choose this option to recalculate a price based on an exchange rate.
- UoM 'REDUCED BY %': Choose this option to multiply, divide, add, subtract, or set a price based on a factor to quickly update the REDUCED BY % field, which we saw in the price management module when UoM GROUP is involved.

9.8 Pick and Pack

Pick and Pack is a powerful feature to prioritize the allocation of the stock to sales orders, reserve invoices, production orders, and inventory transfer requests.

9.8.1   Pick and Pack Manager

In the Pick and Pack Manager shown in Figure 9.41, a document could have one of three statuses:

▶ Open: The document is ready to be picked.

▶ Released: The pick list is created but not picked.

▶ Picked: The pick list has been picked and the next step can be executed, which could be—depending on the base document type—a delivery, an invoice, an inventory transfer, an issue for production, or a receipt from production.

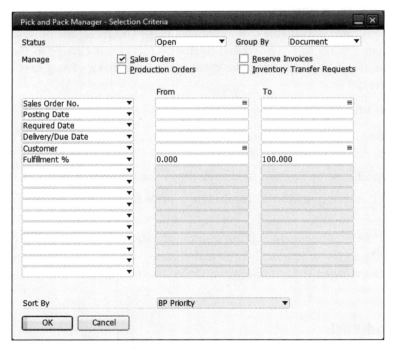

Figure 9.41 Pick and Pack Manager Selection Criteria

In the PICK AND PACK MANAGER window, you can:

▸ Filter with criteria

▸ Group by document or display the details of each document

▸ Sort by the delivery/due date, business partner code, document number, or business partner priority

Once you've made your selection, click OK to start the allocation process. Depending on the status selected in the first field, the window opens in one of the three corresponding drawers shown in Figure 9.42.

Figure 9.42 Drawers in the Pick and Pack Manager

Tips and Tricks: Merging or Splitting Documents

You can merge or split document; for example, one sales order could be divided into two pick lists, or two sales orders could combined into one pick list.

From the OPEN drawer, you can create a pick list with the RELEASE TO PICK LIST button or use the CREATE button to create a delivery, an invoice, an inventory transfer, an issue for production, or a receipt from production (depending on the base document type). In both cases, you'll need first to select line items by checking their respective checkboxes.

From the RELEASED drawer, you can drill down to the pick list using the golden arrow in the PICK NO. column or select lines by checking their respective checkboxes and use the CREATE button to create a delivery, an invoice, an inventory transfer, an issue for production, or a receipt from production (again, depending on the base document type).

From the PICKED drawer, you can drill down to the pick list using the golden arrow in the PICK NO. column or select lines by checking their respective checkboxes and use the CREATE button to create a delivery, an invoice, an inventory transfer, an issue for production, or a receipt from production (depending on the base document type).

9.8.2 Pick List

When first accessing the PICK LIST window shown in Figure 9.43, the window will open in Find mode by default. Only the Find mode (and not the Add mode) is available, so you will not be able to create new pick lists from this menu. If you want to create a new pick list, you'll need to use the PICK AND PACK MANAGER window.

To find a pick list, you can use all the fields in yellow or use the navigation icons in the toolbar.

Once you've selected the pick list, you can update the PICKED column or use the PICK ALL button and then use CREATE buttons shown in Figure 9.43 to create a delivery, an invoice, an inventory transfer, an issue for production, or a receipt from production (depending on the base document type).

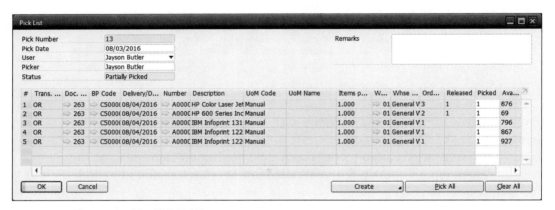

Figure 9.43 The Pick List Screen

9.9 Inventory Reports

SAP offers a variety of inventory reports that will provide the information needed for the warehouse management and the finance. These reports can be previewed in SAP Business One, printed as a PDF file, or exported to Excel.

You can access these inventory reports by following the menu path INVENTORY • INVENTORY REPORTS. Note that all of these reports can be filtered by certain selection criteria, such as posting dates, document dates, item code, item group, property, warehouse code, and so on.

9.9.1 Items List Report

Access the Items List Report shown in Figure 9.44 by following the menu path INVENTORY • INVENTORY REPORTS • ITEMS LIST. For each item, this report provides the quantity in stock, the unit of measure, the manufacturer number, and the price for each price list.

#	Item No.	Item Description	In Stock	Bar Code	Item Group	Manufacturer	Inventory UoM	Last Eval. Price	Last Purchase Price	Base Price	Discount Purchase Price	Regular Purchase Price	Distributor Sales Price	Regular Sales Price	Small Account Sa...
1	A00001	J.B. Officeprint 1420	1,122		J.B. Printers	J.B.	Each	$400.00	$300.00	$400.00	$200.00	$300.00	$500.00	$280.00	
2	A00002	J.B. Officeprint 1111	1,109		J.B. Printers	J.B.		$148.72	$150.00	$150.00	$75.00	$112.50	$187.50	$280.00	
3	A00003	J.B. Officeprint 1186	1,201		J.B. Printers	J.B.		$222.31	$225.00	$300.00	$150.00	$225.00	$375.00	$435.00	
4	A00004	Rainbow Color Printer 5.0	1,131		Rainbow Printers	Rainbow		$375.68	$375.00	$500.00	$250.00	$375.00	$625.00	$725.00	
5	A00005	Rainbow Color Printer 7.5	1,243		Rainbow Printers	Rainbow		$286.00	$300.00	$400.00	$200.00	$300.00	$500.00	$580.00	
6	A00006	Rainbow 1200 Laser Series	70		Rainbow Printers	Rainbow		$325.57	$300.00	$400.00	$200.00	$300.00	$500.00	$580.00	
7	B10000	Printer Label	500		Items	LeMon		$0.82	$0.75	$1.00	$0.50	$0.75	$1.25	$1.45	
8	BATCH		2		Accessories	- No Manufacturer -			$5.00					$7.50	
9	BATCH2		1		Items	- No Manufacturer -			$10.00					$15.00	
10	C00001	Motherboard BTX	1,525		Items	A+ Electronics		$301.42	$200.00	$400.00	$200.00	$300.00	$500.00	$580.00	
11	C00002	Motherboard MicroATX	1,480		Items	A+ Electronics		$223.37	$225.00	$300.00	$150.00	$225.00	$375.00	$435.00	
12	C00003	Quadcore CPU 3.4 GHz	1,180		Items	PCM		$93.20	$65.00	$130.00	$65.00	$97.50	$162.50	$186.50	
13	C00004	Tower Case with Power supply	1,294		Items	J-Tech		$24.80	$26.25	$35.00	$17.50	$26.25	$43.75	$50.75	
14	C00005	WLAN Card	1,166		Items	J-Tech		$44.26	$45.00	$60.00	$30.00	$45.00	$75.00	$87.00	
15	C00006	Gigabit Network Card	1,137		Items	J-Tech		$10.38	$7.50	$15.00	$7.50	$11.25	$18.75	$21.75	
16	C00007	Hard Disk 3TB	1,391		Items	J-Tech		$356.90	$375.00	$500.00	$250.00	$375.00	$625.00	$725.00	
17	C00008	Computer Monitor 24" HDMI	1,211		Items	A+ Electronics		$144.42	$150.00	$200.00	$100.00	$150.00	$250.00	$290.00	
18	C00009	Keyboard Comfort USB	1,193		Items	A+ Electronics		$14.19	$15.00	$20.00	$10.00	$15.00	$25.00	$29.00	
19	C00010	Mouse USB	1,185		Items	PCM		$14.35	$15.00	$20.00	$10.00	$15.00	$25.00	$29.00	
20	C00011	Memory DDR RAM 8GB	1,159		Items	A+ Electronics		$30.18	$20.00	$40.00	$20.00	$30.00	$50.00	$58.00	
21	FIFO_ITEM	FIFO ITEM	11		Accessories	- No Manufacturer -		$19.50	$10.00					$15.00	
22	I00001	Blu-Ray Disc 10-Pack	1,074		Items	PCM		$2.15	$2.25	$3.00	$1.50	$2.25	$3.75	$4.35	
23	I00002	Blu-Ray DL Disc 10-Pack	1,028		Items	PCM		$8.53	$9.00	$12.00	$6.00	$9.00	$15.00	$17.40	
24	I00003	USB Flashdrive 128GB	941		Items	PCM		$14.65	$15.00	$20.00	$10.00	$15.00	$25.00	$29.00	
25	I00004	USB Flashdrive 256GB	973		Items	PCM		$21.74	$22.50	$30.00	$15.00	$22.50	$37.50	$43.50	
26	I00005	J.B. Laptop Batteries X1 series	1,013		Items	J.B.		$61.59	$45.00	$90.00	$45.00	$67.50	$112.50	$130.50	
27	I00006	J.B. Laptop Batteries X2 series	981		Items	J.B.		$57.96	$40.00	$80.00	$40.00	$60.00	$100.00	$116.00	
28	I00007	Rainbow Printer 9.5 Inkjet Cartridge	951		Items	Rainbow		$19.65	$21.00	$28.00	$14.00	$21.00	$35.00	$40.60	
29	I00008	Rainbow Nuance Ink 6-Pack and Photo Paper Kit	979		Items	Rainbow		$27.21	$29.25	$39.00	$19.50	$29.25	$48.75	$56.55	
30	I00009	SLR PreciseShot FX1500	978		Items	PCM		$108.69	$112.50	$150.00	$75.00	$112.50	$187.50	$217.50	
31	I00010	SLR M-CAM 40C	1,098		Items	PCM		$435.75	$450.00	$600.00	$300.00	$450.00	$750.00	$870.00	$1
32	I00011	KG USB Travel Hub	1,056		Items	PCM		$8.35	$9.00	$12.00	$6.00	$9.00	$15.00	$17.40	
33	I00012	KG PC-to-Mac Transfer Kit	1,092		Items	PCM		$31.90	$33.75	$45.00	$22.50	$33.75	$56.25	$65.25	
34	I00013	SDHC 64 GB CLASS 10			Storage	- No Manufacturer -			$30.00		$15.00	$22.50	$37.50	$43.50	
35	L10001	Labor Hours Production			Items	J-Tech			$5.00		$2.50	$3.75	$6.25	$7.25	
36	LB0001	Daily Service Labor Charge			Items	J-Tech			$200.00		$100.00	$150.00	$250.00	$290.00	
37	LB0002	Hourly Service Labor Charge			Items	J-Tech			$50.00		$25.00	$37.50	$62.50	$72.50	
38	LM4029	LeMon 4029 Printer	254		Items	LeMon		$196.36	$120.00	$240.00	$120.00	$180.00	$300.00	$348.00	
39	LM4029ACA	LeMon 4029 Printer AC Adapter	664		Items	LeMon		$7.35	$7.50	$10.00	$5.00	$7.50	$12.50	$14.50	
40	LM4029APCD	LeMon 4029 Printer AC Power Cord	668		Items	LeMon		$3.83	$3.75	$5.00	$2.50	$3.75	$6.25	$7.25	
41	LM4029D	LeMon 4029 500 sheet paper drawer	793		Items	LeMon		$23.83	$17.50	$35.00	$17.50	$26.25	$43.75	$50.75	
42	LM4029MC	Memory Chip	616		Accessories	A+ Electronics		$37.58	$37.50	$50.00	$25.00	$37.50	$62.50	$54.38	
43	LM4029PH	LeMon 4029 Printer Head	792		Items	LeMon		$13.79	$10.00	$20.00	$10.00	$15.00	$25.00	$29.00	

OK   *You can only select one price list for printing

Figure 9.44 Item List Report

9.9.2 Open Items List Report

The Open Items List Report shown in Figure 9.45 is an important control tool used by many users to get a list of every open document in SAP Business One, for every document type. An *open document* is a document that has not been copied completely into a destination document. For example, an inventory counting document that was not copied into an inventory posting will appear in the Open Item List Report.

Access this report by following the menu path INVENTORY • INVENTORY REPORTS • OPEN ITEMS LIST.

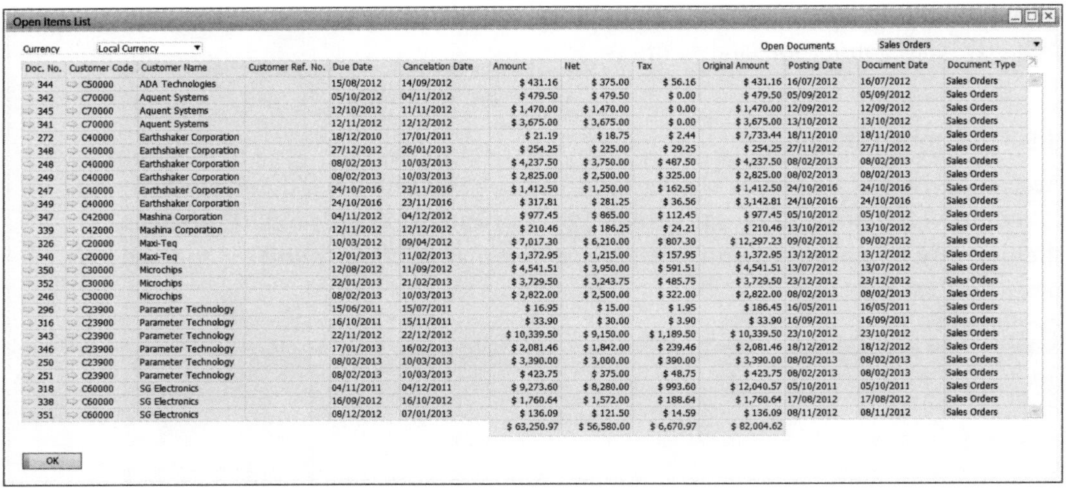

Open Items List

Currency: Local Currency — Open Documents: Sales Orders

Doc. No.	Customer Code	Customer Name	Customer Ref. No.	Due Date	Cancelation Date	Amount	Net	Tax	Original Amount	Posting Date	Document Date	Document Type
344	C50000	ADA Technologies		15/08/2012	14/09/2012	$ 431.16	$ 375.00	$ 56.16	$ 431.16	16/07/2012	16/07/2012	Sales Orders
342	C70000	Aquent Systems		05/10/2012	04/11/2012	$ 479.50	$ 479.50	$ 0.00	$ 479.50	05/09/2012	05/09/2012	Sales Orders
345	C70000	Aquent Systems		12/10/2012	11/11/2012	$ 1,470.00	$ 1,470.00	$ 0.00	$ 1,470.00	12/09/2012	12/09/2012	Sales Orders
341	C70000	Aquent Systems		12/11/2012	12/12/2012	$ 3,675.00	$ 3,675.00	$ 0.00	$ 3,675.00	13/10/2012	13/10/2012	Sales Orders
272	C40000	Earthshaker Corporation		18/12/2010	17/01/2011	$ 21.19	$ 18.75	$ 2.44	$ 7,733.44	18/11/2010	18/11/2010	Sales Orders
348	C40000	Earthshaker Corporation		27/12/2012	26/01/2013	$ 254.25	$ 225.00	$ 29.25	$ 254.25	27/11/2012	27/11/2012	Sales Orders
248	C40000	Earthshaker Corporation		08/02/2013	10/03/2013	$ 4,237.50	$ 3,750.00	$ 487.50	$ 4,237.50	08/02/2013	08/02/2013	Sales Orders
249	C40000	Earthshaker Corporation		08/02/2013	10/03/2013	$ 2,825.00	$ 2,500.00	$ 325.00	$ 2,825.00	08/02/2013	08/02/2013	Sales Orders
247	C40000	Earthshaker Corporation		24/10/2016	23/11/2016	$ 1,412.50	$ 1,250.00	$ 162.50	$ 1,412.50	24/10/2016	24/10/2016	Sales Orders
349	C40000	Earthshaker Corporation		24/10/2016	23/11/2016	$ 317.81	$ 281.25	$ 36.56	$ 3,142.81	24/10/2016	24/10/2016	Sales Orders
347	C42000	Mashina Corporation		04/11/2012	04/12/2012	$ 977.45	$ 865.00	$ 112.45	$ 977.45	05/10/2012	05/10/2012	Sales Orders
339	C42000	Mashina Corporation		12/11/2012	12/12/2012	$ 210.46	$ 186.25	$ 24.21	$ 210.46	13/10/2012	13/10/2012	Sales Orders
326	C20000	Maxi-Teq		10/03/2012	09/04/2012	$ 7,017.30	$ 6,210.00	$ 807.30	$ 12,297.23	09/02/2012	09/02/2012	Sales Orders
340	C20000	Maxi-Teq		12/01/2013	11/02/2013	$ 1,372.95	$ 1,215.00	$ 157.95	$ 1,372.95	13/12/2012	13/12/2012	Sales Orders
350	C30000	Microchips		12/08/2012	11/09/2012	$ 4,541.51	$ 3,950.00	$ 591.51	$ 4,541.51	13/07/2012	13/07/2012	Sales Orders
352	C30000	Microchips		22/01/2013	21/02/2013	$ 3,729.50	$ 3,243.75	$ 485.75	$ 3,729.50	23/12/2012	23/12/2012	Sales Orders
246	C30000	Microchips		08/02/2013	10/03/2013	$ 2,822.00	$ 2,500.00	$ 322.00	$ 2,822.00	08/02/2013	08/02/2013	Sales Orders
296	C23900	Parameter Technology		15/06/2011	15/07/2011	$ 16.95	$ 15.00	$ 1.95	$ 186.45	16/05/2011	16/05/2011	Sales Orders
316	C23900	Parameter Technology		16/10/2011	15/11/2011	$ 33.90	$ 30.00	$ 3.90	$ 33.90	16/09/2011	16/09/2011	Sales Orders
343	C23900	Parameter Technology		22/11/2012	22/12/2012	$ 10,339.50	$ 9,150.00	$ 1,189.50	$ 10,339.50	23/10/2012	23/10/2012	Sales Orders
346	C23900	Parameter Technology		17/01/2013	16/02/2013	$ 2,081.46	$ 1,842.00	$ 239.46	$ 2,081.46	18/12/2012	18/12/2012	Sales Orders
250	C23900	Parameter Technology		08/02/2013	10/03/2013	$ 3,390.00	$ 3,000.00	$ 390.00	$ 3,390.00	08/02/2013	08/02/2013	Sales Orders
251	C23900	Parameter Technology		08/02/2013	10/03/2013	$ 423.75	$ 375.00	$ 48.75	$ 423.75	08/02/2013	08/02/2013	Sales Orders
318	C60000	SG Electronics		04/11/2011	04/12/2011	$ 9,273.60	$ 8,280.00	$ 993.60	$ 12,040.57	05/10/2011	05/10/2011	Sales Orders
338	C60000	SG Electronics		16/09/2012	16/10/2012	$ 1,760.64	$ 1,572.00	$ 188.64	$ 1,760.64	17/08/2012	17/08/2012	Sales Orders
351	C60000	SG Electronics		08/12/2012	07/01/2013	$ 136.09	$ 121.50	$ 14.59	$ 136.09	08/11/2012	08/11/2012	Sales Orders
						$ 63,250.97	$ 56,580.00	$ 6,670.97	$ 82,004.62			

OK

Figure 9.45 Open Item List Report

9.9.3 Document Drafts Report

Access the Document Drafts Report shown in Figure 9.46 by following the menu path INVENTORY • INVENTORY REPORTS • DOCUMENT DRAFT REPORT. This report provides the list of all draft documents, opened or closed, for every document type, organized by user.

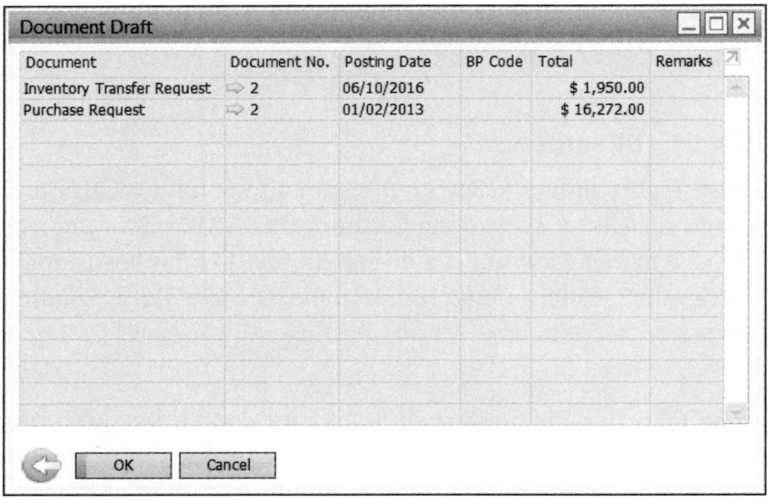

Document Draft

Document	Document No.	Posting Date	BP Code	Total	Remarks
Inventory Transfer Request	2	06/10/2016		$ 1,950.00	
Purchase Request	2	01/02/2013		$ 16,272.00	

OK Cancel

Figure 9.46 Document Draft Report

9.9.4 Last Prices Report

The Last Prices Report shown in Figure 9.47 provides, for a given customer and item, the last prices sold for each type of A/R transaction (from sales quotations to A/R credit memos).

Access this report by following the menu path INVENTORY • INVENTORY REPORTS • LAST PRICES REPORT. You can also call this report from the UNIT PRICE field of a marketing document or from the summary menu.

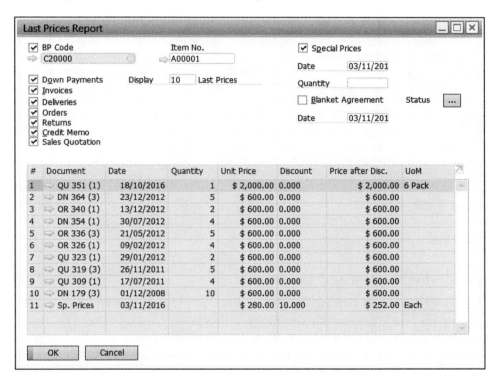

Figure 9.47 Last Prices Report

9.9.5 Inactive Items Report

The Inactive Items Report shown in Figure 9.48 lists what hasn't been sold since a given date or, more properly, the items that are not part of any documents since a specified date, among the following document types: sales quotations, sales orders, deliveries, A/R invoices, and A/R down payments. Each of these documents types can be deselected from the options. For each item, the report provides the quantity in stock, the preferred vendor, and the UoM.

Access this report by following the menu path INVENTORY • INVENTORY REPORTS • INACTIVE ITEMS.

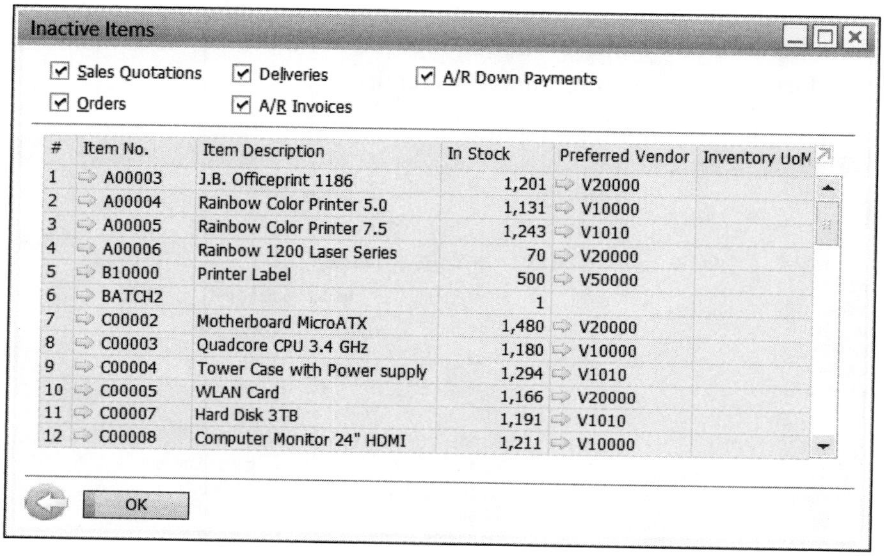

Figure 9.48 Inactive Items Report

9.9.6 Inventory Posting List Report

Access the Inventory Posting List Report shown in Figure 9.49 by following the menu path INVENTORY • INVENTORY REPORTS • INVENTORY POSTING LIST. This report will list of all the transactions that impact accounting. These transactions include deliveries, A/R invoices not based on deliveries, goods receipt POs, A/P invoices not based on goods receipt POs, goods issues, goods receipts, inventory transfers, inventory revaluations, and all the possible transactions linked to production. This report offers a great variety of filters and options.

Inventory Posting List									
Posting Date	Document	Doc. Row	Whse	G/L Acct/BP Code	G/L Acct/BP Name	Inventory UoM	Qty	Price after Disc.	Balance
A00001					J.B. Officeprint 1420				
28/09/2016	SO 1	1	01	13500000	Inventories of Finished Goods	Each	-1	$ 303.71	-1
05/10/2016	SO 2	1	01	13500000	Inventories of Finished Goods	Each	-1	$ 300.00	-2
05/10/2016	IM 1	2	01	13500000	Inventories of Finished Goods	Each	-1	$ 380.00	-3
05/10/2016	IM 1	2	02	13500000	Inventories of Finished Goods	Each	1	$ 380.00	-2
05/10/2016	IM 2	2	01	13500000	Inventories of Finished Goods	Each	-6	$ 400.00	-8
05/10/2016	IM 2	2	02	13500000	Inventories of Finished Goods	Each	6	$ 400.00	-2
06/10/2016	IM 3	2	01	13500000	Inventories of Finished Goods	Each	-6	$ 400.00	-8
06/10/2016	IM 3	2	02	13500000	Inventories of Finished Goods	Each	6	$ 400.00	-2
07/10/2016	SI 140	1	05	13500000	Inventories of Finished Goods	Each	1	$ 300.00	-1
									-1
A00002					J.B. Officeprint 1111				

Figure 9.49 Inventory Posting List Report

9.9.7 Inventory Status Report

The Inventory Status Report shown in Figure 9.50 provides, for each item, the quantities in stock, committed, ordered, and available. These quantities are totaled for all the warehouses selected in the selection criteria. You can access this report by following the menu path INVENTORY • INVENTORY REPORTS • INVENTORY STATUS.

Inventory Status						
Item No.						
Double-click row number to open following report			Normal ▼			
#	Item No.	Item Description	In Stock	Committed	Ordered	Available	Inventory UoM
1	A00001	J.B. Officeprint 1420	1,122	18	12	1,116	Each
2	A00002	J.B. Officeprint 1111	1,109	6	8	1,111	
3	A00003	J.B. Officeprint 1186	1,201	9		1,192	
4	A00004	Rainbow Color Printer 5.0	1,131	9	1	1,123	
5	A00005	Rainbow Color Printer 7.5	1,243		10	1,253	
6	A00006	Rainbow 1200 Laser Series	70			70	
7	B10000	Printer Label	500			500	
8	BATCH		2			2	
9	BATCH2		1			1	
10	C00001	Motherboard BTX	1,525	1	5	1,529	
11	C00002	Motherboard MicroATX	1,480	-	16	1,496	
12	C00003	Quadcore CPU 3.4 GHz	1,180		3	1,183	
13	C00004	Tower Case with Power supply	1,294	3	14	1,305	
14	C00005	WLAN Card	1,166		10	1,176	
15	C00006	Gigabit Network Card	1,137	15	12	1,134	

OK

Figure 9.50 Inventory Status Report

9.9.8 Inventory in Warehouse Report

The Inventory in Warehouse Report shown in Figure 9.51 provides, for each item, the quantities in stock, committed, ordered, and available, detailed per warehouse.

This report also provides the total value of inventory in stock based on a selected price list.

Access this report by following the menu path INVENTORY • INVENTORY REPORTS • INVENTORY IN WAREHOUSE.

Inventory in Warehouse Report (Detailed)

#	Item No.	Item Description	Inventory UoM	First Bin Location	In Stock	Committed	Ordered	Available	Default Bin Location	Enforced Def. Bin Loc.	Item Price	Total	Confirmed
	Whse:	*01*											
1	A00001	J.B. Officeprint 1420	Each		1,008	18	6	996		No	$ 300.00	$ 302,400.00	
2	A00002	J.B. Officeprint 1111			1,009	6	7	1,010		No	$ 150.00	$ 151,350.00	
3	A00003	J.B. Officeprint 1186			1,151	9		1,142		No	$ 225.00	$ 258,975.00	
4	A00004	Rainbow Color Printer 5.0			1,078	9	1	1,070		No	$ 375.00	$ 404,250.00	
5	A00005	Rainbow Color Printer 7.5			1,193		10	1,203		No	$ 300.00	$ 357,900.00	
6	A00006	Rainbow 1200 Laser Series			70			70		No	$ 200.00	$ 14,000.00	
7	B10000	Printer Label			500			500		No	$ 0.75	$ 375.00	

Figure 9.51 Inventory in Warehouse Report

9.9.9 Inventory Audit Report

The Inventory Audit Report is probably the most-used report in the Inventory module. It provides back-datable information about cumulative quantities and values as well as all details about the transactions that impacted the quantities or values of stock. Information can be grouped by item or G/L account and by warehouse.

Access the Inventory Audit Report shown in Figure 9.52 by following the menu path INVENTORY • INVENTORY REPORTS • INVENTORY AUDIT REPORT.

Inventory Audit Report

Date From 01/09/2015 Date To
Currency Canadian Dollar
Items All
Warehouses All

#	Item No.	Description	System Date	Posting Date	Document	Whse	Quantity	Cost	Trans. Value	Cumulative Qty	Cumulative Value
1	A00001	J.B. Officeprint 1420								1,122.000	350,386.36
2					Opening Balance					1,123.000	350,693.78
3			28/09/2016	28/09/2016	SO 1	01	-1.000	303.71	-303.71	1,122.000	350,390.07
4			05/10/2016	05/10/2016	SO 2	01	-1.000	303.71	-303.71	1,121.000	350,086.36
5			05/10/2016	05/10/2016	IM 1	01	-1.000	303.71	-303.71	1,120.000	349,782.65
6			05/10/2016	05/10/2016	IM 1	02	1.000	303.71	303.71	1,121.000	350,086.36
7			05/10/2016	05/10/2016	IM 2	01	-6.000	303.71	-1,822.25	1,115.000	348,264.11
8			05/10/2016	05/10/2016	IM 2	02	6.000	303.71	1,822.25	1,121.000	350,086.36
9			06/10/2016	06/10/2016	IM 3	01	-6.000	303.71	-1,822.25	1,115.000	348,264.11
10			06/10/2016	06/10/2016	IM 3	02	6.000	303.71	1,822.25	1,121.000	350,086.36
11			07/10/2016	07/10/2016	SI 140	05	1.000	300.00	300.00	1,122.000	350,386.36
12	A00004	Rainbow Color Printer 5.0								1,131.000	431,112.07
13					Opening Balance					1,130.000	430,737.07
14			05/10/2016	05/10/2016	SI 135	01	1.000	375.00	375.00	1,131.000	431,112.07
15			05/10/2016	05/10/2016	IM 1	01	-1.000	375.68	-375.68	1,130.000	430,736.39
16			05/10/2016	05/10/2016	IM 1	02	1.000	375.68	375.68	1,131.000	431,112.07
17			05/10/2016	05/10/2016	IM 2	01	-1.000	375.68	-375.68	1,130.000	430,736.39
18			05/10/2016	05/10/2016	IM 2	02	1.000	375.68	375.68	1,131.000	431,112.07
19			06/10/2016	06/10/2016	IM 3	01	-1.000	375.68	-375.68	1,130.000	430,736.39
20			06/10/2016	06/10/2016	IM 3	02	1.000	375.68	375.68	1,131.000	431,112.07

Figure 9.52 Inventory Audit Report

9.9.10 Batches and Serials Inventory Audit Report

The Batches and Serials Inventory Audit Report shown in Figure 9.53 lists all the transactions linked to serial number or batch number: transaction type, transaction number, posting date, warehouse code, quantity, cost of the transaction, cumulative quantity, and serial or batch number. The selection criteria to run the reports are the posting date, item code, batch number, serial number, and warehouse code.

Please note that this report lists only items that are managed by serial/batch accounting valuation method, which is determined in the INVENTORY DATA tab of the ITEM MASTER DATA screen, which we discussed in Section 9.1.4.

Access this report by following the menu path INVENTORY • INVENTORY REPORTS • BATCHES AND SERIALS INVENTORY AUDIT REPORT.

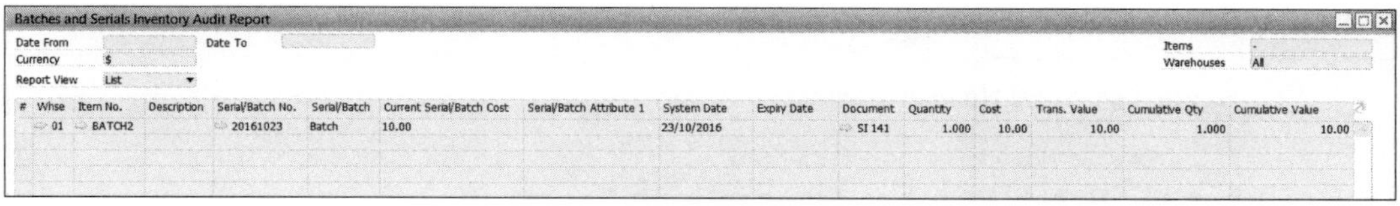

Figure 9.53 Batches and Serials Inventory Audit Report

9.9.11 Inventory Valuation Simulation Report

Access the Inventory Valuation Simulation Report by following the menu path INVENTORY • INVENTORY REPORTS • INVENTORY VALUATION SIMULATION REPORT. This report, shown in Figure 9.54, provides a valuation of the inventory if we were using a different valuation method. For example, if the inventory valued as a moving average, we can simulate the value of the inventory if we were in FIFO. The simulation can also be created against any price list.

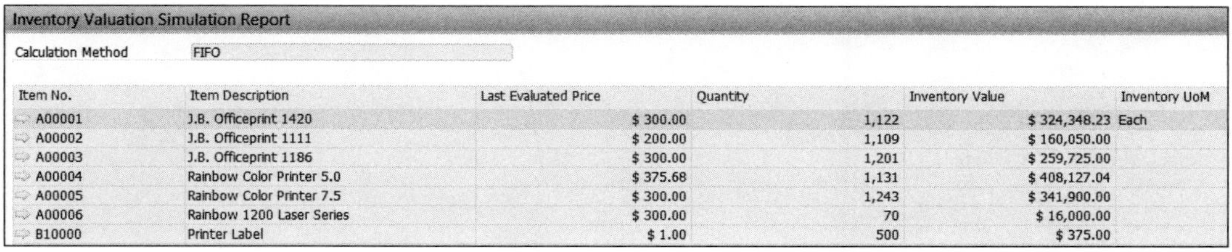

Figure 9.54 Inventory Valuation Simulation Report

9.9.12 Serial Number Transactions Report

Access the Serial Number Transactions Report shown in Figure 9.55 by following the menu path INVENTORY • INVENTORY REPORTS • SERIAL NUMBER TRANSACTION REPORT. This report lists all the serial numbers that were created in SAP Business One, their creation dates, their expiration dates, and more details about each serial number. The report also provides information about the documents that are linked to the inventory movements for production, purchase, or sales.

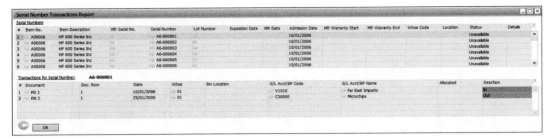

Figure 9.55 Serial Number Transaction Report

9.9.13 Batch Number Transactions Report

The Batch Number Transactions Report shown in Figure 9.56 lists all batch numbers that were created in SAP Business One, including their creation dates and their expiration dates as well as more details about the batch. The report also provides information about the documents that are linked to the inventory movements for production, purchase, or sales.

Batch Number Transactions Report												

Batches

#	Item No.	Item Description	Batch	Whse	Quantity	Allocated	Batch Attribute 1	Batch Attribute 2	Status	Expiration Date	Manufacturing Date	Admis...
1	BATCH		Test1	01					Released			07/10/20
2	BATCH		Test2	01	1				Released			07/10/20
3	BATCH		TEST3	01	1				Released			07/10/20

2

Transactions for Batch: Test1

#	Document	Doc. Row	Date	Whse	First Bin Location	G/L Acct/BP Name	Qty	Allocated	Direction
1	SI 139	1	07/10/2016	01		Gain/Loss Inventory Variance	1		In
2	IN 343	1	07/10/2016	01		Maxi-Teq	-1		Out

☐ Display All Transactions for Selected Batches
☑ Display Batches with Zero Qty

Whse From [ ] ▼ To [ ] ▼

OK

Figure 9.56 Batch Number Transactions Report

Access this report by following the menu path INVENTORY • INVENTORY REPORTS • BATCH NUMBER TRANSACTION REPORT.

9.9.14 Bin Location List Report

Use the Bin Location List Report to get a list of the existing bin locations as well as the number of items and the quantities in each bin. This report is shown in Figure 9.57; access the report by following the menu path INVENTORY • INVENTORY REPORTS • BIN LOCATION LIST.

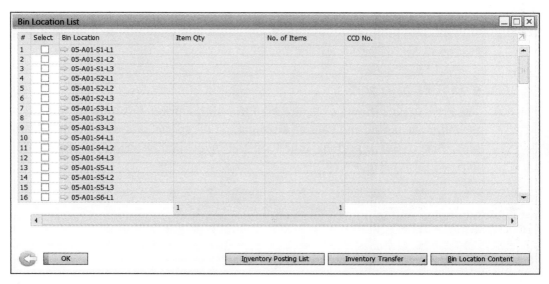

Figure 9.57 Bin Location List

9.9.15 Bin Location Content List Report

The Bin Location Content List Report is shown in Figure 9.58. Offering a great variety of filters, this report provides a list of items in each bin location and also provides shortcuts to create bin replenishment or transfers.

Access this report by following the menu path INVENTORY • INVENTORY REPORTS • BIN LOCATION CONTENT LIST.

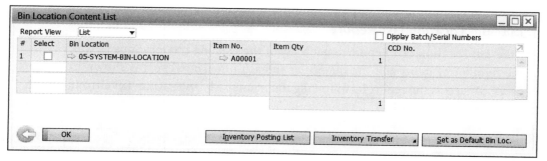

Figure 9.58 Bin Location Content List

9.9.16 Price Report

The Price Report shown in Figure 9.59 lists all the prices linked to the price list, as well as the period and volume discount and the special prices for business partners. Access this report by following the menu path INVENTORY • INVENTORY REPORTS • PRICE REPORT.

#	Source of Price	Item No.	Item Description	Primary Currency - Unit Price	Discount %	UoM	Quantity	Active	Valid From	Valid To	Display in Marketing Doc.
1	Last Evaluated Price	A00001	J.B. Officeprint 1420	$ 300.00		Each					
2	Last Evaluated Price	A00002	J.B. Officeprint 1111	$ 200.00		Manual					
3	Last Evaluated Price	A00003	J.B. Officeprint 1186	$ 300.00		Manual					
4	Last Evaluated Price	A00004	Rainbow Color Printer 5.0	$ 375.68		Manual					
5	Last Evaluated Price	A00005	Rainbow Color Printer 7.5	$ 300.00		Manual					
6	Last Evaluated Price	A00006	Rainbow 1200 Laser Series	$ 300.00		Manual					
7	Last Evaluated Price	B10000	Printer Label	$ 1.00		Manual					

Figure 9.59 Price Report

9.9.17 Discount Group Report

The Discount Group Report shown in Figure 9.60 lists all discount groups. Access this report by following the menu path INVENTORY • INVENTORY REPORTS • DISCOUNT GROUP REPORT.

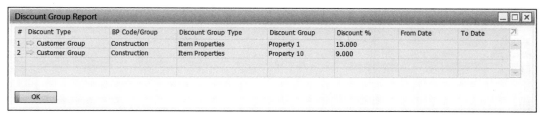

Figure 9.60 Discount Group Report

9.9.18 Inventory Counting Transactions Report

Access the Inventory Counting Transactions Report shown in Figure 9.61 by following the menu path INVENTORY • INVENTORY REPORTS • INVENTORY COUNTING TRANSACTION REPORT. This report provides information about inventory posting transactions that were created in SAP Business One. The report also keeps track of the quantities before and after the posting. The information can be filtered by employee or user.

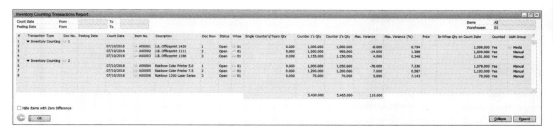

Figure 9.61 Inventory Counting Transaction Report

9.9.19 Inventory Valuation Method Report

Access the Inventory Valuation Method Report shown in Figure 9.62 by following the menu path INVENTORY • INVENTORY REPORTS • INVENTORY VALUATION METHOD REPORT. This report lists, per item group, the number of items that belong to each inventory valuation method (moving average, FIFO, or standard cost).

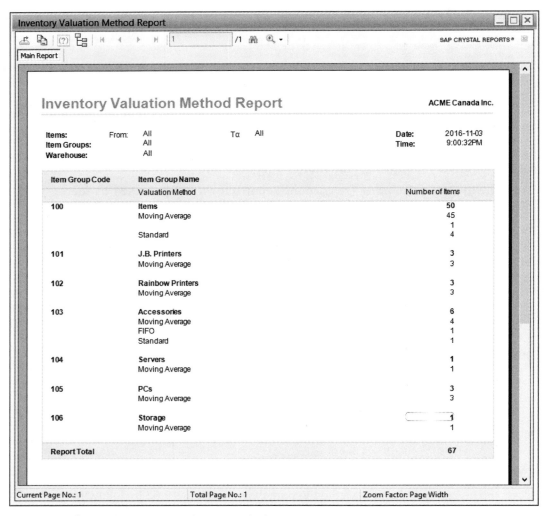

Figure 9.62 Inventory Valuation Method Report

9.9.20 Inventory Turnover Analysis Report

For a period of time selected in the selection criteria, the Inventory Turnover Analysis Report shown in Figure 9.63 provides information about opening inventory, closing inventory, quantity sold, days of inventory, minimum quantity, lead time, inventory turnover, and the next reorder point.

Access this report by following the menu path INVENTORY • INVENTORY REPORTS • INVENTORY TURNOVER ANALYSIS.

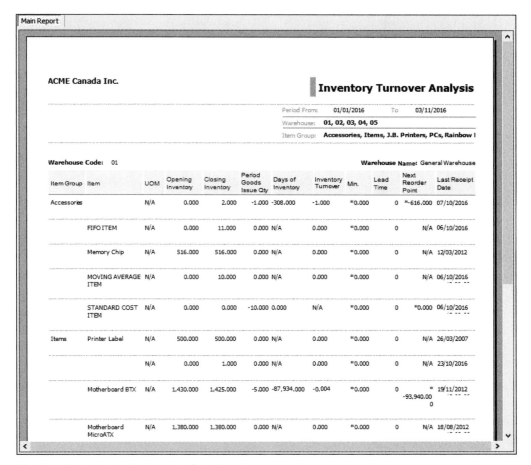

Figure 9.63 Inventory Turnover Analysis Report

To produce finished items, your organization will need the resources that contribute to them, such as labor and machinery. Let's explore how SAP Business One helps you manage data about your resources.

10 Resources

Resources—or the available capacity for labor and machinery—are key to your production processes and, in fact, work in conjunction with the production orders we'll discuss in Chapter 11. For now, though, let's take a look at how you can place resources on your bills of materials (BOMs) to accurately capture the full costs of your final product.

We'll begin this chapter by discussing how to add master data for resources in the RESOURCE MASTER DATA window and its subordinate tabs. We'll conclude by discussing how you can showcase the resources you have available when planning your production processes and how to make changes to your resources during a batch process.

10.1 Resource Master Data

To use resources on your bills of materials (and ultimately, on your production orders), you'll need to first define the data in the RESOURCE MASTER DATA screen shown in Figure 10.1. You can access this screen by clicking on RESOURCES • RESOURCE MASTER DATA.

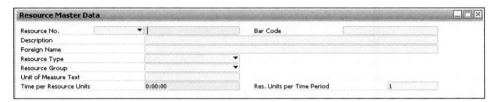

Figure 10.1 The Resource Master Data Header

Table 10.1 lists the important fields in the RESOURCE MASTER DATA screen that you should fill out.

Field	Details/Use
RESOURCE NO.	This field displays a unique value that you will use on your bills of materials and marketing documents to pull up your resource information. This numbering can be defined in ADMINISTRATION • SYSTEM INITIALIZATION • DOCUMENT NUMBERING, but following the initial SAP Business One implementation, is typically automatically created.
RESOURCE DESCRIPTION	This field displays a brief description of the resource you are adding. You can edit it as necessary.
FOREIGN NAME	Use this optional field if you need two different names for your resource.
RESOURCE TYPE	For this field, you have three options: ► LABOR (employee hours) ► MACHINE (machine hours) ► OTHER (resources other than labor or machinery, such as transportation or warehouse resources)
RESOURCE GROUP	This field is used to group together machinery, labor, etc. that have similar costs. You can define resource groups under ADMINISTRATION • SETUP • RESOURCE GROUPS SETUP.
UNIT OF MSR. TEXT	This field specifies the unit of measure associated with the resource that is being added to calculate costs and capacity. The default unit of measure for labor and machine is an hour.
TIME PER RESOURCE UNITS	This field reflects the amount of time the resource will be used to reach the unit of measure. This amount is measured in hours, minutes, and seconds.
RES. UNITS PER TIME PERIOD	This field reflects the number of resources produced per time period and is normally set to "1".

Table 10.1 Fields in the Resource Master Data Header

Resource groups are used to group together like resources that have similar costs. Resource groups are also used for resource reporting and analysis; these groups are similar to those used on items and business partners. To set up a resource group, go to ADMINISTRATION • SETUP • RESOURCE GROUPS SETUP. Figure 10.2 shows the RESOURCE GROUP SETUP screen, and Table 10.2 outlines its fields.

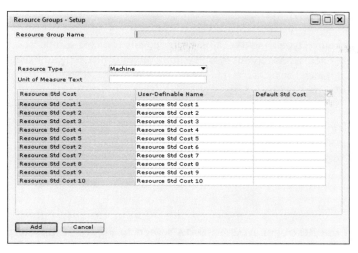

Figure 10.2 The Resource Groups Setup Screen

Field	Details/Use
RESOURCE GROUP NAME	In this field, input a unique name assigned to your group.
RESOURCE TYPE	This resource type will match what is listed on your resource master data, so your options are as follows: ▸ MACHINE ▸ LABOR ▸ OTHER
UNIT OF MEASURE TEXT	This field displays the unit of measure assigned to your group, which will then carry over to the master data.
RESOURCE STD. COST (user-defined name)	In this field, you can rename the resource's standard cost to be more user friendly. In Figure 10.2, we used HOURLY EMPLOYEE RATE and AMORTIZATION, for example.
DEFAULT STD. COST	This field displays the cost associated with one unit of measure for your group.

Table 10.2 Fields in the Resource Groups Setup Screen

You can set up ten different user-defined cost components, which will be the default costs associated with each resource; however, you can change the costs at the resource level as needed. Using this screen, you will also define a resource standard cost name in the first column of the table as seen in Figure 10.2.

> **Tips and Tricks: Resource Type**
>
> When you choose the resource type MACHINE, a new tab appears for fixed assets. You can then link one or more fixed assets to your resource, but you must first activate fixed assets by checking the ENABLE FIXED ASSETS checkbox by following the menu path ADMINISTRATION • SYSTEM INITIALIZATION • COMPANY DETAILS and clicking on the BASIC INITIALIZATION tab.
>
> If you choose resource type LABOR, a new tab will appear for employee. You can then link one or more employees to the resource.
>
> For other resources, no additional tabs are created.

10.1.1 General Tab

On the GENERAL tab of the RESOURCE MASTER DATA screen in Figure 10.2, select the issue method from the ISSUE METHOD dropdown. Next, you'll have two options: *Backflush items* will automatically be removed from inventory on a production order when the finished parent item is received. *Manual issue* allows for more control over which items you choose to issue at a specific time. Manual issue is also the only method if your items are serial or batch controlled; this allows you to choose the batch or serial number.

Resource allocation is the way capacity will be calculated for the production order. You have four choices for determining your resource allocation via the RESOURCE ALLOCATION dropdown list in Figure 10.3:

▶ If you choose ON START DATE, all of the time needed will be allocated to the start date on your production order if even the resource is not available—which could cause your resource availability to fall into the negative. Resource availability can be seen in the AVAILABLE column of your production order.

▶ If you choose ON END DATE, all of the time needed will be allocated to the end date listed on the production order. Again, similar to the ON START DATE function, this choice can cause the availability to fall into the negative amounts.

▶ The START DATE FORWARD option will spread out your resource over the given period list on your production order from start to end date, using up all available resource time for each day starting with the start date.

▶ Finally, using the END DATE FORWARD option, you are also spreading out the resource over the time period given on the production order but going back only as far as needed from the end date. Choosing this option will tell you when, based on your availability, you need to begin working on the finished good in order to finish the products by the end date listed on the production order.

To deactivate a resource, you can click on the INACTIVE button on the bottom of the GENERAL tab. The default is set to ACTIVE.

The RESOURCE STD. COST and DEFAULT STD. COST fields will populate automatically after they're set up during resource group setup.

General	Capacity Data	Planning Data	Fixed Assets	Properties	Attachments	Remarks

			Resource Std Cost	Default Std Cost	
Issue Method	▼				
Resource Allocation	▼		Resource Std Cost 1		0.00
			Resource Std Cost 2		0.00
			Resource Std Cost 3		0.00
			Resource Std Cost 4		0.00
			Resource Std Cost 5		0.00
			Resource Std Cost 6		0.00
			Resource Std Cost 7		0.00
			Resource Std Cost 8		0.00
			Resource Std Cost 9		0.00
			Resource Std Cost 10		0.00
			Total Std Resource Cost		
Active					
Inactive					
Advanced					

Figure 10.3 The General Tab of the Resource Master Data Screen

Now that we've covered the GENERAL tab, let's move onto the more specific resource-related tabs, beginning with CAPACITY DATA.

10.1.2 Capacity Data Tab

The items on the CAPACITY DATA tab can be set to defaults by going to ADMINISTRATION • SYSTEM INITIALIZATION • GENERAL SETTINGS. On this screen, click on the RESOURCE tab, as shown in Figure 10.4.

Figure 10.4 The Resource Tab under General Settings

In this tab, assign the default warehouse from which your resources will be pulled. If needed, you can change the default warehouse in the user defaults or on the CAPACITY DATA tab.

If you check the AUTO ADD ALL WAREHOUSES TO NEW RESOURCES box, all of the warehouses in your system will be listed, which will allow you to change your warehouse default for that resource. If the box is left unchecked, the only warehouse that will be presented on the CAPACITY DATA tab will be the default warehouse set in the general settings.

The DEFAULT CAPACITY PERIOD is where you will set the capacity range on the capacity tab of the master data. In the GENERAL SETTINGS screen, you will set the range where capacity starts from (today), and then you can add months or days to the current date to determine your range. The numbers defined can be both positive and negative numbers, and the timeframe cannot exceed one year.

Select from the following three choices to determine your capacity period:

► TODAY: This selection means that your timeframe is one day. Production will start today and end today.

► MONTH START: Your timeframe will start with the current date and end with the first day of the current month plus a user-defined number of months and/or days.

► MONTH END: Your timeframe will start with the current date and end with the last day of the current month plus a user-defined number of months and/or days.

Tips and Tricks: Default Warehouse

Your production order will pull in a default warehouse based on the defaults set up in a predetermined order:

► The default warehouse set on the CAPACITY DATA tab of the resource master data (see Figure 10.5)

► The default warehouse set in the user defaults

► The default warehouse set in the general settings at the company level

The intent is to be as specific as possible, so the warehouse at the resource CAPACITY DATA tab is the most specific and, if available, has the highest priority.

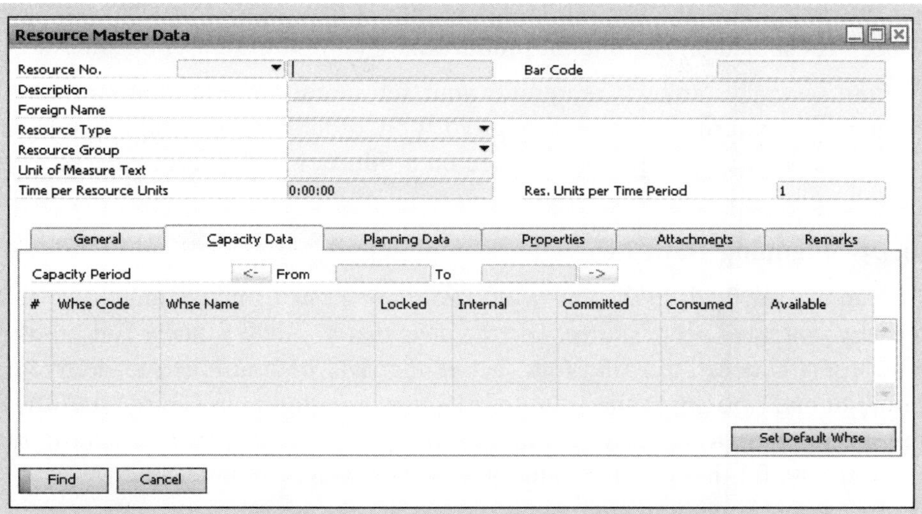

Figure 10.5 The Capacity Data Tab of the Resource Master Data Screen

The CAPACITY DATA tab of the resource master data displays the data you set as default when creating a new resource. To change the capacity period, you can use the backward and forward arrows to change the time period. The period will change using the same timeframe set up in the default data in the general settings.

If you left the AUTO ADD ALL WAREHOUSES TO NEW RESOURCES box unchecked, you can still add additional warehouses as needed by clicking on the LIST icon (three horizontal lines), which will open a new window listing your available warehouses. To add a new one, double-click the desired line. Once the warehouse has been added, you can click the SET DEFAULT WHSE button to make the newly added warehouse your new default.

If you select the checkboxes in the LOCKED column on the warehouse level, the system will stop you from adding that resource to your production order.

From the CAPACITY DATA tab, you will see the availability of your selected resource, divided by the following four columns:

▶ INTERNAL: This amount was set for your resource while configuring it.

▶ COMMITTED: This amount represents resources on planned and released production orders.

▶ CONSUMED: This amount represents resources that you set that have already been consumed on an issue for production.

▶ AVAILABLE: This amount represents your set number of resources (INTERNAL) minus your resources on open production orders (COMMITTED) minus resources that have already been issued on production orders (CONSUMED).

10.1.3 Planning Data Tab

You can use the fields in the PLANNING DATA tab to calculate how much available capacity you have per resource. For the days that you will actually run production, insert between one and four factors that will be multiplied to determine your planned capacity in the 1, 2, 3, and 4 columns shown in Figure 10.6. Or, if you do not want to figure your capacity in terms of factors, you can add in the total capacity for that resource into the DAILY CAPACITY column.

To determine what factors you will put in the four columns, think of them in terms of the number of shifts, the number of machines, the number of employees, the number of hours, etc. For example, you may have one shift and run two machines for 6 hours per machine per day. Using the REMARKS field, you can make notes to remind yourself and your employees of how capacity was determined.

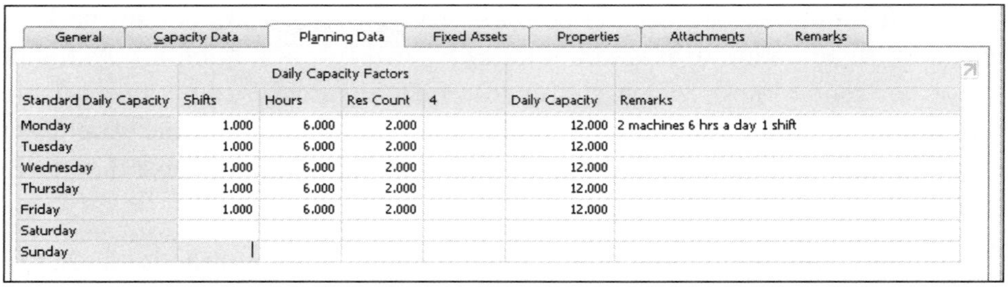

General	Capacity Data	Planning Data	Fixed Assets	Properties	Attachments	Remarks

	Daily Capacity Factors					
Standard Daily Capacity	Shifts	Hours	Res Count	4	Daily Capacity	Remarks
Monday	1.000	6.000	2.000		12.000	2 machines 6 hrs a day 1 shift
Tuesday	1.000	6.000	2.000		12.000	
Wednesday	1.000	6.000	2.000		12.000	
Thursday	1.000	6.000	2.000		12.000	
Friday	1.000	6.000	2.000		12.000	
Saturday						
Sunday						

Figure 10.6 The Planning Tab of the Resource Master Data Screen

10.1.4 Properties, Attachment, and Remarks Tabs

As with the business partner and item master data records, you can use the PROPERTIES, ATTACHMENT, and REMARKS tabs on the resource master data.

The PROPERTIES tab includes sixty-four properties that you can use to filter the reporting related to a resource. Once you set up the properties in ADMINISTRATION •

Setup • Resources • Resource Properties, you can then return to your resource master data and check the box next to the filter(s) that apply for that resource.

To add to attachments using the Attachment tab, you have two options: browsing for files saved on your computer or by holding down the left mouse button while dragging the file on to the Attachment tab. For the drag-and-drop method to work, you do not have to have the Attachment tab open—just the correct master data.

In the Remarks tab, you can add any additional notes relevant to your resource item.

10.1.5 Fixed Assets Tab

The Fixed Assets tab will only appear if you chose Machine as your resource type. Recall that, to enable the Fixed Assets tab, you must first check the box for Enable Fixed Assets in the Administration module under Company Settings, as seen in Figure 10.7.

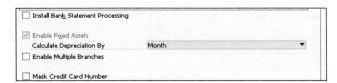

Figure 10.7 Enabling the Fixed Assets Checkbox in the Company Settings Screen

When you check the box, the system will trigger an error message stating that this function cannot be undone once updated. Once you confirm that you agree to enable fixed assets, the field will be grayed out, as shown in Figure 10.7. If you go back to the Fixed Assets tab in the resource master data, you can now choose the fixed assets you would like to assign to your resource. The rest of the tab will automatically populate with the information configured under the Fixed Assets tab.

Tips and Tricks: The Fixed Assets Tab
Each resource can be assigned multiple fixed assets, but each asset can only be assigned to one resource.
To learn more about configuring fixed assets, return to Chapter 3 of this book.

10.1.6 Employees Tab

The EMPLOYEES tab will only be visible if the resource type selected is LABOR.

In the EMPLOYEE NO. field of the EMPLOYEES tab, choose the LIST icon (three horizontal lines) to open a new table that displays the available employees from the employee master data list. Double-click the row to choose the employee or employees you would like to add to your resource; in our example in Figure 10.8, an employee named Bill Levine is highlighted.

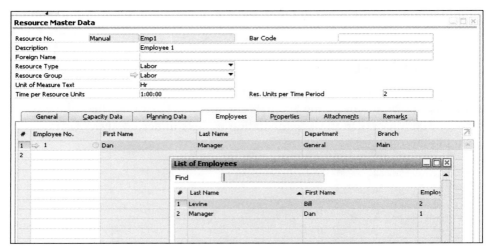

Figure 10.8 The Employees Tab of the Resource Master Data Screen

Tips and Tricks: The Employees Tab

You can assign employees to multiple resources, and multiple employees to one resource.

10.2 Resource Capacity

To reach the RESOURCE CAPACITY screen, go to RESOURCES • RESOURCE CAPACITY. The screen will always open to your last search criteria (except for the capacity period dates, which open to the default from the general settings). On this screen, you'll use the header information as seen in Figure 10.9 to filter your results.

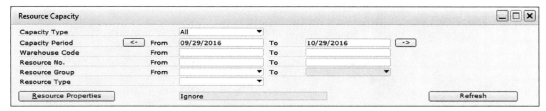

Figure 10.9 Resource Capacity Search Criteria

Table 10.3 describes the fields available as filters in your search. If all the fields are left blank, the system will retrieve all resource data. Any fields that are filled in will be used as part of your search.

Fields	Details/Use
CAPACITY TYPE	Choose from the following types of capacity: ▶ INTERNAL ▶ COMMITTED ▶ CONSUMED ▶ AVAILABLE ▶ ALL When you choose the ALL option, all resource capacity data will be listed. Two new buttons on the right corner bottom of your screen will appear. Use the EXPAND and COLLAPSE buttons to see more or less detail.
CAPACITY PERIOD	The default as defined in the general settings will determine the date range. Starting with today's date, SAP Business One will calculate the end date based on your default settings. You can change the dates manually in this field or use the arrows to move your dates backward or forward based on the time range needed.
WAREHOUSE CODE	This field reflects the warehouses where you want to search for available resources. Note this can be a single warehouse or a range of warehouses. The warehouse is listed in the master data for each resource.
RESOURCE NO.	Search for a specific resource or range of resources by entering numbers in the To and FROM fields.
RESOURCE GROUP	Search by a single resource group that you set up in the master data or by a range of resources.

Table 10.3 Resource Capacity Search Criteria Fields

Fields	Details/Use
RESOURCE TYPE	Search by one of the following types of resources: ▶ MACHINE ▶ LABOR ▶ OTHER This field will bring up all the resources that match the type chosen. A secondary search on another field would narrow your results.
RESOURCE PROPERTIES	Like items and business partners, you can click this button to search by any number of properties you have selected for each resource on the resource master data.

Table 10.3 Resource Capacity Search Criteria Fields (Cont.)

Tips and Tricks: Expand and Collapse Buttons

Once you have determined which fields you want to search, click the REFRESH button to populate the table on the screen. If you choose the ALL CAPACITY type, you can now use the EXPAND button to see more details, as shown in Figure 10.10. If you have expanded your data and now want to see summary data, use the COLLAPSE button to hide the expanded data.

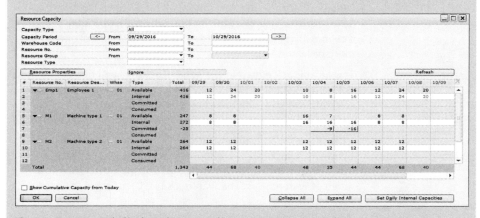

Figure 10.10 Expanded, Filtered Data on the Resource Capacity Tab

The data that is displayed for capacity is from the PLANNING DATA tab of the resource master data. This data can be changed on the RESOURCE CAPACITY screen manually for the timeframe listed in the search criteria, which is an easy way to make simple changes based on things like vacation or machine maintenance. If you need to make changes over the whole capacity period, click on the SET DAILY INTERNAL CAPACITIES button on the lower right side of the screen. You would use this function to make a more widespread change that affects your entire capacity period (for example, if you are temporarily running a weekend shift and you need to account for labor and machinery). We'll discuss this in more detail in Section 10.3.

Figure 10.10 shows the data for Employee 1, which is set up as a LABOR type resource. The INTERNAL row shows us total resource capacity in hours. Because the COMMITTED row lacks data, we know that no production orders that list this item have been planned or released with a start or end date that fits into the capacity period. The CONSUMED row is also blank, indicating that we also have not issued any Employee 1 resources to a production order within the capacity period. As you begin your production using this resource, you'll see these numbers change by clicking on the REFRESH button in the header of the RESOURCE CAPACITY screen.

In the example shown in Figure 10.11, on the first line of the table, we can see that production orders exist that require the resource for Machine 1 (M1). Based on the resource allocation chosen on the production order, we can see where the resource is needed. In row 3, we can see that, on 10/2, Machine 1 needs to run for 25 hours, but we can also see that we don't currently have any resources available on this date because the INTERNAL line is empty—signifying that zero hours are available.

Resource Capacity

Capacity Type			All									
Capacity Period	<-	From	10/02/2016		To	11/02/2016		->				
Warehouse Code		From			To							
Resource No.		From			To							
Resource Group		From			To							
Resource Type			Machine									

Resource Properties   Ignore

#	Resource No.	Resource Des...	Whse	Type	Total	10/02	10/03	10/04	10/05	10/06	10/07	10/08	10/09
1	▼ M1	Machine type 1	01	Available	254	-25	16	7		8	8		
2				Internal	304		16	16	16	8	8		
3				Committed	-50	-25		-9	-16				
4				Consumed									
5	▼ M2	Machine type 2	01	Available	276		12	12	12	12	12		
6				Internal	276		12	12	12	12	12		
7				Committed									

Figure 10.11 The Resource Capacity Screen Showing the Production Capacity for the Machine 1 Resource

In Figure 10.12, we can see the production order that created the commitment for the Machine 1 resource. Based on the resource allocation of the ON END DATE field, the resource is committed to the due date of 10/2, causing the amount in the AVAILABLE column to fall into the negative.

Because there are only 24 hours in a day, we know it won't be possible to meet this due date. If we change the resource allocation in the START DATE FORWARD field and move our due date out a few days, we'll be able to use any available resources over the next few days to complete this item.

However, based on the data in Figure 10.11, we can see that same resource M1 has been committed on 10/4 and 10/5, which means we may not be able to finish this product based on the normal availability per the resource master data. The resource capacity that has been already consumed on 10/4 and 10/5 is what we'd need in order to meet the deadline for an item with a 10/5 deadline in another production order.

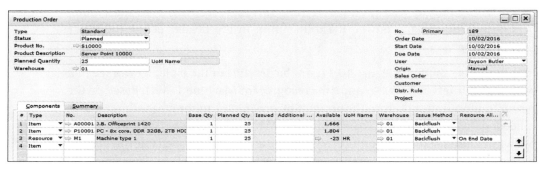

Figure 10.12 Production Order Showing the Committed Resource Due on 10/2

To look at that production order, double-click on the committed number to bring up a screen for resource capacity details (see Figure 10.13). Click on the golden arrow next to the source number to open the production order. Now, you can make changes to your production order, either to the resource allocation, due date, or resource item—whatever makes sense to get the item produced. In this case, we have two machines available, and Machine 2 is currently not in use; we know this because the committed line of the RESOURCE CAPACITY screen has no data, as seen in Figure 10.11.

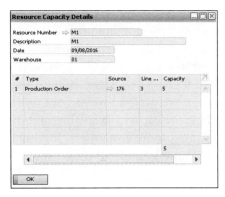

Figure 10.13 The Resource Capacity Details Screen

Another function on the RESOURCE CAPACITY screen is to show cumulative capacity from today, which adds up all the columns from day to day. In Figure 10.14, we can see the capacity after the box has been checked on lower left of the screen.

#	Resource No.	Resource Des...	Whse	Type	Total	0/20	10/21	10/22	10/23	10/24	10/25	10/26
1	Emp1	Employee 1	01	Available		8	16	36	36	44	52	60
2				Internal		8	16	36	36	44	52	60
3				Committed								
4				Consumed								
5	M1	Machine type 1	01	Available		8	16	16	16	40	56	72
6				Internal		8	16	16	16	40	56	72
7				Committed								
8				Consumed								
9	M2	Machine type 2	01	Available		12	24	24	24	48	60	72
10				Internal		12	24	24	24	48	60	72
11				Committed								
12				Consumed								
	Total					28	56	96	96	152	188	224

☑ Show Cumulative Capacity from Today

Figure 10.14 The Resource Capacity Screen after the Cumulative Total from Today Box Is Checked

As of 10/2, we see that no resource capacity is available, and based on the resource allocation and due dates of the production orders, there are no production orders listing resources committed against the zero internal capacity. On Monday, 10/3, we have 24 hours of internal capacity available and a production order using all 24 of those hours, which would leave 0 hours available for any other production to use. Now, on Tuesday 10/4, if we pretend we did not finish any production, we now have 40 hours of internal capacity available and 34 hours of committed time based on the two existing production orders, leaving 6 hours available. As the weeks go on, we can see what is available if we do not produce any items.

10.3 Set Daily Internal Capacities

To access the DAILY INTERNAL CAPACITIES, click on the left side of your screen and go to RESOURCES • DAILY INTERNAL CAPACITIES or click on the button at the bottom of the RESOURCE CAPACITY screen in the lower right corner. Either method will open the SET DAILY INTERNAL CAPACITIES screen shown in Figure 10.15.

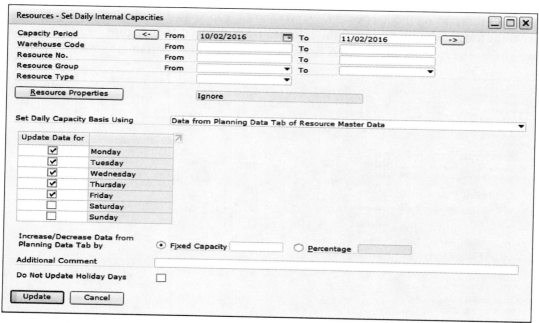

Figure 10.15 The Set Daily Internal Capacities Screen

In the header of this screen, you'll have the same filters that you had in the RESOURCE CAPACITY screen. The capacity period will open from today's date to the end date as figured by the date configured in the general settings.

To change the data on your RESOURCE CAPACITY screen for the capacity period defined in the filter in the header details, choose one of the two following methods from the SET DAILY CAPACITY BASIS USING dropdown list:

▶ DATA FROM PLANNING DATA TAB OF RESOURCE MASTER DATA: Use this option if you have to change the data on the RESOURCE CAPACITY screen and you want to set them back to your defaults on the resource master data PLANNING DATA tab. You can also increase or decrease the data presented from the master data by a fixed amount or a percentage. For example, if you have 8 hours on Monday listed as your daily capacity, and you want to increase that to 10 hours for the capacity period, you'd enter "2" in the FIXED CAPACITY field shown in Figure 10.15. Or, if you want to increase the hours for Monday–Wednesday by 25%, you would choose the bubble for percentage and type in "25."

▶ MANUAL DATA AS ENTERED BELOW FOR EACH WEEKDAY: When using this option, you'll be presented with a screen that mimics what you have on the PLANNING tab of the master data screen. You can manually change the capacity for the range chosen in the filter by adding in a total capacity, or you can have the system determine capacity by entering in your factors as described in the resource master data section. This option is useful, for example, if you want to change all Mondays in your capacity period range from 8 to 10 hours without having to manually change each one. In our example in Figure 10.16, we changed MONDAY to have a daily capacity of 24 hours—which will then be represented on the RESOURCE MASTER DATA window.

Both options offer you a field for leaving an additional comment and a checkbox used to exclude holiday days. To exclude holidays, you must have them set in your company master data. Set holidays by going to ADMINISTRATION • SYSTEM INITIALIZATION • COMPANY DETAILS. Once you are on the COMPANY DETAILS screen, click on the golden arrow next to holidays to update your data.

Tips and Tricks: Manual Data as Entered Below for Each Weekday

If you leave the UPDATE DATA FOR box checked next to a day but do not enter in any data into the daily capacity field, your resource capacity data will be zero.

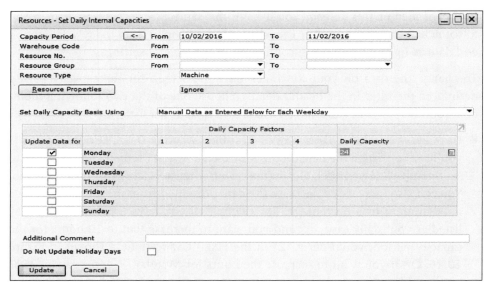

Figure 10.16 The Set Internal Capacity Screen: Manual Data as Entered Below for Each Weekday

Tips and Tricks: Capacity Period

When using the SET INTERNAL DAILY CAPACITY screen, the days affected will be over the entire period listed in the filter. If you want to change to a smaller date range, either change this value manually on the RESOURCE CAPACITY screen or manually change your dates in the capacity period filter of the SET INTERNAL DAILY CAPACITY screen.

The Production module is useful for companies that have light manu-facturing processes or that sell items together in a bundle. This chapter will take you through the process to make and receive items in your inventory.

11   Production

Companies who use SAP Business One for their production processes must create bills of materials (BOMs) and production orders, must manage goods issues and receipts, and so on. In this chapter, we'll discuss how to create BOMs for sales, assembly, template, and production and then turn those BOMs into production orders and retrieve finished goods from inventory—while at the same time removing the raw components. This chapter will then explain a method to turn your sales orders and quotations into production orders without having to manually enter them. Finally, we'll cover a few reports you can use to update your BOMs, pricing, and items in batches as well as to verify that items are set up correctly.

11.1   Bills of Materials

All BOMs are composed of a parent item and one or more child items. The *parent item* is your finished good, and your *child item* can be either a raw component or a finished good.

11.1.1   Types of Bills of Material

SAP Business One manages four types of BOMs.

The *sales BOM* can only be created for parent items (items that will be sold). The parent item must be a noninventoried item and should be marked as a sales item in the item master data. Child items can be marked either inventoried items or sales items. When the parent item is entered on the sales marketing document, all the child items will be listed to check if inventory is available.

This type of BOM is useful if your customers need to see the bundled details of their order. If you would like to hide the child items when printing your documents, you may select the HIDE BOM COMPONENTS IN PRINTOUT checkbox. This checkbox only becomes available when you change your BOM to a sales type. On a marketing document, the quantities can be changed for the child items, but they cannot be deleted or added.

Pricing in a sales BOM is used to determine the sale price for your customers. Gross profit is configured at the child level.

The *assembly BOM* is like the sales BOM, except that, on marketing documents, the only item listed is the parent item. Use this type of BOM when you do not need your customers to see details about the bundled items. Pricing in an assembly BOM is used to determine pricing for your customers. The gross profit is calculated at the parent level by totaling up the child components.

The *template BOM* has no restrictions regarding what type of items can be entered. Items can be sales, purchase, or inventoried items or any combination of the three. A template BOM can be used with both sales and purchasing marketing documents. When the parent item is used on a marketing document, you can make any changes you need to items or quantities. A template BOM is useful if your customer needs to see what items are in the bundle you are selling to them or if you need to swap out items on the BOM for any reason.

Pricing in a template BOM is used to determine pricing for your customer. Gross profit is calculated on the child item level.

Finally, *production BOMs* are used when a production order is needed. The parent item is a finished good, and the children items are component items. The production BOM is used as an instruction manual for your production area on how to create the finished items. Because you won't be selling the parent item as part of bundle pricing, it is not used on the production BOM.

The costs on the component items listed in the item master will be used to determined finished cost of the parent item. Labor and overhead can be added to a production BOM as items with a standard cost. Gross profit is calculated at the item level. Only the parent items are listed on marketing documents. The parent items will all be included in the MRP run.

11.1.2   Header and Line Item Data

Once you determine which type of BOM you need, you can begin creating your BOM. To open the BILL OF MATERIALS screen, go to the MODULES tab and click on PRODUCTION • BILL OF MATERIALS, as shown in Figure 11.1. The BILL OF MATERIALS screen will open in Find mode.

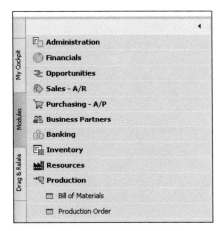

Figure 11.1 Navigating to the Bill of Materials Screen

To switch to Add mode, click on the FIND icon (the binoculars) in the toolbar or press ⌨Ctrl+⌨A. In Add mode, begin adding your data to the fields in the header shown in Figure 11.2 and listed in Table 11.1.

Figure 11.2 The Bill of Materials Screen Header

Field	Description/Use
PRODUCT NO.	This field displays the finished goods item you are making or selling.
PRODUCTION DESCRIPTION	This field will fill in once an item is entered in the PRODUCT NO. field in the item master data.

Table 11.1 Fields in the Bill of Materials Header

Field	Description/Use
BOM TYPE	Choose one of the four types of BOMs we described in the beginning of this section: ▶ SALES ▶ ASSEMBLY ▶ TEMPLATE ▶ PRODUCTION
PRODUCTION STD. COST	This static field displays information from the item master data under the PRODUCTION tab.
PLANNED AVERAGE PRODUCTION SIZE	This field displays the average quantity of your finished item that is produced when a production order is finished; by default, this field is set to "1."
QUANTITY	The field displays the quantity that will be produced by this BOM.
WAREHOUSE	This field displays the warehouse where this item will be sent after being produced.
PRICE LIST	This field displays the price list you would like to use as the basis for your items. (When creating a production BOM, the price list does not apply.)
DISTRIBUTION RULE	This field is used for shared expenses by all departments and can be set up under FINANCIALS • COST ACCOUNTING • DISTRIBUTION RULES.
PROJECT	This field is related to financial projects and can be set up under ADMINISTRATION • FINANCIALS • PROJECTS.

Table 11.1 Fields in the Bill of Materials Header (Cont.)

Below the header, you'll notice a table that organizes line item data on your BOM, as shown in Figure 11.3. Once the header is complete, begin adding information here, as listed in Table 11.2.

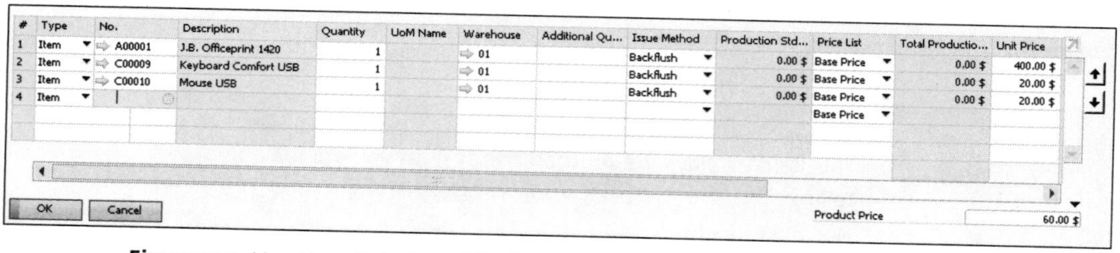

Figure 11.3 Line Item Data for a Bill of Materials

Field	Description/Use
Type	On the lines of your table, you can choose different item types from the dropdown list: ▸ Item: Use this type for raw component items from the item master data. ▸ Resource: Use this type for resources that are needed to complete your finished good item. ▸ Text: Use this type to allow additional notes to your production staff regarding a line on your BOM.
No.	This field displays the item that will be used in either a finished product or a sales item.
Description	This field displays the item description from the item master data.
Quantity	This field displays the quantity needed for a component to create the quantity produced on the BOM.
Unit of Measure Name	This field displays the unit of measure as defined in the resource master data (as discussed in Chapter 10).
Warehouse	This field designates the warehouse from which the component item will be pulled; the BOM will default to the item master default warehouse.
Additional Quantity	This field displays any additional quantity of the component item needed to create the finished good.
Issue Method	Identify the issue method here: ▸ Backflush: Components will be issued automatically when the receipt of the finished good is done. ▸ Manual: Items are manually issued to the production floor.
Production Std. Cost	This static value is pulled from the item master data under the Production tab.
Price list	Price list used as the basis for your price determination. Note that this value is not used on a production BOM.
Unit Price	On sales, assembly, and template BOMs, this field displays the price on the associated price list. Note that this value is not used for a production BOM.
Total	This field displays the quantity times the unit price.
Production price	This field displays the total of all component items.

Table 11.2 Raw Data Fields in the Bill of Materials Screen

Once you have entered all the raw data for your BOM, click on the ADD button in the lower left corner of the BILL OF MATERIALS screen and then click OK. You are now ready to use your BOMs.

Tips and Tricks: Bill of Material Data from Other Sources

On your BOMs, any field that is grayed out will be pulled in from master data or calculated based on information provided in the rows of your bill of material.

Tips and Tricks: Batch- or Serial-Controlled Items

If your items are batch or serial controlled, you will need to set those items to MANUAL so you can choose the correct serial/batch number.

If you would like to have more control over when your items are released to the warehouse set all of your items to MANUAL.

Now that we've looked at the process of creating BOMs, in the next section, we'll discuss how to create production orders in the Production module.

11.2   Production Orders

A *production order* is a set of instructions for the production floor for planning and making a finished good item. A production order is used to track all costs associated with the production process including resources such as labor.

In this section, we'll first walk through the field information for the header and line item data of a production order and then look at the steps for adding and disassembling a production order.

11.2.1   Header and Line Item Data

Under the PRODUCTION module in the main menu of the MODULES tab (see Figure 11.1), select PRODUCTION • PRODUCTION ORDER. Your production order will open, presenting you with header and line item data information. The screen will be blank; to enter a new production order, fill in the fields shown in Figure 11.4 and listed in Table 11.3.

Figure 11.4 The Production Order Screen

Field	Description/Use
TYPE	Choose from the following types of available production orders: ▶ STANDARD: Use this type for normal production orders that will bring the finished item into inventory. ▶ DISASSEMBLY: Use this type for reversals of standard production orders. This type will take the finished item out of inventory and put it back the raw components. ▶ SPECIAL: Use this type when the items are put together as the production order is created. (These are not brought in from a BOM.)
STATUS	The following options indicate the production order's status: ▶ PLANNED: Used when in the planning stage. ▶ RELEASED: Components are ready to be released to the production floor. ▶ CLOSED: Components have been issued, and finished good items have been received into inventory. ▶ CANCELED: Used when you decide not proceed with production order.
PRODUCT NUMBER	This field indicates the parent item you are making.
PRODUCT DESCRIPTION	This field displays the description of item master data for the parent item.
PLANNED QUANTITY	This field displays the quantity of the finished good item you will make in this run.
WAREHOUSE	This field displays the warehouse where the finished good will be sent after production.
NO.	This field displays the sequential document number assigned to the production order.

Table 11.3 Fields in the Production Order Screen

483

Field	Description/Use
ORDER DATE	This field displays the date the production order is entered in the system (POSTING DATE).
START DATE	This field displays the date to begin production.
DUE DATE	This field displays the date the production is due.
USER	This field indicates the person responsible for the production, which is the person entering the production order by default.
ORIGIN	You have three options for determining how this production was created: ▶ MRP ▶ SALES ORDER ▶ MANUALLY This field will fill in automatically depending on how you arrive on the PRODUCTION ORDER screen.
SALES ORDER	This field displays the sales order related to the production order when the origin is one or more sales orders.
CUSTOMER	This field displays the business partner code associated with the production order if the origin is a sales order.
DISTRIBUTION RULE	This field will default to what was chosen on the BOM.
PROJECT	This field indicates the financial project this production order is linked to; it defaults to what is on the BOM.

Table 11.3 Fields in the Production Order Screen (Cont.)

When you fill in the parent item on the production order, the line item data will autopopulate with data from the BOM associated with that item, as shown in Figure 11.5. Let's walk through the line item data we see in this screen in Table 11.4. You're welcome to change any of the details in the line item data *until* the production order is released and the component items have been issued.

Field	Description/Use
TYPE	Each line item on the production order will populate with the type chosen on the BOM. If you need change or add a line, you can choose one of the following from the dropdown list: ▶ RESOURCE ▶ ITEM ▶ TEXT

Table 11.4 Line Item Data Fields for a Production Order

Field	Description/Use
No.	This field displays the component item number.
DESCRIPTION	This field displays the description of the component item from the item master data.
BASE QUANTITY	This field displays the quantity listed on the BOM line item that is required to make the BOM quantity.
PLANNED QUANTITY	This field displays the base quantity times planned quantity in the header data.
ISSUED	This field displays the amount of component items that have been issued. This field will be filled after you have issued components to the production order.
ADDITIONAL QUANTITY	This field displays any additional quantity from the BOM or any additional quantity you will need to finish production.
AVAILABLE	This field displays the available quantity for components in the inventory that is available for use.
WAREHOUSE	This field displays the warehouse for component items that will be removed from inventory. This field defaults to the warehouse listed on the BOM, which is usually the default warehouse on the item master, but can be changed.
ISSUE METHOD	The issue method will autopopulate from the BOM, but if you want to change the method, then choose either the BACKFLUSH or the MANUAL issue method from the dropdown list.
OPEN QUANTITY	This field displays the quantity still open on the line item data after the items have been issued.

Table 11.4 Line Item Data Fields for a Production Order (Cont.)

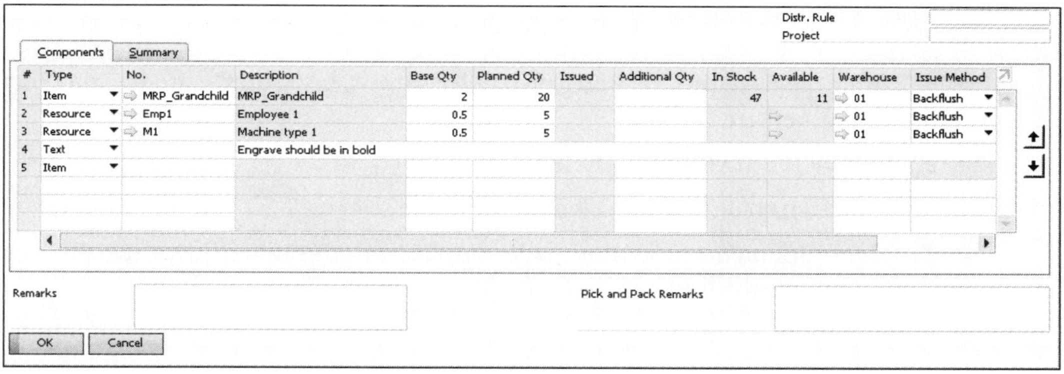

Figure 11.5 Line Item Data on a Production Order

11.2.2 Adding a Production Order

To add a finished goods inventory using a production order, follow these steps:

1. Follow the menu path PRODUCTION • PRODUCTION ORDER.

2. The PRODUCTION ORDER screen will open. Select SPECIAL or STANDARD from the TYPE dropdown list; this field will default to STANDARD.

3. Leave the STATUS as PLANNED.

4. Enter the parent item in the PRODUCT NO. field. The default BOM will now be filled on the production order.

5. Change the PLANNED QUANTITY to the quantity that will be produced with this production order.

6. Change the START DATE and DUE DATE if necessary.

7. Click on the ADD button at the bottom of your screen, as shown in Figure 11.6.

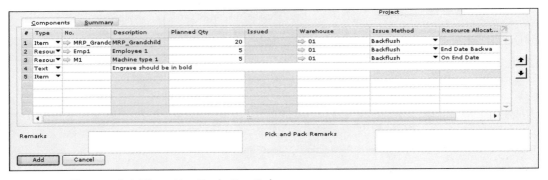

Figure 11.6 Adding a New Production Order

8. Using the PREVIOUS RECORD icon (the left arrow), bring up the production order you just entered.

9. Change the STATUS to RELEASED.

10. Click UPDATE in the lower left corner of the screen.

11. Right-click on the production order and select ISSUE COMPONENTS. (Do this step if you have the ISSUE METHOD of the items marked as MANUAL.)

12. A new table will open titled Issue for Production. Once you have issued the components for production, close the screen to return to your production order.

13. Back on the Production Order screen, click on the Refresh button to verify that all the manual components have been issued. If all the items have been issued, the Issued column will contain a quantity, the open quantity will be zero, and the line will be grayed out.

14. Right-click to bring up the context menu and click on Report Completion to bring up the Receipt from Production screen where the finished good item will be listed. When you add this receipt from production, the backflush items on your production order will be issued, and the parent item will be entered into inventory.

15. Close the report completion document and return to the Production Order screen. Click the Refresh button. If all the lines have been issued, they will all be grayed out now.

16. Once you are sure that all lines are completed, change your selection in the Status field from Planned to Closed.

17. Click the Update button in the lower left corner of your screen, as shown in Figure 11.7.

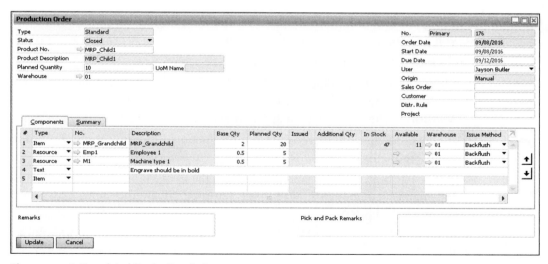

Figure 11.7 A Completed Production Order

Until the production order is closed, you can issue one or more receipts from production against a production order. Each of these will update inventory levels as appropriate.

11.2.3   Disassembling a Production Order

To remove finished goods and add raw components back into inventory, follow these steps, referring back to Figure 11.7:

1. To access this functionality, navigate through the menu path PRODUCTION • PRODUCTION ORDER.

2. Just as when you added a production order, the PRODUCTION ORDER screen opens. Select DISASSEMBLY from the TYPE dropdown list, rather than the default (STANDARD).

3. Leave the selection in the STATUS dropdown list as PLANNED.

4. Enter the parent item in the PRODUCT NO. field. The default BOM will now fill in on the production order.

5. Change the PLANNED QUANTITY value to the quantity that will be removed from inventory.

6. Click on the ADD button at the bottom of your screen.

7. Using the PREVIOUS RECORD icon (left arrow), bring up the production order you just entered. Change the STATUS from PLANNED to RELEASED.

8. Click UPDATE in the lower left corner of the screen,

9. Right-click on the production order and bring up the context-sensitive menu. Choose RECEIPT COMPONENTS (again, this step is done if you have the ISSUE METHOD of the items marked as MANUAL).

10. A new table opens for a receipt from production. Once you have received in the components, close the screen to return to your production order

11. On the PRODUCTION ORDER screen, click on the REFRESH button to verify that all the manual components have been returned. If all the items have been returned, the ISSUED column will now contain a quantity, the open quantity will now be zero in the OPEN QUANTITY column, and the line will be grayed out.

12. Right-click to bring up the context menu and click on REPORT COMPLETION, which will open a screen called RECEIPT FROM PRODUCTION where the finished good item will be listed. Upon adding this receipt from production to the

system, the backflush items on your production order will be issued, and the parent item will be removed from inventory.

13. Close the report completion message screen. Return to the PRODUCTION ORDER screen and click on the REFRESH button. If all the lines have been issued, they will all be grayed out now.

14. Once you are sure all lines are completed, change the STATUS to CLOSED.

15. Click UPDATE.

11.3 Procurement Confirmation Wizard

The Procurement Confirmation Wizard is used to turn your sales demand into a production or purchasing document. You already saw this wizard in Chapter 6, Section 6.4, and used it for your purchasing workflow. In this chapter, we'll focus on using the Procurement Confirmation Wizard for production documents. As sales orders and quotations are entered for items that have a production bill of materials, you can use the wizard to create the production order automatically from one or more sales orders/quotations, speeding up the process of creating production orders manually. To use this functionality, you must have access to both the Sales (A/R) and Production modules.

Figure 11.8 shows the main screen of the Procurement Confirmation Wizard, where you'll see a brief description of what the wizard can do.

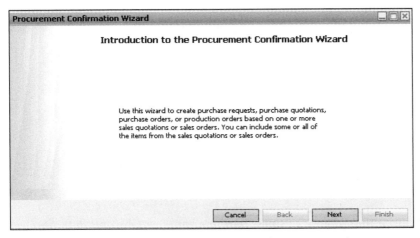

Figure 11.8 The Main Screen of the Procurement Confirmation Wizard

To begin using the wizard, proceed with the following steps:

1. Access the wizard by following the menu path PRODUCTION • PROCUREMENT CONFIRMATION WIZARD. Click on the NEXT button shown in Figure 11.8 to get going.

2. The first step is to choose the base document type and the corresponding customers. From the BASE DOC. dropdown list shown in Figure 11.9, choose the type of document you would like to create for your production order: either SALES ORDER or SALES QUOTATION.

3. Once you have decided, choose the customers that have ordered the items you would like to produce by clicking the ADD button to the right of the table. Using the selection criteria window that appears, you can filter by customer, customer group, or business partner property, or you have the option to select all.

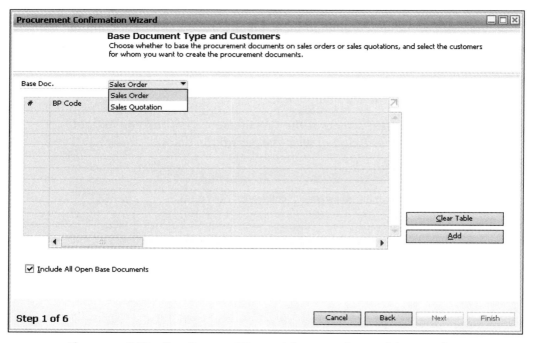

Figure 11.9 Setting Base Document Type and Customers (Step 1 of the Wizard)

4. After you have chosen your business partners, you have the option to unselect those that fit into a specific customer group but are not part of the orders you

would like to include in the production order demand. To do this, uncheck the checkbox in the third column next to the customer name. In our example in Figure 11.10, we've unchecked the boxes for Parameter Technology and the Mashina Corporation.

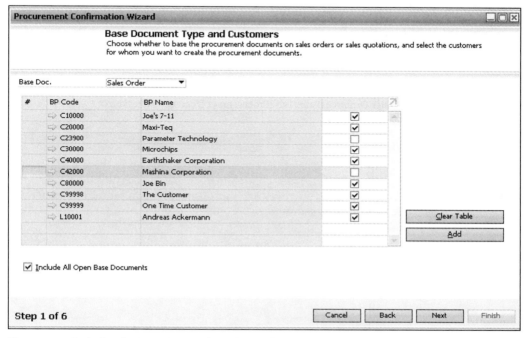

Figure 11.10 Excluding Business Partners from the Production Order Demand

5. Notice the INCLUDE ALL OPEN BASE DOCUMENTS checkbox underneath the table. If you leave the box checked (which is its default mode), the wizard will pull in all documents with open sales orders for any item that is linked to the current production BOM. If you uncheck the box, the system will only look at the documents where you checked the PROCUREMENT DOCUMENT checkbox under the LOGISTICS tab of your sales order or quotation (see Figure 11.11).

6. Now that you have chosen your criteria, click NEXT to proceed to Step 2 of the wizard.

7. The BASE DOCUMENTS screen displays documents that have open items for the customers you chose. Highlight the lines you would like to include in your production order. Click NEXT to proceed to Step 3 of the wizard.

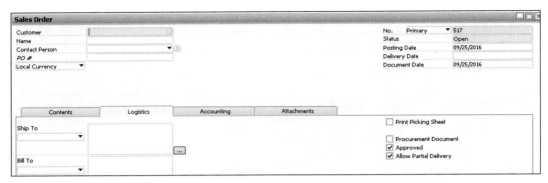

Figure 11.11 The Sales Order Logistics Tab (Procurement Document Checkbox)

Tips and Tricks: Choosing Multiple Rows

To choose all of the lines, highlight the top row and scroll down to the last row; now, while holding down the `Shift` key, click on the last row. If you want to include only certain lines, hold down the `Ctrl` key and then, using your mouse, click on each row you would like to include, as shown in Figure 11.12.

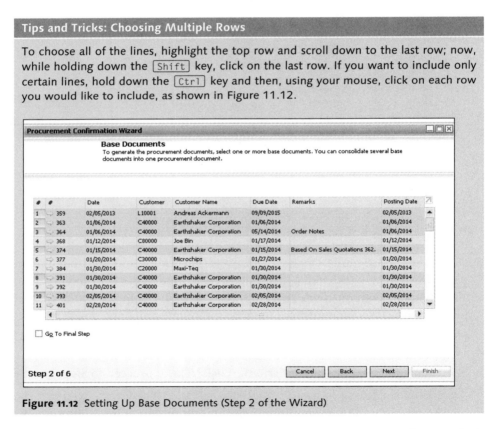

Figure 11.12 Setting Up Base Documents (Step 2 of the Wizard)

8. In the BASE DOCUMENT LINE ITEMS screen shown in Figure 11.13, choose which document you would like to create and how many items will be planned based

on the open quantity on the sales order. (In our example, we've chosen PRO-DUCTION ORDER from the TARGET DOCUMENT list.)

When you enter into this screen, all items listed will be highlighted; if you choose not to make an item, you can remove the highlighting by clicking on the row.

Once you have decided which items you will produce, click NEXT to proceed to Step 4 of the wizard.

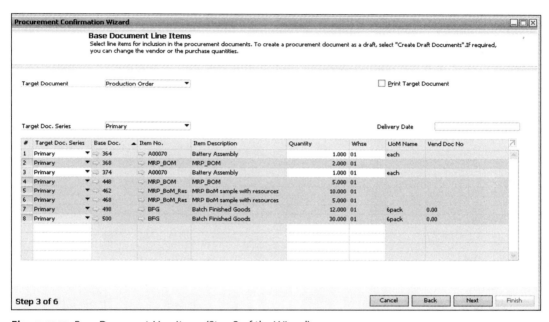

Figure 11.13 Base Document Line Items (Step 3 of the Wizard)

9. The next step is performed in the CONSOLIDATION screen, shown in Figure 11.14. You have two options, shown as radio buttons:

   ▸ NO CONSOLIDATION: If you decide not to combine like line items, then the SAP Business One system creates a single production order for every open line item on the sales order/quotation.

   ▸ CONSOLIDATED BY: You can consolidate line items by item or target document; you can also select from a list of advanced options by clicking on the dropdown lists.

After you have chosen your consolidation option, determine what to do if an error occurs by selecting either STOP THE EXECUTION or SKIP TO THE NEXT ITEM. Click NEXT to continue.

Tips and Tricks: Consolidation Using the Procurement Confirmation Wizard

Consolidating by item and target document can be helpful if you are targeting a purchasing document. If you have multiple items that will made by the same vendor, consolidation would result in one purchase order.

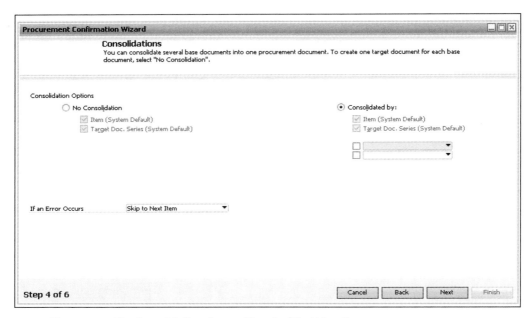

Figure 11.14 The Consolidations Screen (Step 4 of the Wizard)

10. The PREVIEW RESULTS screen shown in Figure 11.15 displays the results that will be turned into one or more *planned* production orders, based on the consolidation method you select. Click NEXT to proceed.

11. The Procurement Confirmation Wizard will now execute the production orders and present you with any errors in a detailed summary report (shown in Figure 11.16).

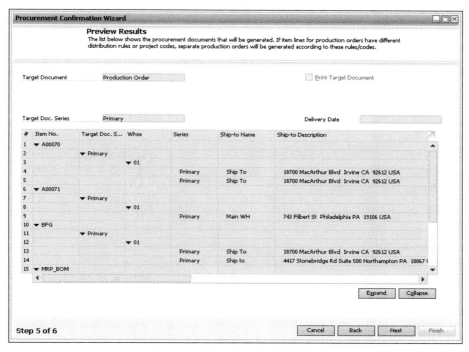

Figure 11.15 Previewing Results (Step 5 of the Wizard)

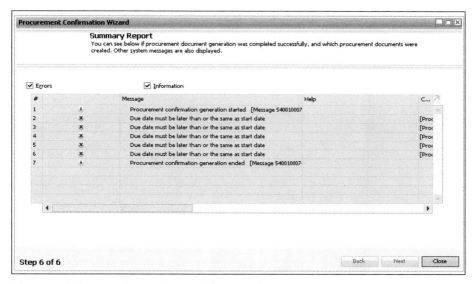

Figure 11.16 Summary Report (Step 6 of the Wizard)

11.4   Receipt from Production

The RECEIPT FROM PRODUCTION screen will bring in the finished good inventory on both standard and special production orders. If you are doing a disassembly, the RECEIPT FROM PRODUCTION screen will return the raw component items to inventory.

You can reach the RECEIPT FROM PRODUCTION screen in one of two ways:

▶ On the PRODUCTION ORDER screen, right-click and select REPORT COMPLETION to open the RECEIPT FROM PRODUCTION screen. This screen shows the finished good item you are producing.

▶ Follow the menu path PRODUCTION • RECEIPT FROM PRODUCTION. The screen that opens will be blank; you will need to manually enter the production order number on the line or click on the PRODUCTION ORDER button in the lower right-hand corner to bring in the data from the production order.

You can now change any quantities in the RECEIPT FROM PRODUCTION header and body shown in Figure 11.17 and Figure 11.18 as necessary; we list the relevant fields in Table 11.5 and Table 11.6. Once the quantities are correct, click on the ADD button. When the warning message pops up, click OK and close the document.

Figure 11.17 The Receipt from Production Screen

Field	Description/Use
NUMBER	This is the sequential document number assigned to the receipt from production
SERIES	This is the numbering series assigned to production in the Administration module
POSTING DATE	This is the transaction posting date; this field defaults to today's date.
REFERENCE 2	Any additional details needed for the receipt from production are entered here.

Table 11.5 Fields in the Receipt from Production Header

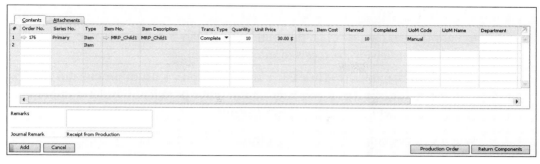

Figure 11.18 The Receipt from Production Screen

Note that the fields listed in Table 11.6 are all autopopulated by the system.

Field	Description/Use
ORDER NUMBER	This field displays production order number.
SERIES	This field displays numbering series set for production in the Administration module.
TYPE	This field displays the item type.
ITEM NO.	Enter the parent item being produced.
ITEM DESCRIPTION	This field displays an item description from the item master data.
QUANTITY	Enter the quantity being received into inventory, which can be modified if necessary.
UNIT PRICE	This field displays the cost of items being received into warehouse based on rolled up cost of components.
TOTAL	This field displays the total (unit price times quantity).
WAREHOUSE	This field displays warehouse where parent items are being received.
PLANNED	This field displays the quantity that was planned on the production order.
COMPLETED	This field displays the quantity that was completed on the receipt from production.
REMARKS	Use this field for any additional notes about the receipt from production.

Table 11.6 Fields in the Receipt from Production Screen

Take note of two buttons at the bottom of the RECEIPT FROM PRODUCTION screen:

▶ PRODUCTION ORDER: Click this button to display a list of available production orders that need to be received into the system.

▶ RETURN COMPONENTS: Click this button to display a list of production and disassembly orders. Once you have chosen your production order number, you can choose which items you want to return.

When you've completed the receipt from production data, click ADD.

11.5   Issue for Production

An *issue for production* issues your components in the system that are marked as MANUAL on a standard and special production order. In our example in Figure 11.19, two LeMon 4029 printers are marked MANUAL in the ISSUE METHOD column of a production order. If you are doing a disassembly, the issue for production will remove your finished goods from inventory.

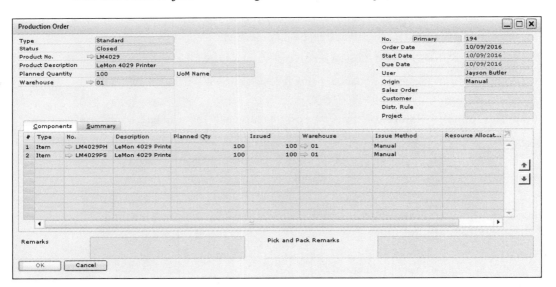

Figure 11.19 Items Marked as Manual in the Issue Method Column

You can reach the Issue for Production in one of two ways:

▶ On the production order, right-click to bring up the context menu, then click on Issue Components to open the Issue for Production screen. This screen shows the finished good item you are producing.

▶ Alternatively, follow the menu path Production • Issue for Production. The screen that opens will be blank; manually enter the production order number in the Number field or click on the Production Order button in the lower right-hand corner to import the data from the production order.

You can now change any quantities in the Issue for Production header and body shown in Figure 11.20 and Figure 11.21 as necessary; the relevant fields are listed in Table 11.7 and Table 11.8. Once the quantities are correct, click on the Add button. When the warning message pops up, click OK and close the document.

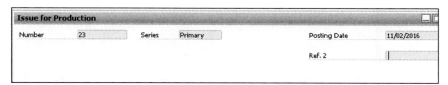

Figure 11.20 The Issue for Production Header

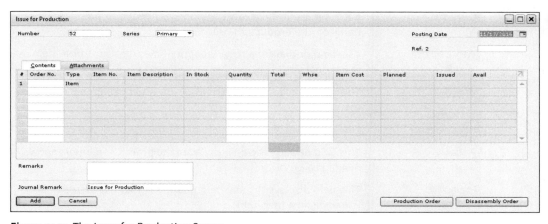

Figure 11.21 The Issue for Production Screen

Field	Description/Use
NUMBER	This field displays a sequential issue for production number assigned in the Administration module.
SERIES	This field displays the series set in the Administration module for the Production module.
POSTING DATE	This field displays the transaction posting date, which defaults to today's date.
REF 2	Use this field for additional notes about an issue for production.

Table 11.7 Fields in the Issue for Production Screen

Field	Description/Use
ORDER NO.	This field displays the production order number.
TYPE	This field displays the item type.
ITEM NO.	Enter the component items that need to be manually issued.
DESCRIPTION	This field displays the item master description of the component item.
IN STOCK	This field displays the quantity of components items on the shelf before production. (This quantity is different from the available quantity.)
QUANTITY	Enter the quantity of raw components needed to produce the items on the production order.
TOTAL	This field displays the total (quantity times item cost from item master data).
WAREHOUSE	This field displays the warehouse from which components will be removed.
ITEM COST	This field displays the current cost of this item in inventory.
PLANNED	This field displays the quantity from the production order that was needed to produce the finished good quantity.
ISSUED	This field displays the any item quantities that have already been issued against that item.
AVAILABLE	This field displays the available inventory for the item.

Table 11.8 Fields in the Issue for Production Screen

11.6   Update Parent Items Globally

The Update Parent Items Globally functionality is used to update parent item prices in the price list entered on the BOM header when a child component item price has changed in the same price list.

To access this function, follow the menu path PRODUCTION • UPDATE PARENT ITEMS GLOBALLY to open the UPDATE PARENT ITEMS PRICES selection criteria screen shown in Figure 11.22.

Figure 11.22 Update Parent Item Prices Selection Criteria

On this screen, you can narrow your search for items that need to be updated, for example, by filtering by price list using the FROM and TO dropdown lists next to PRICE LIST. To search by item number, enter a part number in the FROM and TO fields next to CODE. This selection is a range of values; to search for a single item number, enter the item number in both the TO and FROM fields.

The SELECTION CRITERION radio buttons will both bring up parent items that need to be updated, but you have a choice here:

▸ The PARENT ITEMS radio button brings up a list of parent items that have a child item that has been changed.

▸ The COMPONENT ITEMS radio button brings up the component items that have been changed that are then rolled up into the parent item.

Therefore, if you know the price of a component item number has changed on the price list associated with the BOM, you can enter both the component item number and use the radio button for components to bring up the parent item. If you have updated all items or a portion of items in an item group, you can bring them up by selecting the item group. You can also use item properties from the item master data as a filter.

Once you have selected your filters, choose OK. If you encounter an error message that says "No parent item prices to be updated found [Message 65020-3]," either you do not have the correct criteria checked or no items need to be updated.

When the UPDATE PARENT ITEM PRICES GLOBALLY screen shown in Figure 11.23 opens, you'll be presented with the parent items, their current prices, and the suggested list price based on the prices of the components in the corresponding price list. To see details about the price change, click the EXPAND button in the lower right corner; the current price of the components as well as the new price will be displayed. The DIFFERENCE column will give you the variance between the two prices and will alert you to which items have been changed in the price list.

If you have approved all the suggested prices, click UPDATE, and your prices will be changed in the price list listed on the UPDATE screen. If you choose *not* to approve a price, you can override the update by unchecking the UPDATE checkbox next to the items.

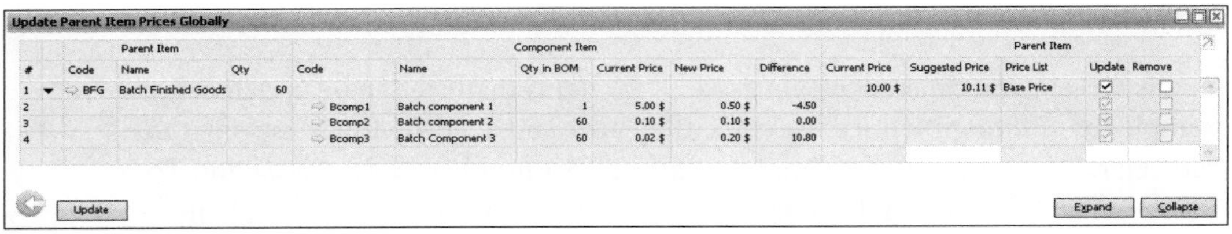

Figure 11.23 Results Based on Criteria in the Update Parent Item Prices Screen

11.7 Production Cost Recalculation

The Production Cost Recalculation Wizard changes your inventory cost for a batch of items already in inventory using the serial/batch valuation method. In order to run the Production Cost Recalculation Wizard, the item must meet the following criteria:

▶ The product to be revalued must use the batch/serial valuation method.

▶ The production order must be closed.

▶ One or more of the component items on the closed production order must use the serial/batch valuation method.

Currently, not much written documentation on how to use this function in SAP Business One is available since the function is still new, but you should proceed with the following steps:

1. When the wizard opens, click NEXT to view what options are available in the wizard:

    ▸ RUN PRODUCTION COST RECALCULATION SIMULATION: This option will run the wizard to determine what costs SAP Business One recommends you change.

    ▸ START PRODUCTION COST RECALCULATION RUN: This option will run the wizard to make the changes as proposed by SAP Business One.

    ▸ LOAD A SAVED PRODUCTION COST RECALCULATION RUN: This option will run the wizard using a saved parameter from the START PRODUCTION COST RECALCULATION RUN option.

    Click NEXT to move ahead—but remember that, if you do not have your items marked with the serial/batch valuation method, you won't be presented with data.

2. In the WIZARD PARAMETERS screen shown in Figure 11.24, determine which items you would like to examine. If you click the SEARCH button, all the items marked as serial/batch valuation will appear in the table on the left.

3. Highlight the items on the left side of the table that you would like to run through the Production Cost Recalculation Wizard and move them to the table on the right using the double-right arrow. (This method is similar to choosing a batch or serial number in the batch transaction.) Click NEXT.

4. The next step of the wizard displays the items whose production costs need to be adjusted to the current cost of the product components. Highlight the items you would like to adjust and click NEXT again.

5. The MATERIAL REVALUATION DETAILS screen summarizes the items that will be adjusted; once you are satisfied with your selection, click NEXT.

6. Finally, the SAVE AND EXECUTE OPTIONS screen gives you three options:

    ▸ You could click EXECUTE to run the simulation.

    ▸ You could click SAVE AND EXIT to save the wizard parameter and exit without running the simulation.

    ▸ You could click SAVE AND EXECUTE to save the simulation that has been executed and then exit.

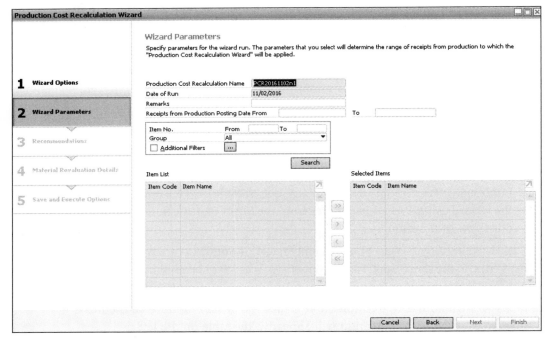

Figure 11.24 The Wizard Parameters Screen (Step 2 of the Wizard)

11.8 Component Management

The Component Management function in the Production module is used to change, add, or delete information from a BOM. In this section, we'll look at the steps for performing each of these functions.

To access the Component Management function, follow the menu path Production • Bill of Materials – Component Management. In the selection criteria screen that opens, in the Management Task dropdown list, choose from three options: Add BOM Lines, Change BOM Lines, or Delete BOM Lines. Your selection in this small header will impact the rest of the fields on the screen; we'll walk through all of these tasks now and consider the corresponding fields to complete the process.

If you need to add lines to your BOM, choose the Add BOM Lines option and then proceed with the following steps (see Figure 11.25):

1. Use the filters in the SELECT BOMs area of the screen to narrow your selection down to the correct BOM(s).

2. In the SELECT BOM LINES TO ADD dropdown list, select the type of component you will be adding: either RESOURCE, ITEM, or TEXT.

3. Go to the BOM LINE DETAILS TO BE ADDED section and fill in all the appropriate information:

   ▸ If the component type is either ITEM or RESOURCE, enter the quantity needed, any additional quantities, warehouse, issue method (either backflush or manual), and the associated work-in-progress (WIP) account.

   ▸ If the component type is TEXT, you will be given a large text box to add your text to each BOM that is selected in the above criteria.

4. After you click OK, a new screen will open with a list of BOMs that meet your criteria. Select those you wish to update and click OK to approve the BOMs to be changed. Your BOM will now have a new component item.

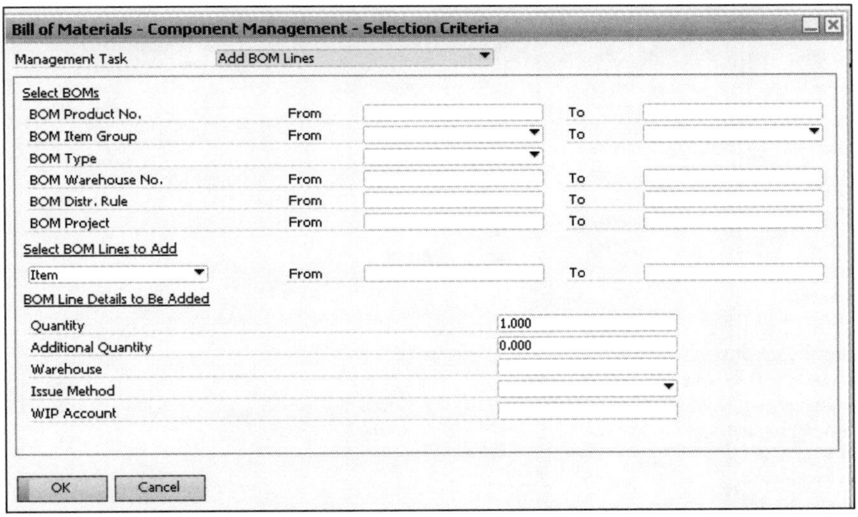

Figure 11.25 Adding BOM Lines

If you need to change lines in your BOM, choose the CHANGE BOM LINES option and then follow these steps (see Figure 11.26):

1. Use the filters in the SELECT BOMs area of the screen to narrow your selection down to the correct BOM(s).

2. In the SELECT BOM LINES TO ADD dropdown list, select the type of component you will be adding: either RESOURCE, ITEM, or TEXT.

3. Go to the SELECT PROPERTIES FOR BOM LINES TO BE CHANGED section and fill in all the appropriate information:

   ▶ If the component type is either ITEM or RESOURCE, you will be able to check the boxes next to the lines you would like to change on the BOM: the REPLACEMENT BOM COMPONENT checkbox and the NUMBER OF REPLACEMENT COMPONENTS PER EXISTING COMPONENTS field; CHANGE ADDITIONAL QUANTITY checkbox and corresponding field; CHANGE WAREHOUSE checkbox; CHANGE ISSUE METHOD checkbox; and CHANGE WIP ACCOUNT checkbox.

   ▶ If the component type is TEXT, you will need to type in the text to be replaced and, in a separate larger area, type in the text that you would like the current tab changed to.

4. After you click OK, a new screen will open. Click OK if you approve of the BOMs to be changed. Your BOM will now be changed.

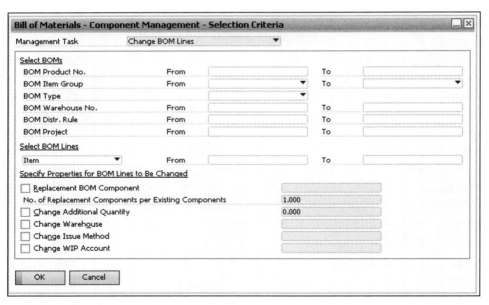

Figure 11.26 Changing BOM Lines

If you need to delete lines from your BOM, choose the DELETE BOM LINES option and then proceed with the following steps (see Figure 11.27):

1. Use the filters in the SELECT BOMs area of the screen to narrow your selection down to the correct BOM(s).

2. In the SELECT BOM LINES TO ADD dropdown list, select the type of component you will be adding: either RESOURCE, ITEM, or TEXT.

3. Once you have determined your component type, tab to add the component item(s):

   ▸ If the component type is either ITEM or RESOURCE, type in the part(s) that need to be deleted from your BOM(s).

   ▸ If the component type is TEXT, type in the text to be deleted from each BOM that is selected in the above criteria.

4. After you click OK, a new screen will open. Click OK if you approve of the BOMs to be changed. Your components will now be deleted from your BOM(s).

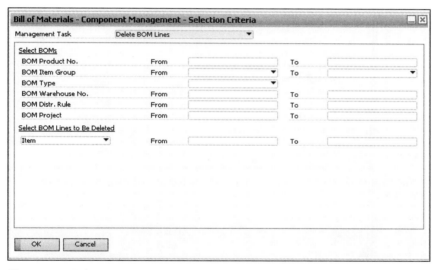

Figure 11.27 Deleting BOM Lines

11.9   Production Standard Cost Management

This section will explain the procedure to roll up the standard costs of the item master listed in the Production module or to update the standard costs as found at the default warehouse level of the item master data on the INVENTORY tab.

11.9.1 Production Standard Cost Rollup

The PRODUCTION STANDARD COST ROLLUP screen takes the standard cost amount listed on the PRODUCTION DATA tab of the item master data (see Figure 11.28) and rolls it up in to the total cost on the BOM under the PRODUCTION STD. COST field shown in see Figure 11.29.

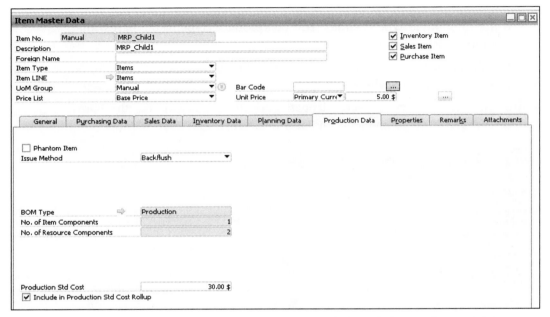

Figure 11.28 The Item Master Data Production Tab with the Include in Production Std. Cost Rollup Box Checked

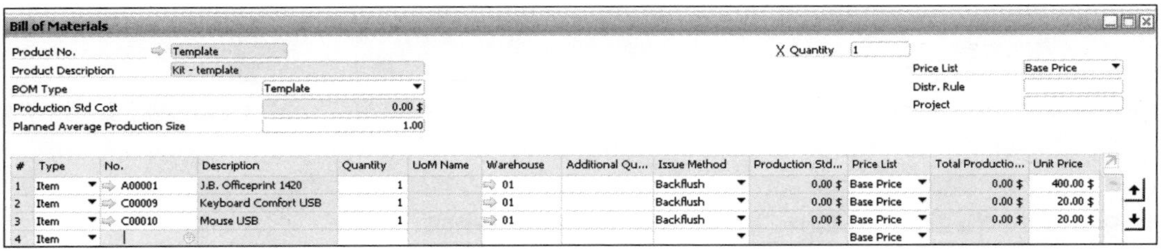

Figure 11.29 The Sum of the Total Production Standard Cost in the Production Standard Cost Header Field

If any of your items has a child BOM, make sure they have items set to a standard cost on the item master as well; otherwise, when you check the INCLUDE IN PRODUCTIONS STD. COST ROLLUP checkbox on the PRODUCTION tab of the item master, your total for that item will roll up to zero.

If you choose not to include a budgeted standard cost on the PRODUCTION tab for the raw components in a child BOM, you can uncheck the box (see Figure 11.30). As a result, the cost will not be changed to zero.

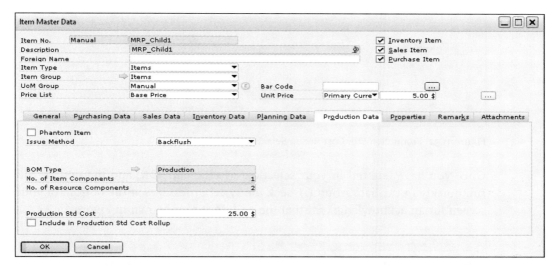

Figure 11.30 The Production Tab in the Item Master Data Record with the Include in Production Std. Cost Rollup Box Unchecked

Now that your child component has a budgeted amount, as shown in Figure 11.31, you can run the production standard cost rollup procedure, and your production standard cost total will now include this amount.

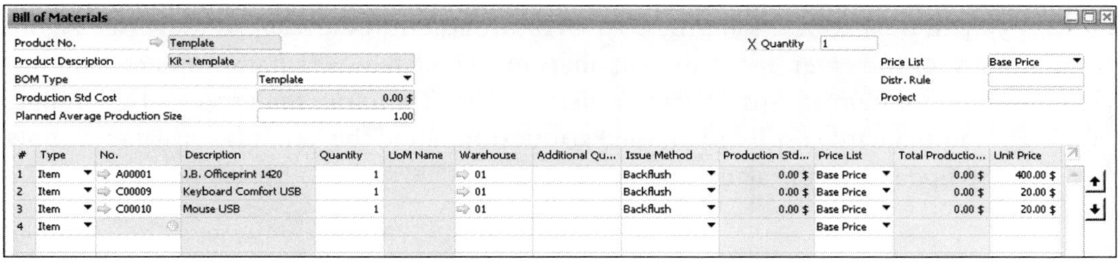

Figure 11.31 An Updated BOM with Production Standard Cost Updated after Item Master Data

509

To run the production standard cost rollup function, click on PRODUCTION • PRO-DUCTION STD. COST ROLLUP and enter the selection criteria, as shown in Figure 11.32. You have several choices when deciding how to update the budgeted production standard cost. You can update by item number, item group number, or by any item properties you have stated on your items.

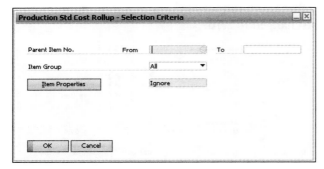

Figure 11.32 Production Std. Cost Rollup Selection Criteria

Once you have entered in your selection criteria, click OK, and the update will run quickly in the background. Check the system messages at the bottom of your screen for an acknowledgment that the update ran, as shown in Figure 11.33.

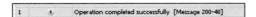

Figure 11.33 Successful Completion Message for Updating Budgeted Standard Cost

11.9.2 Production Standard Cost Update

You can use the Production Standard Cost Update function to update the PRODUCTION tab standard production cost from actual item cost listed in the item master data.

Open the PRODUCTION STD. COST UPDATE SELECTION CRITERIA window (see Figure 11.34) and enter in the item numbers to be updated (both parent and child items) or enter item groups or item properties. Click OK to run the process. The production standard cost listed on the PRODUCTION tab of the item master data will now be updated to the actual costs.

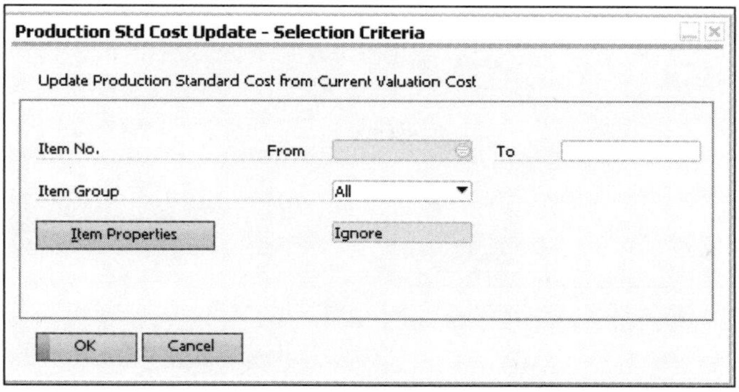

Figure 11.34 Production Std. Cost Update Selection Criteria

Once all your costs have been updated with the actual costs on the PRODUCTION tab of the item master data, you can now run the production standard cost rollup to update the BOM with standard costs. This can be used as a benchmark against the future actual costs of your items.

11.10 Production Reports

We want to call your attention to two key production reports: the Bill of Materials Report and the Open Items Report.

11.10.1 Bill of Materials Report

The Bill of Materials Report examines multiple bills of materials at one time. To access the report, follow the menu path PRODUCTION • PRODUCTION REPORTS • BILL OF MATERIALS REPORT. Identify the required selection criteria in the screen shown in Figure 11.35 to filter your report.

Once you have opened the Bill of Materials Report, you'll be presented with a listing of all available BOMs based on your filter. By clicking the EXPAND button on the report screen, you can drill down into the data associated with each bill of materials, as shown in Figure 11.36. From there, you can use the arrows to open the BILL OF MATERIALS window and make any additions, deletions, or modifications that are needed.

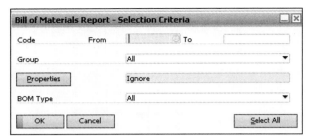

Figure 11.35 Selection Criteria in the Bill of Materials Report Screen

Item	Item Description	UoM	Quantity	Whse	Price	Depth	BOM Type
▼ ⇨ Assembly	Sales Assembly		1 ⇨	01	600.00 $	1	Assembly
⇨ AsComp3	Assembly component		1 ⇨	01	25.00 $	2	N
⇨ AsComp1	Assembly component		1 ⇨	01	30.00 $	2	N
⇨ AsComp2	Assembly component		1 ⇨	01	45.00 $	2	N
⇨ LB0001	Daily Service Labor C		1 ⇨	01	200.00 $	2	N

Bill of Materials Report

Figure 11.36 The Bill of Materials Screen, with Filters

Tips and Tricks: Bill of Materials Report

Using the expanded view is a good way to view all BOMs that have the same component items at once.

11.10.2 Open Items Report

The Open Items Report can be accessed through any of the report modules in the main menu. If you access this report through the Production module, you will see the open production order list, as shown in Figure 11.37. In this screen, you can click the golden arrows to drill into the production order document and modify, add, or delete information as necessary.

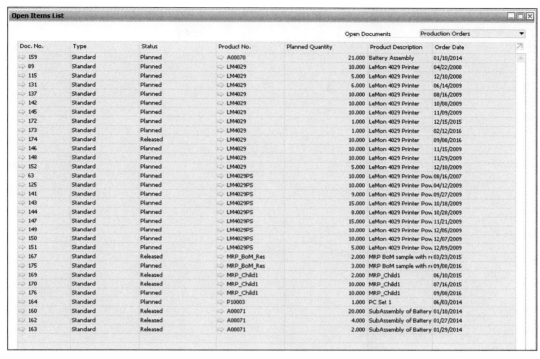

Figure 11.37 An Open Items List Report

Tips and Tricks: Open Items List

If you arrive on the open items list from any of the other report modules in your main menu, use the OPEN DOCUMENTS dropdown list in the upper right-hand corner to choose the open documents you would like to see.

Materials requirements planning (MRP) is used in the manufacturing processes to plan, schedule, and control inventory and to plan production schedules so you can meet your customers' needs. MRP allows you to maintain lower inventory levels by recommending the appropriate raw material and finished good items to be made or purchased.

12 MRP

SAP Business One's MRP module uses three tools to help you run your MRP recommendations: forecasts, the MRP Wizard, and order recommendations.

However, before you can use these tools, you'll need to set up some data on the item master data records. In Section 12.1, we'll show you how to set up this data for each item or at the item group level. We'll then cover how to use SAP Business One's tools for MRP tasks and transactions: forecasts in Section 12.2, the MRP Wizard in Section 12.3, and order recommendations in Section 12.4.

Note that unlike the other modules you've seen in this book, the MRP module does not have a separate report section because it is already a reporting tool for planning, scheduling, and controlling inventory in a manufacturing environment. The MRP sections described throughout the chapter will be used for creating your MRP reports.

12.1 Planning Master Data

To access the ITEM MASTER DATA, follow the menu path INVENTORY • ITEM MASTER DATA and click on the PLANNING DATA tab shown in Figure 12.1.

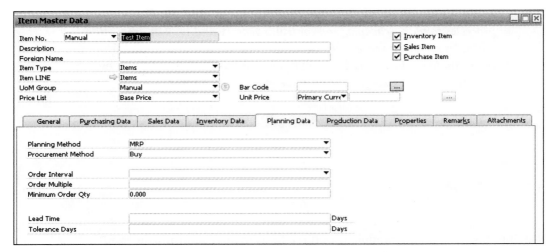

Figure 12.1 The Planning Data Tab of the Item Master Data Screen

On the PLANNING DATA tab, you'll need to enter the information as described in Table 12.1.

Field	Description/Use
PLANNING METHOD	In the PLANNING METHOD dropdown list, choose from the following options: ▶ MRP: This option will add this item to your MRP calculation. ▶ NONE: This option excludes the item from the MRP calculation; this item will not be planned.
PROCUREMENT METHOD	Once an item is chosen for MRP, you will need to determine its procurement method from two choices: ▶ BUY: These items will be recommended on purchase orders. Buy items will be your child items on a BOM or other items that do not appear on a BOM. ▶ MAKE: These items will be recommended on production orders. In an MRP calculation, all of your parent items must be set to MAKE.

Table 12.1 Fields in the Planning Data Tab

Field	Description/Use
ORDER INTERVAL	The order interval is the time between your MRP calculation and your next calculation date. You have the following three pre-defined time frames available to you, but you can click ADD NEW to add your own: ▶ WEEKLY: Choose which day of the week to begin your MRP run from the dropdown list. ▶ MONTHLY: Choose what month to begin your MRP run from the dropdown list. ▶ EVERY "X" DAYS: Set your own number of days between MRP runs.
ORDER MULTIPLE	Enter the factor used in calculating how many of the item may be made or purchased in one run.
MINIMUM ORDER QUANTITY	Enter the lowest quantity that you can purchase from your vendor.
LEAD TIME	Enter the amount of time needed to make or buy the item.
TOLERANCE DAYS	Enter the amount of time you are willing to wait outside of the lead time for the item before fulfilling your customer's orders.

Table 12.1 Fields in the Planning Data Tab (Cont.)

MRP calculates your requirements by first determining the inventory levels for your parent items, followed by the inventory level for your child items. MRP looks at the in-stock number combined with the receipts from purchase orders, production orders, inventory transfers to the parent warehouse, A/P reserve invoices, and recurring transactions on the A/P side. The system then subtracts the demand as defined by forecasts, sales orders, production orders for child items on a BOM, A/R reserve invoices, blanket sales order agreements, recurring orders, inventory transfers from the parent warehouse, and negative inventory levels.

Based on this supply and demand, MRP then uses the information we set up on the item master data to make its recommendations regarding production orders, purchase orders, or even inventory transfers, if appropriate.

Now that the planning data has been established, let's examine the first MRP tool: forecasts.

12.2 Forecasts

A *forecast* is a way to predict future demand for your finished items. Since not all sales orders come in on a set schedule, which would allow for a constant production or purchase schedule, supply chain departments must rely on a forecasts to ensure on-time delivery to their customers. Forecasts are built on historical sales data, current sales data, and data about any future sales that the sales team might have.

In SAP Business One, you can enter a forecast manually or automatically. If you choose the automatic method, SAP Business One will build a forecast based on historical sales from sales orders or deliveries and A/R invoices. Multiple forecasts can be added as needed; however, in an MRP run, you may only choose one forecast.

To build a forecast, follow the menu path MRP • FORECAST. Click on the ADD NEW icon (the sheet with a yellow star) in your taskbar.

To begin compiling your forecast, enter the information listed in Table 12.2 into the FORECASTS screen shown in Figure 12.2.

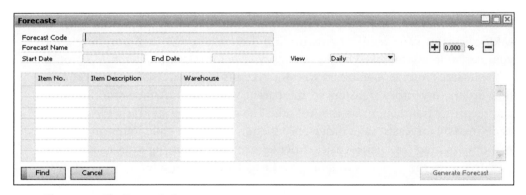

Figure 12.2 The Forecasts Screen

Field	Description/Use
FORECAST CODE	Enter a unique code for this forecast.
FORECAST NAME	Enter a description of your forecast. This description does not have to be unique.

Table 12.2 Fields in the Forecasts Screen

Field	Description/Use
START DATE	Enter a start date for your forecast horizon (in other words, the date you want to start planning on).
END DATE	Enter the end date for your forecast (in other words, how far in advance from your start date you will plan).
VIEW	You have three options for displaying your data: ► DAILY: If you choose this method, each day in the date range will have a column. ► WEEKLY: If you choose this method, SAP Business One will list the columns by the week number in the year. For example, January 1–7 is week 1, January 8–15 is week 2, etc. ► MONTHLY: If you choose this method, each month in the date range will have a column. The start and end dates will adjust automatically based on which view you choose. If you enter values on weekend days and have deselected the checkbox to set weekends as workdays, then SAP Business One will schedule recommendations so that they fall on the last workday of the week. To adjust for holidays and weekends, go to ADMINISTRATION • SYSTEM INITIALIZATION • COMPANY SETTINGS, click on the ACCOUNTING DATA tab and then on golden arrow next to HOLIDAYS.
+ and − percent	When items have been added to your table, you can highlight a line or lines to change the quantities by a certain percent by using the + and − buttons.

Table 12.2 Fields in the Forecasts Screen (Cont.)

To add items manually to the forecast, enter the item number(s) and add a quantity in the FORECAST PERIOD columns. To delete items manually from your forecast, highlight the part number and right-click to bring up the context menu. Choose DELETE ROW.

Tips and Tricks: Forecast Columns

You don't have to add a value in every column of the forecast; you only need to enter data into the columns where you can foresee sales being made based on history, current sales, or future sales communicated to your department.

To automatically enter in a forecast, click the GENERATE FORECAST button in the far-right corner. The GENERATE FORECAST SETUP screen shown in Figure 12.3 will pop up; here you can define how the forecast will be generated.

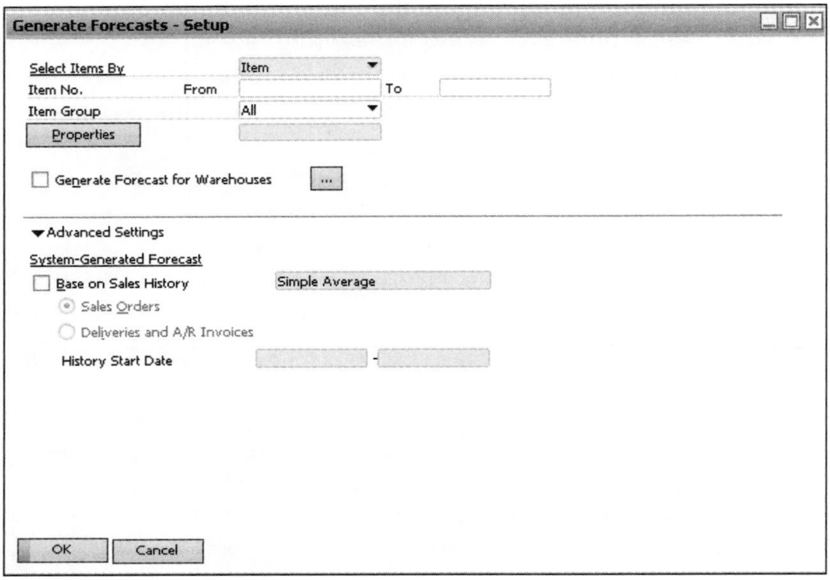

Figure 12.3 The Generate Forecast Setup Screen

First, choose one of these options from the SELECT ITEMS BY dropdown list:

▶ ITEM: You can either bring in items by item number, item group, or item property or some combination of all three.

▶ PREFERRED VENDOR: You can choose to add items by vendor code, vendor group, business partner property, or some combination of all three.

▶ DEFAULT WAREHOUSE: You can choose a FROM warehouse and a TO warehouse. If you only would like to choose one warehouse, enter the same number in the FROM and TO fields.

To choose specific warehouses for your forecast, check the GENERATE FORECAST FOR WAREHOUSE box or click the BROWSE icon (the ellipsis). The WAREHOUSE SELECTION screen shown in Figure 12.4 will list the available warehouses. If no warehouses are selected, then the default warehouse will be used for that item.

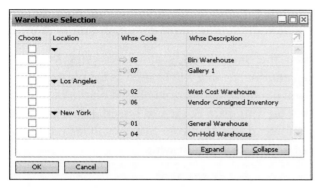

Figure 12.4 The Warehouse Selection Box When Automatically Creating a Forecast

Click OK to save your selection and return to the GENERATE FORECAST SETUP screen, where you can now enter the advanced settings shown in Figure 12.5.

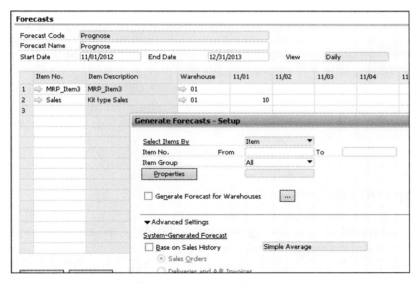

Figure 12.5 Advanced Settings in the Generate Forecast Setup Screen

Let's look first at the SYSTEM-GENERATED FORECAST section. Clicking the BASE ON SALES HISTORY checkbox gives you two options. The SIMPLE AVERAGE option uses total quantities of either sales orders or deliveries and invoices, which you will choose in the next step, per day, averaged out over the forecast horizon defined in the header. The MONTHLY AVERAGE option uses the total number of sales orders or deliveries and A/R invoices for a month, averaged out over the forecast horizon.

Next, you can choose between the SALES ORDERS and DELIVERIES AND A/R INVOICES radio buttons and then enter a date that will be used as the starting point of your history. The end date will populate automatically based on the range you chose in your start and end dates on your main FORECASTS screen. For example, if you only choose a three-month forecast window, your history will look at three-month increments regardless of what date you start with.

> **Tips and Tricks: History Dates**
>
> SAP Business One uses the following dates when figuring history dates:
>
> ▸ If you checked SALES ORDER, SAP Business One will look at the proposed delivery date listed in the header.
>
> ▸ If you checked DELIVERIES AND A/R INVOICES, SAP Business One will look at the actual delivery date in the header.

After you have entered all your data into the setup screen, click OK to return to the FORECASTS screen, where you'll see the data that was generated by SAP Business One. If any data needs to be adjusted, you can use the + and – buttons to adjust by a certain percentage, or you can manually adjust the numbers in the table. Click ADD to finish your forecast—which you can now use in the MRP Wizard.

12.3   MRP Wizard

The MRP Wizard is a set of parameters you define to run MRP recommendations. You can define several different scenarios, but you may only use one of those scenarios at a time. Let's walk through how to use the MRP Wizard.

Navigate to the MRP Wizard by going to MRP • MRP WIZARD. As shown in Figure 12.6, the wizard will open to the first screen, which describes the MRP Wizard; click NEXT to begin your scenarios.

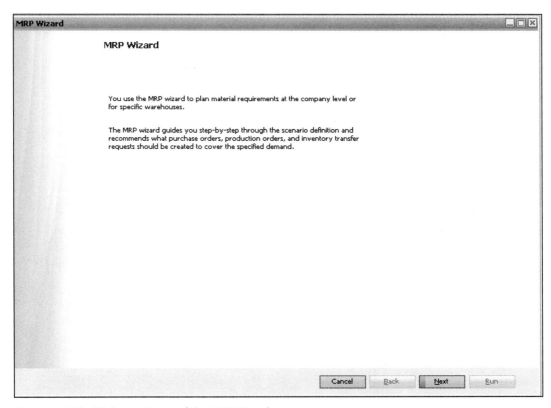

Figure 12.6 The Welcome Screen of the MRP Wizard

1. In the first step of the MRP Wizard, choose whether you want to run a predefined scenario or create a new scenario using the corresponding radio buttons. If you choose a predefined scenario, you will be presented with a list of defined scenarios. You will only need to change your start and end date dates and click RUN to see your MRP recommendations.

   To define a new scenario, click on the CREATE A NEW SCENARIO radio button; the screen will prompt you to enter a unique scenario name and corresponding description, as shown in Figure 12.7. After entering the information, click NEXT to proceed to Step 2.

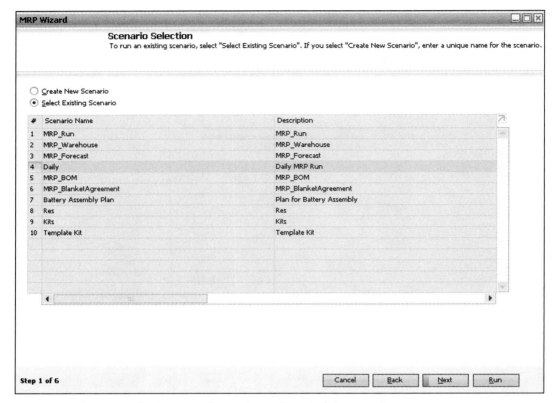

Figure 12.7 The Scenario Selection Screen (Step 1 of the Wizard)

Tips and Tricks: Scenario Description

The description you enter in to the MRP Wizard does not have to be unique. In fact, the name can be the same as the scenario name you gave in the previous field, as in our example.

2. The second step of the MRP Wizard is dedicated to scenario details. In the SCENARIO DETAILS screen shown in Figure 12.8, you will define your *planning horizon*, which is defined as the amount of time your organization will look into the future (forecast) for planning purposes.

Fill out the SCENARIO DETAILS page with the data listed in Table 12.3.

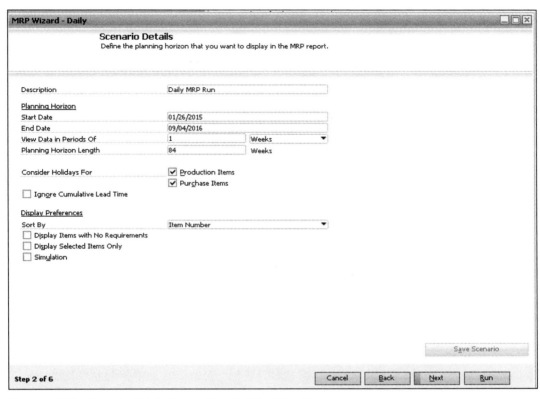

Figure 12.8 The Scenario Details Screen (Step 2 of the Wizard)

Field	Description/Use
START DATE	Enter the start of your planning period for your MRP recommendations. This date must be equal to the current date or a prior date but cannot be in the future. MRP will look at all receipts and requirements that have a due date that is equal to or greater than your start date.
END DATE	Enter the end date, which is the last day of the period for which you want MRP recommendations. This date must be in the future. MRP will look at all receipts and requirements that have a due date prior to your end date.

Table 12.3 Fields in the Scenario Details Screen

Field	Description/Use
VIEW DATA IN PERIODS OF	Choose one of the following options from this dropdown list: ▶ DAYS: Select this option to set your start date to the actual date you enter. The screen will then show you every day of the week including weekends. ▶ WEEKS: Select this option to set your start date to the first day of the week and set your end date to the last day of the business week as defined in your company settings. ▶ MONTHS: Select this option to set your start date to the first day of the month that falls on a business day and set your end date to the last day of the month that falls on a business day. If you enter dates as start and end dates that fall mid-week or mid-month, the VIEW DATA IN PERIODS OF field will automatically change your dates to accommodate your selection.
PLANNING HORIZON LENGTH	This field is automatically calculated for you based on your previous selections and displays the length of time you are looking to plan your items. If you manually change your planning horizon, SAP Business One will also adjust your end date to match the number of days entered.
CONSIDER HOLIDAYS FOR	Use the PRODUCTION ITEMS and PURCHASE ITEMS checkboxes to plan for items on weekends and holidays if checked. Leave these checkboxes unchecked to exclude holidays from your planning horizon.
IGNORE CUMULATIVE LEAD TIME	Select this checkbox to make the MRP calculation only look at the lead time on the parent item as listed in the item master data. This option relates only to items on a BOM.
SORT BY	Select the order in which the items you've selected are listed in the recommendation: ▶ ASSEMBLY SEQUENCE (from the highest level on a BOM to the lowest) ▶ ITEM NUMBER ▶ ITEM GROUP ▶ ITEM DESCRIPTION
DISPLAY ITEM WITH NO REQUIREMENTS	Select this checkbox to display items with that do not currently need to be planned because of current level of in-stock inventory.

Table 12.3 Fields in the Scenario Details Screen (Cont.)

Field	Description/Use
DISPLAY SELECTED ITEMS ONLY	Select this checkbox so that you can determine which items to display; you'll select the desired items themselves in the next few steps.
SIMULATION	Select this checkbox to create a test simulation.

Table 12.3 Fields in the Scenario Details Screen (Cont.)

Once all the data has been entered, you can save your scenario to use in later MRP runs, click NEXT to move on to the next step and further refine your MRP scenario or click RUN to run the scenario. If you choose to run your scenario, the system will use all items in your item master data marked as "MRP" to make recommendations.

Let's proceed with our example and click NEXT to define more data. The next screen is the ITEM SELECTION screen shown in Figure 12.9.

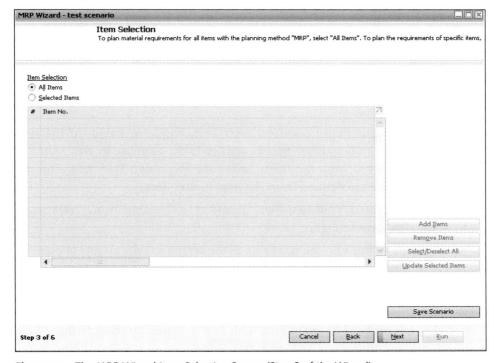

Figure 12.9 The MRP Wizard Item Selection Screen (Step 3 of the Wizard)

3. By default, when you enter the ITEM SELECTION screen of the MRP Wizard, the radio button for ALL ITEMS will be already checked. If you want to plan for all items, you can save your scenario and then click NEXT to define your scenario further or click RUN your scenario.

However, if you only want to plan *certain* items, then select the radio button for SELECTED ITEMS; this action activates the buttons on the lower right side of the screen: ADD ITEMS, REMOVE ITEMS, SELECT/DESELECT ALL, and UPDATE SELECTED ITEMS. To add items to your table for planning, click the ADD ITEMS button; a selection criteria screen like the one shown in Figure 12.10 will open.

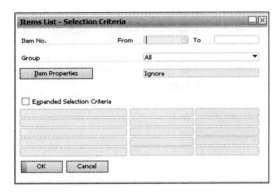

Figure 12.10 The Items List Selection Criteria Screen

4. Next, choose your items based on their item numbers, based on the item group, or based on item properties as defined in the item master data. Another option is to choose from the fields below the EXPANDED SELECTION CRITERIA checkbox, which are defined from the item master data.

Click OK to proceed. Your items will be added to the table on the ITEM SELECTION screen shown in Figure 12.11.

5. Next, use the buttons on the right side of the screen to select items to plan for. You have three options:

▶ REMOVE ITEMS: Click this button to remove all items from your table.

▶ SELECT/DESELECT ALL: Click this button to change all items at once. Alternatively, uncheck the boxes in each item row to manually select items.

▶ UPDATE SELECTED ITEMS: Click this button to update your items based on selection criteria, which we'll further define next.

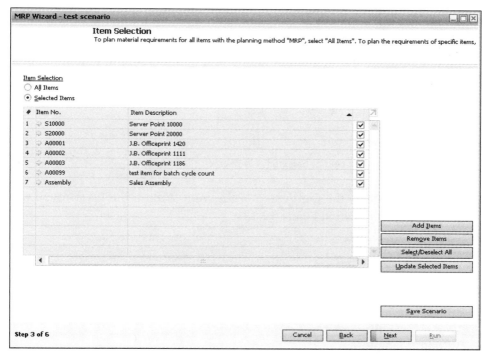

Figure 12.11 Items Selected Based on Criteria

If you click on the UPDATED SELECTED ITEMS button, the system will open a new criteria screen in which you can further refine your scenario. By default, the screen will open with the UPDATE WITH SPECIFIC VALUES radio button checked (see Figure 12.12). You can then check the boxes next to the items you want to update: MRP PROCUREMENT METHOD, MRP COMPONENT METHOD, MRP ORDER INTERVAL, MRP ORDER MULTIPLE, MRP MINIMUM ORDER QUANTITY, MRP LEAD TIME, and MRP TOLERANCE DAYS. The values in the dropdown lists are the same values we set up in the item master data. As a result, you can update a large group of items with new values for this MRP run.

If you want to set them all to their values from the item master data, then select the radio button for UPDATE VALUES FROM ITEM MASTER DATA. When you click OK to update, you'll be returned to the ITEM SELECTION screen where you can save your scenario. Click NEXT to continue to refine your search or click RUN to run your scenario.

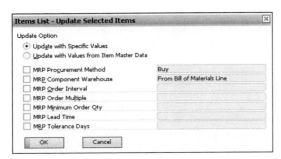

Figure 12.12 The Items List Update Selected Items Screen

Click NEXT to go to the fourth step of the MRP Wizard: the INVENTORY DATA SOURCE screen shown in Figure 12.13.

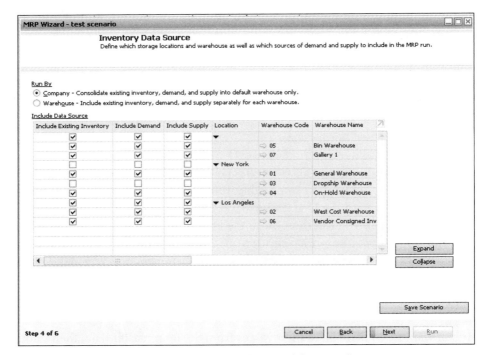

Figure 12.13 The Inventory Data Source Screen (Step 4 of the Wizard)

6. The INVENTORY DATA SOURCE screen identifies which storage locations or warehouses you'll use in your MRP run. In the RUN BY section at the top of Figure 12.13, you can select from two options:

► COMPANY: The system will sum up the on-hand inventory, demand, and supply for all warehouses and then create a recommendation for the default warehouse. When using this option, you cannot include inventory transfer requests as a document type.

► WAREHOUSE: The system will sum up the on-hand inventory, demand, and supply for all warehouses, but then it will make recommendations separately for each warehouse. Because this option gives you a recommendations by warehouse, SAP Business One will tell you to make an inventory transfer if available inventory exists in another warehouse.

In the screen shown in Figure 12.14, you can check or uncheck the data as needed for your calculation by warehouse. You can choose to include or exclude data for existing inventory, demand, and supply.

Once you have selected your data, click the SAVE SCENARIO button to save your scenario. Click NEXT to advance to another step to further refine your search or click RUN to run your scenario. For our scenario, let's choose NEXT to further specify the documents' data source.

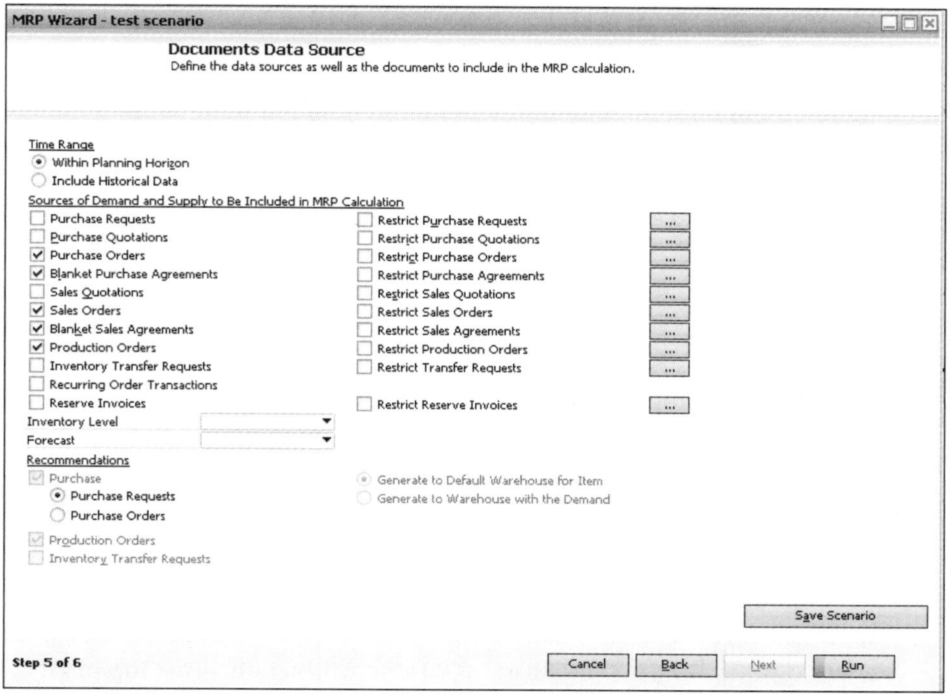

Figure 12.14 The Documents Data Source Screen (Step 5 of the Wizard)

This Documents Data Source screen has abundant options. In the first section, you will choose your time range from the following two options:

▶ Within the Planning Horizon: This option will show data based on the planning horizon as defined in Step 2. If your start date is prior to the current date, a new column for past due data will be added to the recommendation with a sum of all data prior to the current date.

▶ Include the Historical Data: This option will consider all supply and demand before your start date. A new column for historical data will be created in your recommendation table.

The next section of the Documents Data Source screen is called Sources of Demand and Supply to be Included in MRP Calculation. Here you can decide which sources of demand and supply to include into your MRP calculation, among these options:

▶ Purchase Orders: Purchase orders used for MRP calculation must be open documents. If you need to narrow your search to only a few purchase orders, click on the Browse icon (the ellipsis) to restrict the purchase orders option.

▶ Blanket Purchase Agreements: These documents must be of type *Specific* and *Unapproved* and must be open. If you need to narrow down your criteria, click on the Browse icon (the ellipsis) to restrict the Blanket Purchase Agreements option.

▶ Sales Orders: The sales orders used for MRP calculation must be open documents. If you need to narrow down your search to only a few sales orders, click on the Browse icon (the ellipsis) to restrict the sales orders option.

▶ Blanket Sales Agreements: These documents must be of type *Specific* and *Unapproved* and document must be open. If you need to narrow down your criteria, click on the Browse icon (the ellipsis) for the restrict the blanket sales agreements option.

▶ Production Orders: Production orders must be in "released" or "planned" status only. If you need to narrow down your criteria, click on the Browse icon (the ellipsis) to the restrict production order option. Parent items are considered supply, and child items are considered demand; the reverse is true if you are doing a disassembly.

▶ Reserve Invoices: The document must be open. If you need to narrow down your criteria, click on the Browse icon (the ellipsis) for the restrict reserve invoices option. A/R invoices are considered demand, and A/P invoices are considered supply.

▸ INVENTORY TRANSFER REQUESTS: The document must be open. If you need to narrow down your criteria, click on the BROWSE icon (the ellipsis) for the restrict transfer request option. The warehouse specified in the FROM field is considered demand, and the warehouse specified in the TO field is considered supply.

▸ RECURRING ORDER TRANSACTIONS: The document must be open with a next executable date, an item quantity, and a warehouse listed on each item level.

Underneath these options, you'll find two dropdown lists:

▸ INVENTORY LEVEL: Choose from one of the following: REQUIRED, MINIMUM, MAXIMUM, or MINIMUM-MAXIMUM as defined in the item master data.

▸ FORECAST: Choose one of the forecasts you created. If you only have one warehouse listed in Step 4 of the MRP Wizard, the demand of the forecast is listed on that warehouse. If you have multiple warehouses listed and one is the default for that item, then the system will place the demand on the default warehouse. If multiple warehouses are listed and none is the default, then the system will place the demand at the first warehouse listed.

The last section of the screen is RECOMMENDATIONS, where you'll choose the output method for the recommendation when the procurement method is set to BUY. You can either choose PURCHASING REQUEST or PURCHASE ORDER, depending on your business practices.

The PRODUCTION ORDER checkbox is always checked by default because MRP will always recommend production orders if required. If you want SAP Business One to suggest inventory transfers instead of purchase orders, choose the INVENTORY TRANSFER REQUESTS checkbox. This box will only be available when you chose to run MRP by warehouse in Step 4 of the wizard.

If you are running MRP by warehouse, choose one of the following options: GENERATE TO DEFAULT WAREHOUSE FOR ITEM or GENERATE TO WAREHOUSE WITH THE DEMAND. If you're running MRP by company, the recommendation is automatically configured to the default warehouse.

Save the scenario by clicking the SAVE SCENARIO button and then click the RUN button to execute your wizard. Step 6 will present you with the results screen, as shown in Figure 12.15.

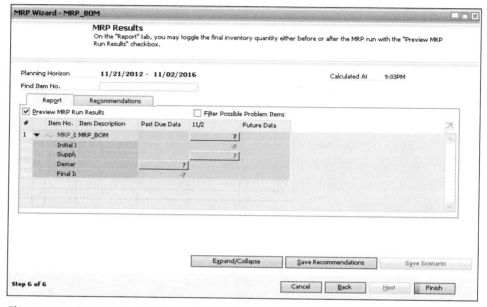

Figure 12.15 The MRP Results Screen (Step 6 of the Wizard)

In the MRP RESULTS screen, the REPORTS tab shows the schedule for the MRP demand, while the RECOMMENDATIONS tab shows you what SAP recommends you purchase or make to supply the demand.

To create documents, you must save these recommendations; then you can proceed to the order recommendations in the next section to create your documents.

12.4 Order Recommendations

Once you have saved your recommendations in the MRP Wizard in Step 6, you can now use order recommendations to follow up on any recommendations as needed and then add the document to the system.

To use order recommendations, go to MRP • ORDER RECOMMENDATIONS. The ORDER RECOMMENDATIONS SELECTION CRITERIA window shown in Figure 12.16 will open. Based on the order type chosen from the ORDER TYPE dropdown list, your screen will include or omit the VENDORS section at the bottom of Figure 12.16.

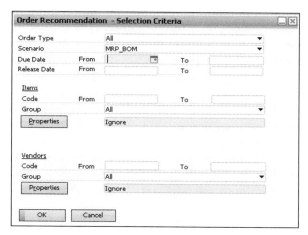

Figure 12.16 The Order Recommendation Selection Criteria Screen

Input data into the fields shown in Table 12.4.

Field	Description/Use
ORDER TYPE	From this dropdown list, select the type of document you want to create that was recommended to you. Choose from the following options: ► ALL ► PRODUCTION ORDERS ► PURCHASE ORDERS ► INVENTORY TRANSFER REQUESTS ► PURCHASE QUOTATIONS ► PURCHASE REQUESTS
SCENARIO	To use a previously saved scenario created in the MRP Wizard, choose the appropriate scenario from the dropdown list.
DUE DATE	Insert data into the DUE DATE fields if you want to see only certain documents within a certain due date range.
RELEASE DATE	Enter the date the order is to be released or to make or buy the item ahead of the due date.
ITEMS: CODE	Enter criteria to filter by item number.
ITEMS: GROUP	Enter criteria to filter by item group.

Table 12.4 Fields in the Order Recommendation Selection Criteria Screen

Field	Description/Use
ITEMS: PROPERTIES	Enter criteria to filter based on item properties.
VENDORS: CODE	Enter criteria to filter by vendor number.
VENDORS: GROUP	Enter criteria to filter by vendor group.
VENDORS: PROPERTIES	Enter criteria to filter by business partner properties.

Table 12.4 Fields in the Order Recommendation Selection Criteria Screen (Cont.)

> **Tips and Tricks: Vendor Information**
>
> Vendor information can only be filtered if you choose ALL or a PURCHASING DOCUMENT as the ORDER TYPE field.

Once you have your criteria chosen in the table, click OK to generate the ORDER RECOMMENDATION window shown in Figure 12.17. Now, you can change any data that needs to amended. If your data is accurate, choose the checkbox next the documents you would like to create and click UPDATE. To select all, double-click on the header titled CREATE; to deselect all selected items, double-click the header again.

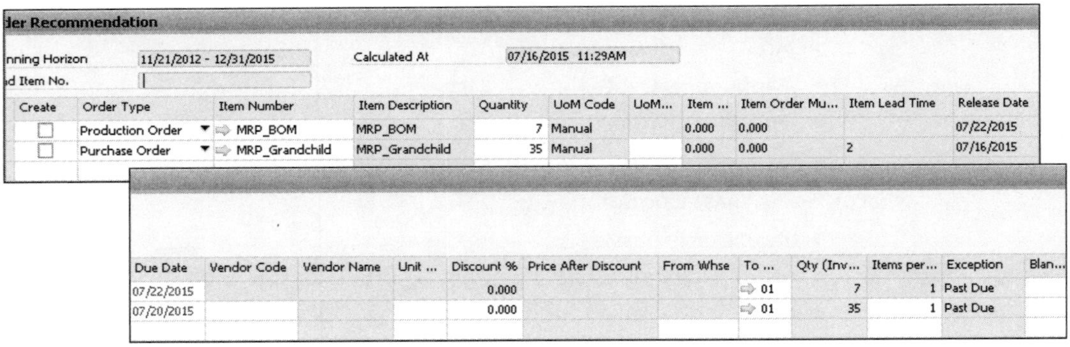

Figure 12.17 The Order Recommendation Screen

> **Tips and Tricks: Consolidating Vendor Documents**
>
> If you have multiple purchasing documents with the same preferred vendor and you have checked the boxes for all the documents at once, the system will create one document.

The SAP Business One Service module is a powerful but easy-to-use tool that can be used to track calls and provide the best possible service to customers and vendors.

13   Service

Organizations that sell goods and services, offer contracts or support agreements to customers, receive calls from customers or vendors requesting action within the company (like quotes or complaints) can all benefit from the Service module in SAP Business One.

The Service module can help you monitor pending calls, track overdue tasks, and measure workloads by groups of technicians, which will help you improve the customer service. Once a call has been entered into SAP Business One, all expenses, activities, and related documents can be registered against the call—creating a single source of data for all employees within the organization. This feature reduces the need for emails and phone calls and increases the productivity significantly.

In this chapter, we'll teach you how to handle service calls, equipment cards, service contracts, and more with SAP Business One. We'll close the chapter by outlining some common reports you'll use in providing customer service.

13.1   Service Calls

A *service call* can be initiated by a customer or a vendor through a phone call, an email, a web portal, or any other way of communication. The SERVICE CALL screen shown in Figure 13.1 has a header and few tabs to keep track of activities, solutions, resources, expenses, documents, and so on, as we'll explain in this section.

Once a call is received, you can check for open or previous calls from the customer or vendor, as the call could be related to a previous one.

Let's look at the top half of the screen shown in Figure 13.1. This header displays the contact information for the customer or vendor and an optional business partner reference number. If the call is about a specific machine or equipment previously sold to the customer, enter the item code and serial number the service call applies to in the ITEM and SERIAL NUMBER fields. If the item/serial number is covered by a service contract, the CONTRACT NO. field on the right side will be populated automatically.

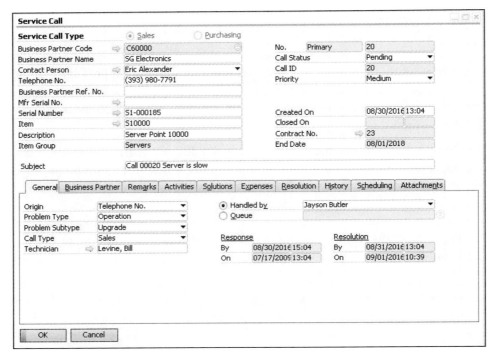

Figure 13.1 The Service Call Screen

Tips and Tricks: Start with the Serial Number

If you know the serial number, enter that information into the SERIAL NUMBER field first; information about the customer that owns the item will be populated automatically, along with the number of the contract that covers the equipment.

On the right side of the screen, the CALL ID and PRIORITY fields will be set by default. The status and the creation date and time will be populated automatically, but these details can be changed by users with proper authorization, which you can set up by following the menu path ADMINISTRATION • SYSTEM INITIALIZATION • AUTHORIZATIONS • GENERAL • SERVICE.

Most of the fields in the SERVICE CALL screen are straightforward, but we want to draw your attention to a few in particular, which we'll describe in Table 13.1.

Field	Description/Use
SERVICE CALL TYPE	Choose from between the SALES and PURCHASING radio buttons.
BUSINESS PARTNER CODE AND NAME	Enter the code and name of the customer or vendor.
MFR SERIAL NO. and SERIAL NUMBER	Enter the manufacturer and internal serial number of the item the service call refers to.
ITEM, DESCRIPTION, and ITEM GROUP	Enter the item number; the description and item group will be populated automatically.
SUBJECT	Enter a brief description of the service call, which will display on reports.
NO.	This field will display the number of the service call, automatically assigned by the system.
CALL STATUS	Choose a status for the call. The default statuses are OPEN, PENDING, or CLOSED, but new statuses can be defined by clicking on the DEFINE NEW option.
PRIORITY	Choose a priority for the call: LOW, MEDIUM, or HIGH. You cannot modify these values.
CREATED ON	This field displays the date of creation.
CLOSED ON	This field displays the date of closing, which is updated automatically.
CONTRACT NO.	This field displays the contract number, if the item/serial number is covered by a support contract.
END DATE	This field displays the end date of the contract.

Table 13.1 General Fields in the Service Call Screen

The bottom half of Figure 13.1 shows the GENERAL tab, which is where you can classify the service call using the ORIGIN, PROBLEM TYPE, PROBLEM SUBTYPE, and CALL TYPE fields for reporting purposes. All these classifications can be defined as needed by opening a list and adding a new entry or from the ADMINISTRATION • SETUP menu.

The fifth field in the GENERAL tab is the TECHNICIAN field, from which you can select a technician from the list of employees that are flagged as technicians. Two radio buttons are on the right side: Choose the HANDLED BY radio button to assign the service call to one individual or choose the QUEUE radio button if there are multiple people who can take care of the service call request. For example, the company in Figure 13.2, which sells computers, could define one queue for miscellaneous equiment, another for personal computers, and another for printers. The queues and their members, which monitor the workload and track pending calls for each category of merchandise, are maintained by following the menu path ADMINISTRATION • SETUP • SERVICE • QUEUES.

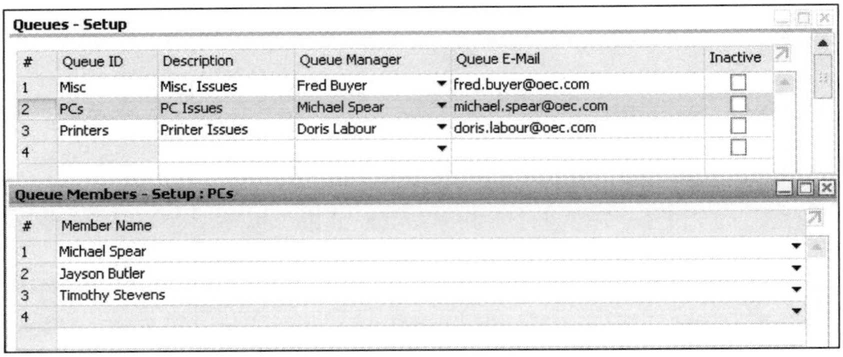

Figure 13.2 Setting Up Service Call Queues

Back in the GENERAL tab shown in Figure 13.1, the system updates the RESPONSE fields when the first action is taken and updates the RESOLUTION fields when information is entered into the RESOLUTION tab.

Let's look at a few more visible tabs in the SERVICE CALL screen. The BUSINESS PARTNER tab includes more details of the customer, like addresses and contact details. The REMARKS tab is a free text field where additional information can be typed in. On the ACTIVITIES tab shown in Figure 13.3, you can register any SAP Business One activity linked to the service call, like tasks, phone calls, notes, and so on. In this example, an activity was assigned to the sales rep Jim Boswick to order and invoice a part needed to resolve a service call.

Tab over to the SOLUTIONS tab. The Service module in SAP Business One maintains a knowledge-based database called the Solutions Knowledge Base that can be used to find solutions to problems based on previous experience and the symptoms of the issue. Any solution selected and applied is linked on this tab on the service call (see Figure 13.4). We'll go into more detail about the Solutions Knowledge Base in Section 13.4.

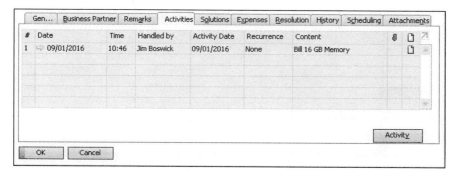

Figure 13.3 An Activity Linked to a Service Call

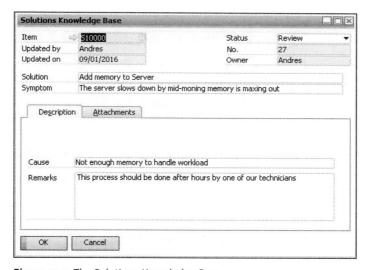

Figure 13.4 The Solutions Knowledge Base

After the SOLUTIONS tab comes the EXPENSES tab shown in Figure 13.5. In this tab, you can register any invoice that has billable expenses, or you can register the time spent working on a call. If you bill the customer for labor but that labor is covered by the service contract, then a warning will be displayed asking for confirmation.

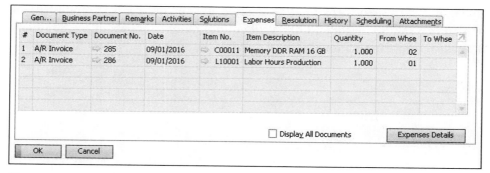

Figure 13.5 Parts and Labor Billed to Customer, Linked to a Service Call

Click on the EXPENSES DETAILS button to open the SERVICE CALL EXPENSES screen shown in Figure 13.6, where you can record billable invoices, vendor invoices, and time spent. The expenses will be split based on the type of items being invoiced: either ITEMS (at the top) or LABOR AND TRAVEL (at the bottom).

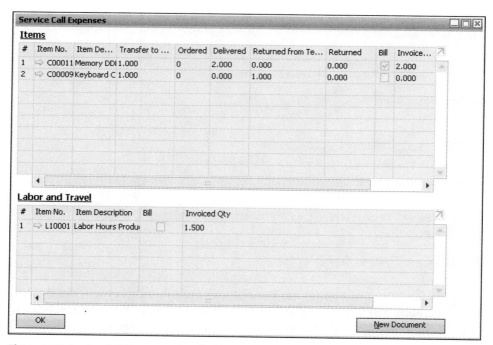

Figure 13.6 Service Call Expenses Classified by Item Type

Click on the NEW DOCUMENT button in the bottom right of the screen to access the DOCUMENT TYPE screen shown in Figure 13.7. In this screen, you can register a transaction and link it to the service call. On the DOCUMENT TYPE dropdown list, select ALL DOCUMENTS, A/R DOCUMENTS, or A/P DOCUMENTS to get the list of available transactions. Please note that, if you select A/R DOCUMENTS, then the A/P documents will be grayed out.

If you select TRANSFERRED TO TECHNICIAN, the expense will be listed on the service call expenses, or the item quantity will be listed on the DELIVERED column, but will not be flagged as "Billable." If you select RETURNED FROM TECHNICIAN, the item quantity will show on the RETURN FROM TECHNICIAN column.

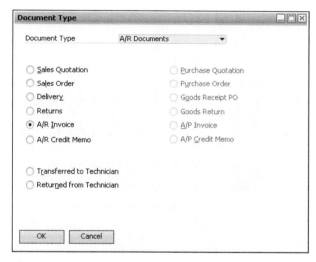

Figure 13.7 Service Call Document Types

Technicians can register any comments about how the service call was resolved in the RESOLUTION tab. Once something is entered and updated on this tab, the resolution dates will be updated by the system on the GENERAL tab.

On the HISTORY tab shown in Figure 13.8, the system displays any previous transactions for the equipment linked on the service call. This tab shows the time and date of service call, the user, the description, and the previous and new values of the relevant fields. You can expand or collapse these entries using the COLLAPSE ALL and EXPAND ALL buttons on the bottom right of the screen.

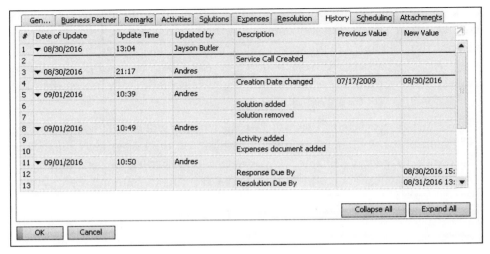

Figure 13.8 Service Call History

The SCHEDULING tab shown in Figure 13.9 displays the information of the technician or queue the service call was assigned to. You can input the start and end times, the duration of the appointment, the meeting location, and any relevant address details.

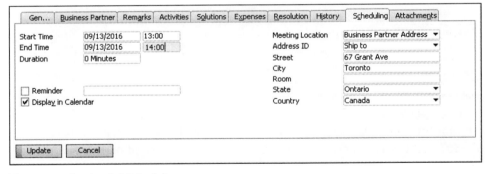

Figure 13.9 Service Call Scheduling

Finally, as in most of the master records and transactions of SAP Business One, you can easily link any document relevant to the service call in the ATTACHMENTS tab (see Figure 13.10) or by clicking on the BROWSE button (the ellipsis) and selecting the document. For each attachment, the system will show the path, the name of the file, and the date the file was included as an attachment.

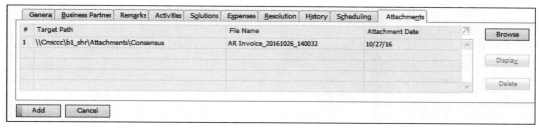

Figure 13.10 Service Call Attachments

13.2 Equipment Cards

The EQUIPMENT CARD screen displays all data associated with specific equipment that has been purchased, sold, or loaned by the company, including sales and purchasing transactions, service contracts or agreements that cover the equipment, and any service calls for the equipment. You can create the equipment card manually if you prefer; alternatively, you can configure the system to create the equipment card automatically for every piece of equipment delivered by the company. Configure equipment cards by following the menu path ADMINISTRATION • GENERAL SETTING • INVENTORY • ITEMS; note the activated AUTO. CREATE CUSTOMER EQUIPMENT CARD checkbox in Figure 13.11.

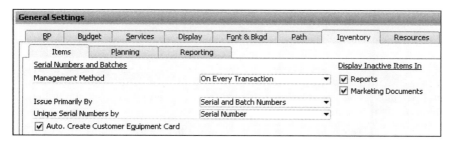

Figure 13.11 Selecting the Auto. Create Customer Equipment Card Checkbox

Let's look at the EQUIPMENT CARD screen itself, which contains all the static information of the unit plus some additional tabs with information relevant to the equipment, as shown in Figure 13.12.

Let's dive into the equipment card by exploring its key fields more closely in Table 13.2.

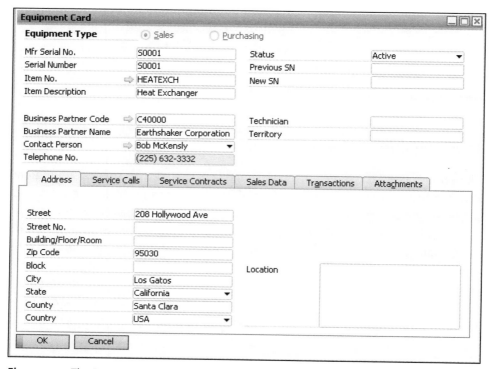

Figure 13.12 The Equipment Card Screen

Field	Description/Use
MFR SERIAL NO. and SERIAL NUMBER	This field displays the manufacturing and internal serial numbers, respectively.
ITEM NO.	This field displays the item code. Click on the golden arrow to drill down into the item master data.
ITEM DESCRIPTION	This field displays the item description.
BUSINESS PARTNER CODE AND NAME	This field displays the customer code. Click on the golden arrow to drill down into detailed information about the business partner.

Table 13.2 Fields in the Equipment Card Screen

Field	Description/Use
CONTACT PERSON	This field displays the contact name.
STATUS	In this dropdown list shown at the top right corner of Figure 13.12, choose from among the following options: ▶ ACTIVE ▶ RETURNED ▶ TERMINATED ▶ LOANED ▶ IN REPAIR LAB
PREVIOUS SN	This field displays the previous serial number if the item serial number has changed.
NEW SN	This field displays the new serial number if the item serial number has changed.
TECHNICIAN	This field displays the technician assigned to the equipment.
TERRITORY	This field displays the territory where the unit is installed.

Table 13.2 Fields in the Equipment Card Screen (Cont.)

Tips and Tricks: Deleting an Equipment Card

The equipment card can be deleted manually *unless* it is currently referenced in sales transaction, a service contract, or a service call.

The equipment card shown in Figure 13.12 is divided into six tabs. The ADDRESS tab shows the address where the equipment is physically located.

Next, the SERVICE CALLS tab shown in Figure 13.13 displays information about any service calls, historic or current, that have been placed for this equipment, including the creation date and the statuses of those calls. In the event that a call is received, you can check any previous incidents related to this unit by clicking the VIEW RELATED SERVICE CALLS option visible from the YOU CAN ALSO menu in the bottom right. From the YOU CAN ALSO menu, you can start a new service call as well.

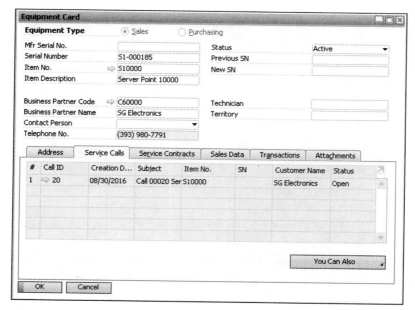

Figure 13.13 Service Calls Placed for This Equipment

The SERVICE CONTRACTS tab shown in Figure 13.14 shows all contracts associated with the equipment, either current or historic, including dates and the service type of the contract. Equipment service contracts are discussed in more detail in Section 13.3.

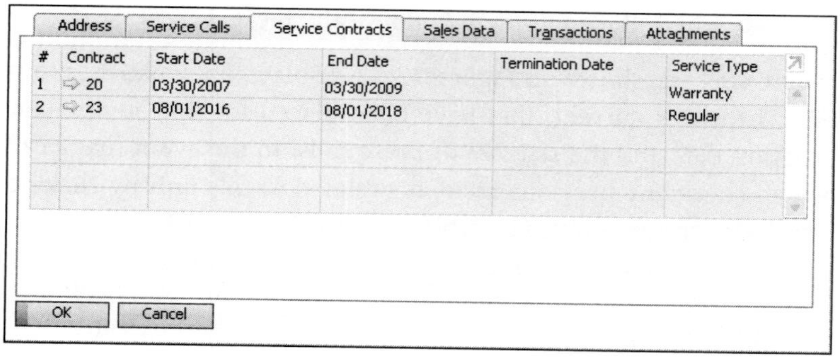

#	Contract	Start Date	End Date	Termination Date	Service Type
1	⇨ 20	03/30/2007	03/30/2009		Warranty
2	⇨ 23	08/01/2016	08/01/2018		Regular

(Tabs: Address | Service Calls | Service Contracts | Sales Data | Transactions | Attachments)

OK   Cancel

Figure 13.14 Equipment Service Contracts

The SALES DATA tab shown in Figure 13.15 displays the buyer's name and code and the delivery and invoice numbers of the equipment.

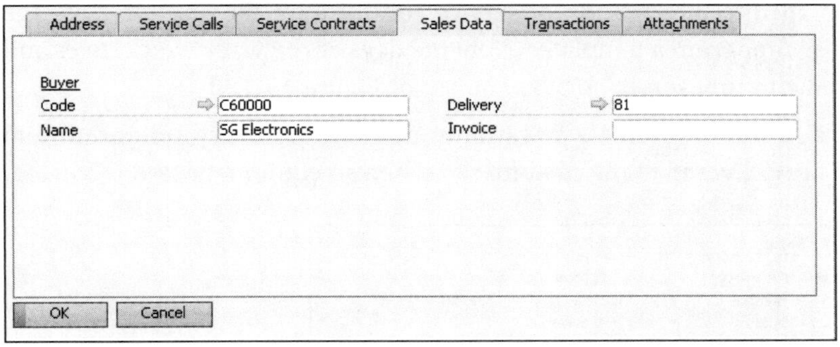

Figure 13.15 Equipment Card Sales Data

In the TRANSACTION tab, you'll find all the transactions where the equipment was included. In our example in Figure 13.16, the equipment was received with the Goods Receipt (PD) 78 from Vendor Lasercom on March 6 and was shipped to customer SG Electronics with Delivery (DN) 81 on March 30.

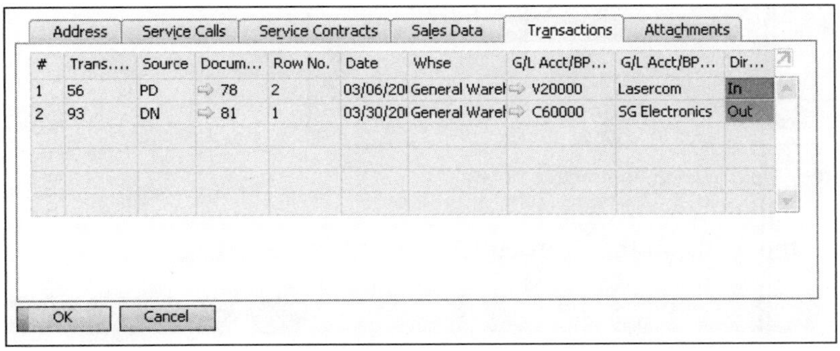

Figure 13.16 Equipment Card Transactions

13.3   Service Contracts

The *service contract* is used to define the coverage offered for a single unit or a group of units by either customer or item group. This contract also stipulates the service level and expected response time agreed upon for this customer or item group.

You can either create a service contract manually or use a service contract template previously defined on the ADMINISTRATION • SETUP • SERVICE • CONTRACT TEMPLATES. Contract templates have two main purposes:

▶ Templates expedite the creation of service contracts by copying the coverage and response time from a template. (Note the days of the week checkboxes and the start and end times in the COVERAGE tab of Figure 13.17.)

▶ Templates automatically create a warranty contract for every serialized item once items are delivered to the customer or when an equipment card is created.

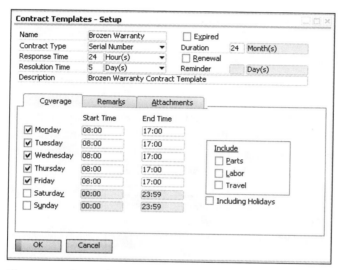

Figure 13.17 Setting Up a Service Contract Template

Table 13.3 lists the fields on the CONTRACT TEMPLATE SETUP screen.

Field	Description/Use
NAME	Enter the name of the contract or a short description.
CONTRACT TYPE	Define the type of template you want to use by choosing one of the following options from the dropdown list: ▶ CUSTOMER: Defines a service contract that applies to all items sold to a customer, regardless of the item group or serial numbers ▶ ITEM GROUP: Defines the coverage for all items in one item group for a customer ▶ SERIAL NUMBERS: Defines the coverage for specific units

Table 13.3 Fields in the Contract Templates Setup Screen

Field	Description/Use
RESPONSE TIME	Enter the expected response time for a call placed for equipment covered by this type of contract. In this example, some type of response should be given in the next 24 hours.
RESOLUTION TIME	Enter the period of time for resolving a service call. In our example, a resolution should be provided within 5 days. If this time is not met, the call will be considered overdue and will show up on monitoring reports and alerts.
DESCRIPTION	Enter a long description for the contract template.
EXPIRED	Select this checkmark if you want the contract template to be inactive. Templates cannot be deleted if any contracts are linked to them. However, by checking this box, you prevent this template from being used to create new contracts.
DURATION	Enter a default duration for the contract before it has to be renewed by the customer.
RENEWAL	If you select this checkbox, new fields related to the reminder will be enabled. Use this functionality to notify the customer that the contract will be expiring soon and will need to be renewed.
REMINDER	Enter the number of days, weeks, or months ahead of contract expiration to send a reminder to the customer to renew the contract.
COVERAGE	For every day of the week that you select with the checkboxes on the left, enter the start and end times of the contract coverage. Four checkboxes can be used to define what else is INCLUDED as part of the contract: ▶ PARTS ▶ LABOR ▶ TRAVEL ▶ HOLIDAYS
REMARKS	Enter any additional notes for this template.
ATTACHMENTS	Attach any documents relevant to the contract template, like an agreement that needs to be signed or disclaimers, for example.

Table 13.3 Fields in the Contract Templates Setup Screen (Cont.)

You can create a service contract manually or use a contract template as a basis, but we recommend using contract templates to achieve some type of standardization across your contracts. After a new contract is generated from a template, that contract can be further modified to reflect the specific agreements made with the customer or vendor.

Figure 13.18 shows the GENERAL tab of the SERVICE CONTRACT screen.

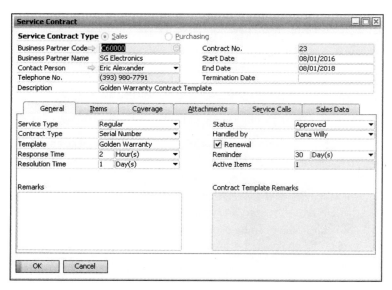

Figure 13.18 The General Tab of the Service Contract Screen with Contract Coverage

Table 13.4 lists the main fields of the service contract.

Field	Description/Use
SERVICE CONTRACT TYPE	Choose either CUSTOMER or PURCHASING. The ability to manage service contracts from vendors, not just for customers, makes this capability very useful.

Table 13.4 Fields in the General Tab of the Service Contract Screen

Field	Description/Use
BUSINESS PARTNER CODE, NAME, CONTACT, and TELEPHONE	These fields display the details for the customer or vendor related to this service contract.
CONTRACT NO.	This field displays a contract number automatically assigned by the system.
START DATE, END DATE, and TERMINATION DATE	Enter the range of dates during which the contract will be in effect as well as the termination date, if the contract was finalized.
DESCRIPTION	Enter a long description of the service contract.
SERVICE TYPE	Use this dropdown list to define if the contract is a REGULAR contract or a WARRANTY. If the service type is WARRANTY, before you can add an invoice or a charge for a service provided to an item covered by the agreement, the system will display a warning.
CONTRACT TYPE	Use this dropdown list to define the type of template. You can choose from the following options: ▶ CUSTOMER: This option defines a service contract that applies to all items sold to a customer, regardless of the item group or serial numbers. ▶ ITEM GROUP: This option defines the coverage for all items in one item group for a customer. ▶ SERIAL NUMBERS: This option defines the coverage for specific units.
TEMPLATE	Enter a template name to use when creating this service contract. In this example, SG Electronics has a contract based on a Golden Warranty template.
RESPONSE TIME	Specify the time frame during which the customer should get a response.
RESOLUTION TIME	Specify the time frame during which a resolution should be provided; otherwise, the service call will be overdue.
STATUS	Select a status for the contract among the following: ▶ APPROVED: The contract is in full standing. ▶ ON HOLD: No service is allowed under this contract. ▶ DRAFT: The contract needs approval to take effect. ▶ TERMINATED: The contract is not valid anymore.

Table 13.4 Fields in the General Tab of the Service Contract Screen (Cont.)

Field	Description/Use
HANDLED BY	Select the employee that will handle the contract from the dropdown list.
RENEWAL	If you select this checkbox, new fields related to the reminder will be enabled. Use this functionality to notify the customer that the contract will be expiring soon and will need to be renewed.
ACTIVE ITEMS	This field displays the number of different items covered by the contract. In our example, only one item is covered.
REMARKS	Enter additional remarks into this free text field.
CONTRACT TEMPLATE REMARKS	This field displays remarks from the template used to create this contract. If the remarks change on the template, this field will reflect those changes.

Table 13.4 Fields in the General Tab of the Service Contract Screen (Cont.)

The ITEMS tab on the SERVICE CONTRACT screen shown in Figure 13.19 displays all the items covered by the contract. Details include item numbers, item descriptions, and serial numbers as well as the start, end, and termination dates.

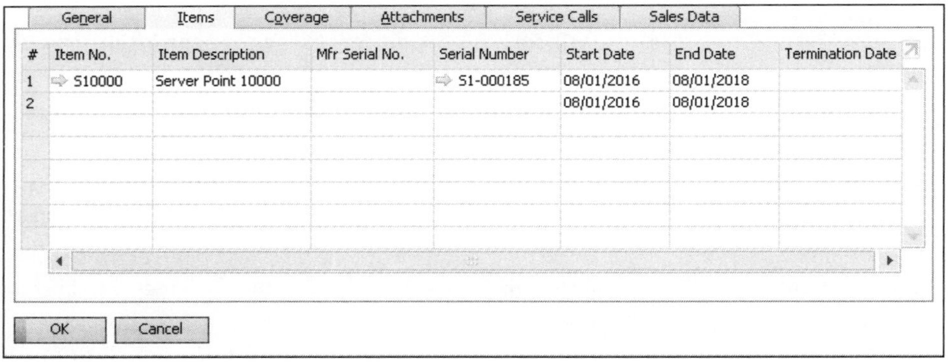

Figure 13.19 The Items Tab in the Service Contracts Screen

The COVERAGE tab shown in Figure 13.20 displays what type of service components and hours are included under this particular contract. In our example, all days of the week and holidays are included, and our contract covers PARTS, LABOR, and TRAVEL.

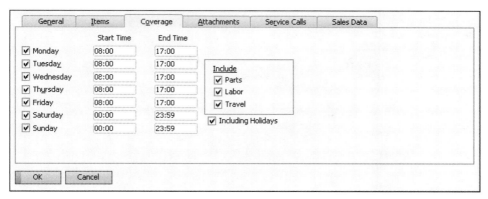

Figure 13.20 Service Contract Coverage Details

On the SERVICE CALLS tab shown in Figure 13.21, you'll find details about the service calls placed under this contract. Details include call IDs, creation dates, subjects, item numbers, customer names, and statuses.

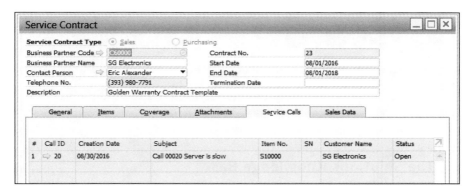

Figure 13.21 Service Contract Service Calls

The last tab is the SALES DATA tab, where the system keeps track of A/R invoices for service contract renewals. Notice in Figure 13.22 that the sales data is separated into the RECURRING TEMPLATES section on the left side and the RECURRING TRANSACTIONS section on the right side.

On the RECURRING TEMPLATES on the left, select the dropdown icon and the screen shown in Figure 13.23 will open to list the recurring templates.

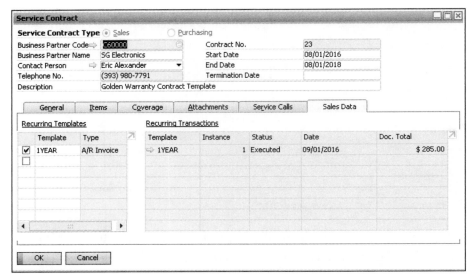

Figure 13.22 The Sales Data Tab of the Service Contract Screen

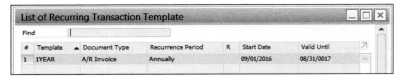

Figure 13.23 Recurring Templates for Renewing Service Contracts

13.4 The Solutions Knowledge Base

The Solutions Knowledge Base is a simple and yet powerful repository of common problems and their solutions that can be shared among the technicians in charge of service calls.

For a given item, the SOLUTIONS KNOWLEDGE BASE screen lists the item, the user who last updated the entry and the date of that update, the unique item number, and the owner who initially created the entry in the Solutions Knowledge Base. The STATUS dropdown list offers the following options: INTERNAL, PUBLISH, and REVIEW; you can also add new statuses using the DEFINE NEW option. Make sure you add as much information as would be helpful to the SOLUTION and SYMPTOM fields underneath these items. In our example, the technician is sharing knowledge about application settings for a particular printer.

The main DESCRIPTION tab gives plenty of room for you to add details about the cause of a problem or its solution as well as any remarks that would benefit the team of technicians. You can also attach documents related to the solution in the ATTACHMENTS tab. Recall from Section 13.1 that this solution can be linked to a service call; notice that the first line of the list of service calls in Figure 13.25 lists the solution shown in Figure 13.24.

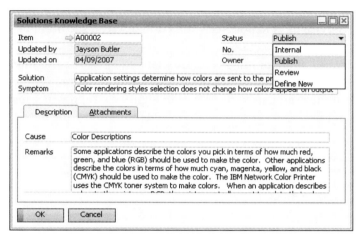

Figure 13.24 The Solutions Knowledge Base

#	Created on	Owner	Solution	Status	Item No.
1	04/09/2007	Jayson Butler	Application settings determine how colors are sent to the printer	Publish	IBM Infoprint 1222
2	04/09/2007	Jayson Butler	Check parallel cable	Publish	IBM Infoprint 1226
3	04/09/2007	Jayson Butler	Pull the page from the paper input tray until it is fully removed	Publish	IBM Infoprint 1226
4	04/09/2007	Jayson Butler	Clean Sensors	Publish	IBM Infoprint 1226
5	04/09/2007	Jayson Butler	Additional random access memory (RAM) is installed on the PostScript(R) / PCL 5C per	Publish	Memory Chip
6	04/09/2007	Jayson Butler	The printer language determines how memory is utilized	Publish	Memory Chip
7	04/09/2007	Jayson Butler	Some HP printer CD-ROMs include network installation software	Publish	HP 600 Series Inc
8	04/09/2007	Jayson Butler	Clean electrical contacts on print head	Publish	HP 600 Series Inc
9	04/09/2007	Jayson Butler	Replace color cartridge	Review	IBM Infoprint 1312
10	04/09/2007	Jayson Butler	Reconnect electric cable	Review	IBM Infoprint 1312
11	04/09/2007	Jayson Butler	Refill paper try	Review	IBM Infoprint 1222
12	04/09/2007	Jayson Butler	Clean printer cartridge	Review	IBM Infoprint 1222
13	04/09/2007	Jayson Butler	Restart printer and printer server	Review	IBM Infoprint 1226
14	04/09/2007	Jayson Butler	Replace toner	Review	IBM Infoprint 1226
15	04/09/2007	Jayson Butler	Wait for Display Language menu to appear	Publish	HP Color Laser Jet 5
16	04/09/2007	Jayson Butler	Print demonstraton page	Publish	HP Color Laser Jet 5

Figure 13.25 The List of Service Call Solution Screen

13.5   Service Reports

SAP Business One offers several reports to monitor the performance of the service department as a whole, by queue, or by individual to identify areas of improvement. Information about service contracts and equipment cards is also available. Most of these reports offer multiple filters as well as the ability to sort the information as needed.

Let's take a look at the Service Calls Report selection criteria screen shown in Figure 13.26. In this screen, you can select ranges by dates, customer codes, the user who handled the service call, item, or queue ID. Alternatively, you can also filter by problem type, origin, priority, status, call type, and overdue status. Finally, you can also make use of the SORT checkbox shown in Figure 13.26; if you select this checkbox, the system will provide the fields available for sorting the data in the report.

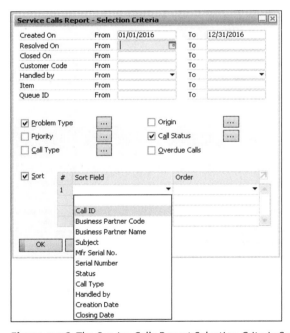

Figure 13.26 The Service Calls Report Selection Criteria Screen

You have the following service reports at your disposal.

13.5.1 Service Calls Report

The Service Calls Report shown in Figure 13.27 includes all service calls based on the filters and sorting options. Our example here shows that one service call is open, three are pending, and two have been closed.

Access the Service Calls Report by following the menu path SERVICE • SERVICE REPORTS • SERVICE CALLS.

#	Call...	Customer Name	Customer Code	Item	Mfr Serial No.	Serial No.	Subject	Status	Handled by	Priority	Type	Creation Date	Creation Time	Closure Date	Closure Time	Overdue	Resolv...
20	20	SG Electronics	C60000	S10000		S1-000185	Call 00020 Server is slow	Open	Jayson Butler	Medium	Sales	08/30/2016	13:04			☑	10/01/2016
19	19	Earthshaker Corporation	C40000	A00006		A6-000283	Call 00019	Pending	Jayson Butler	Medium		07/17/2009	13:04			☐	07/17/2005
18	18	Earthshaker Corporation	C40000				Call 00018	Pending	Jayson Butler	High		07/17/2009	13:04			☐	07/17/2005
17	17	Microchips	C30000				Call 00017	Pending	Jayson Butler	Medium		07/17/2009	13:04			☐	07/17/2005
16	16	Parameter Technology	C23900				Call 00016	Closed	Jayson Butler	Low		07/17/2009	13:04	07/17/2009	13:04		07/17/2005
15	15	Mashina Corporation	C42000				Call 00015	Closed	Jayson Butler	High		07/17/2009	13:04	07/17/2009	13:04	☐	07/17/2005

Figure 13.27 A Service Calls Report

13.5.2 Service Calls by Queue Report

The Service Calls by Queue Report shown in Figure 13.28 offers you the ability to arrange by queue; for our example organization, we have separated the calls into the MISCELLANEOUS and PCs queues.

Access the Service Calls by Queue Report by following the menu path SERVICE • SERVICE REPORTS • SERVICE CALLS BY QUEUE.

#	Queue	No. of Calls	Call ID	Time in Queue	Customer Name	Customer Code	Item	Mfr Serial No.	Serial No.	Status	Priority	Type	Assign Date	Assign Time
1	▼ Misc	2												
2			17	2662.34 Days	Microchips	C30000				Pending	Medium		07/17/2009	21:15
3			20	61.34 Days	SG Electronics	C60000	S100		S1-000185	Open	Medium	Sales	07/17/2009	21:17
4	▼ PCs	1												
5			19	2662.34 Days	Earthshaker Co	C40000	A00C		A6-000283	Pending	Medium		07/17/2009	21:17

Figure 13.28 A Service Calls by Queue Report

13.5.3 Response Time by Assigned To Report

The Response Time by Assigned To Report shown in Figure 13.29 displays the service calls grouped by responsible person. All of the calls in our example report were managed by Jayson Butler.

Access the Response Time by Assigned To Report by following the menu path
SERVICE • SERVICE REPORTS • RESPONSE TIME BY ASSIGNED TO.

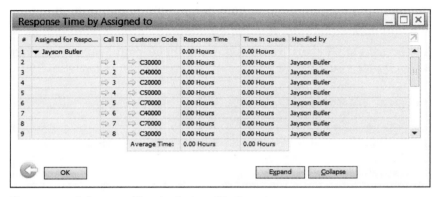

Figure 13.29 A Response Time by Assigned To Report

13.5.4 Average Closure Time Report

The Average Closure Time Report shown in Figure 13.30 works as a key performance indicator by showing details about service calls that have been closed.

Access the Average Closure Time Report by following the menu path SERVICE •
SERVICE REPORTS • AVERAGE CLOSURE TIME.

#	Call ID	Customer Name	Customer Code	Items	Subject	Handled by	Priority	Type	Creation Date	Creation Time	Closure Date	Closure Time	Time for Closure
1	1	Microchips	C30000		Call 00001	Jayson Butler	Low		07/17/2009	13:04	07/17/2009	13:04	0.00 Hours
2	2	Earthshaker Corporation	C40000		Call 00002	Jayson Butler	Medium		07/17/2009	13:04	07/17/2009	13:04	0.00 Hours
3	3	Norm Thompson	C20000		Call 00003	Jayson Butler	High		07/17/2009	13:04	07/17/2009	13:04	0.00 Hours
4	4	ADA Technologies	C50000		Call 00004	Jayson Butler	Low		07/17/2009	13:04	07/17/2009	13:04	0.00 Hours
5	5	Aquent Systems	C70000		Call 00005	Jayson Butler	Medium		07/17/2009	13:04	07/17/2009	13:04	0.00 Hours
6	6	Earthshaker Corporation	C40000		Call 00006	Jayson Butler	High		07/17/2009	13:04	07/17/2009	13:04	0.00 Hours
													0.00 Hours

Figure 13.30 An Average Closure Time Report

13.5.5 Service Contracts Report

The Service Contracts Report shown in Figure 13.31 can show all service contracts or, optionally, just the valid service contracts. To see only the valid service contracts, check the DISPLAY VALID SERVICE CONTRACTS ONLY box at the top of Figure 13.31.

Access the Service Contracts Report by following the menu path SERVICE • SERVICE REPORTS • SERVICE CONTRACTS.

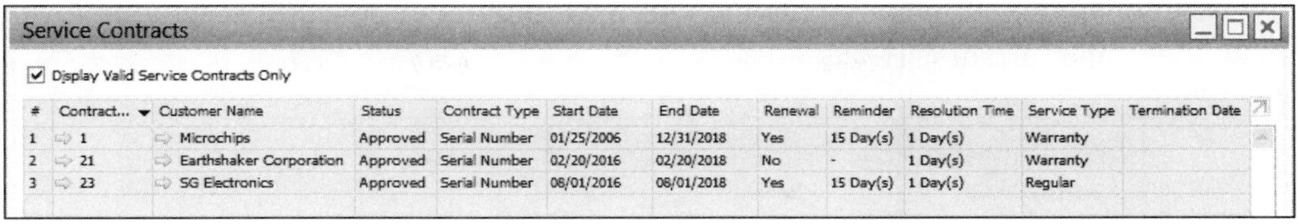

Service Contracts

☑ Display Valid Service Contracts Only

#	Contract...	Customer Name	Status	Contract Type	Start Date	End Date	Renewal	Reminder	Resolution Time	Service Type	Termination Date
1	1	Microchips	Approved	Serial Number	01/25/2006	12/31/2018	Yes	15 Day(s)	1 Day(s)	Warranty	
2	21	Earthshaker Corporation	Approved	Serial Number	02/20/2016	02/20/2018	No	-	1 Day(s)	Warranty	
3	23	SG Electronics	Approved	Serial Number	08/01/2016	08/01/2018	Yes	15 Day(s)	1 Day(s)	Regular	

Figure 13.31 A Service Contracts Report Showing Valid Contracts Only

13.5.6 Customer Equipment Card Report

The Customer Equipment Card Report shown in Figure 13.32 displays details about all equipment cards.

Access the Customer Equipment Card Report by following the menu path SERVICE • SERVICE REPORTS • CUSTOMER EQUIPMENT CARD REPORT.

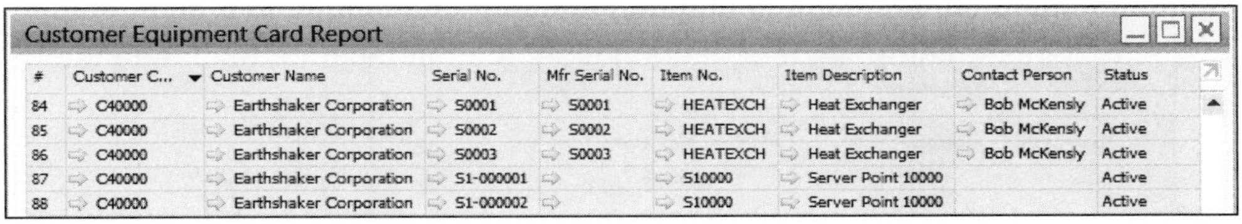

Customer Equipment Card Report

#	Customer C...	Customer Name	Serial No.	Mfr Serial No.	Item No.	Item Description	Contact Person	Status
84	C40000	Earthshaker Corporation	S0001	S0001	HEATEXCH	Heat Exchanger	Bob McKensly	Active
85	C40000	Earthshaker Corporation	S0002	S0002	HEATEXCH	Heat Exchanger	Bob McKensly	Active
86	C40000	Earthshaker Corporation	S0003	S0003	HEATEXCH	Heat Exchanger	Bob McKensly	Active
87	C40000	Earthshaker Corporation	S1-000001		S10000	Server Point 10000		Active
88	C40000	Earthshaker Corporation	S1-000002		S10000	Server Point 10000		Active

Figure 13.32 A Customer Equipment Card Report

13.5.7 Service Monitor

Shown in Figure 13.33, the Service Monitor is a graphical display of service calls open and overdue and can be set up to refresh as often as needed using the REFRESH field and dropdown list in the lower right corner. Click on the DETAILS button to a get a list of the open or overdue service calls.

Access the Service Monitor by following the menu path SERVICE • SERVICE REPORTS • SERVICE MONITOR.

A few more reports are worth mentioning; note that these are specific to the current user rather than *all* users.

- The My Service Calls Report shows the service call for the current user.
- The My Open Service Calls Report displays all open service calls for the current user.

▶ The My Overdue Service Calls Report includes service calls that are overdue for the current user.

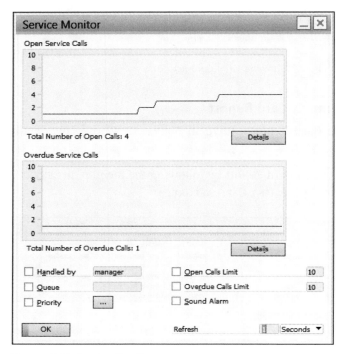

Figure 13.33 Service Monitor

In addition to the standard reports, SAP Business One, version for SAP HANA, offers a dashboard, shown in Figure 13.34, that includes the following information:

▶ Incoming calls by queue and calls to close by due date at the top left

▶ Graphical representations of calls per queue, with the ability to select different period lengths

▶ The workload per queue, with the ability select a queue and period range at the bottom left

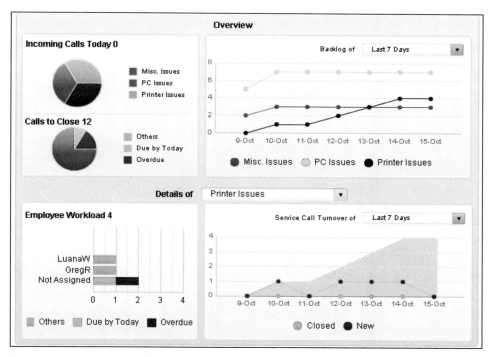

Figure 13.34 The Service Call Dashboard in SAP Business One, Version for SAP HANA

SAP Business One's human resources (HR) system supports staff management, including employee details, contact information, and salary information.

14   Human Resources

This chapter on the Human Resources module in SAP Business One will teach you how to maintain employee data, time sheets, and workforce analysis reports using step-by-step instructions and screenshots.

14.1   Employee Master Data

The employee master data allows you to capture pertinent information about each employee so you have one place to maintain and manage your employee records and data.

14.1.1   Creating the Employee Master Data

To start creating your employee master data, choose EMPLOYEE MASTER DATA from the HUMAN RESOURCES dropdown list. Once the EMPLOYEE MASTER DATA window shown in Figure 14.1 opens, start by clicking the button ADD on the menu bar under DATA or by using the convenient ADD icon on the toolbar.

You can register all pertinent information about your employees in the EMPLOYEE MASTER DATA screen, including pictures and related files or documents. The top right field, EMPLOYEE NO., in the header of Figure 14.1, is an automatic number that the system assigns to each new employee registered in the employee master data.

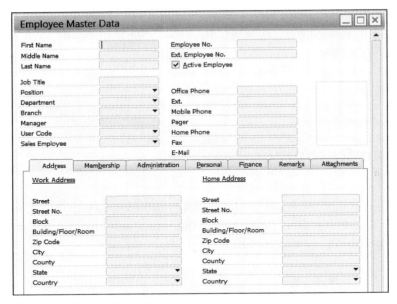

Figure 14.1 The Employee Master Data Screen

On the employee master data GENERAL tab, you will register all contact information like phone numbers and email addresses, as well as the employee's job title, position, department, and branch. Table 14.1 outlines these fields and provides tips for filling them out.

Field	Description/Use
FIRST NAME, MIDDLE NAME, and LAST NAME	Specify the name of the employee. Each part of the name may be up to 50 characters long.
EMPLOYEE NO.	This field displays an automatically assigned, unique sequential number that identifies an employee.
POSITION	Define the post that the employee occupies within the organization.
DEPARTMENT	Specify the division in which the employee works.
BRANCH	Enter an additional organizational division in which the employee works.
MANAGER	Define the employee's supervisor.

Table 14.1 Employee Master Data Fields

Field	Description/Use
USER CODE	Select an appropriate user code for the employee or define the employee as a new user in the application.
SALES EMPLOYEE	Specify an employee in the sales and distribution department of the company.
EXT.	Specify the extension of the employee's office phone number.
PAGER	Specify the employee's pager number.
IMAGE icon (camera)	Opens a window from which you can select an image file (i.e., an employee's photo) to add to the record.

Table 14.1 Employee Master Data Fields (Cont.)

If you are registering a sales employee, you should establish his or her particular sales commission level in the SALES EMPLOYEE dropdown list. As shown in Figure 14.2, make sure that you've already defined the different types of sales employees commission structures by following the menu path ADMINISTRATION • GENERAL • SALES EMPLOYEES/BUYERS, before trying to add employees from this dropdown list.

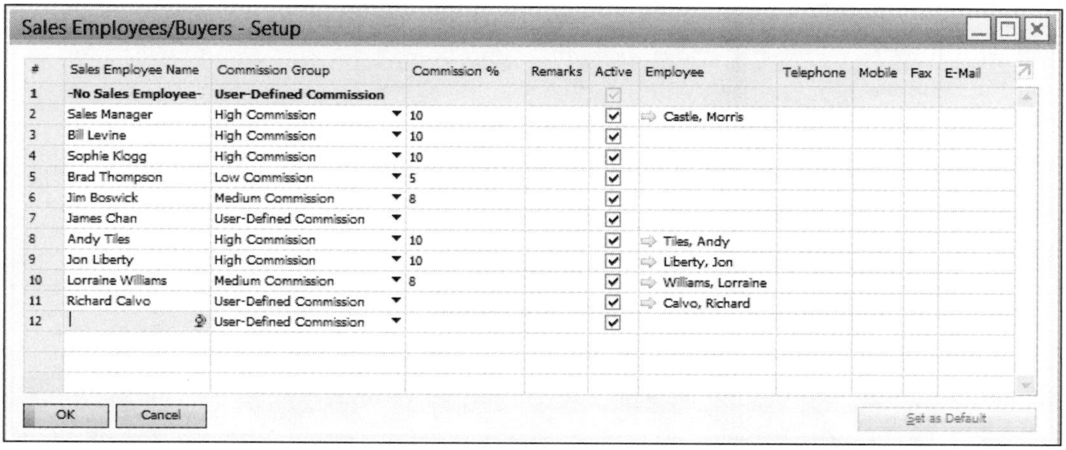

Figure 14.2 Setting Up Sales Employees/Buyers

Notice that, underneath the header in Figure 14.1, this master data window is divided into seven tabs: ADDRESS, MEMBERSHIP, ADMINISTRATION, PERSONAL, FINANCE, REMARKS, and ATTACHMENTS. Let's look at each of these now.

Address Tab

The ADDRESS tab shown in Figure 14.3 allows you to specify the work and home address details on the left and right side of the screen, respectively, including zip code, city, and state.

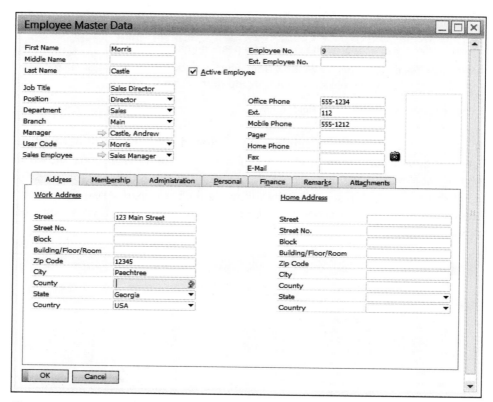

Figure 14.3 The Employee Master Data Address Tab

Tips and Tricks: Defining a New User

As you define a new user in the EMPLOYEE MASTER DATA screen, the following fields in the USER • SETUP window are filled automatically with their corresponding values from the employee master data: USER CODE, USER NAME, EMPLOYEE, E-MAIL, MOBILE PHONE, FAX, BRANCH, and DEPARTMENT.

Membership Tab

Use the MEMBERSHIP tab shown in Figure 14.4 to describe how an employee fits into the company. Table 14.2 outlines the fields that are available in this screen.

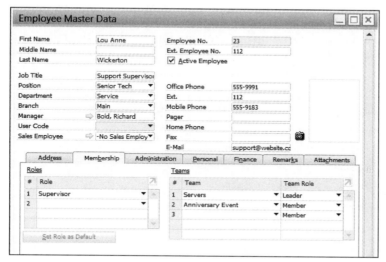

Figure 14.4 The Employee Master Data Membership Tab

Field	Description/Use
ROLES	Each employee could have one or several roles within the company. Assign one of the predefined roles or add new ones.
SET ROLE AS DEFAULT	Select this checkbox to make the selected role for the employee the default role.
TEAMS	Assign one or more teams to the employee or define a new team. Teams enable employees who otherwise have no relationship to share tasks, comments, and opportunities.
TEAM ROLE	Select either LEADER or MEMBER from this dropdown list to further specify the employee's role in the team.

Table 14.2 Fields in the Employee Master Data Membership Tab

Let's put these fields to use. In our example, the employee Lou Anne Wickerton's job title is "Support Supervisor," and her position is "Senior Technician" in the service department. Look closely at the left side of the MEMBERSHIP tab; at the bottom, we have created a new role named "Supervisor," and we set this role as default for Lou Anne by clicking the SET ROLE AS DEFAULT button.

Our sample company, OEC Computers, has various projects, and different teams have been created to work towards those specific goals. One the right side of Figure 14.4, we have designated Lou Anne as a leader in the "Servers" team, which reviews the configuration of the company's servers for scheduled upgrades, but she is also a member of the company's anniversary event team. You can add or create as many roles or teams as needed for each employee.

Tips and Tricks: Predefined Roles

By default, the following roles are predefined in SAP Business One:

▶ Sales employee: Responsible for sales documents

▶ Purchasing: Responsible for purchasing documents

▶ Technician: Assigned as a technician in a service call

You can use these roles or create any new roles as needed.

Administration Tab

Use the ADMINISTRATION tab shown in Figure 14.5 to register when an employee started/stopped working for the company as well as the employee's current status.

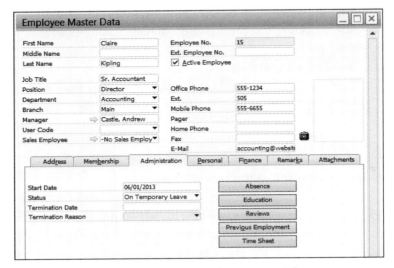

Figure 14.5 The Employee Master Data Administration Tab

Our employee Claire Kipling began working for OEC Computers in June 2013, and at this moment, she is on temporary leave. Five key buttons are available on this screen to allow you to enter, view, delete, or update information about the employee:

▶ ABSENCES: Use this button to enter details about an employee's absence.

▶ EDUCATION: Use this button to register details about the employee's education.

▶ REVIEWS: This button opens the REVIEW window, where you can enter details about the employee's professional reviews.

▶ PREVIOUS EMPLOYMENT: Use this button to enter information about the employee's work history.

▶ TIME SHEET: Use this button to record times of activities for an employee.

Let's briefly focus on absences. As of SAP Business One, version 9.2, the ABSENCE TYPE column has been newly added to the ABSENCE INFORMATION window shown in Figure 14.6 in the employee master data ADMINISTRATION tab.

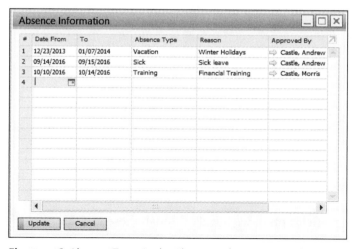

Figure 14.6 Absence Types in the Absence Information Window

Only activity types that are defined as ABSENCE in the ACTIVITY TYPE • SETUP window are available. To learn how to create activity types, skip ahead to Section 14.2 in this chapter.

To define a time for an absence in the time sheet, follow these steps:

1. Enter the date range of employee's absence in the DATE FROM/TO fields.
2. From the ABSENCE TYPE dropdown list, select the relevant activity type.
3. Enter the reason for the absence in the REASON field.
4. From the APPROVED BY dropdown list, select the relevant employee who approved the absence.
5. To save the changes, choose UPDATE.

Finance Tab

Use the FINANCE tab shown in Figure 14.7 to record the employee's financial information.

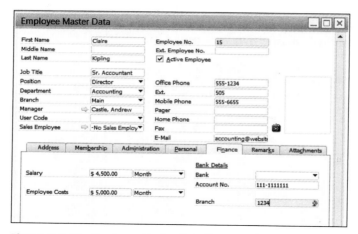

Figure 14.7 The Employee Master Data Finance Tab

This screen only has a few fields on it; we'll walk through these in Table 14.3.

Field	Description/Use
SALARY	Specify the employee's salary and select the relevant payment basis.
EMPLOYEE COSTS	Enter the employee's actual costs (i.e., salary, company car, and meals) and select the relevant payment basis.
BANK	Specify the bank where the employee has an account.

Table 14.3 Fields in the Employee Master Data Finance Tab

Field	Description/Use
ACCOUNT NO.	Enter the employee's bank account number.
BRANCH	Specify the branch number or name of the bank.

Table 14.3 Fields in the Employee Master Data Finance Tab (Cont.)

Personal, Remarks, and Attachment Tabs

The PERSONAL tab is used to specify personal information about the employee such as marital status, date of birth, etc. The fields are self-explanatory.

The REMARKS tab can be used to enter, update, or delete any freestyle text regarding the employee, such as additional comments, notes, and relevant details.

Finally, you can use the ATTACHMENTS tab shown in Figure 14.8 to enter and display attachment files associated with the employee. Two key fields are available in this tab: The ATTACHMENT DATE column shows when the existing file was attached, and the BROWSE button, which opens a window where you can select the file(s) you want to attach.

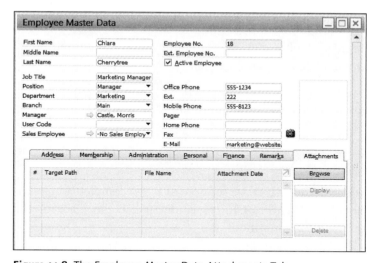

Figure 14.8 The Employee Master Data Attachments Tab

Tips and Tricks: Attachment Tab

To attach files, you must define the attachments folder by using the PATH tab in ADMINISTRATION • SYSTEM INITIALIZATION • GENERAL SETTINGS.

14.1.2 Viewing and Editing the Employee Master Data

To change or update information about an employee record that already exists, choose EMPLOYEE MASTER DATA from the HUMAN RESOURCES dropdown list. Once the EMPLOYEE MASTER DATA window opens, search for the required employee record using standard search functions, modify the information as required, and then choose UPDATE • OK.

To delete a record, choose DATA • DELETE.

14.1.3 Using Relationship Maps for Human Resources

Beginning with SAP Business One, version 9.2, you can now work with the relationship map in the Human Resources module by using the right-click context menu.

This functionality allows you to do three key things:

► You can view employee master data records, including embedded photos of employees.

► You can visualize the manager and subordinates of each employee.

► You can display teams and the roles of company employees.

Once in a relationship map, double-click on any employee to access their information, including any embedded photos uploaded on their profile.

When viewing a human resources relationship map, you can choose one of three options from the dropdown list menu at the bottom left of your screen:

► The EMPLOYEES: HIERARCHY option displays the employee's manager and subordinates. Figure 14.9 shows that our example employee, Lou Anne Wickerton reports to Richard Bold.

► The EMPLOYEES: ORGANIZATIONAL CHART option displays complete organizational chart, as shown on Figure 14.10, to contextualize the place of the employee within the whole organization.

► The EMPLOYEES: TEAMS AND ROLES option displays the teams and roles assigned to your employee. Lou Anne is a Senior Technician whose role by default has been defined as Support Supervisor. In our example in Figure 14.11, you can see that Lou Anne is, at the moment, involved in two different teams: the "Servers" team and the "50th Company Anniversary" team.

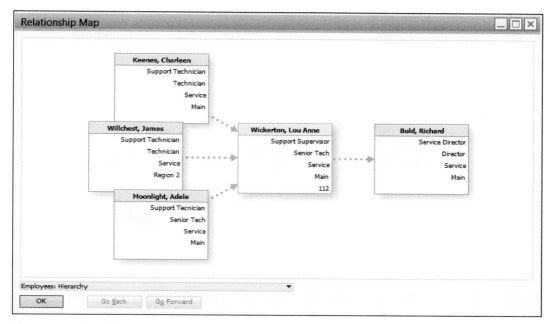

Figure 14.9 Selected Employee's Hierarchy Relationship Map

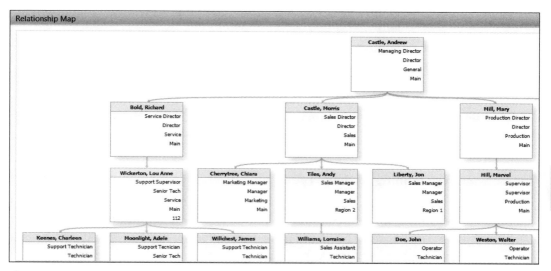

Figure 14.10 Organizational Chart Relationship Map

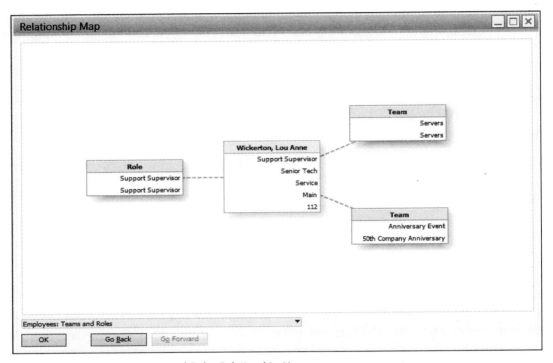

Figure 14.11 Teams and Roles Relationship Map

14.2 Time Sheet

The Time Sheet feature in the Human Resources module allows you to record the times of activities by an employee, user, or other. Before you start working with the time sheets, you'll need to define your activity types.

14.2.1 Defining Activity Types

To define the activity types that you'll use in your time sheets, go to MAIN MENU • ADMINISTRATION • SETUP • PROJECT MANAGEMENT • ACTIVITY TYPES. The ACTIVITY TYPES SETUP window shown in Figure 14.12 appears. Right-click in the next available row and choose ADD ROW to specify the fields listed in Table 14.4.

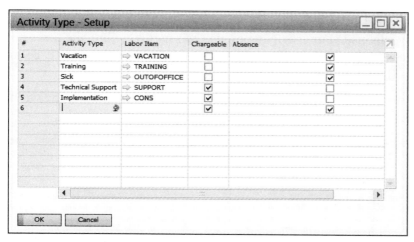

Figure 14.12 The Activity Types Setup Screen

Field	Description/Use
ACTIVITY	Specify the name of the activity.
LABOR ITEMS	If a labor item is related to this activity type, select the relevant item from the dropdown menu.
CHARGEABLE	Some projects have activities that are passed on to customers; select this checkbox if the activity type is chargeable or billable.
ABSENCE	Select this checkbox if the activity type represents an absence.

Table 14.4 Fields in the Activity Types Setup Screen

To save your changes, choose OK.

Note that you can also delete an activity type in this screen by right-clicking the desired row and choosing DELETE ROW instead of ADD ROW.

> **Tips and Tricks: Activity Type Setup**
>
> You won't be able to define activity types if the Project Management module is not enabled in your system. To enable the Project Management module in SAP Business One, go to ADMINISTRATION • SYSTEM INITIALIZATION • COMPANY DETAILS. Scroll down to the bottom to find and select the ENABLE PROJECT MANAGEMENT checkbox. For more information on the Project Management module, please see Chapter 15.

14.2.2 Defining Time Sheets

Once you have defined your activity types, you can start recording the times for those activities for an employee, user, or other. To define a time sheet, go to MAIN MENU • HUMAN RESOURCES • TIME SHEET.

Table 14.5 lists the time sheet fields you'll need to fill in the header shown in Figure 14.13.

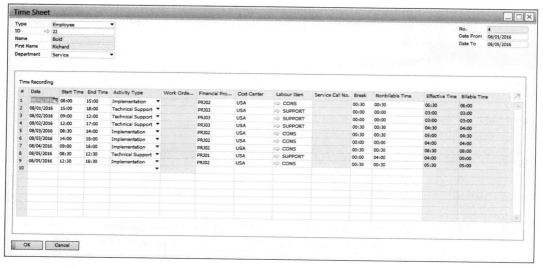

Figure 14.13 Defining a Time Sheet Template

Field/Checkbox	Description/Use
TYPE	Select a choice from the dropdown list from the available options: EMPLOYEE, USER, or OTHER.
ID	From the dropdown list, select the employee for whom you want to define the time sheet.
DATE FROM and DATE TO	Specify the range to which the time sheet applies. The DATE FROM field is the current date by default, but you can change it to a different date.
DEPARTMENT	Select the relevant department.

Table 14.5 Fields in the Time Sheet Screen

In the TIME RECORDING table shown in Figure 14.13, you'll specify the fields listed in Table 14.6.

Field/Checkbox	Description/Use
DATE	Enter the date of the activity.
START/END TIME	Specify the time range of the activity.
ACTIVITY TYPE	Select the activity type from the dropdown menu.
WORK ORDER NUMBER	Enter the work order number if the employee is assigned to one.
FINANCIAL PROJECT	Select the relevant financial project.
COST CENTER	Select the relevant cost center if no work order or service was specified for the activity.
LABOR ITEM	This field displays the default labor item if defined in the ACTIVITY TYPES SETUP window.
SERVICE CALL NO.	Select the relevant service call number.
EFFECTIVE TIME and BILLABLE TIME	This field displays the effective and billable times based on the information you provided.

Table 14.6 Fields in the Time Recording Table

To save your changes, choose UPDATE.

14.3 Human Resources Reports

Depending on your selection criteria, you can generate reports to display the contact details for every company employee, view employee absences for the entire organization or a particular department, or print phone books or employee lists in various combinations. Let's look at these three key reports.

14.3.1 Employee List Report

To access general information about employees from the different branches and departments in the company according to your selection criteria, follow the menu path MAIN MENU • HUMAN RESOURCES • REPORTS • EMPLOYEE LIST to use the Employee List Report.

In the example shown in Figure 14.14, we used selection criteria to filter the employee list to include only those that worked at the main branch in the production department, regardless of role.

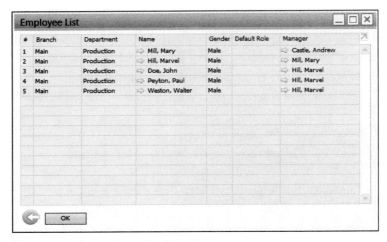

Figure 14.14 An Employee List Report

14.3.2 Absence Report

The Absence Report shown in Figure 14.15 shows the amount of time employees have been absent. Access this report by following the menu path MAIN MENU • HUMAN RESOURCES • REPORTS • ABSENCE REPORT.

You will need to enter your criteria for the content of the report, including branch, department, manager, and the range of dates.

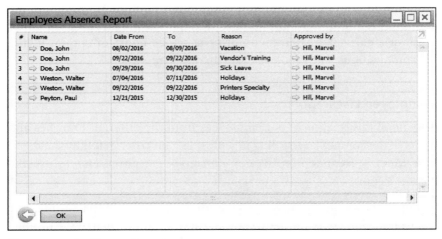

Figure 14.15 An Absence Report

14.3.3 Phone Book

Company phone books can be helpful for communicating information with employees. To create a company phone book according to your selection criteria, follow the menu path MAIN MENU • HUMAN RESOURCES • REPORTS • PHONE BOOK. In our example in Figure 14.16, the report was limited to six employees in the service department; in row 3, notice that the system lacks contact information for one of our employees, Bill Levine.

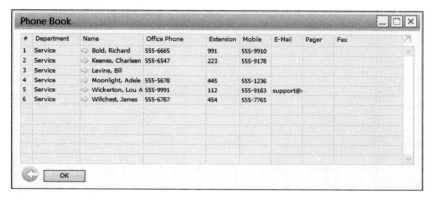

Figure 14.16 A Phone Book

Effective project management requires planning, communication, and coordination among the project members so they can track project execution and identify any deviations from the plan. SAP Business One functionality is available for these kinds of tasks.

15 Projects

Any company, regardless of its size and type of operation, manages internal and external projects, which requires planning, budgeting, and execution control to identify deviations and make prompt adjustments to meet goals. These projects can vary in complexity, value, and time span.

SAP has supported projects for financial purposes for many years, which allows you to register any transaction with a project code and utilize it later to obtain financial reports. SAP Business One introduced the Project Management functionality in version 9.2 to manage projects, subprojects, tasks, documents, transactions, resources, estimated and actual costs, and other relevant information.

In addition to a main project, SAP Business One allows you to set up subprojects (and even subprojects of an existing subproject), each with its own description, owner, dates, tasks, and so on. Figure 15.1 shows a project to launch a new product (a "Heat Exchanger") that the engineering department has developed and tested in the market. You can see that there are two main subprojects: heat exchanger production and marketing campaign production launch, which itself has its own subproject (event launch).

Main Project: Product Launch

Tasks:

- ▸ Management approval of project
- ▸ Communicate to project members
- ▸ Production setup
- ▸ Marketing campaign
- ▸ First customer orders
- ▸ Evaluate product performance on the market

Subproject: Heat Exchanger Production

Tasks:

- ▸ Presentation to plant personnel
- ▸ Train shop floor operators
- ▸ Start production, monitor process
- ▸ Monitor process and perform quality checks
- ▸ Approval of process

Subproject: Marketing Campaign Production Launch

Tasks:

- ▸ Prepare newsletter and mailing list
- ▸ Execute social media communication strategy
- ▸ Prepare and execute launch event

Subproject: Event Launch

Tasks:

- ▸ Define and contract venue and menu
- ▸ Obtain list of attendees
- ▸ Send invitation
- ▸ Call to confirm attendance
- ▸ Prepare presentation and supporting materials
- ▸ Event day
- ▸ Follow up with leads

Figure 15.1 Multiple Levels of Related Project and Subprojects, Including Tasks

15.1   Setting Up and Initializing Project Management

To activate the Project Management module in SAP Business One, you must select the ENABLE PROJECT MANAGEMENT checkbox shown in Figure 15.2. Follow the menu path ADMINISTRATION • SYSTEM INITIALIZATION • COMPANY DETAILS and scroll down to the bottom.

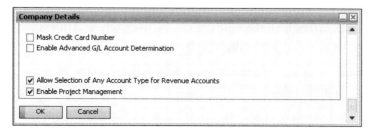

Figure 15.2 Enabling Project Management

Once the module has been enabled, two options will open up under ADMINISTRATION • SETUP • PROJECT MANAGEMENT called STAGES and ACTIVITY TYPES. Because activity types are used on time sheets in the Human Resources module, refer to Chapter 14 for coverage of that functionality; we'll focus on STAGES in this chapter.

SAP Business One uses *stages* to define the phases the project will go through. A stage can be added to a project multiple times if needed, so that different tasks can be aligned with each stage. Our example in Figure 15.3 shows five stages: CONCEPTION/INITIATION, DEFINITION/PLANNING, LAUNCH/EXECUTION, PERFORMANCE AND CONTROL, and the FINISHING STAGE.

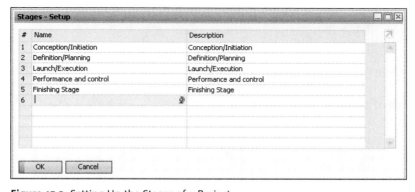

Figure 15.3 Setting Up the Stages of a Project

15.2   Creating and Managing Projects

Setting up a project in SAP Business One is easy. The project object can handle almost any level of complexity. Creating new subprojects is done from the parent project or subproject; we recommend that you plan the general structure and hierarchy of subprojects carefully because changing the levels of subprojects is not possible.

In this section, we'll walk through all the fields of the PROJECT screen. Unless otherwise noted, these fields also apply to subprojects.

As in most of the master data and transactions in SAP Business One, a project includes a header and multiple tabs.

The header in Figure 15.4 displays static information about the project and provides a link to the financial project assigned to it, which will be used to track financial transactions and enable you to create financial reports for the project. (In the FINANCIAL MODULE • REPORTS • FINANCIAL REPORTS, one of the filtering options is by financial project.)

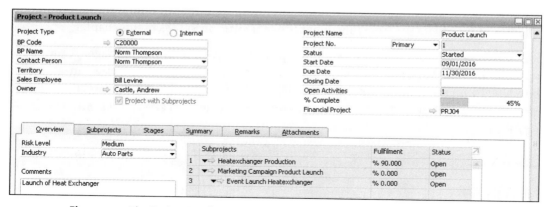

Figure 15.4 The Project Header and Overview Tab of the Project Screen

The main fields of this screen are explained in Table 15.1.

Field	Description/Use
PROJECT TYPE	Choose the project type from the two available radio buttons: ▶ EXTERNAL: Choose this option if the project is linked to a business partner (a customer or a vendor). ▶ INTERNAL: Choose this option if the project is not linked to a business partner.
BP CODE, BP NAME, CONTACT PERSON, and TERRITORY	These fields contain information about the customer or vendor associated with the project. If the project is an internal one, then the BP CODE, BP NAME, and CONTACT PERSON fields are not used.
SALES EMPLOYEE	This field displays the salesperson associated with this project and is used for reporting purposes.
OWNER	Enter the project manager's name in this field.
PROJECT WITH SUBPROJECT	Select this checkbox to allow subprojects, which will enable a new tab called SUBPROJECTS.
PROJECT NAME	Enter a project name in this mandatory field, where you can register a description of the project.
PROJECT NO.	Enter a unique project identification number in this field, if needed.
STATUS	Choose a status from these four options: ▶ STARTED ▶ PAUSED ▶ STOPPED ▶ FINISHED These statuses are for information only and have no limitations; for example, you can change a finished project to STARTED if needed, and even if the project is STOPPED, you can register transactions to it.
START DATE, DUE DATE, and CLOSING DATE	Enter the start and end dates manually. The CLOSING DATE field is updated once the project status is changed to FINISHED.
OPEN ACTIVITIES	This field displays the number of activities that are pending for the project. We'll walk through these activities in Section 15.2.3.
% COMPLETE	This area of the screen displays a colored bar for the percentage of completion of the project, based on the percentages assigned to each stage.

Table 15.1 Fields in the Project Header

Field	Description/Use
FINANCIAL PROJECT	Every project is linked to a financial project. However, this financial project must be added manually to every document in the system that is linked to the project, in order to get financial statements based on the project.

Table 15.1 Fields in the Project Header (Cont.)

Tips and Tricks: Calculating the Percent Completion

The percentage of completion is based on the percentages assigned to the stages and the percentages of contributions from the subprojects; we'll discuss these percentages further when we discuss the STAGES and SUBPROJECTS tabs in Section 15.2.3 and Section 15.2.4, respectively. The system will ensure that the total percentages between stages and subprojects does not exceed 100%.

15.2.1 Overview Tab

The OVERVIEW tab gives you a summary of the status of the project, as shown in Figure 15.4. Table 15.2 lists the fields in this tab.

Field	Description/Use
RISK LEVEL	Choose a risk level for the project from the following options in the dropdown list: ▶ LOW ▶ MEDIUM ▶ HIGH
INDUSTRY	Select one of the options from the dropdown list, but you can also leave this optional field empty. You can add a new entry to the INDUSTRY table by selecting DEFINE NEW. You can also delete an existing entry by right-clicking on the line number and selecting REMOVE.
COMMENTS	Enter a long description of the project.
SUBPROJECTS	The area displays an indented list of subprojects on the right side of the OVERVIEW tab, and for each one of them, the percentage of completion is displayed in the FULFILLMENT and STATUS columns.

Table 15.2 Fields in the Overview Tab

15.2.2 Subprojects Tab

If the PROJECT WITH SUBPROJECTS checkbox is selected in the header, then the SUB-PROJECTS tab shown in Figure 15.5 is enabled.

Tips and Tricks: Adding Subprojects

You cannot link an existing project as a subproject of another existing project. Only sub-projects can be added from this screen.

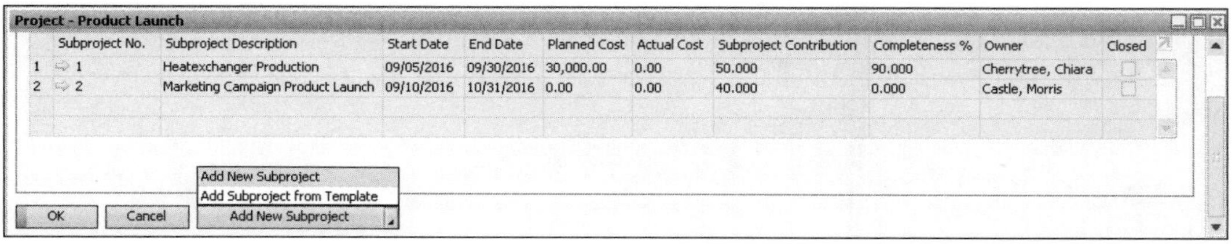

	Subproject No.	Subproject Description	Start Date	End Date	Planned Cost	Actual Cost	Subproject Contribution	Completeness %	Owner	Closed
1	1	Heatexchanger Production	09/05/2016	09/30/2016	30,000.00	0.00	50.000	90.000	Cherrytree, Chiara	
2	2	Marketing Campaign Product Launch	09/10/2016	10/31/2016	0.00	0.00	40.000	0.000	Castle, Morris	

Figure 15.5 Details in the Subprojects Tab

First, take note of the ADD NEW SUBPROJECT button on the bottom of the screen. Clicking this button will bring up a dropdown list; your options here are to add a new subproject or add a subproject from a template.

In the subprojects list for our example in Figure 15.5, we have two subprojects: HEATER EXCHANGE PRODUCTION and MARKETING CAMPAIGN PRODUCT LAUNCH. The top table of the screen has a number of columns that display subproject data, including the following:

- Subproject descriptions
- Start and end dates
- Planned and actual costs (updated manually on the header of the subproject)
- Subproject contributions to the completion of the parent project
- Completeness percentages
- Owners

Note that you can click on the golden arrow to drill down into any of these sub-projects.

15.2.3 Stages Tab

You'll enter the different stages of your project into the STAGES tab shown in Figure 15.6. This list, which can be edited at any time, has a header at the top and then other subtabs that can be used once a stage is selected by clicking on the number of the list.

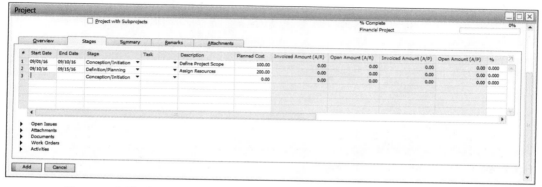

Figure 15.6 The Project Stages Tab

Let's walk through the fields in the STAGES tab in Table 15.3.

Field	Description/Use
START DATE and END DATE	Enter start and end dates for the subproject. Please note the system checks that the date of each stage falls within the overall project start and end dates.
STAGE	Choose a stage from the dropdown list. Stage definitions are mandatory, but you can edit them as necessary.
TASK	This is an optional field and can be selected from a dropdown list; edit the dropdown options by clicking on DEFINE NEW.
DESCRIPTION	Add a brief description of the task.
PLANNED COST	Enter the planned cost for the stage manually here.
INVOICED AMOUNT (A/R) and OPEN AMOUNT (A/R)	These fields are updated automatically. Every time a delivery is linked to the project through the financial project, the OPEN AMOUNT (A/R) field is updated. Also, every time an A/R invoice is linked to the project, the INVOICED AMOUNT (A/R) field increases.
INVOICED AMOUNT (A/P) and OPEN AMOUNT (A/P)	If a goods receipt PO is linked to project, the OPEN AMOUNT (A/P) field increases. If an A/P invoice is linked, the INVOICED AMOUNT (A/P) field is updated.

Table 15.3 Fields in the Projects Stages Tab

Field	Description/Use
%	This column shows the percentage of completion that each task will add to the project at this level. The system will prevent the sum of these percentages and the percentage contribution of the subprojects from exceeding 100%.
OWNER	Select the employee responsible for this task.
STAGE DEPENDENCE (1) TO (4)	Select the stages that should be finished before this task can be finished. Note that there is no restriction with starting these stages.

Table 15.3 Fields in the Projects Stages Tab (Cont.)

Open Issues

Once a stage line is selected, you can expand the OPEN ISSUES pane at the bottom of the STAGES tab to add or edit issues that have arisen in a given stage. The OPEN ISSUES pane is shown in Figure 15.7, and its columns are explained in Table 15.4.

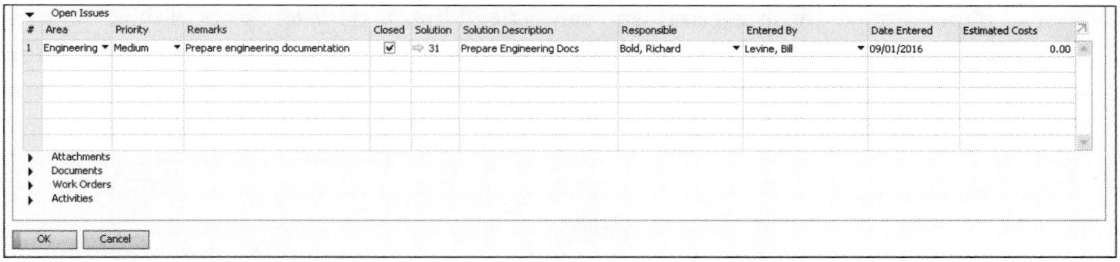

#	Area	Priority	Remarks	Closed	Solution	Solution Description	Responsible	Entered By	Date Entered	Estimated Costs
1	Engineering	Medium	Prepare engineering documentation	✓	31	Prepare Engineering Docs	Bold, Richard	Levine, Bill	09/01/2016	0.00

Attachments
Documents
Work Orders
Activities

OK   Cancel

Figure 15.7 The Open Issues Pane

Field	Description/Use
AREA	Select the area of the organization responsible for this issue.
PRIORITY	Choose a priority level for the project from the following options in the dropdown list: ▶ LOW ▶ MEDIUM ▶ HIGH
REMARKS	Enter any helpful remarks using this free text field.

Table 15.4 Fields in the Open Issues Pane

Field	Description/Use
CLOSED	For each issue, place a checkmark in the CLOSED column once the issue has been addressed. The stage can't be closed until all issues for the task have been closed.
SOLUTION	Select a solution from the Solutions Knowledge Base (described in Chapter 13) once the issue has been addressed. Please note that a solution is mandatory to close the issue.
RESPONSIBLE	Select the employee responsible for the issue.
ENTERED BY	Select the employee that entered the issue.
DATE ENTERED	Register the date the issue was added.
ESTIMATED COST	This field displays the cost that is expected from addressing the issue.

Table 15.4 Fields in the Open Issues Pane (Cont.)

Documents

Once a stage line is selected, you can expand the DOCUMENTS pane at the bottom of the STAGES tab to link an SAP Business One document to the project. Our example in Figure 15.8 shows that three documents—a sales order, a delivery, and an A/P invoice—have been linked to the project. Table 15.5 lists key fields in this screen.

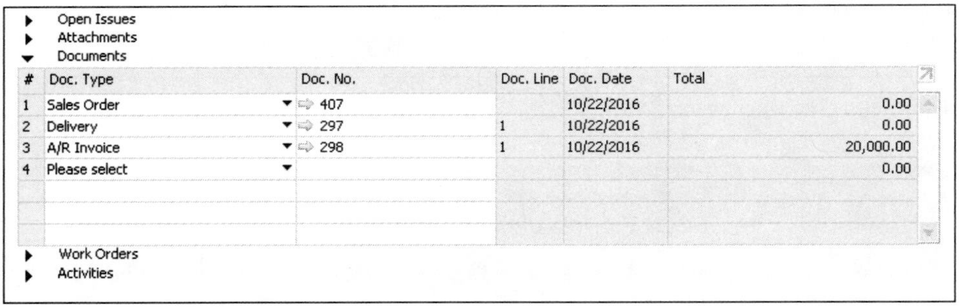

		Doc. No.		Doc. Line	Doc. Date	Total	
▶	Open Issues						
▶	Attachments						
▼	Documents						
#	Doc. Type			Doc. Line	Doc. Date	Total	⌐
1	Sales Order	▼ ⇨ 407			10/22/2016	0.00	▲
2	Delivery	▼ ⇨ 297		1	10/22/2016	0.00	
3	A/R Invoice	▼ ⇨ 298		1	10/22/2016	20,000.00	
4	Please select	▼				0.00	
							▼
▶	Work Orders						
▶	Activities						

Figure 15.8 The Documents Pane

Field	Description/Use
DOC. TYPE	Select the type of document to link. The available document types are SALES, PURCHASE, INVENTORY TRANSACTIONS, JOURNAL ENTRIES, or SERVICE CALLS.

Table 15.5 Fields in the Documents Pane

Field	Description/Use
Doc. No.	This field displays the document's number. You can use the golden arrow to drill down into the transaction.
Doc. Line	This field displays the line of the document that applies to the project.
Doc. Date	This field displays the date of the document.
Total	This field displays the amount of the document that applies to the project. This amount will update the amounts of the stage at the top of the screen.

Table 15.5 Fields in the Documents Pane (Cont.)

As we've discussed, every project has a financial project associated with it. Once the document is added, SAP Business One will suggest adding documents that reference the financial project of the project.

In our example in Figure 15.9, materials have been issued to a work order that has the same financial project as the project. On the right side, you can see the project and subprojects that have the same financial project, to facilitate the assignment to the correct stage. You can assign (or unassign) these to the project using the left and right arrows in the center of the screen.

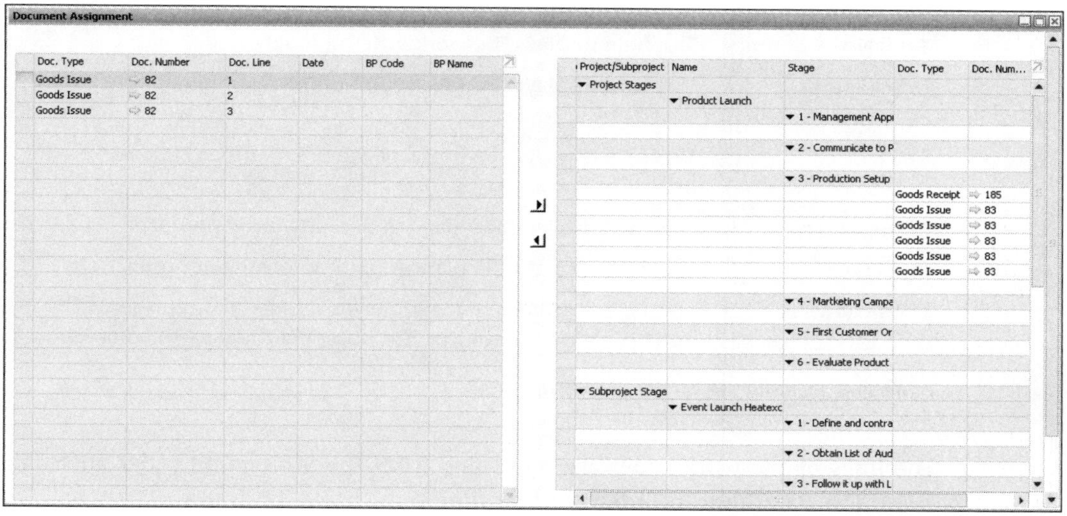

Figure 15.9 Transactions Associated to the Project Based on the Financial Project

Work Orders

Open the WORK ORDERS pane shown in Figure 15.10. You can use a project to group multiple work orders or just add a production order to a more general project.

In Figure 15.10, we can see that the work order 204 for 20 units of the Heat Exchanger was linked to the project. This work order shows three sample lines: two for components and one for a resource utilized in the production process, the Cutting Machine. For each line, the system displays the base and planned quantities, the issued quantity, additional quantity and available quantity, the unit of measure, and the issue method (manual or backflush).

▶	Open Issues															
▶	Attachments															
▶	Documents															
▼	Work Orders															
#	Doc. No.	Description	Status	Planned Qty	Due Date	Days Overdue	Type	No.	Description	Base Qty	Planned Qty	Issued	Additional Qty	Available	UoM Name	Warehouse	Issue Method
1	204	Heat Exchanger	Closed	20.000000	09/30/2016	22											
2							Item	STEELROD	STEEL ROD	3.000	60.000	60.000	0.000	50.000	FT	01	Backflush
3							Item	STEEL	STEEL PLATE	10.000	200.000	200.000	0.000	225.000	SF	01	Backflush
4							Resource	CUTTING	Cutting A	0.250	5.000	5.000	0.000	0.000		01	Manual

Figure 15.10 The Work Orders Pane

Table 15.6 describes the columns shown in the WORK ORDERS pane. Note that these fields are populated from data in the production order.

Field	Description/Use
DOC. NO.	This field displays the work order number.
DESCRIPTION	This field displays the description of the main item being produced.
STATUS	This field displays the status of the order, either PLANNED, RELEASED, or CLOSED.
PLANNED QTY.	This field displays the planned quantity to be produced.
DUE DATE	This field displays the planned date to complete production.
DAYS OVERDUE	This field is calculated from the work order and represents the number days between the due date and the date of completion.

Table 15.6 Fields in the Work Orders Pane

The lines of the work order are populated from the production order automatically. The data here includes the line type (which can be ITEMS, RESOURCES, or TEXT). Each line has an ITEM or RESOURCE NO.; a DESCRIPTION; and several fields for

QUANTITY, BASE, PLANNED, ISSUED and ADDITIONAL QUANTITY. For more details, please refer to the Chapter 11 on the Production module. The work order should have the same financial project as the project, and after the transactions are processed in the Production module, the system will suggest these transactions be linked to the project and assigned to a task.

Activities

SAP Business One lets you link activities to most of the master data and transaction documents, and the Project Management module is no exception. In the ACTIVITIES pane shown in Figure 15.11, you can link activities to the stage selected by clicking on its number. The activity has to be closed before the stage associated with it can be reported as closed.

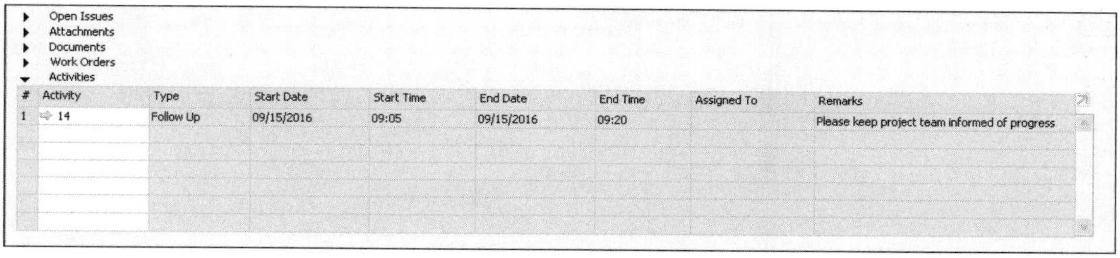

#	Activity	Type	Start Date	Start Time	End Date	End Time	Assigned To	Remarks
1	14	Follow Up	09/15/2016	09:05	09/15/2016	09:20		Please keep project team informed of progress

Figure 15.11 The Activities Pane

The fields listed in Table 15.7 are updated for connected activities when the activity is closed and the project is updated.

Field	Description/Use
ACTIVITY	This field shows the activity number; you can drill into the activity using the golden arrow.
TYPE	This field shows the activity type (e.g., NOTE, TASK, FOLLOW UP, CALL, etc.).
START DATE, START TIMES, END DATE, and END TIMES	These fields display dates taken from the activity itself.
REMARKS	This field gives a description of the activity.

Table 15.7 Fields in the Activities Pane

15.2.4 Summary Tab

The SUMMARY tab shows the financial summary for the project, organized in six sections that show the budget for this project; the budget for the subprojects; the profits for this project; the accumulated profit for this project; and its subprojects, work order costs, and dates.

As shown in Figure 15.12, the BUDGET and ACCUMULATED BUDGET sections of the SUMMARY tab have the same type of data; the difference is that the top refers to the budget for all stages of the current project, while the bottom accumulates the budget from all the stages of the subprojects. Please note that the actual and planned cost of the header of the subprojects are not added to the summary; these fields, described in more detail in Table 15.8, are for information purposes only.

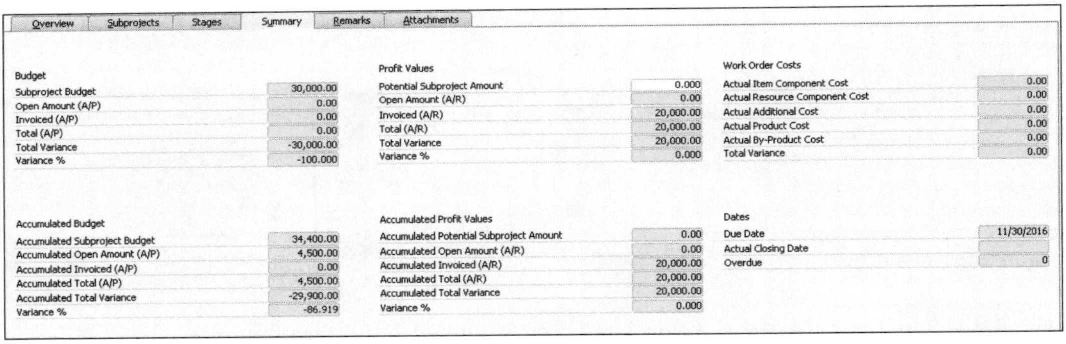

Figure 15.12 The Financial Summary for the Project

Field	Description/Use
SUBPROJECT BUDGET and ACCUMULATED SUBPROJECT BUDGET	These fields display the budget for this project's stages and for all the stages of the subprojects accumulated, respectively.
OPEN AMOUNT (A/P) and ACCUMULATED OPEN AMOUNT (A/P)	These fields display the open payables not yet invoiced by vendors but accrued based on goods receipts not yet invoiced.
INVOICED (A/P) and ACCUMULATED INVOICED (A/P)	These fields display invoices received from vendors linked to the project or subprojects.

Table 15.8 Budget and Accumulated Budget Fields

Field	Description/Use
TOTAL (A/P) and ACCUMULATED TOTAL (A/P)	These fields display the sum of open and invoiced amounts.
TOTAL VARIANCE and ACCUMULATED VARIANCE	These fields display the difference between the budget and the total amount.
VARIANCE %	This field shows the variance in percentage.

Table 15.8 Budget and Accumulated Budget Fields (Cont.)

While the BUDGET section refers to expenses, the PROFIT VALUES and ACCUMULATED PROFIT VALUES sections of the SUMMARY tab refer to the revenue component of the project or subprojects. Table 15.9 lists these fields.

Field	Description/Use
POTENTIAL SUBPROJECT AMOUNT and ACCUMULATED POTENTIAL	These fields estimate the potential revenue for the project or subproject, which will be used to estimate variance.
OPEN AMOUNT (A/R) and ACCUMULATED OPEN AMOUNT (A/R)	These fields display the value of deliveries not invoiced yet to customers.
INVOICED (A/R) and ACCUMULATED INVOICED (A/R)	These fields display the amount invoiced to customers as part the project or subprojects.
TOTAL (A/R) and ACCUMULATED TOTAL (A/R)	These fields display the total open and the total invoiced amounts.
TOTAL VARIANCE and ACCUMULATED TOTAL VARIANCE	These fields display the difference between the potential subproject amount and the total A/R.
VARIANCE % and ACCUMULATED VARIANCE %	This field shows the percentage of the variance compared to the potential amount.

Table 15.9 Profit Values and Accumulated Profit Values Fields

As shown in Figure 15.13, the Work Order Costs area from the Summary tab shows the costs for the work orders linked to a project.

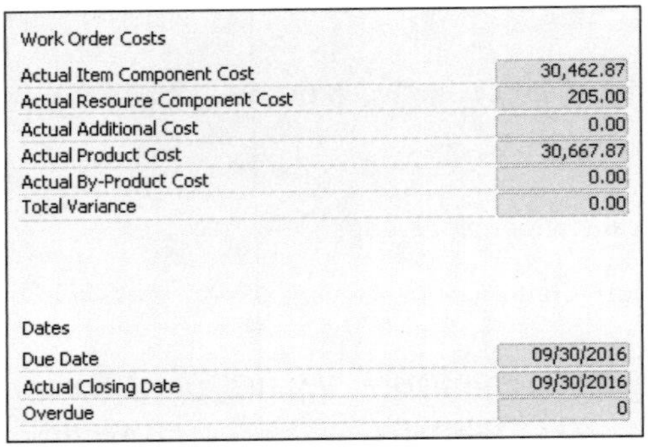

```
Work Order Costs
Actual Item Component Cost               30,462.87
Actual Resource Component Cost             205.00
Actual Additional Cost                       0.00
Actual Product Cost                      30,667.87
Actual By-Product Cost                       0.00
Total Variance                               0.00



Dates
Due Date                                09/30/2016
Actual Closing Date                     09/30/2016
Overdue                                          0
```

Figure 15.13 Work Order Costs Section on the Summary Tab

These fields are explained in Table 15.10.

Field	Description/Use
ACTUAL ITEM COMPONENT COST	This field displays the costs of all items consumed in the production order.
ACTUAL RESOURCE COMPONENT COST	This field displays the cost of the resources, such as labor and machines, used in the production order.
ACTUAL ADDITIONAL COST	This field displays any additional costs charged to the production order.
ACTUAL PRODUCT COST	This field combines the previous three costs from the ACTUAL ITEM COMPONENT COST, ACTUAL RESOURCE COMPONENT COST, and ACTUAL ADDITIONAL COST fields.
ACTUAL BY-PRODUCT COST	If there is a by-product produced as part of the work order, this field will display the value of the by-product here.
TOTAL VARIANCE	This field displays the difference between the planned cost and the actual cost of the production order.

Table 15.10 Fields in the Work Order Costs Section

The DATES section displays the dates in reference to the current project or subproject; these fields are explained in Table 15.11.

Field	Description/Use
DUE DATE	This field displays the due date for the project or subproject.
ACTUAL CLOSING DATE	This field displays the closing date for the project or subproject.
OVERDUE	This field displays the difference in days between the closing and the due date.

Table 15.11 Fields in the Dates Section

15.3 Project Reports

SAP Business One offers several useful reports with multiple filtering capabilities to monitor the status of the projects, their open issues, and their resource utilization.

15.3.1 Stage Analysis Report

The Stage Analysis Report shows a list of the projects in the system that meet the criteria you select. Access this report by following the menu path PROJECT MANAGEMENT • PROJECT REPORTS • STAGE ANALYSIS. The selection criteria screen is shown in Figure 15.14; we'll walk through the fields in this screen in Table 15.12.

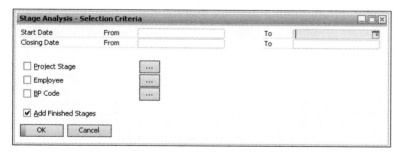

Figure 15.14 Stage Analysis Report Selection Criteria

Field	Description/Use
START DATE	Enter a date range for start dates in the FROM and To fields.
CLOSING DATE	Enter a date range for closing dates in the FROM and To fields.

Table 15.12 Fields in the Stage Analysis Report Selection Criteria

Field	Description/Use
PROJECT STAGE	Click on the BROWSE icon (the ellipsis) to select the stages that will be included on the report.
EMPLOYEE	Click on the BROWSE icon (the ellipsis) to select the projects that are related to one or more sales employees.
BP CODE	Click on the BROWSE icon (the ellipsis) to select the projects for one or more customers or vendors.
ADD FINISHED STAGES	Check the ADD FINISHED STAGES checkbox to include stages that have been finished already.

Table 15.12 Fields in the Stage Analysis Report Selection Criteria (Cont.)

Figure 15.15 shows a sample of the report, and as usual on SAP Business One, the columns that are displayed can be modified by using the FORM SETTINGS (a blank sheet with a green gear) icon. At the top, you'll find the name of the project, the type, whether it has subprojects, and the number of open activities as well as other data.

Stage Analysis

#	Project/Sub...	Project/Subproject Name	External/Internal	Type	Project with Subprojects	Level	Parent	Open Activities	Financial Project	Business Partner Code	Business Partner Name	Contact Person	Sales Emplo...
1	4	Setup Production	External	Project	No	1		0		C20000	Norm Thompson	1	Bill Levine
2	10	Office Lease agreement	Internal	Project	No	1		0	PRJ05				Andy Tiles
3	9	Move to new location	Internal	Project	Yes	1		0	PRJ05				Andy Tiles
4	3	Product Launch	External	Project	Yes	1		0	PRJ04	C20000	Norm Thompson	1	Bill Levine
5	1	Heatexchanger Production	External	Subproject	Yes	2	3	0	PRJ04	C20000	Norm Thompson	1	Bill Levine
6	2	Marketing Campaign Product Launch	External	Subproject	Yes	2	3	0	PRJ04	C20000	Norm Thompson	1	Bill Levine
7	3	Event Launch Heatexchanger	External	Subproject	Yes	3	2	0	PRJ04	C20000	Norm Thompson	1	Bill Levine

Stages

#	Project/Subproject	Position	Start Date	Closing Date	Task	Stage Description	Planned Cost	Invoiced ...	Open Amo...	Invoiced ...	Open Amo...	% Complete	F...
1	Product Launch	1	09/01/2016	09/02/2016	Planning	Concept Management	0.0	0.0	0.0	0.0	0.0	5.000000	
2	Product Launch	2	09/03/2016	09/04/2016	Kick-off	Definite Communicate	0.0	0.0	0.0	0.0	0.0	0.0	
3	Product Launch	3	09/05/2016	09/30/2016	Realization	Launch/Production	3500.000000	0.0	0.0	0.0	0.0	0.0	
4	Product Launch	4	09/10/2016	10/31/2016	Realization	Launch/Martketing Ca	0.0	0.0	0.0	0.0	0.0	0.0	
5	Product Launch	5	11/01/2016	11/15/2016	Realization	Perform First Customer	0.0	20000.000000	0.0	0.0	0.0	3.000000	
6	Product Launch	6	11/16/2016	11/30/2016	Evaluation	Finishing Evaluate Prod	0.0	0.0	0.0	0.0	0.0	2.000000	

Figure 15.15 A Stage Analysis Report

If you double-click on the row number, a new window will open up to display the stages for the project or subproject, as shown in Figure 15.15. In our example, the PRODUCT LAUNCH project is selected, and the stages for this project are displayed in an additional window, which includes the date, the task, description, costs, and so on.

15.3.2 Open Issues Report

Tracking open issues is paramount for effective project management. Remember that open issues are activities that require special attention, are assigned to one person or team, and need to be resolved before a due date so that the project deadline is not affected.

The Open Issues Report will display information about the project, its subject, its current stage, and other relevant information. Access this report by following the menu path PROJECT MANAGEMENT • PROJECT REPORTS • OPEN ISSUES REPORT, and then use the selection criteria screen shown in Figure 15.16 to generate the report. Table 15.13 provides further details about the selection criteria.

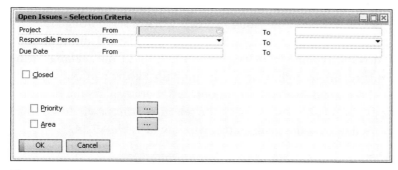

Figure 15.16 Open Issues Report Selection Criteria

Field	Description/Use
PROJECT FROM/TO	Define a range of projects or leave blank to display the open issues of all projects.
RESPONSIBLE PERSON FROM/TO	Select the persons responsible for solving the issues.
DUE DATE FROM/TO	Select the range of due dates for the issues.
CLOSED	Check this option to include issues that have been closed already.
PRIORITY	Click on the BROWSE icon (the ellipsis) to open up the screen to choose a priority for the issue. Your options are LOW, MEDIUM, or HIGH.
AREA	Click on the BROWSE icon (the ellipsis) to select the department areas the issue belongs to.

Table 15.13 Open Issues Report Selection Criteria Fields

Figure 15.17 shows an example of an Open Issues Report that lists eight open issues related to product launch.

Open Issues

#	Project	Subproject	Stage	Area	Priority	Remarks	Responsible	Entered By	Date	Due Date	Effort
1	Product Launch	Marketing Campaign Product Launch	Launch/Execution	Marketing	Medium	Obatin mailing list	Castle, Morris	Levine, Bill	09/02/2016	11/30/2016	0.0
2	Product Launch	Marketing Campaign Product Launch	Launch/Execution	Marketing	Medium	Prepare Newsletters x 3	Castle, Morris	Levine, Bill	09/02/2016	11/30/2016	0.0
3	Product Launch	Marketing Campaign Product Launch	Launch/Execution	Marketing	Medium	Send Newsletters once per week	Castle, Morris	Levine, Bill	09/02/2016	11/30/2016	0.0
4	Product Launch	Marketing Campaign Product Launch	Launch/Execution	Marketing	Medium	Prepare video clip	Castle, Morris	Levine, Bill	09/02/2016	11/30/2016	0.0
5	Product Launch	Marketing Campaign Product Launch	Launch/Execution	Marketing	Medium	Prepare short notes for FB	Castle, Morris	Levine, Bill	09/02/2016	11/30/2016	0.0
6	Product Launch	Marketing Campaign Product Launch	Launch/Execution	Marketing	Medium	Publish every week on FB and YouTube	Castle, Morris	Levine, Bill	09/10/2016	11/30/2016	0.0
7	Product Launch	Event Launch Heatexchanger	Definition/Planning	Marketing	Medium	Contract with Hotel	Castle, Morris	Levine, Bill	09/10/2016	11/30/2016	0.0
8	Product Launch	Event Launch Heatexchanger	Launch/Execution	Marketing	Medium	Calls to confirm attendance	Keenes, Charleen	Levine, Bill	09/10/2016	11/30/2016	0.0

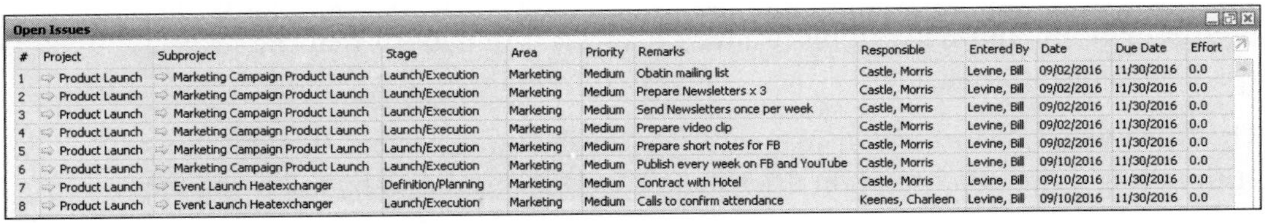

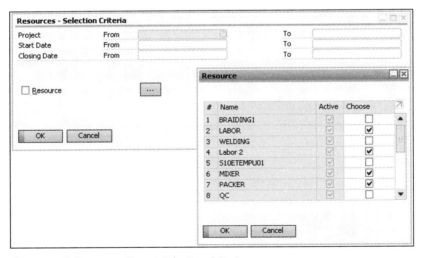

Figure 15.17 An Open Issues Report

15.3.3 Resources Report

Within a project in SAP Business One, you can create work orders through the Production module; these work orders will include items to be issued and consumed in production and resources like labor and machines used in the manufacturing process. Access this report by following the menu path Project Management • Project Reports • Resources Report. The Resources Report displays the resources that are used in a project or subproject, using the selection criteria window shown in Figure 15.18. We'll discuss the fields in this window in Table 15.14.

Figure 15.18 Resources Report Selection Criteria

Field	Description/Use
PROJECT FROM/TO	Define a range of projects or leave blank to display the open issues of all projects.
START DATE FROM/TO	Select the range of start dates for the report.
CLOSING DATE FROM/TO	Select the range of closing dates for the report.
RESOURCE	Click on the BROWSE icon (the ellipsis) to open up the screen to mark the resources to be included in the report. This is useful when you want to focus on resources in certain areas of the shop floor.

Table 15.14 Resources Report Selection Criteria Fields

Once you've entered your criteria, a report similar to the one shown in Figure 15.19 will be displayed. This report outlines the resources used for the Heat Exchanger project, with resources segmented into LABOR, CUTTING, and WELDING.

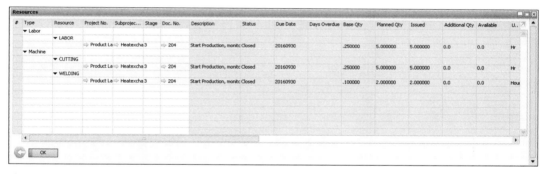

Figure 15.19 A Resources Report

Perhaps nothing delivers greater value than the ability to produce mean-ingful reports with your ERP system. Unfortunately, querying the data and returning the sought-after answers quickly and accurately is some-times outside the reach of most business users. SAP Business One offers several out-of-the-box tools that make these reporting inquiries easier than ever before.

16 Reporting

In your typical daily routine as a business user, reporting is more than just convenience; it is an imperative, whether you are an SAP Business One user or a user of any other software.

SAP Business One delivers reports out of the box that will probably satisfy 70% of the reports your company might need, but sometimes, you might need to create your own for your own unique business needs. To go beyond the reports already explained in this book and to satisfy these specific needs, SAP Business One has delivered several reporting solutions: queries, Drag and Relate, the Print Layout Designer, and SAP Crystal Reports. We'll show you how to use each of these tools in this chapter.

16.1 Queries

One of the most unique features of the SAP Business One solution is the concept of queries.

In general, to *query* means to ask a question about something, especially to express one's doubts about it or to confirm the validity or accuracy of a hypothesis. In the enterprise world, many users who have past experience with other ERP systems claim that SAP Business One's ability to query the database is the best, easiest, and most powerful of any ERP system ever produced. The most popular reporting solution, queries result in onscreen reports, which are designed to be interactive via SAP Business One's golden arrow icon.

To access the query functionality in SAP Business One, click on the TOOLS menu item to reveal the TOOLS menu shown in Figure 16.1. Scroll down and click on the QUERIES selection; the system will display the query options shown in Figure 16.2: QUERY MANAGER, QUERY GENERATOR, and so on.

Figure 16.1 The Tools Menu with the Queries Submenu Selected

Figure 16.2 The Queries Submenu

Although queries have a lot of ground cover, the easiest way to learn is to jump to the second menu option to open the Query Generator, which we'll use to create a simple query that we'll call "Credit Report."

Once you select the QUERY GENERATOR button, the system will open the QUERY GENERATOR screen shown in Figure 16.3.

Finding the data we need for this simple little credit report is fairly straightforward in SAP Business One. Keeping in mind that a query is just a question, let's start our report by asking, "What is the available credit for all of my customers?" and "Where can I find that information displayed in SAP Business One?"

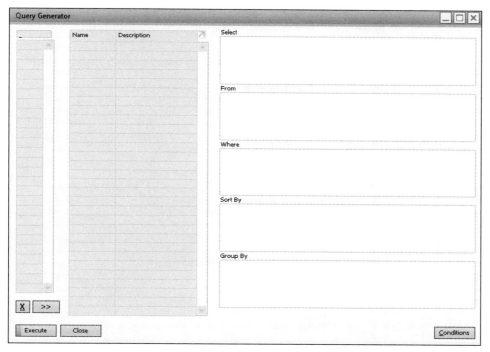

Figure 16.3 The Query Generator Screen

We already know that we'll find information about customers in the BUSINESS PARTNER MASTER DATA screen, which you can access by following the menu path BUSINESS PARTNERS • BUSINESS PARTNERS MASTER DATA. Notice that Figure 16.4 is focused on the PAYMENT TERMS tab for our credit report query because the CREDIT LIMIT field is located on this tab.

While you can see the necessary information in the BUSINESS PARTNER MASTER DATA screen, to reference the data in the Query Generator, we'll need to discover the table name and the field name for this data location. First, select the VIEW menu, which will deliver us the viewing options available, as shown in Figure 16.5. From these options, click on SYSTEM INFORMATION to activate this feature. You could alternatively use the keystrokes $\boxed{\texttt{Ctrl}}+\boxed{\texttt{Shift}}+\boxed{\texttt{I}}$.

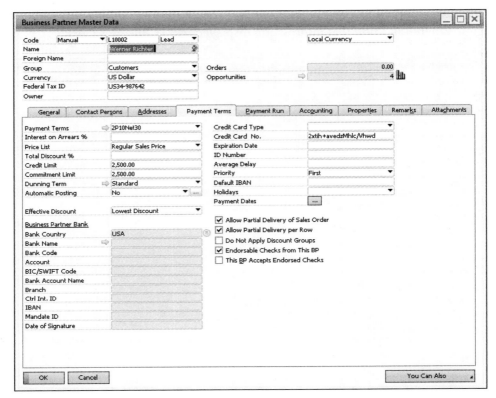

Figure 16.4 The Payment Terms Tab of the Business Partner Master Data Screen

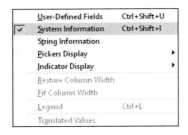

Figure 16.5 The View Options in the View Menu Selection

With the BUSINESS PARTNER MASTER DATA screen open and the PAYMENT TERMS tab visible in Figure 16.6, hover your mouse over the CREDIT LIMIT field to see additional information (the table name and field name) about where the data resides in the database.

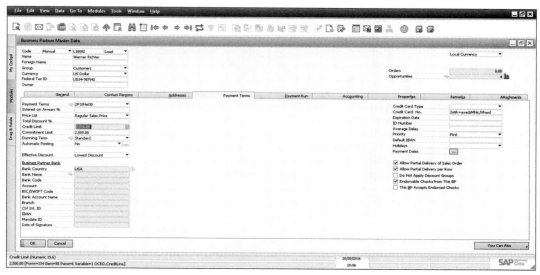

Figure 16.6 The Payment Terms Tab of the Business Partner Master Data Screen

You can see details about the CREDIT LIMIT field in the lower left corner of Figure 16.7. The last two pieces of information on the bottom line are what we are looking for: OCRD is the name of the database table where the actual field name CREDITLINE exists.

Figure 16.7 Credit Limit Details

With this information, we can return to the Query Generator and enter the table name "OCRD" into the left column, as shown in Figure 16.8. This column lists the tables that are a part of a particular query.

Press the [Tab] key to automatically populate the middle column with all of the fields within the OCRD table (or whichever table name is highlighted in that left column). Figure 16.9 shows the results when the OCRD table name is highlighted.

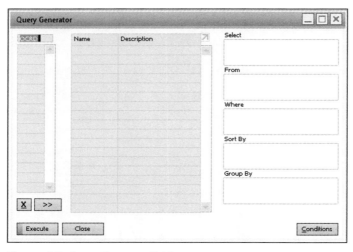

Figure 16.8 Query Generator Tables

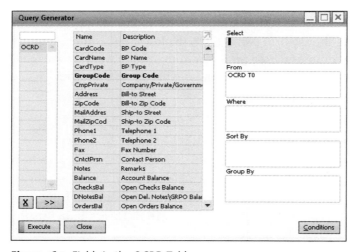

Figure 16.9 Fields in the OCRD Table

Tips and Tricks: Getting a List of All SAP Business One Tables

To generate a list of *all* SAP Business One tables, open the Query Generator as if you're starting a new query. Place your cursor in the dialog box on the top of the leftmost column of the QUERY GENERATOR screen and press the Tab key. The system will return a list of all SAP Business One tables, as shown in Figure 16.10.

Figure 16.10 A Complete List of Tables in SAP Business One

Tips and Tricks: Sorting an SAP Business One List

Take a closer look at Figure 16.10 and notice that SAP Business One has a default sort order based upon the first column in the list. You can easily change the "focus" of the sort order by clicking on the column heading that you wish to sort by. In Figure 16.11, we chose the DESCRIPTION column for the sort order by double-clicking on the column header.

Figure 16.11 Sorting the Tables for a Query

To keep refining your search, you can type a keyword into the Find field. In our example, we searched for sales-related tables by typing "sales" in the Find field.

Once you find the tables you're looking for (in our case, the Sales Employee table), highlight the table name and click the Choose button. The system will automatically bring that table into the query you are working on.

Let's return to our example query in Figure 16.9. We now have the list of all the fields in the OCRD table to potentially use in our query.

The next step is to select which of these fields you would like to include in your credit report query. You can add fields to the query report by adding them into the Select box at the top of the right column of the Query Generator. Simply place your cursor inside the Select box and then locate the field you wish to add to the query report and double-click on it.

In our simple example, let's add the following fields from the OCRD table to our query report (Figure 16.12 shows the final result):

- CardName (the Business Partner Name field)
- CntcPrsn (the default Contact Persons Name field)
- Phone1 (one of two primary telephone fields in the business partner master record)
- Balance (the open invoice balance of the business partner)
- CreditLine (the Business Partners Credit Limit field)

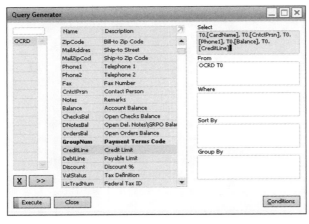

Figure 16.12 Fields Selected from OCRD Table for the Credit Report Query

The objective of reports is to find and organize relevant information—and for this example, we can identify two additional fields you might like to add to this little report:

- The group each business partner belongs to
- The sales person responsible for this business partner

However, we have a small problem. Scrolling up and down the middle column in Figure 16.12, you can see the GROUPCODE field is available. You can add this field to the credit report, but you'll most likely receive a code or number—not the description or actual name for this field, as shown in Figure 16.13. Most of us can't remember numbers for this type of information, so this doesn't help us achieve our goal of gaining insights into business partner groups.

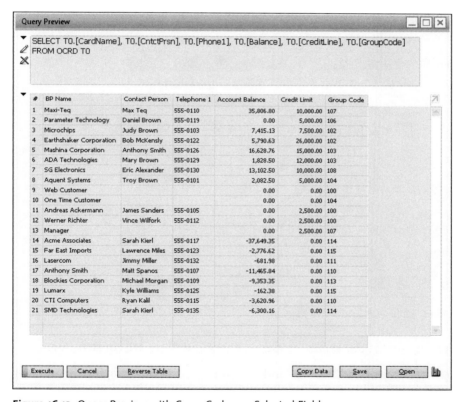

Figure 16.13 Query Preview with GroupCode as a Selected Field

So how can we actually add the name of the group, rather than its number?

If you look closely at the Query Generator, you'll notice that some of the fields in the list of fields available in the OCRD table are bold, which indicates that they are *related tables* that are linked to the OCRD table based upon their primary keys. In our example, the GROUPCODE field exists in the OCRD table and *also* exists in another table where GROUPCODE is the primary key. In order to access the name of the group instead of the number, we need to join that table and our OCRD table to the same query.

SAP Business One makes seemingly complex SQL queries easy. Just click on the GROUPCODE field and hold; once the cursor highlights the field with a box, drag the GROUPCODE field into the left column underneath the OCRD table. The result—the addition of a new table named OCRG to our query—is shown in Figure 16.14.

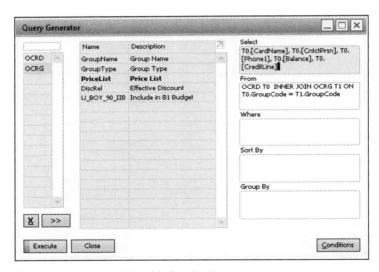

Figure 16.14 Table OCRG Added to the Query

A couple important things just happened in the query we are constructing:

▶ A new table name (OCRG) was added to the left column, bringing the number of tables in our query to two.

▶ The OCRG table has been highlighted in the left column.

▸ The fields available for the query from the OCRG table have populated the middle column. Notice that one of them is GROUPNAME.

▸ SAP Business One has automatically written the SQL that joins these two tables together in the FROM box in the right most column (under the SELECT box).

Next, you can add the GROUPNAME field to the query by following these steps:

1. Place your cursor at the end of the last field you added to the SELECT box. (Alternatively, you could place the cursor at a more appropriate location between any two fields using the keyboard.)

2. Highlight the OCRG table in the left column.

3. Double-click on the GROUPNAME field to add it to the SELECT box, as shown in Figure 16.15.

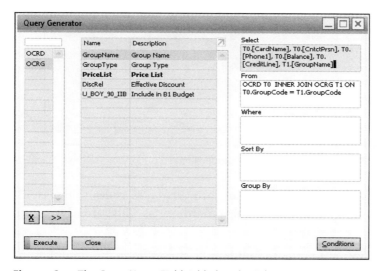

Figure 16.15 The GroupName Field Added to the Select Box

Figure 16.16 shows what happens when you click the EXECUTE button: the actual group names—and not their numbers—are displayed in your report. This information is far easier to consume for most users.

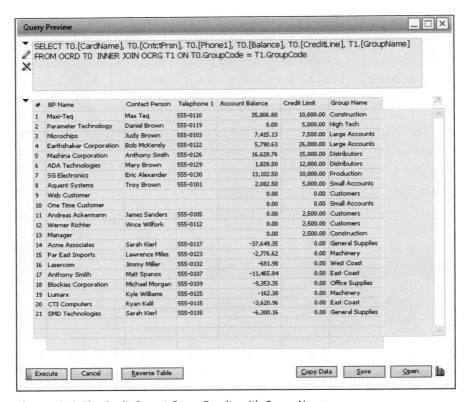

Figure 16.16 The Credit Report Query Results with Group Names

To add the salespersons' names rather than their employee codes to our credit report, you would follow the exact same procedure, as illustrated by Figure 16.17:

1. Highlight the OCRD table in the left column.

2. Locate the SLPCODE field for the sales employee code in the middle column, and drag it into the left column.

3. Place the cursor in the SELECT box at the desired position.

4. Double-click the SLPNAME field to add it to the SELECT box.

Now, when we execute our credit report query, we'll see a screen like the one shown in Figure 16.18.

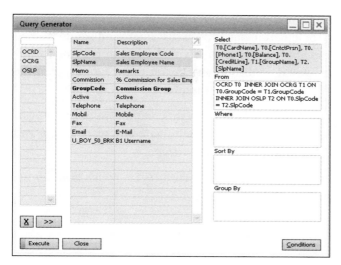

Figure 16.17 Tables OCRD, OCRG, and OSLP Joined in the Query

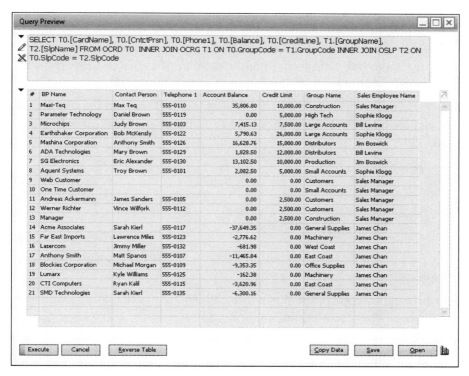

Figure 16.18 The Credit Report Query Results with Group and Salesperson Names Added

If you were to examine the data in the business partner query closely, you would notice that the query has a problem: it includes both customers and vendors—and probably leads as well. Although it's conceivable you'd want to get this list for either customers *or* vendors, you'd probably never want to include leads in the report. How can we identify leads and remove them?

By turning our attention to the WHERE box of the right column, we can refine our query. The first thing we will do is permanently eliminate any place that a lead would infiltrate the credit report by following these steps:

1. Place the cursor into the WHERE box shown in Figure 16.19, which is under the FROM box shown on the right side of Figure 16.17.

Figure 16.19 The Where Box

2. Click on the CONDITIONS button at the bottom right corner of the screen.

3. Highlight the OCRD table in the left column.

4. Locate the CARDTYPE field in the middle column of available fields from the OCRD table.

5. Make certain the cursor is inside the WHERE box and then, in the middle column, double-click on the CARDTYPE field to add it to the WHERE box in Figure 16.20.

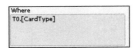

Figure 16.20 The CardType Field in the Where Box

6. Again, click on the CONDITIONS button. The system will display the CONDITIONS box, which is shown in Figure 16.21.

7. Make sure the cursor is in the WHERE box immediately to the right of the CARD-TYPE field.

8. In the CONDITIONS column of the CONDITION CONTROL box, double-click on the NOT EQUAL condition, which will enter <> into the WHERE box following the CARDTYPE field.

Figure 16.21 The Condition Control Center

9. In SAP Business One, the CARDTYPE field of the OCRD table has three possible answers: L for lead, S for supplier or vendor, and C for customer. Just to the right of the <>, enter "L".

The QUERY GENERATOR screen now looks like Figure 16.22.

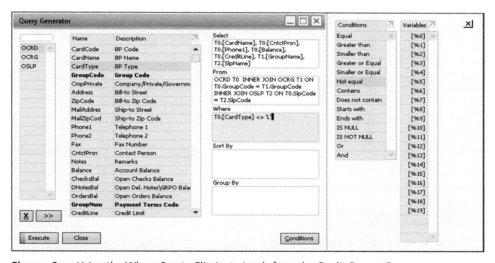

Figure 16.22 Using the Where Box to Eliminate Leads from the Credit Report Query

Now, clicking the EXECUTE button will return the data shown in Figure 16.23. Notice that only nineteen records are listed, whereas the previous execution of the query in Figure 16.18 contained twenty-one records. This difference is because two records (two leads) have been successfully eliminated from the query.

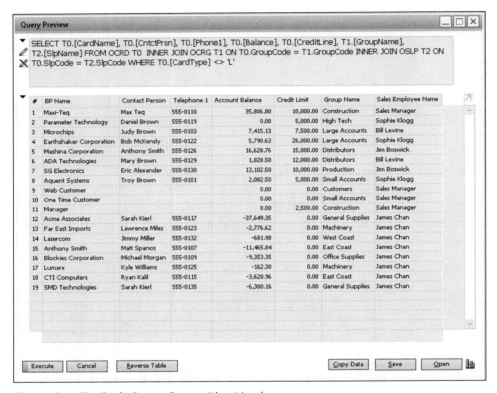

Figure 16.23 The Credit Report Query without Leads

Now, let's say we want the option to include either customers *or* vendors the next time we run the report. We will want to return to our query (which is still under construction) and add additional conditions.

Tips and Tricks: Returning to the Edit Mode in Query Generator

A query is rarely absolutely correct the first time. Typically, you will execute the query multiple times on the way to the finish line, so going back and continuing work on the query is almost a guarantee for most users.

To simply go back and continue working on the query, click the CANCEL button from within the QUERY PREVIEW window. Notice the location of the button in Figure 16.23—adjacent to the EXECUTE button.

So let's return to our query and make some changes to start the new optional conditions choice:

1. Place the cursor immediately to the right of the previously created condition in the CONDITIONS box.

2. If the Conditions Control Center isn't already open, click the CONDITIONS button to open it.

3. In the CONDITIONS column, double-click on the condition AND.

4. Make certain that the focus in the left column is still on the OCRD table by highlighting OCRD and that the cursor in the WHERE box is after the condition AND. The entire condition at this point should read T0.[CardType] <> 'L' AND.

5. Double-click on the CARDTYPE field to add it again to the WHERE box after the condition AND. The entire condition at this point should read T0.[CardType] <> 'L' AND T0.[CardType].

6. Now, let's step into new territory: the VARIABLES column. In any SAP Business One query, you can have as many as twenty different variables, which are labeled [%0], [%1], and so on.

7. With the cursor in the WHERE box immediately to the right of the T0.[CardType], select the EQUAL condition by double-clicking on it. The entire condition at this point should read T0.[CardType] <> 'L' AND T0.[CardType] =.

8. With the cursor in the WHERE box immediately to the right of the T0.[CardType]=, double-click on the first variable [%0]. The entire condition at this point should read T0.[CardType] <> 'L' AND T0.[CardType] =[%0].

At this point, the QUERY GENERATOR screen should look like Figure 16.24.

With little effort, we can also sort the query by the BALANCE field. Simply make certain the OCRD table is highlighted in the left column and then place the cursor in the SORT BY box and double-click on the BALANCE field in the middle column, as shown in Figure 16.25. Remember that sorting in the Query Generator is by default in ascending order. If you wish to sort in descending order, add the phrase "DESC" after the sorted field in the SORT BY box.

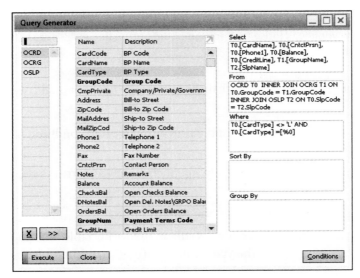

Figure 16.24 Permanently Removing Leads and Conditionally Selecting Either Customers or Vendors

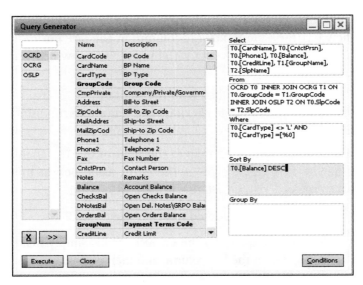

Figure 16.25 The Credit Report Query with a Sort-By Clause

Now, when you execute our query, you'll see the QUERY SELECTION CRITERIA prompt shown in Figure 16.26. The system automatically fills the dropdown list with the potential answers: C for customer, S for vendor, and L for lead. Of course, we've already permanently eliminated leads, so if we select LEADS, no data will be available.

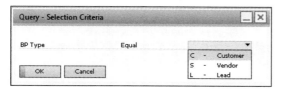

Figure 16.26 Query Selection Criteria Prompt

But if we select CUSTOMERS, we'd see only customers and what they owe us, as shown in Figure 16.27.

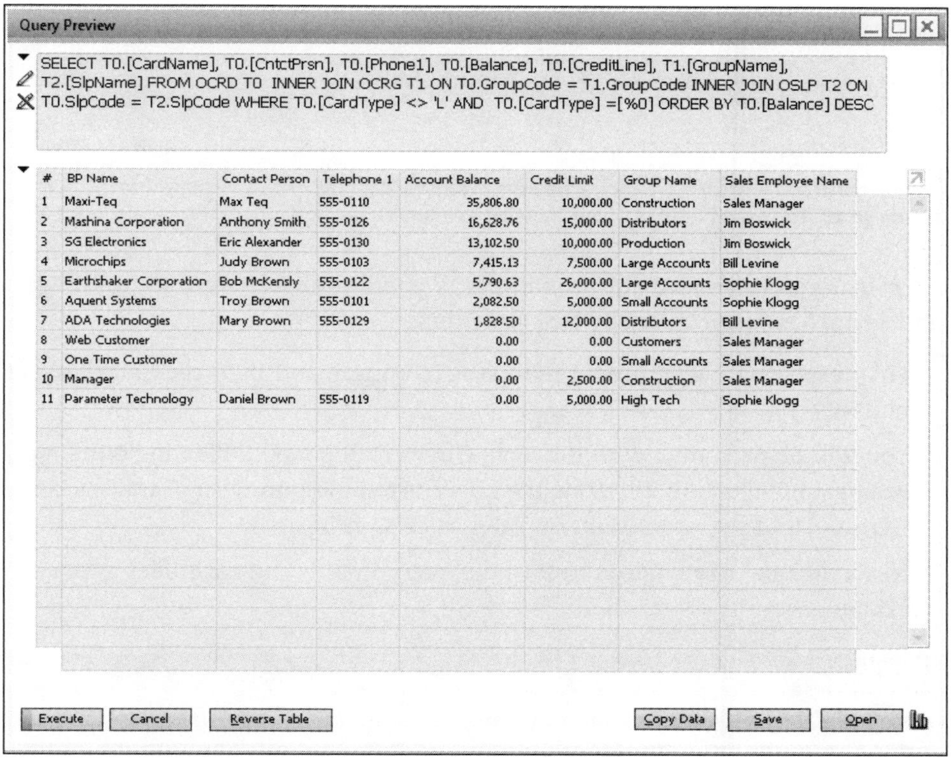

SELECT T0.[CardName], T0.[CntctPrsn], T0.[Phone1], T0.[Balance], T0.[CreditLine], T1.[GroupName], T2.[SlpName] FROM OCRD T0 INNER JOIN OCRG T1 ON T0.GroupCode = T1.GroupCode INNER JOIN OSLP T2 ON T0.SlpCode = T2.SlpCode WHERE T0.[CardType] <> 'L' AND T0.[CardType] =[%0] ORDER BY T0.[Balance] DESC

#	BP Name	Contact Person	Telephone 1	Account Balance	Credit Limit	Group Name	Sales Employee Name
1	Maxi-Teq	Max Teq	555-0110	35,806.80	10,000.00	Construction	Sales Manager
2	Mashina Corporation	Anthony Smith	555-0126	16,628.76	15,000.00	Distributors	Jim Boswick
3	SG Electronics	Eric Alexander	555-0130	13,102.50	10,000.00	Production	Jim Boswick
4	Microchips	Judy Brown	555-0103	7,415.13	7,500.00	Large Accounts	Bill Levine
5	Earthshaker Corporation	Bob McKensly	555-0122	5,790.63	26,000.00	Large Accounts	Sophie Klogg
6	Aquent Systems	Troy Brown	555-0101	2,082.50	5,000.00	Small Accounts	Sophie Klogg
7	ADA Technologies	Mary Brown	555-0129	1,828.50	12,000.00	Distributors	Bill Levine
8	Web Customer			0.00	0.00	Customers	Sales Manager
9	One Time Customer			0.00	0.00	Small Accounts	Sales Manager
10	Manager			0.00	2,500.00	Construction	Sales Manager
11	Parameter Technology	Daniel Brown	555-0119	0.00	5,000.00	High Tech	Sophie Klogg

Execute   Cancel   Reverse Table   Copy Data   Save   Open

Figure 16.27 The Credit Report Query Showing Customers Only

If we select VENDORS, we'd see only vendors and what they owe us, as shown in Figure 16.28. Notice that the numbers here are negative, meaning that we owe our vendors, not the other way around!

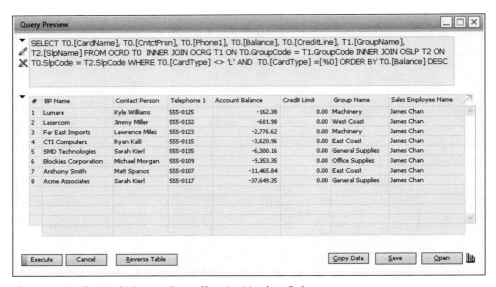

Figure 16.28 The Credit Report Query Showing Vendors Only

Now that you've created this useful query, you'll probably want to use it again and again. Save your query by following these steps:

1. First, execute the query with the EXECUTE button, and then click on the SAVE button.

2. You will be presented with the SAVE QUERY dialog box. Following our simple example in Figure 16.29, name the query "Credit Report Query" and select the GENERAL folder to store it there. Then, click SAVE again.

3. Now, click the SAVE button to save the query in the GENERAL folder as per our example.

Tips and Tricks: Manage Categories

Using the MANAGE CATEGORIES button, you can create other folders and control what folders various users will be able to execute. This control is created by assigning queries to groups in SYSTEM INITIALIZATION • ADMINISTRATION • AUTHORIZATIONS • GENERAL AUTHO-RIZATIONS • USER tab.

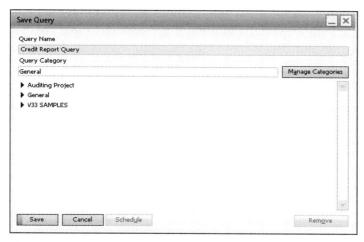

Figure 16.29 The Save Query Dialog Box

4. To check your work, close the Query Generator and open QUERY MANAGER TOOLS • QUERIES • QUERY MANAGER.

5. Click on the GENERAL folder to expand it and see its contents. Confirm that the credit report query is there. Double-click it to run the query from this location.

Tips and Tricks: Getting a Total the Easy Way

One complaint many users have is that their queries do not automatically total columns that are either numerical or in a currency. One valuable trick is to hold down the `Ctrl` key and click on the column header you wish to total. The total of the column will appear at the bottom.

Tips and Tricks: Filter and Sort

Once you've executed a query, you can further sort and filter the query without re-creating it. You simply click on either the FILTER icon (the funnel) and/or the SORT icon (an A and Z in a box) located in the menu bar ribbon at the top of the SAP Business One screen. Just remember—these tools are limited to the data already present within the query.

Many more complicated queries are available using the Query Generator, but in this section, we've covered the basics, which should convince you of how valuable queries can be. In fact, queries are particularly versatile in a well-designed SAP Business One system; they can be deployed in alerts, approval procedures, formatted searches, SAP Crystal Reports, and query print layouts; exported to Excel; and even permanently embedded into Excel spreadsheets for up-to-the-minute analytics. Learning and developing more in-depth Microsoft SQL skills will help not only you as an SAP Business One user but will also deliver great benefits to your company.

> **Tips and Tricks: Organizing Queries in Folders**
>
> Within no time, you may have forty or more queries. We recommend that you organize them into folders that help to locate them for editing or use at a later date. A best practice is to create query folders or categories for such things as alerts, approval procedures, scheduled reports, formatted searches, and more.

Another tool in SAP Business One to help with creating queries is the Query Wizard. (Typically, you may prefer to use either the Query Wizard or the Query Generator.) While we won't go into the same detail for the Query Wizard as we did for the Query Generator, note that the Query Wizard may also be a tool you wish to investigate.

Also note that Microsoft SQL Management Studio also has a more complete query generation and writing tool. Most advanced query creators prefer this tool because creating complex queries can be difficult using more basic tools. You can copy and paste queries created in the Microsoft SQL Management Studio into the Query Generator to use in SAP Business One.

16.2 Drag and Relate

Drag and Relate is SAP Business One's ad-hoc report writer. Ad-hoc reports are "one-and-done" reports used for a specific purpose without consideration of wider applications. This limitation is both a strength and a weakness of the reporting tool: you can't save anything you create with Drag and Relate for another day.

Another Drag and Relate weakness is security and authorizations. Every user with authorization to use Drag and Relate has full access to all the data provided by Drag and Relate (which is substantial), no matter what license type that user may have. Sadly, unscrupulous users may use this weakness to view sensitive data. As a result, many organizations only allow a few highly trusted individuals to use Drag and Relate altogether.

In SAP Business One, version 9.2, the main menu has three tabs: My Cockpit, Modules, and Drag and Relate. Selecting Drag and Relate will bring up the tab shown in Figure 16.30.

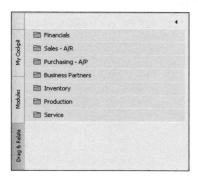

Figure 16.30 The Drag and Relate Tab

To practice with Drag and Relate, click on the Sales – A/R menu selection, which will reveal the subtopics shown in Figure 16.31. You'll remember these from Chapter 5.

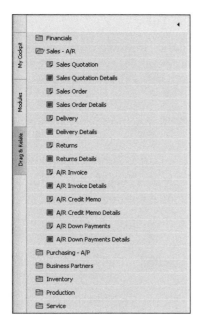

Figure 16.31 Sales A/R Subareas in Drag and Relate

To drill down further, double-click on A/R Invoice Details, which will display the screen shown in Figure 16.32.

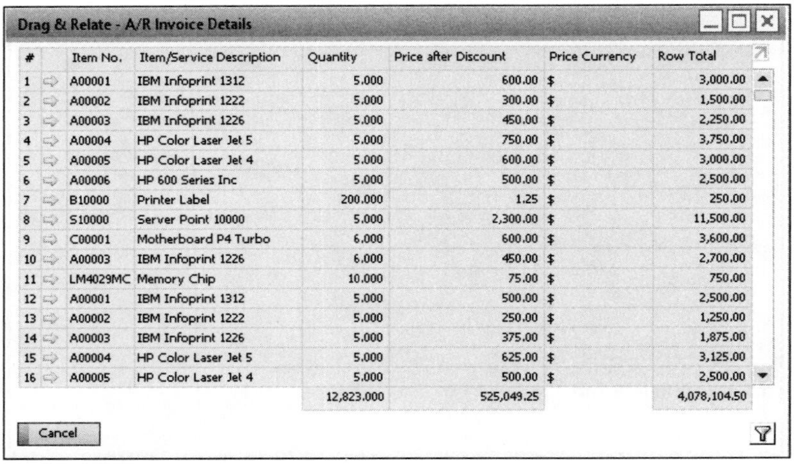

#	Item No.	Item/Service Description	Quantity	Price after Discount	Price Currency	Row Total
1	A00001	IBM Infoprint 1312	5.000	600.00	$	3,000.00
2	A00002	IBM Infoprint 1222	5.000	300.00	$	1,500.00
3	A00003	IBM Infoprint 1226	5.000	450.00	$	2,250.00
4	A00004	HP Color Laser Jet 5	5.000	750.00	$	3,750.00
5	A00005	HP Color Laser Jet 4	5.000	600.00	$	3,000.00
6	A00006	HP 600 Series Inc	5.000	500.00	$	2,500.00
7	B10000	Printer Label	200.000	1.25	$	250.00
8	S10000	Server Point 10000	5.000	2,300.00	$	11,500.00
9	C00001	Motherboard P4 Turbo	6.000	600.00	$	3,600.00
10	A00003	IBM Infoprint 1226	6.000	450.00	$	2,700.00
11	LM4029MC	Memory Chip	10.000	75.00	$	750.00
12	A00001	IBM Infoprint 1312	5.000	500.00	$	2,500.00
13	A00002	IBM Infoprint 1222	5.000	250.00	$	1,250.00
14	A00003	IBM Infoprint 1226	5.000	375.00	$	1,875.00
15	A00004	HP Color Laser Jet 5	5.000	625.00	$	3,125.00
16	A00005	HP Color Laser Jet 4	5.000	500.00	$	2,500.00
			12,823.000	525,049.25		4,078,104.50

Figure 16.32 The A/R Invoice Details Screen in Drag and Relate

We should call your attention to a few universal Drag and Relate principles that govern any object for which Drag and Relate returns data:

- Drag and Relate handles what we refer to as *raw data*—in other words, all data, without a filter or criteria of any kind. Thus, in our example, every line of every A/R invoice, in other words, all the rows of all the A/R invoices from the beginning of time, are included.
- This data is presented, by default, according to the transaction order (basically date order) of the system.
- The golden arrow in this A/R Invoice Details selection will open the A/R invoice that this particular line item was a part of. Notice that the first column, denoted by the # column header, contains the invoice number.
- To change the sort order of the screen, double-click on a different column header.
- Any column representing containing numbers is automatically totaled at the bottom of the column.
- You can also filter the results by clicking on the Filter icon (the funnel). The system will return a new filter table, as shown in Figure 16.33.

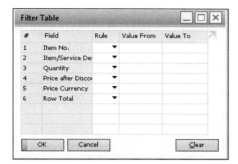

Figure 16.33 Filter Table for the Sales A/R Invoice Details Selection

Let's look at a complex example of using Drag and Relate to look at vendor data.

1. With your cursor on the ITEM NO. field in any row, click and hold the ITEM NUMBER field.

2. With the PURCHASING – A/P section expanded, drag and drop the ITEM NO. field on top of the PURCHASING – A/P INVOICE section as shown in Figure 16.34. Drag and Relate will return all the A/P invoices where this item has ever appeared. Double-click on the CUSTOMER/VENDOR CODE column header to get a quick list of the vendors from which you previously ordered this item.

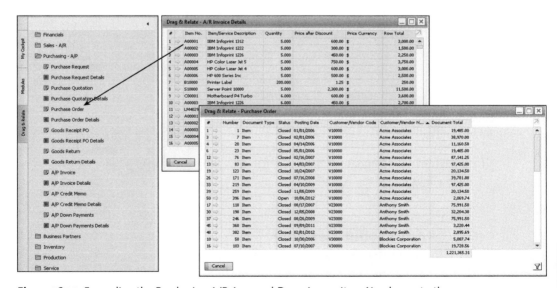

Figure 16.34 Expanding the Purchasing A/P Area and Dropping an Item Number onto the Purchase Order Subsection

You can also open another master data record such as the BUSINESS PARTNER MASTER DATA screen. With the BUSINESS PARTNER MASTER DATA screen open, confirm that the DRAG AND RELATE menu tab is selected and open to the PURCHASING – A/P section. Be sure a vendor is in the BUSINESS PARTNER MASTER DATA screen, then drag and drop the VENDOR CODE field on top of the PURCHASE ORDER menu section of Drag and Relate, as shown in Figure 16.35. Drag and Relate will return a list of all purchase orders in the system for the vendor you selected.

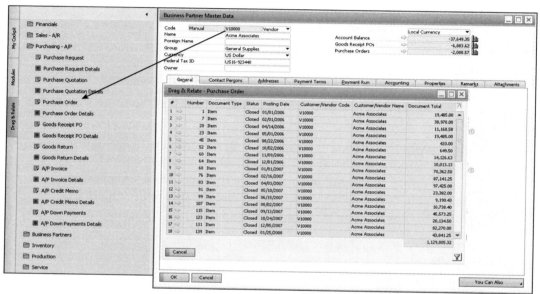

Figure 16.35 Dragging and Dropping the Vendor Code from the Business Partner Master Data Screen to the Purchase Order Menu Section in Drag and Relate

This short lesson on how to use the Drag and Relate ad-hoc reporting feature of SAP Business One covers just the basics. With just a little trial and error, you'll find many more ways to deliver useful data with Drag and Relate in just a few mouse clicks.

16.3   Print Layout Designer

The Print Layout Designer was the original reporting tool delivered with SAP Business One. But, to this day, many SAP Business One customers count on the Print Layout Designer day in and day out for layouts. *Layouts* refer to printouts and document previews that are generated from marketing documents in SAP Business One, such as sales orders, invoices, and delivery quotations. Most of the out-of-the-box "reports" from early versions of SAP Business One were also based upon the Print Layout Designer. For many users, the Print Layout Designer is the fastest way to preview the look and feel of a marketing document.

While Print Layout Designer isn't a difficult reporting and editing tool to learn for basic uses, true mastery can be difficult, as is the case with most reporting tools. While there has been no date announced for the permanent retirement of the Print Layout Designer as a reporting tool within SAP Business One, SAP Crystal Reports is its replacement. As of the time of this writing, the Print Layout Designer is still operational within all the latest versions of SAP Business One.

Because many users of SAP Business One had invested significantly in the Print Layout Designer for both reports and layouts, SAP created a tool to transform Print Layout Designer designs to SAP Crystal Reports. This tool is available on the SAP Community Network (SCN) in the SAP Business One section.

A complete explanation of Print Layout Designer falls outside the scope of this book, but numerous documents are available from which you can learn to use Print Layout Designer. The best way to learn is to do everything you can on your own and, when you get stuck, ask for help. Stay close to your consultant, especially those that have many years of experience with SAP Business One. These consultants likely found it necessary to master the Print Layout Designer.

16.4   SAP Crystal Report Designer

When SAP Business One was introduced to the marketplace, the only report writing option within the application was the Print Layout Designer. But perhaps the most popular and far-reaching report writer for small and medium-sized enterprises has been SAP Crystal Reports.

Many early adopters of SAP Business One were disappointed that the report writer they had previously invested in (Crystal Reports) was not included in their new ERP experience. Still, because SAP Crystal Reports was compatible with Microsoft SQL databases, users were able to create SAP Crystal Reports from their SAP Business One data. However, these reports were not integrated with their ERP systems, and all report designs and specification were stored completely outside of SAP Business

One. When SAP asked customers what report writer they would most like to use, Crystal Reports easily rose to the top of customers' reporting wish lists. SAP Business One resellers even collected samples of country-specific marketing documents and submitted them to SAP as targets for future designs within SAP Business One. As you can imagine, everyone was anticipating being able to more easily use Crystal Reports within SAP Business One.

In the meantime, SAP acquired the parent company of Crystal Reports, Business-Objects, which set the stage for quick integration through the development of SAP Crystal Reports, as well as other SAP BusinessObjects software within the overall footprint of SAP Business One. Because of SAP's acquisition, SAP Business One users enjoy close integration with SAP Crystal Reports, which is not available in any other ERP system. SAP Crystal Reports integration within SAP Business One is truly unique.

16.4.1 Installation

Today's technology has led us to the cloud. Greater numbers of SAP Business One users are deploying their ERP systems with cloud-based technologies in one way or another. As of the time of this writing, SAP recently released a new web client for SAP Business One, making it easy—even necessary—to jump into the cloud.

As a result, SAP Crystal Reports Designer should be installed on a cloud-based terminal server for most customers. Doing this will make SAP Crystal Reports Dsigner easily accessible to users no matter where they are located when writing reports.

Two installations are important for your SAP Business One system:

▶ SAP Crystal Reports Designer: As a separate installation from SAP Business One, SAP Crystal Reports Designer is not installed using the SAP Business One Installation Wizard. Make sure you use the SAP Crystal Reports Designer version recommended for your specific version of SAP Business One. You should validate this with your SAP Business One reseller.

▶ SAP Crystal Reports Add-in: Also a separate installation from SAP Business One, the SAP Crystal Reports Add-in should be installed after SAP Business One and SAP Crystal Reports Designer have been installed. This add-in will be located within the folder structure of your SAP Business One software. Look for the installation package in the PACKAGES folder and then under the SAP CR ADD-IN INSTALLATION subfolder.

Keep in mind that this installation process is separate from the installation of SAP Business One and is not trivial. If you are not 100% certain of the procedures for this installation, you should seek help from a qualified consultant capable of assisting you. We recommend that you work with your reseller on this project!

16.4.2 Integration

Once both the SAP Crystal Reports Designer and the add-in have been installed in the cloud, launch SAP Crystal Reports using the Windows shortcut the installation created. Everyone's system is a little different. The shortcut could be in the Windows START menu, on the desktop, or in the taskbar—maybe even on all three. Your SAP Crystal Reports Designer application will look similar to Figure 16.36.

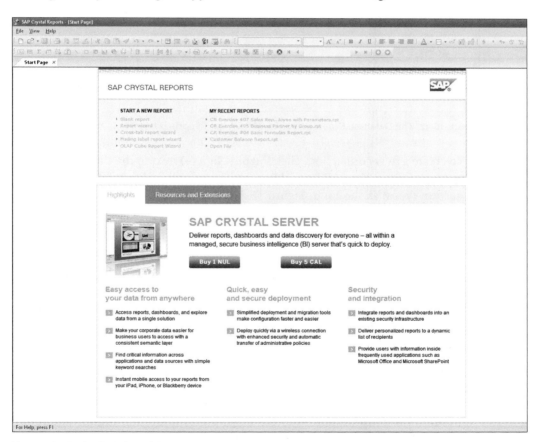

Figure 16.36 The SAP Crystal Reports Designer Start Screen

16.4.3 Report Creation

Follow these steps to create reports using the SAP Crystal Reports Designer but note that these reports will be viewed by other users via the SAP Crystal Reports Viewer.

1. In the gray area under START A NEW REPORT, click BLANK REPORT to open the DATABASE EXPERT screen in SAP Crystal Reports Designer (as shown in Figure 16.37). In this screen, you'll acquire a new connection to your SAP Business One database.

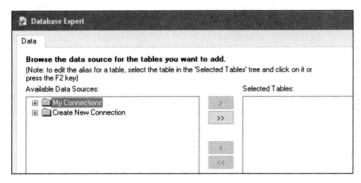

Figure 16.37 The Database Expert Screen in SAP Crystal Reports Designer

2. To create a new connection, click the plus sign (+) next to the CREATE NEW CON-NECTION folder. The SAP Crystal Reports Designer will display the possible connection types, as shown in Figure 16.38.

The SAP Crystal Report Designer can be used with many, many different types of databases—but most users of SAP Business One focus on two of these connection options:

▸ OLE DB (ADO): Prior to the new integration with SAP Business One, this type of connection was used by everyone for reports related to SAP Business One and, in fact, might still be used today. These reports can also be exported from one SAP Business One system and imported into another without any issues.

▸ SAP BUSINESS ONE: This new integration tool is part of SAP's unique integration between SAP Business One and the SAP Crystal Reports Designer. If the SAP Business One connection type is not visible in this selection screen in Figure 16.38, then the SAP Crystal Reports Add-in installation did not execute correctly. Return to Section 16.4.1 and try to install the add-in again.

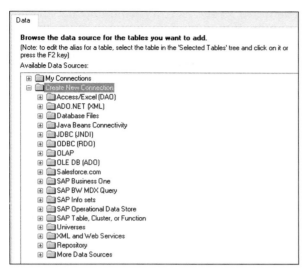

Figure 16.38 Possible Connection Types for SAP Crystal Reports Designer

3. To create an SAP Business One connection, click the plus sign (+) next to the SAP BUSINESS ONE folder. The connection type connection details screen shown in Figure 16.39 will be displayed.

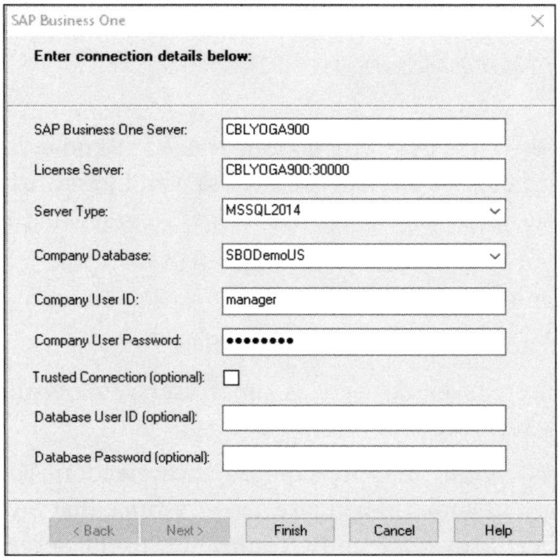

Figure 16.39 SAP Business One Connection Details

Table 16.1 lists each field in Figure 16.39 and its entry requirement. Note that all but the last three fields are required to make the connection.

Field	Use/Description
SAP BUSINESS ONE SERVER	Enter the name of your SAP Business One server.
LICENSE SERVER	Enter the name of your SAP Business One server, a colon, and the port number that was assigned to your license server for SAP Business One. By default, the port number is typically 30000.
SERVER TYPE	Enter your database type, such as "MSSQL2008," "MSSQL2012," "MSSQL2014," or "SAP HANA."
COMPANY DATABASE	Select the database you wish to create a report for from the drop-down list.
COMPANY USER ID	Enter your SAP Business One user name.
COMPANY USER PASSWORD	Enter your SAP Business One password.
TRUSTED CONNECTION (optional)	For security reasons, we recommend ensuring this box is unchecked.
DATABASE USER ID (optional)	Enter your database user name. This field isn't needed when using the new SAP Business One connection type.
DATABASE PASSWORD (optional)	Enter your database user password. This field isn't needed when using the new SAP Business One connection type.

Table 16.1 SAP Business One Connection Type Connection Fields

With new integration with SAP Business One, you no longer need to know the Microsoft SQL system administrator user name (typically "sa") and password, even if you are using the SAP Business One connection type. Now all that is required is the following:

▶ An SAP Business One user name and password

▶ A professional SAP Business One license assigned to the user

▶ The designation as a super user; to mark users as super users, follow the menu path ADMINISTRATION • SETUP • USERS

4. Click the FINISH button shown in Figure 16.39 to acquire the connection. The system will then return a screen that looks like Figure 16.40. Notice that SAP Business One data source has been expanded and a connection to the server and database (symbolized by an electrical plug to the left of the server name)

has been activated. Also notice that a plus sign (+) appears next to the database name to which we requested a connection.

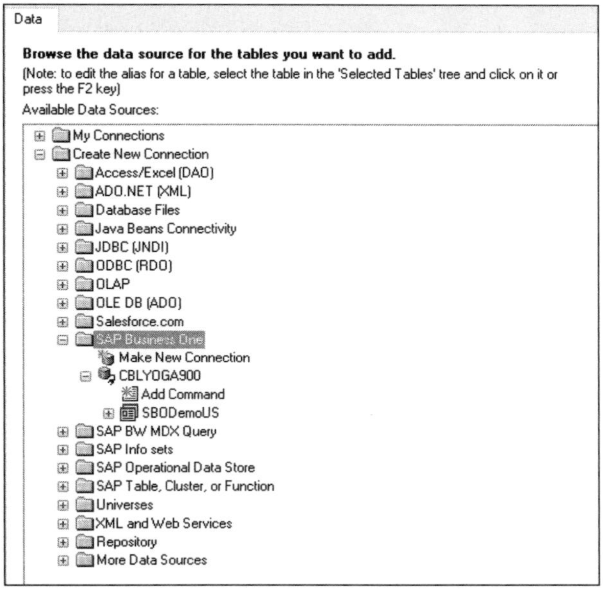

Figure 16.40 Connection to SAP Business One Database

5. To select data for your report, click the plus sign (+) just to the left of the database. As shown in Figure 16.41, the system will now list additional database branches for potential use in our report creation. For the purposes of our example, let's focus on B1 TABLES and DBO.

Figure 16.41 Expansion of the Database Tree

The DBO menu branch is often used in the creation of SAP Crystal Reports. As you can see in Figure 16.42, the DBO menu branch is the pathway to the entire list of tables, views, and stored procedures used by SAP Business One. Views and stored procedures may be delivered out of the box from SAP or may be created unique to your implementation of SAP Business One by a consultant, an add-on software solution provider, or users themselves.

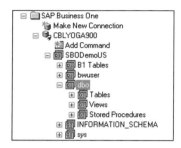

Figure 16.42 Expanding the DBO Menu Branch to Show Tables, Views, and Stored Procedures

6. To expand the SAP Business One tables, click the plus sign (+) to the left of the B1 TABLES menu branch. As shown in Figure 16.43, since SAP Business One, version 8.8, this new integration enables even a novice SAP Crystal Reports creator to find the data they need by replicating the SAP Business One main menu structure within this new connection type. As a result, if you know where the data is located in SAP Business One, you'll know where to find it in SAP Crystal Reports Designer.

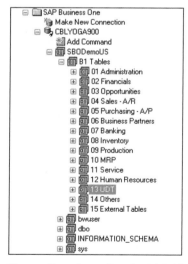

Figure 16.43 Expanding the B1 Tables Branch

7. Before you add data/tables to the report, think about which tables you need. For our purposes, let's focus on the following:

   ▸ The master data table for business partners

   ▸ The salespersons table

   ▸ The business partner groups table

   A brief aside is necessary here: We are demonstrating the simplest way that data can be connected to a report—by connecting various tables from within the database. Alternate methods include using a command (query), a view, or a stored procedure. Each of these alternative methods requires ever-increasing SQL skills.

Tips and Tricks: SAP Crystal Reports Commands

Once you have mastered creating a report using the method we illustrated—using direct connections to SAP Business One tables—as soon as possible, you should next learn how to use a *command*.

A command may sometimes be preferable to other methods because the command always travels with the report specification, whereas a view or a stored procedure, while also originating in an SAP Business One database, may need to be re-created in the target database. An SAP Crystal Report based on a command can simply be exported from one SAP Business One system and then imported into the next system using the Report and Layout Manager found under ADMINISTRATION • SETUP • GENERAL • REPORT AND LAYOUT MANAGER.

In fact, copying a query created in SAP Business One is easy: Instead of clicking the plus sign (+) next to the database name to start the selection process, simply double-click the word COMMAND. In the window that appears, paste the query, as shown in Figure 16.44. This query becomes the dataset for your new report, instead of many tables and many fields.

Over time, high data volumes may slow down the report's productivity, but a command is a much more productive and long-term solution.

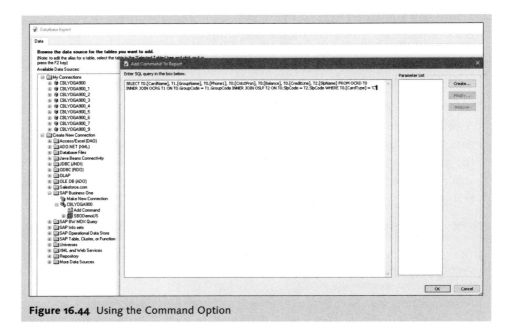

Figure 16.44 Using the Command Option

8. In our example, the tables we want to add are as follows:

> OCRD: The master data table for business partners

> OSLP: The salespersons table

> OCRG: The business partner groups table

First let's add the OSLP table, which is located in the menu path ADMINISTRA-
TION • SETUP • GENERAL – SALES EMPLOYEES/BUYERS. For our example in Figure
16.45, let's navigate to the menu in that exact fashion using the DATABASE
EXPERT screen and add the OSLP table to our report. First, move the table into
the right half of the screen (the SELECTED TABLES pane) in one of three ways:

> Double-clicking

> Dragging and dropping

> Using the arrow controls between the two halves of the DATABASE EXPERT
screen

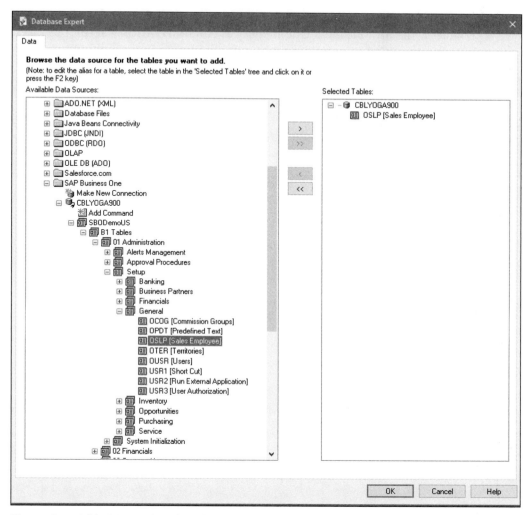

Figure 16.45 Table OSLP in the Selected Tables Pane

Now select OCRG as shown in Figure 16.46. Notice that the location for this table in the SAP Business One menu was ADMINISTRATION • SETUP • BUSINESS PARTNERS • OCRG (CARD GROUPS).

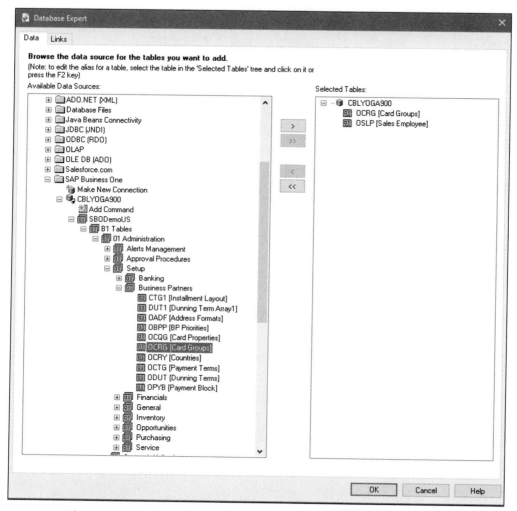

Figure 16.46 Customer Groups OCRG in the Selected Tables Pane

Now, add the OCRD table to the SELECTED TABLES pane, as shown in Figure 16.47. Notice that the OCRD table is located at BUSINESS PARTNERS • BUSINESS PARTNERS MASTER DATA • OCRD (BUSINESS PARTNER).

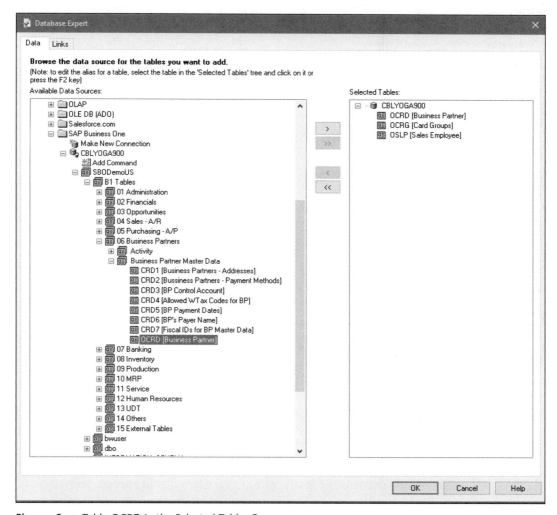

Figure 16.47 Table OCRD in the Selected Tables Pane

Now, click on the LINKS tab at the upper-left corner of the DATABASE EXPERT screen. Figure 16.48 shows how SAP Business One and its handy SAP Crystal Reports integration automatically created the links between the tables you selected for the report. This functionality was built especially for users of SAP Business One and makes even novice report writers highly proficient.

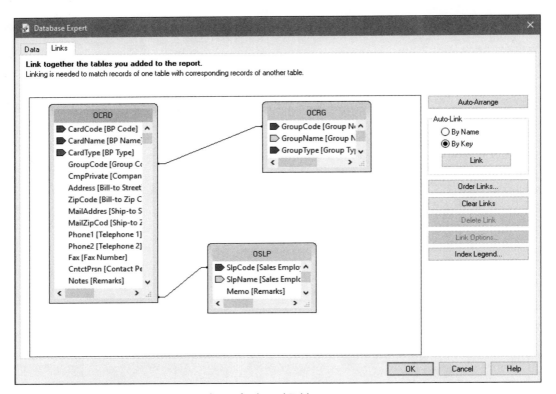

Figure 16.48 Automatic Linking of Selected Tables

Once you click OK, you're ready to start using the SAP Crystal Reports Designer application to truly design, present, and manipulate data with our new report. The FIELD EXPLORER toolbar is the primary tool used for managing data in these reports. SAP Crystal Reports Designer can also use formulas, SQL expressions, parameter fields, running totals, group name fields, and special fields.

Figure 16.49 shows the SAP Crystal Reports Designer with the default FIELD EXPLORER toolbar displayed on the right; Figure 16.50 shows a close-up of the same toolbar. Notice that the toolbar now has our three tables listed OCRD, OCRG and OSLP; we can now select fields from each of the tables to add them to our report. You can expand each table by clicking on its plus sign (+).

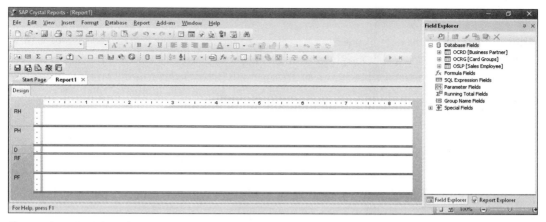

Figure 16.49 SAP Crystal Reports Designer with the Field Explorer Toolbar

Figure 16.50 The Field Explorer Toolbar

9. Expand OCRD with the plus sign and add the CardName, CntctPrsn, Balance, and Credit-Line fields to the report by dragging them into the details row of the SAP Crystal Reports Designer.

10. Expand OCRG with the plus sign and add the GroupName field to the report by dragging and dropping it into the details row of the SAP Crystal Reports Designer.

11. Expand OSLP with the plus sign and add the SLPName field to the report by dragging and dropping it into the details row of the SAP Crystal Reports Designer.

> **Tips and Tricks: Change to Landscape Mode**
>
> The vast majority of SAP Crystal Reports will require additional space, which means that managing space is one of the most critical aspects of report creation.
>
> We recommend that you change the layout to landscape mode prior to adding any data fields to your report, especially before adding groups and subtotals. You'll save a great deal of effort that would go to rearranging and keeping your columns lined up from top to bottom.

12. One way to make sense of your data is to pay attention to its presentation and field names. If you changed your SAP Crystal Reports Designer screen to landscape mode and successfully added the six fields from the three tables, your screen should look like Figure 16.51.

   But notice that, when you drag and drop data fields into the details section/row, SAP Crystal Reports Designer tries to name the columns automatically. Unfortunately, this automatic naming is seldom satisfactory. In our example, we've edited the column heading to make more sense. You can simply double-click on a column heading and then, when you see a visible cursor, delete the heading name and type what you would like as a replacement title for the column.

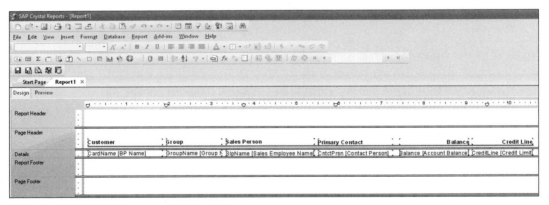

Figure 16.51 Fields Added and Column Titles Edited in the SAP Crystal Reports Designer

You can also preview the report you are creating and get a much more what-you-see-is-what-you-get (WYSIWYG) view of the report you are creating. From the VIEW menu, select PRINT PREVIEW. The SAP Crystal Reports Designer will create a new PREVIEW tab for your report. You can see the tab in Figure 16.51; the preview result itself is shown in Figure 16.52, which is a much more realistic representation of what the report will actually look like when printed.

Customer	Group	Sales Person	Primary Contact	Balance	Credit Line
Maxi-Teq	Construction	Sales Manager	Max Teq	35,806.80	10,000.00
Parameter Technology	High Tech	Sophie Klogg	Daniel Brown	0.00	5,000.00
Microchips	Large Accounts	Bill Levine	Judy Brown	7,415.13	7,500.00
Earthshaker Corporation	Large Accounts	Sophie Klogg	Bob McKensly	5,790.63	26,000.00
Mashina Corporation	Distributors	Jim Boswick	Anthony Smith	16,628.76	15,000.00
ADA Technologies	Distributors	Bill Levine	Mary Brown	1,828.50	12,000.00
SG Electronics	Production	Jim Boswick	Eric Alexander	13,102.50	10,000.00
Aquent Systems	Small Accounts	Sophie Klogg	Troy Brown	2,082.50	5,000.00
Web Customer	Customers	Sales Manager		0.00	0.00
One Time Customer	Small Accounts	Sales Manager		0.00	0.00
Andreas Ackermann	Customers	Sales Manager	James Sanders	0.00	2,500.00
Werner Richter	Customers	Sales Manager	Vince Wilfork	0.00	2,500.00
Manager	Construction	Sales Manager		0.00	2,500.00
Acme Associates	General Supplies	James Chan	Sarah Kierl	-37,649.35	0.00
Far East Imports	Machinery	James Chan	Lawrence Miles	-2,776.62	0.00
Lasercom	West Coast	James Chan	Jimmy Miller	-681.98	0.00
Anthony Smith	East Coast	James Chan	Matt Spanos	-11,465.84	0.00
Blockies Corporation	Office Supplies	James Chan	Michael Morgan	-9,353.35	0.00
Lumarx	Machinery	James Chan	Kyle Williams	-162.38	0.00
CTI Computers	East Coast	James Chan	Ryan Kalil	-3,620.96	0.00
SMD Technologies	General Supplies	James Chan	Sarah Kierl	-6,300.16	0.00

Figure 16.52 Credit Report Query Preview

Tips and Tricks: Out-of-the-Box Changes

Exploring everything you can do in the SAP Crystal Reports Designer would require an entire book devoted to the topic. What we do want to emphasize, however, is how the SAP Crystal Reports Designer has been uniquely configured to work with SAP Business One.

But, before we move on to the next SAP Business One-specific topic, let's make a few changes to the report behind the scenes, such as the following:

▸ Filter out vendors and leads

▸ Add a logo to the report header

▸ Add a report title to the report header

▸ Add a print date to the report header

▸ Add page number to the page footer

▸ Add a group for sales person

▸ Add a subtotal for the sales person group and a grand total

Once we have made these modifications using the SAP Crystal Reports Designer's out-of-the-box features, the DESIGN tab should look something like Figure 16.53 and the PREVIEW tab should look like Figure 16.54. The result is a neat little report regarding our customers' available credit.

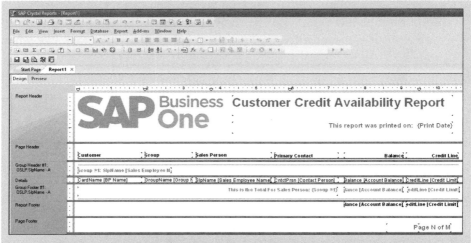

Figure 16.53 The Design Tab of our Customer Credit Availability Report

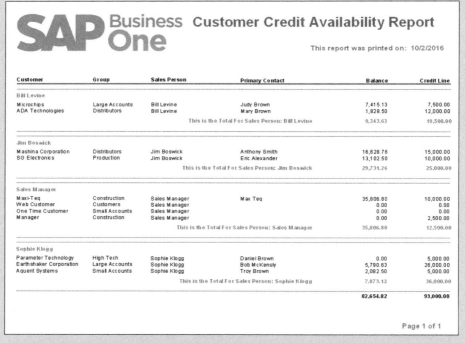

Figure 16.54 Preview of Our Customer Credit Availability Report

First, let's see what the report will actually look like inside of SAP Business One. In the SAP Crystal Reports Designer, click on SAP BUSINESS ONE • PREVIEW IN SAP BUSINESS ONE from the ADD-INS menu shown in Figure 16.55. The resulting screen is how SAP Business One users will see the report on a daily basis.

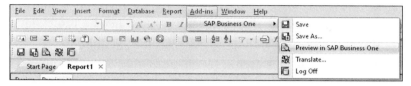

Figure 16.55 The SAP Crystal Reports Viewer

When you select the PREVIEW IN SAP BUSINESS ONE menu option, you will see a message that says, "Waiting for external add-in command to complete." When the message disappears, switch to SAP Business One and notice the SAP Crystal Reports Viewer has been opened, as shown in Figure 16.56.

SAP Business One — Customer Credit Availability Report

This report was printed on: 10/30/2016

Customer	Group	Sales Person	Primary Contact	Balance	Credit Line
Bill Levine					
Microchips	Large Accounts	Bill Levine	Judy Brown	7,415.13	7,500.00
ADA Technologies	Distributors	Bill Levine	Mary Brown	1,828.50	12,000.00
			This is the Total For Sales Person: Bill Levine	9,243.63	19,500.00
Jim Boswick					
Mashina Corporation	Distributors	Jim Boswick	Anthony Smith	16,628.76	15,000.00
SG Electronics	Production	Jim Boswick	Eric Alexander	13,102.50	10,000.00
			This is the Total For Sales Person: Jim Boswick	29,731.26	25,000.00
Sales Manager					
Maxi-Teq	Construction	Sales Manager	Max Teq	35,806.80	10,000.00
Web Customer	Customers	Sales Manager		0.00	0.00
One Time Customer	Small Accounts	Sales Manager		0.00	0.00
Manager	Construction	Sales Manager		0.00	2,500.00
			This is the Total For Sales Person: Sales Manager	35,806.80	12,500.00
Sophie Klogg					
Parameter Technology	High Tech	Sophie Klogg	Daniel Brown	0.00	5,000.00
Earthshaker Corporation	Large Accounts	Sophie Klogg	Bob McKensly	5,790.63	26,000.00
Aquent Systems	Small Accounts	Sophie Klogg	Troy Brown	2,082.50	5,000.00
			This is the Total For Sales Person: Sophie Klogg	7,873.13	36,000.00
				82,654.82	93,000.00

Page 1 of 1

Figure 16.56 SAP Crystal Reports Viewer Inside of SAP Business One

Now, make sure you save/publish your report in SAP Business One so that it can be used by others by following these steps:

1. To place the report in the SAP Business One menu, click ADD-IN • SAP BUSINESS ONE • SAVE. You will be greeted with a logon screen for SAP Business One, as shown in Figure 16.57. This logon screen makes certain that you are authorized to connect to SAP Business One. (Remember that you'll need a professional SAP Business One license and need to be designated as a super user!)

   You must enter the name of the license server (including the port number), select your database server type from the dropdown list, and enter the name of your database server. Then click the CONNECT TO SERVER button. (In Figure 16.57, we have already connected, so the button displayed is CHANGE SERVER.) Once connected to the server, you can select your database from the dropdown list and enter your SAP Business One user name and password; then click OK.

Figure 16.57 The SAP Business One Login Screen

2. The next step is to give the report a name and make sure you select whether what we are saving in SAP Business One is a *report* or *layout* using the radio buttons; the wizard shown in Figure 16.58 will change based on your selection.

   When we select REPORT, the system will check to see if a report with our chosen report name already exists and show us a list of all SAP Crystal Reports in the system. We can either give our report a unique name or select a name from the list and overwrite the old report. If we overwrite an old report, the revised report is still located in its previous folder location in SAP Business One. If it's a new report being imported for the first time, it will be placed in the LOST REPORTS folder in the Report and Layout Manager.

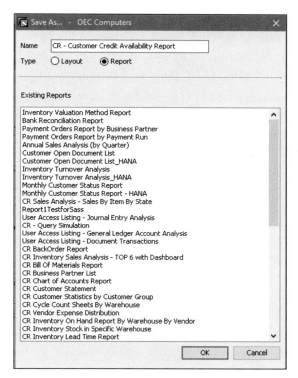

Figure 16.58 Existing Reports Displayed

But first, we must click the OK button, which will trigger the two messages shown in Figure 16.59: "Waiting for external add-in command to complete" and "Operation succeeded." Click OK.

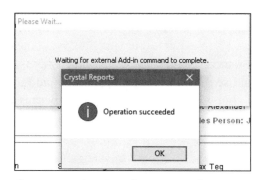

Figure 16.59 SAP Crystal Reports Confirmation Messages

3. Next, log in to SAP Business One and navigate to ADMINISTRATION • SETUP • GENERAL • REPORT AND LAYOUT MANAGER. Once you have opened the Report and Layout Manager, scan down the list and locate the LOST REPORTS folder. If you expand the folder, you will see that your report has been placed in this location.

The right half of this utility screen allows you to pick a menu location in SAP Business One where the report should be located. As shown in Figure 16.60, we chose the BUSINESS PARTNERS REPORTS folder.

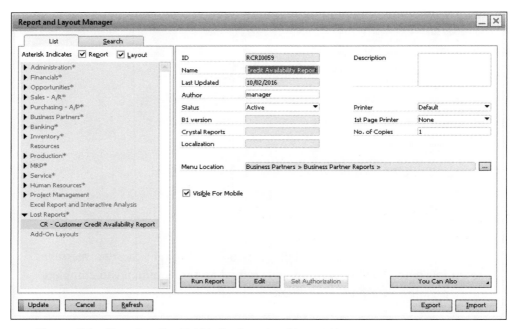

Figure 16.60 Menu Location Field in the Report and Layout Manager

Figure 16.61 drills down into the BUSINESS PARTNERS • BUSINESS PARTNER REPORTS subfolder. Notice that you can use the NEW FOLDERS button to add to the SAP Business One menu structure—but we don't advise doing this because these added folder names may not be edited or deleted.

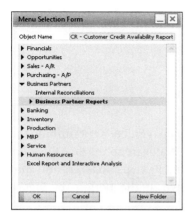

Figure 16.61 Business Partner Reports

4. Returning to the Report and Layout Manager, click the UPDATE button to move your report to its new location. We recommend that you click the REFRESH button and then navigate to the BUSINESS PARTNERS menu in the Report and Layout Manager. Take a look at Figure 16.62, which shows that our report is now in the BUSINESS PARTNER REPORTS menu.

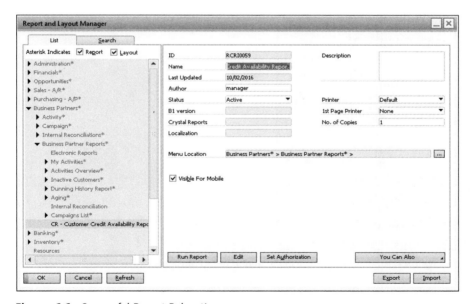

Figure 16.62 Successful Report Relocation

From this screen in the Report and Layout Manager, you can do the following:

▸ Run the report

▸ Edit the report

▸ Set authorizations for the report

▸ Export the report

For now, click OK and close the Report and Layout Manager. Let's try running the report from SAP Business One's main menu instead. Navigate to the SAP Business One main menu then to BUSINESS PARTNERS • BUSINESS PARTNER REPORTS and spot the new Customer Credit Availability Report shown at the bottom of Figure 16.63.

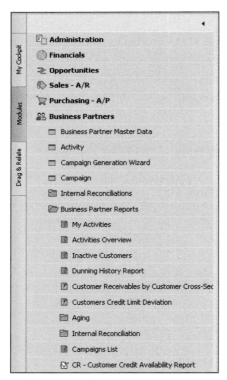

Figure 16.63 CR Customer Credit Availability Report in SAP Business One

Clicking on the report from this location will run the report and preview it in the SAP Crystal Reports Viewer as it will be seen by the typical SAP Business One user, as shown in Figure 16.64. In this preview, the GROUPS panel has been toggled on. Click on any group name within the panel to immediately navigate to that section of the report.

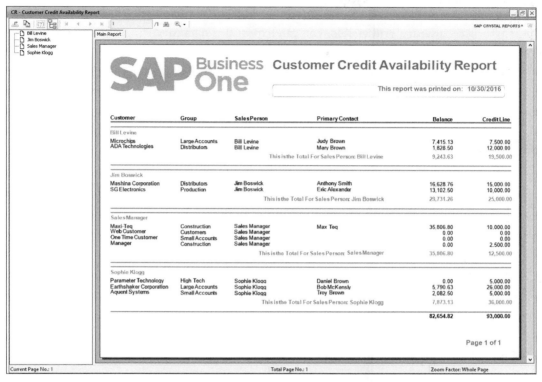

Figure 16.64 CR Customer Credit Availability Report in SAP Crystal Reports Viewer

This small introduction to SAP Crystal Reports and how it works with SAP Business One is a basic illustration of the integration between the two systems. This integration, available since SAP Business One, version 8.8, has delivered a useful tool into the hands of normal business users.

But much more is possible with SAP Crystal Reports and its integration to SAP Business One. For example, you could create *parameters*, which present themselves at runtime and ask the report writer to select values to include or exclude data and much more. For more advanced instruction, we encourage you to seek out deeper training and exposure to SAP Crystal Reports Designer.

16.5 Integration with Microsoft Excel

Integration with Microsoft Excel has always been one of great conveniences delivered out of the box with SAP Business One. Any time a grid appears in SAP Business One, whether a query that has been run or even a document on the screen with a grid visible, you can export this data to Microsoft Excel with a simple procedure.

To transfer a query to Microsoft Excel for further investigation, formatting, emailing, or report designing, click the EXCEL icon (a page with a green X), as highlighted in Figure 16.65, and follow the prompts.

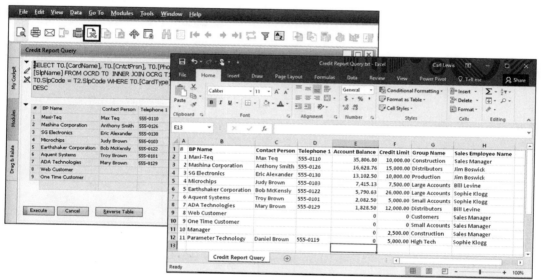

Figure 16.65 Microsoft Excel/SAP Business One Integration

For example, Figure 16.66 shows what would happen if an A/R invoice is open and you click the EXCEL icon.

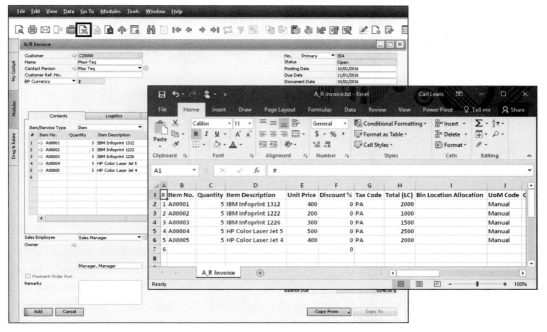

Figure 16.66 An A/R Invoice Being Exported and Presented in Microsoft Excel

One important enhancement to the Microsoft Excel integration in SAP Business One arrived in SAP Business One, version 9.1: cutting and pasting from Excel into an SAP Business One screen. Make sure that the order of the fields in Microsoft Excel is identical to the order of the fields in the SAP Business One screen.

Let's look at an example. In Figure 16.67, we will use the same spreadsheet as Figure 16.66 to create a new invoice in SAP Business One. Perhaps you received this spreadsheet from your customer, and you have decided to cut and paste the data in order to reduce data entry time and potential errors.

First, copy the items and the quantity. You can alternately copy additional fields if they are needed for your document in SAP Business One or are required for the uniqueness of the customer, vendor, journal voucher, and so on.

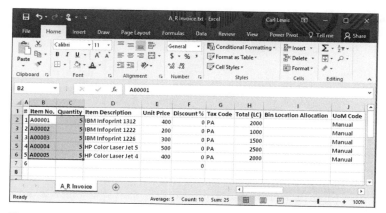

Figure 16.67 Copying Items from Microsoft Excel

Then, open a new A/R invoice (in our example), making certain that the customer has been selected in the A/R invoice header, as done at the top of Figure 16.68. Notice that the cursor is in the first column and row of the A/R invoice grid and that the first two fields are ITEM NO. and QUANTITY, just as they are in our Microsoft Excel spreadsheet in Figure 16.67.

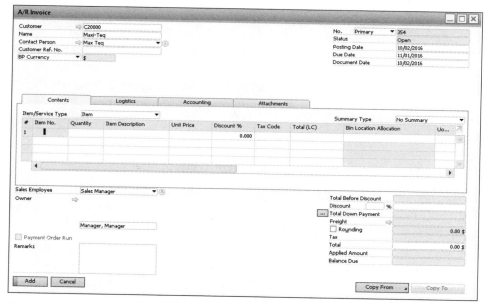

Figure 16.68 A Blank Invoice with the Required Customer in the Header

Making certain that you have copied those five items and their respective quantities into the buffer, place the cursor into that first grid field and then right-click and choose PASTE. Notice in Figure 16.69 that the A/R invoice has now been populated automatically.

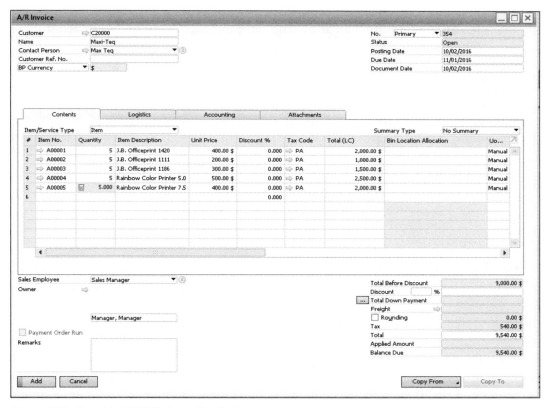

Figure 16.69 Populated SAP Business One System

Why was it important to have a customer in the header? Because the system uses this information to identify other required information for the grid, such as pricing assigned to this customer, and uses the customer connection to both validate and populate those additional fields automatically.

This new cut-and-paste feature has the potential of being a real time-saver for many users of SAP Business One. Many organizations make hundreds of journal entries at the end of every month. These entries are almost always prepared in

659

Excel, but before SAP Business One, version 9.1, they had to be re-entered by hand into the journal voucher data entry screen. Now, they can just be cut and pasted into SAP Business One.

Even more exciting integration with Microsoft Excel is available in the SAP Business One, version for SAP HANA. The new analytics functionalities based on Microsoft Excel are truly amazing, and we encourage readers to learn about these from their consultants and resellers.

If your company has not yet taken the dive into mobile and reaped its benefits, the time is now. SAP Business One makes mobile access easier than ever before with three powerful solutions.

17   Mobile

From its early days, SAP Business One has been integrated with the websites, stores, and shopping carts used by the customers of companies running SAP Business One, but other than through a terminal services-style connection, the solution didn't initially enable business users to conduct their work outside of the office.

In the past several years, SAP has delivered three exciting ways to extend SAP Business One to mobile workers: the SAP Business One mobile application; the SAP Business One Web Client; and the SAP Business One Sales mobile app. Let's look at each of them now.

17.1   SAP Business One Mobile Application

The SAP Business One mobile application gives you access to your SAP Business One business processes anytime, anywhere. Available since SAP Business One, version 8.8, patch level 12 (and improved in releases thereafter), the mobile application offers key functionalities from your core SAP Business One system in a helpful and concise solution.

Using the SAP Business One mobile application has several benefits:

- CRM capabilities are embedded to help with customer, vendor, and lead contact management; scheduled sales activities; and opportunity management driven by quotations and sales orders.
- Alerts and approvals provide the ability to stay in touch with important developments and keep workflows moving.
- Live reporting easily turns SAP Crystal Reports into a live, real-time connection to the data.

- ▶ Inventory information communicates up-to-the-minute inventory levels and detailed product information.
- ▶ Pricing detail for every customer and vendor, including volume discounts and special prices, are made easily visible.
- ▶ Service contracts and their statuses are visible to field workers and support staff.
- ▶ Key performance indicators (KPIs) report up-to-the-minute business metrics.
- ▶ The product catalog capability can create quotations and orders during trade shows and customer-facing events.

As shown in Figure 17.1, the application interface is straightforward and user friendly.

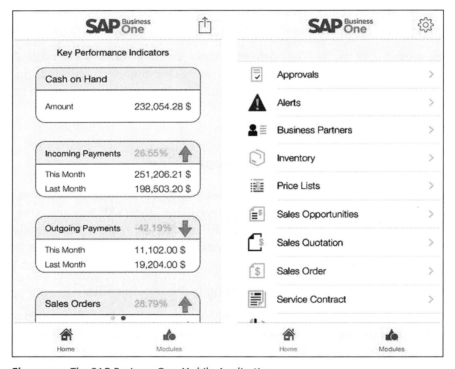

Figure 17.1 The SAP Business One Mobile Application

We recommend that you visit the store specific to your Apple or Android device and download a trial version of the application for evaluation. You can connect to a demo system hosted by SAP for an in-depth test drive. When you're ready to adopt the SAP Business One mobile application, keep in mind a few considerations:

▶ Licensing: A mobile application user must have either a professional license or a limited SAP Business One license.

▶ Compatibility: The mobile application works on both Apple and Android devices; its user interface (UI) is very similar in both formats.

▶ Internet connection: The mobile application requires an active Internet connection

▶ Extensibility: KPIs may be customized, but the application itself can't be modified by the user or your company's development team.

▶ Setup: Significant setup is required in SAP Business One to activate the mobile application and includes setting up both the SAP Business One Client and the SAP Business One Integration Framework.

With these considerations in mind, if you determine that the SAP Business One mobile application can add value to your organization, remember it's free! Consult your SAP Business One consultant or vendor to go through the necessary steps to configure the application to connect to your database(s) and system for productive use.

17.2   SAP Business One Web Client

Targeted at users on the go, the SAP Business One mobile application was never intended to handle 100% of the functionality of your desktop-based system.

But the new SAP Business One Web Client released with SAP Business One, version 9.2, will deliver increased functionality and behave much more like the SAP Business One desktop client than the SAP Business One mobile application. As shown in Figure 17.2, the web client replicates the look and feel that most SAP Business One users already know. The significant difference is that the web client is built on HTML5 and designed to run in a browser.

The SAP Business One Web Client greatly reduces the IT management demands and the overhead required to administer an SAP Business One system and its overall environment. You'll no longer need to maintain client installations on multiple workstations; instead, you can maintain only a single instance of the "client" and make it available to all users, no matter their location, device, or browser.

Keep in mind, however, the two following caveats:

▸ Remember that the web client is new. As functionality progresses, you're likely to continue relying on your desktop client for a while to perform some "administrative" functions in SAP Business One, even if, in the long term, the goal may be for a 100% replacement of the desktop client with the web client.

▸ Note that, since the database and client server(s) are no longer accessed through a local domain network, the web client relies on the Internet, and bandwidth is of vital importance to the user experience. This bandwidth requirement will be much more easily addressed by deploying your SAP Business One system in the cloud.

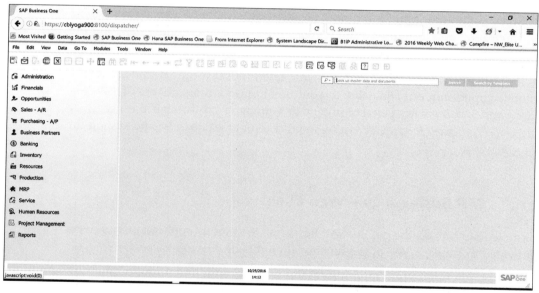

Figure 17.2 The SAP Business One Web Client

Using the SAP Business One Web Client has several benefits:

▸ Although still a work in progress, the web client will always be platform neutral and accessible with any device. As a result, the everyday user will be able to access a full replica of the desktop client from any location.

▸ All processing is performed on the server, thus reducing load and increasing performance.

▸ Mobile report distribution is an out-of-the-box functionality.

Keep in mind a few considerations:

- Licensing: A user of the SAP Business One Web Client must have either a professional or a limited SAP Business One license.

- Compatibility: The intent of the web client is to provide platform-neutral access; in other words, the web client will work with any device (smartphones and tablets, PCs and desktops, etc.) using any browser. As of the writing of this book, the SAP Business One Web Client works best with the Firefox browser. In the near future, SAP expects that the web client will work with a variety of web browsers, such as Safari and Microsoft Edge. Add-on products supplied by the network of software solution providers in the SAP Business One ecosystem are still in the process of gaining compatibility with the web client.

- Internet connection: The mobile application requires an active Internet connection

- Setup: The web client is installed automatically when SAP Business One is installed or upgraded and requires minimal configuration. You do not need to install, maintain, or upgrade an app on your mobile device; instead, you access the web client going to a web URL address in your browser.

- Versions: For SAP Business One, version for SAP HANA, the web client may also be deployed as an SAP Fiori-style desktop.

17.3 SAP Business One Sales Mobile App

The competitive marketplace is increasingly investing in applications that address the needs of a single user profile. In the case of the SAP Business One Sales application shown in Figure 17.3, the focus is on the sales professional, whose major concerns center on pipeline management, inventory review, price quotations, and order placement.

Because the SAP Business One Sales mobile app requires the SAP HANA platform, users have constant access to the information they need. In the growing digital economy, the advantages of SAP HANA deliver truly instant access to data with a greatly enhanced user experience, so sales professionals can remain online all the time.

Keep in mind a few considerations:

- Versions: You must be running SAP Business One, version 9.2 PL1, version for SAP HANA, or higher.

- ► Compatibility: The app runs only on the Apple iPhone 5 or newer (and running iOS 8.0 or higher), but other devices will be available in the future.

- ► Downloading: You can download a trial version of the SAP Business One Sales mobile app from the Apple App Store.

- ► Requirements: You must have a service layer running as well as SAP Business One analytics and the app framework installed.

- ► Licensing: The professional, limited CRM, starter package, and mobile sales users (new!) are supported.

- ► Security: The app provides simple security access with logons, license-based function levels and user-based data-level authorizations (data ownership), valid SSL certificates, and Apple Touch ID.

- ► Languages: All twenty-seven languages available in SAP Business One are available in the mobile app.

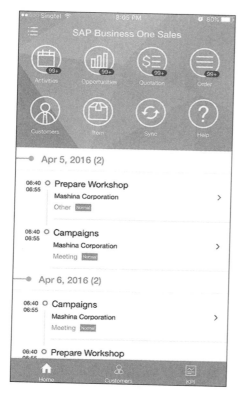

Figure 17.3 SAP Business One Sales Mobile App

A   Supplemental Materials

One of the goals for this guide is to make certain that we provide you with supplemental materials, especially how-to documents, that can help you complete tasks outside of your routine transactions. Our goal is for the book to be helpful to the casual user as well as the more technically capable individual.

While these pages are by no means a 100% complete orientation to the topic of SAP Business One, it is a good place to start. SAP is always adding new features and functions to the application to remain current and to make life easier for users.

To keep abreast of these movements, there are a few generic resources you should familiarize yourself with, as follows:

▶ **SAP Community Network (SCN)**
SCN is SAP's official user community (*http://go.sap.com/community.html*). It contains official product documentation, forums, and help documents. The official landing page for SAP Business One on SCN is *https://go.sap.com/community/topic/business-one.html*. The central page for the SAP Help Portal for SAP Business One can be found here: *http://help.sap.com/businessone*.

▶ **SAP Business One Academy**
The SAP Business One Academy is located in the SAP BUSINESS ONE section of SCN. This academy provides extremely valuable information such as training videos specific to navigation and design or single modules.

Currently this site doesn't require a username or password, though you can choose to become a registered user. If you don't wish to register, and you receive any sort of a prompt for credentials, just hit CANCEL to access the public site.

▶ **SAP Business One YouTube channel**
The official SAP Business One YouTube channel (*https://www.youtube.com/user/businessonesap*) contains product demos, how-to videos for multiple product versions, customer success stories, information on SAP Business One's mobile capabilities, and more.

▶ **Vision33 support documents**
Vision33, an SAP Business One implementation partner, hosts a number of helpful documents on its "Tips and Tricks" page located here: *http://www.vision33.com/b1tips*. You can sort by area or view all the documentation at once.

While we will call out specific materials that may be of interest to you from these resources throughout this appendix, we encourage you to fully explore the resources available. We have divided the resources into a number of categories, as follows:

- **Cockpits, dashboards, and widgets**
  Available at *http://www.vision33.com/b1tips*
  - "Activating Cockpits (excluding Dashboards)"
  - "Working with the Cockpit"
  - "Working with Dashboards"

- **SAP Business One, version for SAP HANA**
  - SAP Business One. "Fiori-Style Cockpit in SAP Business One 9.1, version for SAP HANA - Feature Clip." YouTube video, 06:08. Posted July 2014. *https://www.youtube.com/watch?v=BTWQyO7Zu00&feature=youtu.be*
  - "Working with Key Performance Indicators (KPIs) in SAP Business One, version for SAP HANA," *http://www.vision33.com/b1tips*
  - "Designing Pervasive Dashboards Using the Dashboard Designer," *http://help.sap.com/saphelp_sbo901/helpdata/en/48/ dac76f6e534647b8df5adbec5b3067/content.htm*

- **General administration resources**
  Available at *http://www.vision33.com/b1tips*
  - "SAP Business One Administrator's Guide Version 9.2 PL04 – SQL"
  - "SAP Business One Administrator's Guide Version 9.2 PL04 – HANA"
  - "Administrator's Guide for SAP Business One analytics powered by SAP HANA"

- **How-to guides**
  Available at *http://www.vision33.com/b1tips*
  - "How to Perform Year-End Closing in SAP Business One"
  - "How to Prepare for and Perform Master Data Cleanup"
  - "How to Setup Advanced G/L Account Determination"
  - "How to Work with SAP Business One Sales, mobile app for iOS"
  - "How to Work with SAP Business One Sales, mobile app for Android"

- "How to Set Up and Manage a Perpetual Inventory System"
- "How to Set Up and Manage a Nonperpetual Inventory System in SAP Business One 9.1"
- "How to Set Up and Use Serial/Batch Valuation Method SAP Business One 9.1"
- "How to Work with Project Management in SAP Business One"
- **Business Processes**
  - SAP Business One. "Sales Opportunities." YouTube video, 23:21. Posted September 2014. *https://www.youtube.com/watch?v=De_pVNExI-g*
  - SAP Business One. "Campaign Management." YouTube video, 11:59. Posted September 2014. *https://www.youtube.com/watch?v=mZXQNtn4JAY& list=PLMdHXbewhZ2Sglcoj5nU6mmz1ACExV7FM&index=5*
  - SAP Business One. "Data Ownership." YouTube video, 06:13. Posted December 2015. *https://www.youtube.com/watch?v=ZImQOjYexcc*
  - SAP Business One. "SAP Business One 9.2." YouTube playlist. Last updated September 2016. *https://www.youtube.com/playlist? list=PLMdHXbewhZ2QFUvOJ4uWYH-oqPmu9RTer* SAP Business One. "Inventory Counting in SAP Business One 9.0 - Feature Clip." YouTube video, 07:13. Posted December 2012. *https://www.youtube.com/watch?v=x_-mTrlc9iQ&hd=1*
  - SAP Business One. "Multiple Unit of Measures in SAP Business One 9.0 - Feature Clip." YouTube video, 07:23. Posted December 2012. *https://www.youtube.com/watch?v=0omysY1mrqA&hd=1*
  - SAP Business One. "Bin Locations in SAP Business One 9.0 - Feature Clip." YouTube video, 08:02. Posted December 2012. *https://www.youtube.com/watch?v=bgAFgdKyuao&hd=*
  - SAP Business One. "Price Update Wizard." YouTube video, 06:07. Posted December 2015. *https://www.youtube.com/watch?v=kFblQv4bdqg*
  - SAP Business One. "SAP Business One Service System Demonstration." YouTube video, 21:26. Posted September 2014. *https://www.youtube.com/watch?v=hnbNqqEtMis*
  - SAP Business One. "SAP Business One Project Management 9.2." YouTube video, 13:15. Posted December 2015. *https://www.youtube.com/watch?v= eObm8eHueZQ&index=5&list=PLMdHXbewhZ2QFUvOJ4uWYH-oqPmu9RTer*

▸ **Reporting**

- ▸ "How To Define Use Formatted Search 2005," *http://www.vision33.com/ b1tips*

- ▸ SAP Help Portal. "Demo 1: Query Wizard Tool." Video, 04:33. *http://help.sap.com/saphelpiis_hc/B1_Image_Repository/Consultant_Training/ Basic/B1_90_TB1200_03_01_Demo02/index.htm*

- ▸ Leverage Technologies Pty Limited. "SAP Business One Query Generator Video," YouTube video, 5:03. Posted September 2010. *https://www.youtube.com/watch?v=4Wlhe7G_VU8*

- ▸ SAP Help Portal. "Demo 4: Saving and Managing Queries." Video, 03:13. *http://help.sap.com/saphelpiis_hc/B1_Image_Repository/Consultant_Training/ Basic/B1_90_TB1200_03_01_Demo04/index.htm*

- ▸ "How To Create Query Print Layouts," July 2009, *http://www.tegrous.com/wp-content/uploads/2011/07/HowTo_QPrintLs_88.pdf*

- ▸ "How to Customize Printing Layouts with the Print Layout Designer," August 2009, *http://www.pioneerb1.com/wp-content/uploads/2012/04/ HowTo_PrintLayouts_PLD_88.pdf*

- ▸ "How to Customize Printing Templates with the Print Layout Designer," June 2006, *http://ktrs.vision33.com/media/5432/howto-customizepldtemplates.pdf*

- ▸ "How To Use The PLD Variables File," *http://www.vision33.com/b1tips*

- ▸ *"How To Work With Crystal Reports in SAP* Business One, Applicable Release: SAP Business One 8.8," January 2010, *http://www.pioneerb1.com/wp-content/ uploads/2012/04/How-to-work-with-Crystal-Reports-8.8.pdf*

- ▸ "How To Work With Crystal Reports 8.82," *http://www.vision33.com/b1tips*

- ▸ "How to Work with SAP Crystal Reports in SAP Business One," September 2014, *http://www.vision33.com/b1tips*

- ▸ "How To Integrate SAP Crystal Server with SAP Business One," *http://www.vision33.com/b1tips*

- ▸ "How To Set Up Data Sources for Crystal Reports in HANA," *http://www.vision33.com/b1tips*

- SAP Help Portal. "Manage SAP Crystal Reports for SAP Business One". Video, 02:00. *http://help.sap.com/saphelpiis_hc/B1_Image_Repository/ Consultant_Training/Additional/B1_88_CR_Manage/content/index.htm*

- SAP Help Portal. "Analyze the Business Need." Video, 01:04. *http://help.sap.com/saphelpiis_hc/B1_Image_Repository/Consultant_Training/ Additional/B1_88_CR_Analyze_Need/content/index.htm*

- SAP Help Portal. "Create a Report from an SAP Business One Data Source." Video, 00:59. *http://help.sap.com/saphelpiis_hc/B1_Image_Repository/ Consultant_Training/Additional/B1_88_CR_Create_Report/content/index.htm*

- SAP Help Portal. "Refine a Report using Modes, Sections, and Tools." Video, 01:25. *http://help.sap.com/saphelpiis_hc/B1_Image_Repository/ Consultant_Training/Additional/B1_88_CR_Refine_Report/content/index.htm*

- SAP Help Portal. "Add Filters, Parameter and Selection Criteria." Video, 01:15. *http://help.sap.com/saphelpiis_hc/B1_Image_Repository/ Consultant_Training/Additional/B1_88_CR_Add_Filters/content/index.htm*

- SAP Help Portal. "Add Formulas." Video, 01:08. *http://help.sap.com/saphelpiis_hc/B1_Image_Repository/Consultant_Training/ Additional/B1_88_CR_Add_Formulas/content/index.htm*

- SAP Help Portal. "Present Your Report Visually." Video, 01:20. *http://help.sap.com/saphelpiis_hc/B1_Image_Repository/Consultant_Training/ Additional/B1_88_CR_Present_Report/content/index.htm*

- *businessonenews*. "What is Drag and Relate in SAP Business One." YouTube video, 03:24. Posted December 2010. *https://www.youtube.com/watch?v=PSrtOVtc9IE*

- **Reporting in SAP Business One, version for SAP HANA**

  - *"How to Work with Excel Report and Interactive Analysis in SAP B1 HANA," http://www.vision33.com/b1tips*

  - *"How To Work with Pervasive Analytics in SAP Business One HANA," http://www.vision33.com/b1tips*

  - *"How To Work With Semantic Layers in SAP Business One HANA," http://www.vision33.com/b1tips*

  - *"How To Work With The Fiori Style Cockpit in SAP Business One HANA," http://www.vision33.com/b1tips*

SAP Business One Customer Portal

Lastly, be sure and check out the SAP Business One customer portal at *http://service.sap.com/smb/sbocustomer*. Registration is required for this portal and your SAP Business One business partner can help you with access.

B   The Authors

Carl Britton Lewis is the chief SAP Business One ambassador for Vision33, the largest reseller of SAP Business One globally. For many years, Carl has been a global influencer working to enhance the experience of every customer and user of SAP Business One.

Due in part to his work as the program chair for the SAP Business One Special Interest Group (SIG) for the Americas' SAP Users' Group (ASUG), Carl's professional endeavors extend beyond Vision33's more than 700 SAP Business One customers. It has been Carl's personal mission to create and grow the SAP Business One Summit, now an annual ASUG-driven event where more than 500 attendees from SAP, customers, resellers, and software solution providers gather for education and networking. He served as the first chairman of the North America Partner Advisory Council, which consists of the most significant SAP Business One resellers in North America. No longer the chairman, Carl remains an active member of the council.

Juanita Karan graduated from Louisiana State University with a degree in finance and has been working in corporate finance since 2009. After graduation, she worked as a controller for Allbrands, a regional sewing and home appliance company, where she worked with SAP Business One for two years. During that time, she restructured the inventory management and purchasing process for the company in order to increase inventory accuracy. Juanita also worked for Woman's Hospital as a financial analyst. As lead analyst, she assisted hospital departments with reporting, budgeting, and new initiatives. Additionally, she worked as a controller for Auger Services where she audited all business processes, prepared yearly budgets, and prepared monthly financials for reporting. Using her extensive financial background, she became an SAP Business One consultant; she now implements SAP Business One for manufacturing companies.

Andres D. Castrillon is the president and founder of Consensus International LLC in 2007 and founder of Consensus S.A. in Colombia in 1990; these organizations have helped hundreds of companies in the U.S. and Latin America become more efficient and profitable through the use of SAP Business One systems. Before working for Consensus, Andres worked for ten years in Florida as Exact Software/Macola's general manager for Latin America and as general manager for multinational sales for Exact Software North America. He has also worked for IBM and Philips Colombia, where he started as an IT manager and later became the F&A director and member of the board of Philips Major Domestic Appliances. He contributed to taking the company from a 14% market share to a leading 37% in less than two years.

Andres graduated as a systems and computer engineer from the University of Los Andes in Bogotá, Colombia, and received his master's degree in industrial administration from Purdue University.

Derin Hildebrandt is vice president and a founding co-owner of ProjectLine Solutions, Inc., a Canadian-based business software and consulting firm in operation since 2001. His experience includes senior project management for large-scale international software projects, ERP sales, consulting, and software development. Derin has been instrumental in the growth and expansion of the organization, including the establishment of its SAP Business One practice in 2004. Under his leadership, ProjectLine has grown to become a highly respected Gold-Certified SAP Channel Partner that is ranked in the top five in the nation. He has served on the North America Partner Advisory Council (PAC) for SAP Business One since its inception, has been a guest speaker at SAP customer events, and is routinely sought out by both SAP and its partners for in-house and customer consultations.

Robert (Rob) Peterson-Wakeman is the client relationship manager of western Canada for ProjectLine Solutions, Inc. Rob has been with ProjectLine since 2012 and, prior to that, was an SAP Business One customer and power user. Rob has a bachelor's degree and a master's degree of science from the University of Saskatchewan. His analytical training in the sciences drives a natural curiosity for business performance analysis; over the years, he has also accumulated many skills and much experience in small business management and entrepreneurship. At ProjectLine, Rob is enthusiastic about delivering blog content and webinars that instruct the SAP Business One end user community. Rob is also a regular contributor to educational sessions at the annual Americas' SAP Users' Group (ASUG) conference for SAP Business One.

Ryan Howe is a managing director at Clients First Business Solutions, which has more than twenty years of ERP industry expertise. Ryan is a graduate of Michigan State University and began his professional career as a certified public accountant for PricewaterhouseCoopers. There, he worked with global clients and gained exposure with how large and small companies operate in complex business environments. During this time, Ryan learned the importance of business processes and how business management software can benefit companies when a proper solution is effectively utilized.

This business experience allowed Ryan to become an active member of the SAP Business One community, in which he works diligently to provide value to all its members. Ryan actively participates in ASUG events and is currently the vice-chairman of the North America Partner Advisory Council (PAC). Ryan is known as a friendly face in the SAP Business One community that is always willing to go above and beyond to assist however he can.

Jennifer Schmitt is an SAP Business One solution expert at Clients First Business Solutions. After graduating from Grand Valley State University, Jennifer spent several years in the banking industry before joining a manufacturing company as its order management and shipping supervisor. During her tenure, the company purchased SAP Business One to allow for continued exponential year-over-year growth. Jennifer was actively involved in the implementation and became the lead SAP Business One resource for the company. Jennifer's continued passion for SAP Business One led her to take on her current role as an SAP Business One solution expert with Clients First Business Solutions.

Keith Taylor is an APICS-certified manufacturing and distribution operations professional whose background includes more than twenty-two years working with a large manufacturer/distributor, where he held several positions including marketing manager and vice president of materials and purchasing. Keith joined Long Business Systems, Inc., (LBSI) in 1995 and has managed hundreds of SAP Business One projects, including implementations, upgrades, additional training, enhancements, and assistance with business process optimizations, customizations, and reporting. Keith is the vice president of consulting services and a partner in the ownership of LBSI.

Keith has been a charter member and active participant in the North America SAP Business One Partner Advisory Council (PAC) since 2009 and has been its chairman since January 2014. As an SAP Business One program committee member and speaker for the ASUG SAP Business One user group, Keith contributes and shares his vast expertise in project management, business processes, manufacturing, distribution, and accounting with the SAP Business One community.

With more than twenty-five years of experience in business management solutions for small and medium-sized enterprises (SMEs), **Bertrand Tougas** is skilled at project management, communication, and work organization. Having worked as a consultant, analyst, trainer, and business owner, he joined SAP Canada in 2005 as the software solution partner manager for SAP Business One. In 2011, he became the general manager of Forgestik, Inc., a professional services company dedicated to software implementation and computer support. Its primary focus is on the installation of SAP Business One; with more than twenty-five years of experience, Forgestik sees itself as the Canadian reference in the deployment of ERP solutions for SMEs in the distribution, food, pharmaceuticals, and production industries.

After graduating from HEC Montréal with a bachelor's degree in business administration with a specialization in operation and production management, **Christophe Contat** started his career as a procurement officer and project manager. In 2008, he joined Forgestik, Inc.; as a certified SAP Business One consultant, he supports significant companies of various sizes in their growth.

James Gibbons has been a certified public accountant (CPA, CMA) since 1991 and received his master's of business administration degree in 1985. He has previously held positions as controller, business process consultant, system implementation project manager, vice president of finance and chief financial officer, and college professor and university lecturer. Recently, he decided to see things from the other side and joined Forgestik, Inc., as an SAP Business One consultant in charge of Ontario's market.

Hired in 2000, **Frédéric Marchand** is the SAP Consulting Director at Forgestik, Inc., where he is responsible for leading and managing a group of professional consultants. Over the years, Frédéric has proven his expertise in business process management, project management, and SQL reporting. He holds a BTS degree in accounting and management, has completed a short-term program in computer programming, and has a professional project management certification.

Michal Raczka has a bachelor's degree in business administration from HEC Montréal and a professional project management certification. Since graduation, Michal has applied his expertise to the ERP industry. He joined Forgestik, Inc., in 2011 as a consultant; since then, he progressed as a specialist in logistics and operations and, most recently, as a full-time project manager.

Index

Interested in reading more?

Please visit our website for all new
book and e-book releases from SAP PRESS.

www.sap-press.com